The Real Estate Professional

YOUR MASTER GUIDE TO PREPARING
FOR A CAREER IN REAL ESTATE

REVISED EDITION

The Real Estate Professional

YOUR MASTER GUIDE TO PREPARING FOR A CAREER IN REAL ESTATE

William M. Shenkel
The University of Georgia

DOW JONES-IRWIN
Homewood, Illinois 60430

© DOW JONES-IRWIN, 1976 and 1978

ISBN 0-87094-159-3
Library of Congress Catalog Card No. 78–52950
Printed in the United States of America

1 2 3 4 5 6 7 8 9 0 K 5 4 3 2 1 0 9 8 .

Preface

A s noted in the first edition, real estate salespersons and brokers must meet increasing educational requirements. Further, real estate continues to be more closely regulated. And since this book appeals to persons preparing for a professional career, this second edition has been considerably revised. The new material is believed especially helpful to applicants preparing for real estate salespersons and brokers examinations.

First, the multiple-choice questions now appear at the end of each chapter with an answer key. This arrangement makes it much more convenient for the reader to complete a self-test and to review chapter material.

Second, attention is invited to the new Appendix: "How to Take Real Estate License Examinations." The Appendix describes the main features of the most frequently used license examinations. Not only are suggestions offered to help pass multiple choice questions, the Appendix provides space for the addition of pertinent information on your particular state's license laws and regulations, which are usually covered by license examinations.

Third, coverage of new federal legislation that affects local real estate operations (and is usually found in state license examinations) has been added to this edition. Of particular importance is the explanation of *tenant-landlord* legislation added to Chapter 10, "Commercial and Residential Leases." Chapter 20 reviews certain federal legislation not covered in other chapters. This new chapter presents relevant material on *fair housing regulations*, the *Equal Credit Opportunity Act*, and *truth in lending requirements*. The current national *flood insurance program* and the many *environmental laws* enacted by Congress are also dealt with Chapter 20.

Finally, two new chapters with a more practical orientation also have been added: Chapter 14 discusses the _evaluation of energy conservation techniques_ including current data on solar energy. Chapter 17 provides a survey of _real estate selling techniques_ considered important to applicants for the salesperson license. In other chapters, material has been updated.

Note that the book is divided into four parts. Part I consists of four chapters that introduce the reader to the nature and structure of the real estate industry. Chapter 4 describes the provisions and general specifications of real estate licensing laws.

Part II, which consists of seven chapters, provides thorough coverage of real estate transactions. Chapter 7, "Reading Legal Descriptions," evolved from my observation of a very real need among real estate professionals for a guide to understanding the legal descriptions of real property. Chapter 9, "Closing Statements," is based on practical examples derived from my experience in writing and grading state real estate licensing examinations.

Part III prepares the reader for real estate specialization. Besides explaining energy conservation techniques, the chapters introduce the reader to activities and functions of the typical real estate office: real estate appraising, finance, management, and selling. Chapter 12, on mathematics, is derived from the author's many years of teaching this material to real estate students.

Part IV, the last section of this book, consists of three chapters that discuss the critical issues of government regulation and control. The chapter on subdivision regulations includes a discussion of the Interstate Land Sales Full Disclosure Act. The final chapter provides a survey of new federal legislation that affects real estate. It is difficult to operate as a real estate agency without observing state, local, and federal controls.

In preparing this work, I am grateful for the assistance of many real estate experts. I am particularly indebted to Percy E. Wagner of Chicago for his contributions. Mr. Wagner has been a very successful Realtor® for over 50 years. He is an author in his own right and is acknowledged throughout the United States as one of the leading proponents of rigorous standards for real estate professionals. His invaluable suggestions have improved both the presentation and chapter content.

Dr. Eugene F. Dunham, Jr., of the University of South Florida also provided in-depth guidance and I express to him my sincere thanks. Dr. James P. Gaines of the University of South Carolina added considerable input to the final manuscript. My colleague, Dr. Hans Isakson, made several helpful comments on Chapter 14.

A special note of appreciation is extended to others who have submitted material and reviewed the text. Gaylord Wood, attorney-at-law, Fort Lauderdale, Florida, and Franklin H. Spitzer, of the law offices of Wolf, Block, Schorr and Solis-Cohen, Philadelphia, have both contributed material for the text. Others who have provided material include E. A. Isakson, president of Northside Realty Associates, Inc., of Atlanta and former chairman of the Georgia Real Estate Commission, and Wade Manning, of the Land Department, Georgia Power Company.

My secretarial assistant, Sue Hoy, and her able graduate assistant, Janice Clark, were responsible for manuscript typing—an exacting task which was undertaken with high professional skill.

April 1978   *William M. Shenkel*

Contents

The Origin of Private Land Ownership: *Land Titles. Developing a Land Ownership Policy. Real Property Rights Unlike Personal Property Rights. Public Rights in Private Property.* Estates in Real Estate. Freehold Estates: *Estates of Inheritance. Estates Not of Inheritance. Legal Estates.* Less than Freehold Estates: *Estates for Years. Periodic Tenancies. Tenancy at Will. Tenancy by Sufferance.* Easements: *Easement in Gross. Easements Appurtenant. Easements by Prescription. Other Property Interests.* Ownership Interests: *Joint Tenancy. Tenancy in Common. Tenancy by the Entireties. Multiple Ownership.* Real and Personal Property: *Real Property Defined. Fixtures.*

Relation of Real Estate Markets to Economic Conditions: *Population. Income and Employment.* Determinants of Community Growth: *Economic Base Analysis. Patterns of Urban Growth.* The Nature of Real Estate Markets: *The Highest and Best Use. Real Estate Markets Imperfect. Real Estate Submarkets.* The Residential Market: *The Residential Occupancy Market. The Rental Housing Market.* Commercial Real Estate Markets: *Market Characteristics.* Industrial Real Estate. Real Estate Market Indicators: *Local Information.* Published Sources.

tion. The Conveyance Clause. The Legal Description. Proper Signatures. Delivery and Acceptance. Reservations, Exceptions and Encumbrances. Elements of a Deed: The Premises. The Habendum. The Testimonium. Restrictive Deed Covenants. Adverse Possession. The Unauthorized Practice of Law: The Deposit Receipt and Contract for Sale Limitation. Legal Advice. Conveyance Instruments Incidental to Business. Unauthorized Law Practice Summarized.

Part III
The Practice of Real Estate

Foot Conversions. Real Estate Commissions. Interest Rate Problems: *The Mortgage Constant. Simple Interest Calculations.*

The Appraisal Process: *Definition of the Problem. Appraisal Data. Valuation Approaches.* The Cost Approach: *The Land Value Estimate. The Cost New Estimate. Per Unit Costs. The Depreciation Allowance. The Cost Approach Evaluated.* The Market Comparison Approach: *Field Data Sources. Advantages of Market Comparisons.* The Income Approach: *The Gross Income Estimate. Net Operating Income. The Capitalization Rate.* Capitalization Techniques: Residual Methods: *Land-Residual Capitalization. Building-Residual Capitalization. Property-Residual Capitalization.*

Retrofitting Single-Family Dwellings: *Retrofitting Feasibility. Energy Cost Reduction for Apartments.* Solar Heating: *Solar Systems for Domestic Heat. Solar System Feasibility. Solar Property Rights.*

Government Intervention in the Mortgage Market: *The Supply of Mortgage Money. The Demand for Loanable Funds.* Real Estate Mortgages: *Mortgages Classified by the Repayment Plan. Special-Purpose Mortgages. Rights of the Mortgagor. Rights of the Mortgagee.* New Mortgage Plans: *Flexible-Payment Mortgages. Variable Rate Mortgages. Partially Amortized Mortgages.* Sources of Mortgage Funds: *Savings and Loan Associations. Mutual Savings Banks. Life Insurance Companies. Mortgage Bankers. Commercial Banks. Other Loan Sources.* Government Assistance: *Federal Housing Administration. Veterans Administration. Federal National Mortgage Association. Governmental National Mortgage Association. Federal Home Loan Bank Board.* Private Mortgage Insurance.

Functions of a Real Estate Manager: *Marketing and Budgeting. Rehabilitation, Modernization, and Conversions. Rent Collection.* The Management Agreement: *Duties of the Managing Agent. Owner Grant of Authority.* Tenant-Owner Relations: *Tenant Relations.* Management Accounting Systems. The Management Survey. Physical Real Property Inventory: *Neighborhood Analysis. Market Analysis. Gross Income Analysis. Operating Expense Analysis, Short and Long Term. Economics of Alternative Plans.* Management of Income Properties: *Managing Apartment Properties. Apartment Financial Ratios. Shopping Center Management. Office Management.*

Selling the Listing: *Unsolicited Listings. Solicited Listings.* Qualifying the Buyer: *Buyer Qualification Forms. Showing the Prospect.* Meeting Buyer Objections. Negotiating the Sale: *Realistic Offers. Counteroffer.* Closing the Sale: *Presenting the Final Offer. Closing the Negotiations.*

Part IV
Real Estate and the Community

Local Subdivision Regulations: *Local Approval. The Preliminary Plan. Preparation of the Final Plat. The Recording of Plats.* State Administered Subdivision Controls: *Blanket Encumbrances. Contracts of Sale. Grounds for Denial of Public Report.* Subdivision Covenants: *Land Use and Aesthetic Covenants. Enforcement.* The Interstate Land Sales Full Disclosure Act: *Statement of Record. The Property Report.*

Public Land Use Controls: *General Powers of the State. The General Plan. Zoning Regulations. Housing Codes. Building Codes.* Private Controls: *Deed Restrictions. Subdivision Covenants. Planned Unit Developments.* Environmental Controls.

Fair Housing Administration: *Fair Housing Regulations. Affirmative Marketing Plans.* Equal Credit Opportunity. Truth in Lending: *The Right of Rescission. Advertising.* The National Flood Insurance Program: *Insurance Coverage. Administrative Requirements.* Environmental Laws: *The Environmental Protection Agency. Air Pollution. Water Pollution. The Coastal Zone Management Act. Noise Pollution.* The Federal Impact on Local Environmental Controls: *Zoning Environmental Controls. Other Local Controls.*

License Examination Content: *The California Multistate Examinations. The Educational Testing Service Examinations.* State Test Questions: *State Real Estate License Laws. Real Estate Instruments.* How to Take Multiple-Choice Examinations: *Examination Preparation. The Examination Technique.* Suggested Completions or Answers.

List of Illustrations

Part I

The Real Estate Industry

1

Real Estate and Ownership Interests

P rofessional activity in the real estate industry is a relatively recent development. Before the organization of the National Association of Real Estate Boards in 1908 (now the National Association of Realtors), the real estate business was largely unorganized. Transactions were negotiated directly between seller and buyer, and lawyers attended to financial and legal details. Real estate salespersons' and brokers' licenses were not required, and no national organization encouraged professional or educational development. In fact, real estate textbooks were not available until 1920, nor did colleges and universities as late as then offer real estate courses.

By contrast, persons currently interested or engaged in the real estate business have many opportunities to raise their professional status. A professional practices a profession, and *a profession is an occupation based on specialized, continuing study to supply skilled service and expert advice for compensation.* In brief, a professional provides a unique, essential service. What this means in the real estate industry is that formal technical knowledge and a dedication to excellence are both required.

Professionalism can also be identified with a self-governing organization that undertakes a program of education for its members, such as the National Association of Realtors. Its various divisions enforce a code of ethics governing its members in their conduct with the public.

A review of educational facilities supported by the real estate industry shows the trend towards higher professional status in an increasing emphasis on educational facilities. Preparation for a real estate career may start with attendance at short courses offered by real estate boards and schools which specialize in preparing novices for state salesman and broker

3

examinations. The organized real estate associations and public and private accredited schools also offer advanced courses of study.

The real estate associations affiliated with the National Association of Realtors sponsor courses that usually result in industry-supported special designations. The designations are earned after a prescribed series of courses, examinations, and experience credits that qualify a person for special recognition. Virtually every community has these courses available from state and national real estate groups. The affiliate members of the National Association of Realtors that promote increased professionalism include:

American Institute of Real Estate Appraisers.

American Society of Real Estate Counselors.

American Chapter, International Real Estate Federation.

Institute of Real Estate Management.

Realtors National Marketing Institute (Formerly National Institute of Real Estate Brokers).

National Institute of Farm and Land Brokers.

Real Estate Securities and Syndicate Institute.

Society of Industrial Realtors.

Women's Council of Realtors.

Today, universities and colleges regularly support real estate courses leading to a real estate major with a bachelor or advanced degree. Supplementing these courses of study are the noncredit extension courses serving the adult educational needs of real estate. Indeed, the license laws of the respective states, if not directly favoring such courses of study, may require adult courses as a prerequisite to a salesperson's or broker's license, and state legislation increasingly requires a minimum of required courses to practice in the real estate industry.

A brief review of the origin of real property will show why these developments have occurred.

THE ORIGIN OF PRIVATE LAND OWNERSHIP

Private rights in personal property preceded property rights in land. Jewels, weapons, slaves, women, and household goods were items that were first subject to private ownership. These were followed by private property rights in burial grounds, springs, and wells. As agriculture assumed more significance, property rights in land developed from a system of communal rights in grazing areas—for instance, nomadic desert tribes historically had no concept of private property and land, though they recognized private ownership of man-made wells. Agriculture made little progress until communal groups recognized and protected the right of an owner to a specific site, giving the owner the right to reap his harvest.

Land Titles

European explorers, following the directions of their sovereigns, established their title claims by discovery or settlement. Usually some ceremonial act established the right of the sovereign to land. Employing the appropriate ceremonial rites, Balboa claimed title to all land touched by the Pacific Ocean. In the same manner, La Salle standing at the mouth of the Mississippi, and with much pomp and ceremony, claimed all lands drained by the river for Louis XIV. Other explorers, such as Drake in California and Biddle of the U.S. Navy, formally established claims for California and lands drained by the Columbia River.

Titles were evidenced by various monuments placed on the land—placed with sacred ceremonial words which were then written on paper and set in a book of public record. By these acts title was established in perpetuity to a given land area, much as title abstracts or deeds are placed on record at the courthouse today. Much of the land in the United States may be traced to the formal rites initiated by Western European discoverers; other portions were established by conquest or purchase.

For the most part, if you own land in the United States today, the original title has been carried forward from ownership policies developed in Colonial times. Starting with the ownership of 13 colonies by Great Britain (which were acquired by discovery and conquest), land rights were administered by appointed governors and proprietors who acted on behalf of the Crown. The right of occupancy by Indians was recognized in treaties and by the outright purchase of Indian titles. While 13 separate governments were established by Great Britain, the colony boundaries were poorly defined. They overlapped and they were mixed with Indian claims of occupancy.

Thomas Jefferson was a leader in denying the right of the Crown to halt land grants given by colonial governors, to raise quitrents, and to require that lands be sold at public auction at a minimum price per acre. With the Declaration of Independence, the question of land ownership became a question between the sovereign states and the emerging federal government.

Developing a Land Ownership Policy

The laws of the United States respecting the transfer of land title after death follow European practices. They therefore reflect a concern about the right of an individual to private property. And when the federal government adopted a policy of disposing of the public domain, settlers who went westward developed a strong commitment to private property.

To some extent, our ownership interests today may be traced to the need for federal revenue. Originally, land acquired outside the original 13 colonies and under control of the federal government, totaled some 3 million square miles, at one time encompassing Alaska and the states of Florida, Alabama, Mississippi, and all other conterminous states except Texas lying north and west of the Ohio and Mississippi rivers. Facing the urgent task of disposing of this public domain, the government had to extinguish Indian titles, survey the land and offer land at public auctions. The successful bidder was issued a deed granting title from the government. The early sales priced land at $1 per acre plus surveying costs. By 1796 land of the public domain was available for $2 per acre, with a year's time allowed to complete the payment. Later, the credit provision was repealed and the price of land was reduced to $1.25 per acre. The Homestead Act of 1862 permitted the purchase of 160 acres for the cost of a filing fee and five years' residence. Very few people today would balk at such purchase terms.

The problem of disposing of the public domain led Congress between 1785 and 1880 to enact some 3,500 laws dealing with public lands. As land passed into private ownership, the present system of property rights in land, with all its legal limitations, formed a private system of land tenure. Thus, our concept of property, defined as the exclusive right to control an economic good, was firmly settled. But of course this right cannot be effective without a society with instruments of enforcement.

Real Property Rights Unlike Personal Property Rights

Private property calls for control by individuals or organizations. Thus property rights and society have developed together, and thus real estate ownership calls for a complex set of laws.

Why? The answer lies in the basic difference between real property and personal property, the most outstanding of which relates to the fixed location of land. Land cannot be moved and it cannot be concealed. Another difference is the high value of land relative to personal property. In Colonial times most wealth was in the form of land, not personal property, giving rise to special laws controlling real property which had their basis in English common law stemming from the feudal system of land tenure. In the feudal system, land was possessed and used with permission of the manor lord, but personal property was free of this restriction.

Special rules govern the ownership of real property:

1. Title in real estate is transferred by a written document. Personal property, on the other hand, is conveyed by delivery of the object, an impossibility in the case of real estate.

2. Legal estates of the surviving spouse apply to real estate but not personal property.
3. Rules governing the inheritance of real property differ from the division and inheritance of personal property.
4. The laws giving creditors the right to attach real property are more restrictive than the rights of creditors against personal property.
5. The law of the state in which real property is located governs ownership rights; the state in which the legal residence of the owner of personal property is established governs ownership in personal property.

Though private property rights in real estate are quite definite, they are also subject to certain public rights. Therefore, while a person may claim absolute title to real property, giving him exclusive rights of use and possession, such rights are secondary to four recognized rights of the government and its administrative agencies. We will now discuss these.

Public Rights in Private Property

Federal, state, and local governments have certain rights falling under (1) the police power, (2) the right of eminent domain, (3) the right of taxation, and (4) the right of escheat.

Under the *police power*, government has the inherent right to regulate property in the public interest, convenience, necessity, health, safety, and morals. Such rights must be exercised reasonably, they cannot be discriminatory, and they must be applied uniformly. The exercise of police power limits an owner's right to the use and enjoyment of his property, but such restrictions are justified by the promotion of the general welfare. For example, zoning ordinances, building codes, and housing codes fall under the general police powers of governments to regulate the use of property for the public good.

Eminent domain may be traced back to the Magna Carta of 1215 and later to the 5th and 14th Amendments of the U.S. Constitution. The right of eminent domain gives government (and regulated public utilities) the right to take private property upon payment of just compensation. The taking must be in the public interest and it must compensate the owner for the value of his property acquired. Under this concept, land is acquired for the construction of highways, public buildings, water reservoirs, irrigation systems, and other public improvements.

The *right of taxation* relates primarily to the property tax, which is usually state or locally administered and, again, constitutes a restraint on private property ownership. Taxation is administered by governments according to constitutional, statute and common law.

It is fairly apparent that all real estate in the United States must be owned by someone. It is inconceivable in our land tenure system to have land which is not owned, controlled, or administered by some public, private, or personal entity. Yet on occasion, property owners die without any traceable heirs or without a last will and testament. In these circumstances, property ownership vests with the state under the *right of escheat.* Without this power, persons dying without any heirs or a will would leave the property without ownership.

ESTATES IN REAL ESTATE

In large measure, success in real estate depends on a knowledge of real estate ownership interests. The appraising, financing, developing, and—more significantly—the sale of real estate must deal with a specific type of real estate interest, and a knowledge of the legal vocabulary is essential to communicate with buyers, sellers, lenders, and government agencies. In addition, it is not unusual for the practicing salesman to be the first contact a client has with a real estate specialist. Therefore it is also essential that the salesman know when legal counsel is necessary. For this reason, too, the salesman must have a working knowledge of the basic elements of real property interests (and a knowledge of the legal vocabulary used in real estate).

For these reasons, then, virtually every state requires a familiarity with estates in real estate and ownership interests as qualification for a salesman or broker license. To cover this subject, the rest of this chapter is organized in three parts: (1) estates in real estate—freehold and non-freehold estates; (2) easements; and (3) ownership interests.

FREEHOLD ESTATES

Figure 1–1 diagrams the division of estates in real estate. Thus a person may hold either a *freehold estate* or a *less than freehold estate*, the latter referring to various leases. Leases convey exclusive rights of use for a definite period. (Their use is discussed in Chapter 10.) Freehold estates relate to two other main divisions: *estates of inheritance* and *estates not of inheritance.*

Estates of Inheritance

An estate that continues after the death of the owner and descends to his heirs is known as an estate of inheritance. While Figure 1–1 shows two divisions—the *fee tail* and the *fee simple*—only the fee simple estate is widely accepted. The fee tail, which now exists in only four states, has been eliminated by some 36 states which originally recognized a fee tail

FIGURE 1–1

Estates and Interests in Real Estate

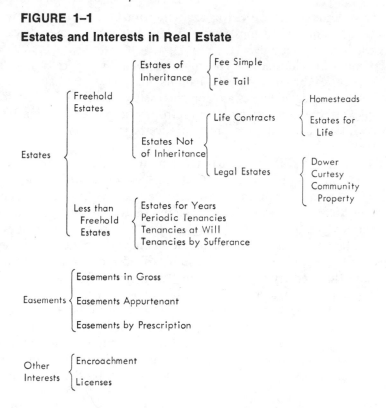

estate. It refers to the practice of granting the right of an inheritance only to the lineal descendants of the owner. Usually the eldest son, representing an heir of the body, has the right to possession of the inherited fee but may convey it only to his lineal descendants.

The more common estate subject to inheritance is the fee simple estate. Though subject to regulation and other powers of the state, the fee simple estate constitutes the most complete form of ownership. Provided the owner observes public and private laws regulating land use, he has virtually an absolute ownership, giving him the right to dispose of his interest by sale or gift. Under our form of ownership this is the most extensive legal estate in land, including all rights of real property ownership. Title to the fee simple absolute may be willed, or on death of the owner without a will (i.e., intestate), title will pass to surviving heirs. With no heirs, the property escheats to the state.

Estates Not of Inheritance

As shown in Figure 1–1, estates not of inheritance are subject to considerable classification. The two main divisions cover formal life contracts and three legal estates created by legislation or by operation of law. The former are common to most states, while the legal estates depend on differing laws of each state.

Formal Life Contracts. The most familiar life contract is the *life estate* acquired by deed or will. Parents may deed real estate to their children, reserving a life estate for themselves. With a life estate, for example, a father may establish an estate in the property during his lifetime, while at his death the property reverts to his son, the designated grantee.

The owner of a life estate has most rights associated with fee simple title—but only during the owner's lifetime. In other words, the owner's death determines when the life estate ceases. To distinguish between rights of the parties to a life estate, the person who receives the life estate is identified as a *life tenant.* The party who acquires title on the death of the life tenant is called the *remainderman.* On the death of the life tenant, the remainderman, in some states called the *reversioner* (a person to whom the property reverts), is entitled to possession.

On this point it is fairly clear that possession reverts to the remainderman upon death of the tenant even if a third party holds a valid lease from the life tenant. A farmer who orally leased 160 acres from a life tenant refused to give possession to the remainderman until his lease expired. The court held a life tenant cannot make a lease for a longer period than his own term (his life) unless joined by the remainderman. (*Craig et al.* v. *Launer et al,* 104 N.E. 2d 830 [Ill. 1952].)

There are certain common features of the life estate that distinguish this interest from a fee simple estate. Though the life tenant has the exclusive right to possess, enjoy, and use the property, these rights are subject to the interest of the remainderman. For example, a life tenant has rights of ownership subject to passing the property to the remainderman in approximately the same condition prevailing at the time of conveyance. The life tenant may not use the property so as to diminish its value or to flagrantly commit waste. The life tenant may not cut trees or extract an unreasonable amount of minerals or oil. Constructing a building or changing the use of the property, say from agricultural to industrial use, may constitute waste.

While the life tenant is charged with maintaining the property and cannot commit waste, an Illinois court held that the life tenant is not required to insure the interest of the remainderman. In the case cited, the life tenant failed to restore a residence damaged by fire, though the tenant recovered $2,000 from the fire insurance. The remainderman, upon death of the life tenant, was unable to recover damages under the claim of waste by the life tenant. In this instance the life tenant was not required to use proceeds of the fire policy to restore premises to their former condition. In the absence of a showing that more than the interest of the life tenant was insured, that the remainderman had been led to believe that his interest was insured, or that some other equitable consideration compelled the life tenant to so use proceeds for the remainderman, the court ruled in favor of the life tenant. (*Honeyman* v. *Heins*, 268 N.E. 2d 907 [1971].)

In the same manner, the right to mortgage the property is subject to certain restrictions. A life tenant may encumber the property with a

FIGURE 1–2
A Diagram of a Life Estate

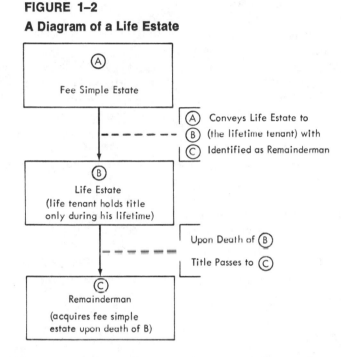

mortgage but upon the death of the life tenant, the mortgage is extinguished. State statutes differ on the right to mortgage life tenant interests. Generally the life tenant is not obligated to pay the principal but only the interest on the mortgage. Similarly, while a life tenant may lease his interest, as mentioned, the lease terminates on the death of the life tenant. In short, any interest conveyed by the life tenant is ended upon his death. The diagram in Figure 1–2 illustrates a typical life estate.

Homestead Rights. Homestead rights should not be confused with the Federal Homestead Act nor property tax exemption coming under the homestead tax exemption common to the states of Florida, Georgia, Texas, and others. The homestead rights dealt with here are those rights created by state law protecting the household from creditors. Under homestead rights, property qualifying as a homestead is not subject to sale for payment of debts. Typically because of homestead rights, both the husband and wife must consent to a sale or mortgage. Even in the event of the husband's death, the surviving widow and children may occupy the premises during the widow's life and while the children are minors.

Homestead rights protect the family from creditors who generally may force the sale of real estate to pay off legal debts. Generally speaking, homestead rights are associated with the following requirements: (1) the homestead must be declared and filed according to state law, and (2) the head of the household must own land which is occupied by the family as their home.

Suppose for example that Mr. Jones, the head of a household who has filed a homestead exemption, owns land worth $15,000 in a state providing for a $5,000 homestead exemption. If creditors force a sheriff's sale to satisfy a $20,000 debt, Mr. Jones would have the right to retain $5,000 worth of land. Creditors may not recover a debt from land subject to a homestead right.

In some states the family unit that qualifies for homestead rights is defined by statute. A divorced wife with custody of children, a bachelor supporting relatives, or a deserted wife with children generally qualify. The states may impose other limitations governing the maximum value attached to the homestead right or, as in Florida, the homestead limitation relates not to value but to the number of acres. A homestead that exceeds the statutory limit is subject to sale to satisfy creditors. Not all states have homestead rights; for example Delaware, Indiana, Maryland, and Pennsylvania do not.

Legal Estates

Legal estates credited by law include dower, curtesy, and community property. While legal estates are unique to the states that have them, usually those that do will have one or more of the three legal estates. They are created not by the parties themselves but by operation of law. The legal estates provide support for the surviving spouse.

Dower. In some states the widow is given an interest in real estate owned by the husband. More commonly it constitutes a life estate in one-third or one-half of the real estate owned by the husband during the marriage, provided: (1) there is a valid marriage, (2) the real estate was owned by the husband during the marriage, and (3) the husband dies before the wife.

Since state statutes govern here, the rule of situs affects claims under dower right. A Florida widow entitled to one third of the fee simple property owned by the husband at the time of his death or which he had before conveyed, to which she had not relinquished her right of dower, failed to support a claim against real property previously conveyed in Michigan. Though the wife did not relinquish her dower rights, the Florida court held that the dower right did not apply to property previously conveyed in Michigan. (*Johnson* v. *Johnson*, 240 So. 2d 840 [1970].)

During the life of the husband, the dower right is said to be *inchoate*. That is, it is a conditional right based on the possibility of the husband's death. The conditional status of an inchoate dower right means that the wife's dower interest is unknown and undefined until the husband's death. The Florida court has stated "since the wife's dower interest is inchoate, uncertain and remote, it does not constitute an estate or interest." (*U.S.* v. *Griffin*, 164 So. 2d 883 [Fla. 1964].) Consequently, it is not transferable and may only be released to a purchaser by the wife signing the deed covering property owned by the husband.

A surviving widow is said to have a *consummate* right, which is an interest similar to a life estate, subject to existing mortgages, liens, and other encumbrances at the time of the husband's death. If, however, the wife joined with the husband in deeds, mortgages, or other encumbrances, her dower interest may be released for such encumbrances if they were created after marriage. Dower rights are extinguished by divorce. (*Busch* v. *Busch*, 68 So. 2d 350 [Fla. 1953].)

Curtesy.   Curtesy extends virtually the same rights to the husband as the wife enjoys under dower. In states where curtesy is practiced, the husband should sign conveyances with the wife if his right is to be extinguished. Like dower, curtesy is ended by mutual agreement, divorce, or death of the husband.

In brief the husband is given a life estate in real estate owned by the wife during the marriage. It requires a marriage and in some states birth of a living child during the marriage. Both the dower and curtesy have been largely eliminated in states that provide for joint tenancy and community property.

Community Property.   Community property, tracing its origin to Spanish law, is found in the western states of Arizona, California, Idaho, Nevada, New Mexico, Texas, and Washington. In these states married couples have two kinds of property: separate property and community property. The first represents property owned by either party before marriage. Community property must be acquired during marriage. If a property is separate property, it is free from claims on the part of the other spouse and completely under the ownership and management of the owning husband or wife.

Under community property, it is reasoned that marriage partners should share equally in property acquired by their joint efforts. Consequently, the husband shares equally in property acquired by the wife, just as she is entitled to share equally in acquisitions of the husband; each partner owns one half of gains earned by the other. Generally the husband and wife each have a vested, undivided one half interest in the community property. Each spouse may dispose of his interest by will. Either may convey his interest to the other during marriage. (*Silverstein* v. *U.S.* 424 F. 2d 1148 [Ariz. 1970].)

It should be noted, however, that property purchased with separate funds remains separate property of the husband or wife, while property purchased with community funds is community property. In preparing deeds, it is presumed that the ownership of the property vests in the husband and wife any community property, regardless of whether the deed is in the name of the husband or wife. Hence ownership does not depend on the party mentioned in the deed. In some states the husband has the sole control over the community property and may sell or mortgage without the wife's consent. Community property states require both the husband's and the wife's signatures on real estate conveyances and mortgages involving community property.

In conveying property subject to community property laws, the intent of the parties affects disposition of community property. Thus in Arizona a deed executed by a wife who conveyed her community property interest to her mother-in-law for tax purposes was set aside. Since she did not intend to give up her community property interest, the deed was held invalid. (*Armer* v. *Armer*, 463 P. 2d 818 [Ariz. 1970].)

LESS THAN FREEHOLD ESTATES

Less than freehold estates are estates held by the lessor (owner) and tenant (lessee) under a lease. The lease creates a possessory interest in real estate for a definite time. Under the lease the tenant gains exclusive rights of possession, but unlike the freehold estate the right is not held in perpetuity but according to the time specified in the lease. The estate held by the owner constitutes the *leased fee* while the tenant has a *leasehold interest*. These estates may be either oral or written. Under the Statute of Frauds, a lease for more than one year must be in writing. The four types of estates created by a lease are classified as: (1) estates for years, (2) periodic tenancies, (3) tenancies at will, and (4) tenancies by sufferance.

Estates for Years

While an estate for years is common to all states, circumstances under which a tenant holds an estate for years vary. Simply stated, an estate for years refers to a lease for a fixed time—a month, a year, or longer. It has a definite beginning and ending date stated in the lease. Because Massachusetts enacted a statute holding that leases for more than 100 years automatically transferred the freehold estate to the lessee, custom has dictated that leases have a maximum term of 99 years. The owner, in giving up possession for such an unusually long time, virtually transfers all his rights of a fee owner to the tenant. However, under a lease the tenant pays for the use of the property by periodic payments (rent). The alternative—purchase of the freehold estate—involves a one-time payment at the time of conveyance in exchange for property rights held in perpetuity.

The main complication arising under an estate for years occurs when the tenant holds over after the lease terminates. A tenant remaining in possession after termination of the lease may either extend the lease term antomatically, or he could be held as a trespasser. It depends on state law and the language of the lease. Some leases have an automatic renewal clause so that a tenant holding over renews the lease on the same terms and conditions for an additional period. A Texas court has ruled that in the absence of an agreement, a tenant holding over is presumed to be in possession under terms of his previous contract in the reference to the amount of rent paid. (*Rogers* v. *Kolp* 272 S. W. 2d 793 [Texas 1954].)

Generally if the landlord accepts rent from a holdover tenant, it is implied that he has accepted extension of the lease for the period covered by the rent. This issue is sufficiently complex to require a legal opinion on the effect of a holdover tenant, given a specific state and an enforceable lease.

Periodic Tenancies

A tenancy that is renewed indefinitely from month to month or year to year by payment of rent constitutes a periodic tenancy. Ordinarily, if the tenant is in possession and pays rent monthly, he has a periodic tenancy running from month to month. The significance of this type of tenancy is that both parties must observe statutory notice. That is, the tenant must continue to pay rent unless he or she gives the landlord statutory notice—usually 30 days notice for a month-to-month tenancy. By the same token, the owner is barred from evicting the tenant unless statutory notice is given terminating the tenancy. While these leases are often based on an oral agreement, both parties must observe statutory notice required by state law. In at least one case it has been held that a periodic tenancy is not terminated by mere abandonment. A tenancy at will, according to a Texas ruling, may be terminated by surrender and acceptance. It is not terminated by the mere act of the tenant vacating the premises, where the landlord does not accept surrender, unless proper legal notice is given by the tenant of intention to terminate tenancy. (*Achille* v. *Baird* 361 S. W. 2d 439 [1962].)

Tenancy at Will

An agreement between the owner and tenant which may be terminated at the will of either party is a tenancy at will. Even though the lease term is uncertain, the tenant continues possession with the knowledge of the owner. Proper statutory notice must be given under a tenancy at will. This tenancy normally is created by a tenant holding over at the end of a lease with permission of the owner. Under these circumstances, a five-year lease terminating on December 31 might revert to a tenancy at will if the owner continues to accept monthly rent payments on an indefinite basis from the tenant remaining in possession. Such a rule was applied to a used car dealer who occupied a lot for 14 years. The lease expired in the earlier years, but the dealer continued in possession under an oral agreement by paying $300 a month rent. The court held the tenant had no assignable interest holding a tenancy at will on a month-to-month basis. (*Mossler Acceptance Company* v. *Martin* 322 F. 2d 183 [Fla. 1963].)

Tenancy by Sufferance

Tenancy by sufferance is actually a misleading phrase. A tenant classified in this way has no rights in real estate. Typically a tenant falls in this category if he originally occupied the premises lawfully but remains in possession unlawfully when the lease expires. Until the owner accepts rent or by some other act implies continuation of the tenancy, the tenant by sufferance may be dispossessed immediately; he has no rights of possession and he is not entitled to notice. In some states the owner may impose penalty rent as damages against a tenant at sufferance.

Even acceptance of the rent for an additional month after the lease expires may not destroy a tenancy by sufferance. In a lease of a jewelry store in the Miami air terminal building, the Miami Port Authority accepted rent for a 30-day period after a lease terminated. The tenant in possession lost to a higher bidder for a new lease. The Port Authority granted the tenant in possession—and with permission of the new tenant —not more than 30 days to vacate the premises, even though rent was accepted for the month to come. The tenant in possession argued that a tenancy at will was established by acceptance of the month's rent. The court held however, that the 30-day holdover was a mere convenience to the tenant, and that the tenant continued to occupy the premises at sufferance. (*Leaders International Jewelry, Inc.* v. *Board of County Commissioners of Dade County Fla.*, 183 So. 2d 242 [1966].

EASEMENTS

An easement is a nonpossessory interest in real estate. Legally, the owner of an easement has an interest in the real estate owned by another.

FIGURE 1–3

An Easement Agreement for an Electric Distribution Line

1974—2M—7-22-70

EASEMENT FOR RIGHT-OF-WAY

DUCKTOWN-MATT TRANSMISSION _____ LINES

STATE OF GEORGIA,
Forsyth _____ COUNTY.

For and in consideration of the sum of   ten dollars and other valuable consideration

($ 10.00) Dollars, in hand paid by GEORGIA POWER COMPANY, a corporation (hereinafter called the Company),

the receipt and sufficiency whereof is hereby acknowledged, the undersigned,

Billy McBrayer

whose Post Office address is   Route #1, Highway 19 North Cumming , Georgia
for himself, his heirs, legal representatives and assigns, does hereby grant to said Company, the right to, from time to time, construct, operate, maintain and renew overhead and underground electric transmission, distribution and communication lines, with necessary or convenient towers, frames, poles, wires, manholes, conduits, fixtures and appliances, protective wires and devices

in connection therewith upon or under, a strip of land _____ XXXXXXXXXXXXXXXX

XXXXXXXX _____ XXXXXXXXXXXXXXXXXXXXXXXXXXXXXXXXXXXXXXX
and described below; together with all rights and privileges necessary or convenient for the full enjoyment or use of said strip for the purposes above described, including the right of ingress and egress to and from said strip and the right to cut away and keep clear, remove and dispose of all trees and undergrowth and to remove and dispose of all obstructions now on said strip or that may hereafter be placed thereon by the undersigned, his heirs or assigns or any other person, and to cut, remove and dispose of danger trees on lands adjacent thereto, which now or may hereafter, injure or endanger any of the works on said strip provided that on future cutting of such danger trees the Company shall pay to the undersigned, his successors or assigns, the fair market value of the merchantable timber so cut; timber so cut to become the property of the Company; and the right to install, maintain and use anchors and guy wires on lands adjacent to said strip.

Said strip is a part of that tract of land situated in Land Lot _____ 709 _____ of the _____ 3rd _____ District

of 1st Section of Forsyth _____ County, Georgia, said tract being described as follows: Bounded on the North by

lands of _____ James A. McBrayer

on the South by lands of _____ Laura Tallant Pirkle

on the East by lands of _____ Jim Roger and lands of Mrs. Jay S. Holbrook

and on the West by lands of _____

XXXXXXXXXXXXXXXX said strip is more fully described as follows: BEGINNING at a corner common to lands of Mrs. Jay S. Holbrook and lands of Jay L. Holbrook and lands of Laura Tallant Pirkle and lands of the Undersigned, said corner also being common to Land Lots 708, 709, 702 and 733 of the 3rd District, 1st Section of Forsyth County; thence from said Point of Beginning South 89° 30' West 100.09 feet to a point; thence North 01° 53' East 1305.50 feet to a point and lands of James A McBrayer; thence along the dividing line between lands of James A. McBrayer and lands of the Undersigned North 89° 30' East 100.09 feet to lands of Jim Roger; thence along the dividing line between lands of Jim Roger and continuing along the dividing line between lands of Mrs. Jay S. Holbrook and lands of the Undersigned South 01° 53' West 1305.50 feet to lands of Laura Tallant Pirkle and the Point of Beginning.

XXXXXXXXXXXXXX said strip being shown on plat made by or for said Company, and on file in the Office of said Company.

Said Company, its successors and assigns, shall pay or tender to the owner thereof a fair market value for any growing crops, fruit trees or fences cut, damaged or destroyed on said premises by the employees of said Company, its agents, successors, or assigns, in the construction, reconstruction, operation and maintenance of said transmission lines, except those crops and fruit trees which are an obstruction to the use of the right-of-way as herein provided or which interfere with or may be likely to interfere with or endanger said lines or their proper maintenance and operation, provided the Grantors herein shall give the Company written notice thereof within thirty (30) days after said alleged damage shall have been done. Any growing crops or fruit trees so cut or damaged on said premises in the construction, reconstruction, operation and maintenance of said transmission lines to remain the property of the owner of said crops or fruit trees.

It is agreed that part of the within named consideration is in full payment for all timber cut or to be cut in the initial clearing and construction of said transmission lines; timber so cut to become the property of the Company.

The Grantors reserve the right to use the land hereinbefore described upon which the said transmission line or lines may be erected, for agricultural or any other purposes not inconsistent with the rights hereby granted, provided such use shall not injure or interfere with the proper operation, maintenance, or repair of, or extensions or additions to, the said line or lines; and provided further, that no buildings or structures other than fences may be erected upon the said strip of land.

Because it is recognized that there is the absolute necessity for the Company, in the safe and proper utilization of the rights, privileges, and interests herein granted, to have, from time to time and at all times, the following rights, powers, and interests, the same are hereby expressly granted to the Company, to-wit: To, by any action in law, or in equity, by injunction, ejectment, or otherwise, prevent the erection, or after erection to cause the removal, of any building or other structures, other than fencing, on or from said strip whether the offending party be a successor in title to the undersigned or not.

Said Company shall not be liable for or bound by any statement, agreement or understanding not herein expressed.

TO HAVE AND TO HOLD forever, unto said Company, its successors and assigns, the rights, powers, and interests herein granted, which shall be a covenant running with the title to the lands above described.

IN WITNESS WHEREOF, the said _____ undersigned _____ has _____

hereunto set   his   hand   and seal , this the   8   day of   May   , 1974 .

Signed, sealed and delivered in the presence of:

Billy M. Bryan (SEAL)

(signature) (SEAL)

(signature) (SEAL)

Notary Public

More specifically, an easement covers the right to enter and use another person's real estate for a special purpose. The purpose may include a right of way over another person's land or a right of way for a power line, pipeline, underground cables, drainage ditches, and the like. Customarily, an easement is conveyed under an easement deed or an easement agreement. Figure 1–3 represents an easement agreement covering a right of way for an electric distribution line. Easements consist of two types: an easement in gross and an easement appurtenant.

Easement in Gross

An easement in gross is a *personal right* acquired by one party to use land of another for a specific purpose. The acquisition of land to erect public transmission towers usually constitutes an easement in gross which is a personal right of the power company to use private lands for the construction and maintenance of an electric distribution line. The owner retains the ownership and use subject to the easement. Similarly billboard companies frequently acquire billboard sites under an easement in gross.

Such easement rights are acquired by parties who do not own land; yet an easement in gross is not revocable at the will of the property owner. An owner must observe rights of the utility company for pipelines, telephone lines, or power lines as stated in the easement agreement. In return for giving up property rights, the owner is paid according to the value of the easement.

Easements Appurtenant

An easement appurtenant is attached to the land benefiting from the easement. An easement appurtenant runs with the land receiving the benefit. Associated with an easement appurtenant are two estates: the *servient estate* and the *dominant estate*. A right of way over Parcel A to Parcel B, for example, identifies Parcel B as the dominant estate—the land receiving the benefit of the right of way. Parcel A represents the servient estate, which is the land used or enjoyed for the benefit of Parcel B. An easement appurtenant automatically passes to owners of the dominant estate (Parcel B) when it is conveyed to subsequent grantees. It is not a personal right and the owner of the dominant estate cannot separate the easement rights from the dominant estate (see Fig. 1–4).

Easements by Prescription

While public utilities, private owners, and government jurisdictions normally acquire easements by a contract agreement or deed, easements may also be acquired without a conveyance instrument. Suppose A uses

FIGURE 1–4

An Easement for a Right of Way Showing the Dominant and Servient Estates

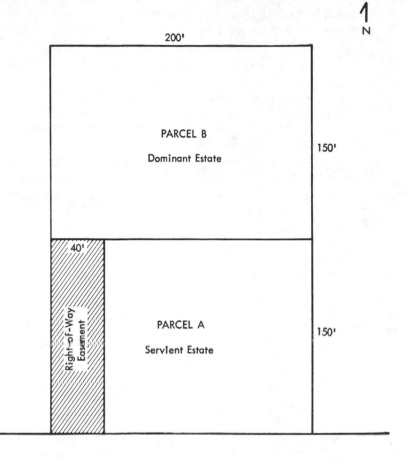

a portion of *B*'s property to gain access to a landlocked parcel. Provided certain statutory conditions are met, A may acquire an easement without a written document. Such an easement is called an easement acquired by prescription.

Generally, easements by prescription must be used in a manner that is (1) hostile to the use or enjoyment of the fee owner, (2) open and notorious, and (3) continuing for the minimum statutory period. In other words, the right of way must be visible, continuous, and uninterrupted such that it is presumed that the owner knows of the hostile use, and by his implied permission over the statutory time, effectively grants an easement by prescription. The period of time in which the use must be uninterrupted and continuous varies, but it typically ranges from 5 to 20 years. According to the Washington State court:

> To establish an easement by prescription, the claimant must prove that his use of the right of way has been, for a period of ten years, open, notorious, continuous, uninterrupted, over a uniform route, adverse to the owner of the subservient estate, and with the knowledge of such owner at a time he was able in law to assert and enforce his rights. (*Northwest Cities Gas Co.* v. *Western Fuel Co.*, 123 P. 2d 771 [1942].)

In other instances, easements may be acquired by necessity. These cases arise in the case of parcels that are virtually landlocked with no means of access. If the only means of access is over an adjoining parcel, the owner may have an easement of necessity across adjoining land to a public road. To establish this type of easement, the need must be real and reasonable. Mere convenience is insufficient.

There remains the establishment of an *easement by implication*. For example, a parcel of land in the state of New York was conveyed with a legal description describing the land as bordered on one side by a private road owned by the grantor. The grantee claimed use of the road under an easement which was "implied" in the conveyance. On the facts, the court concluded that the legal description did not establish an easement entitling the grantee to use the road. (*Tarolli* v. *Westvale Genosee, Inc.* 187 N.Y.S. 2d 762 [1959].)

Other Property Interests

There remain two other property interests which should be differentiated from easements. The first relates to a license. Without a license or easement, an unauthorized entry on land constitutes a trespass and subjects the trespasser to damages. If a real estate owner grants permission to enter for hunting purposes, the owner has effectively granted a temporary license. Tickets for ball games, concerts, and theaters also represent licenses for the use of real estate. Licenses are personal; the right does not run with the land and it cannot be sold with the property. In contrast, an easement is not revocable. It is permanent unless changed by mutual agreement and it runs with the land.

To determine whether an encroachment or lease applies, legal opinion may be required. For example, if a building encroaches on adjoining land, the title is unmarketable. Without a survey and appropriate contract language, a buyer might acquire land and a building that encroaches on adjoining streets or on adjoining property. Unless the encroachment qualifies for an easement by prescription or title by adverse possession, the buyer could be subjected to damages or loss of title.

OWNERSHIP INTERESTS

Under the U.S. system of ownership, land must be owned by an individual, corporation, or other entity such as a government agency. The ownership interest itself may be owned by a single person or other entity. Separate or sole ownership is also known as *ownership in severalty*. Ownership in severalty means that benefits of property ownership accrue to a sole owner subject to public and private benefits. The alternative is to hold ownership concurrently with others, each of whom hold simultaneous ownership in a single property. *Concurrent ownership* refers to ownership by two or more persons which may assume characteristics of (1) joint tenancy, (2) tenancy in common, and in some states (3) tenancy by the entireties. Besides these forms of concurrent ownership, title may be taken in other legal entities grouped under the general heading of multiple ownership.

Joint Tenancy

The main feature of joint tenancy is the right of survivorship which provides, upon the death of one joint tenant, that the surviving joint tenant or tenants become sole owners. As a result, property held by a joint tenant may not be willed nor can property of a joint tenant be subject to probate. Because of the rule of survivorship, some states specifically call for language that states "as joint tenants and not as tenants in common." In still other states, right of survivorship has been abolished by the state legislature.

Usually a joint tenancy must include four requirements or "unities": the unities of interest, title, time, and possession. The first unity means that persons owning as joint tenants have an equal and undivided interest in the title. A unity of title means that the joint tenancy is created by the same conveyance and establishes the unity of time by originating each joint tenancy at the same time. The last unity requires possession by one and the same possession. In effect, joint tenants hold real property jointly as if they were one person. Joint tenancies are controlled by statutes and vary considerably between the states.

Tenancy in Common

If two or more persons own title to an undivided share of real estate *without* the right of survivorship, they hold a tenancy in common. In contrast to a joint tenancy, tenants in common may hold unequal shares in the whole estate. They may have acquired their interest at different times under different conveyances. Moreover, a tenancy in common may be willed; title passes to lawful heirs in the absence of a will. Tenants in common have the right to partition their interests, converting the tenancy in common to sole ownership. If the property is impractical to divide, tenants in common may force the sale by filing an action known as a *partition action.*

Tenancy by the Entireties

In some states such as Florida, husband and wife hold property as tenants by the entireties. This resembles joint tenancy in that each tenancy has the right of survivorship. In these instances, neither the husband nor the wife have the power to sever the tenancy by sale or mortgage without the signature of the spouse. Generally speaking, community property estates do not recognize tenancy by the entireties. To be valid, deeds, conveyances or mortgages held in tenancy by the entireties must be executed by both husband and wife.

Multiple Ownership

Besides owning title as a sole owner or concurrently with others, property owners have the option of holding real estate in special legal entities. Here we will show the legal liability in electing multiple ownership status and identify the responsibility for real estate documents. This brief description will make clear certain financial advantages of ownership in multiple form.

Partnerships. Ownership in a partnership allows investors to pool their assets and thereby acquire property they might not be able to afford individually. Larger enterprises make professional management feasible and partnerships allow investors to diversify their investments. Further, pooling capital into a partnership tends to attract capital in relatively small amounts into real estate investments that otherwise would be invested in nonreal estate assets.

Partnerships can be formed by two or more persons operating as co-owners for profit. If property is purchased with partnership funds, it is usually held that partners have a "tenancy in partnership." If a partner dies, his interest reverts to the remaining partners, though his estate is entitled to reimbursement for the value of his interest. Though the partnership agreement is controlling, generally a partner may dispose of his interest to other partners or to strangers if not prohibited by agreement. Moreover, in a general partnership, ownership of real estate must be taken in the name of the partners individually and conveyed by the partners, each of whom participates in the execution of the conveyance instrument. If other partners empower a single partner to take the title in his name for the partnership, other partners need not participate in the execution of real estate documents. In real estate, special care must be taken to insure that partners are acting within the scope of their authority. If it is proven that a partner is acting wrongly, transacting business which is not a part of the partnership, the partnership will not be bound.

Some states provide for a limited partnership which includes *general partners* and *limited partners*. The general partner usually assumes the management and the control of the property, sharing in the profits and losses with liability to the partnership and creditors. The limited partner is usually an investor who has no power over property management. His liability to creditors is limited to the amount of capital actually invested. The limited partner ordinarily has no power to contract for mortgages, or to purchase or convey partnership real estate.

Corporate Ownership. A corporation formed to own real estate enjoys all the benefits of the corporate entity: liability limited to the ownership share of stock, perpetual life, spreading the risk among individual stockholders, and gaining liquidity of ownership to the extent that shares may be exchanged more readily than real estate assets. Against these advantages is the liability of a corporation for the federal corporate net income tax which is imposed before distribution to shareholders. As income is received by the shareholders, it is taxed again under the federal personal net income tax. Many states also administer a corporate net income and personal income tax.

Title to real estate may be taken in the name of the corporation according to the certificate of incorporation, which normally would grant the corporation the right to acquire, hold, and convey real personal property. The articles of incorporation may restrict purchase, mortgage, or sale of corporate realty by requiring consent of the stockholders. In other cases real estate corporations engaged in real estate as a business may hold authority for real estate operations by resolution of the stockholders. Or the articles may grant authority to the board of directors or selected officers to execute real estate documents. Real estate documents involving corporations should be reviewed for the authority granted to the officer or persons executing instruments for the corporation.

Cooperative Ownership. In the larger metropolitan cities a cooperative form of ownership has been used to acquire ownership rights in multiple-family units. Under these arrangements an apartment building will be owned by a nonprofit cooperative that sells ownership shares equal in value to the apartment unit conveyed. The cooperative shareowner is then granted a proprietary lease from the corporation and pays his pro rata expense of operation according to the value of his apartment as stated in the cooperative agreement. The main attraction of cooperative ownership, it is contended, lies in (1) the lower average vacancy that helps to reduce operating expenses relative to straight rental; (2) operation of the cooperative on a cost basis, thus eliminating the operator's profit; (3) the control of apartment services by the owners; and (4) income tax advantages gained through the deductibility of mortgage interest and property taxes on individual cooperative units, as opposed to straight apartment rental, which does not provide these advantages.

Cooperative ownership is not without its disadvantages, however. First, very little flexibility in financing is available since the cooperative is financed by a single mortgage covering the apartment building, with the same terms extended to each cooperative owner. Under a cooperative each owner is liable for the debts of the cooperative. If the cooperative is unsuccessful, the remaining shareholders must bear the burden of operation. Moreover, most cooperatives do not allow for capital gains on resale of a cooperative share. Usually the cooperative buys back the ownership at the original cost. For the most part, cooperative ownerships are limited to apartment dwellings.

Condominium Ownership. The concept of condominium ownership is used mostly in multiple-family housing, but it is also found in the development, operation, and management of office buildings, industrial property, and medical clinics. The condominium form of ownership gives the advantages of single ownership with all of the benefits of a multiple-unit structure. In essence, the owner of a condominium unit acquires the ownership of a three-dimensional space with a pro rata ownership share in the common elements of the property: namely, land, hallways, and building structure owned in common with other condominium owners.

In contrast to cooperative ownership, each condominium owner is liable for debts and liens of the condominium and its operating expenses *only* to the share stated in the condominium agreement. Moreover, the financing of a condominium purchase is unique to each owner in the same manner as in a single-family dwelling. The resale of the property is not unlike the transfer of a single-family dwelling. The owner may experience capital gains or losses as in other property. Furthermore, the condominium gives the purchaser an income tax deduction for the mortgage interest and property taxes that he would receive under a like ownership in a single-family dwelling. The legal and financial implications of condominium ownership is treated in greater detail in a later chapter.

Other Forms of Multiple Ownership. Other forms of ownership encountered in real estate, though with less frequency, are *syndications* and *trusts*. In syndications, ownership is generally placed in a partnership and therefore is not truly a separate form of ownership. Ordinarily ownership rests in a limited partnership to avoid the double taxation of a corporation while still limiting the liability of investing partners.

A trust occurs when title is held by a trustee for the benefit of the owner (called the *beneficiary*). The powers of the trustee are provided by a trust agreement which delegates management to the trustee who acts for property owners who are generally inexperienced in real estate matters.

Still another form of trust arises from the Real Estate Investment Trust Act of 1960. This act exempts a real estate investment trust from the corporate net income tax on distributed earnings. To gain the tax advantages of a real estate investment trust, certain minimum requirements must be met:

1. Management must be in the hands of one or more trustees.
2. Ownership must be held by 100 or more persons.
3. Property must be held for investment and not for the purpose of selling to brokers and buyers in the ordinary course of business.
4. No five persons may own more than 50 percent of the trust, directly or indirectly.
5. At least 90 percent of the gross income is derived from investment sources.
6. A minimum of 75 percent of gross income must be derived from real estate.
7. No more than 30 percent of annual gross income is derived from sales of stock, or securities held less than 6 months and real property held less than 4 years.
8. At least 75 percent of the trust assets must be in real estate, cash, or government securities.
9. Not more than 25 percent of the trust assets may be in securities other than real estate, cash, cash items, or government securities.

The real estate investment trust tends to attract the savings of small investors who pool their assets for the purpose of investing in large-scale properties. At the same time, they avoid tax liabilities of corporations organized for profit. In recent years investment trusts have constituted an important source of real estate capital since they are not governed by restrictive legislation placed on financial institutions such as savings and loan associations, life insurance companies, and commercial banks. Provided they conform to special laws governing a real estate investment trust, they operate in real estate transactions as other corporations.

REAL AND PERSONAL PROPERTY

A clear understanding of the legal differences between real and personal property eliminates a common source of misunderstanding, controversy, and a considerable volume of litigation.

Real Property Defined

It should be emphasized that the concept of property does not refer to the physical thing owned but to the *rights* of ownership. Ownership in the absolute sense includes the right to possess, to use, to mortgage, and to dispose of the thing owned. For the present purpose, real property consists of ownership rights to land and anything permanently affixed to land.

While real property refers to the rights of ownership, the concept of land refers to the physical thing itself. In a larger sense, land refers to space. Space which is fairly fixed in quantity is largely indestructible. Thus ownership of land includes the right to use the surface and even the space beneath the surface which is sometimes conveyed separately (i.e., subsurface rights or rights to coal, oil and minerals). In another sense, land also refers to space above the surface area. It is sometimes convenient to acquire air rights above the land surface separate and apart from the surface area.

Things permanently attached to the land become part of the land itself. Lumber stacked on a residential lot would be regarded as personal property legally referred to as "chattel." Once the lumber is made part of a newly constructed building attached to the foundation and land, it becomes real estate and is conveyed with the land.

Therefore, personal property is all nonreal estate property. Personalty is not attached to land or buildings; it is generally movable property such as household furniture, automobiles, and other personal articles.

The issue is not too clear for specialized property such as house trailers. In Pennsylvania a local assessor taxed a house trailer as part of the real estate. On appeal it was determined that the trailer rested on loose concrete blocks and that sewer and water connections could be disconnected in ten minutes time. In ruling that the trailer was not permanently attached to the land the court held "the fact that the landowner intends to reside in the present trailer or in a trailer which might replace it either permanently or for an indefinite period of time, does not change the character of the trailer from personal property to real estate." (*Hartman v. Fulton County*, Adams County, L. J., II 127 [1960].)

Fixtures

A fixture is an item of personal property classified as real estate. For example, a combination television and stereo music system would normally be regarded as personal property. But if a living room is constructed with built-in cabinets and speaker system, these items may assume the form of a fixture and, therefore, become a part of the real estate.

If an item is classified as personal property, usually it will not be conveyed as part of the real estate (i.e., draperies, rugs, curtains, and the like). But if the item represents a fixture, it *is* conveyed with the real estate. The classification of fixtures rests on four tests: (1) the intent of the parties, (2) method of attachment, (3) the relation of the parties, and (4) adaptation of the article.

Clearly it must be the intent of the parties to assume that these items become part of the real estate. The courts will rule on this point according to a finding of facts. If a hi-fi-TV system is specially attached to a building in cabinets forming part of the interior wall, it probably could not be removed without substantial damage. In the same manner, bathroom plumbing and lighting fixtures, which are personal property before being attached to the building, represent fixtures and are conveyed with the land. Attached items qualifying as fixtures are further illustrated by a built-in intercom and music system, window screens, storm windows, and the like.

The relation of the parties controls where there is doubt concerning the classification of the fixture. In a dispute about an overhead chandelier, the law generally favors a buyer because of the relation between buyer and seller. In the same manner, the law favors the tenant over landlord and in the case of heirs, the law tends to view articles as fixtures passing with the real estate to the heir.

In Pennsylvania the "assembled plant doctrine" controls the classification of fixtures. Here it has been held that

> . . . all machinery, equipment and fixtures, whether loose or detached, which are vital to unit and permanent installation therein are to be considered a part of the realty under assembled economic unit doctrine. . . .

But under the same rule a grocery store owner failed to support a claim that movable fixtures represented a part of the real estate. (*Singer* v. *Redevelopment Authority of the City of Oil City*, 261 A. 2d, 594 [1969].)

The rule of adaptation concerns the purpose for the article in question. If the article is necessary to the building operation, it would be regarded as a fixture. Therefore, in dealing with land, one must consider those items attached to the land which become real estate and fixtures, which change their form from personalty to real estate.

Special provisions of state law may interpret the rule of adaptation differently—especially on trade fixtures installed by tenants. The Pennsylvania court ruled "such structures, placed by a tenant on demised premises for the purpose of carrying on his business, may be removed by him, or may be replevied or levied on by a writ of execution, during the term of the lease; being built on leased land and therefore on a chattel estate they are themselves chattels in regard not only to the lessor but to everyone else. The criterion is not one of physical annexation. . . ." (*First Nat. Bank of McAdoo* v. *Reese et al.*, 356 Pa. 175, 179, 51 A. 2d 806 [1947].)

QUESTIONS FOR REVIEW

_____ 1. A knowledge of real estate interests is helpful
  a. to appraise real estate.
  b. to enable the salesman or broker to direct his client to professional counsel when needed.
  c. to finance and develop real estate.
  d. all of the above.

_____ 2. Real estate may be defined as
  a. space.
  b. land and its attachments.
  c. only the land surface and attached buildings.
  d. chattels.

_____ 3. Which of the following does *not* relate to fixtures?
  a. The intent of the parties.
  b. Method of attachment.
  c. The value of the chattel.
  d. Adaptation of the article.

_____ 4. A chattel is
  a. more commonly known as realty.
  b. personal property.
  c. the same as a fixture.
  d. conveyed by a deed rather than a bill of sale.

_____ 5. A chattel estate refers to
  a. the items the lessee installs on the leased land that do not become part of the leased land.
  b. property subject to a leasehold estate.
  c. land conveyed by a deed.
  d. a life estate.

_____ 6. Which of the following would be considered a freehold estate?
  a. Estate for years.
  b. Periodic tenancy.
  c. Tenancy at will.
  d. Estate for life.

_____ 7. Which of the following is the most commonly accepted estate of inheritance?
  a. Fee simple.
  b. Fee tail.
  c. Community property.
  d. Curtesy.

_____ 8. The person who receives the life estate is identified as a
  a. remainderman.
  b. revisioner.

       c.   designated grantee.
       d.   life tenant.

_____ 9.   _____ refers to the person to whom real property reverts to after expiration of the life estate.
       a.   Remainderman
       b.   Designated grantor
       c.   Revisionee
       d.   All of the above

_____10.   Which of the following requirements are associated with homestead rights?
     I.   The homestead must be declared and filed according to state law.
     II. The head of the household must own land which is occupied by the family as their home.
       a.   I only.
       b.   II only.
       c.   I and II.
       d.   Neither I nor II.

_____11.   Legal estates created by law do *not* include
       a.   dower.
       b.   curtesy.
       c.   community property.
       d.   life contracts.

_____12.   In some states a dower constitutes a life estate of one third or one half of the real estate owned by the husband during the marriage unless
       a.   there is a valid marriage.
       b.   the real estate was owned by the husband during the marriage.
       c.   the husband dies before the wife.
       d.   the wife dies before the husband.

_____13.   The rule of situs affects claims under
       a.   quitclaim rights.
       b.   community property.
       c.   dower right.
       d.   legal estates.

_____14.   During the life of the husband the dower right is said to be
       a.   consummate.
       b.   governed by the rule of situs.
       c.   inchoate.
       d.   exempt from a lis pendens action.

_____15.   Referring to dower rights, the consummate right of a surviving widow is similar to a
       a.   fee simple estate.
       b.   fee tail estate.

    c. legal estate.
    d. life estate.

___16. Dower rights are extinguished by
    a. death of the wife.
    b. death of the husband.
    c. divorce.
    d. recording.

___17. In states that have community property, which of the following principles apply?
    a. After marriage, partners should share equally in property acquired by their joint efforts.
    b. After marriage, all property owned by either party becomes jointly owned property.
    c. Property is owned by either the husband or wife before or after marriage, but is never a joint venture.
    d. Community property rights are similar to dower rights.

___18. Which of the following represents less than a freehold estate?
    a. Fee simple.
    b. Homestead.
    c. Tenancy at will.
    d. Dower.

___19. The legal instrument that is used in an estate for years is called
    a. a deed.
    b. a bill of sale.
    c. a lease.
    d. either *a* or *b*.

___20. _____ refers to a lease for a fixed time, such as a month, a year, or longer.
    a. Estate for years
    b. Periodic tenancy
    c. Tenancy at will
    d. Tenancy at sufferance

___21. A(n) _____ is renewed indefinitely from month to month or year to year by payment of rent.
    a. estates for years
    b. periodic tenancy
    c. tenancy at will
    d. tenancy at sufferance

___22. An agreement between the owner and the tenant which may be terminated at the discretion of either party describes the
    a. estate for years.
    b. periodic tenancy.

     c. tenancy at will.

     d. tenancy at sufferance.

_____23.   _____ refers to a nonpossessory interest in real estate.

     a. Dower

     b. Curtesy

     c. Tenancy at sufferance

     d. Easement

_____24. A(n) _____ is a personal right acquired by one party to use land of another for a specific purpose.

     a. easement in gross

     b. easement appurtenant

     c. encroachment

     d. license

_____25. An easement in gross is

     a. revocable at the will of the property owner.

     b. an easement in which the owner does not retain ownership of the property.

     c. an easement in which the owner may use the property subject to the easement.

     d. created if the property owner is not paid for granting the easement.

_____26. A right of way over parcel *A* to parcel *B* identifies parcel *B* as the

     a. servient estate.

     b. dominant estate.

     c. appurtenant estate.

     d. encroachment estate.

_____27. An easement appurtenant automatically passes to the owners of the

     a. servient estate.

     b. dominant estate.

     c. servient and the dominant estate.

     d. leasehold estate.

_____28. An easement acquired without a conveyance instrument is called

     a. an easement in gross.

     b. an easement appurtenant.

     c. an easement by prescription.

     d. a dominant easement.

_____29. Generally, easements by prescription must be used in a manner that is

     a. hostile to the use or enjoyment of the owner.

     b. open and notorious.

     c. continuing for a minimum statutory period.

     d. all of the above.

_____30. Without _____ an unauthorized entry on land constitutes a trespass and subjects the trespasser to damages.

    a. a license

    b. an estoppel certificate

    c. encroachment

    d. *a* and *b*

_____31. A license is

    a. revocable.

    b. not revocable.

    c. made through mutual agreement.

    d. an interest that runs with the land.

_____32. Under certain circumstances an encroachment may constitute

    a. an easement by prescription.

    b. title by adverse possession.

    c. a mortgage.

    d. both *a* and *b*.

_____33. Which of the following is *not* a concurrent form of ownership?

    a. Joint tenancy.

    b. Tenancy in common.

    c. Tenancy by the entireties.

    d. Ownership in severalty.

_____34. The main feature of _____ is the right of survivorship.

    a. joint tenancy

    b. tenancy in common

    c. tenancy by the entireties

    d. ownership in severalty

_____35. Which of the following is *not* one of the four unities required for a joint tenancy?

    a. Unity of interest.

    b. Unity of title.

    c. Unity of place.

    d. Unity of time.

_____36. If two or more persons own title to an undivided share of real estate *without* the right of survivorship, they hold title as

    a. joint tenants.

    b. tenants in common.

    c. concurrent owners.

    d. owners in severalty.

_____37. Which of the following statements is correct?

    I. A limited partner is usually an investor with no power over property management.

    II. A general partner usually assumes control of the property and shares in the profits and losses of the partnership.

    a. I only.
    b. II only.
    c. I and II.
    d. Neither I nor II.

_____38. One of the advantages of cooperative ownership relates to
    a. the higher average vacancy that helps to reduce operating expenses relative to single rental.
    b. operation of a cooperative to maximize profit.
    c. the control of apartment services by the owners.
    d. income tax advantages gained through the deductibility of mortgage principal payments, insurance, and property taxes on individual cooperative units.

_____39. Which of the following represents a disadvantage of cooperative ownership?
    a. The inflexibility of financing of the cooperative.
    b. The liability for debts of the cooperative.
    c. Restrictions on resale.
    d. All of the above.

_____40. In comparing condominium with cooperative ownership, which of the following statements is true?
    a. The condominium owner is liable for debts and liens for the entire complex.
    b. The condominium owner does not receive income tax deductions for mortgage interest.
    c. Cooperative ownership may lead to substantial capital gains.
    d. Condominium ownership provides for single ownership in addition to advantages of a multiple-family dwelling.

ANSWER KEY

1. (*d*)	11. (*d*)	21. (*b*)	31. (*a*)
2. (*b*)	12. (*d*)	22. (*c*)	32. (*d*)
3. (*c*)	13. (*c*)	23. (*d*)	33. (*d*)
4. (*b*)	14. (*c*)	24. (*a*)	34. (*a*)
5. (*a*)	15. (*d*)	25. (*c*)	35. (*c*)
6. (*d*)	16. (*c*)	26. (*b*)	36. (*b*)
7. (*a*)	17. (*a*)	27. (*b*)	37. (*c*)
8. (*d*)	18. (*c*)	28. (*c*)	38. (*c*)
9. (*a*)	19. (*c*)	29. (*d*)	39. (*d*)
10. (*c*)	20. (*a*)	30. (*a*)	40. (*d*)

SUGGESTED ADDITIONAL READING

Atteberry, William; Pearson, Karl; and Litka, Michael. *Real Estate Law.* Columbus, O.: Grid, Inc., 1974, chaps. 3, 7, and 16.

Creteau, Paul G. *Principles of Real Estate Law.* Portland, Me.: Castle Publishing Co., 1977, chaps. 3 and 5.

Hebard, Edna L., and Meisel, Gerald S. *Principles of Real Estate Law.* Cambridge, Mass.: Schenkman Publishing Co., 1967, chaps. 4 and 5.

Kratovil, Robert. *Real Estate Law.* 6th ed. Englewood Cliffs, N.J.: Prentice-Hall, Inc., 1974, chaps. 6 and 16.

Lusk, Harold. F., and French, William B. *Law of the Real Estate Business.* 3d ed. Homewood, Ill.: Richard D. Irwin, Inc., 1975, chaps. 2 and 4.

2

Real Estate Markets

A familiarity with real estate markets minimizes the probability of investment losses. With a knowledge of real estate markets, investors can use real estate in the most efficient way. While some factors affecting real estate markets are unpredictable, a study of market characteristics helps not only to minimize losses but also enables investors to recognize conditions leading to a favorable market.

In this chapter, the real estate market is explained in terms of its relationship to general economic conditions. Next, determinants of community growth that affect real estate are discussed in relation to the demand and supply of real estate. Finally, the balance of the chapter deals with unique features of real estate markets for three main property types: residential, commercial, and industrial.

RELATION OF REAL ESTATE MARKETS TO ECONOMIC CONDITIONS

Like other markets found in the durable goods industries, such as automobiles, furniture, and home appliances, the real estate market interacts with employment, household formation, and variations in family income.

Population

Obviously, population trends affect the quantity of real estate demanded. Especially in residential property, the number of people is less significant than the number of households. For example, as the number of single adult individuals increases, the number of required housing units

35

increases. The number of single adult individuals can increase when young persons leave home, when people divorce or separate, or when they are widowed. Thus, the number of households needed may increase with no net change in the absolute population. Moreover, as population characteristics change, so does the demand for housing. The type of housing required for a community of retirees (Sun City, Arizona, or St. Petersburg, Florida, for example) is quite different than the housing required for young married couples. In large measure, general trends in household formation determine general housing demand.

Population changes are not only closely related to residential markets, but they also partly control the demand for commercial and industrial real estate. Shopping centers and other retail and service businesses follow the population. In this respect, commercial real estate tends to be a derived demand—a demand derived from the buying power of the local population. Similarly, a considerable proportion of industry locates near consumer and industrial markets or near low-cost or skilled labor. Hence, a study of population forces is the first step in judging real estate markets.

Income and Employment

A family with an income of $20,000 will of course demand a different type of housing than a family with an income of $50,000. But in real estate the issue is more complex than this simple comparison would suggest. Buyers enter the housing market according to their future expectations of income. A wave of optimism stimulates the demand for real estate, which, in turn, generates more income throughout the economy. As more jobs are created, the general wave of optimism continues to favor real estate and other markets. With a rising level of expectations and general business expansion, new subdivisions, shopping centers, and industrial parks are created to satisfy increasing demands.

The converse is also true. A rising level of unemployment and lower personal incomes are magnified by waves of pessimism as consumers postpone decisions to purchase housing and durable goods such as automobiles, home appliances and furnishings, and similar products. Unemployment increases, creating further pessimistic projections. Even though a local community may show an impressive prospect for favorable growth, the interaction of the real estate market with national trends in gross national product, employment, and personal incomes partly controls the demand and supply of residential, commercial, and industrial real estate.

Indeed, as explained in the chapter on real estate finance (Chapter 15), a favorable real estate market is also dependent on the flow of savings into financial institutions that grant mortgages. Credit availability and the prevailing interest rate on real estate loans may encourage or discourage new real estate developments. And even under the most favorable national or regional conditions, the market for real estate is closely tied to community growth.

DETERMINANTS OF COMMUNITY GROWTH

Community growth is related to the source of employment and personal income. An analysis of these factors comes under the heading of economic base analysis. The economic base refers to activities in which people make their living. The economic base probably affects the real estate market more than any other single factor.

Economic Base Analysis

The importance of the economic base lies in its effect on employment and personal income. Some students of economic base analysis hold that businesses that manufacture goods or services for sale outside the boundaries of a local community provide a flow of income into the community. Other types of employment—those that produce goods and services consumed within the community—are viewed as less important to community growth. Experience shows that both types of employment are important in maintaining employment, personal income, and a favorable real estate market.

Economic base studies classify employment according to the type of business: manufacturing, retailing, real estate and finance, wholesaling, government employment, and other sources. Such analysis would usually take the following form:

1. List sources of employment by major groups showing the number of persons employed in each industry.
2. List the number of firms in each major category (i.e., manufacturing, retailing, and the like).
3. Identify the markets served by local firms. For example, local markets, regional markets, national or international markets.

The trends in each of the industries and the prospects for their growth depend on their competitive position and their respective markets. Projections may be made on probable future employment. By looking at past records, industries showing a steady growth for long periods may be affected by trends that show a high degree of continued growth in the future. National and international conditions may lead to upward or downward adjustments of past trends.

Besides the source of employment, the diversity of employment affects prospects for community growth. A community dependent on a single plant or a single industry is vulnerable to changes in consumer preference,

unique economic conditions that affect particular industries, and technological obsolescence. A community with a high degree of employment
diversity is likely to show more stable real estate values over the business
cycle.

Economic base analysis is supplemented by a study of physical, social,
and economic data. Population trends are reviewed to determine the
reason for upward or downward trends and the likelihood of their continuation. At the same time, the analyst studies the probable impact of
economic activity on property values. The answer to the following questions on these points helps to reveal probable trends in property values.

1. Does the community have a diversified employment base including
    manufacturing, service, and government activities?
2. Has employment shown a stable pattern of past growth?
3. Do local businesses and manufacturing firms serve local, national, or
    international markets? What are the prospects for growth in these
    market areas?
4. Is the labor supply adequate for local needs in terms of skills, wage
    levels, and education?
5. Are state and local governments adaptable to expansion of govern-
    ment services, zoning, and land planning?
6. Is the community served with amenities such as quality schools,
    churches, adequate utility systems, recreation, and suitable housing?
7. Is a community dependent on economic activities that are likely to
    increase or decrease in the future?

Patterns of Urban Growth

Considerable importance is attached to the *manner* in which urban
centers grow. Economic base analysis may predict the degree of growth
or decline but it will not indicate the direction of growth nor identify
changes in specific real estate markets. In this respect, the record shows
that urban centers tend to grow in four ways, and that the way any given
community grows is related to its geography and to its historical patterns
of growth.

First, urban areas, according to some observers, grow in clusters of
multiple nuclei. Such groupings refer to property uses that concentrate
around a dominant land use. In this view, the real estate market tends to
be stratified into clusters of special-purpose properties. For example, consider the hotel and motel districts of Phoenix, Arizona, Palm Springs,
California, or Miami Beach, Florida, that form a separate nuclei of
property uses. To cite another example, medical services tend to attract
land uses centering around hospital and medical centers. The resulting

complex produces a land area dominated by pharmacies, medical supply houses, medical and dental clinics, housing for hospital personnel, nursing homes, and other retailing and service establishments catering to medical and dental services and their patrons. Industrial parks represent another land use illustrating the multiple nuclei concept. Retail uses grouped around a shopping center and its surrounding residential districts, serve as further examples of the multiple nuclei concept.

Predicting the real estate market, then, would require identification of land uses that cluster around the dominant use. Such a clustering results from (1) the mutual attraction of special-property uses, and (2) the tendency to separate incompatible property uses. Certainly the prediction of demand and supply of certain types of real estate must recognize the tendency of land uses to group in mutually exclusive areas.

Second, urban growth has been explained in terms of *concentric circles* originating from a central point—usually the downtown. Observers have explained past growth patterns in the older cities in these terms. In these cases casual observation discloses that cities grew away from the downtown area, which historically was the center for government, shopping, and office use. Less intensive uses surround the main street, such as second-hand stores, wholesale establishments, budget stores, pawn shops, and other less intensive land uses that require a location near the major traffic generators of the downtown.

Multiple-family and single-family dwellings formed in concentric circles away from the city center. Industry concentrated along routes of transportation, especially near railroads. Thus, in this view, as the city grew it expanded in concentric circles from a central point as modified by topography.

Third, city growth has been observed to radiate outward along lines of transportation starting from an initial point. Growth would be predicted along main lines of transportation from the city center to more outlying districts. Here, satellite neighborhood centers were established, forming a star-like pattern from the city center. In this explanation, the *central axial theory*, geographic limitations and the availability of transportation were claimed as the leading determinants of urban growth patterns. Even today the importance of transportation and access partly explains the location of residential property, shopping centers, industry, and other main land use types.

Yet another way of predicting land use centers on growth that proceeds in *wedge-shaped sectors*. As explained by Homer Hoyt, a land use economist, the personal incomes of residents dictate the formation of residential districts; high income groups tend to move outward from the city center in wedge-shaped sectors. According to this view, residential districts of middle- and lower-income groups tend to follow neighborhoods occupied by high-income groups. The direction of city growth depends on the location of high-income residential districts.

Probably no single theory helps explain local growth for each community. It is also equally true that some aspects of each of these theories is present in virtually every community. The main problem is to identify those factors that affect the direction of growth. The maximum land value enhancement and stable property values occur for land lying in the direction of growth.

THE NATURE OF REAL ESTATE MARKETS

Land use and its value are not static. Market values change. Property uses undergo a continual transition. As land utility and market conditions change, land may revert to a lower use or, typically, it assumes a higher value because of a change in its potential use-capacity. Under our system, land tends to be rationed among competing uses according to the highest economic return. Consequently, expanding areas reveal shifts in land use (e.g., from agricultural to single-family subdivisions). Rural land will be devoted to commercial or industrial use if returns on alternative employments create higher values and higher rents.

Figure 2–1 illustrates the general tendency of land to assume higher land values as the productivity of land increases according to its highest use. The least productive uses—desert, swamplands, mountain areas—have the lowest land value, since the economic returns from such land is at the lowest level.

As soil and climate characteristics improve, certain lands will be used for timber or grazing since they represent the highest economic return. Dry land farming use assumes a higher value by reason of greater land productive capacity. Figure 2–1 suggests that as the population expands, agricultural land, which is often intensively developed for irrigated row crops near urban centers, succeeds to low density, single family dwelling use. As land becomes scarcer or in greater demand, space is allocated to multiple family and commercial use. Generally speaking, the centrally located industrial, retail, and office space assumes the highest value in the larger urban centers.

Though the ranking of land use and values of Figure 2–1 is highly generalized (and there is much overlapping), the figure demonstrates the idea that land value and its use are not fixed permanently. Further, there are many exceptions (oil deposits under deserts, for example). Yet the point is clear: land use responds to changes in public laws, public construction of highways and transportation, and changing population characteristics. Land use reacts to technological change that accelerates even more the movement of land use patterns. In short, there is a

FIGURE 2–1

Land Ranked by Type of Use Showing Relative Land Values

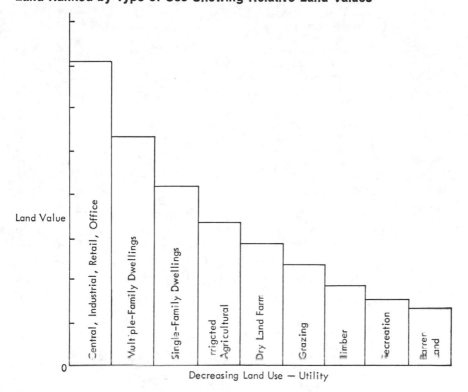

tendency for land to be devoted to its most urgent use—or the highest and best use.

The Highest and Best Use

The central idea is that land tends to be put to the use earning the highest economic return permitted by land use regulations. Technically, the highest and best use is the legal use that produces the highest net income to the land. The concept is qualified by referring only to the use that may be reasonably expected at the time of appraisal. The main point remains that the highest market value of the land results from the use which earns the maximum net income to land.

To illustrate this point, let us take as an example a 7.2-acre site suitable for an office building or a small shopping center. The projected net income from the proposed office building reveals a potential net income, before depreciation, of $458,850.

```
Gross income
  95,000 square feet rentable,
    @ $7.50 per square foot.........................  $712,500
    Less 5 percent vacancy...........................  −35,625
    Effective gross income...........................  $676,875
  Less expenses
    Real estate taxes.....................  $61,750
    Insurance.............................   4,750
    Cleaning..............................  47,500
    Heating and air conditioning..........  42,750
    Water and sewer.......................   2,850
    Electric..............................   9,500
    Snow removal and landscaping........   3,800
    Repairs and maintenance..............   9,500
    Payroll...............................   8,550
    Management........................  27,075
                                                      −$218,025
  Net income......................................  $458,850
```

Starting with the net income from land and building, the land value may be estimated by capitalizing that portion of net income allocated to land. The proposed building has 107,000 square feet and an estimated construction cost of $3,210,000. Allocating the income to the building on the basis of a 12 percent overall capitalization rate produces a capitalized land value of $736,500.

```
Net income...........................  $  458,850
Less income to building
  $3,210,000 × .12 (107,000
  square feet × $30.00)................  −385,200
Income to land.......................  $   73,650
Land value, 7.2 Acres $73,650/.10.......  $  736,500
Add building value....................   3,210,000
Estimated market value...............  $3,946,500
```

The alternative is to develop the 7.2 acre site as a shopping center with a $2-million building. Income to the land is estimated at $65,000, which if capitalized at 10 percent, produced a land value of $650,000.

```
Net income...........................  $  305,000
Less income to building
  $2,000,000 × .12......................  −240,000
Income to land.......................  $   65,000
Land value $65,000/.10..................  $  650,000
Add building value....................   2,000,000
Estimated market value...............  $2,650,000
```

The office building use will earn *a higher income from the land*. Capitalizing this income gave a higher value than the alternative of developing the property for a neighborhood shopping center. Investors considering alternatives tend to ration land according to its highest and best use. In practice, investors in rental property are guided by the use that earns the highest economic return to the land.

Real Estate Markets Imperfect

If land is allocated according to that use earning the highest return or developing the highest land value, land would be allocated efficiently among the most urgently needed uses. The fact that land is not rationed in this way attests to the imperfections of the real estate market. For under a more perfect market, land uses would assume their optimum use. To help explain the irrational land use pattern, compare the characteristics of the actual real estate market to criteria assumed for perfectly competitive markets. Recognizing the imperfections *assists* in predicting —in a local market—the most probable land use.

Many Buyers and Sellers. A competitive market includes a sufficient number of buyers and sellers so that the decision of a single buyer or seller to enter (or leave) the market has no effect on the price. Certainly this is true of the market for wheat, eggs, or generally for stocks offered on the New York Stock Exchange. Superficially, real estate markets would appear to conform to this criteria.

But if this criteria is applied to real estate, say single-family dwellings, this first competitive condition is generally absent. For instance, consider a realistic situation. Each house has a unique location. The sale of a single residence in a subdivision tends to influence the asking price of adjoining owners who later place their property on the market. In this sense, the decision of the seller to accept an offer tends to affect the asking price of surrounding properties. Partly this is because houses are not perfect substitutes, that is, a house on a given street is not a perfect substitute for a similar house two miles away.

Likewise, buyers of single-family dwellings are not sufficiently numerous in a *given* neighborhood so that they can operate without influencing surrounding prices. In the residential market, the many buyer and seller criteria does not apply to prices of houses in selected neighborhoods.

Reasonable Knowledge. For supply and demand to adjust under competitive conditions, buyers and sellers must have a knowledge of market prices. In the real world the buyer and seller have highly imperfect knowledge. The imperfection lies both in knowledge of the product and of the going market price.

The seller of a single-family dwelling generally has superior knowledge of his property, especially its advantages and limitations, relative to the buyer's knowledge. In this respect, the seller has a bargaining advantage. On the other hand, the buyer, in his search for the best buy, acquires a better knowledge of going real estate prices than the seller has. The seller of a dwelling enters the market over intervals of several years and normally has only a vague acquaintance with current prices. Because of these unequal advantages in knowledge, real estate prices and land use do not assume their perfectly competitive ideal.

Standardized Products. Buyers and sellers are able to compare values if the product is standardized, but the nature of real estate violates this rule. Properties have different types of construction, workmanship, and material, and they are in different states of repair. To the layman it is most difficult to evaluate a $60,000 offer of a three-bedroom house with a family room, two fireplaces, air conditioning, and a two-car enclosed garage with a $55,000 offer of a three-bedroom house with basement, one fireplace, and a one car carport. A different location, in itself, complicates the price comparison. Thus, the inherent differences in the real estate product leads to noncompetitive market adjustments both in land use and in prices.

Freedom of Entry. Theoretically, as prices increase, producers enter the market and increase the supply. Likewise, an increase in supply with subsequent lower prices encourages more sales so that supply and demand vary according to market needs. But real estate seldom conforms to this pattern. In single-family dwellings, a shortage of housing will not be met by more than a 2 or 3 percent annual increase in supply. The lead time for new construction causes time lags that prevent quick adjustment of supply to market conditions.

Buyers also operate under restrictive conditions. The purchase of real estate is highly dependent upon the availability of credit and its cost. An urgent demand of housing will go unsatisfied if buyers do not have the opportunity to finance a purchase within their means. A change in the supply and demand of loanable funds, government policy, and even international conditions may quickly frustrate buyers. It is fairly clear that this last item, credit availability, together with other market imperfections, prevents the smooth adjustment of supply and demand. As a consequence, real estate markets are characterized by a high degree of imperfection. A more detailed discussion of the real estate submarkets supports this view.

Real Estate Submarkets

In the final analysis, there is no single real estate market; there is no separate housing market. Instead, the real estate market is a highly stratified series of submarkets. The division of the supply and demand for real estate into many subclassifications partly accounts for price distortion, fluctuation in real estate values and inefficient land allocation. Market values of real estate tend to be influenced by the operation of these separate submarkets. For instance, the real estate market may be stratified by:

1. The residential market.
    a. Occupancy.
    b. Rental.

2. The commercial market.
   a. Retail.
   b. Office.
   c. Industrial.

Within each of these subdivisions, real estate can be further subdivided into innumerable submarkets, each having its own supply and demand characteristics.

For example, the housing market may be stratified according to the diagram in Figure 2–2. In this case, houses constructed for owner-occupancy contrast with housing produced for the rental market. The *occupancy* market is divided into three broad categories: single-family residence, mobile homes, and condominiums and cooperatives. Each of

FIGURE 2–2

Stratification of the Housing Market

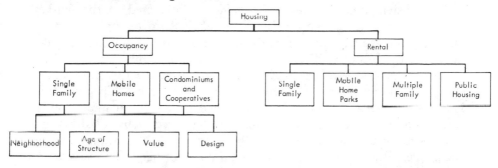

these classifications could be further subdivided. Single-family dwellings, for example, may be differentiated by neighborhood, by the age of the structure, by value, and by architectural design. Each of these subgroups has its own potential buyers and a limited number of suppliers.

By the same token, mobile homes, condominiums, and cooperatives may be similarly grouped in submarkets. For example, there are luxury condominiums in central city areas, condominiums in resort areas, or owner-occupancy in condominiums for the retirees, low-income groups, and the like. Within this group the market could be further stratified by location, type of construction, age, and condition.

The *rental* market is equally complex. Rental housing includes single-family dwellings that have reverted from owner-occupancy to rental status. Mobile homes are rented; further, rental occupancy includes multiple-family structures of many groupings: walk-up apartments, elevator high rise, garden court apartments, among others. Public housing occupies a small proportion of the rental occupancy market.

Because of these stratifications, a given dwelling or property serves as an inadequate substitute for like property that falls in a different sub-group. A 3,000-square-foot house 5 years old in the north end of the city may not be an equal substitute for the same type of house in the south end. The overlapping of these submarkets creates many interactions and distortions in the free movement of prices in response to supply and demand.

THE RESIDENTIAL MARKET

The residential market includes owner occupancy and rental occupancy. Market forces are different enough in both cases to deserve separate treatment. First we will discuss the characteristics of the owner-occupancy market and supply and demand forces that affect the ownership market.

Observers have described the owner-occupancy market as a disorganized market. (1) There is no *central market place* to exchange price information. On the contrary the owner-occupancy market is highly localized, highly differentiated, and relatively inefficient compared to the market for personal goods. (2) Real estate is *immobile*. An oversupply of single-family dwellings in Sarasota, Florida, does not satisfy a housing shortage in St. Louis, Missouri. The immobility creates a highly geographically structured market. (3) Real estate is *durable*. Consequently, an oversupply of new houses cannot be withdrawn from the market. They must be held by the owner, the investor, or the lender until the market absorbs vacant property. In this respect real estate differs substantially from other types of production in which the supply may be withdrawn from the market as demand decreases. (4) Real estate is *highly diverse*. Properties are not easily substitutable. In fact, the diversity contributes to price variation and confusion among buyers and sellers who have little technical knowledge of construction, financing, or the legal aspects of real estate.

The Residential Occupancy Market

In this discussion no analysis of the demand for second homes, the vacation home, or resort property is offered. Instead, the material relates only to occupancy by owners of their main residence. With this qualification, the market for residential real estate depends on determinants of demand and supply.

The Demand for Owner Occupancy. It will be recalled that the local demand for dwellings is closely related to changes in population and the rate of household formation. To be sure, the number of households is usually associated with population growth, yet it is possible that the population will decline while the number of households increases. This relationship occurs because average household size is decreasing. More single households, children departing from the family at an earlier age, a larger number of elderly setting up separate households, early marriages, and an increase in longevity add to the trend towards a smaller average household. As the number of households varies, the demand for owner occupancy generally moves in the same direction.

Income and employment determines the ability of households to purchase housing. As employment varies, so does the demand for housing. The level of family income determines the type of dwelling demanded, its location, and the price level demanded.

Given the rate of household formation, income, and employment, the financing of residential property determines the effective demand. Financing includes the amount of liquid assets held by potential homebuyers. The liquid asset position largely controls the type of loan available to most households—the down payment, the length of mortgage, and the interest rate. Credit availability has a direct bearing on the ability of buyers to bid for the available housing stock.

Consumer housing preferences determine the type of space demanded. Buyers may turn to new subdivisions and avoid older districts with obsolete architectural styles, for example. Changes in housing preferences must be added to other factors affecting housing demand. To put it differently, a dwelling that does not meet taste preferences of the buying public in the market for a specific location and price bracket will suffer a decline in value.

The Supply of Owner Occupancy Dwellings. The supply of the residential housing stock is a product of complex forces, some political and some economic. The components of supply deal with the additions and subtractions from the housing inventory. Those houses added to the existing housing stock may come about by conversion of existing structures to dwelling use. Though statistically unimportant in relation to new construction, conversions of nondwelling structures to dwelling use provides a quick means of adjusting to changing market conditions. Besides new housing construction, which accounts for the largest addition to the housing inventory, local housing may be increased by transfer of units from outside the community and by moving mobile homes.

Offsetting these additions are losses from demolition. Demolition occurs by condemnation of private houses for public purposes such as limited access highways, urban renewal and private demolition for new nonresidential construction. Houses are also lost through public condemnation for health or safety reasons. New construction is the most volatile of factors affecting supply. Construction may be stimulated by a general increase in housing prices which increases profit opportunities for builders and investors.

The Rental Housing Market

The housing market is characterized by a high rate of turnover. Nationally, unfurnished elevator apartments have experienced an average annual tenant turnover rate of 25.3 percent. The annual tenant survey by the Institute of Real Estate Management indicates that one-half of all tenants of furnished elevator apartments change their residence each year. Tenants, as a group, are well-informed of the rental housing market. Accordingly, the demand for rental space is subject to fairly rapid change. The supply, in contrast, changes slowly with new construction and demolition. The characteristics of tenants determines the nature of the rental housing market.

Tenant Characteristics. The rental market serves a special segment of the population that prefer to be renters. In some cases rental housing is virtually the sole means of satisfying housing needs. The majority of apartment dwellers fall in one of the following groups:

1. *Newly married couples.* These households require minimum housing space. Their incomes and liquid asset position typically does not justify immediate home ownership. Moreover, these groups tend to be young and highly mobile, with developing careers that place them in the rental market, not the occupancy market.
2. *Single households.* This group includes widows and widowers, divorcees, and the young pursuing the early years of a career. They show strong preferences for rental housing.
3. *Mobile workers.* Certain occupations necessitate frequent moving. Entertainers, members of the heavy construction industry, and even high-level executives fall in this group. Their assignments are temporary, and their preferences favor the convenience of rental occupancy. Their tastes do not run to the chores of maintaining owner-occupancy housing.
4. *Seasonal workers.* Certain types of employment are too uncertain for long-term mortgage credit. Musicians, entertainers, salesmen, agricultural workers, and construction workers prefer rental occupancy over the responsibilities of home ownership. Households within this group require the flexibility of short-term rental occupancy.
5. *Luxury apartments.* Professional workers, highly-paid executives, and the well-to-do single household gravitate to the urban centers offering the maximum convenience of entertainment, restaurants, cultural activities, and closeness to employment. Their demands lean toward urban rental units rather than owner-occupancy.
6. *Low-income groups.* To a large proportion of the population, home ownership is not an available alternative. Welfare recipients and low-income workers rent space on a permanent basis.

The rental market, serving the specialized needs of these groups tend to be volatile and subject to fairly rapid changes in local economic conditions. To many of these groups, the rental market for housing is related to the comparative cost of home ownership.

Rental and Ownership Costs. The preference for renting turns partly on the cost of renting versus the cost of home ownership. In this regard, some renters erroneously compare rental payments with mortgage payments. In comparing rental occupancy with ownership, a distinction must be made between (1) monthly out-of-pocket expenses of home ownership, and (2) the economic costs of ownership. The former is of interest to the mortgage lender who must be certain that family income is sufficient to cover the mortgage payments. The latter should be considered by the prospective purchaser, assuming personal assets and monthly income meet mortgage credit standards.

The *monthly out-of-pocket expenses* include five items:

1. monthly mortgage payments;
2. property taxes per month;
3. average monthly utility expenses (electricity, heating fuel, water, cable TV);
4. home owner's insurance policy converted to the cost per month;
5. average monthly maintenance expense (allow 1 percent per year on the building cost for a new house).

The list is based on certain annual expenses converted to a monthly charge—primarily, annual property taxes and insurance. Besides the direct monthly charge of mortgage payments and utilities, some allowance must be made for normal upkeep and repair (e.g., interior and exterior painting and carpet replacement).

Calculating the economic cost of home ownership is more complex. To start, certain assumptions must be made before the true economic cost can be estimated. Since certain costs must be allocated over the period of ownership, some assumption must be made with respect to the expected period of ownership. Given an anticipated ownership of, say, five years, the next necessary assumption calls for an estimated selling price at the end of the ownership. Suppose a house originally costs $50,000. At the end of five years, assume that the expected sale price will be $60,000. Though this figure is not much more than a guess, historically, housing has undergone recent price inflation. Probably this trend will continue.

With these two assumptions, calculation of the economic costs of ownership requires:

1. Amortizing closing costs over the expected period of ownership and converting these costs to a monthly basis. For a 5-year ownership, monthly closing costs would be 1/60th of total closing costs.
2. Adding interest foregone on the down payment. A $9,000 down payment on a house might be invested in a certificate of deposit paying 7.5 percent interest. This interest cost must be converted to a monthly basis.

3. Converting annual property taxes to a monthly expense.
4. Calculating the monthly insurance cost.
5. Adding monthly mortgage payments.
6. Adding an allowance for annual maintenance and repair expenses per month.
7. Allocating appreciation (or depreciation) expected over the term of ownership on a monthly basis. If property is estimated to appreciate $12,000 over 60 months, the monthly appreciation would be $200.
8. Mortgage interest and property taxes are deductible against personal income taxes. If personal income taxes are paid at the rate of 36 percent of taxable income, take 36 percent of annual property taxes and mortgage interest as the annual saving arising from home ownership.

While the projections called for in calculating the economic costs of home ownership are highly subjective, items on this list represent the true costs of home ownership. Actual ownership costs are unknown until the property is sold and the true costs are known. In short, the rental housing market is closely interrelated with projections of home ownership costs. General business conditions, building cost trends, anticipated price increases or decreases, and the availability of credit all affect the market for rental housing.

COMMERCIAL REAL ESTATE MARKETS

Commercial space tends to be dominated by office and retail properties. Office space tends to be highly specialized by location, construction, and ownership. Most retail locations fall in one of three locations: shopping centers, the downtown areas, and highway or arterial sites. The market for commercial space in these main categories is a product of forces largely unrelated to the housing market. Before treating characteristics of the market for commercial space, however, we will discuss the adjustment in the market to changing demands.

Assume an increase in demand for rental space. (1) As vacancies decline, tenants compete for increasingly scarcer space, causing owners to increase rents. The higher rent level induces investors and builders to construct additional space. (2) The supply of rentable space increases if investors anticipate that rents have increased to the point that they will earn a profit on new buildings. Part of this equation depends on the cost of mortgage capital and the required equity.

Given these circumstances favoring new investment, the supply of rentable space increases, let us say, for offices or retail stores. (3) As new construction adds to the local supply of rentable space, vacancies increase. With increasing vacancies, rents fall, causing foreclosures and losses. (4) If at the same time the increased construction activity results in higher land values, labor, and material costs, builders and investors withdraw from the market. Normally, the least desirable buildings will be abandoned, encouraging demolition and redevelopment to other purposes.

In this way the market is continually undergoing transition. New construction progresses to the point where vacancies center in the least desirable properties, making their continued use unprofitable. The market tends to equate supply and demand such that property tends to revert to the most profitable use; over time the unprofitable uses are discontinued.

Market Characteristics

There is a marked tendency to allocate too much land for office, retail, and other commercial uses, with the result that there is often an oversupply of commercial land. Yet if attention is directed to the quality of space demanded for nonresidential purposes, supply may be viewed as inadequate for the current demand. A review of demand and supply factors tends to verify this judgment.

Office Buildings. The supply of office space includes the single-tenant building. These buildings are usually subsidized to improve the corporate image. They are viewed as good company advertising. More important, are the multiple-tenant buildings which include the high rise elevator or low rise, office park buildings. Older downtown office buildings follow the alphabet style—they were built in the form of alphabetic letters. The newer office towers fill the current demand for multiple-tenant buildings. Add to this special use buildings such as medical and dental clinics, and within these categories you would judge the supply of office space according to the following commonly accepted standards:

1. Office sites must have space for a parking garage.
2. Office buildings should be constructed in the path of development.
3. Office buildings should be built in areas of compatible land use.
4. The office site must be convenient to public transportation and should be built with respect to the future traffic plan.
5. Certain office sites, depending on the tenant market, should be built within walking distance of public buildings.

While the supply of office space may meet these criteria, existing use may not satisfy the current demand. Deficiencies observed in existing buildings may warrant additional new construction. For example, the appearance of surroundings, public transportation, and the location with respect to other buildings have a bearing on office building efficiency. The exterior appearance, attractiveness of the lobby, elevator service, size of the corridors, in addition to building services, management competence, and the type of existing tenants, largely control the quality of office space.

Retail Space. Since the market for commercial space depends on a derived demand, investors in shopping centers forecast prospects for net rental income for shopping center operation. Such an analysis includes factors that bear on total purchasing power within the shopping center trade area. The trade area may be affected by numerous factors, including the highway traffic pattern, the population distribution, and natural geographic boundaries. The estimation of the primary trade area, since it accounts for generally 85 percent of the sales volume, is made with considerable care. The remaining 15 percent of the sales volume comes from widely scattered areas.

Given the trade area, the next step is to estimate family or per capita income. These data are taken from census sources, planning surveys, retail sales tax collections, state employment records, and other sources. An estimate of the total purchasing power of the trade area allows the investor to determine the proportion of total retail expenditures in the trade area that may accrue to the proposed shopping center. With these estimates, the projected rental income is capitalized to test the feasibility of the project in the light of anticipated land and construction costs. In this sense, the demand for commercial rental space is based on secondary sources: namely, population, buying habits, and purchasing power. It should be noted further that there are certain economic advantages in relocating out of the downtown area. Because of federal income tax depreciation allowances, owner-occupants have an incentive to invest in lower-price land, thereby qualifying for a proportionately larger income tax depreciation deduction.

For instance, a greater income tax advantage accrues to a $1,000,000 land-and-building investment with a $900,000 building and a $100,000 site in contrast to a $100,000 building and a $900,000 site. In addition, higher property taxes for more central locations historically have operated against downtown locations. Poor public parking and the relocation of customers probably are leading reasons for preferring suburban sites.

Shopping Centers. Though subject to much variation, shopping centers group together on the basis of size. For instance, a *regional shopping center* generally requires a 35-acre to 100-acre site. Such a center will require at least one leading department store of about 100,000 square feet. Another 15 to 100 retail establishments will be added. Regional centers are supported by a population of some 200,000. The *community center* occupies a site of 15 acres to 40 acres. A community center will have a gross leasable area of about 100,000 to 400,000 square feet. Approximately 100,000 people or more are served by a community center. The *neighborhood center*, beginning with a minimum of about 5 acres to 20 acres or so, has up to 10 or 15 stores selling primarily convenience goods. The retail space totals around 50,000 to 100,000 square feet. Depending on the size of the center, a population up to 35,000 is required.

The success of a shopping center partly depends on proper tenant selection. Among the list of suitable tenants are the so-called key tenants, because they attract retail trade that benefits other shopping center tenants. Without the leading attraction of key tenants, the shopping center has little prospect for success. The record proves that each type of center has a different mix of key tenants:

Type of Center	Key Tenants
Regional.................	Department stores
Community..............	Junior department stores, variety stores
Neighborhood...........	Supermarket stores, drug stores

With the selected key tenants, other tenants that have a mutual attraction for each other complete the shopping center complex.

INDUSTRIAL REAL ESTATE

Industrial real estate occupants have many locational options. Certain industries select locations near the downtown fringe near railroads and low-income housing. Old style, multiple-story industrial buildings are found in this district. The central space has utility for industries that must locate near low priced labor in congested areas or that must be near downtown customers.

Urban renewal sites and the industrial park provide attractive open space for industrial use. Industrial parks, in particular, cater to assembly, storage, and distribution industries, and industries that employ skilled and professional labor. They prefer industrial parks because of their services, attractive surroundings, and ideal location.

Industrial acreage represents a supply of real estate for industries that have resources to develop their own utility systems. Other industries require large tracts. They prefer limited access locations with proximity to suburban labor—or they prefer low-priced land.

Generally speaking, industrial land demonstrates a relatively low rate of absorption. Characteristics of the demand for industrial space suggest reasons for this. First, most communities will require industrial space for at least three types of industry: printing, construction, and food processing and its distribution. These industries tend to be market-oriented. They must locate near customers. Transportation costs and the need to maintain day-to-day contact with customers limits the space suitable for these industries. To the extent that improvement in transportation gives convenient access to customers from more distant points, these industries have a wider choice of sites.

Second, certain industries are independent of customer location, requiring instead a location near raw materials and fuel. Firms processing raw materials, the extractive industries, furniture manufacturers, and others using basic raw materials of large bulk generally prefer locations near the source of supply in order to minimize transportation costs.

Third, add to this group industries that characteristically favor locations near a preferred labor supply; e.g., the Southern textile mills that locate in outlying areas near low-cost labor. The hardware industry of New Britain, Connecticut, benefits from that area's pool of skilled machinists and other workers experienced in prefabricated metal work. There are many other examples of labor-oriented industries that demand sites for this particular advantage.

There is one other point. Industries purchasing new sites generally buy in advance of need. Anticipating future expansion, an industry requiring 5 acres today may buy 20 acres, allowing 15 acres for future expansion. After adding space for parking, offstreet loading, landscaping, and future expansion, an industry may require 10 acres for every 1 acre of floor area. Given one-story construction, industries may observe a stated land-to-building ratio as a matter of policy. Moreover, building setback and side-yard requirements, together with room for off-street parking, truck maneuvering, and landscaping usually require a minimum of four square feet of land for every square foot of building area. Table 2–1

TABLE 2–1

Acreage Requirements according to Size of Structure and the Land-to-Building Ratio

Square Feet of Building	Acres Required for Selected Land-to-Building Ratios (one-story construction)									
	1 to 1	*2 to 1*	*3 to 1*	*4 to 1*	*5 to 1*	*6 to 1*	*7 to 1*	*8 to 1*	*9 to 1*	*10 to 1*
5,000......	.23	.34	.46	.57	.69	.80	.92	1.03	1.15	1.26
10,000......	.46	.69	.92	1.15	1.38	1.61	1.84	2.07	2.29	2.52
20,000......	.92	1.38	1.84	2.29	2.75	3.21	3.67	4.13	4.59	5.05
30,000......	1.38	2.07	2.75	3.44	4.13	4.82	5.51	6.20	6.89	7.57
40,000......	1.84	2.75	3.67	4.59	5.51	6.43	7.35	8.26	9.18	10.10
50,000......	2.29	3.44	4.59	5.74	6.89	8.03	9.18	10.33	11.48	12.63
60,000......	2.75	4.13	5.51	6.89	8.26	9.64	11.02	12.40	13.77	15.15
70,000......	3.21	4.82	6.43	8.03	9.64	11.25	12.85	14.46	16.07	17.68
80,000......	3.67	5.51	7.35	9.18	11.02	12.85	14.69	16.53	18.36	20.20
90,000......	4.13	6.20	8.26	10.33	12.40	14.46	16.53	18.59	20.66	22.73
100,000......	4.59	6.89	9.18	11.48	13.77	16.07	18.36	20.66	22.96	25.25
200,000......	9.18	13.77	18.36	22.96	27.55	32.14	36.73	41.32	45.91	50.50
300,000......	13.77	20.66	27.55	34.43	41.32	48.21	55.10	61.98	68.87	75.76
400,000......	18.36	27.55	36.73	45.91	55.10	64.28	73.46	82.64	91.83	101.01
500,000......	22.96	34.43	45.91	57.39	68.87	80.35	91.83	103.30	114.78	126.26
1,000,000......	45.91	68.87	91.83	114.78	137.74	160.70	183.65	206.61	229.57	252.52

shows the land area required for a given floor area under different build-ing ratios. In illustration, an industry proposing to construct a 40,000 square foot building would require a 5.51-acre site, assuming a 5-to-1 land-to-building ratio. The additional land would provide for off-street parking, truck loading, landscaping, and a limited area for later expansion.

REAL ESTATE MARKET INDICATORS

To a large degree, real estate activity is closely associated with general economic conditions. If a community shows continued growth, optimism generally leads to new real estate development. And as employment declines or population decreases, real estate generally follows the same trend. For real estate, certain economic indicators are helpful in predict-ing real estate trends. Certain of these indicators are immediately re-sponsive to market conditions and more useful than published sources, which generally lag behind current trends. Some of these indicators may be obtained from state and local offices, while others are available from public sources.

Local Information

The local county office responsible for recording deeds and mortgages is probably the best current source to measure the direction of change. In the larger metropolitan areas, deed and mortgage recordings, some-times by property type and financing details, are available from local subscription sources.

If these records are compared to the same month of the preceding year, or are collected on a cumulative basis each month for reference to preceding months, they provide an immediate indication of real estate sales and transfers. Mortgage recordings move in a similar direction. If data are available on conventional and FHA and VA financing, trends in mortgage credit are readily known.

A related series are building permits, listed by number, type of property, and value. While the value stated on building permits is suspect, their number by type of property are strong indicators of real estate activity. Building permit data have certain limitations, however. For example, they cover public construction, which, in terms of dollars, falsely repre-sents activity in the private market.

Further, building permits in smaller communities may show incorrect trends because of the influence of a single project on the total. The smaller the total volume, the more building permit data is affected by a large project. It is also helpful to compare local records with a published series showing state and national trends.

Vacancy surveys are invaluable. Some professional trade organizations, planning agencies, and FHA surveys are also invaluable sources to show changing market conditions. On this point, it is important to note the type of vacancies occurring—in older units, in new construction, and in old or new neighborhoods—and the relative length of vacancy.

If information is desired on apartment houses, vacancies should be classified by the type of vacancy available. The inventory of new houses, vacant and for sale, if it is locally available, provides a measure of how housing supply compares to the demand for housing. Some real estate experts are guided by changes in the volume of classified newspaper advertisements. Another qualitative judgment relates to changes in the terms of sale, mortgage financing, interest rates, and down payment requirements.

Other local series indicative of real estate market trends include the number of

1. Mortgage foreclosures.
2. Water meters installed.
3. New telephone installations.
4. Electric meters installed.

Published Sources

Annual surveys conducted by trade associations report cumulative data showing main trends in real estate activity. The more widely circulated reports are issued by:

Institute of Real Estate Management	Apartments, cooperatives, and condominiums
Building Owners and Managers Association	Office buildings
Urban Land Institute	Shopping centers
Mobile Home Manufacturers Association	Mobile homes
Apartment Owners and Managers Association	Apartments

The Superintendent of Documents, Washington, D.C., issues federally-sponsored reports important to real estate analysis. A representative list includes:

Construction Review	Department of Commerce
Federal Reserve Bulletin	Federal Reserve System
Survey of Current Business	Department of Commerce
Economic Indicators	
Federal Home Loan Bank Board Journal	Federal Home Loan Bank Board

There are many more national publications specializing in real estate data. The series above are useful in measuring construction trends and real estate credit information that bear on real estate development. Several of these series report data by state, county, metropolitan area. They are useful in comparing regional and national trends with local trends.

QUESTIONS FOR REVIEW

_____ 1. In estimating the demand for residential property, which of the following items is most significant?
   a. The total population.
   b. The number of households.
   c. The number of single individuals under 30 years of age.
   d. The number of retirees over 65.

_____ 2. Which of the following statements is correct?
   a. The market for commercial and industrial real estate is related to the property tax level.
   b. The demand for shopping center space is independent of population.
   c. The population partly controls the demand for commercial and industrial real estate.
   d. The study of the real estate market must be undertaken independently of a study of population forces.

_____ 3. A favorable real estate market is dependent on
   a. the flow of savings into financial institutions that grant real estate mortgages.
   b. the willingness of consumers to postpone the purchase of consumer goods.
   c. employment in basic or primary industries.
   d. a relatively high interest rate that attracts a high level of savings.

_____ 4. Economic base studies
   a. identify employment sources by industry, and markets served by local firms.
   b. analyze the population age distribution.
   c. identify the market served by local firms and determine the educational level of the local population.
   d. list the number of persons employed by industry and their consumer preferences.

_____ 5. Which of the following is relevant to estimating the probable impact of economic activity on property values?
   a. A diversified employment base.
   b. A stable pattern of past growth in employment.

    c. An adequate labor supply in terms of skills, wage levels, and education.
    d. All of the above.

_____ 6. An explanation of urban growth that refers to property uses concentrating around a dominant land use describes the
    a. multiple nuclei theory.
    b. central axial theory.
    c. concentric circle theory of urban growth.
    d. wedge-sector theory.

_____ 7. Which of the following statements best describes the nature of real estate markets?
    a. Land uses and values in urban centers are fairly static.
    b. Land use and its value are not static.
    c. It is unlikely that property uses undergo transition in urban centers.
    d. A change in the potential use capacity does not lead to a change in property value.

_____ 8. Under our system of land ownership,
    a. zoning prevents a shift in land use.
    b. higher land values and higher rents result from a static land use plan.
    c. land tends to be rationed among competing uses according to the highest economic return.
    d. increases in land productivity lead to lower land use.

_____ 9. Land represents a _____ product.
    a. heterogeneous
    b. homogeneous
    c. standardized
    d. noncompeting

_____10. The real estate market tends to be imperfect because
    a. it is primarily a seller's market.
    b. it is primarily a buyer's market.
    c. land is not always rationed efficiently among the most urgently needed uses.
    d. it is so closely related to the mortgage market.

_____11. Which of the following is an indicator of local real estate market conditions?
    a. Deed recordings.
    b. Building permits.
    c. Mortgage recordings.
    d. All of the above.

_____12. The feasibility of a shopping center would depend on
    a. trends in property taxes.
    b. general economic conditions.

c. natural geographical barriers.

d. national business trends.

_____13. Generally speaking, the primary trade area of a shopping center accounts for _____ percent of the sales volume.

a. 33

b. 50

c. 75

d. 85

_____14. The economic cost of home ownership includes

a. an amortization of closing costs.

b. foregone interest on the equity.

c. appreciation or depreciation of the dwelling.

d. all of the above.

_____15. Which of the following would *not* be considered a monthly out-of-pocket expense of home ownership?

a. Monthly payments on the mortgage.

b. Economic depreciation.

c. Property taxes.

d. Property insurance premiums.

_____16. Which of the following is a classification of typical apartment dwellers?

a. Newly married couples.

b. Single households such as widows and widowers.

c. Transient workers.

d. All of the above.

_____17. Experience indicates that the rental housing market is characterized by a

a. rising demand for unfurnished apartments.

b. rising demand for furnished apartments.

c. high rate of tenant turnover.

d. rate of tenant turnover less than 10 percent.

_____18. Over time, the real estate market equates supply and demand so that

a. properties tend to revert to their most profitable use.

b. the least desirable buildings will be the first to be abandoned.

c. rents are stabilized.

d. a and b.

_____19. _____ industries tend to locate near customers.

a. Hardware

b. Furniture

c. Steel processing

d. Food processing

_____20. Without the attraction of _____, shopping centers have little prospect for success.
   a. low rents
   b. high depreciation schedules
   c. key tenants
   d. low land costs

_____21. Shopping centers locate on sites that
   a. are near commercial and retail districts.
   b. maximize annual sales per square foot.
   c. are close to downtown shopping centers.
   d. are outside city political boundaries.

_____22. The demand for commercial or industrial space is said to be a(n) _____ demand.
   a. derived
   b. variable
   c. highly predictable
   d. stable

_____23. Which of the following statements explains the shift in retail space from central to suburban sites?
   a. A shift of population to suburban areas.
   b. Poor public parking facilities in downtown areas.
   c. Tax advantages from proportionately high building values relative to land values.
   d. All of the above.

_____24. Which of the following statements is *incorrect?*
   a. There is a general tendency to allocate too much land for commercial uses.
   b. The quality of downtown property is generally inadequate.
   c. Property values are unaffected by industrial or commercial zoning.
   d. The factors of supply and demand for industrial space are significantly different from the factors of supply and demand for retail space.

_____25. The market for commercial land is a product of forces _____ to the housing market.
   a. internal
   b. parallel
   c. external
   d. none of the above

_____26. The local demand for owner-occupied dwellings is closely associated with
   a. the availability of mortgages.
   b. the number of households.

    c. population in-migration into an area.

    d. all of the above.

_____27. The diversity of real estate means that properties are not easily

    a. sold.

    b. created.

    c. substitutable.

    d. mortgaged.

_____28. The _____ of real estate creates a highly geographically structured housing market in which a shortage of housing in one area will not relieve housing shortages in other areas.

    a. immobility

    b. durability

    c. expensiveness

    d. heterogeneity

_____29. The market for single-family dwellings may be stratified by

    a. neighborhoods.

    b. age of dwellings.

    c. architectural design.

    d. all of the above.

_____30. Which of the following is associated with a perfectly competitive market?

    a. Reasonable knowledge, free egress and ingress, adequate zoning, and low property taxes.

    b. Many buyers and sellers, reasonable knowledge, low interest rates, and free egress and ingress.

    c. A heterogeneous product, free egress and ingress, reasonable knowledge, adequate financial resources.

    d. Many buyers and sellers, reasonable knowledge, a homogeneous product, free egress and ingress.

_____31. Observers have described real estate markets as highly disorganized because

    a. there is no central place to exchange price information.

    b. real estate is widely owned.

    c. land does not depreciate.

    d. of government regulations.

_____32. In estimating monthly out-of-pocket expenses and the economic cost of home ownership, which of the following would be included in both estimates?

    a. Property taxes and mortgage interest.

    b. Property appreciation.

    c. Maintenance and repair expenses.

    d. Amortization of the closing costs.

_____33. The demand for retail space depends on
   a. the local population.
   b. the market area.
   c. the purchasing power in the market area.
   d. all of the above.

_____34. Which of the following statements is correct?
   a. The rental market tends to be more responsive to changes in supply and demand than the occupancy market.
   b. The market for owner-occupied housing conforms to a competitive model.
   c. The demand for industrial acreage and. centrally located industrial land is created by the same industries.
   d. The utility of a shopping center site is unaffected by the quality of access.

_____35. Trends in the local real estate market may be indicated by
   a. graphing changes in the stock market.
   b. noting changes in the consumer price index.
   c. comparing deed recordings to those of preceding periods.
   d. counting the number of retail stores in the area.

_____36. The local real estate market is
   I.   closely associated with general economic conditions.
   II. affected by changes in the interest rate and down payment requirements.
   a. I only.
   b. II only.
   c. Both I and II.
   d. Neither I nor II

_____37. Which of the following statements is correct?
   a. The office of the real estate broker is the central market place for exchange of price information in the real estate market.
   b. Like properties are easily substitutable.
   c. The immobility of real estate contributes to the tendency of builders to oversupply the housing market.
   d. Because real estate is highly diverse, properties are not easily substitutable.

_____38. The stratification of real estate markets
   I.   creates interactions and distortions in the free movement of prices in response to supply and demand.
   II. allows a given property to serve as an adequate substitute for a like property in a different market.
   a. I only.
   b. II only.
   c. Both I and II.
   d. Neither I nor II.

_____39. If the real estate market conformed to the four assumptions of a perfectly competitive market,

  a. the decision of a single buyer to enter the market would only have a small effect on the price.
  b. land would be allocated to its highest and best use.
  c. the resulting land use pattern would be irrational.
  d. buyers would be required to operate under more restrictive conditions.

_____40. The economic cost of home ownership

  a. includes a deduction of the down payment divided by the period of the ownership in months.
  b. is unknown until the property is sold.
  c. does not include mortgage interest and property taxes because they are deductible for personal net income tax purposes.
  d. includes interest foregone on closing costs.

ANSWER KEY

1. (b)	11. (d)	21. (b)	31. (a)
2. (c)	12. (b)	22. (a)	32. (d)
3. (a)	13. (d)	23. (d)	33. (d)
4. (a)	14. (d)	24. (c)	34. (a)
5. (d)	15. (b)	25. (c)	35. (c)
6. (a)	16. (d)	26. (d)	36. (c)
7. (b)	17. (c)	27 (c)	37. (d)
8. (c)	18. (d)	28. (a)	38. (a)
9. (a)	19. (d)	29. (d)	39. (b)
10. (c)	20. (c)	30. (d)	40. (b)

SUGGESTED ADDITIONAL READING

David, Philip. *Urban Land Development,* part III. Homewood, Ill.: Richard D. Irwin, Inc., 1970.

Land Development Manual. Washington, D.C.: National Association of Home Builders, 1969, chaps. 16 and 17.

Maisel, Sherman J., and Roulac, Stephen E. *Real Estate Investment and Finance.* New York: McGraw-Hill, 1976, chaps. 23 and 24.

McMahan, John. *Property Development.* New York: McGraw-Hill, 1976, chaps. 6, 7, and 8.

Roulac, Stephen E. *Case Studies in Property Development.* Menlo Park, Calif.: Stephen E. Roulac, 1973, chap. 31.

3

Real Estate Brokerage

The real estate broker serves as an agent. To the extent that he acts as an agent for his principal (the property owner), he must observe general laws controlling agent-principal relations. In addition he must comply with state real estate license laws. Accordingly, this chapter concentrates on agency relationships that are important to real estate brokers. The next chapter concentrates on real estate license law.

In explaining the special role of real estate brokers, the first task is to define the real estate broker and his salespeople as viewed by the courts and the statutes. At this juncture, the functions of the real estate broker are relevant topics for review. In covering the law of agency, there are specific laws covering the conduct of the broker in relation to his principal and his prospects. Given these introductory topics, the next crucial issue relates to brokerage operations that develop from the agency, including broker relations with salesmen. There remains also the question of when the broker is entitled to a real estate commission.

REAL ESTATE BROKER DEFINED

In the simplest terms, a broker is defined as an agent who serves his principal. In this sense the broker must conform to the common law governing relations between the agent and his principal. Yet because real estate brokers and their salesmen must confrom to the real estate license laws of the respective states, the statutory definition is much broader. State license laws range from those with a fairly narrow definition of a real estate broker to those with an all-inclusive list of real estate operations coming under license regulations.

The National Association of Realtors Pattern License Law 71969 defines a broker as follows:

> "Broker" shall mean any person who for a fee, commission or any other valuable consideration, or with the intent or expectation of receiving the same from another, negotiates or attempts to negotiate the listing, sale, purchase, exchange, lease or option for any real estate or of the improvements thereon, or collects rents or attempts to collect rents, or who advertises or holds himself out as engaged in any of the foregoing. "Broker" also includes any person employed by or on behalf of the owner or owners of lots or other parcels of real estate, at a salary, fee, commission, or any other valuable consideration, to sell such real estate or any part thereof, in lots or parcels or other disposition thereof; it also includes any person who engages in the business of charging an advance fee or contracting for collection of a fee in connection with any contract whereby he undertakes primarily to promote the sale of real estate either through its listing in a publication issued primarily for such purpose, or for referral of information concerning such real estate to brokers, or both.
>
> "Person" shall mean and include individuals, corporations, partnerships or associations, foreign and domestic.

Statutory Definitions

Virginia defines a real estate broker in the following terms:

> A real estate broker within the meaning of this chapter is any person, partnership, association or corporation, who for a compensation or valuable consideration sells or offers for sale, buys or offers to buy, or negotiates the purchase or sale or exchange of real estate, or who leases or offers to lease, or rents or offers for rent, any real estate or the improvements thereon for others, as a whole or partial vocation.

This definition is pretty much confined to persons who buy, sell, exchange or lease real estate. The other extreme is illustrated by the Florida law that defines property managers and real estate appraisers as brokers who must observe the state real estate license law.

> Every person who shall, in this state, for another, and for a compensation or valuable consideration directly or indirectly paid or promises, expressly or impliedly, or with an intent to collect or receive a compensation or valuable consideration thereof, *appraise, auction, sell, exchange, buy or rent,* or *offer, attempt or agree to appraise auction* or *negotiate the sale, exchange, purchase or rental* of any real property, or any interest in or concerning the same, including mineral rights or leases . . . shall be deemed and held to be a real estate broker or a real estate salesman . . . (Ch. 475.01, Real Estate License Law).

Some states, like Florida, define brokers to include not only those directly selling, leasing, managing or appraising property but those who assist in these activities. Or, as in California, the legal definition of broker includes parties charging, receiving, collecting or contracting for advanced fees in both the sale and lease of property, dealing in business opportunities, or obtaining a loan on such properties.

These same provisions are extended to include real estate salespeople working for compensation or expecting compensation and employed by a licensed real estate broker to do one or more of the acts set forth in the statutory definition of a broker. In sum, the salesperson is defined as one who is employed by a broker as statutorily defined.

Statutory Exclusions

While the definitions cited specifically define activities regarded as real estate brokerage, the statutes usually exempt certain activities from the real estate license law. The main exclusions may be listed under five categories.

1. Anyone who directly performs any acts within the scope of the real estate law with reference to his own property or in the case of a corporation which, through its regular officers receiving no special compensation therefore, perform any of the acts with reference to corporate property.
2. Anyone holding a duly executed power of attorney from the owner.
3. Services rendered by an attorney-at-law performing his duties as such attorney-at-law.
4. Any receiver, trustee in bankruptcy or any person acting under order of any court.
5. Any trustee selling under a deed of trust.

The first exclusion covers those instances in which the property owner is acting for himself and not as an agent. The second exclusion delegates the acts of the owner to a power of attorney who is legally exempt from laws governing agency. Another common exclusion covers attorneys, who practice law on real estate matters, and legally appointed trustees or others acting under the direction of a court of law. Trustees are appointed or act under trust agreements and normally do not act as agents.

It will be recognized that real estate brokers are members of a three-party transaction. First, the broker, serving as agent to his principal—the selling property owner—is charged with negotiating a transaction between the buyer and seller. If the seller hires the broker to act as an agent, the broker must deal with a third party or the prospect. The commission is earned when the broker successfully negotiates a sale between the buyer and seller. This arrangement varies from the usual two-party transaction representing only the agent and principal. An explanation of the law of agency emphasizes the importance of the three-party arrangement. A brief review of the functions of the broker illustrates even more the many complications facing a broker.

FUNCTIONS OF A REAL ESTATE BROKER

The definition of a real estate broker given by statute suggests the scope of brokerage operations. While some states license auctioneers, appraisers, and property managers under license laws, most real estate broker operations focus on procuring buyers for the owner-principal. In this regard, the lay public tends to oversimplify the selling function.

Indeed, the industry is handicapped by the casual preparation of prospective real estate salespersons who regard their education in real estate as fairly complete once they pass the salesperson license examination. Such a group typically includes people who intend to sell part-time, retired persons who look to other sources of income for their main livelihood, and others who have only a transitory interest in real estate.

Disappointed licensees do not realize that past sales experience in goods and services, while helpful, is no guarantee of success in selling real estate. Moreover, experience has shown that the same qualities that insure success in other occupations are the qualities required for success in real estate. The converse is also true. A history of an unsuccessful career indicates a strong probability of a similar fate in real estate.

Skills Required

The difficulties facing the lay person entering real estate brokerage for the first time stem in part from the special knowledge and skills demanded of the salesperson. Consider some of the minimum areas of knowledge demanded of competent salespersons: (1) they must know the city and neighborhood and the advantages and limitations of the area in which they hope to negotiate sales. (2) Before showing a house to a prospect, they must know details of the floor plan, construction quality, condition of the neighborhood environment, and other intimate details of the property. (3) Because each property is unique, the selling task is more complex compared to other types of selling. The salesperson does not deal in the standardized products of other industries. (4) Further, the time to complete a sale extends over several weeks. Frequently the property must be sold to more than one party because prospective buyers may not qualify for mortgage credit. (5) Buyers are cautious because of the large financial commitment; buyer indecision leads to numerous property inspections and time-consuming delays. (6) Real estate financing, appraising, and title transfer call for highly specialized technical knowledge. It takes advanced training and months of experience to gain competence in the more specialized real estate operations. (7) Real estate salespersons must be experts in interpersonal relations. Since the buyer faces all the complexities confronting the salesperson—and with less know-how—the consummation of the sale depends on buyer confidence in the selling agent. Few selling jobs are so demanding.

Brokerage Operations

Because brokers and their staff are highly oriented to sales, the office operation develops around functions not found in other types of businesses. First, the broker must *secure listings* of properties for sale. Personal contacts, direct solicitation, and advertising represent an important phase of this brokerage function. *Soliciting buyers*, the second main function, requires skill in spending advertising funds wisely, in the placement of signs, and in developing referrals and other sources of buyer prospects. The third function deals with actual *negotiation*. Seldom does the buyer agree to the exact terms specified by the seller. The skill of the sales staff in completing the sale to the mutual satisfaction of buyer and seller is, in itself, an exacting task requiring diplomacy and knowledge of the local real estate markets. The last function, *closing the sale*, calls for an assemblage of complicated legal documents and an exchange of funds with a written statement and oral explanation of closing costs, financing, and disposition of funds.

To pursue real estate brokerage operations successfully, these functions require a highly developed ability in handling people and designing and maintaining a record system with a file of standard legal forms for mortgages, deeds, closing statements, and records for local, state, and federal tax and licensing requirements. Indeed, functions undertaken by brokers lead to considerable specialization within the office. The lay view of easy and high real estate commissions earned with a minimum of effort are unrealistic views of real estate brokerage practice.

LAW OF AGENCY

Real estate brokers acting as agents of their principal must qualify under state license laws. While most of their transactions represent an employment by a property owner to sell real estate for a commission, the nature of the real estate industry places the real estate broker and his employees in positions of trust not found under more common agency-principal roles. To develop this point, certain types of employment falling outside the agency definition warrant mention.

Nonagency Relationships

Because real estate brokers are licensed to serve as agents, special importance is attached to other roles they may assume as a consequence of their special position in the real estate industry. Brokers, who have more than the usual knowledge of real estate, may themselves act in an investment capacity. In still another area, brokers serve as consultants acting either as an employee or an independent contractor. In other cases, they employ subagents. The license laws generally restrict the role that brokers may play in these nonreal estate agent activities.

Brokers Acting on Their Own Account. Real estate license laws prohibit real estate brokers from acting as principals or under their own account without a full disclosure of their status. In fact, they must take special precautions to insure that all parties are fully aware of their position. The use of printed forms and advertising signs present the broker as an agent serving his principal. Unless steps are taken to dispel the implied agency, the broker may be in violation of the state license law. For instance, it is not enough to inform the buyer that the broker has an interest in the property or that he has control of the property in question. The broker must prove that he has informed third parties of his status as principal so that it is obvious that the broker is negotiating as a principal and not as an agent.

To be more specific, brokers are cautioned not to accept employment as an ageny and at the same time accept an option to purchase the property. Under this arrangement the broker is serving in a dual position —he assumes the status of an agent and potential purchaser—which is against the statute and common law. He must not exercise an option without divorcing his relationship with the principal as agent.

Not only is a broker required to disclose his role as a principal, but he must also report all facts that have a bearing on the transaction to the principal and disclose all facts concerning the prospect of sale to others. Indeed, the combination of a listing and option contract requires that the broker exercise extreme caution so as not to violate his duties as agent.

Employer-Employee Relationship. To be sure, the broker is employed by the principal, but as an agent not as an employee. The difference is that an employee renders services to his employer; an employee legally assumes a master-servant relationship. The broker must not only serve his principal but he must act for the principal in relations with third persons. In contrast, the independent contractor constitutes a relationship markedly different from an agency or an employee.

Independent Contractor. Brokers also serve as independent contractors if they are employed as a consultant; here the broker is responsible only for the results of his work. The employer has no control over the method of work performed.

In this regard, salesmen are also said to be employed by brokers as independent contractors. Brokers must exercise supervision over their activities. Since the salesman works in his own way on his own time and is paid by commission and pays his own expenses, he is regarded as an independent contractor. The question assumes critical importance in determining liability for employee income tax deductions and unemployment taxes.

Subagents. Subagencies are created if the selling broker cooperates with other brokers in completing a sale. Yet the cooperating broker normally would not sue the principal for a commission. Ordinarily, the cooperating broker is only responsible to the listing broker and not to the seller.

The main point is that the agent serving as a broker for a listing seller may not assign his duties to a subagent unless authorized by the principal. The final determination is governed by the listing agreement, which in most cases allows the broker to enlist the cooperation of other licensed brokers.

While the listing broker has a duty in performance to his principal, he is usually authorized to delegate actual performance to others. The rules are fairly clear in preventing the delegation of discretionary powers by agents unless authorized by the principal. Generally speaking, the broker may delegate his authority if the delegation is customary, if delegated performance covers duties the agent cannot perform himself, and if the delegation is for purely mechanical operations not involving discretionary powers.

Creation of an Agency

Though an agency may be created by an oral or a written contract, some 15 states require the employment of a real estate broker to be in writing. And even where the written contract is not required, good business practice advises a written contract of employment. The written contract helps to enforce the payment of real estate commissions. Without written evidence of employment, the facts are difficult to determine.

Written or oral contracts are called creation of an agency by *express contract.* Real estate brokers may also be employed under an implied contract. *Implied contracts* occur as a result of a special circumstance existing between the agent and the principal. Thus an agent may be given authority in case of an emergency calling for immediate action to protect the interest of the principal. Because the nature of the incident may not allow time to contact the principal, the agent usually is held responsible for acting with authority to protect the interest of the principal. With respect to third parties, if the broker makes statements on intentions of the principal and the principal does not act to refute the statements, the principal may be estopped from denying the implied authority given the broker.

A distinction is often made between the general agency and a special agency. Suppose the real estate broker is employed to manage a 100-unit apartment building. As property manager he acts for his principal, the property owner, and he must operate the property according to the management agreement which gives the broker *general authority* over the property.

This arrangement differs markedly from a *special agency* normally created when the broker agrees to sell a house for a commission. In this latter instance, the authority and jurisdiction of the broker is limited only to acts consistent with finding a qualified buyer. General agency authority is much broader in that he must do those acts in the normal course of the year which fall within the scope of the property manager.

In creating the agency, normal requirements of a contract are present. However, the consideration paid is not like other contracts. For under the usual listing contract, the owner gives the listing to the broker and promises compensation for services; that is, for finding a buyer willing and able to buy. The broker promises "to use due diligence" in finding a purchaser. The promise constitutes consideration for contract purposes. It should be added that creation of the agency authorizes the broker to find a willing buyer, but the agency does not give the broker authority to bind the owner or sign listing forms or other contracts.

Termination of an Agency

The question of termination often determines whether a broker is entitled to a commission. Like other contracts the parties may mutually agree to terminate a listing agreement. Similarly, a broker may revoke the agency or the principal may cancel the agreement. For instance, Crescent Realty Company, a real estate management firm, held a written agreement to manage the Frank Leu Building in Montgomery, Alabama, under a contract which could be terminated upon 30 days' notice. The court ruled that the agent could not claim a 5 percent commission on monthly rents after the building owner gave proper notice of termination. According to the Alabama court, after due notice of cancellation, Crescent had no authority to collect rents and having no right to collect rents "certainly it could claim no commission." (*Homeland Insurance Co. v. Crescent Realty Co.*, 168 So. 2d 243 [1964].)

Normally termination is likely to occur by expiration of the agency, the death of either party, or destruction of the subject of the agency. In the event of termination, there remains the question of liability for contract performance.

It is an accepted point of law that the principal may revoke a listing agreement before the agreement has expired. However, the principal may be liable for damages. Suppose for example, the principal terminates the listing agreement by revoking a contract under a 90-day listing. The principal may notify the broker he no longer wishes to offer his property for sale.

If the listing contract has been terminated before the 90-day termination date, this constitutes a breach of employment and either party is liable for damages to the other. For instance, if the principal wrongfully terminates the agency and the broker has incurred time and effort on behalf of the principal, he will have a valid claim for damages equal to the broker's services plus expenditures paid on behalf of the principal such as advertising expenses. If the breach is on the part of the broker, the principal may recover damages equal to his loss by a reason of the broker's failure to perform.

However, if the owner terminates an agency, he may not claim that the broker at a later date violates a fiduciary relationship. In a New York case, the owners terminated a listing on June 1st, and at the time forwarded a sales contract for $11,700,000 with the name of the purchaser left blank. The owner gave the broker four days to complete the contract and stated no commission was to be paid. After the broker purchased the property in his own name, the seller was unable to claim the broker violated a fiduciary relationship because the principal agent relationship was terminated by the owners. (*Midcourt Builders Corp.* v. *Eagan,* 319 N.Y.S. 2d 286 [1971].)

The point is equally clear that a principal may not revoke the agency after the broker has procured a purchaser ready, willing, and able to buy. That is, the owner may not revoke the agency merely to avoid payment of a commission. Moreover, in the case of an open listing in which several brokers are employed to sell the same property, the sale by one broker automatically terminates the agency.

Agency Relationships

Agency relationships include (1) the general authority of the agent; (2) duties to the principal; and (3) duties to the prospect.

Authority of the Agent. A real estate broker in the ordinary course of acting as agent of the seller has no authority to act in his own name. Moreover, he has no authority to commit an act which would defraud his principal. On the contrary by accepting an agency, the broker is required to do everything necessary and customary in his business to carry out the purpose of his agency.

The authority of an agent arises from three sources: (1) express authority which may be written or oral unless required to be in writing; (2) implied authority; and (3) apparent authority. The *express* authority, especially in real estate, usually assumes the form of written instructions —for example, a listing agreement. In less restrictive cases, an agent such as a property manager may have express authority to undertake certain acts under an oral agreement. Unless the statute requires that the agency be in writing, the principal is bound by the agent's acts undertaken as a consequence of an expressed, oral authority.

The *implied* authority comes about from authority granted to an agent to accomplish a particular task. For example, a written management agreement may call for certain implied authority which follows from his management role. That is, under the management agreement (which is an express authority), it is also implied that an agent has the authority to purchase supplies, undertake repairs, hire custodial employees, and undertake other more specific duties which are incidental to building management.

In the case of *apparent* authority, acts of the agent must be apparent to third persons. The authority arises from acts which a third party might reasonably expect and attribute to an agent. The cases of authority granted from this source usually follow from the acts and conduct of the principal. That is, if the principal by his words or conduct, holds his agent out as having certain authority, he is prevented from denying that the agent has actual authority to bind the principal.

Care should be taken in distinguishing between actual and apparent authority. Suppose, for example, that X writes Y directing him to sell a 100-acre farm. X sends a copy of this letter to Z, a prospective buyer. This arrangement illustrates actual authority of Y to sell X's 100 acres.

In states that permit oral listing agreements, suppose that X asks Y to sell his 100-acre farm but he directs Y not to accept any offers without X's approval. If a prospect asks Y about the property, and Y tells Z that he should work out a deal with X, here Y has *no actual* authority to sell but to Z he does have *apparent authority*. Consequently, X is likely to be bound if Y accepts an offer to purchase from Z. These conflicts between express authority, implied authority, and apparent authority are sufficiently technical to require legal counsel if the authority of an agent is in question.

The importance of a written contract is illustrated in the case of a Fort Worth, Texas, broker who was unable to recover a commission because the employment was not under a written contract as required by Texas law. The case involved the Ford Motor Company which wished to acquire a site for a truck dealership and to conceal their identity until final settlement. The broker secured an option to purchase under an alleged oral agreement to be compensated by the spread if he could buy the property at a price below what Ford approved. The court ruled against the broker's claim for compensation on grounds that the agreement was unenforceable because it was not in writing. (*Roquemore* v. *Ford Motor Company*, 290 F. Supp. 130 [1967].)

In states requiring the wife to sign deeds with the husband, a listing agreement may not be binding on the wife if she does not sign the listing agreement with the husband. In the state of Washington, the court held that the wife and the community property were not bound by a listing agreement signed only by the husband. (*Geohegan* v. *Dever*, 30 Wash. 2d 877 [1948].) In a similar case in Arizona, the court viewed a listing agreement as only a contract for personal services which did not require the wife's signature to bind the husband for a commission. In this case Mr. Vance signed an exclusive listing agreement with Management Clearing, Inc. The agreement covered community property and was not signed by the wife. When the broker secured a purchaser who signed a purchase contract and receipt on terms identical with the listing agreement, Mr. and Mrs. Vance refused to sign the purchase agreement on grounds the wife did not sign the listing agreement. The court stated: "Since the brokerage contract is a contract for personal services, and a debt incurred by the husband is presumed to be for the benefit of the community, . . . we hold that the listing contract is not a conveyance or encumbrance. . . ." (*Management Clearing, Inc.* v. *Vance*, 464 P. 2d 977 [1970].) Therefore, in Arizona when the broker performed, he was entitled to a commission though the wife did not sign the contract of employment.

Duties to the Principal. An agent's duty to the principal is quite clear. These duties are subject to much regulation and little question remains on the responsibilities of an agent to the principal. In fact, duties of the agent to the principal probably override most other activities of the usual real estate office. Authorities are in general agreement that duties of the agent include, as a minimum, the following seven points.

1. *The broker must be loyal to his principal.* As a practical matter, the broker who accepts a listing to sell property acts like a trustee who serves the beneficiary. In this respect, the broker directs his skills to serving the purpose of the agency—primarily finding a buyer, willing and able to purchase the property listed. He must not gain any advantage over his principal by reason of his agency and he must not make the slightest misrepresentation or exercise concealment.

The law regards the agent as working with the principal's confidence; the agent must not enjoy any undue financial gain arising from the confidential relationship. The position of trust requires that the broker inform the seller of his option on offering prices or any information such as new public improvements, proposed new highways, or other facts that may affect the value of the principal's property. He must not mislead or deceive the principal in any way.

This issue is demonstrated by an Arizona broker who represented both the buyer and seller. The broker induced a widow and long-time family friend to purchase a restaurant after showing her a false net operating statement which reported a profit of $83,000. It was later proven that the claimed profit was five times greater than the actual profit. The widow was able to have her purchase contract rescinded with payment of monetary damages because of the false representations of the real estate broker. (*Jennings* v. *Lee*, 461 P. 2d 161 [1969].)

2. *The broker acts as a fiduciary.* A fiduciary relationship exists when good conscience requires one to act at all times for the sole benefit and interest of another with loyalty to those interests. The agency relationship requires good faith on the part of the real estate broker; the broker must do not only what is best but he must make no personal profit out of the subject matter of the agency. As a general rule, the fiduciary relationship prevents the agent or his employees from competing with his employer in any way that violates the agency agreement. To put it differently, the broker has no right to hold an interest adverse to his principal.

An apparent exception to this rule was illustrated by a Georgia case which dealt with a broker who held a deed to secure a debt, an option to purchase, and an exclusive listing on a farm. The owner, who was in financial difficulty, sold at a reduced price under the option to purchase held by the broker who later sold the farm at a higher price. The owner claimed damages for fraud and deceit because the broker made a profit on the resale. The owner held that the broker breached a fiduciary relationship since it was argued that the broker had a prospective purchaser for the property at the time he held an option to purchase and a listing agreement. The broker replied that at the time of purchase, he had no prospective buyer. The court, on a finding of facts, agreed with the broker. The fundamental rule remains: the fiduciary relationship of the broker requires that his principal be made aware of the true situation, especially as to prospective purchasers. (*Smith* v. *Blackshear*, 189 S.E. 3d 99 [1972].)

3. *The broker must account for money and deposits.* It is universally true that a broker acting as agent for a seller must account for earnest money deposits and other money entrusted to him in a separate trust account which is not commingled with personal funds. The authority to accept money offered by the buyer as a deposit is usually granted in listing forms which authorize the broker to accept earnest money deposits.

In this capacity, the broker holds the money as an agent of the buyer and not the seller. Brokers must observe the rule that deposit money is not the property of the broker. He accepts it in trust for the buyer. On close of the sale or default by the buyer, the seller has a claim to the deposit money according to the listing agreement. Real estate agencies are directed to place trust funds in special accounts immediately upon receipt. If the sale does not materialize, through no fault of the buyer, the money must be returned.

4. *The broker must obey instructions of his principal.* In the listing agreement, the principal gives special instructions on terms of sale; namely, the minimum down payment, other conditions acceptable to the seller,

and items of personal property to be included with the real estate. The broker has not earned his commission unless he procures a buyer willing to meet the terms of sale established by the seller. Failure to obey lawful instructions of the principal subjects the broker to damage suits as a result of injuries suffered by the principal. For example, a broker accepting a personal check when he is under instructions only to accept cash makes the agent personally responsible if the check is returned for insufficient funds.

5. *The broker must act in person.* This statement means that the person employing the broker relies on his personal services. If the broker has delegated his authority to another broker, the employing broker remains responsible for acts of a cooperating broker. For example, if A employs broker B who in turn shares a listing with broker C, and C later commits fraud against the seller, broker B may be held accountable to the seller. For listings that contemplate services of a cooperating broker, which is quite common for large-scale industrial properties that have a national market, the listing agreement will usually grant authority to delegate or to enlist the services of cooperating brokers.

In other respects, the broker may delegate only mechanical, clerical, or bookkeeping duties to others. The main idea is that the seller enlisted the personal services of the broker on the basis of his expertise and reputation and, therefore, it would be unjust to allow the broker to avoid his responsibility by delegating his appointment to others.

6. *Without full disclosure to his principal, the broker may not have any personal interest in property for which he acts as a broker.* This duty is violated if the broker purchases property on his own account which he has listed for sale with his principal. The broker may assume an interest in the property listed only if he discloses his interest to the principal. The rule prevents the agent from gaining secret profits from the principal.

The courts have interpreted this rule strictly, allowing the principal to repudiate a sale in which the broker sold property to relatives, employees, or used a straw man to gain a personal profit. Clearly the agent is prohibited from overstating the purchase price, then personally buying the property at a lower price, and later selling it at a higher price. Or in representing a seller, he cannot falsely state that the property is overpriced and then buy the property at a lower price in his own name. If the broker has an interest or contemplates an interest in the property in which he acts as broker, he must disclose his interest to the principal.

The rule is illustrated by a broker, Jack A. Patton, in Atlanta, Georgia, who accepted a listing to sell land for $2,000. The broker on March 27, presented the owner with a contract for sale from S. A. Kellett for $1,600 which was accepted by the owner. On the same date, S. A. Kellett conveyed the same property to R. M. Crane for $3,000. The facts disclosed that the broker and the first purchaser, without knowledge of the principal, were in fact partners in real estate doing business as Kellett and Patton. The plaintiff owner won an award of $1,400 representing the difference in price he received as owner and the price received by the broker. The court concluded: "The law is uniform and well settled that an agent who has been engaged to sell real estate for the owner may not, either directly or indirectly, purchase it himself, without the express consent of the principal after a full knowledge of all the facts." (*Kellett* v. *Boynton*, 75 S.E. 2d 292 [1953].)

The foregoing rule does not prevent the broker from buying and selling real estate when he is not acting as an agent. But if he does act on his own account, it is important that the broker reveal his identity as an owner-buyer and not as an agent. Again, if the broker acts as an agent, he is not entitled to make undisclosed profits from the principal.

7. *The broker may not act for the buyer and seller without full disclosure.* Suppose the broker is offered a commission by both the buyer and seller. Unless both parties are informed and both consent, the broker cannot accept a commission from the principal and a third party. Even if the third party is willing to pay a commission, the broker is still responsible to the principal and without consent of both parties he violates the agency-principal relationship by serving a third party.

In Wisconsin, two brokers represented a buyer in the purchase of an $80,000 farm for which they each received a $1,000 commission from the buyer after telling the buyer that the seller would pay no commission. The facts revealed that, in truth, the brokers had an undisclosed purpose to collect a further commission from the seller. The seller shortly after the settlement paid the brokers a $1,833.34 commission. The court awarded the commission paid by the seller to the buyer. The court held that an agent who makes a profit in connection with transactions conducted by him on behalf of his principal is under duty to give such profit to his principal. It was the duty of the broker to account to the buyer when he received a commission from the seller without the consent of the buyer. (*Degner* v. *Moncel*, 93 N.W. 2d 857 [1959].)

In other words, the agent must not assume a position in which he represents the conflicting interests of the buyer and seller. Dual agencies undertaken without permission of both parties is universally prohibited by statute and the courts. Some states have revoked or suspended real estate licenses for violation of this principle.

In the final analysis, the broker acting as an agent of the principal assumes responsibilities not found in the usual employer-employee relationship. In most respects these duties of the agent to the principal follow rules of common sense and ordinary business ethics. Clearly, the agent must be loyal, in that an agent acts as a fiduciary and must act in the best interest of the employing principal. An agent must account for all monies of the principal, obey instructions, and act in person. An agent must not have any interest in property subject of the agency and must not act for the principal without full disclosure to third parties. Besides these responsibilities, the broker must observe certain responsibilities to third parties, primarily buyer-prospects.

Duties to the Prospect. While brokers owe loyalty to the employing principal, they also owe certain duties to third parties. As an agent, the broker acts with all the authority of the agency in dealings with third parties. This issue arises if false representations are made by the broker. In this respect, brokers may be liable to third parties if they misrepresent facts which are known to be false. Such misrepresentations are fraudulent and may void the contract for sale. Even silence on material facts which the broker knows affect the desirability of a property may subject the broker to criminal, civil, or disciplinary action.

It should be borne in mind that the usual task of a broker is to find a purchaser, to make statements about the property for sale, and to accept an earnest money deposit. In the conduct of this agency, the broker may make statements such as "this is the best house available" or that the neighborhood is "superior" to other neighborhoods. These are mere statements of opinion and fall in the category of "puffing of goods" and are usually not classified as misstatements of facts.

The rule is illustrated by the purchaser of a house in Portland, Oregon, who claimed damages of $2,500 as a result of the supposed fraudulent misrepresentations of the broker. Statements made by the broker such as "this house was a new home and of good quality and that it was constructed in a good and workmanlike manner" were held to be mere opinion. The court viewed commendatory statements by a seller of the thing which he is trying to sell are not actionable even though false. (*Holland* v. *Lentz*, 397 P. 2d 787 [1964].)

If the broker makes false promises, such as that the property could be sold for $10,000 more in 12 months, it would constitute a misrepresentation, a false promise, and would be a violation against the buyer. The duty of the agent-broker, to be sure, is directed primarily to serving the principal-employer. It is also true that the broker must observe duties to third parties to avoid an action for fraud, misrepresentation, false promises, or other acts constituting negligence or criminal action by the agent.

BROKER RELATIONS WITH SALESPERSONS

The law regards the acts of salespersons as acts made on the broker's behalf. Salespersons who violate the agency relationship jeopardize the interest of the broker and may subject both the salesperson and broker to loss of their licenses.

The Status of Salespersons

Generally, salespersons must act only by direction of the broker; they have no authority to accept money in their own behalf; they have no claims against the principal and must seek compensation through the real estate broker. In brief, the salesperson must follow the same duties and responsibilities enforced against a broker. While they act as an agent serving the principal, they do so only through the employing broker. There is no direct relationship between the salesperson, the principal, or the prospect. For this reason, brokers must give instructions to salespersons and in other respects supervise them as other employers supervise employees.

The Broker-Salesperson Agreement

Leading brokers recognize the strong mutuality of interest between brokers and their salespersons. Though the broker is the employing party, salespersons legally assume the status of an independent contractor. Accordingly, they are highly dependent on services provided by the broker. It is equally true that the broker is dependent on the successful endeavors of salespersons. To define these relations more closely, some offices use an agreement signed by both parties as a condition of employment. Such an agreement is reproduced in Figure 3–1 taken from the *Idaho Real Estate Manual*.

Duties of the Brokers and Salesmen. The first two points in the agreement shown in Figure 3–1 require that the broker provide sales-

FIGURE 3–1

Broker-Salesman Agreement

BROKER-SALESMAN AGREEMENT

THIS AGREEMENT, made and entered into this ....*fifteenth*.... day of........*May*........, 19........, by and between....*Henry A. Johnson*...., hereinafter referred to as broker, and........*Lyle J. Keithly*........, hereinafter referred to as salesman.

WITNESSETH:

WHEREAS, broker is now and for many years last past has been engaged in business as a real estate broker in the City of........*Happytown*........, County of........*Sunnyvale*........, Idaho, and is duly licensed to sell, offer for sale, buy, offer to buy, list or solicit prospective purchasers, negotiate the purchase, sale or exchange of real estate, negotiate loans on real estate, lease or offer to lease, and negotiate the sale, purchase or exchange of leases, rent or place for rent, or to collect rent from real

FIGURE 3–1 (continued)

estate or improvements thereon for another or others, has and does enjoy the good will of and a reputation for fair dealing with the public, and

WHEREAS, broker maintains an office in said City and County, properly equipped for furnishings and other equipment necessary and incidental to the proper operation of said business, and staffed with employees suitable to serving the public as a real estate broker, and

WHEREAS, salesman is now and for some time past has been engaged in business as a real estate salesman, duly licensed by the State of Idaho, and has enjoyed and does enjoy a good reputation for fair and honest dealing with the public as such, and

NOW, THEREFORE, in consideration of the premises and the mutual agreements herein contained, it is understood and agreed as follows:

1. Broker agrees to make available to salesman all current listings of the office, except such as broker may find expedient to place exclusively in the temporary possession of some other salesman, and agrees to assist salesman in his work by advice, information, and full cooperation in every way possible.

2. Broker agrees that salesman may share with other salesmen in all the facilities of the office now operated by broker in connection with the subject matter of this contract, which office is now maintained at ....*1131 Greenbriar, Happytown*........, Idaho.

3. Salesman agrees to work diligently and with his best efforts to sell, lease or rent any and all real estate listed with broker, to solicit additional listings and customers of broker, and otherwise promote the business of serving the public in real estate transactions to the end that each of the parties hereto may derive the greatest profit possible.

4. Salesman shall read and be governed by the Code of Ethics of the National Association of Real Estate Boards, the real estate law of the State of Idaho and the bylaws of the local real estate board, and any future modifications or additions thereto. Each party acknowledges receipt of a copy of the said Code of Ethics and of the local board bylaws.

5. The usual and customary commissions shall be charged according to the commission schedule adopted by this office. Broker shall advise salesman of any special contract relating to any particular transaction which he undertakes to handle. When salesman shall perform any work hereunder whereby a commission is earned, said commission shall, when collected, be divided between broker and salesman, in which division salesman shall receive a proportionate share as set out in the current commission schedule as set forth in the broker's policy book and broker shall receive the balance. In the event of special arrangements with any client of broker or salesman on property listed with broker or controlled by salesman, a special division of commission may apply, such rate of division to be agreed upon before completion of the transaction by broker and salesman and outlined in writing.

FIGURE 3–1 (*continued*)

6. In the event that two or more salesmen participate in such work, or claim to have done so, the amount of the commission over that accruing to broker shall be divided between the participating salesmen according to agreement between them or by arbitration.

7. In no case shall broker be personally liable to salesman for any commission not collected, nor shall salesman be personally liable for any commission not collected. When the commission shall have been collected from the party or parties for whom the service was performed, broker shall hold the same in trust for salesman and himself to be divided according to the terms of this agreement. Complying with Section 10138 Business and Professions Code, all compensation shall be delivered to broker to be paid as per this agreement.

8. The division and distribution of the earned commissions as set out in Paragraphs 5, 6, and 7 hereof shall take place as soon as practicable after collection of such commissions.

9. Broker shall not be liable to salesman for any expenses incurred by him or for any of his acts, nor shall salesman be liable to broker for office help or expense. Salesman shall have no authority to bind broker by any promise of representation unless specifically authorized in writing in a particular transaction. Expenses which must by reason of some necessity be paid from the commission, or are incurred in the collection of, or in the attempt to collect the commission, shall be paid by the parties in the same proportion as provided for herein in the division of commissions.

10. This agreement does not constitute a hiring by either party. The parties hereto are and shall remain independent contractors bound by the provisions hereof. Salesman is under the control of broker as to the result of salesman's work only and not as to the means by which such result is accomplished. This agreement shall not be construed as a partnership and broker shall not be liable for any obligation incurred by salesman.

11. Salesman agrees that any and all listings of property, and all employment in connection with the real estate business, shall be taken in the name of broker. Such listings shall be filed with broker within twenty-four hours after receipt of same by salesman. All listings shall be and remain the separate and exclusive property of broker.

12. This contract and the association created hereby, may be terminated by either party hereto at any time upon written notice given to the other. The rights of the parties to any commission earned prior to said notice shall not be divested by the termination of this contract.

13. When this agreement has been terminated for any reason, the salesman's regular proportionate share of commission on any sales the salesman has made that are not closed shall be considered his property, and upon closing of said sales, said proportionate share of the commission shall be paid to him; and salesman shall receive agreed listing commission on his listings if sold within the life of such listings, and commission re-

FIGURE 3–1 (concluded)

ceived by broker. This shall not apply to any extension of the said listings beyond the original listing period.

14. In the event salesman leaves and has sales or listings pending that require further work normally rendered by salesman, the salesman and broker, or broker alone, shall make arrangements with another salesman in the organization to perform the required work, and the salesman assigned shall be compensated for taking care of pending deals or listings from the portion of the commission due the selling or listing salesman.

15. Arbitration—In the event of disagreement or dispute between salesmen in the office or between broker and salesman arising out of or connected with this agreement which cannot be adjusted by and between the parties involved, such questions shall be submitted to the local real estate board committee governing such disputes or, if this is not agreed upon, the problem must be submitted to a temporary Board of Arbitration for final adjustment. Such board shall be selected in the following manner: Each of the parties to the disagreement or dispute shall select one member who shall be a licensed broker or licensed salesman. Such selection shall be made within five days from the time notice is given in writing by either party to the other, that arbitration is desired. The two arbitrators thus selected, in case they cannot reach a decision after a single conference, or adjustment thereof, shall name a third arbitrator who shall be a person not licensed by the Idaho Real Estate Brokers Board. Such arbitration may follow the provisions of Sections 1280 through 1293 of the Code of Civil Procedure for the State of Idaho. Broker and salesman hereby agree to be bound by the decision of the above described arbitration body.

16. Salesman shall not after the termination of this contract use to his own advantage, or the advantage of any other person or corporation, any information gained for or from the files or business of broker.

WITNESS the signatures of the parties hereto the day and year first above written. In duplicate.

....

....

Broker

....

....

Salesman as Independent Contractor

persons with listings and otherwise assist them by advice, information, and office cooperation. The agreement lists duties of the salesperson: "to work diligently and with his best efforts to sell, lease or rent any and all real estate listed with the broker and to solicit additional listings. . . ." Salespersons are directed to read and be governed by the code of ethics of the National Association Real Estate Boards (now National Association of Realtors).

Commissions. Agreement on division of the commission is covered in the next four paragraphs. While not subjecting the broker to payment of a commission unless the commission is collected, the agreement states that distribution of earned commissions shall take place as soon as practicable after collection. On expenses incurred by salespersons, the agreement states that the broker is not liable for expenses nor can the salespersons bind the broker unless authorized in writing. By agreement, paragraph 10 defines salesmen as independent contractors under control of the broker.

Salesperson's Ethics. In the same way that the broker must be loyal to his principal, paragraph 11 requires a salesperson to act in the name of the broker, filing all listings with the broker within 24 hours of receipt, and these remain the property of the broker. In the event of disagreement, the agreement of Figure 3–1 includes a clause providing for arbitrators or settlement of disputes under the state real estate license law. The last point prohibits a salesperson from changing brokers and using listings and prospect files to his advantage in working for a new broker.

LIABILITY FOR COMMISSIONS

Controversies relating to the earning of commissions are settled by four requirements observed among the 50 states. Related commission controversies concern the sharing of commissions and the disposition of deposit money.

Requirements for Earning a Commission

The broker is particularly vulnerable to buyers and sellers who may conspire to avoid payment of a commission. In addition, real estate transactions are dependent on financing, title searches, and the completion of surveys, appraisals, and other matters. Consequently, the time between commitment to buy and the closing of the sale may extend over several weeks. During the ensuing interval, the buyer or seller may have a change of heart and, though the broker has acted in good faith and performed according to his agency, he might be forced to take legal action if a buyer or seller change their mind before closing. The four elements necessary to enforce payment of a commission, therefore, are critical to the broker who must initiate action for payment of earned commissions.

The Broker Must Be Licensed. Though it is unlawful to engage in real estate brokerage without a license, disputes arise among brokers who do not timely renew their licenses or who may not hold a valid license at the time a listing is accepted or at the time a contract for sale is executed.

To enforce payment of a commission in Florida, real estate brokers and salesmen must hold a registration certificate issued by the Florida Real Estate Commission:

> No contract for a commission or compensation for any act or service enumerated in subsection (2) of 475.01 shall be valid unless the broker or salesman shall have complied with this chapter in regard to registration and renewal of the certificate at the time the act or service was performed (*Florida Real Estate Handbook*).

However, if a broker is not the holder of a current registration certificate but was formerly registered and has timely applied for renewal of the expired certificate which has not yet been physically issued, he is not precluded from collecting a commission. If the state requires a bond in addition to the license, the collection of a commission may be endangered if the broker does not hold a valid license at the time of performing any act or service for the payment of the commission.

Procuring Cause of the Sale. To enforce payment of a commission, the broker must prove that he was the efficient and procuring cause of the transaction. In the case of a listing agreement in which seller lists his property with several brokers, this point would be difficult to prove. Under this type of listing, the owner reserves the right to sell the property through his own efforts without payment of the commission.

Suppose for example, that under a listing agreement the broker shows a buyer a single-family dwelling. While inspecting the property, the buyer makes no offer to the broker but later buys directly from seller. In this instance, the broker probably could enforce payment of the commission, since the transaction followed as a direct result of the broker's efforts. The broker was the first to show the property and by his other acts introduced the buyer to the seller. The evidence would probably be sufficient to enforce payment of the commission.

To provide evidence of "procuring cause of sale," brokers may inform the seller in writing of the date and name of a prospect who was shown the property. By keeping a copy for future reference, broker provides evidence that he was the procuring cause of the sale in disputes with other brokers or principals.

In contracts listing the broker's services, the broker must perform within the time specified in the contract. It is not enough that the broker introduces a purchaser to a seller. If the broker abandons his efforts and the property is sold by a competing broker, the first broker may not claim the commission merely because he was the first broker to show the property to the purchaser. The evidence must show that the broker was the efficient and procuring cause of the sale and the facts must show that the first broker clearly abandoned the sale while the second broker must show that through his efforts the sale was consummated.

For instance, a broker in New York failed to enforce payment of a commission under an implied agency because he did not prove that the sale was completed through his efforts. In this instance the broker failed to obtain a store lease and purchase of fixtures for the principal. After several months the same building was leased to the same party by another broker. Because the original principal had a right to engage another broker and because the plaintiff broker failed to show that the transaction took place through his efforts, no commission was earned. (*Adams and Co. Real Estate* v. *E. and B. Supermarkets, Inc.* 274 N.Y.S. 2d 776 [1966].)

In still other instances, the broker who introduces the purchaser to a seller and, through the broker's efforts, the parties complete the transaction, the broker may be entitled to a commission. It should be emphasized that the commission does not rest on the amount of work done but on the question of whether the broker has performed his agency—to find a buyer willing and able to purchase under terms acceptable to the seller.

A related issue concerns the time in which the commission is earned. Most jurisdictions hold that a broker has completed his services when he accepts a deposit money receipt or negotiates and executes a contract for sale. If he has performed within the contract period, the broker has earned his commission. If the owner refuses to sign a contract of sale or cannot convey title, generally the seller is liable for a commission since the broker has performed.

Listing agreements generally provide for forfeiture of the deposit, if the buyer revokes a contract for sale. Typically the listing agreement provides that the broker and seller share the deposit equally in the event of a forfeiture. The listing contract may alter this arrangement by giving the broker a right to a commission only after transfer of title from seller to buyer. Other cases have stated that the full commission was earned when broker completed performance and is not dependent on the seller's ability to deliver title or execute a deed.

The Broker Must Be Employed. There is no liability for a commission unless the broker proves he was employed. In states that require a broker's employment to be in writing, controversies on this point are less frequent, especially in states that require an expiration date on exclusive listing contracts. In those states that permit an oral listing, it is more difficult to prove employment. Though the broker may have influenced a buyer to purchase, the broker is not entitled to a commission unless he was employed by the owner. Merely discussing the possibility of a sale with an owner would not in itself constitute employment if the broker later secures a willing and able buyer.

A Willing and Able Buyer. Provided other requirements for enforcement are present, the broker has not earned his commission unless he secures a buyer ready, willing, and able to purchase on terms acceptable to the principal. Though the broker may have secured a deposit receipt or contract for sale, the buyer may not qualify for the required loan and be unable to complete this transaction. In this case no commission would be earned. Or suppose the buyer tenders an offer to the seller that is less than the asking price or offers different terms of purchase. If the seller accepts the offer, the broker has found a buyer willing and able to purchase on terms acceptable to the seller. A buyer who has signed an earnest money deposit receipt or paid the asking price and is financially able to complete the transaction constitutes strong evidence of a buyer ready, willing, and able to purchase.

QUESTIONS FOR REVIEW

_____ 1. The employment contract between an agent and a principal creates:
I. an agency.
II. a fiduciary relationship.
a. I only.
b. II only.
c. Both I and II.
d. Neither I nor II.

_____ 2. A real estate broker is
a. a fiduciary to a person interested in buying property that he has listed.
b. an attorney-in-fact.
c. an agent who serves his principal under a duly executed power of attorney.
d. none of the above.

_____ 3. A principal in an agency contract must
a. have reached maturity.
b. be competent.
c. possess the authority he is conveying.
d. all of the above.

_____ 4. An agent must always
a. be loyal to his own interests.
b. obey instructions of the principal.
c. do what is best for the principal provided the agent makes a personal profit out of the subject matter of the agency.
d. assume a personal interest in the sale of each property for which he acts as a broker.

_____ 5. Funds of others which are received by a salesperson must be
I. deposited into an escrow account by the salesperson.
II. turned over to a broker for deposit in an escrow account.

      a. I only.

      b. II only

      c. Either I or II.

      d. Neither I nor II.

_____ 6. A salesperson authorized to negotiate a sale of property has no implied authority to

      a. accept payment on the purchase price subsequent to the initial down payment.

      b. permit a purchaser to take possession of the premises before the deal is closed.

      c. permit the purchaser to enter the premises for the purpose of painting or decorating.

      d. all of the above.

_____ 7. Unless the owner-seller has consented, the salesperson violates his fiduciary relationship to his principal if he accepts _____ as a down payment.

      a. cash

      b. a check

      c. a note

      d. a money order

_____ 8. A salesperson negotiated a sale for his employing broker and demanded that the seller pay the commission to the firm. The seller refused to pay and the employing broker refused to be involved in a litigation regardless of the merits of the salesperson's claim. Therefore, the salesperson sued the seller in his own name. Which of the following statements is correct?

      a. The salesperson may sue in his or her own name and collect a portion of the commission.

      b. The salesperson may sue in court but must collect the commission for the broker also.

      c. It will not be necessary for the salesperson to go to court to obtain his or her commission. He or she may do so by attaching the property that was sold.

      d. None of the above.

_____ 9. To a real estate broker, the listing property owner is known as the

      a. agent.

      b. fiduciary.

      c. prospect.

      d. principal.

_____10. One who has the right to sign the name of the principal to a contract is

      a. a broker.

      b. a special agent.

      c. an auctionee.

      d. an attorney-in-fact.

_____11. If a broker accepts a postdated check as a down payment on a real estate transaction and the check is not honored, the seller can
   a. declare the contract void.
   b. bring criminal action against the buyer.
   c. hold the broker responsible.
   d. file a complaint with the local credit bureau.

_____12. A real estate broker is a special agent with _____ authority.
   a. limited
   b. unlimited
   c. special
   d. privileged

_____13. In the absence of a prior agreement defining when the broker's commission is earned, the commission is earned when the
   a. deal is consummated.
   b. buyer and seller have a meeting of minds.
   c. broker introduces the buyer to the seller.
   d. deed is delivered.

_____14. For his acts as a real estate salesperson, the salesperson is responsible to the
   a. owner of the property (principal).
   b. prospective buyer.
   c. employing broker.
   d. prospective mortgagees.

_____15. Generally speaking, no person shall bring or maintain any action in the courts for the collection or compensation for the performance of any of the acts of a real estate salesperson unless the salesperson
   a. is employed on a full-time basis by the property owner for the purpose of selling, buying, leasing, managing, auctioning, or otherwise dealing with such property.
   b. was acting as a referral agent who was not involved in the actual negotiations.
   c. proves that he or she was a duly licensed real estate salesperson at the time the alleged cause of action arose.
   d. obtains written permission from the real estate commission.

_____16. With regard to representations made to prospective purchasers, a salesperson may be held liable for
   a. statements of the owner.
   b. puffing of goods.
   c. statements of fact.
   d. an honest mistake.

_____17. Without the knowledge of his employing broker, salesman A sold a $70,000 house with the cooperation of salesman B who works for another agency. Salesman A paid half of his commission to salesman B. Which of the following statements is correct?

   a. Salesman *A* has no right to recognize anyone other than his employing broker.
   b. Salesman *B* may not keep half of the commission.
   c. Salesman *B* has violated his duty to his employing broker.
   d. All of the above.

_____18. In order to recover a commission in a court of law, it is necessary for a broker to prove that he or she was
   a. properly licensed.
   b. employed.
   c. the efficient and procuring cause of the sale.
   d. all of the above.

_____19. When acting on his or her own behalf in buying or selling real estate, a broker or salesperson must indicate his or her true position by a clause inserted in the
   a. sales agreement.
   b. deed.
   c. security deed.
   d. listing agreement.

_____20. An exclusive listing should include
   a. an estimate of the fair market value.
   b. a definite closing date.
   c. an acknowledgment.
   d. provision for recording.

_____21. The contract which provides for payment of a commission to a broker even though the owner makes a sale without the aid of the broker is called an
   a. exclusive listing.
   b. open listing.
   c. exclusive right to sell.
   d. agency coupled with an interest.

_____22. The exclusive right to sell
   a. is the same thing as an exclusive agency.
   b. is a contract of employment between a broker and his or her principal.
   c. gives the property owner the right to sell property without payment of commission to the broker.
   d. must include a "holdover" clause.

_____23. Jordan, a salesman, would be judged negligent or incompetent in his fiduciary relationship if he
   a. did not advertise a house for at least six weeks.
   b. showed the house only by appointment.
   c. did not disclose the annual property tax.
   d. waited one week to transfer an earnest money deposit to his broker in order to give the seller time to accept or reject the offer.

_____24. The salesperson, on showing a client's property to a prospect, should

    a. make an office memorandum.

    b. confirm the interview by a memo to the buyer.

    c. notify the seller as to the prospect's identity.

    d. wait until the prospect makes a deal with the owner.

_____25. The maximum monetary commission that may be paid in an agency relationship is determined by the

    a. seller.

    b. broker.

    c. real estate commission.

    d. parties involved.

_____26. John Adams, a real estate broker, employs Jane Welford as a real estate salesperson. Welford listed the home of Mr. and Mrs. Charles Thomas and found a buyer for the home within two weeks of the listing date. Which of the following statements correctly describes this situation?

    a. Mr. and Mrs. Thomas will pay the real estate commission to Mr. Adams.

    b. Mr. and Mrs. Thomas will pay the real estate commission to Ms. Welford.

    c. Mr. and Mrs. Thomas will pay half of the real estate commission to Mr. Adams and half of the real estate commission to Ms. Welford.

    d. The buyer will pay Ms. Welford's commission.

_____27. Which one of the following persons is universally exempt from the licensing law?

    a. A trustee in bankruptcy.

    b. A person handling leases only.

    c. A salesman employed by a builder.

    d. A person employed to sell subdivision lots.

_____28. _____ must be licensed to sell real property.

    a. An executor

    b. An attorney-in-fact

    c. A receiver

    d. A partnership

_____29. A real estate salesperson in most states may lawfully pay a part of a commission to

    a. any person who assisted in performing the services for which the commission was paid.

    b. the buyer as a refund.

    c. the seller as a bonus.

    d. none of the above.

_____30. Generally, a salesperson
    a. has no authority to accept money in his or her own behalf.
    b. has no claims against the principal.
    c. must seek compensation through the real estate broker.
    d. all of the above.

_____31. Which of the following statements is true?
    a. The broker is employed by a principal.
    b. The salesperson is not employed by principals who list property for sale.
    c. The salesperson is employed by the broker.
    d. All of the above.

_____32. Sarah Findley, a real estate salesperson for the Bentley Realty Company, succeeded in finding a buyer for a home listed by the Bentley Realty Company. As a general rule, she will receive her commission
    a. as soon as the contract for sale of realty is signed.
    b. at the end of each month, along with any other commissions she may have earned in the month.
    c. from the broker as soon as practicable after collection.
    d. from the seller at closing.

_____33. Which of the following represents a primary function of real estate brokers?
    a. Soliciting buyers.
    b. Negotiating a sale.
    c. Closing a sale.
    d. All of the above.

_____34. Real estate license law prohibits real estate brokers from acting as principals on their own account without
    a. the approval of the state regulatory agency.
    b. the approval of the local real estate board.
    c. full disclosure of their status.
    d. reservations.

_____35. A subagency is created if the selling broker
    a. assigns selling responsibilities to a salesperson.
    b. cooperates with another broker in completing a sale.
    c. participates in a sale by exercising an option.
    d. assigns the selling responsibilities to another broker.

_____36. Written or oral contracts are said to create agency by
    a. implied contract.
    b. express contract.
    c. contract in fact.
    d. none of the above.

_____37. _____ occurs as the result of a special circumstance existing between the agent and a principal.

    a. An implied contract
    b. An expressed contract
    c. A contract in fact
    d. An ostensible contract

_____38. Normally, termination of an agency may occur by
    I. expiration of the agency.
    II. destruction of the subject of the agency.
    a. I only.
    b. II only.
    c. Both I and II.
    d. Neither I nor II.

_____39. The authority of an agent may be created by
    a. authority expressed or implied by contract.
    b. apparent authority.
    c. authority arising from an agency relationship.
    d. all of the above.

_____40. The agent must attempt to follow instructions of the principal unless
    a. the principal makes an unreasonable demand, such as over-pricing the property.
    b. the instructions are illegal.
    c. the instructions are oral.
    d. the listing principal has grossly underpriced the property.

ANSWER KEY

1. (*c*)	11. (*c*)	21. (*c*)	31. (*d*)
2. (*d*)	12. (*a*)	22. (*b*)	32. (*c*)
3. (*d*)	13. (*b*)	23. (*d*)	33. (*d*)
4. (*b*)	14. (*c*)	24. (*c*)	34. (*c*)
5. (*b*)	15. (*c*)	25. (*d*)	35. (*b*)
6. (*d*)	16. (*c*)	26. (*a*)	36. (*b*)
7. (*c*)	17. (*d*)	27. (*a*)	37. (*a*)
8. (*d*)	18. (*d*)	28. (*d*)	38. (*c*)
9. (*d*)	19. (*a*)	29. (*d*)	39. (*d*)
10. (*d*)	20. (*b*)	30. (*d*)	40. (*b*)

SUGGESTED ADDITIONAL READING

Beaton, William R., and Bond, Robert J. *Real Estate*. Pacific Palisades, Calif.: Goodyear Publishing Co., Inc., 1976, chap. 5.

Harwood, Bruce. *Real Estate Principles*. Reston, Va.: Reston Publishing Co., Inc., 1977, chap. 18.

Real Estate Office Management: People, Functions, Systems. Chicago, Ill.: Realtors® National Marketing Institute of the National Association of Realtors®, 1975, chap. 9.

Shenkel, William M. *Modern Real Estate Principles.* Dallas, Tex.: Business Publications, Inc., 1977, chaps. 16 and 17.

Unger, Maurice A. *Real Estate: Principles & Practices.* 5th ed. Cincinnati, O.: South-Western Publishing Co., 1974, chap. 17.

4

Real Estate License Laws

Real estate license statutes of the 50 states require persons acting as real estate salespersons or brokers to be licensed by a state agency. Though these laws vary in their administrative procedures, they are fairly uniform in regulating the conduct of real estate brokers and their employees. The laws are in fairly close agreement, moreover, on acts considered to be in violation of the real estate license law. Further, most states require prospective licensees to be familiar with a well-defined code of ethics. Several states incorporate the code of ethics of the National Association of Realtors in their rules and regulations.

The most important issues to be reviewed relate to the rationale of license laws and their general content. The next section of this chapter covers regulations that are fairly common to the majority of the states. Even if the items noted are not covered specifically by statute or rules and regulations of the licensing agency, they constitute good business practice. A special section on the code of ethics completes the topical material normally required of prospective licensees.

GENERAL PROVISIONS OF REAL ESTATE LICENSE LAWS

To understand the content of license laws, it is worthwhile to trace the origin of real estate license laws. A review of their main elements shows the general purpose of regulating salespersons and brokers.

The Rationale of Real Estate License Laws

Real estate license laws originated with a 1917 California act which was declared unconstitutional. In 1919 the California legislature amended the

94

original act, resulting in a successful test of its constitutionality. The 1919 act was introduced by the real estate industry to regulate those engaged in the real estate brokerage activity. The justification was the protection of the public in real estate transactions employing the services of real estate brokers. In the words of a New York court, "the license laws were designed to protect dealers in real estate from unlicensed persons who acted as brokers and to protect the public from inept, inexperienced or dishonest persons who might perpetrate or aid in the perpetration of frauds upon it and to establish protective or qualifying standards to that end." (*Dodge v. Richmond*, 173 N.Y.S. 2d 786 [1958].)

Earlier opponents of the law viewed it as deprivation of individual private property rights without due process of law. It was argued that the state cannot legally prohibit a person from following his trade. The courts had ruled that the state has the right to regulate real estate brokers and salesmen under the police power; that is, the right to regulate in the interest of the public health, convenience, welfare, and safety.

Though all states have enacted real estate license laws, they vary widely in their educational requirements. For instance, the Kentucky license law was first enacted in 1924 but declared unconstitutional in 1925. A reenactment of the real estate license law of 1938, however, did not require a written examination for broker and salesmen until enactment of a 1952 amendment. Licenses were required in Kentucky for only first, second, and third cities within a radius of five miles until 1956 when the act was amended to include the entire state. Similarly, it was not until 1963 that the real estate license law applied to all 95 counties of Tennessee. In each instance the legislative purpose of license laws was to protect the general public. In protecting the public, moreover, competent persons engaged in the real estate business benefit by increased public confidence in real estate agencies.

Educational Requirements

The philosophy of license law regulation has materially changed from its inception. Before World War I, a Milwaukee real estate board member stated it was easier to become a real estate man than to qualify as a barber. Initially, real estate license laws were merely administered as occupational licenses introduced for revenue purposes and not for qualifying competent salespersons and brokers. To eliminate the unscrupulous, some communities raised license fees and—as did Louisiana (in 1900)—required a $5,000 security bond.

Of special importance are the educational activities of the National Association of Real Estate License Law Officials. Through this organization, license law officials are encouraged to work with their legislatures to support real estate education. This support has assumed many different forms.

In California, an educational fund of some $8 million has accumulated from license fees for educational purposes. These funds are used to support research and university real estate courses. Today California brokers must have a minimum of six college courses.

1. In Ohio, a portion of the license law fee supports an education and research fund. Grants are made to universities and colleges for real estate education. Brokers and salespersons must have 120 and 60 hours of instruction.

2. In Texas, one-half of all renewal fees supports an education and research center at Texas A&M University. License officials supervise real estate courses in 50 universities and colleges.

3. In Kentucky, license fee monies support an education and research fund that currently totals over $200,000.

4. The Pennsylvania Real Estate Commission has approved courses 1A, 1B, and 1I given by the American Institute of Real Estate Appraisers toward qualification for a broker's license.

These are current developments which show an increasing trend toward higher educational standards for licensed personnel. These trends may be expected to continue, requiring even higher educational standards as a prerequisite to holding a real estate license. Numerous universities offer a bachelor degree with a real estate major. A few schools such as Ohio State University, American University, the University of California, and the University of Georgia offer a Doctor of Philosophy degree with emphasis on real estate subjects. Graduates with higher degrees are active in advanced real education and research. This growing emphasis on real estate education makes one thing clear: Prospective licensees—more than ever before—have an opportunity (and the responsibility) to increase their competence in real estate activities.

General License Law Administration

The license laws, though subject to different orders of presentation, generally cover certain common administrative points:

1. Creation of the regulatory agency: the real estate commission, boards, or other designated body.
2. Persons requiring a real estate license.
3. Qualifications of prospective licensees.

Besides these points, administrative provisions detail specific procedures that must be followed by licensees. For the present purpose, the most important aspect of real estate license laws relates to the direct regulation of salespersons and brokers. Directives of the license law generally concentrate on:

1. Positive directions, requiring compliance of all licensees, salespersons, and brokers.
2. Specific acts prohibited licensees under the license law.

As an expedient in enforcing real estate license law, real estate commissions may enact rules and regulations under authority granted by the state legislature. Though most of the listed grounds for revocation or suspension of licenses are found among the respective states, state references must be consulted for a more detailed review.

Creation of the Regulatory Agency. Typically the real estate commission, the real estate board, or other designated body is made up of real estate brokers who have had several years experience. The real estate license act in Georgia, for example, creates a commission appointed by the governor with the approval of the secretary of state and confirmed by the senate. The commission meets at least once a month or as often as necessary to undertake the business of the commission. Each commission member must be a licensed real estate broker or salesperson, a resident of the state and actively engaged in the real estate business. Since the states show much variation and because these details are covered by license examinations, individual state license manuals should be studied for information respecting each state.

Persons Requiring a Real Estate License. To regulate real estate activity, the laws may define real estate brokers or those subject to license examination to include agencies and related activities. Some of the occupations coming under license law regulation include:

Real estate auctioneers	Advance fee agents
Real property managers	Real estate appraisers
Mortgage lenders	Salespersons of cemetary lots
Real estate salespersons	Corporations selling lots
Real estate schools	Business opportunity brokers
Officers of corporations performing as brokers	Real estate brokers

The licensing requirement has been tested by persons seeking commissions from an isolated transaction not undertaken as the regular activity of a real estate broker. A salesman for an Arizona beer distributor agreed to find a buyer for tavern fixtures and a tavern lease. He was to receive any amount over $6,000 paid to the seller. When he found a buyer who paid $9,000, he sued for a $3,000 real estate commission, claiming a real estate license was unnecessary for an isolated transaction. The court replied: "The underlying public purpose is not served in subjecting an unsuspecting public to untested, unregulated practitioners of isolated transactions. (*Bonasera* v. *Roffe*, 442 P. 2d 165 [1968].)

To illustrate further, the Stapleton Insurance and Realty Company, an Alabama corporation, was unable to enforce payment of a $21,250 commission because none of the corporate officers held a broker's license. The fact that the corporation employed a licensed broker did not constitute compliance with the license law. (*Faulkner* v. *Stapleton Insurance and Realty Corp.*, 96 So. 2d 761 [1957].)

In still other states, license regulations apply only to parties receiving a commission acting as agent for a principal. The trend, however, is to include others serving the public in a consulting, fiduciary, or other agent classification such as a property manager.

Qualifications of Prospective Licensees. Qualifications for prospective salespersons and brokers usually include a minimum age, citizenship, residency in the state, and a minimum educational requirement. Broker applicants must have, as a rule, some experience as a salesperson to qualify for the broker examination. Educational requirements may include a minimum number of classroom hours of instruction given by noncredit private or public institutions. The subject content, the quality of instruction, and copies of the examination usually must be submitted to the regulatory agency for approval.

Some states such as Georgia permit three five-credit-hour real estate courses in an accredited university or college as qualification for prospective broker examinees. In Georgia salespersons must complete an approved course of instruction on subjects selected by the real estate commission or have satisfactorily taken real estate courses offered by an accredited college or university. The state legislatures are tending to raise real estate educational requirements before applicants are allowed to take real estate license tests.

Administrative Provisions

License laws are unique to each state. The term of the license, the license fee, examination fees, and rules for submitting documents, application forms, and letters of recommendation are subjects covered in state license manuals. Other features of state license laws tend to be fairly common. They are noted here because experience indicates that certain administrative requirements are necessary for the protection of the public.

First, the license laws require brokers to maintain a place of business. Generally, brokers may not use post office box numbers; they must have an office that can be readily located by the public. They must display their own licenses and the licenses of employee-salespersons. In this regard, brokers may not imply a relationship to a large corporation. That is, they must present their services as independent agents without implying that they have a relationship with a national corporation or in any other way indicate that they are not an independent, free agent. In addition, most states require that branch offices must be supervised by a licensed broker. Changes of location and transfers of salespersons are closely regulated and require strict observance of standard forms and procedures.

Other features of real estate license laws cover the administration of inactive licenses of salespersons and brokers who maintain their status while temporarily inactive in the real estate business.

Subdivision Sales. Some license authorities are charged with protecting the public from false representation and deceit in the sale of lots both in and out of state. Thus, in Oregon no person shall offer any subdivided land for sale or lease without having complied with all applicable provisions of ORS 92.21 to 92.390 (Oregon Subdivision Control Law). The act is similar to legislation in Georgia, Pennsylvania, California, and other states that require that subdividers identify their organization, the names and addresses of licensees, and other persons selling in the state.

The legal description of the land and locality, title information, potential use of property, a complete statement of utility availability and occupancy restrictions are other criteria necessary for compliance. With this information, the approving authority issues a public report which must be given to potential purchasers. Salespersons and brokers engaged in the sale of subdivision lots according to the Oregon statute are in violation of a law if they commit any of the prohibited acts listed in the statute:

(1) Employ any device, scheme or artifice to defraud;

(2) Make any untrue statement of a material fact or fail to state a material fact necessary to make the statement made, in the light of the circumstances under which it is made, not misleading;

(3) Engage in any act, practice or course of business which operates or would operate as a fraud or deception upon any person;

(4) Issue, circulate or publish any prospectus, circular, advertisement, printed matter, document, pamphlet, leaflet or other literature which contains an untrue statement of a material fact or fails to state a material fact necessary in order to make the statements therein made, in the light of the circumstances under which they are made, not misleading;

(5) Issue, circulate or publish any advertising matter or make any written representation, unless the name of the person issuing, circulating or publishing the matter or making the representation is clearly indicated;

(6) Make any statement or representation, or issue, circulate or pub-

lish any advertising matter containing any statement to the effect that the real estate subdivision has been in any way approved or endorsed by the commissioner.

Regulation of Real Estate Schools. Real estate schools are licensed and regulated for the protection of prospective licensees. Among the states imposing fairly strict regulations are California, Pennsylvania, Wisconsin, Oklahoma, Illinois, and Georgia.

Indiana has approved a course for salesmen and women to be administered by the Indiana Real Estate Commission in cooperation with the University of Indiana. The law requires that the course extend over 2-½ hours per week for 16 weeks. The course covers real estate practice, which includes bookkeeping, ethics, and a review of the Indiana real estate license act. California has a similar program requiring the broker to take four college-level courses on the legal aspects of real estate, real estate practice, real estate finance, and real estate appraisal before taking the real estate examination.

The regulations of schools is illustrated by Pennsylvania, which requires Real Estate Commission approval for schools other than accredited universities and colleges. Schools must be owned by persons of moral character and financial responsibility as evidenced by a surety bond. The director of each school must devote at least one half the school day to administration and be qualified as an instructor in real estate.

Teaching loads are limited to one teacher for 60 students per hour and 300 students daily. No instructor is allowed to teach more than 20 50-minute classes a week. Student fees, records, advertising, and the curriculum are subject to commission approval. Instructors must have had at least five years active real estate practice, hold a college degree with college credits in courses they propose to teach, or have an equivalent education as approved by the commission. The school plant must conform to standards of the commission. Standards set by Pennsylvania parallel similar regulations of other states that protect the novice from false representation, excessive fees and incompetent instruction.

Real Estate Recovery Fund. Some states have eliminated the bonding requirement of real estate brokers, substituting instead a real estate recovery fund. In some states, the law authorizes a fund from which any person aggrieved by any act, representation, transaction, or conduct of a licensed broker or salesperson who acts in violation of the license law to recover through the courts actual damages resulting from the violation. In Georgia a limit of $10,000 per transaction is imposed on each case.

To illustrate further, the Georgia Act does not cover salespersons acting on their own account. In lieu of the bonding requirement, the broker pays in addition to his original fee, a $20 deposit into the real estate recovery fund. Each salesperson pays an additional fee of $10. If the balance remaining in the real estate recovery fund is less than $200,000 on December 31 of each year, brokers in renewing their license, shall pay an additional renewal fee of $10 into the real estate recovery fund, and salespersons must pay in addition to the license fee a $5 deposit into the real estate recovery fund.

A party claiming a violation of the license act must secure a valid judgment in a court of competent jurisdiction against the broker or salesperson. By filing a verified claim in the court and upon ten days' written notice to the commission, the person may apply to the court for an order directing payment out of the real estate recovery fund for the amount unpaid upon the judgment after the complaining party has taken all reasonable steps to collect the judgment and exhausted all remedies available for recovering the court award.

If the Real Estate Commission is directed to pay the claim toward satisfaction of the judgment against a licensed broker or salesperson, the license of such broker or salesperson is automatically terminated. The license will not be renewed unless the recovery fund is repaid with interest. Therefore, in the event the licensee does not have sufficient assets to pay claims, parties suffering damages as a result of violation of the real estate license law have a means to recoup their losses, up to the limit of $10,000.

Escrow Regulations. A review of license laws shows that the states publish detailed directions on the handling of real estate trust funds. Trust funds are defined as money or things of value received by the broker or his salespeople on behalf of the principal or any other person, not belonging to the broker but being held for the benefit of others. Trust funds are normally received from four sources:

1. Earnest money and down payments.
2. Collection of rents, security deposits, payments on land contracts, mortgages, tax and insurance escrow money.
3. Advance fees.
4. Receipts relating to the sale, exchange, purchase, or rental of business properties.

The broker typically must identify the name of the bank, the trust account for deposit of all real estate trust funds, and authorize state authorities to audit trust accounts. His personal funds must not be commingled with those held in trust. A bookkeeping system must be provided listing dates, names of parties to the transaction, amount of receipts, and disposition of funds received. Wisconsin requires the withdrawal of fees and commissions earned by the broker within 24 hours after the transaction is completed.

While the broker may delegate bookkeeping duties, he is held strictly accountable for the management of the trust account. He is advised to instruct salespeople to issue receipts for all trust funds taken on behalf of the broker, preferably using only consecutively numbered down payment receipts in a bound receipt book. By reviewing carbon copies of the receipt book, and by bonding salespeople, the broker may more closely supervise his employees.

Failure to observe this rule subjects the broker to civil and criminal action and possibly a suspension and revocation of license. He cannot rationalize the misappropriation of funds by replacing funds, claiming that "everything is back in order." Any misappropriation violates rules of licensing agencies.

To demonstrate, the license of an Illinois broker was revoked by his failure to return a purchaser's deposit of $1,100 after the seller refused to go through with the sale. The broker sold property in Chicago owned by Mr. and Mrs. Cooper to Mr. and Mrs. Coleman, who deposited $1,300 with the broker, turning $200 over to the sellers. Subsequently Mr. Cooper died and Mrs. Cooper decided not to sell, returning $200 to the buyer. The broker refused to return the deposit, claiming he was entitled to a commission. Though the broker was entitled to a commission, his action should have been directed to the defaulting principal, the seller. The broker had no right to retain the purchaser's deposit, who was not in default. After a hearing, the Illinois Department of Registration and Education revoked the broker's license upon a finding that the broker "had neglected, failed and refused to return the earnest money deposit of $1,100. . . ." (*Huff* v. *Department of Registration and Education,* 180 N.E. 2d 460 [1962].)

GROUNDS FOR SUSPENSION OR REVOCATION

Provisions of the real estate license law that identify acts of a salesman or broker causing the commissioner to suspend or revoke a license are known as the "thou shall not" provisions. Licenses shall be suspended or revoked if it is proven that the licensee has been guilty of committing any of the listed grounds for revocation or suspension. Many of these provisions are taken from court litigation on these points.

It should be noted that courts support revocation to preserve proper standards of conduct and character. For example, in New York a conviction for a felony is grounds for revocation. In the case of a salesman who had been convicted of a felony and subsequently appealed, the New York Supreme Court ruled that revocation was improper while the conviction for a felony was under appeal. (*Colombo* v. *Lomenzo,* 321 N.Y.S. 2d 1000 [1971].)

Relations to Public

Most grounds for disciplinary action deal with the broker's relation to the public. His or her conduct toward other members of the industry may also serve as ground for suspension or revocation. An explanation of the more frequent causes of disciplinary action indicates how the broker must strictly serve the license laws.

Substantial Misrepresentations. The type of misrepresentations included under "substantial" usually result from the failure of a licensee to disclose material facts to the principal. However, a New Jersey broker's license was suspended when he was accused of falsely signing a corporate check to meet a payroll. His misrepresentation and false denials before the commission were ruled as demonstrations of unworthiness and incompetency, a violation of the license act. The court upheld the license suspension. (*Middleton v. Division of New Jersey Estate Commission*, 120 A 2d 789 [1956].) It should be noted that the misrepresentations to the public must be interpreted as "substantial" and not the mere "puffing of goods."

False Promises. A false promise is a statement about what a promisor is going to do in the future. Usually these cases cover promises that are impossible to fulfill; they are false because the person making the promise knows that they are impossible of performance. The failure to carry out an oral promise by a broker served as sufficient grounds to revoke a license. The broker, as part of the sale agreement, orally promised to share equally with the buyer the cost of a landfill on land sold to the buyer. On findings of the Division of the New Jersey Real Estate Commission, the broker was accused of making a false promise, causing his license to be revoked. (*Maple Hill Farms, Inc. v. Div. of N.J.R.E. Comm.*, 170 A. 2d 461 [1961].)

Acting for More than One Party. The licensing authority usually has authority to discipline an agent if he acts for more than one party without full disclosure. This provision is in agreement with agency law.

Commingling. The license laws provide that funds of a principal and money entrusted to the broker be held in a separate bank account. If the broker fails to observe this rule and mixes personal funds with funds of the principal, the broker risks license revocation. A related problem represents conversion, which constitutes a personal spending of a deposit. Conversion for personal use and misappropriation of money belonging to others may be subject to civil and criminal penalties.

Secret Profits. Revocation and suspension may follow if a licensee uses a dummy purchaser to buy listed property for a low price and then later sells at a higher price to an undisclosed buyer. Secret profits result from the spread between these two prices. Such an action is against most real estate license laws.

A salesperson was censored by the commission and discharged by her broker for making an undisclosed profit against the interest of a principal. The facts revealed that this salesperson purchased property listed with her broker for $6,000 through her parents, and collected a commission on the sale. Two days later she conveyed title to another purchaser, profiting $1,196 on the resale. The complaint charged the salesperson with a violation of Rule 6, prohibiting brokers from buying on their own account, directly or indirectly, without informing the listing owner. (*Cochrane* v. *Wittbold*, 102 N.W. 2d 459 [1960].)

Agreements to Sell and Options to Buy. Suspension and revocation is avoided (1)·if the licensee obtains the written consent of..the principal indicating the amount of profit he may make by exercising the option, or (2) if the broker or salesperson uses the option without listing the same property. Otherwise, suspension or revocation follows because the licensee violates the fiduciary relationship if he makes an undisclosed profit at the expense of his principal by exercising the option.

Dishonest Dealing. Some license laws include dishonest dealing as grounds for suspension to cover dishonest acts not mentioned specifically in other rules and regulations or the license law.

In some instances the dishonesty need not arise from acts of a real estate broker. In New Jersey a real estate license was revoked after a broker, acting as a principal and not as a broker, unlawfully refused to return a deposit to a purchaser who could not obtain the necessary mortgage to complete the sale. In upholding the commission, the court stated:

> . . . acts of a licensed broker comprehended by the statute in its specifications which are determined by the Commission to disqualify the real estate broker from the retention or renewal of his license are not necessarily restricted to those committed in the pursuit of the privileges accorded by the license. (*Division of New Jersey Real Estate Commission* v. *Ponsi*, 121 A 2d 555 [1956].)

Real Estate Appraising. The real estate commission in Georgia has the power to revoke or suspend a licensed salesperson or broker who appraises real estate contingent upon the reporting of a predetermined value. Or if the appraisal report is completed on property on which the broker has an undisclosed interest, the licensee is subject to disciplinary action. This does not bar real estate brokers from appraising property which they later accept as a listing. The regulation only applies to appraisals that are directed to a given value or that cover property in which the broker may have intentions of purchasing or selling to other undisclosed buyers.

Free Lot Schemes. Free lot schemes, though subject to much variation, are methods of giving low-value lots to a party as an inducement to purchase adjoining property. For example, the victim may be informed that he is the winner of a lottery giving him title to a free lot, say Lot 1. This letter is followed by a generous offer to purchase Lot 1 and Lot 2 by a fictitious corporation. The victim is induced to purchase Lot 2 because he anticipates a profitable resale to the corporation. After the second lot is purchased, the corporation disappears or withdraws its offer. Generally it is a violation of license laws to "solicit, sell or offer for sale real estate by offering free lots or conducting lotteries for the purpose of influencing a purchaser or respective purchaser of real estate."

Sharing Commissions. It is universally true that the license laws prohibit sharing of commissions or paying compensation for services of a salesperson or broker to unlicensed persons. The regulation covers part-time people who solicit listings or unlicensed office personnel who show property during the absence of salespersons and brokers. Payments for tips on prospective buyers or listings to unlicensed persons are similarly prohibited.

To cite a related issue, consider the salesperson who, unknown to his broker, held himself out as a broker. While employed by another broker, the salesperson filed a certificate of doing business under the "Nicholas Agency," advertising in the newspaper and posting signs in this name. He obtained listings for sale on his own account and not in the name of his broker. The New York Court upheld the revocation of the salesman's license. (*Triolo* v. *Department of State*, 322 N.Y.S. 2d 328 [1971].)

Copies of Sales Documents. In states requiring a written listing agreement, and in states that require an expiration date for listings, it is a violation of the license act not to give a copy of listing agreements to the principal. Moreover, state law usually directs the real estate broker to deliver to the seller and to the buyer complete and detailed closing statements showing receipts and disbursements relating to the transaction. The accounting must show the disposition of all costs and monies received by the broker. Copies of statements must be retained for audit.

Real Estate Commissions Not a Lien. Real estate brokers can not file a lien against the property sold to recover a commission. The agent must bring proceedings against the principal as other creditors act against defaulting debtors. Despite this rule, occasionally real estate brokers, violating rules of ethics and license laws, wrongfully place liens on real estate, which effectively cloud the owner's title.

Consequently, rules and regulations frequently list this activity as grounds for suspension or revocation of the license. In Georgia a broker's license may be revoked if the broker files "a listing contract or any document or instrument purporting to create a lien based on a listing contract for the purpose of casting a cloud on the title of real estate when no valid claim under said listing contract exists."

Demonstrated Incompetence. The broker in holding out as a real estate agent is charged with serving the principal in a competent, businesslike manner. Failure to observe this requirement may subject the broker to civil, criminal, and disciplinary action. Real estate commissions charged with safeguarding the interests of the public may revoke or suspend the license in the light of demonstrated unworthiness or incompetency to act as a real estate broker or salesperson, or for any other conduct constituting dishonesty or deceit.

Though not losing his license, a Louisiana broker accused of incompetence lost a commission of $3,000 and was required to pay $1,386 damages to his principal. The broker sold a 138-acre tract to a subdivider without mentioning a 50-foot easement for a power line that restricted access to the site to not more than four streets. The principal refused to take title and to pay a commission. The court required the broker to pay $1,386 in surveying fees which the principal paid after the contract for sale was executed. The broker in stating that there were no easement restrictions misrepresented the facts. (*Norgren* v. *Harwell*, 172 So. 2d 723 [1965].)

Relations to Other Brokers

Unethical practices with respect to salespersons and brokers can also be grounds for suspension or revocation of a license.

Dealing Direct with Owner Represented by Another Broker. If a licensee knowingly negotiates with an owner in the sale, exchange, or lease of real estate knowing that such owner has an unexpired listing contract for an exclusive agency or right to sell, the licensee has committed an unethical practice. This provision discourages brokers from inducing property owners to revoke binding listing contracts with others. (The same principle is extended to illegal competition for listing contracts.) The licenses of a broker and salesperson were revoked by the state of New York for similar conduct, termed "demonstrated untrustworthiness." The salesperson and broker induced an owner to breach a prior contract of sale and to substitute a new contract of sale with themselves as purchasers. License revocation was founded on "a reasonable basis in law and was neither arbitrary or capricious." (*Tegeler* v. *Department of State*, 258 N.Y.S. 2d 850 [1965].)

Illegal Solicitation of Listing Contracts. If a licensee knows that another broker has an exclusive listing on a property, he is typically prevented from obtaining an exclusive listing or sales contract covering the same property. To proceed in this fashion, he must have written permission from the broker holding the unexpired exclusive listing agreement. The unethical practice is that of encouraging others to violate contracts. Not only does this constitute grounds for suspension or revocation of the license, but the broker may suffer other court awarded damages.

Sharing Commissions. While brokers may share listings and cooperate in sales, it is usually against the license law to share a commission or compensation for performing as a real estate broker with one who is not licensed in the state in which his services are performed. The cooperative broker must be licensed as a nonresident broker or otherwise conform to rules governing nonresident, cooperating licensees.

Discrimination against Minorities

Real estate licensees are required to observe common and statutory law, federal, state and local, dealing with the purchase and sale of real estate, especially housing. For example, in Georgia, the licensee, if found guilty of discriminatory practices, may have his license suspended or revoked. Grounds for suspension include "refusing, because of race, color, national origin or ethnic group, to show, sell or rent any real estate for sale or rent to prospective purchasers or renters."

Thus a broker had his license suspended for 90 days for violating the Chicago Fair Housing Ordinance which makes it unlawful to refuse listings of any real estate because of race, color, religion, or national ancestry. The broker had refused to show an apartment listing to a prospect because of his race. (*Bell Realty and Ins. Agency* v. *Chicago Commission on Human Rel.*, 266 N.E. 2d 769 [1971].)

Some states go further and prohibit "blockbusting" tactics. In Philadelphia, the real estate commission restricts brokers from inducing high-volume sales or lease by appealing to racial, religious, or ethic prejudices. People aroused in this manner are induced to panic selling, causing market values to decline and vacancies to increase. Panic selling is defined as frequent efforts to sell residential real estate in a particular neighborhood as a result of fear of a decline of real estate values, when the fear is not based on facts relating to the intrinsic value of the real estate itself.

To enforce this rule, the real estate broker is directed not to solicit by personal contact, or advertise by phone or mail the sale of real estate in such frequency as to constitute harassment of the owner. The systematic solicitation of listings is viewed in Pennsylvania as conclusive evidence of an attempt to induce panic selling.

THE CODE OF ETHICS

The Code of Ethics, published by the National Association of Realtors, first adopted in 1913, covers 24 articles. Some articles deal with the professional conduct of Realtors as well as their relations with the public. The final four articles cover relations of Realtors with other Realtors. Though adopted and published by the National Association of Realtors, several real estate commissions have published a code of ethics in state manuals. For example, see *The Oklahoma Manual for Real Estate Brokers and Salesmen*, G. Douglas Fox (ed.), Oklahoma Real Estate Commission, Oklahoma City, Oklahoma, January 1969, pages 9–11.

The first few articles guide the Realtor in the professional relationships with the community and clients. In many instances, the Code of Ethics closely corresponds to legal grounds for suspension and revocation of a real estate license.

> **Article 1**   The Realtor® should keep himself informed on matters affecting real estate in his community, the state, and nation so that he may be able to contribute responsibly to public thinking on such matters.*

The first article directs Realtors to advise the public on issues that might affect real estate investments. In the local community, this means that the Realtor would be expected to participate in hearings on new proposals for zoning, planning, environmental controls, and other regulatory measures. On the state level, the Realtor, who observes Article 1, would offer advice to public officials on pending legislation that could affect land use, real estate finance, and real estate investments. On national issues, Realtors observing this article would interpret the effect of proposed legislation on real estate matters. For example, Realtors have been active in interpreting the effect of rent controls on the local housing supply.

> **Article 2**   In justice to those who place their interests in his care, the Realtor® should endeavor always to be informed regarding laws, proposed legislation, governmental regulations, public policies, and current market conditions in order to be in a position to advise his clients properly.

Since property owners often turn to the Realtor for an interpretation of the real estate market, the Realtor must keep informed on public events that may affect real estate investments—for example, a proposal to construct a new highway or new income tax legislation that might affect real estate interests of clients. Any relevant information known to the Realtor should be passed on to the client. Clearly, the Realtor has a responsibility under Article 2 to help clients make decisions on the sale, purchase, lease, and financing of real estate.

> **Article 3**   It is the duty of the Realtor® to protect the public against fraud, misrepresentation, and unethical practices in real estate transactions. He should endeavor to eliminate in his community any practices

---

* Note: Where the word Realtor® is used in this Code and Preamble, it shall be deemed to include Realtor®-Associate. Pronouns shall be considered to include Realtors® and Realtor®-Associates of both genders.

The Code of Ethics was adopted in 1913. Amended at the Annual Convention in 1924, 1928, 1950, 1951, 1952, 1955, 1956, 1961, 1962, and 1974.

Published with the consent of the National Association of Realtors®, author of and owner of all rights in the Code of Ethics of the National Association of Realtors®, © National Association of Realtors® 1974—all rights reserved.

which could be damaging to the public or bring discredit to the real estate profession. The Realtor® should assist the governmental agency charged with regulating the practices of brokers and salesmen in his state.

For the most part, Article 3 agrees with real estate license laws that provide for the suspension or revocation of licenses if licensed real estate personnel commit fraud or make misrepresentations. Note, however, that Article 3 goes beyond the statutory requirement. The act includes unethical practices. That is, the Realtor is directed to help eliminate any practice which could be damaging to the public or bring discredit to the real estate profession. False statements, the act of withholding information considered valuable to a client, or acting in any way against the public interest would fall under this category. Realtor members are encouraged to help regulatory agencies in supervising the conduct of brokers and real estate salespersons.

> **Article 4** The Realtor® should seek no unfair advantage over other Realtors® and should conduct his business so as to avoid controversies with other Realtors®.

Realtors are prevented from actively soliciting listings held by other Realtors or otherwise damaging the reputation of other Realtors. Controversies over real estate commissions would be avoided by insisting on written listing agreements and documentation on the prospects the Realtor has solicited on the part of a client. To observe Article 4, the Realtor must have a close familiarity with real estate legal requirements and know when to seek the advice of legal counsel in conveying, leasing, and managing real property.

> **Article 5** In the best interests of society, of his associates, and his own business, the Realtor® should willingly share with other Realtors® the lessons of his experience and study for the benefit of the public, and should be loyal to the Board of Realtors® of his community and active in its work.

It is clear that Realtors strive for business efficiency. Educational conferences, meetings, and courses of study are regularly sponsored by local, state, and national affiliates of the National Association of Realtors. New techniques are introduced to the membership; the organization circulates changes in laws that might affect Realtor operations. Going beyond technical expertise, real estate boards actively work with community programs to rehabilitate communities and sponsor other non-real estate but important community works.

> **Article 6** To prevent dissension and misunderstanding and to assure better service to the owner, the Realtor® should urge the exclusive listing of property unless contrary to the best interest of the owner.

Realtors strongly endorse exclusive listings—and probably for good reasons. An exclusive listing lessens the chance of controversies over payment of commissions and since the exclusive listing is usually in writing, both the client and the Realtor are guided by a written contract defining the rights and duties of both parties. This is another example showing how the Code of Ethics goes beyond the state license requirements. It would be difficult to promote professional conduct without an organization that sponsors and requires observance of a comprehensive Code of Ethics.

> **Article 7**   In accepting employment as an agent, the Realtor® pledges himself to protect and promote the interests of the client. This obligation of absolute fidelity to the client's interests is primary, but it does not relieve the Realtor® of the obligation to treat fairly all parties to a transaction.

Recall that a Realtor, in accepting a listing to sell a house, establishes a fiduciary relationship with the client. While the Realtor may observe the law, he or she would be in violation of Article 7 unless the Realtor actively promotes the interest of the client. It is equally true that business reputations depend on both buyer and seller satisfaction. While the agency-principal relationship prevails between the listing seller and the Realtor, the broker is reminded that fair treatment is required for both the client and the buyer-prospect.

> **Article 8**   The Realtor® shall not accept compensation from more than one party, even if permitted by law, without the full knowledge of all parties to the transaction.

Though most states prohibit Realtors from accepting compensation from more than one party without notifying both parties, membership in the National Association of Realtors also requires that the Realtor inform both the client and the prospect of the fact that the Realtor is compensated by both parties. If a Realtor is employed by a client to find a suitable property, say a factory site, the broker would earn a commission from the buyer. If at the same time the broker has a property listed that meets the buyer's requirements, the Realtor would be entitled to a commission from the seller according to the listing agreement. Collecting commissions from both parties in this case would be permissible under Article 8 only if the buyer and the seller know of the commission agreement.

> **Article 9**   The Realtor® shall avoid exaggeration, misrepresentation, or concealment of pertinent facts. He has an affirmative obligation to discover adverse factors that a reasonably competent and diligent investigation would disclose.

The Realtor is obligated to explain adverse factors—for instance, the danger of flooding during the rainy season which would not be evident during dry months. Similarly, the Realtor could not represent that a single family dwelling was insulated when in fact it was not. The Realtor could not be a party to concealing structural faults, damaged foundations, termite infestation, or other deficiencies. It would be difficult to meet the requirements of Article 9 without requiring that Realtors conform to a Code of Ethics.

Article 10   The Realtor® shall not deny equal professional services to any person for reasons of race, creed, sex, or country of national origin. The Realtor® shall not be a party to any plan or agreement to discriminate against a person or persons on the basis of race, creed, sex, or country of national origin.

Article 10 represents an intent to comply with federal and state laws on fair housing, credit matters, and nondiscriminatory legislation. A Realtor who docs not observe Article 10 would be subject to censure by the National Association of Realtors in addition to the penalties provided by law.

Article 11   A Realtor® is expected to provide a level of competent service in keeping with the Standards of Practice in those fields in which the Realtor® customarily engages.

The Realtor® shall not undertake to provide specialized professional services concerning a type of property or service that is outside his field of competence unless he engages the assistance of one who is competent on such types of property or service, or unless the facts are fully disclosed to the client. Any person engaged to provide such assistance shall be so identified to the client and his contribution to the assignment should be set forth.

The Realtor® shall refer to the Standards of Practice of the National Association as to the degree of competence that a client has a right to expect the Realtor® to possess, taking into consideration the complexity of the problem, the availability of expert assistance, and the opportunities for experience available to the Realtor®.

Since the Realtor is viewed by the public as an expert in a field, there is the possibility that a Realtor would offer advice on real estate matters for which he or she has no experience. A Realtor would be in violation of Article 11 if clients were advised to accept a technical financing plan. If a broker offered to appraise property for which he had no background (i.e., a shopping center or a complex industrial property) he or she would violate Article 11. Note that if the broker delegates an assignment to a third party, the person employed to provide assistance must be identified to the client.

Article 12   The Realtor® shall not undertake to provide professional services concerning a property or its value where he has a present or contemplated interest unless such interest is specifically disclosed to all affected parties.

This article deals directly with the agency-principal relationship. The client is entitled to know if the Realtor has an interest in the transaction of a client since an undisclosed interest might invite opportunities to violate the agency-principal relationship. The article also includes even contemplated interests which may or may not be realized.

> **Article 13**   The Realtor® shall not acquire an interest in or buy for himself, any member of his immediate family, his firm or any member thereof, or any entity in which he has a substantial ownership interest, property listed with him, without making the true position known to the listing owner. In selling property owned by himself, or in which he has any interest, the Realtor® shall reveal the facts of his ownership or interest to the purchaser.

Article 13 is an extension of Article 12 prohibiting the use of a "straw man." In other words, it would be unethical to purchase a client's property on the Realtor's own account by placing ownership with a family member or other entity in which the Realtor has a personal interest. The Realtor may become personally involved in the client's property, or he may sell property owned by himself provided the facts of the Realtor's interest or ownership are given to the client or prospect.

> **Article 14**   In the event of a controversy between Realtors® associated with different firms, arising out of their relationship as Realtors®, the Realtors® shall submit the dispute to arbitration in accordance with the regulations of their board or boards rather than litigate the matter.

Under this article Realtors have provided machinery to settle disputes over real estate commissions. This self-governing feature avoids unwelcome publicity that might arise in court testimony. Further, clients and prospects are protected by a formally recognized procedure which is less expensive and easily resolved.

> **Article 15**   If a Realtor® is charged with unethical practice or is asked to present evidence in any disciplinary proceeding or investigation, he shall place all pertinent facts before the proper tribunal of the member board or affiliated institute, society, or council of which he is a member.

There are occasions when a Realtor could be acting in agreement with the law and yet commit an unethical practice. This article provides machinery to enforce the Code of Ethics. A Realtor may be charged with an unethical practice if he does not comply with a request to submit the facts as requested.

> **Article 16**   When acting as agent, the Realtor® shall not accept any commission, rebate, or profit on expenditures made for his principal-owner, without the principal's knowledge and consent.

This article is a means of enforcing the agent-principal relationship. It is inconsistent for an agent to make a profit on expenditures made for his principal-owner without the principal's knowledge and consent. For example, the Realtor who purchases supplies and services in managing a client's property may not be allowed to make a profit on purchases or accept rebates from suppliers without the principal's knowledge and consent. This article is consistent with the agency-principal relationship.

Article 17 The Realtor® shall not engage in activities that constitute the unauthorized practice of law and shall recommend that legal counsel be obtained when the interest of any party to the transaction requires it.

The unauthorized practice of law is usually defined by agreements between Realtor organizations and the state bar associations. In other cases, the unauthorized practice of law by Realtors is covered by state statutes. Even if certain acts are regarded as the proper exercise of Realtor activities, the Realtor is required to recommend legal counsel if he believes the interest of a client involves a legal question.

Article 18 The Realtor® shall keep in a special account in an appropriate financial institution, separated from his own funds, monies coming into his possession in trust for other persons, such as escrows, trust funds, clients' monies, and other like items.

Recall that earnest money deposits and down payments given to the Realtor pending closing of a sale, represent other people's money. Accordingly, these funds must be placed in accounts separate from personal funds of the Realtor. Failure to observe this rule subjects the Realtor to an accusation of unethical conduct and, in most states, suspension or revocation of the real estate license.

Article 19 The Realtor® shall be careful at all times to present a true picture in his advertising and representations to the public. He shall neither advertise without disclosing his name nor permit any person associated with him to use individual names or telephone numbers, unless such person's connection with the Realtor® is obvious in the advertisement.

Article 19 for the most part duplicates state license laws. The Realtor who violates this article faces censure by the National Association of Realtors and their affiliates as well as endangering the status of his real estate license.

Article 20 The Realtor® for the protection of all parties, shall see that financial obligations and commitments regarding real estate transactions are in writing, expressing the exact agreement of the parties. A copy of each agreement shall be furnished to each party upon his signing such agreement.

Article 20 requires that Realtors observe good business practices. Presumably an oral listing would violate Article 20. By insisting on written agreements delivered to each party, the Realtor minimizes controversies, disagreements, and the possibility of litigation.

> **Article 21**   The Realtor® shall not engage in any practice or take any action inconsistent with the agency of another Realtor®.

One of the purposes of the Code of Ethics is to control relations with other members. By observing Article 21, each Realtor member may conduct business affairs without being subject to hostile acts by other Realtors. For example, it would be unethical for a Realtor to actively solicit a listing, knowing that another Realtor member had the same property under an exclusive listing. Article 21 would cover co-brokerage arrangements in which Realtors agree to share commissions with cooperating brokers.

> **Article 22**   In the sale of property which is exclusively listed with a Realtor®, the Realtor® shall utilize the services of other brokers upon mutually agreed upon terms when it is in the best interests of the client.

Negotiations concerning property which is listed exclusively shall be carried on with the listing broker, not with the owner, except with the consent of the listing broker.

Realtors who list property that would have an out-of-town market would be advised to solicit cooperation from other real estate brokers. It is a common practice to list industrial property which may have a regional or even a national market. A broker who lists a 500,000 square foot manufacturing plant in New Jersey would be expected to solicit cooperation in selling the property with other Realtors who specialize in industrial property. The New Jersey plant listed by a Realtor in Newark might be sold by a Realtor in Chicago. The last paragraph of Article 22 insures that the exclusive listing will be administered and controlled by the listing broker.

> **Article 23**   The Realtor® shall not publicly disparage the business practice of a competitor nor volunteer an opinion of a competitor's transaction. If his opinion is sought and if the Realtor® deems it appropriate to respond, such opinion shall be rendered with strict professional integrity and courtesy.

Realtors prefer to be judged by their clients and prospects according to the quality of their service. It would be unfair, and under Article 23 unethical, to criticize another Realtor before the public.

> **Article 24**   The Realtor® shall not directly or indirectly solicit the services or affiliation of an employee or independent contractor in the organization of another Realtor® without prior notice to said Realtor®.

The successful Realtor trains staff to serve clients. Under this article a key employee who has benefited from a company training program and who has access to confidential business information could not be ethically approached by a competitor with the idea of gaining business information of a competitor.

In short, legislation is inadequate to deal with business conduct. While state license laws provide minimum standards of competence, the real estate broker could practice unethically and still conform to legal requirements. Virtually the only way to protect the public from unethical practices lies in organizational support, administration, and enforcement of the Code of Ethics. The 24 articles control conduct of a Realtor in his relation with clients listing property for sale and with prospects who utilize services of a real estate broker.

Note further that the Code of Ethics encourages the closest cooperation of Realtors with the public on real estate issues. And finally, brokers look to the Code of Ethics to govern their interrelationships with other Realtors. These articles as a group supplement state, federal, and local regulations guiding real estate brokers and salespersons.

QUESTIONS FOR REVIEW

_____ 1.   Real estate license laws originated with the
   a.   Statute of Frauds, 1476.
   b.   Nebraska Homestead Act, 1867.
   c.   Bill of Rights, 1787.
   d.   California Real Estate Act, 1917.

_____ 2.   The objective of real estate license laws is to
   a.   restrict competition in the real estate industry.
   b.   provide a means of enforcing criminal and civil statutes.
   c.   protect the public.
   d.   promote better planning and zoning administration.

_____ 3.   Which of the following items is _not_ included in real estate license laws?
   a.   Creation of a regulatory agency.
   b.   A listing of persons requiring a real estate license.
   c.   Mortgage collection procedures.
   d.   Qualifications of prospective licensees.

_____ 4.   Though state legislatures differ in their attitudes toward licensing real estate brokers, the trend in the last few years has been toward

Note: The National Association of Realtors® reserves exclusively unto itself the right to comment on and interpret the Code and particular provisions thereof. For the National Association's official interpretations of the Code, see "Interpretations of the Code of Ethics: National Association of Realtors®."

    a. increasing the educational requirements of prospective brokers.

    b. decreasing the educational requirements to become a real estate broker in order to increase the number of brokers.

    c. decreasing the educational requirements to enable more practical-minded people to enter the profession.

    d. increasing the educational requirements to protect agents already licensed.

_____ 5. Which of the following is universally exempt from the license requirement?

    a. Auctioneers.

    b. Salespersons who only list property.

    c. Attorneys-at-law.

    d. Corporations selling cemetery lots.

_____ 6. Proprietary real estate schools, designed to train real estate brokers and salespersons, are generally

    a. organized by the real estate commission.

    b. designed to protect the public from incompetent salespersons or brokers.

    c. regulated to insure that prospective broker and salesperson licensees gain competent instruction.

    d. degree-granting publicly-owned schools.

_____ 7. Some states have eliminated the bond requirement for real estate brokers in favor of

    a. the assumption of liability by the real estate commission for losses suffered by the public.

    b. the rule of caveat emptor.

    c. a real estate recovery fund.

    d. civil and criminal penalties.

_____ 8. In states that have adopted the real estate recovery fund, the aggrieved individual must first

    a. have his attorney send a registered letter to the state real estate commission.

    b. secure a valid judgment in a court of competent jurisdiction.

    c. petition the state real estate regulatory agency for the amount of loss.

    d. petition the broker acting in violation of the license act.

_____ 9. Regulations covering escrow accounts cover

    a. rent payments.

    b. earnest money deposits.

    c. advance fees.

    d. all of the above.

_____10. Ultimately, who is responsible for the trust fund or escrow account of a real estate firm?

I.   The licensed broker or senior broker.
II. The salesman who was responsible for the transaction.
 a. I only.
 b. II only.
 c. Both I and II.
 d. Neither I nor II.

_____11. Which of the following is *not* a ground for license suspension or revocation?
 a. Conviction of a felony.
 b. Making false promises.
 c. Commingling of personal and escrow funds.
 d. A traffic violation.

_____12. "Puffing of goods" means
 a. a false promise.
 b. commingling.
 c. substantially misrepresenting facts.
 d. making overstatements of personal opinion.

_____13. If a broker distributes information about a transaction, part of which cannot transpire, he is subject to license revocation because he has
 a. made a false promise.
 b. commingled funds.
 c. substantially misrepresented the facts.
 d. committed a fraudulent act.

_____14. Which of the following is *not* included in the definition of a trust fund?
 a. Earnest money and down payments.
 b. Collection of rents and insurance escrow money.
 c. A real estate broker's personal account.
 d. Receipts relating to the sale of business property.

_____15. Suppose a broker, knowing that a purchaser was not able to meet the down payment requirement, submitted a loan application to a mortgage company at a higher price than the purchase price, enabling the purchaser to make a lower down payment. His license may be revoked on which of the following grounds?
 a. Commingling.
 b. Acting for more than one party.
 c. Making substantial misrepresentations.
 d. Making secret profits.

_____16. With regard to agreements to sell and options to buy, suspension and/or revocation of licenses is avoided if the
I.   licensee obtains a written consent of the principal indicating the amount of profit he may make by exercising the option.

     II. broker or salesperson uses the option without listing the same
property.

    a. I only.

    b. II only.

    c. Both I and II.

    d. Neither I nor II.

_____17. Which of the following statements is *incorrect?* The 24 articles
adopted by the National Association of Realtors

    a. serve as grounds to revoke a real estate salesperson's license.

    b. represent a code of ethics which Realtors must observe.

    c. closely parallel state laws governing the conduct of real estate
brokers and salespersons.

    d. establish rules of conduct for member Realtors.

_____18. The Code of Ethics published by the National Association of
Realtors has 24 articles that cover relations with

    a. the public.

    b. the client.

    c. other Realtors.

    d. all of the above.

_____19. Which of the following statements is *not* in the Code of Ethics of
the National Association of Realtors?

    a. The Realtor should keep himself informed on matters affect-
ing real estate in his community, the state, and nation so that
he may be able to contribute responsibility to public thinking
on such matters.

    b. The Realtor should seek no unfair advantage over other
Realtors and should conduct his business so as to avoid controversies with other Realtors.

    c. It is not the duty of a Realtor to protect the public against
fraud, misrepresentation, or unethical practices.

    d. None of the above.

_____20. Which of the following statements is *not* part of the Code of
Ethics of the National Association of Realtors?

    a. It is the duty of the Realtor to protect the public against
fraud, misrepresentation, and unethical practices in real estate
transactions.

    b. The Realtor's first objective and responsibility is the comple-
tion of his client's desires.

    c. To prevent dissension and misunderstanding and to assure
better service to the owner, the Realtor should urge the exclusive listing of property unless contrary to the best interest
of the owner.

    d. All of the above.

_____21. Which of the following would constitute an unethical practice?

    a. A Realtor advised all parties in a real estate transaction of their legal rights and indicated to the parties the best legal solution.

    b. A Realtor maintains a special bank account.

    c. A Realtor is especially careful in his advertising to present a true picture.

    d. A Realtor makes sure that financial obligations and commitments regarding real estate transactions are in writing.

_____22. Which of the following statements is correct?

    a. A Realtor should keep escrow trust funds, clients' monies, and other like items in a separate bank account.

    b. In accepting employment as an agent, a Realtor pledges himself to protect the interest of his firm.

    c. Since the Realtor is representing other parties to a transaction, he should be able to accept compensation from more than one party.

    d. Exclusive listing of property should not be urged and practiced by Realtors.

_____23. The Code of Ethics states: When acting as agent, the Realtor shall not accept any commission, rebate, or profit on expenditures made for his principal-owner, without the principal's knowledge and consent. Violation of this article is a

    a. violation on the grounds of commingling funds.

    b. violation of a fiduciary relationship.

    c. violation of agency law.

    d. misrepresentation.

_____24. Which of the following statements is *not* included in the Code of Ethics of the National Association of Realtors?

    a. The Realtor shall not directly or indirectly solicit the services or affiliation of an employee or independent contractor in the organization of another Realtor without prior notice to said Realtor.

    b. Signs giving notice of property for sale, rent, lease, or exchange may be placed on any property by one or more brokers and the owner.

    c. Negotiations concerning property which is listed exclusively shall be carried on with the listing broker, not with the owner, except with the consent of the listing broker.

    d. The Realtor shall be careful at all times to present a true picture in his advertising and representations to the public.

_____25. Which of the following statements complies with the Code of Ethics of the National Association of Realtors?

    a. A broker should use every advantage and should attempt to seek any advantage over his fellow brokers.

b. A broker should, without hesitation, point out the strengths and the weaknesses of fellow brokers.
c. In the event that a broker is charged with unethical practice, he should protect his own civil rights.
d. A broker should accept only written listings.

_____26. Which of the following statements is correct?
  a. A broker may solicit the services of an employee in an organization of a fellow broker without the knowledge of the employer.
  b. A broker may publicly criticize a competitor if it serves his purpose.
  c. A broker should seek every advantage over his fellow brokers.
  d. When a broker is charged with unethical practice, he should voluntarily place all pertinent facts before the proper tribunal.

_____27. Which of the following demonstrates a false promise?
  a. A statement about what a promisor is going to do in the future.
  b. A promise made by a person who knows the promise is impossible to fulfill.
  c. Failure to carry out an oral promise.
  d. All of the above.

_____28. David Jackson, owner of an apartment complex, hired Frank Lane, a Realtor specializing in subdivision property, to appraise his property for him. Lane violated the Code of Ethics if he
  a. revealed to Jackson that he obtained the assistance of an authority on apartment valuation.
  b. revealed to Jackson that he has never made a similar appraisal.
  c. secretly hired an authority on apartment valuation to assist him with the appraisal.
  d. referred Jackson to Tom Jones of Income Properties, Inc., an expert in apartment appraisal.

_____29. A Realtor should keep a special bank account, separated from his own funds, in which he deposits
  I. escrows.
  II. commissions.
  a. I only.
  b. II only.
  c. Both I and II.
  d. Neither I or II.

_____30. An attempt to influence the sale or lease of properties in a neighborhood by informing the residents of that neighborhood of the character, quality, or ethnic background of new residents constitutes
  a. a blockbusting tactic.
  b. harassment.

    c. an unethical practice.
    d. all of the above.

____31. Which of the following statements is correct? A broker may share his commission with

    a. all his employees.
    b. a cooperating broker.
    c. resident brokers only.
    d. out-of-state brokers only.

____32. If a broker has direct evidence as to the incompetence of another broker, he has a duty to report this to

    a. any and all clients that he comes in contact with.
    b. the public as a whole.
    c. the local real estate commission.
    d. the state real estate commission.

____33. Unless the owner-seller has consented, the salesperson violates his fiduciary responsibility to his principal if he accepts _____ as a down payment.

    a. cash
    b. a certified check
    c. cash and a certified check
    d. a note

____34. The Code of Ethics

    a. requires that the Realtor, for the protection of all parties, shall see that financial obligations and commitments regarding real estate transactions are in writing, expressing the exact agreement of the parties.
    b. requires brokers and salespersons to be licensed to enforce payment of a commission.
    c. regulates escrow accounts.
    d. regulates fraudulent conveyances.

____35. A salesperson negotiated a sale for her employing broker and demanded that the seller pay the commission to the firm. The seller refused to pay and the employing broker refused to be involved in a litigation regardless of the merits of the salesperson's claim. Therefore, the salesperson sued the seller in her own name. Which of the following statements is correct?

    a. A salesperson may not sue the principal in her own name and collect her portion of the commission.
    b. A salesperson can sue in court but must collect the commission for the broker also.
    c. It will not be necessary for the salesperson to go to court to obtain her commission. She may do so by attaching the property that was sold.
    d. The salesperson may force her employing broker to bring a court action against the seller of the property.

____36. The Code of Ethics
  a. defines frauds which can be perpetrated by brokers.
  b. sets forth punishment for brokers convicted of fraud.
  c. requires brokers to give legal advice.
  d. none of the above.

____37. A Realtor is a member in good standing with the
  a. state real estate commission.
  b. National Association of Real Estate License Law Officials.
  c. the local real estate board affiliated with the National Association of Realtors.
  d. local real estate commission.

____38. Rick Wiggins has just received his broker's license and is in the process of opening his office. He will violate the Code of Ethics if he
  a. solicits real estate salespeople employed by another broker without first contacting the employing broker.
  b. solicits insurance salespeople to apply for a real estate license.
  c. tries to hire the secretary of a fellow broker with the broker's knowledge.
  d. advertises in the newspaper that he wants to hire four real estate salespeople.

____39. If a broker accepts a postdated check as down payment on a real estate transaction and the check is not honored, the principal can
  a. declare the contract void.
  b. bring criminal action against the buyer.
  c. hold the broker responsible.
  d. legally withhold the deed.

____40. A salesperson is responsible to the
  a. principal.
  b. purchaser.
  c. real estate commission.
  d. employing broker.

ANSWER KEY

1. (*d*)	11. (*d*)	21. (*a*)	31. (*b*)
2. (*c*)	12. (*d*)	22. (*a*)	32. (*d*)
3. (*c*)	13. (*a*)	23. (*c*)	33. (*d*)
4. (*a*)	14. (*c*)	24. (*b*)	34. (*a*)
5. (*c*)	15. (*c*)	25. (*d*)	35. (*a*)
6. (*c*)	16. (*c*)	26. (*d*)	36. (*d*)
7. (*c*)	17. (*a*)	27. (*d*)	37. (*c*)
8. (*b*)	18. (*d*)	28. (*c*)	38. (*a*)
9. (*d*)	19. (*c*)	29. (*a*)	39. (*c*)
10. (*a*)	20. (*b*)	30. (*d*)	40. (*d*)

SUGGESTED ADDITIONAL READING

Dasso, Jerome; Ring, Alfred A.; and McFall, Douglas. *Fundamentals of Real Estate*. Englewood Cliffs, N.J.: Prentice-Hall, Inc., 1977, chap. 3.

Davies, Pearl Janet. *Real Estate in American History*. Washington, D.C.: Public Affairs Press, 1958, chap. 4.

Pearson, Karl G. *Real Estate: Principles and Practices*. 2d ed. Columbus, O.: Grid, Inc., 1977, chap. 2.

Semenow, Robert W. *Questions and Answers on Real Estate*. 8th ed. Englewood Cliffs, N.J.: Prentice-Hall, Inc., 1975, chap. 9.

Part II

Real Estate Transactions

5

Listing Agreements and Contracts for Sale

R eal estate brokers and salespersons continually deal with listing agreements and contracts of sale. The first concern is the listing agreement with the seller wherein the seller agrees to sell under terms of an agreement. The listing agreement constitutes an employment contract which is necessary to enforce payment of the real estate commission and is the basis for a contract of sale between the seller and the purchaser. Accordingly, this instrument must have the essential elements of a valid contract.

LISTING AGREEMENTS

The listing agreement is a personal contract between the broker, who acts as an agent, and the principal, who is typically the seller. When salespersons accept or sign a listing contract, they do so on behalf of their employing broker. Under a listing agreement, the broker assumes certain responsibilities and the seller agrees to perform certain acts.

The real estate broker is obligated under the law of agency to exercise his best efforts on behalf of his principal, the seller. It is understood that the broker, to perform under the listing contract, may advertise and exercise diligency in finding a purchaser. Duties of the real estate broker include retaining money accepted as part of the selling function in a trust account. The seller on his part agrees to pay a stated real estate commission and agrees to grant certain rights to sell. The seller also has the responsibility of furnishing a marketable title at the time of closing. Listing agreements have certain common elements: (1) Listing agreements should be in writing (legally required in some states). (2) The listing agreement, signed by the seller, should preferably show a definite termination date. (3) Good practice dictates that a copy of the listing agreement be given to the seller.

The listing agreement must state the price and the terms of payment acceptable to the seller. The nonreal estate items to be included in the sale should be listed in an inventory. In this respect the listing agreement serves as a preliminary step in completing the contract for sale.

Since the listing agreement is a contract of employment, preferably in writing as legally required in some states, it must contain certain minimum information to expedite the sale. In all respects the format of the listing agreement should agree with normal contract requirements. In addition the listing form should include:

1.   The names and signatures of the party to the listing contract.
2.   A legal description of the real estate to be sold. The street address and the designated legal description should be shown on the listing form.
3.   The terms of sale acceptable to the seller. This should include the acceptable sales price, the down payment required, the acceptability of a second mortgage or purchase money mortgage, and the assumption of outstanding mortgages with their terms and remaining balance noted as of the date of listing.
4.   The duration of the contract.
5.   Definition of rights and duties of the parties. This portion of the listing agreement usually defines the type of listing agreement and circumstances in which the commission will be paid. The right of the seller to list the property with other brokers or to sell it himself without payment of a commission would be stated in the listing agreement.
6.   An agreement to pay a stated commission—usually expressed as a percentage of the actual sale price.

A discussion of the different types of listing agreements shows how critical this contract is to the completed real estate transaction.

Types of Listing Agreements

There is a surprising degree of similarity in listing agreements. With little significant variation most states provide for the following types of agreements: (1) net listings, (2) open listings, (3) exclusive right to sell, (4) exclusive agency, and (5) multiple listings.

Net Listings. The net listing is used only if the seller insists he wants a net amount after closing. For example, the owner would state that the broker may list the property provided the seller nets $30,000 from the sale. The understanding is that a sale in excess of this amount may be retained by the broker as his commission. Such an agreement must be clearly agreed upon and, preferably, shown in a mutually-signed statement.

Such a listing is discouraged by the real estate industry and declared illegal or subject to regulation in some states. These restrictions follow from the basic weaknesses of the net listing: mainly, it violates the duty of the agent to exercise every effort on behalf of his principal.

The fiduciary relationship further requires that the broker have no personal interest in the transaction. For under the listing agreement, the broker presumably exercises his efforts to gain the best price and the best deal for his employing principal. Moreover, the net listing encourages brokers to sell to a strawman, to misrepresent, or to engage in fraud or other abuses. California law holds that if an agent does not disclose the amount of compensation in connection with a net listing, the violation is cause for revocation or suspension of the license. The disclosure must be made before the principal is committed to the sale. In other instances the broker must notify both the buyer and the seller in writing within a stated time of the closing date of the exact amount of the price.

Open Listings. This agreement, in which the broker agrees to act as agent for the sale of real estate, is the simplest form of listing. It may not have any termination date. It is called open because the seller retains the right to list with more than one broker. The seller is not legally required to notify other agents in the case of sale by one of the listing brokers. In the event of a sale, the agreement with other brokers is considered terminated.

The open listing is unique in that the commission is earned by the broker who first finds a buyer who meets terms acceptable to the seller. If the owner sells the property, he is under no obligation to pay a commission to a broker holding an open listing. The main difficulty with this type of listing is the danger that the owner may be subjected to claims of more than one broker for payment of a commission. This could occur if two brokers showed the property to the same prospect.

There is the added problem that brokers will be reluctant to spend personal time and costs on a listing shared with other brokers. Brokers typically complain that the competition with other brokers does not allow sufficient time to find the best prospect. A broker under these circumstances, it is claimed, is more inclined to close the sale in the quickest possible time at a negotiated price that does not serve the best interest of his principal, the seller.

On the other hand, the seller may view the open listing as an opportunity to gain more exposure in the market. He believes that if property is listed by more than one broker, he gains the advantage of reaching the prospects of many listing brokers. Some sellers may prefer the right to sell their own property in competition with the listing brokers with no obligation to pay a real estate commission. These terms stand in marked contrast to other types of listing agreements.

Exclusive Right to Sell. At the other extreme, the exclusive right to sell grants the broker the right to a commission if the property is sold. The seller agrees that the listing broker has an exclusive right to the commission with respect to other brokers. That is, the seller gives up the right to list the property with other brokers during the listing period. If the owner himself sells the property when the agreement is in effect, he is still liable for a commission.

The listing will include a definite termination date. The period of listing will vary according to custom and the reasonable time required to market the property. A period of 60 or 90 days is typical for most properties. For more special-purpose property such as industrial real estate of relatively high value and offered on a national market, the listing may be for a minimum period of six months.

The listing form usually provides for protection to the broker for a sale completed after the termination date. (See Fig. 5–1.) The commission will be paid according to the prevailing rule that if the broker was the procuring cause of the sale, a commission is earned though the sale is completed after the termination date. Such a clause protects the broker from owners who, with the express purpose of avoiding a commission, postpone acceptance of an offer until after the employment contract has terminated. Therefore, if negotiations are started within the stated time, and are completed after the listing period, the broker would normally be entitled to his commission—especially if the delay is the fault of the owner who was unable to deliver the title within the specified time.

Because the broker serves as the sole agency, this type of employment is viewed as the most desirable. In this regard such a contract suits the mutual interest of both parties if the property is listed at a marketable price. The broker is able to freely advertise the property and show the property to a selected group of clients. The seller is protected from casual buyers who have little interest in his property, which might be the case under an open listing. During the employment period the broker is required to exert every effort through advertising, showing the property, and posting the listing in appropriate places to complete the sale under terms acceptable to the seller.

Exclusive Agency. Exclusive agency combines features of the open listing and the exclusive right to sell. Under this agreement the seller gives up the right to list the property with other brokers during the listing period. In this respect the exclusive agency is similar to the exclusive right to sell. But under the exclusive agency *the owner may sell the property by his own efforts* without paying a real estate commission. However, if the seller completes the sale and it is later proven that the broker was the procuring cause of the sale, the seller is liable for a commission. The seller is free of the commission if he completes a direct sale without assistance of a listing broker.

FIGURE 5–1
An Exclusive Right to Sell Agreement

EXCLUSIVE LISTING CONTRACT

NORTHSIDE REALTY ASSOCIATES, INC.
Realtors

BUCKHEAD	4120 ROSWELL ROAD, N.E.	255-8220
SANDY SPRINGS	6090 ROSWELL ROAD, N.E.	255-7631
NORTHEAST	1584 TULLY CIRLCE, N.E.	633-1484
NORTH SPRINGS	700 DALRYMPLE ROAD, N.E.	252-0175
N. PEACHTREE I-285	2310 PERIMETER PARK	458-8211
NORTH RIVER	8975 ROSWELL ROAD	993-8800
	ATLANTA, GEORGIA	
ROSWELL, GEORGIA	10915 HIGHWAY 19	993-9200
MARIETTA, GEORGIA	1584 ROSWELL STREET	427-0171
ALPHARETTA, GEORGIA	200 S. MAIN STREET	475-4541
TUCKER, GEORGIA	2262 COOLEDGE ROAD	939-6765

, 19

In consideration of $1.00 (one dollar) and your acceptance of the terms of this agreement and of your promise to list, to offer for sale and to endeavor to sell my property hereinafter described, to advertise the same in such manner as you may deem advisable and further, to enlist in this behalf the best efforts of your organization in its ordinary course of business, I hereby give and grant you for a period of _____ days commencing on the _____ day of _____ and expiring on _____ 12:00 Midnight, the exclusive right and authority to sell the property hereinafter described, for the price and upon the terms hereinafter set forth.

I hereby further agree, upon the considerations hereinabove mentioned, to pay you a commission calculated under Item _____ of the schedule shown on the reversed side of this contract, which schedule is made a part of this contract by reference, whether such sale be made by you or me, or by any other person acting for me or in my behalf upon the terms hereinafter mentioned, or upon any other terms acceptable to me. If the property is afterwards sold within ninety (90) days from the termination of this agency to a purchaser to whom it was submitted by you during the continuance of said agency, and whose name or names have been disclosed to me in writing during said agency, I agree to pay you the commission above stated unless the property is sold to such purchaser during said ninety-day (90) period by or thru another licensed real estate broker with whom I have made an Exclusive Listing Contract. In this latter event I will not be responsible to you or your representatives for a real estate commission should the property be sold by another broker or salesman to a person or persons to whom it was shown by you or your representatives during the period of your exclusive.

Said property is described as:

Said property is rented as follows.

PRICE for which said property is to be sold is _____ **Dollars.**

TERMS OF SALE:

I grant you the exclusive For Sale sign privilege on said described property and agree to refer to you all inquiries which I may receive during the continuance of this agency.

In any exchange of the aforesaid described property, permission is hereby given to you in negotiating such exchange to collect commissions on all properties involved in the transaction.

(continued on reverse side)

Multiple Listing. There are certain risks assumed by the seller under the exclusive agency or the exclusive right to sell. The risks are that the broker will not actively promote the sale even though he is given a virtual monopoly in the right to earn a commission for a limited time. Similarly, under an open listing brokers are reluctant to actively pursue a sale because of the risk of losing a sale to other competing brokers and the possibility of a contested commission.

The multiple listing supposedly overcomes these limitations. Strictly speaking, a multiple listing is not a separate listing. It usually rests on an exclusive right to sell agreement which is shared by an association of brokers joined in a multiple listing arrangement. Thus the multiple listing is really a service organized by a group of brokers. The group is drawn together by a multiple listing form providing for an exclusive right to sell agreement. Those subscribing to the multiple listing service share their listings with the other members. An example of a multiple listing form is shown in Figure 5–2.

FIGURE 5–2
A Multiple Listing Agreement

EXCLUSIVE LISTING CONTRACT

To ______________________________
REALTOR FIRM DATE

Description of Property:
Lot No. Blk. No. Deed Bk. No. Page No. Plat Bk.

County ____________ State ____________ City ____________

In consideration of your listing and continued endeavors to sell the within described property, I hereby grant to you, for the term of ________ days from the date hereof, and to expire at Midnight on ________, 19____, the exclusive right and privilege to sell or exchange the above described property for the sum of $ ________ or at such lesser price or terms to which I may consent. I acknowledge that you are a member of the ATHENS AREA MULTIPLE LISTING SERVICE, INC. (AAMLS) and give you the privilege of distributing listing information to other members.

I agree to pay you ________% of the Sales price as commission, providing said property is sold, exchanged, or leased with option to purchase before the expiration of this agency or any extension thereof, whether such sale, exchange, or lease with option to purchase is made by you, by me by any member of the AAMLS or anyone else.

Should I contract to sell, exchange, or lease with option to purchase the within described property within three (3) months after the above expiration date or any extension thereof to a purchaser to whom the within described property was offered during the continuance of this agency by you, by me, or any other member of the AAMLS or anyone else, I agree to pay you at the same rate commission.

You are hereby authorized to place your (FOR SALE) sign, on said property, to remove all other "For Sale" signs if any, and to photograph said property and use such photographs in promoting the sale. I further agree to consider your recommendations to enable you to show this property to its best advantage, to allow you to show it at all reasonable hours and otherwise co-operate with you. I hereby acknowledge receipt of a copy of this contract.

SPECIAL STIPULATIONS: ______________________________

I (We) Certify that the above described Property is titled in my (our) name.

______________ REALTOR FIRM

BY: ______________ BY: ______________
OWNER

____
OWNER

WHITE COPY - MLS OFFICE
CANARY COPY - PROPERTY OWNER
PINK COPY - LISTING REALTOR

Address ________ Brs.____ Baths____ Price ________
Owner ________ Res. no________ Bus. no________ Sign____
Tenant ________ Res. no________ App. ________
Date Listed________ Until________ By________ Firm. ________
Area________ Schools________ Bus____ Key____
Builder ________
Const. & Style ________
Lot Size ________
Lot# ________ Block# ________
Age ________ Sq. Ft. ________
Roof ________ TV Ant. ________
Heat ________ Air Cond. ________
Water ________ Sewage ________
Ter Bond ________ Fences ________
Carport ________ Garage ________
Patio ________ Porch ________
Out Buildings ________

Fl. Plan	1	2	Bsmt.	F/P	Fls.	Walls
Liv. rm.						
Din. rm.						
Kitchen						
F. Rm.						
Brs.						
Baths						
Util. Rm.						

EQUIPMENT: Stove ________ Refrig ________ D/W ________ Disp ________ Fan ________
W & D Conn. ________ Water Heater ________
Total Sales Price $________ Loan Bal $________ As of ________ Loan Int. ____%
Cash Equity ________ Yrs. Remain ________ Mo. Pymts ________ T & I ____
Loan With ________ 2nd mtg. Info. ________
Reason for selling ________ Possession ________
MLS Showing date ________
Special Features & Remarks ________

In practice, members must turn over eligible listings to the multiple listing service immediately. The central multiple listing service then distributes the listing to subscribing members. The rules of the organization provide for a share of the commission to be paid to the multiple listing service to cover its cost of operation. The balance of the commission is then paid in two shares: one share to the broker who acquired the listing agreement and another share to the selling broker. Each sale is reported immediately to the central office, which notifies other members.

Multiple listing succeeds for several reasons. First, though this is not universally practiced, properties accepted for multiple listing may be screened by an appraisal board established by the multiple listing service. In this way the multiple listing service avoids listing properties that are overpriced or otherwise unmarketable. In addition, multiple listing gives the seller the advantage of the sales staff of several brokers, each of whom is protected by an exclusive right to sell agreement. If a broker participates in a sale, he will receive a prescribed share of the real estate commission.

The listing broker is induced to secure listings, since if the property is sold, he is rewarded by a share of the commission. In practice, the multiple listing service provides a clearing house for salable properties, reasonably priced, and exposed to prospects of many participating brokers. Based as it is on the exclusive right to sell agreement, the multiple listing service attempts to combine the best features of the open listing and the promotional advantages of the exclusive right to sell agreement.

There is an important precaution to observe in administering a multiple listing service. To avoid accusations of setting commissions "in restraint of trade," the multiple listing service must show that the commission share is the result of individual negotiations. The same rule applies here as is found in commissions which must be negotiated by individual brokers and not by local real estate organizations.

RELATED LISTING ISSUES

Certain other conditions of sale supplement the main elements of contracts for sale and listing agreements. Their importance warrants special mention. For the most part, each of the related listing issues must be dealt with by the practicing real estate broker and his employee-salesmen.

Co-brokerage

Brokers frequently engage in cooperative listing arrangements. This is especially true for large-scale developments, and for properties that have a regional or national market. Co-brokerage refers to informal arrangements in which brokers voluntarily share a real estate commission with other licensed brokers. For example, a broker in Detroit, Michigan, may have a client who wants to buy an apartment house in Miami, Florida.

By giving the listing broker in Miami the terms of the purchase offer, both brokers may agree to divide the commission on a 50–50 basis. Both parties benefit, since the broker with the client who wants to purchase then advises the listing broker, who locates a property fitting the needs of the Detroit buyer.

By the same token, real estate brokers specializing in industrial properties are faced with selling industrial plants that cost several hundred thousands of dollars or more which must be marketed on a national basis to a select group of industrial corporations. It is fairly common in these circumstances for brokers to share their listings and informally agree to divide the commission. While these arrangements are not generally fixed by contract, but are determined by interpersonal relations, they tend to give the exclusive right to sell agreement certain advantages of the multiple listing service. The latter is more of a formalized contractual arrangement providing for a broader exposure of properties to selected prospects.

Termination of Listing Agreements

It is fairly clear that a listing agreement will be terminated upon the sale of property in the case of an open listing and in the case of an owner selling his own property under an exclusive agency listing. In certain other instances the listing is ended without written notification in the case of events that automatically prevent performance of the listing agreement. Insanity or bankruptcy of the property owner listing real estate fall in this category.

Other rules are fairly common to listing agreements: for instance, in a listing agreement for an indefinite period, the owner has the right to terminate the agreement before a purchaser has been found. However, the owner cannot rightfully revoke an agency to avoid payment of a commission. If the broker has found a prospect, ready, able, and willing to buy on the seller's terms, the agency can not be intentionally discontinued to avoid a commission.

If, however, the seller terminates the listing before the date of termination, the broker may claim damages if he has expended money and time in exercising his agency. Though notice of termination is not legally required for an open listing or a listing without a termination date, it is recommended that notice of termination be given to listing brokers. This is especially true for exclusive listings. The listing agreement should require a notice of termination by either party.

The Parol Evidence Rule

The parol evidence rule prevents oral evidence from varying or adding to the terms of a written instrument such as a contract. Only when the contract is indefinite will the courts generally permit outside evidence to supplement the written contract. Thus the effect of the rule is to finalize the written contract and prevent either party from varying the written agreement on the basis of other claimed oral or other written statements. The contract must stand on its own merits. In other words, contracts may not be changed by oral modification. Therefore, oral agreements not a part of the written contract are unenforceable.

Escrow Agencies

Simply stated, an escrow agent is a third person who holds money or a written instrument until certain conditions are met which, according to the instructions, he must deliver or perform as required by the escrow agreement. Elements associated with an escrow require that the agent be a disinterested third party, that he operate under binding contract, or that he act only under written instructions. In a real estate transaction, he favors neither the buyer or the seller; he must operate disinterestedly as a third party.

The escrow arrangement serves conveniently to expedite a real estate transaction, for it frequently occurs that after the parties have mutually agreed to the terms of the sale, defects in the title must be remedied or financing details must be arranged, taxes must be paid, existing liens must be removed, and an endless number of other details must be completed to the satisfaction of both parties before the sale is consummated.

The escrow is a device in which the interests of both the buyer and seller are protected while these events take place. Without this arrangement, a buyer could make a down payment and arrange financing and find that the seller delivered a title subject to liens not known or existing at the time of negotiation.

Therefore, the contract of sale may provide for an escrow that acts as an agent of both parties. The escrow agent must follow instructions of the escrow contract and if the conditions of the escrow agreement are met, then the agent may arrange for the final settlement.

To guard against conflicts, the escrow agreement and the contract of sale must be in agreement. That is, the escrow would normally require certain duties of the seller before title is transferred and call for conditions to be met by the buyer (such as the deposit payment, completion of financing details and payment of closing costs). The complications arising in an escrow have led some states to regulate escrows; for example, California licenses persons or agencies holding themselves out as escrow agents.

Option Contracts

The option contract, like other real estate contracts, must conform to the requirements of enforceable contracts. It is frequently used because with an option the buyer commits the seller to a price for a given period without binding the buyer. In short the seller gives the buyer an exclusive right to purchase upon stated terms and conditions for a specific time.

Ordinarily the option agreement requires the buyer to pay a sum in return for the seller's willingness not to sell property to others during the option period. If at the end of the specified time, the buyer elects not to purchase the property, he forfeits the option payment. Usually, though, if the buyer elects to purchase before the option expires, the consideration paid for the option is applied against the purchase price.

Stated differently, an option is an exclusive right to buy or sell property at a given price within a stated period. It continues an offer which is only binding upon the one who offers to sell but it is not binding on the buyer. Besides the ordinary elements of a contract, the option should include: (1) an expiration date, (2) a statement of conditions under which the option may be exercised, (3) an agreed-upon purchase price and terms of sale, (4) circumstances in which the option payment will be forfeited, (5) rights to assign the option, and (6) an option payment.

The option will be used if the buyer is uncertain about the transaction. His purchase of the property may turn on the availability of credit to finance a major project; further, the option gives the buyer time to undertake feasibility studies for a proposed project. Without the option agreement, there is danger that development plans will become known and have the effect of inducing the seller to increase his price above an economical value. The option fixes the selling price pending a purchase decision.

CONTRACTS FOR SALE

The contract for sale is the most important legal document affecting a real estate sale. It controls the type of instrument conveying title; it provides for the final settlement between buyer and seller; and it governs the manner in which the broker relates to his client, the seller, and his prospect, the buyer. More significantly, it guides the sale from the negotiating stage to the final step—delivery of title and payment of the purchase price. Before describing these relationships in more detail, variations in using a contract for sale should be noted.

Methods of Processing Real Estate Sales

Practices vary among the states in the manner in which listings and contracts for sale are handled. Their main differences lie in the responsibility of the real estate broker and the role played by attorneys or escrow agents. In some states the broker prepares a binder which constitutes a receipt of the deposit given to the seller pending closing or disposition of the offer. The binder constitutes an offer to the seller, describing the terms of sale and the legal description of the property. In a sense, the binder constitutes an offer to buy which must be accepted and signed by the seller. The binder serves as a preliminary contract for preparation of a contract for sale which is prepared by an escrow agent or an attorney. The contract for sale is more detailed and controls the final closing procedure.

In still other states, brokers work with prepared forms and fill in blanks in a document that leads to the final closing operation. Such a document is called the *receipt and agreement to purchase*. In this case no contract for sale is prepared, since the necessary information is covered in this document. It also serves as a receipt of the deposit; it includes the legal description, terms of the sale, and requires the seller's signature.

A third group of states provide for a detailed contract for sale that serves as a receipt of the deposit and describes details of the sale relevant to completing the closing. These three methods of processing real estate transactions are shown in Figure 5–3.

FIGURE 5–3

Methods of Processing a Real Estate Sale

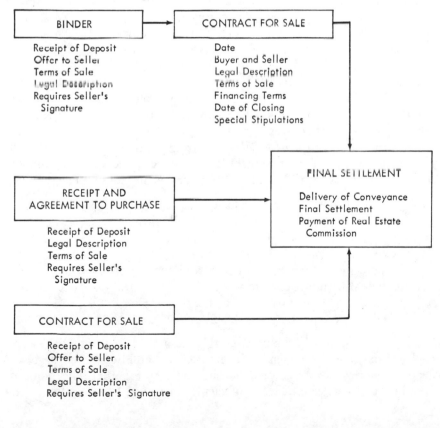

Because of its significance, the contract for sale must meet the requirements of a contract: (1) an offer and acceptance, (2) valid consideration, (3) parties capable of contracting, and (4) a lawful object. As it is true for other real estate instruments, the contract, though not legally required in some states, should be in writing. Besides these usual requirements of an enforceable contract, a contract for sale includes other promises required to complete the transaction.

Minimum Provisions of Contracts for Sale

It will be appreciated that in every transaction the seller outlines the cash requirements, the method of payment, and conditions under which he will sell the property. These seller reservations are known as his offer. If a prospective buyer accepts the stated terms and conditions required by the seller, the sale is formalized in a contract for sale. The contract for sale ends the period of negotiation. It is a written statement of an offer of the seller and an unconditional acceptance by the buyer that a sale has been made.

Suppose Brown offers to sell his property for $50,000 cash. Broker A secures a buyer, Jones, who offers to buy at $45,000 under the following terms: Jones plans to secure a first mortgage of $30,000, pay $10,000 cash, and pay for the balance with a purchase money mortgage from the seller of $5,000, payable in monthly payments over 5 years, 8 percent interest. Jones has not accepted the selling offer of Brown; Jones has made a new offer to Brown which must be accepted before the contract of sale is enforceable. Before Jones accepts the counteroffer, either party may withdraw. A series of counteroffers by both parties may precede acceptance by either the buyer or seller.

Preparing the Contract for Sale. Accordingly, the written contract for sale, signed by both parties, controls the legal steps necessary to complete the transaction. As a minimum, contract provisions must include:

1. The date of the contract for sale.
2. The names and addresses of the buyer and seller.
3. A legal description.
4. The terms of the sale.
5. The agreement for new mortgages and terms and conditions under which existing mortgages are accepted.
6. The date and place of closing the sale.
7. Special agreements unique to the particular sale.

The date is entered because it establishes a time in which the parties have agreed to sell. Frequently the rights and liabilities of the party are dependent on the date entered on the contract for sale. The name of both buyer and seller should be sufficiently identified to show the marital status of each party in the event that common property rights are established under state law. If one of the parties is a minor, details of the guardian appointment should be shown. Other rules provide for the naming of individuals in a partnership and for the full name of the corporation and its home address.

The description should include the legal description in the proper legal form, and the property to be conveyed including chattels, easements, leases, or other reservations to the title.

The terms of the sale normally state the amount of deposit and circumstances in which it is forfeited or returned. The assumption of liens and other liabilities completes this portion of the contract.

If an existing mortgage is to be part of the transaction, it should be stated that the buyer is either *assuming* or buying *subject to* an existing mortgage. A separate discussion later in this chapter explains these terms. In the case of secondary financing, or a purchase money mortgage, terms of the new mortgage should be noted. The buyer may require that the sale be "subject to the buyer's ability to secure a first mortgage."

Common Methods of Payment. Methods of payment are critical to the contract. The method should be described in sufficient detail to avoid misunderstanding. Most closings will fall into one of five categories. Typical terms used to cover these methods of payment illustrate language that describes the intent of the buyer.

1. *Cash at closing.* Purchaser to pay to seller all cash at closing.

2. *Purchaser to obtain new first loan and pay balance in cash.* Under this arrangement the purchaser intends to pay cash to a seller and apply for a new loan. The contract for sale would read:

> Purchaser to apply for and to accept if approved a new first loan in the principal amount of $_____ secured by said property, bearing interest at the rate of _____% per annum and amortized over _____ equal monthly payments of $_____ each including principal and interest. Purchaser to pay balance to Seller in cash at closing.

3. *Purchaser to obtain first mortgage loan, execute second mortgage loan to seller, and pay balance in cash.* In this case, the seller agrees to a second mortgage and cash. Ordinarily the seller reduces the cash requirements of the buyer by making up the difference between the amount of equity paid and the first mortgage loan.

> Purchaser to apply for and to accept if approved a new first loan in the principal amount of $_____ secured by said property, bearing interest at the rate of _____% per annum and amortized over _____ equal monthly payments of $_____ each, including principal and interest. Seller will accept from Purchaser one note secured by Purchase Money security deed, secured by said property, and

subject to first loan described herein, in the principal amount of $_____ bearing interest at the rate of _____% annum and amortized over _____ equal monthly payments of $_____ each, including principal and interest. The first payment of said Purchase Money note shall become due the _____day of the month after closing. Purchaser to pay balance of purchase price to Seller in cash at closing.

4. *Purchaser to assume existing mortgage loan and pay balance in cash.* For properties with fairly recent mortgages, it is often prudent for the buyer to pay the seller the difference between the offering price and the outstanding mortgage. If the purchaser has sufficient money to pay down, he or she may also take advantage of lower interest rates on older mortgages. If this option is selected, the agreement might conform to the following language:

> Purchaser to assume and agrees to pay the first loan now against said property in the original principal amount of $_____ dated _____19_____ in favor of _____, bearing interest at the rate of _____% per annum and amortized over _____ equal monthly payment of $_____ each including principal and interest. Principal balance of said loan which is to be assumed by Purchaser as of _____, 19_____, is $_____. Purchaser to pay balance of purchase price to Seller in cash at closing.

5. *Purchaser to assume existing mortgage loan, execute a second mortgage loan to the seller, and pay balance in cash.* This last option combines mortgage assumption, a second mortgage loan and the cash arrangement. The language below is taken from a contract for sale used by Northside Realty Associates, Inc. of Atlanta, Georgia.

> Purchaser to assume and agrees to pay the first loan now against said property in the original principal amount of $_____, dated _____ 19_____, in favor of _____, bearing interest at the rate of _____% per annum and amortized over _____ equal payments of $_____ each, including principal and interest. Principal balance of said loan which is to be assumed by Purchaser as of _____, 19_____ is $_____ Seller will accept from Purchaser one note secured by a loan described herein, in the principal amount of $_____ bearing interest at the rate of _____% per annum and amortized over _____ equal monthly payments of $_____ each, including principal and interest. Purchaser to pay balance of purchase price to Seller in cash at closing.

In the case of loans insured by the Federal Housing Administration, brokers are advised to add that the purchaser agrees to accept loans at the current interest rate as of the date of closing. In addition, in a contract for sale that provides for a loan guaranteed by the Veterans Administration, the contract should give the purchaser an option to proceed without regard to the amount of reasonable value established by the Veterans Administration. The last option allows the purchaser to finance the purchase without the guarantee in the event the reasonable value is less than the agreed upon sale price.

The date and place of closing the sale may determine whether the sale will be completed. For instance, if either party claims time to be of the essence, notice must be served stating a reasonable time for the contract to be completed. If no time is stated, either party may have a reasonable period before default may be claimed. Other details supplement these minimum requirements. See Figure 5-4 for a deposit receipt and contract for sale form.

Special Contract Agreements

Because the contract for sale is so controlling, it is imperative to direct attention to provisions usually found in it. Failure to cover these topics could invite expensive litigation, delay the sale, and defeat prospects for a commission.

The Real Estate Commission. At some point the agreement must cover the commission clause and also anticipate the disposition of the deposit if the buyer defaults. The contract for sale may state that the deposit will be divided equally between the seller and broker if the buyer withdraws from the agreement. In this case, the buyer agrees to forfeit the deposit as liquidated damages. A typical commission clause might read:

> I hereby agree to pay Broker as commission 6 percent *of* $60,000 of the selling price if said property is sold during the term hereof or any extension thereof by Broker or by me or by another broker or through any other source. If said property is withdrawn from sale, transferred, or leased during the term hereof or and extension thereof, I agree to pay Broker said percent of the above listed price.

Strictly speaking, the real estate commission is earned if the parties have mutually agreed to the sale; that is, accepted an offer and prepared an enforceable contract for sale. Though practices vary, final payment of the real estate commission usually is made at the time of the final settlement.

The Title Clause. Ordinarily to complete the sale, the seller must provide proof of a marketable title subject to stated liens and encumbrances or other reservations cited in the contract. To accomplish this end, the seller may agree to furnish title insurance, an abstract of title, or, in some instances, both an abstract and title insurance. Custom controls these practices. In much of the Midwest, the seller is required to

FIGURE 5–4
Deposit Receipt and Contract for Sale and Purchase

DEPOSIT RECEIPT AND CONTRACT FOR SALE AND PURCHASE

_____ , his wife,

of _____ (Ph. _____) hereinafter called the seller, and

_____ , his wife,

of _____ (Ph. _____) hereinafter called the buyer, hereby agree

that the seller shall sell and the buyer shall buy the following described property UPON THE TERMS AND CONDITIONS HEREINAFTER SET FORTH, which shall include the STANDARDS FOR REAL ESTATE TRANSACTIONS set forth on reverse side of this contract.

1. LEGAL DESCRIPTION of real estate located in_____ County, Florida:

Personal property included: _____

Street address: _____

Seller represents that the property can be used for the following purposes: _____

2. PURCHASE PRICE is: . . . . $_____

   Method of Payment:

   Deposit to be held in trust by _____ $_____

   Approximate principal balance of first mortgage to which conveyance shall be

   subject, if any. Mortgage holder _____ $_____

   Interest _____% per annum; Method of payment_____

   Other:_____ $_____

   Cash, certified or cashier's check on closing and delivery of deed (or such
   greater or lesser amount as may be necessary to complete payment of purchase price after credits, adjustments and prorations). $_____

   TOTAL: $_____

3. SPECIAL CLAUSES:

4. CLOSING DATE: This contract shall be closed and the deed and possession shall be delivered on or before the_____day of_____

_____ 19_____, unless extended by other provisions of this contract or separate agreement.

WITNESSES: (Two, separate, are required)   Executed by Buyer on_____ , 197___

_____   _____ (SEAL)

_____   _____ (SEAL)
                                                                        Buyer

ACCEPTANCE OF CONTRACT & PROFESSIONAL SERVICE FEE: The seller hereby approves and accepts the offer contained herein and recognizes

_____ as the broker in this transaction, and agrees to pay, as a fee _____ %

of the gross sales price, the sum of _____ Dollars ($_____).
or one-half of the deposit in case same is forfeited by the buyer through failure to perform, as compensation for service rendered, provided same does not
exceed the full amount of the agreed fee.

WITNESSES: (Two, separate, are required)   Executed by Seller on_____ , 197___

_____   _____ (SEAL)

_____   _____ (SEAL)
                                                                        Seller

Deposit received on_____ 197____ to be held subject to this contract; if check, subject to clearance.

By: _____   By: _____
        (Broker or Attorney)

BE ADVISED: When this agreement has been completely and correctly executed, it becomes a legally binding instrument.
The form of this "Deposit Receipt and Contract for Sale and Purchase" has been approved by the
Broward County Bar Association and the Greater Fort Lauderdale Board of Realtors, Inc.

FIGURE 5–4 (*continued*)

STANDARDS FOR REAL ESTATE TRANSACTIONS

A. EVIDENCE OF TITLE: The Seller shall, within ____ days (15 days if this blank is not filled in) furnish to Buyer a complete abstract of title prepared by a reputable abstract firm purporting to be an accurate synopsis of the instruments affecting the title to the real property recorded in the Public Records of that county to the date of this contract, showing in the Seller a marketable title in accordance with title standards adopted from time to time by the Florida Bar, subject only to liens, encumbrances, exceptions or qualifications set forth in this contract and those which shall be discharged by Seller at or before closing. Buyer shall have fifteen (15) days from the date of receiving said abstract of title to examine same. If title is found to be defective, the Buyer shall, within said period, notify the Seller in writing, specifying the defects. If the said defects render the title unmarketable, the Seller shall have ninety (90) days from receipt of such notice to cure the defects, and if after said period Seller shall not have cured the defects, Buyer shall have the option of (1) accepting title as it then is, or (2) demanding a refund of all monies paid hereunder which shall forthwith be returned to the Buyer, and thereupon the Buyer and Seller shall be released of all further obligations under this Contract.

B. CONVEYANCE: Seller shall convey title to the subject property to Buyer by Statutory Warranty Deed subject to: (1) zoning and/or restrictions and matters appearing on the plat and/or common to the subdivision, (3) public utility easements of record, provided said easements are located on the side or rear lines of the property and are not more than six feet in width, (4) taxes for the year of closing, and (5) other matters specified in this contract, if any.

C. EXISTING MORTGAGES: The Seller shall obtain and furnish a statement from the mortgagee setting forth the principal balance, method of payment, interest rate, and whether the mortgage is in good standing. If there is a charge for the change of ownership records by the mortgagee, it shall be borne equally by the parties to the transaction. In the event the mortgagee does not accept the Buyer for purposes of assuming the existing mortgage encumbering the subject property, where the mortgage instrument requires such acceptance, then and in that event, the Buyer at his option may cancel the contract and all monies paid on the purchase price shall be refunded to him and the parties shall be released from all further obligations. Any variance in the amount of a mortgage to be assumed from the amount stated in the Contract shall be added to or deducted from the cash payment or the purchase money mortgage, as the Buyer may elect. In the event such mortgage balance is more than three percent (3%) less than the amount indicated in the contract, the Seller shall be deemed to be in default under the Contract.

D. PURCHASE MONEY MORTGAGES: Any purchase money note and mortgage shall follow the forms generally accepted and used in the county where the land is located. A purchase money mortgage shall provide for insurance against loss by fire with extended coverage in an amount not less than the full insurable value of the improvements. In a first mortgage, the note and mortgage shall provide for acceleration, at the option of the holder, after thirty (30) days default and in a second mortgage after ten (10) days default. Second mortgages shall require the owner of the property encumbered by said mortgage to keep all prior liens and encumbrances in good standing and forbid the owner of the property from accepting modifications of, or future advances, under a prior mortgage. Buyer shall have the right to prepay all or any part of the principal at any time or times with interest to date of payment without penalty and said payments shall apply against the principal amounts next maturing. In the event Buyer executes a mortgage to one other than the Seller, all costs and charges incidental thereto shall be paid by the Buyer.

E. SURVEY: The Buyer, within the time allowed for delivery of evidence of title and examination thereof, may have said property surveyed at his expense. If the survey shows any encroachment on said property or that the improvements intended to be located on the subject property in fact encroach on the lands of others, or violate any of the covenants herein, the same shall be treated as a title defect.

F. TERMITE INSPECTION: Prior to closing, at Buyer's expense, the Buyer shall have the right to have the property inspected by a licensed exterminating company to determine whether there is any active termite or wood-destroying organism or rot present in any improvements on said property, or any damage from prior termite or wood-destroying organism or rot to said improvements. If there is any such infestation or damage, the Seller shall pay all costs of treatment and repairing and/or replacing all portions of said improvements which are infested or have been damaged; provided, however, in the event the cost to be incurred is more than three percent (3%) of the purchase price, then either party may cancel the contract within ten (10) days of receipt of the termite inspection report and cost estimate for effecting exterminations and necessary repairs, by giving written notice to the other party.

G. INSURANCE: The premium on any hazard insurance policy in force covering improvements on the subject property, shall be prorated between the parties, or the policy may be cancelled as the Buyer may elect. If insurance is to be prorated the Seller shall, on or before closing date, furnish to the Buyer all insurance policies or copies thereof.

H. LEASES: The Seller shall, prior to closing, furnish to Buyer copies of all written leases and estoppel letters from each tenant specifying the nature and duration of said tenant's occupancy, rental rate, advance rents or security deposits paid by tenant. In the event Seller is unable to obtain said estoppel letters from tenants, the same information may be furnished by seller to Buyer in the form of a Seller's Affidavit.

I. MECHANICS LIENS: Seller shall furnish to the Buyer at time of closing an affidavit attesting to the absence of any claims of lien or potential lienors known to the Seller and further attesting that there have been no improvements to the subject property for 90 days immediately preceding the date of closing. If the property has been improved within said time, the Seller shall deliver releases or waiver of all mechanics liens, executed by general contractors, sub-contractors, suppliers, or materialmen, in addition to Seller's mechanic lien affidavit setting forth the names of all such general contractors, sub-contractors, suppliers and materialmen and further reciting that in fact all bills for work to the subject property which could serve as the basis for a machanic's lien have been paid.

J. PLACE OF CLOSING: Closing shall be held at the office of the Buyer's attorney if located within Broward County; if not, then at the office of Seller's attorney.

K. INSTRUMENTS FOR CLOSING: Seller's attorney shall prepare deed, mechanic's lien affidavit and any corrective instruments that may be required in connection with perfecting the title. Buyer's attorney will prepare closing statement, mortgage and mortgage note.

L. EXPENSES: State surtax and documentary stamps which are required to be affixed to the instrument of conveyance, the cost of recording any corrective instruments, intangible personal property taxes and the cost of recording the purchase money mortgage, if any, shall be paid by the Seller. Documentary stamps to be affixed to the note or notes secured by the purchase money mortgage, if any, and the cost of recording the deed shall be paid by the Buyer.

M. PRORATION OF TAXES (REAL AND PERSONAL): Taxes shall be prorated based on the current year's tax with due allowance being made for the maximum allowable discount and for homestead or other exemptions if allowed for said year. If the closing occurs at a date when the current year's taxes are not fixed, and the current year's assessment is available, taxes will be prorated based upon such assessment, and the prior year's millage. If the current year's assessment is not available, then taxes will be prorated on the prior year's tax, provided, however, if there are completed improvements on the subject premises by January 1st of the year of closing, which improvements were not in existence on January 1st of the prior year, then the taxes shall be prorated to the date of closing based upon the prior year's millage and at an equitable assessment to be agreed upon between the parties, failing which, request will be made to the county tax assessor for an informal assessment, taking into consideration homestead exemption, if any. However, any tax proration based on an estimate may at the request of either party to the transaction, be subsequently readjusted upon receipt of tax bill and a statement to that effect is to be set forth in the closing statement.

N. PRORATIONS AND ESCROW BALANCE: Taxes, hazard insurance, mortgage guarantee insurance, interest, utilities, rents and other expenses and revenue of said property shall be prorated as of date of closing. Seller shall receive as credit at closing an amount equal to the escrow funds held by the mortgagee, which funds shall thereupon be transferred to the Buyer.

O. SPECIAL ASSESSMENT LIENS: Certified, confirmed and ratified special assessment liens as of the date of closing (and not as of the date of this contract) are to be paid by the Seller. Pending liens as of the date of closing shall be assumed by the Buyer.

P. PERSONAL PROPERTY: The Seller represents and warrants that all major appliances and machinery included in the sale shall be in good working order and repair as of the date of closing. Buyer may, at his sole expense and on reasonable notice, inspect or cause an inspection to be made of the appliances and equipment involved prior to closing. Any necessary repairs shall be made at the cost of the Seller and, if appropriate, adequate funds shall be escrowed at time of closing to effect such repairs. Unless otherwise agreed by the parties, the Buyer shall, by proceeding to closing, be deemed to have accepted the property as is.

Q. RISK OF LOSS: If the improvements are damaged by fire or other casualty before delivery of the deed and can be restored to substantially the same condition as now existing within a period of sixty (60) days thereafter, Seller may restore the improvements and the closing date and date of delivery of possession hereinbefore provided shall be extended accordingly. If Seller fails to do so, the Buyer shall have the option of (1) taking the property as is, together with insurance proceeds, if any, or (2) cancelling the contract and all deposits will be forthwith returned to the Buyer and the parties released of any further liability hereunder.

R. MAINTENANCE: Between the date of the contract and the date of closing, the property, including lawn, shrubbery and pool, if any, shall be maintained by the Seller in the condition as it existed as of the date of the contract, ordinary wear and tear excepted.

S. PROCEEDS OF SALE AND CLOSING PROCEDURE: Possession and occupancy will be delivered to Buyer at time of closing, unless otherwise agreed upon in this contract. The Seller shall be entitled to receive the net proceeds of the sale at time of closing, except in cases where mortgagee requires title clearance before disbursing funds, in which event Seller shall be entitled to payment upon receipt of funds from mortgagee. Payment shall be made in the form of cash, cashier's check, certified check or attorney's trust account check. The professional service fee shall be disbursed at the time of closing.

T. ESCROW: The party receiving the deposit agrees by the acceptance thereof to hold same in escrow and to disburse it in accordance with the terms and conditions of this contract.

U. ATTORNEY FEES AND COSTS: In connection with any litigation arising out of this contract, the prevailing party shall be entitled to recover all costs incurred, including reasonable attorney's fees.

V. DEFAULT: If Buyer fails to perform any of the covenants of this contract, all money paid pursuant to this contract by the Buyer shall be retained by or for the account of the Seller as consideration for the execution of this contract, and as agreed and liquidated damages and in full settlement of any claims for damages. If the Seller fails to perform any of the covenants of this contract, all money paid pursuant to this contract by the Buyer, at the option of the Buyer, shall be returned to the Buyer on demand, or the Buyer shall have only the right of specific performance.

W. CONTRACT NOT RECORDABLE: This contract or any reference thereto shall not be recorded in the office of the Clerk of any Circuit Court of the State of Florida.

X. PERSONS BOUND: The benefits and obligations of the covenants herein shall inure to and bind the respective heirs, executors, administrators, successors and assigns (where assignment is permitted) of the parties hereto. Whenever used, the singular number shall include the plural, the plural the singular, and the use of any gender shall include all genders.

Y. SURVIVAL OF COVENANTS AND SPECIAL COVENANTS: The covenants in this contract shall survive delivery of deed and possession. The Seller covenants and warrants (1) that there is ingress and egress to said property over public roads, and (2) that there are no parties in possession other than the Seller.

Z. No agreements or representations, unless incorporated in this contract, shall be binding upon any of the parties. Typewritten or handwritten provisions inserted in this form or attached hereto as addendums shall control all printed provisions in conflict therewith.

furnish an abstract of title to the buyer as standard practice. If title insurance is required, protection will be furnished by the seller in an amount equal to the purchase price. Unless the contract is specific on this point, the seller is not under obligation to furnish proof of title.

Prorating and Closing Expenses. If standard forms are used, there will be a clause providing for prorating of taxes, prepaid insurance, utilities such as water, electricity, garbage collection, and accrued interest, rents, or similar charges. To the seller, the proration clause reimburses the seller for prepaid items. Proration clauses in a similar manner reimburse the buyer for unpaid expenses incurred before the date of closing. The contract for sale should be explicit on items to be prorated.

It is equally important to cover expenses of the closing to be borne by each party. Mutual understanding on these points avoids controversy at the time of closing. Therefore, all expenses of the sale should be anticipated and listed in the contract for sale according to who assumes responsibility for the payment at the time of final settlement.

The Conveyance Instrument. The contract for sale or its substitute determines the conveyance instrument to be furnished by the seller. It makes considerable difference to the buyer whether the transaction is to be completed with a quitclaim deed or a warranty deed. The contract for sale is the point in which this subject should be stated in writing. If standard forms are used that do not agree with the circumstances, legal advice must be obtained to cover this point.

Acknowledgment. Acknowledgment, generally exercised by having the agreement signed by two persons, one of whom may be the selling broker, permits the instrument to be recorded. However, it should be noted that acknowledgement is not necessary for an enforceable agreement. If it later turns out that the buyer desires recording, he is unable to exercise this privilege unless the seller has initially acknowledged the agreement at the time of execution. Good practice recommends that brokers have contracts of sale signed by the seller and witnessed by two persons. With acknowledgment and recording, a contract continues to cloud the title unless the contract is subsequently closed by recording a deed or released by the buyer by executing and recording a quitclaim deed. The alternative would require court action to remove color of title.

Personal Property. Much misunderstanding is avoided by listing articles of personal property in the contract for sale. At closing, the seller should execute a bill of sale for personal property. It is advisable to list items specifically included in the sale. Articles commonly falling in this category include:

Rugs and carpets.

Expensive lighting fixtures that are easily portable.

Draperies and rods, curtains, awnings, and storm doors, windows, and
  screens.

Kitchen equipment, ranges, ovens, refrigerators.

Air conditioning units.

Fireplace accessories.

Built-in stereo, intercom and speaker systems.

Risk of Loss. Though some states follow the Uniform Vendor and Purchaser Risk Act, the question may arise as to who should bear loss or destruction occurring after the contract for sale and before closing. Those states operating under the Act, place the risk of loss in the one having possession at the time of destruction. Under common law, the purchaser bears the risk of loss from the date of the contract. In these circumstances if the property is destroyed by fire or condemnation, the purchaser would receive whatever insurance proceeds or awards were granted. But he would still be obligated to the seller for the amount of the agreed purchase price. The reasoning here is that the seller retains the legal title merely for the buyer's benefit. In these jurisdictions, the buyer is advised to add a protective clause stating that the seller assumes the risk of loss up to and including the time of delivery of the deed. Hence possession is not always necessary to recover.

Existing Mortgages. A mortgage existing at the time of sale represents a lien on the real estate. Therefore, some provision must be made to retire the debt or provide for its payment. In the contract of sale, if the seller agrees to retire the mortgage at the time of sale from proceeds of the purchase price, the title may be delivered free of the mortgage.

If the buyer elects to buy the property with an existing mortgage, he or she has two options: to buy "subject to," or "assume" an existing mortgage which is described in the contract of sale. The words *subject to* mean that the buyer is not personally liable to the lender for the mortgage debt. Unless released by the lender, the seller remains personally liable for the debt and the property described in the mortgage continues to be subject to the mortgage lien. The buyer in this case is not personally liable, though the realty is subject to mortgage foreclosure. By the terms of the mortgage, the lender has the right to foreclose on the real estate. In addition the lender may bring suit on the promissory note against the personal assets of the original borrower or seller.

The alternative allows the buyer to purchase by "assuming" the existing mortgage. Typical language includes clauses to the effect that the buyer "assumes" or "assumes and agrees to pay" the stated outstanding mortgage. With this language, the buyer becomes personally liable for the debt; the property is also subject to foreclosure. Depending upon state law, the buyer may be held for the deficiency between the price received by the lender at foreclosure and the outstanding mortgage balance. If the buyer assumes a mortgage, the seller—the original mortgagor—secures a release from the lender.

QUESTIONS FOR REVIEW

_____ 1. Under listing agreements
  a. the buyer agrees to purchase under terms of the agreement.
  b. the seller agrees to sell under terms of an agreement.
  c. the seller does not have to pay a commission.
  d. the buyer agrees to pay the commission.

_____ 2. The contract for sale
  a. guides the sale from the negotiating state to the delivery of title and payment of the purchase price.
  b. is the most important legal document affecting a real estate sale.
  c. controls the type of instrument conveying title.
  d. all of the above.

_____ 3. A receipt and agreement to purchase document
  a. is a contract for sale.
  b. serves as a receipt of the deposit, includes terms of the sale, and requires the seller's signature.
  c. includes no description of the property.
  d. requires the buyer's signature but not the seller's.

_____ 4. A contract for sale requires
  a. an offer and acceptance.
  b. a valid consideration.
  c. parties capable of contracting.
  d. all of the above.

_____ 5. A(n) _____ is a written statement by the seller and an unconditional acceptance by the buyer that a sale has been made.
  a. contract for sale
  b. negotiation agreement
  c. option
  d. transaction agreement

_____ 6. Frequently the rights and liabilities of a seller are dependent on the
  a. date of recording.
  b. date of closing entered on the contract for sale.
  c. time of possession.
  d. real estate commission.

_____ 7. A contract for sale must include
  a. the names and addresses of the buyer and seller.
  b. a legal description.
  c. the terms of the sale.
  d. all of the above.

_____ 8. If time is of the essence
  a. either party may have a reasonable period of time before default may be claimed.

     b.   notice must be served stating a reasonable time for the contract to be completed.

     c.   neither of the parties may claim default.

     d.   there is a one-month time limit to complete the contract.

_____ 9.   Generally the seller must provide

     a.   title insurance or a title abstract.

     b.   title insurance and a first mortgage release.

     c.   a title abstract and a current tax certificate.

     d.   proof of title and an equity deposit.

_____10.   Proration clauses

     a.   should not be included in the contract.

     b.   benefit the buyer, not the seller.

     c.   reimburse the seller for prepaid items.

     d.   reimburse the seller for the real estate commission.

_____11.   Co-brokerage

     a.   refers to an arrangement in which a broker shares a real estate commission with another licensed broker.

     b.   tends to give the exclusive right to sell agreement certain advantages of the multiple listing service.

     c.   is often used for properties that have a regional or national market.

     d.   all of the above.

_____12.   Acknowledgment permits a real estate instrument to be

     a.   recorded.

     b.   notarized.

     c.   executed.

     d.   transferred.

_____13.   Personal property

     a.   should not be listed in the contract for sale.

     b.   should be listed in the contract for sale to avoid misunderstanding.

     c.   is always sold as part of the real property.

     d.   is never sold with real property.

_____14.   Under common law the _____ bears the risk of loss from the date of the _____.

     a.   seller, closing

     b.   seller, contract

     c.   buyer, contract

     d.   buyer, possession

_____15.   If a property is bought "subject to" a mortgage, the

     a.   buyer is personally liable to the lender of the mortgage debt.

     b.   lender has no recourse in case of default.

     c.   loan is generally refinanced.

    d. buyer is not personally liable to the lender for the mortgage debt.

_____16. In addition to the ordinary elements of a contract, the option should include

    a. an expiration date.
    b. a statement of conditions under which the option may be exercised.
    c. an agreed-upon price and terms of sale.
    d. all of the above.

_____17. A third person who holds money or a written instrument until certain conditions are met is called

    a. a real estate broker.
    b. an escrow agent.
    c. an attorney in fact.
    d. a trustor.

_____18. The Parol Evidence Rule prevents

    a. oral evidence from varying the terms of a written contract.
    b. a parolee from holding a real estate broker's license.
    c. oral evidence from supplementing terms of a written contract.
    d. *a* and *c.*

_____19. A listing agreement for an indefinite period of time may be cancelled by the

    I. owner.
    II. listing broker.

    a. I only.
    b. II only.
    c. Both I and II.
    d. Neither I nor II.

_____20. Multiple listing services are favored because they

    a. combine the best features of an open listing and an exclusive listing.
    b. expose properties to the prospects of many participating brokers.
    c. serve as clearing houses for saleable property.
    d. all of the above.

_____21. A buyer assuming a mortgage

    a. becomes personally liable for the debt.
    b. may be held for the deficiency between the foreclosure price and the outstanding mortgage balance.
    c. usually must be approved by the lender.
    d. all of the above.

_____22. Under a listing contract, the real estate broker must

    a. not advertise without approval of the owner.

    b. exercise diligence in finding a purchaser.

    c. find a purchaser within the period stated in the contract.

    d. advertise if the seller pays an advance fee.

____23. Co-brokerage refers to informal arrangements in which

    a. salespersons work for two brokers.

    b. brokers voluntarily share commissions.

    c. the principal executes two listings.

    d. none of the above.

____24. Under a listing agreement, the

    a. seller is responsible for a marketable title at the time of clos-
ing.

    b. broker agrees to secure a marketable title.

    c. buyer assumes the risk of an unmarketable title.

    d. broker agrees to grant certain rights to sell.

____25. A(n) _____ is used only if the seller wants a net amount after
closing.

    a. open listing

    b. multiple listing

    c. net listing

    d. exclusive agency

____26. Which of the following does not represent a listing agreement?

    a. A leased fee.

    b. An exclusive agency.

    c. An exclusive right to sell.

    d. An open listing.

____27. The net listing

    a. is the most widely used listing agreement.

    b. encourages the agent to exercise every effort on behalf of his
principal.

    c. is encouraged by the real estate industry.

    d. encourages misrepresentation and fraud.

____28. Under a(n) _____ the seller retains the right to list with more
than one broker.

    a. open listing

    b. net listing

    c. closed listing

    d. exclusive right to sell

____29. Under an open listing, the

    a. seller is not legally required to notify other agents in the case
of sale by one of the listing brokers.

    b. owner may sell the property without paying a commission.

    c. seller may be liable for two real estate commissions.

    d. all of the above.

_____30. If the listing owner sells his property when the listing agreement
is valid, he is liable for a commission under a(n) _____ listing
agreement.
   a. net
   b. exclusive right to sell
   c. exclusive agency
   d. open

_____31. Under the exclusive right to sell, the
   a. property may be listed with other members of the local real
      estate board.
   b. owner may not sell his property while the agreement is in
      effect without paying a commission.
   c. seller may list his property with other brokers during the list-
      ing period.
   d. contract is for an indefinite time.

_____32. Under exclusive agency,
   a. other brokers may list the property.
   b. the owner may not sell the property until the contract his
      terminated.
   c. the seller is always liable for a real estate commission if he
      sells his own property.
   d. the seller is liable for the real estate commission even if he
      sells his own property if the broker is the procuring cause of
      the sale.

_____33. Under a multiple listing agreement, the
   a. commission is shared with the listing service, the listing bro-
      ker, and the selling broker.
   b. commission is shared between the listing broker and the sell-
      ing salesperson.
   c. full commission goes to the listing broker.
   d. full commission goes to the selling broker.

_____34. Under _____ brokers are reluctant to pursue a sale actively be-
cause of the risk of losing a sale to competing brokers and the risk
of a contested commission.
   a. an exclusive agency
   b. a net listing
   c. an open listing
   d. a multiple listing

_____35. Multiple listing succeeds because the
   a. properties are screened by an appraisal board.
   b. seller gains the advantage of the services of cooperating bro-
      kers who are protected by an exclusive right to sell agreement.
   c. individual member brokers are induced to secure listings since

if the property is sold they are rewarded by a share of the commission.

    d. all of the above.

_____36. The listing agreement may not be terminated

    a. without compensation if the broker has found a prospect ready, able, and willing to buy on the seller's terms.

    b. because of incompetence of the buyer.

    c. if the seller files for bankruptcy.

    d. if the listing agreement is for an indefinite time.

_____37. An option contract

    a. commits the buyer to buy.

    b. commits the seller to a certain price for an indefinite period of time.

    c. commits the seller to a certain price for a given period of time.

    d. does not have to conform to contract requirements.

_____38. An option should include

    a. an expiration date.

    b. a statement of conditions under which the option may be exercised.

    c. an agreed-upon purchase price.

    d. all of the above.

_____39. The escrow agent is a(n)

    a. disinterested third party.

    b. agent for the seller.

    c. agent for the buyer.

    d. agent that negotiates the terms of sale.

_____40. Consideration paid for an option is

    a. returned if the buyer decides not to buy.

    b. usually applied against the purchase price if the buyer decides to purchase.

    c. forfeited if the buyer decides not to purchase.

    d. *b* and *c.*

ANSWER KEY

1. (*b*)	11. (*d*)	21. (*d*)	31. (*b*)
2. (*d*)	12. (*a*)	22. (*b*)	32. (*d*)
3. (*b*)	13. (*b*)	23. (*b*)	33. (*a*)
4. (*d*)	14. (*c*)	24. (*a*)	34. (*c*)
5. (*a*)	15. (*d*)	25. (*c*)	35. (*d*)
6. (*b*)	16. (*d*)	26. (*a*)	36. (*a*)
7. (*d*)	17. (*b*)	27. (*d*)	37. (*c*)
8. (*b*)	18. (*d*)	28. (*a*)	38. (*d*)
9. (*a*)	19. (*c*)	29. (*d*)	39. (*a*)
10. (*c*)	20. (*d*)	30. (*b*)	40. (*d*)

SUGGESTED ADDITIONAL READING

Atkinson, Harry Grant, and Wagner, Percy E. *Modern Real Estate Practice: An Introduction to a Career in Real Estate Brokerage.* Homewood, Ill.: Dow Jones-Irwin, Inc., 1974, chap. 14.

Bowman, Arthur G. *California Real Estate Principles.* Pacific Palisades, Calif.: Goodyear Publishing Co., Inc., 1972, chap. 6.

Ficek, Edmund F.; Henderson, Thomas P.; and Johnson, Ross H. *Real Estate Principles and Practices.* Columbus, O.: Charles E. Merrill Publishing Co., 1976, chap. 15.

Hines, Mary Alice. *Principles & Practices of Real Estate.* Homewood, Ill.: Richard D. Irwin, Inc., 1976, chap. 12.

Real Estate Sales Handbook. 7th ed. Chicago: Realtors National Marketing Institute of the National Association of Realtors, 1975, chap. 6.

6

Real Estate Contracts

Virtually every real estate *operation* depends on contracts and their enforcement. Unlike other businesses, a real estate sale requires numerous written documents that assume characteristics of enforceable contracts. Accordingly the real estate agent faces the initial problem of learning (1) common contract terms, (2) contract legal requirements, (3) remedies of the buyer and seller in the case of contract default, and (4) the basic features of installment contracts and options. Other contracts unique to real estate are covered in separate chapters. Knowing the main points relating to contracts helps the agent recognize unenforceable or invalid contracts. To be sure, legal advice should be solicited if substantive questions of law arise.

CONTRACTS DEFINED

Simply stated, a contract is a voluntary agreement between two or more parties consisting of promises made in return for a consideration. The promises may be acts which the parties are going to do or to refrain from doing. In short, a contract involves a promise or a set or promises which, if breached, give the parties a legal remedy or establish a performance which constitutes a legal duty. A promise represents an undertaking either that something shall happen or that something shall not happen.

Normally, real estate contracts assume the form of a written document stating the terms, consideration, and intentions of both parties. Such a contract is an *expressed* contract, as opposed to an *implied* contract. An implied contract is evidenced by the conduct of the parties rather than by

153

written or oral agreements. To gain familiarity with contract terminology, given below is an explanation of differences in contracts classified according to their *legality*. The relative significance of real estate contracts is shown by a *functional* classification that indicates the more commonly used real estate contracts. A discussion by this two-fold classification precedes an explanation of legal contract requirements.

Legal Classifications

The vocabulary common to the following legal subclassifications are widely used by laypersons.

Valid Contracts. A valid contract contains all the essential elements required by law. In every respect, it is binding and enforceable against parties to the contract; in case of default, each party benefits from all remedies available under the law. The importance of the available remedies will be discussed later in the chapter.

Unenforceable Contracts. Some contracts may be valid but unenforceable. In these circumstances, neither party may sue under terms of the contract. For example, the time for a performance may exceed the minimum time provided by the statute of limitations. Hence, neither party can enforce the contract even though it was valid at the time of inception.

Or take the case of an owner who was the sole beneficiary of a trust that held legal and equitable title to a two-unit apartment building. Though the owner, Mrs. Madigan, had full power to instruct the trustee to sell her building, she represented herself as the sole owner without the knowledge of the buyer, who paid $4,000 earnest money towards purchase of the duplex. The court held that the contract was unenforceable—only the trustee had the power of sale. (*Madigan* v. *Buehr*, 260 N.E. 2d 431 [Illinois, 1970].)

Void and Voidable Contracts. A contract to commit an illegal act is *void*. It has no effect as a contract. In some states a contract executed by a minor is void and without effect. On the other hand, a *voidable* contract has all the legal requirements of a contract but may be rejected by one or both parties to the contract. Contracts resulting from fraud or a misrepresentation are cases in point. That is, the person subject to the fraud has the option of rejecting the contract (i.e., the contract is voidable).

For example, suppose a buyer purchases a 5-acre parcel of land which is described as having 330 feet of frontage. After the contract is executed, and it turns out that the frontage is actually 230 feet, the buyer has the option of voiding the contract. A similar result follows when there are substantial differences between the acreage described in the contract and the actual acres (i.e., 150 acres described but there are only 100 actual acres).

Bilateral and Unilateral Contracts. A bilateral contract is a mutual agreement between two parties. In illustration, party A may agree to convey title to a $60,000 house and lot provided party B pays $10,000 down and agrees to pay the balance under a purchase money mortgage over 20 years in monthly payments with interest. In a *bilateral* contract, one party makes certain specific promises in exchange for promises of the other contracting party. A purchase of land under an installment contract or a contract with a builder to construct a new house illustrates a bilateral contract: one party promises to act; the other party agrees to make certain payments. The relationship is bilateral.

A *unilateral* contract is a promise given by one party to induce performance by another party. A farmer may execute an open listing promising to pay a commission of $5,000. If a broker finds a buyer meeting the terms of the sale who is willing to pay $50,000, the broker has performed and the owner is obligated to pay the $5,000 commission. In a unilateral contract the second party is not bound to act but if he or she does act under the terms of the contract, the first party is bound to pay the agreed consideration or commission (in this example).

To put it differently, a person listing a house for sale makes a promise to pay a commission as a means of encouraging a broker to find a buyer. The promise to pay a commission qualifies as a consideration. The broker, however, is not compelled to find a buyer, but the prospect of earning a commission serves as a strong inducement to act. If the broker contracted to build a house, he or she would be compelled to perform; that is, would be governed by a bilateral contract, not a unilateral contract illustrated by a listing.

Executed and Executory Contracts. If a contract is completed—that is, its terms have been fulfilled—it is said to be an *executed* contract. A contract for the sale of land would be an executed contract at the date of settlement, which would include the offer and acceptance of the deed and payment of the consideration (purchase price). In essence, an executed contract refers to a completed transaction; all requirements of a valid contract have been completed or executed.

Contracts in which the performance is incomplete are *executory*. A contract for construction of a new building is executory until construction has been completed and the contractor has been paid. Land purchased under a long-term contract calling for annual installment payments over 15 years would be an executory contract until the final payment and delivery and acceptance of the deed. In further illustration, a valid deed is said to be an executed contract, while a contract for sale is regarded as an executory contract. The main differences in these legal classifications are summarized in Figure 6–1.

FIGURE 6–1

The Legal Classification of Contracts

Valid	Includes All Essential Legal Requirements of a Contract

Unenforceable	Valid but Unenforceable against Parties to the Contract

Void	No Contract; a Contract for an Illegal Purpose
Voidable	Parties Have an Option to Reject Contract

Implied	Contract Implied by Conduct
Express	Written or Oral Contract

Bilateral	Promise of One Party in Exchange for a Promise of a Second Party
Unilateral	Second Party Not Bound to Act

Executed	Terms of Contract Fulfilled
Executory	Performance Incomplete

Functional Classification of Contracts

The most common contracts in real estate fall into three categories: (1) listing agreements which are contracts employing a broker to sell real estate for a commission; (2) leases for more than one year; and (3) contracts for the sale of land. These contracts are covered in separate chapters. Two others, the installment contract and the option to purchase are described in this chapter.

The functional classification of contracts common to real estate would include many other special-purpose contracts. The significant point to remember is that all states require a *written* contract for the conveyance of real property. In most jurisdictions, moreover, leases of more than one year must be in writing to be enforceable. The written requirement comes under the statute of frauds requirement.

Statute of Frauds. The statute of frauds refers to statutes that require certain instruments to be in writing; if such agreements are not in writing, they are void. A typical statute, which is enacted in every state in some form, is illustrated by the Oregon Statute of Frauds which requires certain real estate instruments to be in writing:

In the following cases the agreement is void unless the same or some note or memorandum thereof, expressing the consideration, be in writing and subscribed by the party to be charged, or by his lawfully authorized agent; evidence therefor, of the agreement shall not be received other than the writing, or secondary evidence of its contents, in the cases prescribed by law:

(5) An agreement for the leasing for a longer period than one year, or for the sale of real property, or of any interest therein.

(6) An agreement concerning real property made by an agent of the party sought to be charged unless the authority of the agent be in writing.

(7) An agreement entered into subsequent to the taking effect of this Act, authorizing or employing an agent or broker to sell or purchase real estate for compensation or commission; provided, however, that if the note or memorandum of such agreement be in writing and subscribed by the party to be charged, or by his lawfully authorized agent, and contains a description of the property sufficient for identification, and authorizes or employs the agent or broker named therein to sell such property, and expresses with reasonable certainty the amount of the commission or compensation to be paid such agent or broker, such agreement of authorization or employment shall not be void for failure to state a consideration   (ORS 41.580).

Another portion of the law relates to estates and interests in real property other than a lease of one year or less.

No estate or interest in real property, other than a lease for a term not exceeding one year, nor any trust or power concerning such property, can be created, transferred, or declared otherwise than by operation of law, or by a conveyance or other instrument in writing, subscribed by the party creating, transferring, or declaring the same, or by his lawful agent, under written authority, and executed with such formalities as are required by law.

The Supreme Court has denied Oregon brokers any right of recovery of a commission where they have been employed orally to sell real property. After expressing sympathy with their efforts, the court stated, "without a lawful agreement to support the same, no labor, however valuable, by one for another will make the person performing it more than a mere volunteer not legally entitled to compensation" (ORS 93.020).

Not only must contracts covering estates and interests in real estate be in writing, they must conform to all legal requirements of contracts. This aspect of real estate law is in effect in other states as well as Oregon.

Parol Evidence. One further point affecting contract enforceability concerns oral agreements. Assume seller X accepts a written offer to purchase his house according to agreed-upon terms of sale. Assume also that he agrees orally to replace the composition roof before the date of settlement. While the seller may voluntarily honor his oral agreement, his promise is unenforceable unless it is included as part of the written contract of sale.

The point turns on the parol evidence rule providing that oral agreements which vary or change provisions of a written contract are inadmissible as evidence. The inadmissibility of oral evidence renders oral agreements legally unenforceable. The law presumes that a written contract is complete and cannot be varied or added to by oral evidence. Exceptions are made for contracts that are incomplete, ambiguous, or not enforceable because of mistakes, fraud, illegality, or other deficiencies of legal requirements of a contract. With these exceptions, the parol evidence rule treats completed written contracts as final agreements, discouraging fraud and perjury of parties to the contract.

CONTRACT PROVISIONS

If the buyer and seller agree on terms of the sale, it is only necessary to reduce the agreement to writing and to have both the buyer and seller sign. Before this step is reached, the parties may participate in a series of offers and counteroffers. For example, the seller initially establishes the terms of sale and conditions under which he/she will convey his/her interest. This is legally known as an *offer.*

If the buyer agrees to purchase the property under the terms stated by the seller, he/she has accepted the seller's offer, which establishes a contractual relationship. Usually though, the buyer makes a counteroffer which again requires acceptance by the seller. It is immaterial whether the buyer or seller originates the offer, provided the contract is established with an offer and acceptance. To make such a contract enforceable, there must be other common legal requirements.

Legal Requirements

To be enforceable, legal requirements encompass five points: (1) competent parties, (2) an offer and acceptance, (3) a consideration, (4) a legal purpose, and (5) a written contract. The absence of any one of these requirements results in an unenforceable contract.

Competent Parties. No contract is enforceable unless parties to the contract have the authority to act. It is important to remember that competency is a legal status and has no relation to ability. Thus an American Indian holding allotted land on the reservation owns land held for him/her in trust status by the federal government and is judged legally incompetent to convey an ownership held in trust status. Other common competency questions relate to minors who must have legally appointed guardians. Similarly, a corporation taking title to real estate or acting as party to a contract must be represented by an officer holding proper authority to bind the corporation. A similar problem is encountered by parties acting with written power of attorney, executors, and administrators and trustees who act under legal authority. Without legal authority, husbands residing in community property estates cannot bind the wife to an agreement involving community property. In each of these instances the contract would be unenforceable unless both parties to the contract are legally competent.

In the same manner, a Michigan court that ruled on competency said:

> . . . It must appear not only that person was of unsound mind or insane when [the contract] was made but that unsoundness or insanity was of such character that the [seller] had no reasonable perception of nature or terms of contract.

The case referred to a contract for sale covering a $200,000 property signed by a 25-year-old owner who failed to appear at the time of settlement. The buyer, suing for specific performance, lost because of testimony by a psychiatrist confirming lack of competence. (*Star Realty, Inc.* v. *Bower,* 169 N.W. 2d 194 [Michigan, 1969].)

Offer and Acceptance. Without a valid offer and acceptance, a contract is not enforceable. In the normal case, the buyer offers to purchase the property of the seller. If the seller accepts the offer, the agreement should be immediately reduced to writing. In the act of accepting there must be a mutual meeting of the minds; each party should be thoroughly familiar with the terms, the offer, and conditions of the sale.

In a real estate transaction, the seller in effect contends that the title is marketable subject only to the stated encumbrances. In a contract for sale, the buyer is unable to verify the seller's assertion without title search. At the same time, the seller takes the property off the market pending final settlement. Since both parties stand to lose if the agreement is not consummated, the offer of acceptance should be explicit and placed in writing immediately and be drawn with complete familiarity with terms and conditions of sale.

Consideration. An enforceable contract requires that the buyer and seller agree to promises on something that they were not legally required to do at the time the contract was executed. Typically, the seller agrees to sell and convey title, and the buyer agrees to purchase under stated terms and conditions, paying a price which is the consideration. While real estate transactions show consideration as a nominal amount "$10.00 and other valuable consideration," legally, consideration assumes the form of a promise to pay a debt, pay money, or assume the form of a promise to pay a debt, pay money, or assume obligations of the seller, or perform a service. Thus in a contract for sale, both parties promise to do something which in effect represents an exchange of promises. A promise may serve as a valid consideration.

Legal Purpose. A contract that requires some act against federal, state, or local law is unenforceable. A building sold for the specific purpose of running a gambling casino or the sale of land for dog racing where these acts are prohibited by law would be unenforceable. Therefore a contract to be enforceable must have a legal purpose—a purpose which is not expressly forbidden by law or public policy.

Contracts Must Be in Writing. Since the statute of frauds has been enacted in every state, contracts for the purchase or sale of real estate or any interest in real estate must be in writing. It is also implied that both parties to a contract must sign the contract. While most contracts not in writing may be valid, they are not enforceable in a court of law. Because of the parol evidence rule and the statute of frauds, real estate agents are encouraged to make certain that both parties understand the agreement and that legal counsel convert the agreement to a written contract.

Contract Elements

Standard forms adopted for general use in the respective states serve as a guide for contract preparation. Listing agreements, options, leases, mortgages, and promissory notes are typical of standard forms approved for real estate use. A valid, enforceable contract is not required to follow any certain form. Yet in dealing with real estate, there are certain elements that should always be included. While the list here is not to be used as a checklist, the agent should make certain that the minimum information called for is included.

1. Date of the contract.
2. Names and addresses of parties to the contract.
3. A legal description of the property conveyed and the address.
4. The amount of consideration and terms of payment including encumbrances, liens, unpaid taxes, new mortgages and the like.
5. Other special agreements unique to the sale.
6. The date and place of closing the contract.

To stress the importance of the legal form and the necessity of competent legal advice, consider a contract of sale voided by the Wisconsin Supreme Court because the legal description was too indefinite. The purchasers entered into a contract to purchase a tavern described as "the real estate owned by the sellers and located in the Town of Oak Grove, now known as the 'Dobie Inn' and used in the business of the sellers." The description should have described the property fully, including the notation that the property was situated on the east 62 feet of two lots. (*Stuesser* v. *Ebel*, 120 N.W. 2d 679 [Wisconsin, 1963].)

By the same token, an Ohio court found a contract invalid because one of the parties to a contract was to a nonexistent corporation. In brief, "There were lacking two contracting parties necessary to the execution of a valid contract." Though the corporation later came into existence, the contract was invalid since the directors could have rescinded a contract which they had not authorized. (*Macy Corporation* v. *Ramey*, 144 N.E. 2d 698 [Ohio, 1957].)

RIGHTS OF THE BUYER AND SELLER

Certain rights of the parties to a contract fall under the heading of mistakes, misrepresentation, and duress. While the law in the respective states varies, contract law is sufficiently precise to allow certain generalizations to be made that apply in most court jurisdictions.

Mistakes and Misrepresentations

Most common misunderstandings fall under the general category of mistakes, misrepresentations, and fraud. There is also the issue of undue influence, duress, and the risk of loss assumed between execution of the contract for sale and the conveyance of the property at the time of settlement.

Mistakes. Suppose the seller makes an honest mistake in representing details of the property to the buyer. If the buyer has inspected the property, a mistake made in good faith will not necessarily constitute an unlawful act, especially if the buyer has had the opportunity to verify the truth by his personal inspection.

The law presumes that the buyer in inspecting the property is well informed on the condition of the property he is buying. The law further presumes that he has had the opportunity to verify title through public records. If the buyer fails to conduct the usual normal investigations of the property, an honest mistake by the seller will not void the contract.

The case is quite different in the event of a mutual mistake. If there is an honest misunderstanding of the purchase price or of the amount of land to be included in the transaction, either party may cancel or rescind the contract. This principle is subject to the exception that the mistake must be essential and not trivial.

Moreover, it should be emphasized that to set aside a written contract, the mistake must be clear and precise as shown by the evidence. Signing a contract without reading it has been ruled as insufficient grounds to void a contract. For instance, a buyer sued for performance under a written contract to sell and purchase certain farm lands in Butler and Weaver counties, Pennsylvania, for $95,000. The seller failed to convey two farms and a small tract in Beaver County on grounds that the contract was signed in haste, without reading, which constituted a material mistake, making the contract voidable. On this issue the court concluded that an executed contract signed without a reading cannot be voided merely because one of the parties was mistaken as to its meaning. (*Taylor* v. *Wilson*, 31 Beaver 5 [Pennsylvania, 1970].)

Misrepresentation. To void a contract, the misrepresentation must relate to a material fact covering the subject matter of the contract. Misrepresentations on value are generally matters of opinion and are said to be immaterial. The contract is voidable by the buyer if the seller points out one parcel of land and sells a different property than that which he represents as the property for sale.

Fraud. Fraud is the deliberate intent to misrepresent a material fact causing harm or injury. If fraud exists, the contract may be voided by the party subject to the fraud. Common sources of fraud typically fall in one of the following categories:

1. Statement of a fact that is not true by one who does not believe it to be true.
2. The assertion of a fact which is not warranted by the person making it.
3. A nondisclosure of that which is true by one having knowledge of the fact.
4. A promise made with no intention of performance.

Other types of fraud, regarded as *constructive* fraud, result from the failure to act or to undertake a duty with the purpose of gaining an advantage over the person injured. Generally in such an instance, a a contract will be voidable at the will of the victim.

Undue Influence. During contract negotiations, confidential relationships may be violated; contracts may be obtained under undue influence. The relationship of broker and principal, husband and wife, trustee and beneficiary, or guardian and ward may give one party opportunities to take unfair advantage of another's weakness. A person occupying a position of trust or a fiduciary relationship would be guilty of undue influence if a contract was gained as a result of another's stress or dire necessity. Contracts gained under these circumstances are voidable by the person suffering from the act of undue influence. Brokers who practice blockbusting tactics are guilty of using undue influence.

Duress.   Contracts are voidable if they are entered into against a person's own free will. Use of threats or other restraints to force a person to enter a contract are examples of duress and are voidable.

Risk of Loss.   In the sale of real estate, several weeks may pass between the date of the contract for sale and the execution and delivery of the deed. During this time, suppose the property is condemned by government authority under eminent domain proceedings or burns down. Under a contract for sale, the buyer is said to have an *equitable* title and is bound to pay the purchase price and assume property losses that may occur before the deed is issued. The unfairness of this situation is especially apparent if the seller remains in possession until the deed is delivered at the date of final settlement.

To correct this inequity, some states such as Wisconsin and New York have enacted the Uniform Vendor and Purchaser Risk Act.

The relevant language of the New York law in paragraph (*a*) below places the risk of loss on the seller while he remains in possession. Paragraph (*b*) transfers the risk to the purchaser if he holds legal title or assumes possession.

> (a) When neither the legal title nor the possession of the subject matter of the contract has been transferred to the purchaser: (1) if all or a material part thereof is destroyed without fault of the purchaser or is taken by eminent domain, the vendor cannot enforce the contract, and the purchaser is entitled to recover any portion of the price that he has paid; but nothing herein contained shall be deemed to deprive the vendor of any right to recover damages against the purchaser for any breach of contract by the purchaser prior to the destruction or taking; (2) if an immaterial part thereof is destroyed without fault of the purchaser or is taken by eminent domain, neither the vendor nor the purchaser is thereby deprived of the right to enforce the contract; but there shall be, to the extent of the destruction or taking, an abatement of the purchase price.
>
> (b) When either the legal title or the possession of the subject matter of the contract has been transferred to the purchaser, if all or any part thereof is destroyed without fault of the vendor or is taken by eminent domain, the purchaser is not thereby relieved from a duty to pay the price, nor is he thereby entitled to recover any portion thereof that he has paid; but nothing herein contained shall be deemed to deprive the purchaser of any right to recover damages against the vendor for any breach of contract by the vendor prior to the destruction or taking (Chapter 731, Laws of New York, 1936).

In the absence of this statute, the purchaser must insure his equitable title or include provisions in the contract for sale that effectively place the risk of loss on the seller. Contract for sale forms frequently include langauge that places the risk of loss on the seller until the date of settlement. In other instances, the contract of sale transfers the seller's interest in insurance policies on the property to the buyer.

Time of the Essence. If time is stated to be of the essence to the contract, both parties are bound to fulfill their part of the contract by the date of closing. If the seller is unable to deliver title or the buyer is unable to meet the terms of the sale at the specified date of closing, the contract may be forfeited if it is stated that time is of the essence. If no time is specified for performance, the law will assume a reasonable time.

A 1971 New York case illustrates the meaning of the phrase "time is of the essence." In this instance Howard agreed to sell Clifton Park Affiliates, Inc., two parcels of land in Saratoga County subject "to all restrictions, easements, and conditions of record." Title was to close on or before July 1, 1964. Before closing, the buyer objected to two outstanding contracts that allowed the removal of sand from the premises. At this point the seller tried to rescind the contract by returning the down payment, which was refused. Subsequently, the seller agreed to postpone the closing at various times. Finally the seller tried to rescind the contract because the buyer did not perform on time. The court held that the seller voluntarily consented to adjournment of the closing and thereby waived the right to hold the buyer in default in not performing on the settlement date. The court ruled: "time is not of essence of a realty contract unless parties make it so." (*Clifton Park Affiliates, Inc.,* v. *Howard,* 320 N.Y.S. 2d 981 [New York, 1971].)

Breach of Contract

If the buyer changes his mind after signing the contract for sale, usually (by agreement) he/she loses his/her deposit or binder receipt. The seller may accept the breach of contract and take his/her share of the forfeited deposit as damages. Further litigation may be costly and uneconomic to the seller insofar as the amount of possible damages that might be recovered. If, however, either party is unwilling to accept a breach, other remedies are available.

Remedies of the Buyer. Assume that without sufficient justification the seller fails to perform his part of the contract. In these circumstances, remedies of the buyer include (1) the right to rescind the contract and recover the earnest money deposit and other associated costs; (2) sue for specific performance of the contract as agreed; or (3) sue the seller for damages.

The first choice is taken if the seller is unable to deliver a good title and automatically is unable to perform. The buyer in this instance would be entitled to his earnest money deposit with interest and reasonable charges incurred in his efforts to comply with the contract; namely, expenditures for financing fees, appraisal fees, title searches, legal fees, and the like.

If circumstances are such that the seller has a marketable title, the buyer may elect to sue for specific performance of contract. Buyers will elect this route if the land is purchased for a specific purpose such as a shopping center, land for parking, plant expansion, or in situations where the buyer anticipates an increase in value. Specific performance is recommended if the buyer believes the land will gain in value, since it is easier to sue for specific performance than prove damages that might be ruled speculative and uncertain.

If the buyer anticipates profit by reason of the purchase (e.g., an alternative business location is not as suitable), he/she may sue for damages. The court might award personal damages to the buyer in the amount of foregone profits or, if the buyer anticipates a resale, he/she might sue for damages for the amount of capital gain lost as a result of the seller's default.

Remedies of the Seller. Like the buyer, the seller has similar options. As a rule, the seller will select one of the following: (1) he/she may rescind or forfeit the contract; (2) in some jurisdictions, he/she may sue for the purchase price; (3) he/she may elect to sue the buyer for damages; or (4) he/she may sue for specific performance.

In the case of forfeiture, the contract is terminated by the seller, who retains the earnest money deposit according to the contract for sale. In a rescission the seller surrenders all his rights under the contract. In these circumstances the seller must return the buyers' deposits. The reasoning here is that both buyer and seller must be restored—to the extent possible—to the situation existing before they entered into the contract.

If the seller sues for specific performance, the seller must stand ready to perform his/her part of the contract (i.e., delivery of title). If damages are claimed, seller must prove loss suffered because of the buyer's breach of contract. The seller will usually exercise this option if the market value of the property has gone down since the date of purchase.

A suit for damages was elected by the seller of a subdivision tract in Illinois. In brief, the seller sold subdivision land of 337 acres for a base price of $2,000 per lot to be paid in seven installments. In addition, the seller was to receive 40 percent of the lot price over $5,000. When the buyer defaulted on his payments, the seller sued to be relieved of further performance. The seller recovered unsold lots and was awarded damages equal to the unpaid balance of the purchase price for lots sold and delivered. The court reasoned that the seller could elect to be put in the same position he/she would have been had the contract been fully performed. (*Anderson* v. *Long Grove Country Club Estates, Inc.*, 249 N.E. 2d 343 [Illinois, 1969].)

INSTALLMENT LAND CONTRACTS

Installment land contracts are contracts providing for payment of the purchase price in installments. Installment purchases may require no down payments and installments ranging from 3 to even 20 years. This wide flexibility in financing a real estate transaction results from a virtually unlimited number of repayment methods. To illustrate, sellers may agree to accept interest only payments with the final payment due at some future date, or the seller may agree to transfer title and accept a purchase money mortgage with new repayment terms at a point at which the buyer's equity increases to a stated amount.

The installment land contract, which may include the purchase of buildings, income property, and vacant land, is especially adapted to property that does not qualify for mortgage credit. Such installment contracts are commonly used when transferring vacant land—property which is usually not eligible for long-term mortgage credit, or substandard property in a declining neighborhood, or a remote property rejected by institutional investors. These types of property may be sold under a land contract provided that the seller is willing to accept installment payments. There is one other circumstance leading to the installment contract: The installment contract favors buyers who are ineligible for institutional mortgage credit. Persons with high mortgage risk who are unable to secure a long-term mortgage may purchase property under land installment contracts. In still other respects, the land contract has certain advantages over alternative purchasing plans.

Installment Land Contract Advantages

Frequently, either the property or the buyer are ineligible for conventional financing. The land contract meets a need in those cases in which the seller is willing to take the risk of the land contract. In turn, the contract permits the buyer to purchase real estate which he or she could not finance under other arrangements. Moreover, the installment land contract may be combined with other types of credit and leases to satisfy the buyer and seller, tenants, and others. Thus, the installment land contract enables the buyer to acquire land with little or no capital. Three common uses of land installment contracts illustrate this point.

1. Large-tract builders who have a ready market for housing often acquire subdivision land under installment contracts. For example, in

Phoenix, Arizona, builders have purchased former agricultural land with a nominal downpayment, say 1 percent of the purchase price. The builder agrees to pay interest on the unpaid balance of the purchase price. As the property is subdivided and sold, a stated portion of each house and lot price is applied against the unpaid balance. Builders, therefore, have only a nominal land investment. Usually the seller is willing to accept these terms in view of the substantial capital gains resulting from the sale of agricultural land for subdivision purposes.

2. Consider also the seller who transfers commercial land under, say, a ten-year installment plan and who subordinates his interest to a first mortgage. The buyer then is able to secure a first mortgage up to the statutory limit of 75 percent (or even 90 percent) of the market value of land and the proposed building. In the event of default on the first mortgage, the lender has priority over the seller holding only the land contract. The seller typically shifts the risk of loss to the buyer in the form of a higher purchase price relative to the price that would be acceptable under a cash sale.

3. Others sell land under a five-year installment contract with payments of interest only. At the end of the contract, the full purchase price is due. The buyer usually has no intention of holding the property over the life of the contract. He/she holds the land just long enough to make a capital gain on a resale. Proceeds of the resale are used to pay off the installment contract. In each of these instances, the buyer minimizes his/her down payments or installments.

There are certain other advantages to sellers. First, in the event of the buyer's default on installments, the seller gains virtually immediate repossession, since the property is not under the mortgage redemption laws. Second, because the title remains with the seller until the installment payments are completed, the seller retains the *legal* title.

For the buyer, the land contract allows him/her to acquire property with a minimum credit rating and, assuming an agreeable seller, with a minimum down payment. The sale terms are subject to negotiation with the seller. However, these advantages enjoyed by the buyer and the seller are not without certain risks which are not found in a cash purchase or a combination of cash and a mortgage. Some of these risks may be reduced by anticipating them.

Land Contract Installment Risks

Under an installment contract, the buyer acquires the *equitable* title, which generally carries the right of possession and use. The seller retains the *legal* title. The legal title is conveyed from the seller to the buyer by an instrument specified in the contract when the buyer fulfills his/her part of the agreement, generally by making the final payment. At this time, it is anticipated that the buyer will acquire a marketable title. To reduce the risk of not securing title, the buyer is advised to require the seller to furnish an abstract or title insurance policy at the time the contract is executed.

But it is also possible that the seller may not have a marketable title at the time he/she is required to deliver the deed. The risks that the buyer assumes when purchasing under an installment contract are suggested by the following typical reasons why a title is not marketable:

1. Unsettled claims against an estate of a decreased owner.
2. Unpaid judgment of liens on real estate owned by the seller.
3. Mechanic's and materialman's liens.
4. Unsatisfied mortgages.
5. Unpaid special assessments, delinquent property taxes, state and federal income taxes, inheritance or estate taxes.
6. Failure of a spouse to release a community or other interest.
7. Undisclosed easements.
8. Encroachment of buildings on adjoining land.

To protect him/herself against these eventualities, the buyer may record the land contract, where this is allowed. Recording gives the buyer a prior claim against certain creditors. However, not all jurisdictions accept contracts for recording. Further, some prohibit the recording of the contract because of the time and expense of clearing title if the buyer forfeits or defaults on his/her contract.

Another protective measure requires that the seller furnish a title insurance policy. The contract may also permit the buyer to pay liens and encumbrances to clear title and deduct the sum from the purchase price. If the buyer requires the conveyance of title by warranty deed, he/she gains from the added protection afforded by warranties of the seller. This last device is not available under contracts that call for conveyance by a quitclaim deed.

It should be added that an installment contract does not give the buyer protection of the equity of redemption that applies to mortgages. If the buyer misses mortgage payments, state law allows a stated time in which the buyer may redeem property. For instance, in Wisconsin a buyer purchased a building for $5,000 down, with the balance to be paid in $200 monthly installments. Two years later the buyer defaulted in his payments. The seller brought action to void the contract. The court concluded that the purchaser could redeem his interest only by paying the full amount of the remaining purchase price within six months. (*Kallenbach* v. *Lake Publications, Inc.*, 142 N.W. 2d 212 [Wisconsin, 1966].)

In land contracts it is customary for the seller to stipulate that default on payments gives the seller the right to retain all payments and the right to declare the contract forfeited and to repossess the property. In some states the right of the seller to retain payments and repossess is restricted by statutes that treat land contracts as mortgages. Buyers may seek protection from forfeiture by providing in the contract that after a certain sum has been paid, the seller will transfer title to the buyer subject to a purchase money mortgage.

Assignment of Contracts

Given an enforceable contract, rights of the buyer and seller may be assigned to others—provided the contract does not prohibit assignment. In the case of the seller, the assignment is a method by which the seller (the assignor) transfers his/her interest to another (the assignee) for consideration. The assignee acquires all rights of the former seller. By the same token, the assignee must deliver a deed and observe other obligations of the contract.

Likewise, the purchaser, who usually must have the written consent of the seller, may assign his/her rights to a third party. Again the assignee must make payments and observe other duties of the contract. In both the assignment of seller and of buyer interests, care must be taken to insure that parties intend to assign not only their rights but their obligations, for it is well established that obligations assumed by contract may not be assigned without mutual consent. Because of the personal obligation of the buyer to the seller, contracts generally prohibit assignment of the buyer's interest without consent of the seller.

OPTIONS TO PURCHASE

Typically an option is a right to purchase (or lease) real property within a specified time on stated terms in return for a consideration. In every respect the option is a form of contract binding on the seller for a specified time but not binding on the buyer while the option is in effect. It is a unilateral contract; if exercised, the option develops into a bilateral contract for a sale and purchase. Accordingly, the option must meet all requirements of a contract; it must be in writing and it is usually accompanied by a contract for sale to be executed if the option is taken.

In at least one instance it has been settled that an option is an offer and when it is accepted there is a valid and binding contract. In Mercer County, Pennsylvania, a prospective buyer negotiated an option which provided that the option should be exercised within 60 days and that payment for 30 acres was to be $10,000. If the option was not exercised in 60 days, the option would be null and void. Within the 60 days the buyer tendered $1,000, which the seller refused as a partial payment. By this act the buyer evidenced his intention to accept the offer which was tendered within the 60-day limit. Note that the option did not require full payment of the $10,000 within 60 days. Some eight days later on February 2, the seller gave written notice that the option had expired. On February 10th, the buyer offered to pay the full purchase price. Since the option did not require the full payment within 60 days, the court held the option was accepted within the 60 days and constituted a valid and binding contract. (*Taylor* v. *Hartman*, 87 A. 2d 785 [Pennsylvania, 1952].)

Note that the seller under an option does not sell land or any interest. Note also that the person holding an option has no legal obligation to purchase. Under a contract the seller gives up his or her right to sell to others during the time covered by the option. In brief, the option gives the buyer time to buy on stated terms for a specific period. In this way, the buyer postpones his or her decision until questions of zoning, title, financing, and feasibility are resolved before committing himself to the sale. The price of the option is usually considerably less than the sale price and if the option is exercised, the consideration paid for the option is ordinarily applied to the agreed purchase price. Like other contracts, the option may be assigned by either party.

QUESTIONS FOR REVIEW

_____ 1. A real estate contract, which is a written document stating the terms, considerations and intention of the parties, is known as a(n) _____ contract.
  a. implied
  b. express
  c. legal
  d. functional

_____ 2. Judson Roberts signed a contract for sale to buy a house and lot owned by Earl Reardon. Closing and delivery of the deed was scheduled for two months after the date of the contract for sale. However, Mr. Reardon agreed to allow Mr. Roberts to take possession of the house immediately. If the house burns down one month after the date of the contract for sale, in most states,
  a. Mr. Roberts will still be bound to pay the full purchase price.
  b. Mr. Roberts may cancel the contract for sale at his option.
  c. Mr. Roberts will not have to pay the full purchase price agreed on in the contract for sale.
  d. Mr. Roberts will be required to pay Mr. Reardon the fair market rent for one month if he decides to cancel the contract for sale.

_____ 3. Which group below contains three legal requirements of a real estate contract?
  a. Legal purpose.

Monuments.
Consideration.
   b.   Written contract.
Competent parties.
Recitals.
   c.   Offer and acceptance.
Metes and bounds.
Competent parties.
   d.   Offer and acceptance.
Consideration.
Legal purpose.

_____ 4.   A(n) _____ refers to the mutual intention of two persons to enter into a contract affecting their legal status based upon agreed-upon terms.
   a.   contractual status
   b.   bargaining sale
   c.   meeting of minds
   d.   abandonment and possession

_____ 5.   Which of the following situations describes a unilateral contract?
   I.   Sonny Sample executes an open listing promising to pay Bob Broker a commission of $2,000 when he finds a buyer for Sample's farm.
   II.   Sonny Sample gives Jim Wilson a 30-day option to buy his farm for $80,000.
   a   I only.
   b.   II only.
   c.   Both I and II.
   d.   Neither I nor II.

_____ 6.   With regard to representations made to a prospective purchaser, a salesperson may be held liable for
   a.   statements of the owner.
   b.   puffing of goods.
   c.   statements of fact.
   d.   an honest mistake.

_____ 7.   Which of the following is not necessary to the validity of an agreement of sale?
   a.   The names of the parties.
   b.   A description sufficient to identify the property.
   c.   The purchase price to be paid.
   d.   An earnest money deposit.

_____ 8.   Once an agreement of sale is signed, the purchaser has _____ title.
   a.   legal
   b.   equitable

    c. ostensible

    d. corporeal

_____ 9. An oral agreement of sale in real estate may be enforced if the

    a. sales price is less than 10 percent of the value of the property.

    b. down payment is 20 percent of the sales price.

    c. purchaser and his spouse mutually agree with the seller and his spouse.

    d. none of the above.

_____10. A contract in which neither party may sue under the terms of the contract is called

    a. a valid contract.

    b. an unenforceable contract.

    c. a voidable contract.

    d. a bilateral contract.

_____11. A contract to commit an illegal act is

    a. valid.

    b. unenforceable.

    c. void.

    d. permissible.

_____12. A(n) _____ contract has all the legal requirements of a contract but may be rejected by one or both of the parties to the contract.

    a. valid

    b. enforceable

    c. void

    d. voidable

_____13. A promise given by one party to induce performance by another party is a

    I. unilateral contract.

    II. bilateral contract.

    a. I only.

    b. II only.

    c. Both I and II.

    d. Neither I nor II.

_____14. A contract is said to be _____ if all contract terms have been fulfilled.

    a. executed

    b. executory

    c. executionary

    d. voidable

_____15. Contracts in which the performance is incomplete are called _____ contracts.

      a. executed
      b. executory
      c. executionary
      d. all of the above

_____16. Which of the following would *not* be classified as an enforceable contract?

      a. A listing agreement.
      b. An oral contract to convey title.
      c. A contract for the sale of land.
      d. An option to purchase.

_____17. In most jurisdictions, leases for more than _____ must be in writing to be enforceable.

      a. one day
      b. one month
      c. one year
      d. five years or the legal statute of limitations

_____18. The parol evidence rule provides that oral agreements are not admissible as evidence when the contract is

      a. fraudulent.
      b. illegal.
      c. deficient.
      d. complete.

_____19. Among other requirements, an enforceable contract should include

      a. a purchase price over $500.
      b. an offer and an acceptance.
      c. a written contract only if one of the parties is married.
      d. all of the above.

_____20. An unconscious deletion or omission of a material fact not necessarily constituting an unlawful act may void a contract on the grounds of

      a. mistake.
      b. fraud.
      c. misrepresentation.
      d. undue influence.

_____21. An honest mistake will not void a contract if

      a. it applies only to the legal description.
      b. the buyer fails to conduct the usual investigation of the property.
      c. the damage resulting from the mistake is less than $1,000.
      d. none of the above.

_____22. Sue Kersey accepted a written offer to purchase her house according to agreed-upon terms of sale. Before the contract was executed, she asked for a higher purchase price, which the buyers orally agreed to pay. Which of the following statements is correct in the above situation?

a. The buyers must honor the oral agreement.
b. The seller may legally require the buyers to honor the oral agreement.
c. The buyers may voluntarily honor the oral agreement.
d. If the buyers refuse to honor the oral agreement, the seller may rescind the contract.

_____23. A _____ is the deliberate intent to misrepresent a material fact causing harm or injury.

a. mistake
b. fraud
c. misrepresentation
d. duress

_____24. Carlton Greene sold his property to Elton Warren for $100,000. Mr. Warren later tried to void the contract when, as the result of an appraisal, he was told that the value of the property was only $25,000. Which of the following statements applies in the above situation?

a. The contract may be voided because Mr. Greene clearly misrepresented the value of the property.
b. The contract is enforceable because value is generally said to be a matter of opinion.
c. Mr. Warren may recover the difference between the purchase price and the appraised value in a court of equity.
d. Mr. Greene will be convicted of fraudulently misrepresenting the purchase price of the property.

_____25. Which of the following situations is not an example of constructive fraud?

a. Kim Mosley, a salesman, states to a prospective buyer that there are no encumbrances on the land when he knows that there are.
b. Sarah Mosley, wife of the seller, states to a prospective buyer that the roof was replaced last winter, when she knows that the roof was actually replaced seven years ago.
c. Karen Bland, a saleswoman, does not tell a prospective buyer that the basement leaks in rainy weather, even though the sellers informed her of that fact.
d. Sam Smith, the seller, mistakenly tells the prospective buyers the plumbing is 15 years old when it is actually 16 years old.

_____26. A person occupying a position of trust would be guilty of _____ if a contract was gained as a result of another's distress.

a. perjury
b. fraud

    c. risk of loss

    d. undue influence

_____27. The use of threats or other restraints to force a person to enter into a contract are examples of _____ and are _____ acts.

    a. duress; voidable

    b. fraud; voidable

    c. risk of loss; voidable

    d. undue influence; valid

_____28. "Time is of the essence" is a concept of real estate law concerning

    a. conditions of record.

    b. delivery of title.

    c. leases.

    d. performance.

_____29. In the event that a seller is guilty of breach of contract, an option not open to the buyer is the right to

    a. rescind the contract and recover the earnest money deposit and other associated costs.

    b. sue for a specific performance of the contract as agreed.

    c. sue for the purchase price.

    d. sue the seller for damages.

_____30. Land contracts are especially designed for

    a. substandard property in declining neighborhoods.

    b. remote property rejected by institutional investors.

    c. property ineligible for institutional mortgages.

    d. all of the above.

_____31. Under an installment contract, the buyer acquires the _____ title.

    a. legal

    b. ostensible

    c. equitable

    d. cloudy

_____32. Which of the following statements is correct?

    a. Under an installment land contract, the buyer acquires the legal title while the seller retains the equitable title.

    b. The buyer under an installment land contract may not receive marketable title when the seller is required to deliver the deed.

    c. The seller, under an installment land contract, must guarantee that there are no undisclosed easements on the property.

    d. An installment land contract gives the buyer the same statutory period of redemption that applies to mortgages.

_____33. Which of the following statements is not correct?

    a. The buyer, under an installment land contract, is sometimes prohibited from recording the contract because of the time and expense required to clear title if the buyer defaults on his contract.

    b. The buyer, under an installment land contract, may require that the seller furnish a title insurance policy.

    c. All installment land contracts require the conveyance of title by warranty deed.

    d. Unsatisfied mortgages of the seller under a land contract may prevent the seller from delivering a marketable title at the time he is required to deliver the deed.

____34. In the assignment of contracts, the seller is known as the _____ when he transfers his interest to another.

    a. assignee
    b. assignor
    c. vendor
    d. vendee

____35. To assign rights to a third party, a purchaser must generally have the consent of the

    a. assignor.
    b. assignee.
    c. seller.
    d. mortgagor.

____36. An express contract is

    a. a written or oral contract.
    b. a void contract.
    c. not enforceable.
    d. evidenced by the conduct of the parties rather than by an oral agreement.

____37. Simply stated, a contract is

    a. a voluntary agreement between two or more parties consisting of promises made in return for a consideration.
    b. a compulsory agreement between two or more parties consisting of promises made and delivered.
    c. a compulsory agreement with voluntary promises.
    d. a voluntary promise.

____38. In most states a contract executed by a minor is

    a. valid.
    b. voidable.
    c. void.
    d. unilateral.

____39. James Taylor purchased a house and lot which is described as having 150 feet of frontage. After the contract was executed, he found out that the frontage is actually 110 feet. He may

    a. invalidate the contract.
    b. void the contract.

     c. not reject the contract.

     d. legally require the seller to reduce the purchase price by a proportionate amount.

____40. Billy Wright employed Larry Sikes, a real estate broker, to sell his house for $46,000. If Sikes finds a buyer who offers to pay $45,500 for the house

     a. there is an offer and acceptance.

     b. Wright can accept the offer before there is another offer and acceptance.

     c. Wright must list the house at $45,500 and allow other prospective purchasers to see it for at least one week before he accepts Sikes' offer.

     d. Wright must accept the offer because it is within 10 percent of the listing price.

ANSWER KEY

1. (*b*)	11. (*c*)	21. (*b*)	31. (*c*)
2. (*a*)	12. (*d*)	22. (*c*)	32. (*b*)
3. (*d*)	13. (*a*)	23. (*b*)	33. (*c*)
4. (*c*)	14. (*a*)	24. (*b*)	34. (*b*)
5. (*c*)	15. (*b*)	25. (*d*)	35. (*c*)
6. (*c*)	16. (*b*)	26. (*d*)	36. (*a*)
7. (*d*)	17. (*c*)	27. (*a*)	37. (*a*)
8. (*b*)	18. (*d*)	28. (*d*)	38. (*b*)
9. (*d*)	19. (*b*)	29. (*c*)	39. (*b*)
10. (*b*)	20. (*a*)	30. (*d*)	40. (*b*)

SUGGESTED ADDITIONAL READING

Attenberry, William, Pearson, Karl, and Litka, Michael. *Real Estate Law.* Columbus, O.: Grid, Inc., 1974, chap. 11.

Creteau, Paul G. *Principles of Real Estate Law.* Portland, Me.: Castle Publishing Co., 1977, chap. 13.

Lusk, Harold F., and French, William B. *Law of the Real Estate Business.* 3d ed. Homewood, Ill.: Richard D. Irwin, Inc., 1975, chap. 10.

Ring, Alfred A., and Dasso, Jerome. *Real Estate Principles and Practices.* 8th ed. Englewood Cliffs, N.J.: Prentice-Hall, Inc., 1977, chap. 8.

Unger, Maurice A. *Real Estate: Principles & Practices.* 5th ed. Cincinnati, O.: South-Western Publishing Co., 1974, chap. 4.

7

Reading Legal Descriptions

Under our system of land ownership, each parcel of real estate must have a unique legal description. Because land in the United States must be owned by a public agency, an individual, or a private organization, each parcel must be described in a way that distinguishes that particular parcel from other land. In addition, the method of describing real estate must be flexible so that land may be divided or merged and yet retain a separate, unique legal description. Legal descriptions must also be divisible to record partial interests in real estate such as easements, leases, life estates and other methods of dividing property rights.

Fortunately the 2.3 billion acres included in the United States (which covers the gross area of Alaska and Hawaii) may be legally described. Since the American Revolution, the federal government has conveyed approximately 1.1 billion acres to individuals, business, and nonfederal government agencies. The task of disposing of the public domain, primarily to raise revenue for the federal government, led to the present system of legal surveys.

It should be noted that street addresses are not suitable for locating a site. House numbers and street addresses are not always logical; they are not used in rural areas, and they are subject to duplication, omissions, and frequent change by public authorities. The system of legal descriptions developed in the United States overcomes the deficiencies of describing property by street numbers.

Learning to read legal descriptions is not an academic exercise. There are practical reasons for knowing how to follow a legal description. Rural property or even urban vacant land may not be precisely located without reference to a legal description. Moreover, legal descriptions help to avoid mistakes in identifying real estate. Expensive litigation and costly errors are avoided if parties to the transaction know how to read legal descriptions.

An understanding of legal descriptions is also necessary to interpret public records. The local ownership index for tax and mortgage records are filed according to legal descriptions. Not only are public records dependent on the legal description system, but private documents affecting liens, titles, conveyances, and contracts are also. The latter reason alone recommends a working knowledge of real estate descriptions.

TYPES OF LEGAL DESCRIPTIONS

A legal description is a precise way of describing real estate that will be accepted by a court of law. In most states a street address, while it is sufficient to locate a house, will not serve as a legal description. In practice, a legal description in a conveyance instrument may be followed by the words "commonly known as" and then by street address. The street address has less significance than the proper legal description.

In brief, a legal description describes the boundary of a particular site; it describes the land in definite, accurate and detailed terms, enabling competent persons to locate the boundaries. More importantly, a legal description must meet all requirements to pass title. In considering the adequacy of a legal description, conveyance documents should at the very minimum meet the following requirements:

1. In a land transfer, the legal description should show the intent of the parties. Others unfamiliar with the property should be able to determine the intent of buyer and seller.
2. Each parcel of land has a unique location in relation to its surroundings. Thus the legal description must associate the point of beginning to a fixed monument. The fixed monument may be a natural or an artificial feature; for instance, a concrete monument, an iron pipe, the centerline of a street or highway, or other physical object. A legal description is normally referenced to a state, county, or other legal entity and may be part of a larger survey (i.e., a subdivision).
3. The legal description should show a continuous series of courses and distances along boundaries that encircle the land. By using measured lines and angles, any shape of parcel can be identified.
4. Preferably the area within the boundaries of the legal description should be given in acres or square feet within acceptable tolerances.
5. Legal descriptions usually show the identity of persons currently owning the property described.

A study of legal descriptions shows that surveyors avoid subjective terms such as "over," "through," or "across"—reference is given to specific locations that are identified according to well-known points.

Acceptable legal descriptions meeting these standards fall into groups: (1) metes and bounds, (2) U.S. government rectangular surveys, or (3) recorded subdivisions or plats.

METES AND BOUNDS DESCRIPTIONS

A metes and bounds description starts at a point of beginning and locates tract boundaries by a series of linear measurements, directions, and monuments. The line describing boundaries must end at a point of beginning. In this type of description the term "metes" refers to measures and "bounds" refers to the monuments lying between distances. Such monuments are fixed objects such as iron stakes, road intersections, fences, or even natural objects such as stones, large trees, rivers, streams or lakes.

This system of surveying was first established among the original 13 colonies to dispose of the public domain. The method is currently used in Maine, New Hampshire, Vermont, Massachusetts, Connecticut, Rhode Island, New York, Pennsylvania, New Jersey, Delaware, Maryland, Virginia, West Virginia, North Carolina, Georgia, Kentucky, Tennessee, Texas, Hawaii, and portions of Ohio. Even in other states metes and bounds descriptions are used to describe irregularly shaped land not adaptable to other descriptions.

In describing property by metes and bounds, the surveyor must originate the legal description at the point of beginning (POB). Frequently the point of beginning is established by reference to some other point. To avoid confusion, surveyors commonly locate the point of beginning by writing: "Commencing at the northwest corner of the intersection of state highway 78 and county road 4 thence east on the north boundary of state highway 78 100 feet to the *point of beginning.*"

The next problem is to locate the direction of boundaries measured from identified monuments. Directions from each boundary are defined according to the four quadrants of the compass. For example, if the direction of a line falls in the north half of the compass, it will be measured as so many degrees and minutes east or west of *north.* If the compass bearing is measured from the south half of the compass, the variation will be read from *south* so many degrees east or west. Because a line must fall in one of the four compass quadrants, compass bearings never exceed 89 degrees 59 minutes.

Note that in Figure 7–1, the direction illustrated is measured from the north and must be identified as "North 50 degrees East." Similarly, the direction measured from south will read "South 50 degrees West." The same slope may be measured from either north or south, depending on the direction. In practice, more precision is given by referring to directions in degrees, minutes, and seconds. A degree is divided into 60 minutes; a minute is divided into 60 seconds.

Note, too, that directions are preceded by the designation "North" or "South," followed by the number of degrees, then the direction—either "East" or "West." A description reading "North 50 degrees East" describes a line 50 degrees from north moving in an easterly direction. A description reading "South 50 degrees West" describes a line 50 degrees from south moving in a westerly direction.

Figure 7–2 illustrates a parcel of land described by a metes and bounds description. The points to be remembered in reading a metes and bounds description are these: (1) The beginning of the legal description will be identified by the point of beginning. (2) The direction of the line must be identified from the north or south half of the compass. (3) Using this reference, the line will read as so many degrees east or west of north or

FIGURE 7–1

Compass Quadrants for Metes and Bounds Descriptions

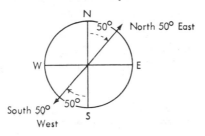

south. Note also, that surveyors typically report distances measured to the closest one-tenth of a foot. (4) A metes and bounds description must always end at the point of beginning—the description must close. A description that does not end at the point of beginning is in error.

Occasionally a conflict will arise between the *actual* distance between two monuments and the *described* distance. The rule is that actual distances prevail over described distances. That is, monuments prevail over reported distances. For example, assume that a description reads "commencing at a point of beginning measured 100 feet south of the northwest intersection of First Avenue and State Highway 3, thence north 50 degrees west 300 feet to an iron pipe. . . ." If a mistake has been made and the actual distance is only 200 feet, the actual distance between the point of beginning and the iron pipe will represent the legal boundary. Though the distance described is 300 feet, the distance between monuments prevails over the "measures" (the 300 feet described).

Frequently a metes and bounds description will end with a phrase noting the number of *acres*, followed by the words "more or less." For example, a description might end with the comment: "containing 140.3 acres more or less." If it later proves that the survey was in error and,

FIGURE 7–2

A Metes and Bounds Description

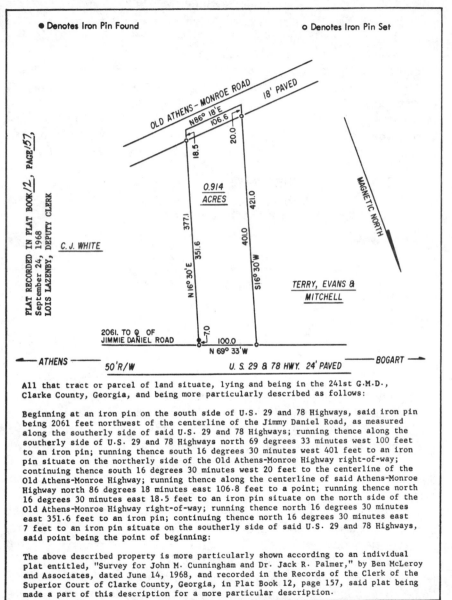

All that tract or parcel of land situate, lying and being in the 241st G.M.D.,
Clarke County, Georgia, and being more particularly described as follows:

Beginning at an iron pin on the south side of U.S. 29 and 78 Highways, said iron pin
being 2061 feet northwest of the centerline of the Jimmy Daniel Road, as measured
along the southerly side of said U.S. 29 and 78 Highways; running thence along the
southerly side of U.S. 29 and 78 Highways north 69 degrees 33 minutes west 100 feet
to an iron pin; running thence south 16 degrees 30 minutes west 401 feet to an iron
pin situate on the northerly side of the Old Athens-Monroe Highway right-of-way;
continuing thence south 16 degrees 30 minutes west 20 feet to the centerline of the
Old Athens-Monroe Highway; running thence along the centerline of said Athens-Monroe
Highway north 86 degrees 18 minutes east 106.8 feet to a point; running thence north
16 degrees 30 minutes east 18.5 feet to an iron pin situate on the north side of the
Old Athens-Monroe Highway right-of-way; running thence north 16 degrees 30 minutes
east 351.6 feet to an iron pin; continuing thence north 16 degrees 30 minutes east
7 feet to an iron pin situate on the southerly side of said U.S. 29 and 78 Highways,
said point being the point of beginning:

The above described property is more particularly shown according to an individual
plat entitled, "Survey for John M. Cunningham and Dr. Jack R. Palmer," by Ben McLeroy
and Associates, dated June 14, 1968, and recorded in the Records of the Clerk of the
Superior Court of Clarke County, Georgia, in Plat Book 12, page 157, said plat being
made a part of this description for a more particular description.

say, the number of acres actually totaled 125.6 acres as determined by a current survey, the phrase "140.3 acres more or less" is not controlling.

Finally, it should be remembered that in reading legal descriptions the bearings or the direction of the line and distances of each course connect the turning points or corners of a tract. They are read in regular order around the perimeter of the parcel surveyed. The point of beginning is sufficiently identified so that a competent surveyor may accurately locate the beginning point.

U.S. GOVERNMENT RECTANGULAR SURVEY SYSTEM

In early colonial times, legal descriptions depended on land settlement patterns. Typically, a group of settlers obtained permission from the King to establish a colonial government and to form a new settlement. After obtaining permission, settlers moved as a group and established a new town, surveying the lands and maintaining title records. Villages were laid out with a common grazing and meeting ground in the center surrounded by a cluster of houses. As fields were cleared, they were divided among the original settlers. The New England states were settled in this way.

In the southern colonies, headrights representing a tract of land, usually 50 acres, were granted to individuals. People who brought in new immigrants were given headrights according to the number of new settlers they brought in. Headrights were based on land surveys and recorded deeds which in practice were often inaccurate and of poor quality. Many southern plantations were formed by the purchase of headrights.

After the American Revolution it was wisely concluded that dependable titles and a system of property descriptions were basic to a system of private land ownership. Accordingly, the federal government adopted a system of rectangular surveys dividing land into square-mile areas. Because survey lines ran north and south, following longitudinal lines, and east and west, following the lines of latitude, the original land surveys affected the patterns of land use. Outside of the original 13 colonies and Texas, the United States developed as a rectangular country, divided into squares like a giant checkerboard.

Thus in the Midwest roads and highways tend to parallel one-mile squares; the roads go over hills rather than around them. In a similar way, farmers tended to plow their lands east and west and north and south and up and down hills rather than around slopes. The results caused much needless erosion that could have been avoided by cultivating land on contours.

The rectangular system, originally introduced in the Land Ordinance of

1785, remains today the basis of our legal descriptions. The ordinance provided that where the Ohio River crosses the Pennsylvania border, a north-south line, which is called a principal meridian and a base line running east and west was to be surveyed. From these lines, other parallel lines running north and south and east and west, at 6-mile intervals established townships of 36 square miles. Each township was surveyed into one-mile squares of 640 acres. Under the ordinance seven ranges were surveyed, a range identifying a six-mile area running north and south.

Private land companies opposed the rectangular system west of the seven ranges surveyed. As a consequence, different survey systems were employed to survey grants of the Ohio and Symmes Companies, the Western Reserve, and the Virginia Military Tract. Ohio soon gained notoriety as a surveyors' museum. However, Congress reestablished the rectangular system in laws enacted in 1796 and 1804. With few changes, the rectangular survey system remains intact where federal lands were originally in the public domain.

Today the system legally describes land in 30 states. The system is based on a system of coordinates. Land is divided into townships of approximately 36 square miles in which each square mile is identified according to a *base line* and a *principal meridian*. In the United States there are 35 principal meridians governing the legal descriptions in 30 states. Because rectangular survey descriptions, like an address, must be read backwards, the key elements must be explained in reverse order.

Principal Meridians

The principal meridians have been established by the Commissioner of the United States General Land Office and follow no set pattern. Because principal meridians represent arbitrarily chosen lines running north and south, they have no relation to lines measured from Greenwich, England, marking areas of the earth in longitude. A principal meridian represents a line running north or south (or in both directions) from the initial point. For example, land in Washington and Oregon is described by the principal meridian and the base line is measured from an initial point near the Willamette River in Portland, Oregon. See Figure 7–3 for a map of principal meridians and base lines.

Ranges

For the principal meridian, *ranges* are established in six-mile intervals representing strips of land running north and south measured from the principal meridian. "Range 2 East of the Willamette Principal Meridian"

Principal Meridians of the Federal System of Rectangular Surveys

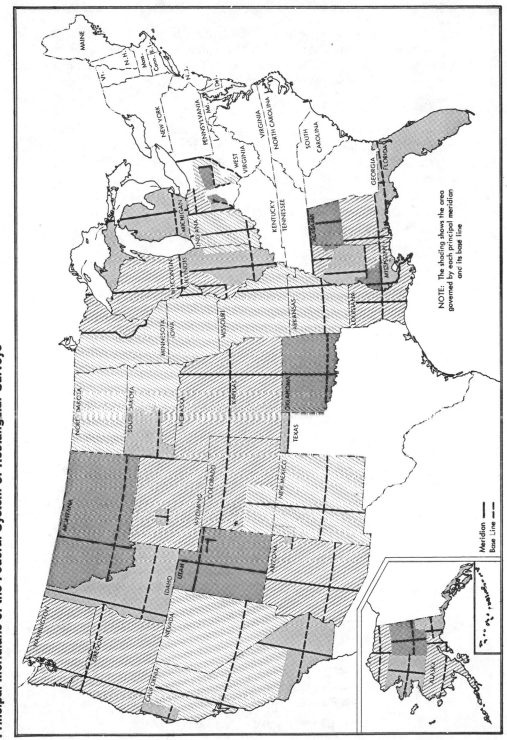

NOTE: The shading shows the area governed by each principal meridian and its base line

Meridian —————
Base Line ———————

refers to land that is located 6 to 12 miles east of the Willamette Meridian. Rectangular surveys end with a reference to the principal meridian and identify the range lying east or west of the principal meridian.

Townships

Starting from a base line extending east and west and associated with each principal meridian, townships lines are drawn in six-mile distances running east and west. "Township 3 North" describes property falling within 12 miles to 18 miles north of the base line. In a similar manner, township lines may be identified as south of the base line.

In practice, reference to the base line is omitted so that the legal description ends with the two elements: "Township 2 North, Range 3

FIGURE 7–4

Township and Range Lines Measured from the Gila and Salt River Meridian (Arizona)

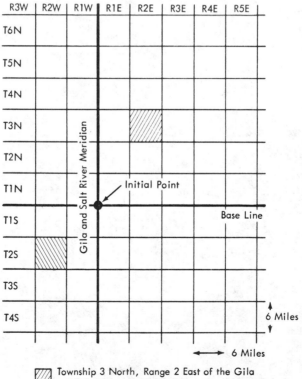

Township 3 North, Range 2 East of the Gila and Salt River Meridian.

Township 2 South, Range 2 West of the Gila and Salt River Meridian.

West of the Willamette Meridian." The land in question must be within an area 6 to 12 miles north of the base line and 12 to 18 miles west of the principal meridian.

To illustrate further, consider the description of land in Arizona. The principal meridian, identified as the "Gila and Salt River Meridian," is located approximately five miles west of the City of Phoenix near Sun City. The base line runs through the south part of Phoenix, Arizona. From the initial point where these two lines meet, 41 townships six miles wide extend north of the base line, while 19 townships extend south of the base line. Land in Arizona extends from range 23 west to 31 east of the Gila and Salt River Meridian. Figure 7–4 illustrates how ranges and townships are identified by reference to the initial point. The two shaded areas describe townships of approximately 36 square miles each.

Sections

Within the townships measuring six miles on each side, sections are numbered from 1 to 36, starting in the upper right-hand corner and numbering left to the end of the row and numbering alternately from left to right. Section numbers are shown in Figure 7–5. Ideally, the

FIGURE 7–5

A Township, Showing the Location of Sections

6 Miles

36	31	32	33	34	35	36	31
1	6	5	4	3	2	1	6
12	7	8	9	10	11	12	7
13	18	17	16	15	14	13	18
24	19	20	21	22	23	24	19
25	30	29	28	27	26	25	30
36	31	32	33	34	35	36	31
1	6	5	4	3	2	1	6

6 Miles

Adjoining Sections of Other Townships

sections describe land measured 5,280 feet on each side, constituting a land area of 640 acres. Within a section, it is customary to identify land according to quarters. For example, land in the "northwest quarter of section 1" describes 160 acres in a northwestern direction measured from the section center. Each quarter may be divided into similar quarters also located by the direction from the section center. A 40-acre parcel in the southwest quarter (SW¼) of section 1 might be designated as the "northwest quarter of the southwest quarter of Section 1" (NW¼ SW¼).

Figure 7–6 shows that this area could be further subdivided by quarters and halves. For instance, the "west half of the northwest quarter of the southwest quarter" describes 20 acres (W½ of NW¼ of SW¼ of Section 1). Notice that identification of areas smaller than one section are located by reading backwards. Besides this rule there is only one

FIGURE 7–6

A Section of Land (640 Acres)

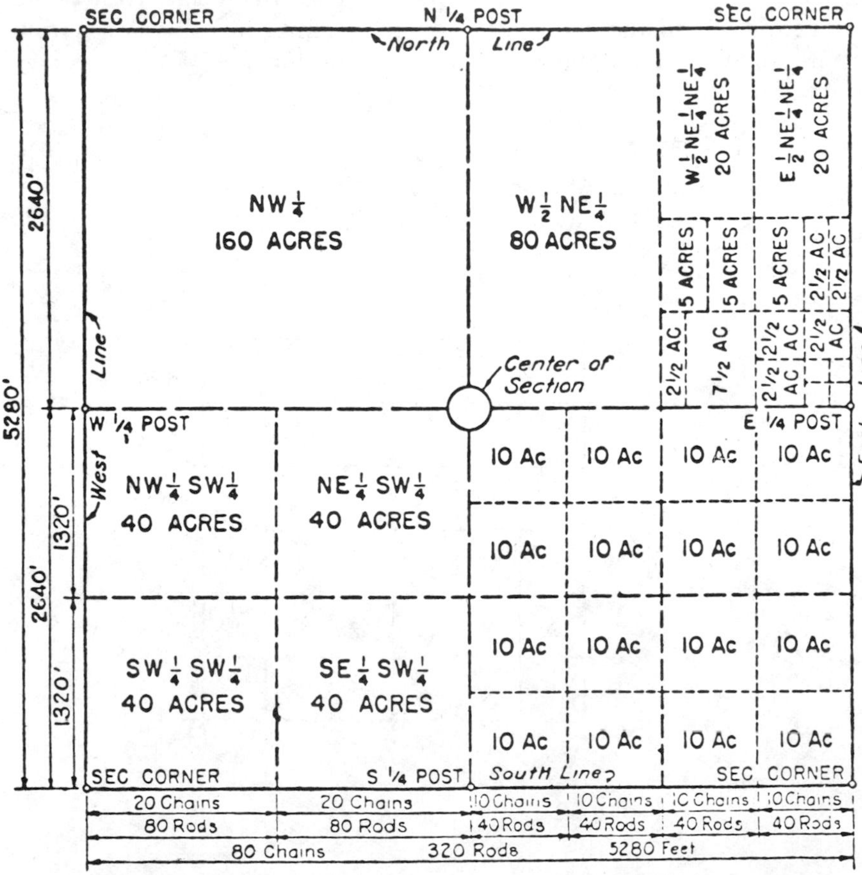

other point to remember. If the legal description includes the word "and," then the designation starts from a new quarter section.

For instance, suppose a legal description reads the "west half of the northwest quarter (80 acres) *and* the northwest quarter of the southwest quarter (40 acres) of Section 1, Township 2 North, Range 3 East of the Principal Meridian." Such a description describes two adjoining parcels in different quarter sections totaling 120 acres. If the preceding description reads the "west half of the northwest quarter *of* the northwest quarter of the southwest quarter," the parcel would identify a five-acre parcel. The words "of" and "and" must be read carefully. Follow the rule of grouping as one unit all parts of the description linked together by the word "of." Separate the groups if the word "and" occurs.

Figure 7–6 describes a section and its dimensions as if land was divided on a flat plain. However, the curvature of the earth requires that these lines converge. Surveyors have compensated for curvature of the earth by defining correction lines in the northern and western tier of sections (sections 5, 6, 7, 18, 19, 30 and 31). In actual practice, land in these sections will not conform to the precise dimensions shown in Figure 7–6.

FIGURE 7–7

Land Description by U.S. Government Rectangular Survey in Riverside County, California

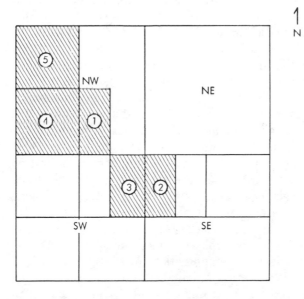

W½ SE¼ NW¼; W½ NW¼ SE¼; E½ NE¼ SW¼; SW¼ NW¼ and NW¼ NW¼, Section 34, Township 4 South, Range 5 East, San Bernardino Base and Meridian.

Moreover, the number of acres will not represent the exact divisions described in a section. For example, near Minneapolis, Minnesota, the two lines forming the east and west line of a township will be 47.9 feet closer together at their northern terminus than at their southern. For this reason, actual acreage must be calculated from dimensions as required in a metes and bounds description.

To illustrate, note the area shaded in Figure 7–7. Identification of this land will start with "Range 5 East of the San Bernardino Base and Meridian." The land located in Riverside County, California is also identified by "Township 4 South of the San Bernardino Base Line." With section 34 identified, the legal description reads:

> Land described as (1) the West half of the Southeast quarter of the Northwest quarter (W½ SE¼ NW¼); and (2) the West half of the Northwest quarter of the Southeast quarter (W½ NW¼ SE¼); and (3) the East half of the Northeast quarter of the Southwest quarter (E½ NE¼ SW¼); and (4) the Southwest quarter of the Northwest quarter (SW¼ NW¼) and the Northwest quarter of the Northwest quarter (NW¼ NW¼) of Section 34, Township 4 South, Range 5 East, San Bernardino Base and Meridian.

To help identify each portion of this description, the numbers in parentheses are added to show the corresponding areas in Figure 7–7. Beginning with the first part of the description, note that you must locate the northwest quarter of section 34—a 160-acre parcel. The first portion is located in the southeast quarter of the northwest quarter and represents only the west half of this area, a 20-acre parcel. The next part of the description starts in the southeast quarter of the section, proceeding next to the northwest quarter of the southeast quarter. The west half of this portion also describes a 20-acre parcel. The third area starts in the southwest quarter and proceeds next to the northeast quarter. The east half of this area also describes a 20-acre area. The fourth item represents land also in the northwest quarter but only the southwest quarter of this area. This adds another 40 acres to the property. The last portion covers the 40-acre parcel in the northwest quarter of the northwest quarter of section 34. Together these areas total approximaely 140 acres. Note that identification of each parcel is possible only by starting from the end of the description and reading backwards.

To cite a further example, consider the land shown in Figure 7–8. After identification of the appropriate rectangular area within a section, occasionally it is necessary to describe land more specifically by the number of feet conveyed. For example parcel A is described as the *"west 200 feet* of the NE quarter of the SW quarter of Section 3, Township 2 N, Range 1 East of the 5th Principal Meridian." Similarly, parcel B would be identified as the *"south 300 feet* of the NE quarter of the SW quarter

FIGURE 7–8

A U.S. Rectangular Survey Description

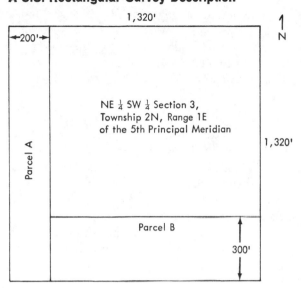

Parcel A: The W 200 feet of the NE¼ SW¼, Section 3, Township 2 N, Range 1 E of the 5th Principal Meridian.

Parcel B: The South 300 feet of the NE¼ SW¼, less the West 200 feet, Section 3, Township 2 N, Range 1 E of the 5th Principal Meridian.

of the NE quarter, less the West 200 feet, Section 3, Township 2 North, Range 1 East of the 5th Principal Meridian."

Qualifications of the Rectangular Survey System

In areas relying on government surveys, section corners are usually identified by concrete posts capped with brass identifiers marked with steel dies. Steel pipe filled with concrete, 30 inches long and 2 inches in diameter has been specified since 1910. In most areas, section corners and quarter-section corners were established by government survey teams. Private surveyors usually add other monuments such as quarter-quarter corners. The usefulness of the government surveys is provided by general rules governing land locations.

1. Boundaries established by government surveyors upon approval of the surveyor general and accepted by the federal government are unchangeable.

2. The corners of townships, sections, and section corners established by government surveyors must stand as originally placed.
3. Corners not established by government surveyors shall be placed on straight lines joining the section and quarter-section corners with exception of the last half mile of section lines closing the north and west boundaries of the township.
4. Lost or obliterated corners will be restored to their original location whenever possible.

A limitation of the government survey is encountered in attempts to survey land crossed by rivers, lakes, and ponds. In these cases meander lines were established generally for land areas of 25 acres or more. The surveyed corner monuments substitute for section corners in these instances. As result of these changes, fractional sections may include numbered government lots, which are the fractional parts resulting from irregularities caused by lakes, rivers, streams, and other bodies of water.

Rectangular surveys are not without other limitations. As surveys were originally undertaken, considerable difficulties were encountered by field surveyors. A surveyor in Indiana reported in 1804 that prairie fires destroyed wooden corner stakes. (He commented further that it was doubtful if settlers would want prairie land anyhow, destitute as it was without water.)

Another surveyor, Thomas Freeman, wrote in 1811 that survey crews could not get into the field until the middle of August or early September because of widespread flooding. Continuing, he said, "few men could be found hardy enough to stand the poisoning effect of half-dried mud, putrid fish, and vegetable matter—almost impenetrable canebrakes, and swarms of mosketoes—with which these low lands abound after the water has withdrawn."

Some improvement was introduced by organization of the General Land Office (now the Bureau of Land Management) in 1812, formed primarily to sell public lands to satisfy debts of the Revolutionary War. Contracts were subsequently placed for the private surveying of the public lands. Today, since an act of June 25, 1910, surveys and resurveys are made by government engineers. Because of the inaccuracies of the original surveys, some areas have been resurveyed several times. In this respect it is not always clear as to which survey the legal description applies. Compounding these difficulties is the problem of attempting to describe land on a flat plain. Because of correction lines and original survey errors, distances and acreages vary considerably from the mathematical standard.

State Coordinate Systems

The state coordinate system of survey is used by the United States Coast and Geodetic Survey in unsurveyed areas. The system is favored by surveyors and engineers since it accurately locates and describes land boundaries. These surveys have a maximum error of 1 foot every 2 miles (1 part in 10,000). While popular among highly-trained technicians, the layperson finds this system largely unuseable because a parcel cannot be located by reference to its immediate surroundings.

The system is based on the proposition that if three parts of a triangle are known, the other three parts may be obtained by calculation. Moreover, the system accounts for the spheroidal shape of the earth. The system provides for each state, representing the surface of the earth as a mathematical projection of cones or cylinders flattened into plains.

The plane coordinates of a point of the earth's surface are expressed in feet and decimals of a foot by two coordinates. The "X-coordinate" pinpoints the location in an east-west direction, while the "Y-coordinate" locates a position in a north-south direction. For every stated position and latitude and longitude determined by the Coast and Geodetic Survey in the states, there is a corresponding plane-coordinate position obtained by accurate and precise calculation. Such positions are marked by monuments serving as starting points for local surveyors. A surveyor using this system finds the position of his corners by getting plane coordinates from the monuments established for the coordinate system.

In that distances are measured in hundreds of thousands of feet or over 1 million feet, the layman has difficulty in verifying the survey corner. In other respects, the legal description based on the state coordinate system reads like a metes and bounds description. For example:

Parcel No. 4—Minnie Wolf, Owner

Situated in Section 9, Township 2, South, Range 3 East, Hamilton County, Ohio and being more fully described as follows:

Beginning at a point in the easterly line of Colerain Avenue, said point being 426,426.73 North and 1,421,136.26 East and being the most southerly corner of the property conveyed to Minnie Wolf by deed recorded in Deed Book 2136, Page 131, Hamilton County Records; thence northwardly along the easterly line of Colerain Avenue to a point in the northerly line of said Wolf property said point being 426,640.19 North and 1,421,049.77 East; thence eastwardly along said northerly line to a point 426,709.99 North and 1,421,255.55 East; thence eastwardly along said northerly line to a point 426,690.90 North and 1,421,460.87 East to most easterly corner of said Wolf property; thence southwestwardly along the southerly line of said Wolf property to a point in the easterly line of Colerain Avenue and the place of beginning.

Being the same premises conveyed to Minnie Wolf by deed recorded in Deed Book 2136, page 131, Hamilton County Records. (*Principles of Right of Way Acquisition*. Los Angeles, California: American Right of Way Association, 1972, p. 121).

Despite their complexity, utilization of electronic instruments to undertake these surveys has made such systems extremely practicable. Solar transits are now the approved instrument for most surveys undertaken by the Bureau of Land Management. As this new surveying technology becomes more widespread, such surveys may be increasingly found in deeds and other instruments of conveyance.

RECORDED SUBDIVISIONS

Lot and block descriptions of recorded subdivisions are not very complicated. Even so, their use requires considerable care in identifying the exact lot, the block, or other designation and the full, precise name of the subdivision. Such a description is truly not complete unless the subdivision is identified by the plat book number, page number, and county in which it is recorded.

Though it is true that the recorded subdivision identifies each lot by a metes and bounds description, such descriptions are not normally de-

FIGURE 7–9

Recorded Subdivision Description

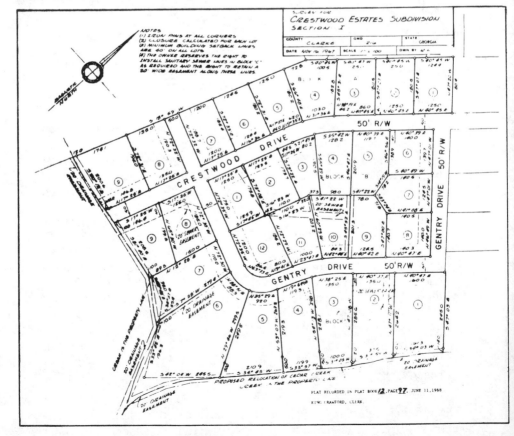

scribed in narrative form like the usual metes and bounds description. For a subdivision covering dozens or even hundreds of lots, this would be a highly burdensome task. Standard procedure is to describe the subdivision by reproducing the plat in map form, identifying metes and bounds on the map by linear measures and bearings with the appropriate identifying monuments. Providing local authorities approve the plat, the plat is then filed with the local recorder of deeds and usually placed in a separate plat book, identified by number and page.

In describing land in a legal instrument conveying land in recorded subdivisions, it is necessary to identify the appropriate plat book, the page number and date of filing, and the office in which it is filed (e.g., "Clarke County"). It is then presumed that the lot conveyed is described fully as if it were identified by a more lengthy metes and bounds description. In this sense, land described by lots and blocks is described by reference to a recorded document, namely a plat filed and recorded in a local government office.

Figure 7–9 is an example of detail included in a recorded plat. A lot in this subdivision would be described as

> Lot 2, Block B, Crestwood Estates Subdivision, Section 1, recorded in Plat Book 12, Page 97, June 11, 1968, Clarke County, Georgia

By referring to this document, which is a permanent record, each property owner can usually identify the boundary, distances, and corners of his land. Buyers of land described in this way have the added protection of plats that comply with professional surveying standards, and other regulations controlling utilities, streets, and other requirements of recorded subdivisions. (These topics are treated in greater detail in a later chapter.)

QUESTIONS FOR REVIEW

_____ 1. In the rectangular survey system, six-mile-wide areas running north and south are called _____ and six-mile-wide areas running east and west are called _____.

    a. townships; ranges.
    b. longitudes; latitudes.
    c. ranges; townships.
    d. chains; rods.

_____ 2. The W½ of the NW¼ of a section contains

    a. 40 acres.
    b. 20 acres.
    c. 160 acres.
    d. 80 acres.

_____ 3. A farm described as "the S½ of the NE¼ and the N½ of the NW¼ of the SE¼ of Section 3, Township 4W, Range 2N of the sixth P.M." contains _____ acres.
    a. 500

    b. 100

    c. 250

    d. 80

_____ 4. According to the numbering system of the U.S. Rectangular Survey, the section adjoining the south boundary of Section 10 is Section _____.

    a. 15

    b. 11

    c. 16

    d. 14

_____ 5. The SE¼ of the SE¼ of the SE¼ of Section 15, Township IN, Range 3E of the Sixth P.M. contains _____ acres.

    a. 40

    b. 5

    c. 10

    d. 20

_____ 6. Correction lines in the government rectangular survey system are used

    a. to compensate for discrepancies caused by geographical boundaries, such as mountains.

    b. to compensate for curvature of the earth.

    c. if base lines are less than 120 miles apart.

    d. if state boundaries do not fall along a principal meridian or base line.

_____ 7. The diagram below shows Section 10, Township 11 South, Range 5 West of the ABC meridian. Which of the following legal descriptions accurately describes the shaded portion of this section?

    a. The NE¼ of the SE¼ and the N½ of the SW¼ of the NE¼ of the S½ of the NE¼.

    b. The SE¼ of the NE¼ and the E½ of the NW¼ of the SE¼ and the N½ of the NE¼ of the SE¼.

    c. The NE¼ of the NW¼ and the W½ of the SE¼ of the SE¼ and the N½ of the NW¼ of the NW¼.

    d. The E½ of the SW¼ of the NW¼ and the W½ of the NE¼ of the SW¼ and the E½ of the SW¼ of the SW¼.

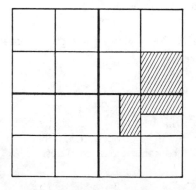

_____ 8. Townships include approximately _____ square miles.
  a. 6
  b. 16
  c. 36
  d. 640

_____ 9. A property described as "Township 5 North" is located between _____ and _____ miles north of the base line.
  a. 6 and 12
  b. 30 and 36
  c. 5 and 10
  d. 24 and 30

_____10. Section 36 of Township 3 North, Range 4 East, would be directly west of
  a. Section 1 of Township 4 North, Range 4 East.
  b. Section 31 of Township 3 North, Range 4 East.
  c. Section 31 of Township 3 North, Range 5 East.
  d. Section 36 of Township 3 North, Range 5 East.

_____11. Land described as the S½ of the N½ of the SE¼ of the NE¼ consists of approximately _____ acres.
  a. 15
  b. 10
  c. 7
  d. 20

_____12. In states using the U.S. Rectangular Survey system, a township is
  a. an incorporated city located at the center of each section.
  b. a 1,280-acre plot of land.
  c. 36 square miles.
  d. 1 square mile.

_____13. The S½ of the NW¼ of the SE¼ of the SE¼ of a section contains
  a. 40 acres.
  b. 5 acres.
  c. 10 acres.
  d. 2.5 acres.

_____14. A government lot refers to
  a. an irregular area fronting on a body of water that does not conform to section lines.
  b. government-owned property.
  c. land acquired by homestead right.
  d. land dedicated to a school district.

_____15. In the diagram below, the shaded area would be described as
  a. the N½ of the S½ of the NE¼ of the NW¼.
  b. the S½ of the N½ of the NW¼ of the NE¼.
  c. the N½ of the N½ of the NE¼ of the NE¼.
  d. the N½ of the S½ of the NW¼ of the NW¼.

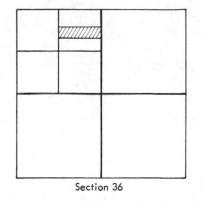

Section 36

_____16. In the section diagrammed below, the land would be described as
   a. the NW¼ of the NE¼ of the NW¼ and the W½ of the
        NW¼ of the NW¼.
   b. the NE¼ of the NE¼ of the NE¼ and the E½ of the
        NE¼ of the NE¼.
   c. the NE¼ of the NE¼ of the NE¼ and the W½ of the
        NE¼ of the NE¼.
   d. the NW¼ of the NE¼ of the NE¼ and the E½ of the
        NE¼ of the NE¼.

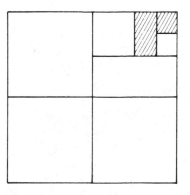

_____17. If a survey of a property shows an actual measurement of the dis-
      tance between two monuments to be three feet shorter than the
      distance given in the legal description in the deed,
   a. a new survey will be ordered by the court.
   b. the actual distance between monuments will take precedence
        over the stated distance between monuments.
   c. the measurements set forth in the description will take prece-
        dence over the actual distance between monuments.
   d. the original survey of the property always takes precedence
        over any later surveys.

_____18. The area shaded in the section below would be described as

  a. the N½ of the NE¼ of the SE¼ and the NE¼ of the NW¼ of the SW¼.

  b. the E½ of the NE¼ of the SW¼ and the NW¼ of the NE¼ of the SW¼.

  c. the E½ of the NE¼ of the SE¼ and the NE¼ of the NW¼ of the SE¼.

  d. the E½ of the NE¼ of the SW¼ and the NW¼ of the NW¼ of the SW¼.

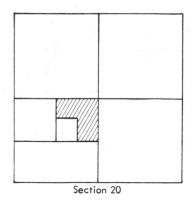

Section 20

_____19. Land shaded in Section 1 below would be described as

  a. the SW¼ of the NW¼ of the NE¼.

  b. the SE¼ of the NE¼ of the NW¼.

  c. the SW¼ of the NW¼ of the NW¼.

  d. the SW¼ of the NE¼ of the NW¼.

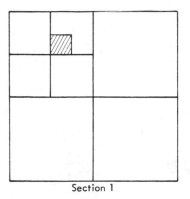

Section 1

_____20. Land shaded in Section 6 below would be described as

  a. the SE¼ of the NW¼ and the SW¼ of the NE¼ and the NW¼ of the SE¼ and the NW¼ of the SW¼.

b. the SW¼ of the NW¼ and the SE¼ of the NW¼ and the NE¼ of the SW¼ and the NE¼ of the SE¼.
c. the SE¼ of the NW¼ and the SW¼ of the NE¼ and the NE¼ of the SW¼ and the NW¼ of the SE¼.
d. the SW¼ of the NW¼ and the SE¼ of the NE¼ and the NE¼ of the SW¼ and the NE¼ of the SE¼.

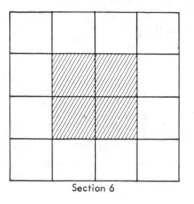

Section 6

_____21. Which of the following descriptions describes the shaded area of the section below?

a. The S½ of the SW¼ of the NE¼ and the NW¼ of the NW¼ of the NW¼ and the S½ of the NE¼ of the NW¼ of the NE¼.
b. The S½ of the NE¼ of the NW¼ of the SE¼ and the NW¼ of the NW¼ of the SE¼ and the S½ of the SW¼ of the NE¼.
c. The NE¼ of the SW¼ of the S½ and the SE¼ of the NE¼ of the NE¼ and the SE¼ of the NW¼ of the S½.
d. The NW¼ of the NW¼ of the SE¼ and the S½ of the SE¼ and the S½ of the N½ of the SE¼.

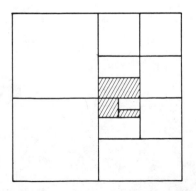

_____22. Which of the following descriptions describes the shaded area of the section below?

  a. The E½ of the NE¼ of the NE¼ and the E½ of the SE¼ of the NE¼.

  b. The W½ of the NE¼ of the NE¼ and the W½ of the SE¼ of the NE¼.

  c. The W½ of the NE¼ of the NW¼ and the W½ of the SE¼ of the NW¼.

  d. The W½ of the NW¼ of the NE¼ and the W½ of the SE¼ of the NE¼.

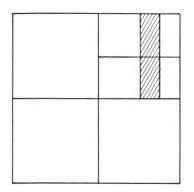

_____23. Which of the following descriptions describes the shaded area of the section below?

  a. The W½ of the SE¼ of the NE¼ and the S½ of the SW¼ of the NE¼ and the S½ of the SE¼ of the NW¼.

  b. The W½ of the NE¼ of the NE¼ and the W½ of the SE¼ of the NE¼ and the S½ of the SW¼ of the NE¼ and the S½ of the SE¼ of the NW¼.

  c. The W½ of the NW¼ of the NE¼ and the W½ of the SE¼ of the NE¼ and the S½ of the SW¼ of the NE¼.

  d. The W½ of the NE¼ of the NE¼ and the W½ of the SE¼ of the NE¼ and the S½ of the SE¼ of the NW¼.

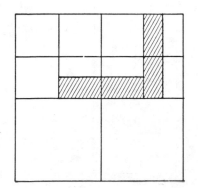

_____24. Which of the following descriptions describes the shaded area of the section below?

    a. The W½ of the NE¼ of the SW¼ and the W½ of the SE¼ of the SW¼ and the W½ of the SE¼ of the NW¼.

    b. The W½ of the SW¼ of the NW¼ and the NW¼ of the SW¼ and the E½ of the NE¼ of the SW¼.

    c. The W½ of the SW¼ of the NW¼ and the NW¼ of the SW¼ and the W½ of the NE¼ of the SW¼.

    d. The E½ of the SW¼ of the NW¼ and the NW¼ of the SW¼ and the E½ of the NE¼ of the SW¼.

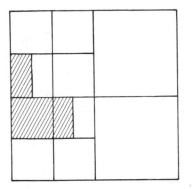

_____25. Which of the following descriptions describes the shaded area of the section below?

    a. The N½ of the SE¼ of the NW¼ and the NE¼ of the SW¼ of the NE¼.

    b. The N½ of the SE¼ of the NE¼ and the NW¼ of the SW¼ of the NW¼.

    c. The NW¼ of the SE¼ of the NW¼ and the N½ of the SE¼ of the NW¼.

    d. The N½ of the SE¼ of the NW¼ and the NW¼ of the SW¼ of the NE¼.

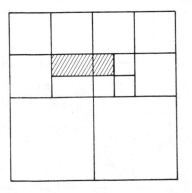

_____26. Assume the following description: Beginning at a point 200 feet east of the intersection of Broad Street and Lumpkin Avenue on the south boundary of Broad Street, thence east 200 feet; thence south 300 feet, thence west 200 feet; thence north 150 feet. Which of the following statements is correct?

   a. The legal description is inadequate because the location of iron pins is not given.
   b. The legal description does not return to the point of beginning.
   c. The description would be complete if the address is added.
   d. The description meets minimum requirements of a metes and bounds description.

_____27. For purposes of defining directions in metes and bounds descriptions, the north and south points on a compass are always _____ degrees while the east and west poles are always _____ degrees.

   a. 270; 90
   b. 90; 360
   c. 0; 90
   d. 360; 180

_____28. The principal direction of a line in a metes and bounds description described as "north 89 degrees east" would be

   a. north.
   b. south.
   c. east.
   d. west.

_____29. A legal description using compass reference points always begins with either the _____ or the _____ as a beginning reference point.

   a. south; east
   b. east; west
   c. north; west
   d. north; south

_____30. The U.S. Rectangular Survey system is not used in

   a. the western states.
   b. states acquired after 1860.
   c. the south central states.
   d. the original 13 colonies.

_____31. To describe real estate legally by lot and block number, which of the following statements is correct?

   a. The subdivision must have at least two blocks.
   b. A plat of the subdivision must be on file in the National Recording Office.
   c. The lot and block numbers must indicate a unique parcel of land.

    d. All of the lots in the subdivision must have been sold by the original owner.

_____32. Which of the following statements is correct?

    a. It is not necessary to specify the city for a recorded subdivision.

    b. After recording, a subdivision cannot be changed.

    c. Descriptions by recorded subdivisions are used in every state.

    d. Lot and block numbers are redundant in states using the U.S. Rectangular Survey system.

_____33. Which of the following statements is correct?

    a. The corners of townships, sections, and section quarters established by government surveyors must stand as originally placed.

    b. Boundaries established by government surveyors upon approval of the surveyor general and accepted by the federal government will be changed only if a subsequent survey finds a mistake in the original survey.

    c. The corners of townships and sections established by government surveyors may be changed only by approval of the state governor.

    d. U.S. governmental rectangular surveys represent the only legally acceptable description in states using this system.

_____34. Land described by lots and blocks is

    a. always surveyed under the U.S. Rectangular Survey system.

    b. described by reference to a recorded plat of a subdivision.

    c. guaranteed to be correct by the state.

    d. always surveyed under the state coordinate system of survey.

_____35. In the township below, how many acres are included in the shaded area?

    a. 480 acres.

    b. 840 acres.

    c. 960 acres.

    d. 1,760 acres.

6	5	4	3	2	1
7	8	9	10	11	12
18	17	16	15	14	13
19	20	21	22	23	24
30	29	28	27	26	25
31	32	33	34	35	36

_____36. The shaded area in the section below represents approximately
  a. 40 acres described as the SW¼ of the NW¼.
  b. 10 acres described as the SW¼ of the NE¼ of the NW¼.
  c. 10 acres described as the SE¼ of the NW¼ of the NE¼.
  d. 40 acres described as the SW¼ of the NE¼ of the NW¼.

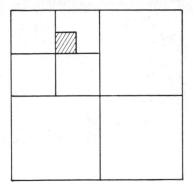

_____37. The system of legal descriptions developed in the United States uses street addresses
  I. for describing land in definite, accurate and detailed terms.
  II. in place of legal descriptions.
  a. I only.
  b. II only.
  c. Both I and II.
  d. Neither I nor II.

_____38. An understanding of legal descriptions
  I. is necessary to interpret tax and mortgage records and private documents affecting liens, titles and conveyances.
  II. allows one to locate a precise site in a rural area.
  a. I only.
  b. II only.
  c. Both I and II.
  d. Neither I nor II.

_____39. The state coordinate system
  a. allows a parcel of land to be located by reference to its immediate surroundings.
  b. provides for surveys without error because the system accounts for surface irregularities.
  c. is based on the proposition that if three parts of a triangle are known, the other three parts may be obtained by calculation.
  d. does not use monuments.

_____40. A recorded subdivision

    a. is described by reproducing the plat of the subdivision in map form, identifying metes and bounds on the map by linear measures and bearings with the appropriate identifying monuments.

    b. must describe each lot in narrative form like the usual metes and bounds description.

    c. must be identified by the plat book number, page number, county in which it is recorded, and the street numbers in the subdivision.

    d. requires a complicated legal description for each lot in the subdivision.

ANSWER KEY

1. (*c*)	11. (*b*)	21. (*b*)	31. (*c*)
2. (*d*)	12. (*c*)	22. (*b*)	32. (*c*)
3. (*b*)	13. (*b*)	23. (*b*)	33. (*a*)
4. (*a*)	14. (*a*)	24. (*c*)	34. (*b*)
5. (*c*)	15. (*a*)	25. (*d*)	35. (*d*)
6. (*b*)	16. (*c*)	26. (*b*)	36. (*b*)
7. (*b*)	17. (*b*)	27. (*c*)	37. (*d*)
8. (*c*)	18. (*b*)	28. (*c*)	38. (*c*)
9. (*d*)	19. (*d*)	29. (*d*)	39. (*c*)
10. (*c*)	20. (*c*)	30. (*d*)	40. (*a*)

SUGGESTED ADDITIONAL READING

Harrington, Earl G. "Cadastral Surveys for the Public Lands of the United States," in *The Public Lands.* Vernon Carstensen, ed. Part I. Madison, Wis.: University of Wisconsin Press, 1962, pp. 35–41.

Moyer, David D., and Fisher, Kenneth Paul. *Land Parcel Identifiers for Information Systems.* Chicago: American Bar Foundation, 1974, chap. 2.

Murray, William G. *Farm Appraisal and Valuation.* 4th ed. Ames, Ia.: Iowa State University Press, 1961, chap. 4.

Wallis, L. J. "Highway and Land Surveying," in *Acquisition for Right-of-Way.* Washington, D.C.: American Association of State Highway Officials, 1962, chap. 13.

8

Deeds

Deeds are written instruments that transfer an interest in real estate. To be legally enforceable, a conveyance of an interest in real estate must be in writing. The written requirement is a carryover from medieval times when real estate was transferred by physically exchanging a clump of dirt or a bundle of sticks with an oral statement of the transfer before witnesses. Later the transfer was evidenced by a written statement which substitutes for the symbolic physical transfer of representative property.

Title to real estate in the United States follows the English version requiring a written document under the Statute of Frauds. The Statute of Frauds is traced to a law enacted in 1676 which stated:

> That no Leases, Estates or Interests, either of Freehold, or Terms of Years, or any uncertain Interest, not being Copyhold or customary Interest, of, in, to or out of any Messuages, Manors, Lands, Tenements or Hereditaments, shall at any Time after the said four and twentieth Day of June be assigned, granted or surrendered, unless it be by Deed or Note in Writing, signed by the Party for assigning, granting or surrendering the same, or their Agents thereunto lawfully authorized by Writing, or by Act and Operation of Law (*Great Britain Statutes*, vol. 3, 1603–98, pp. 384–87).

Therefore a conveyance of real estate is enforceable only if it is in writing evidenced by an instrument of conveyance.

State laws controlling the legal preparation, form and requirements of a deed vary in their detail. Since the deed constitutes an enforceable contract, it has many of the requirements of a land contract. Further, there are certain elements of deeds that tend to be fairly common to all states. In this chapter we will discuss types of deeds in common usage, deed requirements, elements of a deed, restrictive covenants, and adverse possession, concluding with a review of the unauthorized practice of law.

At the outset it should be made clear that licensed salespersons and brokers are not authorized to prepare complex legal documents nor to give legal advice. The topics reviewed here merely help real estate experts decide when to seek legal counsel.

TYPES OF DEEDS

The classification of deeds turns on the kind of title conveyed. Most deeds fall between the warranty deed, which includes five covenants or promises made by the grantor, to the quitclaim deed that conveys only the interest held by the grantor, if any.

Warranty Deeds

The warranty deed may be a *general warranty deed*, sometimes known as the *full covenant and warranty deed*, or a *special warranty deed*. In the former case, the buyer receives maximum protection. Warranties of the grantor include five promises or covenants: (1) the covenant of seizin; (2) the covenant of quiet enjoyment; (3) the covenant against encumbrances; (4) the covenant of further assurances; and (5) the covenant of warranty of title.

Covenant of Seizin. Under the covenant of seizin, the grantor warrants that at the time of delivery, he/she has the right to convey legal title. Thus if the grantor owns only a one-half interest and it turns out that he/she has the title only during his/her life, the covenant of seizin is broken. A violation of this covenant allows the grantee to bring action against the grantor.

Covenant of Quiet Enjoyment. In the case of the covenant of quiet enjoyment, the grantor promises that the grantee will not face eviction from a party claiming title which is superior to that of the grantee. Further the promise runs with the land, meaning that if the grantor does not have good title and subsequently the grantee is evicted, he/she may sue the grantor for damages. The same right applies if an outstanding mortgage is not mentioned in the warranty deed. Foreclosure on an undisclosed mortgage would be equivalent to an eviction, giving the grantee the right to sue the grantor under the covenant of quiet enjoyment.

Covenant against Encumbrances. With the covenant against encumbrances, the grantor warrants that there are no encumbrances against the title other than those noted in the deed. The importance of this promise is increased by the fact that the promise covers all encumbrances even if they are unknown to both grantor and grantee. Encumbrances could cover an unknown lien such as a mortgage, a tax lien, a judgment, a restriction on the use of property, or an outstanding right held by a surviving spouse.

Covenant of Further Assurance. If the grantee's title proves defective, the grantor under the covenant of further assurance promises to execute other documents necessary to perfect the title. Suppose, for instance, that the grantor failed to obtain a satisfaction of a mortgage or failed to release an unrecorded interest in the property of the husband and wife. This covenant protects the grantee from mistakes or oversight that give the grantee an imperfect title. Under this warranty deed, the grantor must voluntarily execute whatever instruments are necessary to give the grantee title which he/she purchased. If the grantor is uncooperative, action may be brought against the grantor under the warranty of further assurances.

Covenant of Warranty of Title. The covenant of warranty of title, also running with the land, requires the grantor to forever defend the grantee's title. Thus the grantor must defend the grantee's title and underwrite the expense if any person establishes a rightful claim to the title.

Special Warranty Deeds

A deed that includes all the statutory covenants but limits the grantor's liability is called a special warranty deed. Here the grantor warrants only against the lawful claims of all persons claiming by, through, or under him (her). The warranties are limited to any defects in the title that occurred *after* the grantor acquired the property. This is a personal covenant that does not run with the land. This type of deed has the effect of protecting the grantor against third parties who claim an interest in the property before he/she acquired title. The states generally require the use of special words such as "special warranty deed" or "warranted specially" to identify the limited liability of the grantor under this instrument.

Quitclaim Deed

The quitclaim deed contains no warranties or guarantees of title. It only conveys an interest that a grantor may have in the property. Therefore the deed passes a valid title if the grantor possesses a valid title. If the intention is to acquire a fee simple estate, the deed will convey this interest to the grantee. If he grantor has no interest whatsoever, he/she conveys nothing and has made no promises regarding his/her title. Typical words of conveyance are "remis, release, and quitclaim."

In the larger sense, the quitclaim deed favors the grantor. Accordingly, buyers are generally reluctant to purchase property under a quitclaim deed. In practice the quitclaim deed is used to clear title by requiring potential claimants to execute a quitclaim deed that effectively releases any interest they may have in the property conveyed.

Bargain and Sale Deeds

Bargain and sale deeds fall between warranty and quitclaim deeds. They convey title but do not include warranties of title. Generally the conveying words "bargain and sell" identify this deed. In most states the bargain and sale deed releases the rights of ownership the grantor may have. In this respect it is an effective way to convey title. Third parties acting for the grantor such as a court-appointed trustee or the executor of an estate prefer this type of deed since they are not held liable for action against warranties arising from events taking place before they acquire control.

Correction Deeds

If parties to a transaction execute a transfer of title and at a later date it is shown that a mistake was made, it is awkward to change the original deed. Erasures, writeovers, and additions to the deed, even though they are agreed upon by both parties, raise questions as to their origin. If the deed has been recorded, alterations are virtually impossible. As an alternative a second deed may include language that "this deed is to correct the deed dated between the named grantor and grantee and recorded in deed book_____, page_____, in _____ County, _____ _____ _____." Correction of the deed must be executed, delivered, and follow the form prescribed for other deeds.

Security Deeds

The states may provide for deeds unique to their jurisdiction. In Georgia, security deeds serve as a substitute for a warranty deed and mortgage. In this instance the security deed is executed to secure a debt in the form of a conveyance by warranty deed that includes the following provisions: (1) a statement that the deed secures payment of a specified debt; (2) establishes a power of attorney authorizing the purchaser or his/her assigns to sell the property upon default and apply the proceeds to the satisfaction of the debt; (3) a statement that upon full payment of the debt, the grantee or his/her assigns will cancel the deed or reconvey the property to the grantor. In short, these provisions constitute the conveyance of a warranty deed to a creditor giving him or her power of a sale without proceeding under a more time-consuming and costly mortgage foreclosure.

Moreover, in the state of Georgia, a mortgage does not vest title in the lender, with the result that the borrower in default subjects the lender's security to a judgment, a mechanic's or a materialmen's lien, and other claims. Note that the security deed becomes null and void on payment of the debt. While this instrument constitutes a conveyance, its real purpose is to provide for real estate financing by the conveyance of title to the lender while the debt remains outstanding.

Trust Deeds

Trust deeds convey real estate that serves as security for a debt. In effect the trust deed substitutes for the first mortgage and the promissory note. Figure 8–1 illustrates the operation of a trust deed. Let us say that

FIGURE 8–1

The Trust Deed Relationship

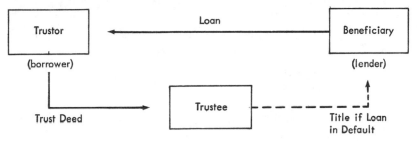

to purchase a new house, a buyer negotiates a long-term loan of $50,000 from a savings and loan association with monthly payments extending over 25 years at 9 percent interest.

In states allowing the trust deed (Arizona and California, among others), the borrower would execute a trust deed that conveys legal title to a third party, the trustee, who holds the title in trust for the beneficiary (the lender) with the power to sell the property if the borrower defaults on the long-term loan according to terms of the trust deed. The trustor or borrower retains possession of the property under an equitable title provided he or she observes terms of the trust deed.

The trustee has no interest in the property until the borrower defaults in his payments or other terms. In such an event, the trustee conveys title to the lender as security for the long-term loan. Hence, a trust deed is not a true conveyance instrument but merely a means of pledging real estate as security for a loan without relying on the mortgage and promissory note. Lenders prefer the trust deed because the statutory right of redemption applying to mortgages is avoided under the trust deed. The lender secures control of foreclosed property at less expense and in a shorter time under a trust deed than if he or she proceeded under the first mortgage foreclosure proceedings.

Sheriff's Deed

A sheriff's deed carries no warranties or guarantees of title. It conveys only the title acquired by the state at the time of foreclosure. Thus the sheriff's deed is given to a party upon foreclosure of the property under court direction for payment of judgments, liens, or mortgage foreclosures.

DEED REQUIREMENTS

Deeds follow a definite format that make them legally enforceable. Most authorities identify seven requirements which must be met before a deed is valid.

1. A designated seller and buyer (grantor and grantee).
2. A lawful consideration.
3. The conveyance clause.
4. A legal description of the property conveyed.
5. Proper signature and form.
6. Delivery and acceptance.
7. A statement of reservations, exceptions, or encumbrances.

Grantor-Grantee

The grantor, who is the seller, must be competent and empowered to convey the real estate described in the deed. The question of competence arises with persons who are not of legal age or who are held to be mentally incapable as determined by law. The question of being empowered to act relates to property conveyed by a guardian, an executor of an estate, or a court-appointed administrator or agent. The authority must be granted according to legal requirements and cited in the deed.

The question of competency may not be used to invalidate a deed which is later proven inequitable to the grantor. Consider a Pennsylvania woman, 78 years old, living alone, who lapsed into a coma and was taken to the hospital by her neighbor. At the hospital the woman directed her attorney to execute a deed granting her house and lot to the neighbor for $1,000. The deed was executed and delivered against the advice of her doctor, friends, and attorney. Later the grantor sued to have the deed set aside on grounds she was incompetent to sign the deed. On a finding of facts, the court ruled that the plaintiff knew what she was doing, that although the price was low, that such price was agreed upon because she wanted to favor her neighbor, the grantee. (*Harman* v. *Huffman*, 5 Lyc. 71 [1955].)

There are certain other rules associated with the naming of the grantor. For example, if an administrator, executor, or agent is acting for someone else, this fact should be stated in the deed. Moreover, if the property is held by more than one person—such as joint ownership by a married couple—each owner should be included in the deed. Because of this requirement, sellers should be identified according to their marital status: bachelor, spinster, married, single, widowed, or divorced and unremarried. In some jurisdictions, the deed may not be recorded unless the name of the grantor and his or her complete address is shown on the instrument. It should be noted also that while the format of the deed is fairly strict, mistakes in spelling, provided the party is properly identified, will not invalidate a deed.

With respect to the buyer, who is always the grantee, the rules are equally clear. To be valid, the deed must show conveyance to a party qualified to take title—a person, a corporation or other legal entity. Thus it has been held that conveyance to a fictitious or nonexistent person is void. If, however, a grantee's name is mistakenly omitted, the deed will be invalid. Nor can a partnership accept title. To be valid, the deed should convey title to the individual partners as joint owners.

A deed without a stated grantee is void. The issue generally arises in the case of a grantee that does not exist at the time of conveyance. For instance, a deed from A to the heirs of B, executed while B is living, would be invalid on grounds that the heirs of B are not identified until B dies. By the same token, a deed conveying an estate to a deceased person or to unborn children will void the deed. For example, a deed from A to the children of B would be improper if at the time B had no children, even though the children were born after delivery of the deed.

Consideration

Consideration represents the price paid to the grantor. Though the actual price paid for real estate may not be shown, every deed should state that a consideration was given for the deed. In practice, it is common to state a nominal consideration of $1 or $10 accompanied by the phrase "and other good and valuable considerations."

Suppose that an individual gives land to a member of the family. No money changes hands. While this deed may be valid between grantor and grantee, creditors may have the deed set aside on grounds that a valuable consideration was not paid, and therefore it defrauds creditors. A "valuable consideration" represents the price paid for the real estate purchased by the grantee. If the deed includes "good consideration," meaning love and affection which substitutes for money, the deed would be valid as between grantor and grantee. A deed executed with "good consideration," however, may be set aside by creditors on grounds that a deed to a third party without valuable consideration defrauds creditors.

The Conveyance Clause

Each state has established specific language showing the intention to convey an interest in real estate. For a warranty deed that includes certain warranties or promises by the seller, the statutes may require words such as "grant and convey," "convey and warrant," or "grant, bargain, sell and convey." The granting clause governs the quality of title conveyed. For instance, a quitclaim deed, which conveys only an interest in real estate and not a warranted title, may call for the words "remis, release and forever quitclaim." State law generally specifies the legal form and words of conveyance that apply to warranties of title.

The Legal Description

Ideally, the deed should include a proper legal description prepared by a surveyor. The legal description must be sufficiently complete to identify the land and its location. While no particular method of describing land is required, the legal description will generally take the form of a metes and bounds description, a lot and block number in a recorded subdivision, or a U.S. government rectangular survey.

Proper Signatures

The main issues relating to proper signatures concern persons who must sign the deed, the requirement for witnesses, and the provision for recording. In each instance laws of the individual states control the way these items must be handled. Certain general practices are fairly common to most jurisdictions, however.

Signing the Deed. Because most states specify the legal division of assets held by married couples, it is advisable to have both the husband and wife sign. The rights of either the husband or wife, or their homestead rights, are such that both signatures are desirable. For example, in states that provide for homestead rights, both husband and wife must sign. In still other states (the minority), the wife cannot convey her own property unless her husband joins in the deed. The more common requirement among those states in which the surviving wife enjoys certain rights in property owned during the marriage calls for the wife's signature. In states that extend these rights to the husband, the husband must sign the deed covering his wife's property. In the western states (Washington, Oregon, California) and other community property states, deeds covering property held as community property must be signed by both husband and wife.

Witnesses. State law generally requires the grantor to sign in the presence of witnesses or, in the case of a corporation, a corporate seal is affixed to the document signed by the duly authorized officer for the corporation. In the latter case a corporate seal is considered a legal signature. In some states the word "seal" or the letters "LS" (*locus sigilli*), meaning place of the seal, entered next to the signatures is sufficient.

In other instances, while witnesses are not required, the signature must be acknowledged before an authorized person such as a notary public or public official who is given the authority to acknowledge signatures. In the state of Georgia, deeds must be signed by two witnesses, one of whom must acknowledge the signatures as a notary public or other official authorized to acknowledge signatures.

If there is more than one grantor, each party to the deed must sign. If a third party signs for the grantor—as executor or with power of attorney—the authority for signing must be stated. While the statutes may require two witnesses to validate a deed, as in Florida (Section 689.01, *Florida Statutes*, F.S.A.), it has been ruled by a Florida circuit court of appeals that witnesses need not sign in the presence of the grantors, or in the presence of each other. (*Medina* v. *Orange County, Fla.*, 147 So. 2d 556 [1962].)

Recording. Recording is the act of placing a deed or mortgage with a local official legally responsible for keeping public records, deeds, mortgages, and other recordable instruments. The title of this official varies among the states—"Recorder of Deeds," "Registrar of Deeds," "County Recorder," "County Auditor," and the like. Their responsibility is to file the instrument for permanent public record.

Deeds are listed (1) in the grantor-grantee index, which is an alphabetical listing of deeds according to the name of the seller, and (2) in the grantee-grantor index which lists the deed alphabetically by the buyer. Besides the name of the grantor and grantee, the two records list the deed book, page number, and date of recording. A facsimile of each instrument is filed in a numbered deed book and given a page number reference which is used to identify the recorded document. By knowing the name of the buyer or seller and the approximate date of recording, the deed book and page number can be identified so that a copy of the instrument can be found.

Deeds do not have to be recorded to be enforceable, but the act of recording gives notice of the transaction to the outside world. Suppose, for example, that A conveys property to B, who does not record the instrument. Later A dies and his heirs, without knowledge of the sale to B, sell the same property to C. If C records the deed prior to B, C's claim is valid against B.

By recording, the buyer gives *constructive* notice that he or she has an interest in the property. In other words recording serves the same purpose as actual notice. Actual notice occurs if the buyer actually occupies, for example, a house that he or she has acquired under a deed. The law assumes that every purchaser or holder with an interest in property has knowledge of public records or knows about actual occupancy.

Because of the importance of filing constructive notice, good practice dictates that as soon as the deed is executed, delivered, and the title transferred, it should be immediately recorded. The grantee is then protected from a subsequent sale by the grantor or his (her) assigns and from mortgages or judgments entered against a seller. The law assumes that subsequent parties have knowledge of the transaction from public records.

Delivery and Acceptance

Title does not pass until the deed is delivered by the seller to the buyer or his or her agent. In some cases a deed may be manually delivered from the grantor to the grantee or certain acts may be interpreted as the intention of the grantor to deliver the deed. Frequently deeds will be delivered by a third party, acting for the grantor. The deed is not delivered, however, until title costs, the real estate commission, and financing have been completed.

The delivery must clearly show the intent of the grantor to deliver the deed. Merely passing the deed to the buyer for inspection or taking the deed without knowledge of the grantor will not constitute delivery. In some jurisdictions, recording of a deed is presumption of delivery even when the deed is recorded without knowledge of the grantor. This rule was stated in litigation of a life estate covered by deed from a father to two sons in 1926. The deed remained in the files of the notary public until his death in 1945. The heirs of the notary delivered the deed to the two sons in 1945, who recorded the deed during the lifetime of their father, the grantor. A surviving daughter petitioned the court to have the deed invalidated on grounds that the deed was never delivered with knowledge of the grantor. The Illinois court ruled that the act of recording constituted delivery:

> . . . Once a deed has been executed and leaves the possession of the grantor, he has no further authority over it, and his consent is not required to authorize a grantee to record the deed unless there is an agreement to the contrary. (*McGhee* v. *Forrester* 15 Ill. 2d 162 [1958].)

At the same time, acceptance, representing voluntary and unconditional acceptance by the grantee, is necessary to a valid delivery. Generally speaking, the law will presume voluntary acceptance if the buyer records the deed or it is recorded at his/her direction, if the grantee possesses the deed or occupies premises described in the deed, or if the buyer mortgages or conveys the deed to third parties. The final rule rests on the intention of the grantee; it must be clear that acceptance was intended.

Reservations, Exceptions, and Encumbrances

Since the buyer is entitled to a marketable title, any item that affects the use or rights of the buyer should be stated in the conveyance document. Reservations affecting title might include coal and mineral rights reserved by the seller. Easements or covenants that affect the buyer's rights—such as "the property conveyed shall be used for a single-family dwelling of not less than 1,600 square feet"—are common deed restrictions. Outstanding mortgages or other liens should be noted. If a warranty deed is used, failure to list outstanding encumbrances violates the seller's warranty.

ELEMENTS OF A DEED

To illustrate the formal arrangement of a full covenant and warranty deed, it is convenient to explain the three main elements: the premises, the habendum, and the testimonium. These sections of the deed are shown in Figure 8–2. The 12 numbered clauses in Figure 8–2 correspond to the numbered paragraphs below.

The Premises

This portion of the deed varies with each transaction and occupies the major portion of the instrument.

1. The Date of the Instrument. This date refers to the date of execution of the deed and is not necessarily the date that the title transfers. Title passes only when the deed is delivered and accepted. The date of recording may also be expected to vary from the date of the deed and the date that title is conveyed (the closing date). Generally, the date of the deed constitutes the date that agreement was reached on the sale.

2. Identification of the Grantor and Grantee. The grantor is identified as the party of the first part. In addition to the name, some states require the address of the grantor before the document is accepted for recording. The grantee is shown as the party of the second part.

3. The Consideration. The clause beginning with the word "WITNESSETH" states that the grantee has paid consideration and received a receipt for the payment before the deed has been signed and delivered. The construction of this clause requires that the consideration be paid before the seller signs the instrument.

FIGURE 8–2
Warranty Deed

WARRANTY DEED

STATE OF GEORGIA,

_____ County

THIS INDENTURE, Made this_____day of_____

in the year of our Lord One Thousand Nine Hundrd and_____

between_____

} 1

of the State of_____and County of_____of the first part,

and _____

of the State of_____and County of_____of the second part,

} 2

WITNESSETH: That the said part____of the first part, for and in consideration of the sum of_____

_____DOLLARS

} 3

in hand paid at and before the sealing and delivery of these presents, the receipt whereof is hereby acknowledged,

ha____granted, bargained, sold and conveyed, and by these presents do____grant, bargain, sell and convey unto

the said part ____of the second part,_____heirs and assigns, all that tract or parcel

of land lying and being in _____

} 4

LEGAL DESCRIPTION·······

} 5

RESERVATIONS OR EXCEPTIONS········
    (Example: "less coal and mineral rights")

} 6

RECITAL CLAUSE········
    (Example: "being all of said land lot formerly conveyed to····

} 7

SUBJECT TO CLAUSE········
    Example: , "subject to security deed from R.E. Kirby to Bank of Cumming,
    dated October 9, 19__, in the principal sum of $5,000, recorded in
    Deed Book 112, page 235, Forsyth County."

} 8

THE PREMISES

TO HAVE AND TO HOLD the said bargained premises, together with all and singular the rights, members and
appurtenances thereof, to the same being, belonging or in any wise appertaining, to the only proper use, benefit
and behoof of____ the said part____ of the second part,_____heirs and assigns forever, IN FEE SIMPLE.

} 9

And the said part____ of the first part, for_____heirs and executors and administrators
will warrant and forever defend the right and title to the above described property unto the said part____ of the
second part,_____ heirs and assigns, against the lawful claims of all persons whomsoever.

} 10

IN WITNESS WHEREOF, The said part____ of the first part ha____ hereunto set_____hand____
and affixed_____our seal, the day and year above written.

} 11

Signed, sealed and delivered in the presence of

_____(SEAL)

_____(SEAL)

_____(SEAL)

_____(SEAL)

_____(SEAL)

} 12

HABENDUM

TESTIMONIUM

4. *The Granting Clause.* Following the clause covering the consideration are the operative words of the deed which actually convey title. The statutory requirements of the state will determine the type of title conveyed (i.e., quitclaim, special warranty deed, bargain and sale deed, or full covenant and warranty deed).

5. *The Legal Description.* At this point, the parties to the transaction have been identified, the consideration stated, and the title has been conveyed. It is logical, then, to cite the property by address and legal description to clearly identify the property being conveyed. Metes and bounds, governmental rectangular survey descriptions, or lots and blocks of property recorded as subdivisions must be entered here so that they can be definitely identified in public documents or by survey. While no specific legal description is required, the parties are advised to use the recognized legal descriptions and the address to avoid misunderstandings.

6. *Reservations or Exceptions from the Fee Simple Estate.* If coal and mineral rights are reserved, the legal description will be followed by the phrase "less coal and mineral rights." Other reservations affecting title will also be shown in this portion of the document; for instance, life estates or partial interests.

7. *The Recital Clause.* The recital clause identifies the previous owner. While the recital clause is not necessary to render a deed valid, it is included as a convenience to title searchers. The typical recital clause would read "being part of the same premises which John Jones, by deed dated December 15, 19_____ and recorded in Clarke County, Georgia, Deed Box 523, Page 183, granted and conveyed to William Smith, grantee."

8. *The Subject to Clause.* Under the warranty of title, it is presumed that title is free and clear of all encumbrances unless they are *stated in the deed*. This portion of the deed cites any existing encumbrances such as mortgages, liens, unpaid special assessments, unpaid property taxes, and the like. Easements for rights-of-way covering pipelines, power lines, or access roads will be described in this section.

The Habendum

9. The habendum defines the interest conveyed. If it is a fee simple title, typical starting words will be "to have and to hold"; typical ending words are "heirs and assigns, forever, in fee simple." If the instrument conveyed only a life estate, then the habendum clause would substitute "life estate" in place of the heirs and assigns clause.

The habendum clause includes language that conveys rights necessary to the use and enjoyment of the property. The usual language reads "with all and singular the rights, members and appurtenances thereof." In this manner, rights that are necessary for the use of the property are provided.

It will be noted that the habendum clause restates the grantor's intention to convey the estate shown in the granting clause. If the two clauses conflict, generally the courts rule that the granting clause prevails. Though many states no longer require this clause, it still appears on some deed forms.

The Testimonium

10. This last portion of the deed includes the covenant of warranty, the testimonium clause, and signatures on the deed. Here the deed states that the grantor will sign the instrument on the given date.

11. In the case of an individual, a testimonium clause states "in witness whereof, the party in the first part hereunto sets his hand in seal the day and year first above written." For the most part, the seal is no longer considered important since individuals no longer wear seal rings or carry an individual seal to be pressed into wax, thereby attesting to their signature. For corporations, in jurisdictions that require a seal, use of the word "seal," or letters "LS" is generally sufficient.

The testimonium clause includes the date of the deed. It will be recalled that dates associated with a deed may vary: the first date refers to the date of execution; the date of acknowledgment may be at a later time, while the date of recording will follow at some later time. If the date of execution is omitted, the deed operates from the date of delivery.

12. The execution of the deed, that is, the signing by the grantors, the witnessing, and the acknowledgment before some authorized person, must follow the laws of each state. Ordinarily, the deed is not signed by the grantee. While witnesses to a deed are not usually necessary to establish its legality, witnesses are helping in proving lawful execution if its legality is later questioned.

The acknowledgment of the deed is usually a requirement for recording. All states require that the deed must be either acknowledged or witnessed before recording. State law specifies persons who are authorized to take acknowledgments. A notary public and state judges, clerks of higher courts, and certain commissioners of deeds and records may be given this power by statute.

RESTRICTIVE DEED COVENANTS

It is an accepted principle that the seller has the right to restrict the use of land conveyed to preserve the value or use of surrounding property. Such restrictions may be personal or real restrictions that run with the land. The latter applies to subsequent owners, while a personal restriction applies only during the life of the grantor. Suppose, for example, that a grantor conveys interest in a retail building under a deed which includes a covenant that the grantor will not engage in a competing business of a similar nature for a given time. Such an agreement will not run with the land—it is personal to the immediate parties.

Take the case of an owner of a 1,200-acre dairy farm on the fringe area of the city, however. Some of the property was potentially valuable for commercial development. Because the owner wanted to protect the character of the neighborhood, he restricted the grantee to buildings constructed with a brick veneer exterior. In this case, such a covenant would run with the land and would be enforceable by subsequent purchasers.

The enforceability of restrictive covenants is an area requiring the advice of legal counsel. First, if the covenant is to be enforceable and run with the land, the intentions of the grantor and grantee must be absolutely clear. Second, the covenant must cover the real estate conveyed without question. Even with these requirements, covenants may or may not be enforceable under certain conditions.

The enforceability issue arises if the purpose is against public policy or if the covenant is against the best interest of the public. If the covenant is not enforced against the violation so that, in effect, the covenant is abandoned by the affected property owners, the covenant will be considered as terminated. Or consider a change in the neighborhood such that the restrictive covenant no longer serves its original purpose. For example, a covenant that requires single-family dwellings of not less than 3,000 square feet would probably be ineffective if the neighborhood has converted to rooming houses and to low-income property. The circumstances affecting each restrictive covenant determine its applicability.

ADVERSE POSSESSION

Conveyance of title by deed establishes a title of record or a "paper" title. Providing statutory requirements are met, a valid title may be acquired by occupation of the land over the minimum period required by statute. Title acquired in this way is a title gained under adverse possession. Under these circumstances, title may be acquired without reference to a deed or other conveyance instrument. Even a holder of title under a deed may not evict a party acquiring title by adverse possession.

Adverse possession is a legal device to vest title where possession results from misplaced fences, boundary lines, and buildings, if they remain undiscovered over the minimum statutory period associated with adverse possession. In other instances, title to property may have been acquired under a defective deed which was not discovered during the statutory period required for adverse possession. Without adverse possession, it would be difficult to obtain a valid title in the case of a defective deed because of the unavailability of witnesses and other parties to the transaction and the difficulty of ascertaining facts that occurred long ago.

The law provides that it is just and fair to grant clear title to one who has been in possession for a long time and who cannot verify his or her legal claim to title without proceeding under adverse possession. If possession arises from a written document, it is said that possession has been taken under a *color of title*. To establish color of title, the claim must come under a conveyance instrument that would appear valid to a person without legal training who believed an actually defective instrument to be legal—for instance, the grantor may have been unauthorized to convey the land (an unauthorized corporate officer), or the signature of the grantor may have been forged, or perhaps the grantor was legally insane or otherwise incompetent at the time of conveyance.

While the statutes do not agree, it is fairly universal to require claimants under adverse possession to prove that their title rests on possession which is (1) actual, (2) continuous, (3) hostile and notorious, and (4) exclusive. In addition, some states require that taxes be paid on the property claimed.

Actual possession must be such that the owner may readily observe the occupation. Actual possession would be evidenced by a fence, farming on a regular basis, or by living on the property. A building that extends over the property line would constitute actual possession.

The general rule is that possession must be *continuous* and uninterrupted over the minimum term required by law ranging from 5 years to 20 years. If the claimant abandons possession and reenters, the minimum time begins from the time of reentry. An occasional visit to the property for firewood or for hunting does not establish continuous possession. Land which was farmed on a seasonal basis would probably qualify as continuous possession even if the land is virtually abandoned during cold winter months.

Hostile possession means that possession clearly is without permission of the owner. This requirement rules out a son occupying land of his father. Hostility is difficult to prove in the case of husband and wife, agent and employer, borrower and lender—cases in which neither party can acquire title by adverse possession since each case covers a relationship of trust and confidence with the holder of the paper title.

The rule of *exclusive possession* is broken if the adverse claimant allows the true owner to remain in possession. Joint occupation does not establish an exclusive claim.

THE UNAUTHORIZED PRACTICE OF LAW

In the preparation of real estate instruments, especially conveyances such as deeds, the question arises as to acts that may be performed by licensed real estate agents and to acts more properly delegated to lawyers. On the one hand, real estate brokers regard the drawing of deeds and the preparation of legal instruments—using printed forms—as essential to closing a real estate deal, and therefore a part of their normal duties. On the other hand, lawyers argue that the public should be protected against laypersons and unskilled advisors in matters relating to the law. On this issue the courts are not in agreement.

The Deposit Receipt and Contract for Sale Limitation

The more restrictive view is illustrated by a Florida company that was enjoined from preparing leases, lease agreements, rental contracts, deeds, mortgages, and contracts for the sale of property (including filling in printed forms), or causing them to be executed unless instruments were drawn on transactions covering their own property.

The Florida Supreme Court observed that when a broker is employed to find a purchaser of property, his or her function is completed when he or she produces a prospective purchaser ready, willing and able to buy, or procures from him a binding contract. Accordingly, the court held that a licensed broker is restricted to drafting deposit receipts or contracts for sale. In Florida the preparation of other instruments, including the filling in of blank spaces on printed forms, is considered the practice of law. Licensed real estate brokers who prepare instruments other than deposit receipts, listing agreements, and contracts for sale are acting illegally, according to the Florida Court. (*Keyes Co.* v. *Dade County Bar Association*, 46 So. 2d 605 [1950].)

In some cases the courts have objected to brokers who complete printed forms incidental to real estate transactions in which they have an interest as a broker. Even though a form is approved by lawyers, in some jurisdictions brokers who complete real estate forms incidental to the completion of a sale are guilty of the illegal practice of law. For example, a court in the state of Washington held:

> . . . Any legal form must be adapted skillfully to the transaction for which it is used, so that it expresses the agreement of the parties and defines their rights and obligations. Doing this is work of a legal nature, and, when it is done by one unqualified, we not only cannot condone its continuance but we must act to prevent it, whether or not it is done for compensation. (*Washington State Bar Association* v. *Washington Association of Realtors*, 41 Wash. 2d 697, 251 P. 2, 2d 619 [1953].)

The same view is expressed in statutes of the various states: for example, in Tennessee, "Any real estate broker who draws any legal document other than contracts to option, buy, sell, or lease real property is engaged in the unauthorized practice of law" (*Tenn. Code Ann.*, Sec. 62–1325, 1955).

Legal Advice

While jurisdictions differ on the legality of filling out printed real estate forms by brokers, it is a universal rule that real estate brokers are prohibited from giving advice or rendering any services requiring the use of legal skills or knowledge such as preparing contracts and real estate instruments which are not incidental to a broker's business.

This point was raised in an action against a real estate broker who advised one of his clients to execute a deed as a substitute for a will. In this case he was charged with advising a client concerning the disposition of real estate and in preparing deeds and other instruments for which he charged a fee. Apparently the broker regarded the preparation of deeds, notes, mortgages, and contracts as being more or less a mechanical routine requiring no legal knowledge or skill. The lower court ruled that the broker was guilty of practicing law in the state of Illinois without a license, for which he should be held in contempt of court. On appeal, the Supreme Court of Illinois agreed, holding the broker in contempt of court subject to fine. (*People ex rel Illinois State Bar Association, et al* v. *Schafer*, 404, Ill. 45 [1949].)

The law is quite definite on the point that real estate brokers are not to give legal advice on real estate matters. A Georgia statute, for instance, is typical of states that prohibit giving legal advice by other than duly licensed attorneys.

> . . . it shall be unlawful for any person other than a duly licensed attorney at law to practice or appear as an attorney at law, for any person other than himself . . . or to render legal services of any kind in actions or proceedings of any nature, or in any other way or manner to assume to be entitled to practice law (*Ga. Code Ann.*, Sec. 9–402, 1936).

Conveyance Instruments Incidental to Business

A different view is taken by other states that permit brokers to fill out blanks on printed forms as *incidental* to their business. In illustration, a Michigan court ruled that licensed realty brokers have the right to engage in conveyancing, without compensation, by completing and filling out printed forms for offers to purchase real estate, warranty deeds, quitclaim deeds, land assignments, and leases and notices including tenancy incidental to their completing realty transactions in which they act as brokers.

The court apparently accepted the argument that the broker was not engaged in the practice of law but was only filling in simple forms, without receiving any extra compensation, as incidental to real estate transactions in which he was engaged.

Under this interpretation, real estate brokers are allowed to execute conveyances to the extent that they are *incidental* to a particular transaction in which they are engaged. It is reasoned that a general deed form is so standardized that to complete them for usual transactions requires only ordinary intelligence rather than legal training. (*Ingham County Bar Association* v. *Walter Neller Co., et al.*, 69 NW 2d 713 [Michigan, 1955].)

A similar case in Arkansas involved a licensed and bonded real estate broker who alleged that it was desirable for him in connection with his business as a real estate broker to be permitted to fill in the blanks on printed, standardized real estate forms prepared by a lawyer, and that he possessed the required knowledge and skill to fill in such blanks on real estate transactions handled by him as a broker. The court ruled that to deny this service would not be in the public interest. (*Creekmore* v. *Izard*, 367 S.W. 2d 419 [1963].)

In at least one instance, the view that completing blank printed forms prepared by lawyers is incidental to real estate brokerage activity has been introduced into a state constitution. Article 26 of the Arizona State Constitution approved in 1962 reads:

> Any person holding a valid license as a real estate broker or a real estate salesman regularly issued by the Arizona State Real Estate Department when acting in such capacity as broker or salesman for the parties, or agent for one of the parties to a sale, exchange, or trade, or the renting and leasing of property shall have the right to draft or fill out and complete without charge, any and all instruments incident thereto including, but not limited to, preliminary purchase agreements and earnest money receipts, deeds, mortgages, leases, assignments, releases, contracts for sale of realty, and bills of sale.

Unauthorized Law Practice Summarized

These conflicting court cases, statutes and regulations lead to the following generalizations:

1. Some states limit brokers to filling in blank spaces on listing forms and contracts of sale.
2. Other states permit brokers to fill in blank spaces on printed forms approved by lawyers for conveyance instruments in which the broker acts for one of the parties as agent as incidental to his or her business.
3. Universally, brokers are prohibited from giving legal advice on real estate matters or on the effect of real estate instruments.
4. Generally speaking, brokers are prohibited from executing conveyance instruments or other real estate documents involving complex legal problems.

The relationship between the right of the broker to complete real estate documents in which he or she has an interest as a broker is defined in the accord reached between attorneys and real estate brokers in Illinois. Figure 8–3 describes duties of the real estate broker with respect to

FIGURE 8–3

The Illinois Real Estate Broker-Lawyer Accord, October 26, 1966

Article I. The Broker

It is the function of the broker to bring the seller and buyer to agreement as to the sale and purchase of a given parcel of real estate.

In order to accomplish this the broker should be governed by the following:

(1) He may complete the preliminary or earnest money contract, as stated by the Court in *The Chicago Bar Association, et al.* v. *Quinlan and Tyson* (hereinafter called "contract") which is customarily in use in the community where the broker does business, by filling in only factual and business details in blanks provided therefor. He may add to or delete from such form only factual statements and business details, furnished by the principals therein, the addition or deletion of which is necessary to conform to the particular factual situation. He may not prepare or complete any document necessary to carry out or implement the contract.

(2) Where it appears prior to the execution of the contract that there are unusual matters involved in the transaction which should be resolved before a binding contract is executed, the broker should advise the parties that each should consult a lawyer of his choice before such contract is executed.

(3) The broker may not give advice on any matter of law, either directly or indirectly, but he should recommend that both the seller and the buyer consult their respective lawyers as to all legal questions and for the preparation of all those documents which may be necessary to implement and carry out the contract.

(4) Where either the seller or the buyer desires to see a lawyer prior to the execution of a contract the broker should not attempt to dissuade such party from legal consultation.

(5) The broker should not minimize the value of the lawyer's services, discuss or comment on the fees of the lawyers, or participate or attempt to participate in the lawyer's fees.

(6) The broker may not directly or indirectly employ a lawyer or pay for the services of a lawyer, to represent either the buyer or the seller.

(7) A broker may refer a buyer or seller to a lawyer if asked to do so by such buyer or seller but in such case the broker should give the party the names of not less than three lawyers who are qualified to perform the legal services involved, without indicating any preference as to any one of the three.

(8) A broker should advise the parties that the contract is binding on them.

(9) Where a broker is also a lawyer, he may not advertise that he can handle the complete details of a real estate transaction including preparation of documents other than the completion of the contract

FIGURE 8–3 *(continued)*

customarily used in the community, or that he can handle the transaction cheaper or better because he is also a lawyer, nor should he act
as a lawyer for either the buyer or the seller in the same transaction in
which he is acting or has acted as the broker.

Article II. *The Lawyer*

It is the function of lawyers to give all legal advice required by the
required parties in a real estate transaction and to prepare all the documents necessary to carry out the contract customarily used in the community. The lawyer may also prepare the contract, if employed to do so
by the buyer, the seller or the broker.

In order to accomplish this function the lawyer should be governed
by the following:

(1) The lawyer who is consulted by either the buyer or the seller
shall use his best efforts to proceed diligently to the conclusion of the
transaction, and if his work load does not permit a prompt conclusion
of the same he should so state at the time of employment.

(2) The lawyer should not minimize the value of the broker's services, discuss or comment on the commission charged, or participate or
attempt to participate in the broker's commissions.

(3) The lawyer in representing the buyer or the seller in a real estate
transaction should not give advice on the physical condition or the market
value of the real estate involved in the transaction.

(4) A lawyer may not accept employment or compensation by the
broker to render services to either the buyer or the seller in the transaction, or to prepare any documents which the broker is not himself
authorized to prepare.

(5) A lawyer may not request a broker to prepare documents for a
buyer or seller which documents the broker is not himself authorized
to prepare even though such documents so prepared are subject to the
lawyer's review.

(6) A lawyer should not represent the broker and the buyer and the
seller, or both of them, or the buyer and the seller, in the same transaction except in those communities where the applicable canons of
ethics clearly permit representation of conflicting interest by a lawyer
after full and complete disclosure of the conflict of interest to the parties
desiring such representation and upon the express consent of the parties
after such full and complete disclosure of the conflict in interest is made
to such parties.

(7) Where a lawyer also holds a broker's license he may not advertise that he can handle a real estate transaction cheaper or better because he is a broker as well as a lawyer nor may he act as a lawyer for the
buyer and seller or either of them, in the same transaction where he is
the broker, even though no charge be made for his services as a lawyer.

completing real estate instruments as agreed to with Illinois lawyers in the Real Estate Broker-Lawyer Accord of October 26, 1966.

In effect, the agreement confines the broker to completion of earnest money contracts by filling in details on printed documents to complete the real estate transaction. Further, the broker is directed to advise parties to consult a lawyer on unusual matters involved in real estate transactions. He or she must not give advice on matters of law. Other terms of the contract refer to ethical relations between brokers and lawyers.

Article II of the Accord covers the duties of the lawyer. Most of these requirements relate to ethical relations between lawyers and brokers: the Accord calls for the lawyer to proceed diligently to the conclusion of the transaction; he or she must not minimize the value of broker services; and the lawyer is directed not to give advice on market value. The last two items separate the function of the lawyer and the broker and prevent conflicts of interest resulting from employment by more than one client without complete disclosure and the express consent of each party.

QUESTIONS FOR REVIEW

_____ 1. Deeds transfer an interest in
    a. personal property.
    b. real estate.
    c. stocks.
    d. bonds.

_____ 2. To be enforceable legally a conveyance of an interest in real estate must be
    a. in writing.
    b. recorded.
    c. witnessed by two disinterested parties for written agreements.
    d. witnessed by two disinterested parties for oral agreements.

_____ 3. Licensed salesmen and brokers
    I. are authorized to prepare complex legal documents.
    II. are not authorized to give legal advice.
    a. I only.
    b. II only.
    c. Both I and II.
    d. Neither I nor II.

_____ 4. In all jurisdictions brokers may
    a. fill out printed real estate forms.
    b. give real estate advice requiring legal knowledge.
    c. not give advice or render services requiring legal knowledge.
    d. draw up contracts.

_____ 5. In some states, a broker who prepares deeds, notes, mortgages, or contracts may be found guilty of

a. practicing law without a license.
b. violating the Statute of Frauds.
c. fraud.
d. violating the covenant of seizin.

_____ 6. Some courts have ruled that licensed brokers may legally prepare
a. offers to purchase real estate.
b. wills.
c. life estate deeds.
d. land assignments.

_____ 7. Which of the following statements is correct?
a. All states limit brokers to filling in blank spaces on listing forms.
b. Some states permit brokers to fill in blank spaces on printed forms approved by lawyers.
c. Brokers can give legal advice.
d. Brokers can execute conveyance instruments.

_____ 8. The agreement governing responsibilities of attorneys and real estate brokers in real estate transactions generally includes:
a. ethical relations between brokers and lawyers.
b. duties of the lawyer in real estate transactions.
c. duties of the broker in real estate transactions.
d. all of the above.

_____ 9. Title to real estate in the United States follows the English version requiring
a. two witnesses for an oral transfer of real estate.
b. all real estate to be transferred by warranty deed.
c. all real estate transfers to be handled by real estate brokers.
d. a written document under the Statute of Frauds.

_____10. The Florida Supreme Court observed that when a broker is employed to find a purchaser of property, his function is completed when he
a. produces a prospective purchaser ready, willing, and able to buy.
b. lists the property at a saleable price.
c. closes the sale.
d. procures from the purchaser a binding contract.

_____11. Which of the following statements is correct?
a. A broker cannot legally advise a client to execute a deed as a substitute for a will.
b. A lawyer may operate as a broker without a license.
c. A broker may prepare any real estate instrument if he charges the usual legal fee.
d. A broker may prepare legal documents only if he does not charge a legal fee.

_____12. Which of the following generalizations on unauthorized law practice is correct?

    a. Some states limit brokers to filling in blank spaces on listing forms and contracts of sale.

    b. Some states permit brokers to fill in blank spaces on printed forms approved by lawyers for conveyance instruments in which the broker acts for both of the parties as agent as incidental to his business.

    c. Brokers are not prohibited from giving legal advice on real estate matters or on the effect of real estate instruments.

    d. Brokers are not prohibited from executing conveyance instruments or other real estate documents involving complex problems.

_____13. Which of the following is *not* a requirement which must be met before a deed is valid?

    a. Delivery and acceptance.

    b. Proper signature and form.

    c. A legal description of the property conveyed.

    d. Adequate consideration.

_____14. The question of competence arises when a person(s) is

    I. 14 years of age.

    II. a corporate officer.

    a. I only.

    b. II only.

    c. I and II.

    d. Neither I nor II.

_____15. Which of the following would invalidate a deed?

    a. A fictitious grantee.

    b. A misspelled name.

    c. A mistake in the legal description.

    d. An unrecorded deed.

_____16. The _____ governs the quality of title conveyed.

    a. conveyance clause

    b. granting clause

    c. warranty clause

    d. release clause

_____17. A _____ conveys only an interest in real estate.

    a. warranty deed

    b. security deed

    c. quitclaim deed

    d. statute deed

_____18. A _____ includes certain warranties or promises by the seller of real property.

    a. warranty deed

    b. security deed

    c. quitclaim deed

    d. statute deed

_____19. In community property states, deeds covering property held as community property must be signed by the

    a. husband.

    b. wife.

    c. husband and wife.

    d. husband or wife.

_____20. Which of the following will *not* invalidate a deed for real property?

    a. Inadequate legal description.

    b. Improper signatures.

    c. Failure to record the conveyance.

    d. All of the above.

_____21. Under the _____ the grantor warrants that at the time of delivery he has the right to convey legal title.

    a. Covenant of Seizin

    b. Covenant of Quiet Enjoyment

    c. Covenant against Encumbrances

    d. Covenant of Further Assurance

_____22. With the _____ the grantor promises that the grantee will not face eviction from a property claiming title which is superior to that of the grantee.

    a. Covenant of Seizin

    b. Covenant against Eminent Domain

    c. Covenant of Quiet Enjoyment

    d. Covenant of Further Assurance

_____23. With the _____ the grantor warrants that there are no encumbrances against the title other than those noted in the deed.

    a. Covenant of Seizin

    b. Covenant against Eminent Domain

    c. Covenant against Encumbrances

    d. Covenant of Further Assurance

_____24. With the _____ the grantor promises to execute another document necessary to perfect the title.

    a. Covenant of Seizin

    b. Covenant against Eminent Domain

    c. Covenant against Encumbrances

    d. Covenant of Further Assurance

_____25. The _____ requires the grantor to forever defend the grantee's title.

    a. Covenant of Seizin

    b. Covenant of Quiet Enjoyment

  c. Covenant against Encumbrances

  d. Covenant of Warranty of Title

_____26. A deed that includes all statutory covenants but limits the grantor's liability is called a

  a. limited warranty deed.

  b. special seizin deed.

  c. special warranty deed.

  d. quitclaim deed.

_____27. The _____ contains no warranties or guarantees of title.

  a. special warranty deed

  b. quitclaim deed

  c. security deed

  d. warranty deed

_____28. A _____ conveys title but generally does not include warranties of title.

  a. quitclaim deed

  b. bargain and sale deed

  c. correction deed

  d. special warranty deed

_____29. Which of the following would be used to convey personal property?

  a. Bargain and sale deed.

  b. Special warranty deed.

  c. Standard warranty deed.

  d. Bill of sale.

_____30. If a security deed is executed to secure a debt from a conveyance, it includes which of the following provisions?

  I. Establishment of a power of attorney authorizing the purchaser or his assigns to sell the property upon default and to apply the proceeds to the satisfaction of the debt.

  II. A statement that upon full payment of the debt the grantee or his assigns will assign the deed or property to the grantee.

  a. I only.

  b. II only.

  c. I and II.

  d. Neither I nor II.

_____31. In states allowing a trust deed, which of the following is *not* true?

  a. A trust deed serves as security for debt.

  b. A trust deed substitutes for the first mortgage and promissory note.

  c. A trust deed conveys legal title to the trustee.

  d. A trust deed conveys legal title to the trustor.

_____32. A _____ is *not* a true conveyance instrument.

  a. bargain and sale deed

  b. sheriff's deed

    c. warranty deed
    d. trust deed

_____33. A _____ carries no warranties or guarantees of title.
    a. special warranty deed
    b. sheriff's deed
    c. warranty deed
    d. security deed

_____34. The premises element in a deed will normally include the
    a. date of recording.
    b. consideration and legal description.
    c. granting clause and the habendum clause.
    d. subject to clause and the testimonium clause.

_____35. The habendum defines the
    a. reservations or exceptions to the fee simple estate.
    b. existing encumbrances on the property.
    c. interest conveyed.
    d. none of the above.

_____36. The testimonium of a deed includes the covenant of warranty, the testimonium clause, and
    a. the recital clause.
    b. the reservations clause.
    c. the signatures.
    d. the identification of the subject property.

_____37. A person acquiring title under adverse possession statutes may lose his title
    a. if the individual who holds paper title comes forward.
    b. if a sheriff's title or eviction notice is issued.
    c. unless a security deed is issued.
    d. if he becomes the grantor in a quitclaim deed.

_____38. While statutes do not agree, it is fairly universal to require claimants under adverse possession to prove that their title rests on possession which is
    a. actual, continuous, hostile, notorious.
    b. exclusive.
    c. granted.
    d. *a* and *b.*

_____39. If the written title to real estate is granted to one who has been in possession for a long time and who cannot verify his legal claim to title without proceeding under adverse possession, it is said that possession has been taken under
    a. adverse occupation.
    b. color of title.
    c. continuous occupation.
    d. hostile occupation.

_____40. Regarding the element of hostile possession in the adverse posses-
         sion statutes, in which of the following cases would hostility be diffi-
         cult to prove?

    a. Husband and wife.

    b. Agent and employer.

    c. Borrower and lender.

    d. All of the above.

ANSWER KEY

1. *(b)*	11. *(a)*	21. *(a)*	31. *(d)*
2. *(a)*	12. *(a)*	22. *(c)*	32. *(d)*
3. *(b)*	13. *(d)*	23. *(c)*	33. *(b)*
4. *(c)*	14. *(c)*	24. *(d)*	34. *(b)*
5. *(a)*	15. *(a)*	25. *(d)*	35. *(c)*
6. *(a)*	16. *(b)*	26. *(c)*	36. *(c)*
7. *(b)*	17. *(c)*	27. *(b)*	37. *(d)*
8. *(d)*	18. *(a)*	28. *(b)*	38. *(d)*
9. *(d)*	19. *(c)*	29. *(d)*	39. *(b)*
10. *(a)*	20. *(c)*	30. *(a)*	40. *(d)*

SUGGESTED ADDITIONAL READING

Atteberry, William; Pearson, Karl G.; and Litka, Michael P. *Real Estate Law.*
      Columbus, O.: Grid, Inc., 1974, chap. 13.

Hebard, Edna L., and Meisel, Gerald S. *Principles of Real Estate Law.* Cam-
      bridge, Mass.: Schenkman Publishing Co., Inc., 1967, chap. 11.

Kratovil, Robert. *Real Estate Law.* 6th ed. Englewood Cliffs, N.J.: Prentice-
      Hall, Inc., 1974, chap. 7.

Lusk, Harold F., and French, William B. *Law of the Real Estate Business.*
      3rd ed. Homewood, Ill.: Richard D. Irwin, Inc., 1975, chap. 5.

Unger, Maurice A. *Real Estate Principles and Practices.* 5th ed. Cincin-
      nati, O.: South-Western Publishing Co., 1974, chap. 5.

9

Real Estate Closing Statements

Closing statements, also known as settlement sheets, show the cash results of a real estate transfer. They must be given to the buyer and seller to show how expenses and proceeds of the sale have been divided. Since certain expenses of owning real estate are paid monthly, annually, or in the case of insurance up to five years in advance, closing statements must show how prepaid or unpaid expenses are allocated between the buyer and seller. Prepaid or accrued rental income must also be divided as of the date of closing.

More important, the closing statement provides a convenient way for salespersons or brokers to explain the final settlement of the transaction. If financial details are listed logically in a closing statement, the salesperson can easily explain settlement figures to inexperienced buyers and sellers. A detailed knowledge of closing statements also helps the salesperson estimate the cash the seller will realize in a given transaction. Moreover, the informed salesperson may advise the purchaser on the amount of money required for closing. The more accurately a salesperson projects the final cash settlement, the more he minimizes the possibility of misunderstanding at the time of closing.

REAL ESTATE SETTLEMENT PROCEDURES ACT (RESPA)

The 1975 amendment to the Real Estate Settlement Procedure Act of 1974 established rules for closing loans on one-to-four-family residential properties. The purpose of the Act was to "ensure that consumers throughout the nation are provided with greater and more timely information on the nature and cost of the settlement process and are protected from unnecessarily high settlement charges caused by certain abusive practices that have developed in some areas of the country" (*Real Estate Settlement Procedures Act of 1974* [Public Law 93–533], as amended by the *Real Estate Settlement Procedures Act of 1975* [Public Law 94–205]).

In operation, the Act applies to one-to-four-family dwellings financed by agencies subject to federal regulation including mortgages on condominiums and cooperatives. Federally regulated mortgage loans are defined to include institutions supervised by the Federal Reserve Board, the Federal Home Loan Bank Board, the Federal Deposit Insurance Corporation, Veterans Administration and federal agencies active in the secondary mortgage market. Though the burden of compliance rests on mortgage lenders, real estate brokers and others must submit data to lenders necessary to comply with the Act.

Exempt Transactions

Certain types of transactions are exempt from provisions of RESPA. Mortgages on property in excess of 25 acres and home improvement loans are among the exempted loans. A loan to finance purchase of a vacant lot to construct a home is exempt. The assumption of an existing loan is exempt if the assumption fee is less than $50. Short-term construction mortgages, land sales, contracts and loans to finance purchase of a property for resale are other exclusions. Generally, crop loans and loans for purposes not involving the transfer of title are not covered.

Duties of the Lender

Duties of the lender follow from the main purposes of the Act:

1. To provide more effective *advance disclosure* of settlement costs to home buyers and sellers.
2. To *eliminate kickbacks or referral fees* that tend to increase unnecessarily the costs of certain settlement services.
3. To *reduce escrow accounts* required of home buyers to insure payment of real estate taxes and insurance.
4. To *modernize recordkeeping.*

To accomplish these purposes, lenders are required to: (1) give borrowers good faith estimates of closing costs at the date of closing, (2) issue settlement costs booklet published by the Department of Housing and Urban Development, (3) at the time of closing, give both buyers and sellers a uniform settlement statement, (4) observe restrictions over payment of fees, kickbacks, or payments as incident to a real estate closing, (5) comply with regulations that prohibit use of a specific title insurance company, and (6) limit monthly escrow deposits only to the amount required for payment of annual property taxes and insurance.

Advance Disclosure of Settlement Costs. Though the lender may use his own form, the borrower must be given (1) an advance disclosure of settlement costs at the time of written loan application and (2) a copy of the settlement booklet. Alternatively, the lender has three days after written loan application to mail these materials to the applicant. The advance disclosure must rest on a "good faith estimate" of probable settlement charges.

FIGURE 9–1

Table of Contents of the Required Settlement Cost Booklet*

Settlement Costs: A HUD Guide. Rev. ed. (Washington, D.C.: U.S. Government Printing Office, June 1976), p. 40.

Settlement Cost Booklet. The 40-page booklet as prepared by the Department of Housing and Urban Development may be reprinted but in no case may lenders make any change, deletion, or addition to its present content. The table of contents shown in Figure 9–1 illustrates how the booklet informs the buyer on the best way of selecting attorneys, lenders, settlement agents, and title services. Home buyer rights are explained in layman terms. Part II of the booklet illustrates settlement statements and the calculation of closing costs, adjustments, and reserve accounts. In short, the booklet encourages the borrower to obtain the most reasonable closing terms.

Uniform Settlement Statement Form. The Act gives the prospective borrower the right to inspect the final settlement statement *on the business day before closing.* The uniform settlement statement as prepared by the Department of Housing and Urban Development shown in Figure 9–2 must be given the buyer *at the time of closing.* The only exceptions to this rule are instances (1) where the borrower or the borrower's agent does not attend the settlement, or (2) where the person conducting the settlement does not require a meeting of the parties for that purpose. In these circumstances, the settlement statement must be supplied "as soon as practicable after settlement."

The settlement statement summarizes the way in which the final settlement cost is calculated. In illustration, assume that the family has purchased a $45,000 house financed by a $36,000 new mortgage. The buyer also agreed to pay $400 for living room draperies. Suppose further that settlement charges totaled $2,000 (note that this is taken from Section L, line 1400, of the Uniform Settlement shown in Figure 9–2). In reality, total settlement charges vary by type of property, financing terms, and geographic area.

Note that in Figure 9–3 under *Section 100* the gross amount due from borrower includes the purchase price, $45,000, the price of personal property, $400, and total settlement charges to the borrower (derived from line 1400 of Figure 9–2) of $2,000 which together amount to $47,400.

This sum is increased by final settlement adjustments; for example, line 108 which shows an unpaid assessment of $20 for one month's dues for the homeowner's association fee of $20—an amount prepaid by the seller and allocated to the buyer. The buyer is also charged for fuel oil remaining in the storage tank (line 109). These sums total $47,432.50 due from the borrower.

Section 200 indicates deductions for the earnest money deposit and amount of the loan, $1,000 and $36,000. In addition, lines 207 and 208 represent unpaid taxes and assessments which are to be paid by the seller and deducted from the amount due the buyer. These totals are shown in lines 301 and 302, indicating the final amount due from the borrower-purchaser, line 303, of $10,082.50.

FIGURE 9–2

A Disclosure/Settlement Statement

A. U.S. DEPARTMENT OF HOUSING AND URBAN DEVELOPMENT	B. TYPE OF LOAN
	1. ☐ FHA 2. ☐ FMHA 3. ☐ CONV. UNINS. 4. ☐ VA 5. ☐ CONV. INS.
DISCLOSURE/SETTLEMENT STATEMENT	6. FILE NUMBER 7. LOAN NUMBER
If the Truth-in-Lending Act applies to this transaction, a Truth-in-Lending statement is attached as page 3 of this form.	8. MORTG. INS. CASE NO.

C. NOTE: This form is furnished to you prior to settlement to give you information about your settlement costs, and again after settlement to show the actual costs you have paid. The present copy of the form is:

☐ ADVANCE DISCLOSURE OF COSTS. Some items are estimated, and are marked "(e)." Some amounts may change if the settlement is held on a date other than the date estimated below. The preparer of this form is not responsible for errors or changes in amounts furnished by others.

☐ STATEMENT OF ACTUAL COSTS. Amounts paid to and by the settlement agent are shown. Items marked "(p.o.c.)" were paid outside the closing; they are shown here for informational purposes and are not included in totals.

D. NAME OF BORROWER	E. SELLER		F. LENDER	
G. PROPERTY LOCATION	**H. SETTLEMENT AGENT**		**I. DATES**	
			LOAN COMMITMENT	ADVANCE DISCLOSURE
	PLACE OF SETTLEMENT		SETTLEMENT	DATE OF PRORATIONS IF DIFFERENT FROM SETTLEMENT

J. SUMMARY OF BORROWER'S TRANSACTION		K. SUMMARY OF SELLER'S TRANSACTION	
100. GROSS AMOUNT DUE FROM BORROWER:		**400. GROSS AMOUNT DUE TO SELLER:**	
101. Contract sales price		401. Contract sales price	
102. Personal property		402. Personal property	
103. Settlement charges to borrower *(from line 1400, Section L)*		403.	
		404.	
104.			
105.		Adjustments for items paid by seller in advance:	
		405. City/town taxes to	
Adjustments for items paid by seller in advance:		406. County taxes to	
		407. Assessments to	
106. City/town taxes to		408. to	
107. County taxes to		409. to	
108. Assessments to		410. to	
109. to		411. to	
110. to			
111. to		**420. GROSS AMOUNT DUE TO SELLER**	
112. to		*NOTE: The following 500 and 600 series section are not required to be completed when this form is used for advance disclosure of settlement costs prior to settlement.*	
120. GROSS AMOUNT DUE FROM BORROWER:			
200. AMOUNTS PAID BY OR IN BEHALF OF BORROWER:		**500. REDUCTIONS IN AMOUNT DUE TO SELLER:**	
		501. Payoff of first mortgage loan	
201. Deposit or earnest money		502. Payoff of second mortgage loan	
202. Principal amount of new loan(s)		503. Settlement charges to seller *(from line 1400, Section L)*	
203. Existing loan(s) taken subject to			
204.		504. Existing loan(s) taken subject to	
205.		505.	
		506.	
Credits to borrower for items unpaid by seller:		507.	
		508.	
206. City/town taxes to		509.	
207. County taxes to		Credits to borrower for items unpaid by seller:	
208. Assessments to			
209. to		510. City/town taxes to	
210. to		511. County taxes to	
211. to		512. Assessments to	
212. to		513. to	
220. TOTAL AMOUNTS PAID BY OR IN BEHALF OF BORROWER		514. to	
300. CASH AT SETTLEMENT REQUIRED FROM OR PAYABLE TO BORROWER:		515. to	
		520. TOTAL REDUCTIONS IN AMOUNT DUE TO SELLER	
301. Gross amount due from borrower *(from line 120)*		**600. CASH TO SELLER FROM SETTLEMENT:**	
302. Less amounts paid by or in behalf of borrower *(from line 220)*		601. Gross amount due to seller *(from line 420)*	
		602. Less total reductions in amount due to seller *(from line 520)*	
303. CASH ☐ REQUIRED FROM OR ☐ PAYABLE TO BORROWER:		603. CASH TO SELLER FROM SETTLEMENT	

FIGURE 9-2 *(continued)*

L. SETTLEMENT CHARGES		PAID FROM BORROWER'S FUNDS	PAID FROM SELLER'S FUNDS
700.	SALES/BROKER'S COMMISSION based on price $ @ %		
701.	Total commission paid by seller Division of commission as follows:		
702.	$ to		
703.	$ to		
704.			
800.	ITEMS PAYABLE IN CONNECTION WITH LOAN.		
801.	Loan Origination fee %		
802.	Loan Discount %		
803.	Appraisal Fee to		
804.	Credit Report to		
805.	Lender's inspection fee		
806.	Mortgage Insurance application fee to		
807.	Assumption/refinancing fee		
808.			
809.			
810.			
811.			
900.	ITEMS REQUIRED BY LENDER TO BE PAID IN ADVANCE.		
901.	Interest from to @ $ /day		
902.	Mortgage insurance premium for mo. to		
903.	Hazard insurance premium for yrs. to		
904.	yrs. to		
905.			
1000.	RESERVES DEPOSITED WITH LENDER FOR:		
1001.	Hazard insurance mo. @ $ /mo.		
1002.	Mortgage insurance mo. @ $ /mo.		
1003.	City property taxes mo. @ $ /mo.		
1004.	County property taxes mo. @ $ /mo.		
1005.	Annual assessments mo. @ $ /mo.		
1006.	mo. @ $ /mo.		
1007.	mo. @ $ /mo.		
1008.	mo. @ $ /mo.		
1100.	TITLE CHARGES:		
1101.	Settlement or closing fee to		
1102.	Abstract or title search to		
1103.	Title examination to		
1104.	Title insurance binder to		
1105.	Document preparation to		
1106.	Notary fees to		
1107.	Attorney's Fees to		
	(includes above items No.:		
1108.	Title insurance to		
	(includes above items No.:		
1109.	Lender's coverage $		
1110.	Owner's coverage $		
1111.			
1112.			
1113.			
1200.	GOVERNMENT RECORDING AND TRANSFER CHARGES		
1201.	Recording fees: Deed $; Mortgage $ Releases $		
1202.	City/county tax/stamps: Deed $; Mortgage $		
1203.	State tax/stamps: Deed $; Mortage $		
1204.			
1300.	ADDITIONAL SETTLEMENT CHARGES		
1301.	Survey to		
1302.	Pest inspection to		
1303.			
1304.			
1305.			
1400.	TOTAL SETTLEMENT CHARGES *(entered on lines 103 and 503, Sections J and K)*		

The Undersigned Acknowledges Receipt of This Disclosure Settlement Statement and Agrees to the Correctness Thereof.

_____   _____
        Buyer or Agent   Seller or Agent

NOTE: Under certain circumstances the borrower and seller may be permitted to waive the 12-day period which must normally occur between advance disclosure and settlement. In the event such a waiver is made, copies of the statements of waiver, executed as provided in the regulations of the Department of Housing and Urban Development, shall be attached to and made a part of this form when the form is used as a settlement statement.

HUD-1 (5-75)   AS & AS (1322)

FIGURE 9–3

A Summary of the Borrower's Transaction

	J. SUMMARY OF BORROWER'S TRANSACTION	
100.	GROSS AMOUNT DUE FROM BORROWER:	
101.	Contract sales price	$45,000.00
102.	Personal property	400.00
103.	Settlement charges to borrower (*from line 1400, Section L*)	2,000.00
104.		
105.		
	Adjustments for items paid by seller in advance:	
106.	City/town taxes to	
107.	County taxes to	
108.	Assessments 6/30 to 7/31	20.00
109.	Fuel oil, 25 gal @ $.50	12.50
110.	to	
111.	to	
112.	to	
120.	GROSS AMOUNT DUE FROM BORROWER:	$47,432.50
200.	AMOUNTS PAID BY OR IN BEHALF OF BORROWER:	
201.	Deposit or earnest money	$ 1,000.00
202.	Principal amount of new loan(s)	36,000.00
203.	Existing loan(s) taken subject to	
204.		
205.		
	Credits to borrower for items unpaid by seller:	
206.	City/town taxes to $600/yr.	
207.	County taxes 1/1 to 6/30 @/	300.00
208.	Assessments 1/1 to 6/30 @	50.00
209.	to $100/yr.	
210.	to	
211.	to	
212.	to	
220.	TOTAL AMOUNTS PAID BY OR IN BEHALF OF BORROWER	$37,350.00
300.	CASH AT SETTLEMENT REQUIRED FROM OR PAYABLE TO BORROWER:	
301.	Gross amount due from borrower (*from line 120*)	$47,432.50
302.	Less amounts paid by or in behalf of borrower (*from line 220*)	$37,350.00
303.	CASH ☒ REQUIRED FROM OR ☐ PAYABLE TO BORROWER:	$10,082.50

Unearned Fees or "Kickback." In frequent instances before RESPA, some title insurance companies were known to pay a fee to others for title insurance specified by the lender. Under the present act this practice is forbidden. Section 8 of RESPA provides:

> No person shall give and no person shall accept any fee, kickback, or thing of value pursuant to any agreement or understanding, oral or otherwise, that business incident to or a part of a real estate settlement service involving a federally related mortgage loan shall be referred to any person.

Accordingly, the Act prohibits payments by an attorney who gives a portion of his or her fee to another attorney, lender, or a real estate agent for referral of clients. Title insurance companies may not pay commissions to others for referral of business.

Selection of Title Companies. Moreover, no seller or lender of property, who must comply with RESPA, may require as a condition of sale that title insurance be purchased by a buyer from a particular title company. Violations of this requirement subjects the violator to damages equal to three times all charges made for such title insurance. This provision permits buyers to shop for the most advantageous policy.

Escrow Deposit. To prevent lenders from collecting excessive monthly sums for payment of annual property taxes and insurance, the Act limits the collection of escrow deposits to sums actually needed for payment of insurance and property taxes—on a monthly basis, equal to $\frac{1}{12}$ of annual property taxes and insurance premiums.

At settlement, however, the lender may charge an initial sum equal to the property taxes due plus two months' advance payment. To illustrate, assume monthly property taxes are $40 per month. If the closing date is June 30 and taxes are due January 1, the lender at time of settlement could charge the buyer $320 ($40 per month × 6 and two months' escrow of $40). The same calculations would be made for the insurance escrow at time of settlement.

TYPES OF CLOSING STATEMENTS

Before describing closing statements, a few preliminary comments are necessary. Typically the salesperson does not prepare a closing statement. In some offices, the broker delegates this task to an accountant or an attorney attached to the office. In still other cases, a bank, trust company, or an independent lawyer handles the closing transaction.

To illustrate the calculation of a closing statement, let us assume that the broker handles all of the money, down payment, and closing details. It should be noted, too, that the broker tries to get a down payment sufficient to cover his or her commission and an amount to cover the cash outlay that he or she spends on the part of the seller. At closing, the purchaser pays directly to the seller the balance due. With this arrangement, the broker then settles with the seller for his or her commission and expenses. If the broker fails to get a down payment sufficient to pay the commission and closing expenses, a settlement statement is presented to the seller and payment is then made to the broker. These procedures are a matter of local practice and vary widely.

Closing statements and other details that complete the transaction may be assigned to an *escrow* agent. The escrow agent is a disinterested third party who must follow written instructions that are necessary to close a real estate transaction. The escrow agent delivers the deed and performs other requirements of the sale and arranges for final settlement between the buyer and seller.

The terms *debit* and *credit* are common to closing statements. These terms identify accounting entries made in two columns. Accounting practice requires that credits be made in the right-hand column and that debits be entered in the left-hand column. Generally, a credit entry operates in favor of each party to the transaction. In this sense, the buyer and seller both receive credit entries on closing statements. A debit on the buyer or seller statement represents a cost or a deduction from the amount due both parties. Expenses of a real estate transaction borne by the buyer and seller are always shown as debits. Credits represent entries in favor of the buyer or seller.

Closing statements include (1) *debit and credit statements* (in some states called the ledger account form), and (2) *the accumulated deduction form.*

Debit and Credit Closing Statements

In the debit and credit format, closing statements are separately prepared for the purchaser and seller. The seller's statement shows the final amount due to the seller; the buyer's statement shows the final balance due from the buyer. Since closing expenses borne by the parties vary, these statements, though showing some common entries, show different balances. In addition, debit and credit statements permit the broker to prepare a cash reconciliation statement. The expense entries from buyer and seller statements are recorded in the cash reconciliation statement. The real estate broker lists the personal receipts and disbursements from the transaction in the cash reconciliation statement. The three statements of the debit-credit approach conform to the debit and credit accounting system.

The Accumulated Deduction Form

In the accumulated deduction form system, a single, summary report is prepared for the buyer, seller, and broker. This requires no knowledge of debit and credit accounting and, consequently, some experts believe that it is more easily understood. Most states favor the debit and credit closing system because each party to the transaction has a separate statement showing his or her final settlement. In both methods, closing statements follow a common procedure in recording expenses and prorating items.

ELEMENTS OF CLOSING STATEMENTS

We will first illustrate closing statements using the debit and credit approach. Each entry, recorded as part of the transaction, must fall in one of four categories: (1) the purchase price: real and personal property; (2) mortgages and other liens; (3) prorated items; and (4) closing expenses. This classification system may be used for both buyer and seller statements.

The Purchase Price: Real and Personal Property

The first entry on both the buyer and seller closing statements is the purchase price. The only complication here is that in some states a separate bill of sale will be prepared for the purchase of furniture, rugs, appliances, or other personal property. In other instances, the buyer and seller may agree on separate prices for the real estate and personal property.

The price paid for personalty will ordinarily be shown separately on the closing statement as an addition to the real estate price. Custom also dictates whether the real estate commission will be based on the consideration paid for personal and real property or for real estate only. With these qualifications, and according to local practice, the purchase price will always be the first entry on a closing statement. Entries following the purchase price represent adjustments to the price necessary to calculate the final settlement.

Mortgages and Other Liens

Mortgages assumed as part of the transaction (or new mortgages) represent the first deduction from the purchase price. In the same manner, tax liens or other unpaid charges against the property are also treated as deductions. For example, the buyer may agree to a $65,000 price and assume a first mortgage of $50,000 and a second mortgage of $9,000. The first and second mortgages would be shown as deductions from the purchase price. Other outstanding liens against the property should be shown in this part of the closing statement as further deductions from the sale price.

Prorated Items

Certain expenses of owning real estate may be prepaid at the time of closing. Normally the seller is responsible for those expenses incurred during his period of ownership. Thus, if property insurance was paid for the month of January and the sale was closed as of January 15, the seller would be entitled to recover the amount of prepaid insurance calculated from January 15 to January 31.

Conversely, certain expenses may be accrued but unpaid at the date of closing. In these circumstances, the buyer may elect to pay accrued expenses and charge the seller for his prorated share. Similarly, rental income prepaid at the first of the month must be allocated between the buyer and seller according to their time of ownership.

Closing Expenses

Ordinarily the expenses associated with a real estate transfer are shared by the buyer and seller. Preferably the expenses to be paid by both parties will be identified in the contract of sale. In the absence of an agreement, expenses will be paid according to local convention. In each instance, expenses of the buyer and seller reduce the amount of cash due the seller and increase the amount of cash due from the buyer. By listing the appropriate expenses on each statement, both parties can follow the final settlement calculation. Before these adjustments may be entered in the closing statement, there must be mutual agreement on closing procedures. Usually these procedures are well understood and follow local practice.

CLOSING PROCEDURES

Certain local practices govern final settlement of the real estate transfer. The buyer and seller, however, may agree on certain closing procedures not covered by local custom. Since these rules govern entries on closing statements, agreement must be reached on general rules accepted by buyer and seller. For the present, the generally accepted procedures are listed for identification. Prorated items are normally based on the following rules:

1. Calculate expenses to and including the day of closing. In a limited number of states—New York, for instance—it is provided that proration shall be made as of the day preceding the day on which title is closed.
2. Proration must be calculated according to (1) an assumed 360-day year and a 30-day month, or (2), alternatively, "the number of days in the calendar month." In the latter case, prorations tend to be

more accurate, especially for higher-valued income property. The sales contract should specify the method to be used.

3. If the real estate commission is paid by the seller, it may be paid from the balance due the seller or by separate arrangement with the seller.

4. Real estate property taxes may be billed after the date of closing and a tax undertaking given by the seller because the amount of the property tax cannot be determined until the tax roll is published. In these circumstances it is customary to prorate on the basis of the property tax of the previous year. The seller provides the undertaking by escrow or letter.

5. Special assessments (e.g., taxes paid for capital improvements such as sewers, streets, sidewalks, and water mains) are ordinarily payable in annual installments over several years. If the current installment remains unpaid at the date of closing, the purchaser usually assumes the payment. All other installments not due at the date of closing are omitted from closing statements. The payment of special assessments by buyer or seller should be determined in the sales contract.

6. Security deposits, including the last month's rent in a lease or damage deposits, are generally transferred by the seller to the buyer.

7. Prepaid rents are payable to the seller up to and including the day of closing. The balance of prepaid rent collected by the seller before the date of closing is prorated to the buyer. Uncollected rent may be covered by special agreement, providing that the buyer will attempt to collect rents and pay the prorated share to the seller. In this latter instance no entries for earned but unpaid rent will be made on the closing statement.

8. Prepaid mortgage interest is credited to the seller for the time he owned the property.

9. Expenses borne by the seller as a general rule, cover the following items: preparing deed instruments in favor of the buyer; state document taxes on the deed; the broker's real estate sales commission; title abstract, title reports and title insurance.

10. Expenses normally charged to the buyer include: instruments drawn in favor of the seller or lender; surveying costs; recording fees for the deed, mortgage, or trust instruments; all costs associated with securing mortgage loans (appraisal fees, credit reports, legal fees); reimbursement of items prepaid by the seller such as taxes and insurance.

While custom may follow generally accepted procedures, the parties to the agreement may vary these arrangements by contract. Accordingly, a careful reading of the sales contract is advised prior to calculating closing statement entries. With these rules in mind, the next most difficult task in calculating the final settlement relates to prorating prepaid and accrued items.

PRORATION ARITHMETIC

Prorating relates to the division of expenses or rental income between the buyer and seller. For example, if the seller has collected a monthly rent of $300 for the month of June and the date of closing is on June 15th, the rent must be prorated—$150 to the seller and $150 to the buyer. Other expenses and prepaid items must be prorated and divided as of the date of closing. For expenses, it must be determined at the date of closing whether the expense item is (1) accrued and payable, or (2) prepaid and, in part, refundable to the seller over his period of ownership. Rental income may be prepaid to the seller and partly refundable to the buyer over his or her period of ownership, or rental income may be earned by the seller and uncollected at the date of closing. If the rent is later collected, the seller is entitled to his share of accrued rent payable.

Accrued Expenses Payable

The accrued expenses payable category covers expenses of property ownership that are due at the time of closing and that have not been paid. Property taxes frequently fall into this category because tax bills are not calculated until the last quarter of the year.

Unpaid Property Taxes.   Assume that property taxes have remained unpaid from January 1 to the closing date of August 11. In this event the seller is responsible for property taxes for 7 months and 11 days (including the date of closing). If the tax bill is not issued until October, the parties must agree on estimated taxes using the preceding year as a guide. If the tax bill for the year is $650 and if the calculation is based on a 30-day month, the monthly tax bill is equal to $54.17 ($650/12). On a daily basis, a monthly charge of $54.17 equals $1.81 ($54.17/30). Therefore, the amount of taxes to be prorated in favor of the seller follows:

$$
\begin{array}{llr}
\text{7 months} \times \$54.17 & = & \$379.19 \\
\text{11 days} \quad \times \$\,1.81 & = & \underline{19.91} \\
\text{Prorated to seller} & = & \$399.10 \\
\text{Prorated to buyer} & & \\
(\$650 - \$399.10) & = & \underline{250.90} \\
\text{Annual taxes} & & \$650.00 \\
\end{array}
$$

Therefore, property taxes of $399.10 would be charged to the seller. The buyer would later receive and pay the annual tax bill of $650 but, in effect, the current property taxes would cost only $250.90, since he or she collected $399.10 from the seller at the time of closing.

If, however, the seller had prepaid the $650 tax *before closing* (i.e., the tax was due and payable July 1 while the closing was August 11), the buyer would be charged $250.90. On the closing statement this entry would increase the amount due from the buyer.

Special Assessments. Special assessments refer to taxes levied against real property to finance local neighborhood improvements. They are levied on a formula related to benefits enjoyed by owners of the affected property. For example, suppose that a new sewer extension has been financed by a special levy of $10 per front foot. Let us say an owner of a 300-foot frontage owes $3,000, payable with interest annually over 10 years. Assume that the first annual payment of $360 is payable August 1 and has not been paid by the date of closing, August 11. In short, the $360 constitutes an accrued item payable at the date of closing.

If the buyer pays $30,000 for the property and assumes the $360 special assessment, the $360 would be charged to the buyer (in effect an increase in the amount due from the buyer). The broker would collect this amount from the buyer as shown on the buyer's statement and pay the $360 shown as a disbursement on the cash reconciliation statement. In subsequent years the buyer would be liable for the balance of the special assessment. These later payments or the remaining lien would not be shown on the closing statement.

Generally speaking, the terms of the contract govern the payment of special assessments. If sewer, water, and streets are installed, and the value of these improvements are included in the sale price, special assessments should be paid by the seller. If their cost is deducted in negotiating the sale price, their cost should be assumed by the purchaser. In this respect special assessments are subject to negotiation and not to a fixed rule.

Prepaid Expenses

Utility expenses such as monthly water charges, insurance, and interest may be prepaid by the seller at the time of closing. For instance, if the closing date is August 11, 1977, and insurance premiums have been prepaid on a three-year contract beginning the 1st of January of 1977, then the seller is entitled to recover the value of the unexpired insurance at the time of closing.

Prepaid Insurance. To illustrate, calculate the number of years, months and days remaining as prepaid from the date of closing. The most convenient method is to establish a format showing the expiration date and the date of closing by year, month and day. Assume a 30-day month.

	Year	Month	Day
Expiration date (December 30, 1979)............	1979	12	30
Date of closing (August 11, 1977)................	1977	8	11
Number of years, months and days remaining............	2	4	19

In this example, start the subtraction with the day column. This practice is recommended because the number of days on the top line may be less than the number of days in the second line. Suppose, for instance, that the expiration date of the outstanding policy falls on July 2, 1979.

	Year	Month	Day
Expiration date (July 2, 1979)............	1979	7	2
Adjusted dates.........	(1978)	(18)	(32)
Date of closing (August 11, 1977)........	1977	8	11
Period remaining.......	1	10	21

Note that in this second example the days on the top lines are less than the days entered on the bottom line. Assuming a 30-day month, increase the days by 30, borrowing from the monthly column. Generally, if the number of months on the top line is less than the bottom line, add 12 months to the month line and subtract one year from the first column. The example shows that the insurance policy has one year, 10 months, and 21 days remaining.

The next step is to prorate the insurance costs over the remaining term. Assuming that insurance for a three-year period costs $240, the remaining insurance to be prorated in favor of the seller would be calculated as follows:

Per Unit Costs

$240	= 3-year cost
80	= 1-year cost
6.67	= monthly cost ($80/12)
.22	= daily cost ($6.67/30)

Proration

1 year................................	$ 80.00
10 months.............................	66.70 (10 × $6.67)
21 days...............................	4.62 (21 × $ .22)
Prepaid insurance in favor of seller............................	$151.32

If closing is to be calculated on the basis of actual days, the daily cost would be $.22 per day times 313 days in addition to the $80 annual cost.

Prepaid Utilities. Assume that the monthly cable TV charge is paid quarterly in advance. If the last payment was made for August, September and October, a prorate must be made in favor of the seller if the closing date is August 11. With a 30-day closing basis, the time left is 19 days plus 2 full months. With a cable charge of $10 per month, the daily charge would be $.33 ($10/30). The cost prorated against the buyer would then be

```
19 days × $.33......................... $ 6.27
2 months × $10.00.....................   20.00
Prorate in favor of the seller...........  $26.27
```

If charges are to be entered on the basis of actual days of the month, then the daily charge will be calculated on the basis of $.32 per day for August ($10.00/31).

Mortgage Interest. Assume that the mortgage payment on the remaining balance of $27,369 is due the first of every month. With a 9-percent annual interest rate and a closing date of August 11, the buyer will be charged with the mortgage payment due September 1 covering interest for the full month of August. To correct for this discrepancy, the seller should be charged interest for the first 11 days of August. With the assumed data, and a 30-day month, this calculation would be made as follows:

```
Monthly interest on the remaining balance
  .09/12 × $27,369                        = $205.27
Daily interest cost $205.27/30            =    6.84
Amount charged to seller 11 days × $6.84  =   75.26
```

Note that the $75.26 prorated charge to the seller is based on a 30-day month. If actual days are to be used, the daily rate would be found by dividing the monthly interest cost of $205.27 by the 31 days of August.

Prepaid Property Taxes. Referring to the former example, assume that the seller had paid the property tax of $650 at the time of closing, August 11. Under these circumstances property taxes are treated as other annual prepaid expenses. The proration calculation, again, assigns the same amounts to the seller and buyer. A 30-day month is assumed.

```
7 months × $54.17 = $379.19
11 days × $1.81   =   19.91
Prorated to seller = $399.10
Prorated to buyer
($650 − $399.10)  =  250.90
                    $650.00
```

The present case differs from the preceding case in assigning these amounts to the buyer and seller. Recall that property taxes of $650 have been prepaid by the seller at the date of closing. Therefore, on the seller's statement an entry of $250.90 will be made in favor of the seller. In accounting terms this would be shown as a *credit* to the seller. On the buyer's statement the $250.90 would be entered as a charge (or *debit*) against the buyer. This procedure effectively increases the amount due from the buyer.

Prepaid Rental Income

It is customary for tenants to pay monthly rent in advance. Assume for example that the monthly rent of $240 has been paid on the first of August. If the closing date is August 11, the seller must reimburse the buyer for rental income during the period of the buyer's ownership.

In the case at hand, it is assumed that the tenant continues to occupy the premises to the end of August. If rent is prorated on the basis of a 30-day month, the prorate against the seller amounts to a daily charge of $8 for 11 days. On the seller's statement this amount would be shown as a charge. The buyer is entitled to 19 days' rent calculated at the rate of $8 per day or $152. On the closing statement of the buyer, the $152 would be entered as a credit in favor of the buyer. These prorations are shown below

```
Rental income per day $240/30          = $  8.00
Amount prorated to seller $8.00 × 11 days = $ 88.00
Amount prorated to buyer $8.00 × 19 days = $152.00
```

Accrued Rent Payable

If rent has not been collected but is due and payable, the parties usually sign an additional agreement permitting the buyer to attempt collection and pay the seller his prorated share. In the present example, if the buyer succeeded in collecting past-due rent, the seller would be entitled to $88 ($8.00 × 11 days). Note that if the unpaid rent remains uncollected at the date of closing, no rental prorate would be shown on the buyer or seller closing statements. It would be unfair to charge the buyer for rent that is past due and uncollectible.

Closing Expenses

Under the debit and credit closing system, only the expenses charged to the buyer and seller are entered on their respective statements. Starting with the seller's statement, the real estate commission will always be shown as a debit to the seller and will not appear on the buyer's closing statement. Similarly, the earnest money deposit is usually shown on the buyer's statement as a credit and is unique to the buyer's statement, never appearing on the seller's debit and credit closing statement.

With these exceptions, closing expenses entered on both statements should follow custom or agreements quoted in the contract of sale. Generally speaking, the closing expenses are out-of-pocket costs necessary to prepare documents for final settlement. In each instance the final adjusting entries—first on the seller's statement—show the amount of *cash due to the seller* and second on the buyer's statement—show the *balance due from the buyer*.

DEBIT AND CREDIT CLOSING STATEMENTS

Certain rules guide the detailed preparation of buyer and seller closing statements. To identify these rules, suppose we turn to facts associated with a real estate transfer. Details on prorating and closing expenses are listed for an actual transaction.

1. Sales price $45,000.
2. The buyer agrees to assume an existing mortgage with a remaining balance at the date of closing of $32,448.96. The mortgage interest rate is 8 percent for a 25-year mortgage. The mortgage payment (interest and principal) of $277.92 is payable the first of every month. Mortgage payments are current. The seller agrees to accept a second mortgage of $5,000. The balance of the purchase price is payable on the date of closing.
3. Earnest money advanced by the buyer at the time of sale is $3,500.
4. The closing date is November 22, 19___ (8 days left in the month —a 30-day month is assumed).
5. The seller has collected rent of $320 for the month of November.
6. A three-year fire insurance policy in effect since January 1, of the same year, has a one-year premium cost of $158. The policy is assigned to the buyer.
7. A street assessment of $360 was outstanding and payable at the date of closing. The seller had paid property taxes of $855.75 for the current year. Taxes were due October 1 and were paid by the seller.
8. The buyer agrees to purchase a refrigerator for $125 and two window air conditioners at $50 each. A bill of sale is to be given at the closing date.
9. Property taxes, insurance, rent, and interest are to be prorated at the date of closing. Prorated items are to be calculated up to and including the date of closing. Prorates are based on 30-day month.
10. Seller agrees to pay the following expenses: real estate commission of 6 percent of the real estate sales price; the real estate transfer tax of $0.10 per $100 on the net consideration; legal expenses for preparation of the warranty deed.
11. Buyer agrees to pay: legal expenses for preparing the second mortgage and promissory note of $25, recording fees of $8; intangible tax on the second mortgage of $1.50 per $500.

Closing Statement for the Seller

The comments below, directed to the closing statement for the seller, relate to the entries shown in Figure 9–4. Entries are arranged in the four categories common to debit and credit closing statements.

Real and Personal Property

a. The purchase price of real estate is credited to the seller. Note that items credited on the seller's statements are entries in favor of the seller.

b. Since the buyer has agreed to pay an additional amount for the refrigerator and two air conditioners, they are also shown as credits—in effect, an addition to the purchase price.

Mortgages and Liens

c. The buyer agrees to assume the outstanding first loan, which actually represents a reduction in the cash due the seller. Therefore, on the seller's

FIGURE 9–4

Closing Statement for Seller

Name of Seller: Joseph S. Smith

Legal Description: Lot 6, Block B, Crestwood Estates, Clarke County, Georgia

Closing Date: November 22, 19___

Real and Personal Property	Debits	Credits
(a) Purchase price of real property................		$45,000.00
(b) Purchase price of personal property		
Refrigerator....................................		125.00
Two window air conditioners.................		100.00
Mortgages and Liens		
(c) First loan assumed.............................	$32,448.96	
(d) Second loan given seller.......................	5,000.00	
Prorated Charges		
(e) Prepaid taxes....................................		90.35
(f) Prepaid insurance..............................		16.69
(g) Prepaid rent.....................................	85.36	
(h) Interest on loan................................	158.62	
Closing Expenses		
(i) Real estate commission........................	2,700.00	
(j) Unpaid street assessment.....................	360.00	
(k) Warranty deed..................................	35.00	
(l) Transfer tax.....................................	12.55	
(m) Title insurance, owners' policy................	157.50	
(n) Balance due seller..............................	4,374.05	
Total..	$45,332.04	$45,332.04

statement the assumed mortgage must be debited to reduce the final amount due the seller.

d. As part of the purchase price, the buyer agrees to give the seller a second mortgage of $5,000. This amount also reduces the cash due the seller and is debited on the seller's statement.

Prorated Charges

e. Taxes of $855.75 have been paid by the seller. The tax calculations are based on a 30-day month.

	Month	Days
Expiration date.........	12	30
Closing date.............	11	22
Proration..................	1	8

$855.75/12	= $71.31 per month
$ 71.31/30	= $ 2.38 per day
1 month × $71.31	= $71.31
8 days × $2.38	= 19.04
Tax prorate due seller	$90.35

The $90.35 property tax prorate entered as a credit to the seller reimburses the seller for the property taxes prepaid over the calendar year.

f. The prepaid insurance of $158.00 is prorated in the manner shown for prepaid property taxes:

$158/12	= $13.17 per month
$13.17/30	= $ 0.44 per day
1 month × $13.17	= $13.17
8 days × $0.44	= 3.52
Insurance prorate	
due seller	$16.69

Since the seller has prepaid insurance for the calendar year, he is entitled to reimbursement for the insurance expenses covering 1 month, 8 days.

g. Because the seller has collected rent for the full month, he must reimburse the buyer for the 8 days of his ownership.

$$\$320/30 = \$10.67 \text{ per day}$$
$$8 \text{ days} \times \$10.67 = \$85.36$$

By showing $85.36 as a debit on the seller's statement, the entry reduces the cash due the seller.

h. On December 1, 19__ (the month following the month of closing), the buyer must pay interest at the rate of 8 percent annually on an outstanding loan balance of $32,448.96. The interest of $216.32 ($32,448.96 × .08/12) is prorated for 22 days against the seller (a debit):

$$\$216.32/30 = \$7.21 \text{ per day}$$
$$22 \text{ days} \times \$7.21 = \$158.62.$$

Closing Expenses

i. The real estate commission of 6 percent is calculated against the purchase price only on real property ($45,000). Expenses on the closing statements are shown as debits or charges against the seller.

j. According to the contract of sale, the seller agrees to pay the $360 street assessment. This is comparable to an additional expense to be shown as a debit with other expenses.

k. By agreement, the seller agrees to pay the legal expenses for warranty deed preparation of $35.

l. The transfer tax applies to the purchase price, less the assumed mortgage:

$$(\$45,000 - \$32,448.96) = \$12,551.04 \text{ net consideration}$$
$$\$12,551.04/100 \times .10 = \$12.55$$

The $12.55 transfer tax, by agreement chargeable to the seller, is shown as a debit on his closing statement.

m. It is customary for the seller to furnish an owner's title insurance policy. This expense of $157.50 is shown as a debit or charge against the seller.

n. The balance due seller is an adjusting entry closed into the broker's cash reconciliation showing the cash due seller as final settlement.

Closing Statement for the Buyer

Figure 9–5 illustrates a closing statement prepared for the buyer. It will be noted that the buyer statement *includes* the earnest money deposit and *excludes* the real estate commission paid by the seller. In other respects, the entries under the heading "Real and Personal Property," "Mortgage and Liens," and "Prorated Charges" are virtually identical to the entries on the statement for the seller.

There is only one difference: Common entries shown on the seller's statement are reversed for the buyer's statement. Furthermore, the closing expenses for the buyer, according to agreement or custom, are unique to this statement.

Real and Personal Property

a. The purchase price of $45,000 is shown as a debit on the buyer's statement. This in effect represents a charge against the buyer.

FIGURE 9–5

Closing Statement for Buyer

Name of Buyer: John T. Brown

Legal Description: Lot 6, Block B, Crestwood Estates, Clarke County, Georgia

Closing Date: November 22, 19__

Real and Personal Property	Debits	Credits
(a) Purchase of real property......................	$45,000.00	
(b) Purchase price of personal property		
Refrigerator.................................	125.00	
Two window air conditioners................	100.00	
(c) Earnest money deposit........................		$ 3,500.00
Mortgages and Liens		
(d) First mortgage assumed......................		32,448.96
(e) Second mortgage to seller....................		5,000.00
Prorated Charges		
(f) Prepaid taxes.................................	90.35	
(g) Prepaid insurance............................	16.69	
(h) Prepaid rent..................................		85.36
(i) Interest on mortgage.........................		158.62
Closing Expenses		
(j) Preparation of second mortgage..............	25.00	
(k) Recording warranty deed & second		
mortgage...................................	8.00	
(l) Intangible tax.................................	15.00	
(m) Balance due from buyer......................		4,187.10
Total...................................	$45,380.04	$45,380.04

b. Personal property, also shown on the seller's statement, constitutes an increase in the amount to be paid by the buyer and must be shown as a debit.

c. The buyer has paid an earnest money deposit of $3,500 to the real estate broker. Since he will be given credit for this amount, this reduces the final amount due from the buyer and should be shown as a credit.

Mortgages and Liens

d. The assumed first mortgage of $32,448.96, since it reduces the cash due from the buyer, is entered as a credit—an entry in favor of the buyer.

e. The second mortgage given to the seller decreases the cash due from the buyer and must be shown as a credit.

Prorated Charges

f. The prepaid taxes, calculated as shown in the section covering the seller's statement, are debited as a charge against the buyer. It will be recalled that taxes of some $90.35 have been prepaid by the seller and are charged back to the buyer as a debit.

g. The prepaid insurance of $16.69 represents the unexpired insurance for the balance of the year. By debiting this amount on the buyer's statement, this sum is charged against the buyer.

h. The prepaid rent of $85.36 is rent due the buyer for the last 8 days of the month. The credit of $85.36 allocates this amount to the buyer.

i. The interest on the mortgage for the month of November (.08/12 × $32,448.96) on the unpaid mortgage balance represents the interest for 22 days of November assignable to the seller. Because the seller is responsible for this amount, the $158.62 is .credited to the buyer. The buyer will pay the full mortgage payment including November interest on December 1.

Closing Expenses

j. Legal fees of $25 for preparing the second mortgage are an expense assumed by the buyer.

k. By agreement, the buyer pays recording expenses of $8 for the warranty deed and second mortgage. The debit charges the buyer for these items.

l. The intangible tax is based on $1.50 per $500 or $15 for a new $5,000 mortgage.

m. The $4,187.10 shown as the balance due from purchaser is closed into the broker's cash reconciliation statement. This is the amount of cash the purchaser must pay at the time of closing.

The Cash Reconciliation Statement

Simply stated, the cash reconciliation statement shows the receipts and disbursements of the real estate broker. The statement is for office use and is not given to the buyer or seller. Its main advantage lies in showing the net result of the transaction to the selling broker. This statement is the easiest to prepare since the entries on the reconciliation statement are taken from the buyer and seller statements. No original entries are shown in this statement.

Figure 9–6 shows the cash reconciliation statement prepared from Figures 9–4 and 9–5.

a. The earnest money deposit of $3,500 is taken from a similar entry recorded as a credit on the closing statement to the buyer.

b. The check for the balance from the buyer, $4,187.10, is the adjusting entry taken from the closing statement to the buyer. These two items constitute the total receipts paid by the buyer, $7,687.10.

c. The amount paid to the seller, shown in the disbursement column,

FIGURE 9–6

Cash Reconciliation Statement

Name of Seller: Joseph S. Smith

Name of Buyer: John T. Brown

Legal Description: Lot 6, Block B, Crestwood Estates, Clarke County, Georgia

Date of Closing: November 22, 19___

From Buyer	*Receipts*	*Disbursements*
(a) Earnest money deposit........................	$3,500.00	
(b) Check for balance............................	4,187.10	
(c) To seller......................................		$4,374.05
Expenses		
(d) Real estate commission......................		2,700.00
(e) Unpaid street assessment....................		360.00
(f) Warranty deed...............................		35.00
(g) Transfer tax.................................		12.55
(h) Title insurance, owners' policy...............		157.50
(i) Preparation of second mortgage..............		25.00
(j) Recording warranty deed and second mortgage.....................................		8.00
(k) Intangible tax................................		15.00
	$7,687.10	$7,687.10

$4,374.05, is from the adjusting entry on the closing statement prepared for the seller.

d. The expenses entered on the cash reconciliation statement are listed on both the buyer and seller closing statements. Each expense item shown on the buyer and seller closing statements should be listed on the cash reconciliation statement. For example, the real estate commission of $2,700 is the first expense listed for the seller on his statement. This sum will be paid into the broker's personal or business account.

e. The unpaid street assessment, entered as a debit on the seller's statement, constitutes a disbursement of the broker.

f. The warranty deed expense of $35 is paid by the seller and corresponds to the similar entry on the seller's statement.

g. The transfer tax of $12.55, shown as one of the seller's expenses, constitutes an additional disbursement by the broker.

h. Similarly, the $157.50 title insurance expense is a disbursement also shown as a debit on the seller's statement.

i. The $25 legal fee for preparation of the second mortgage, another disbursement, compares to a debit entry on the closing statement for the buyer.

j. Recording of the warranty deed and second mortgage, debited to the buyer's closing statement, parallels the same entry in the debit column of the buyer's statement.

k. The $15 intangible tax debited on the buyer's statement is a disbursement to be shown on the cash reconciliation statement.

It will be observed that the balance of the cash reconciliation statement of $7,687.10 has no relation to cash receipts or disbursements. Like the balances shown at the end of the buyer's and seller's statements, these are balancing entries showing the correctness of debits and credits or receipts and disbursements.

Summary: Debit and Credit Closing Statements

By following a uniform list of practices for each of the three statements, difficulties in preparing them can be lessened considerably.

Preparing the Seller's Closing Statement

1. Enter the purchase price of real and personal property as a credit.
2. List other mortgages and other liens as a debit.
3. Prorated items that accrue to the benefit of the seller (i.e., are paid back to the seller) are entered as a credit.
4. Prorated items against the seller (i.e., are charged against the seller) are entered as debits.
5. Closing expenses assumed by the seller are entered as debits. The real estate commission, which appears on the seller's statement and not on the buyer's statement, is shown as a debit.
6. The balance due the seller should be entered as a debit.

Preparation of the Buyer's Closing Statement

1. The prices of real and personal property are shown as debits on the buyer's statement. Note that these entries are opposite to the credit entry of the same amount shown on the seller's statement.
2. The earnest money deposit, which appears only on the buyer's statement, is shown as a credit.
3. Mortgages and liens that reduce the amount due from the buyer are always shown as credits on the buyer's statement.
4. Prorated charges should be identical to the entries shown on the seller's statement with one important difference: debit and credit entries on the seller's statement are reversed on the buyer's statement.
5. Closing expenses shown on the buyer's statement are debited and paid by the buyer. These charges are not shown on the seller's statement. The balance due from the buyer is shown in the credit column.

Preparing the Broker's Cash Reconciliation Statement

1. The receipts of the broker usually include only the earnest money deposit and the final check from the buyer.

FIGURE 9–7

Closing Statement (accumulated deduction)

<u>Joseph S. Smith</u>   <u>John T. Brown</u>
(Seller)   (Purchaser)

<u>Lot 6, Block B, Crestwood Estates, Clarke County, Georgia</u>
(Property Description)

<u>Closing Date: November 22, 19__</u>

		Credit to Purchaser	Credit to Seller
1.	Purchase price...................................		$45,000.00
2.	Personal Property: refrigerator; two air conditioners...................................		225.00
3.	Earnest Money...................................	$ 3,500.00	
4.	Outstanding liens assumed by purchaser:		
	(a) First mortgage............................	32,448.96	
	(b) Second mortgage.........................	5,000.00	
5.	Adjusted (Prorated) Items:		
	(a) Prepaid property taxes for present year....		90.35
	(b) Prepaid insurance.........................		16.69
	(c) Prepaid rent..............................	85.36	
	(d) Interest on mortgage......................	158.62	
6.	Balance due to order of seller..................	4,139.10	
		$45,332.04	$45,332.04

ESCROW MEMORANDUM

Received from the *purchaser* money for the following purposes:
1.	Balance due the seller as per statement................	$4,139.10
2.	Preparation of second mortgage.......................	25.00
3.	Recording warranty deed and second mortgage.........	8.00
4.	Intangible tax...	15.00
	Total received from purchaser.....................	$4,187.10

Received of the *seller* the total amount as shown below, for the following purposes:
1.	Real estate commission................................	$2,700.00
2.	Warranty deed preparation............................	35.00
3.	Transfer tax...	12.55
4.	Title insurance, owner's policy.........................	157.50
5.	Unpaid street assessment.............................	360.00
	Total...	$3,265.05
	Check to seller for balance of purchase price............	4,374.05
	Total ($4,139.10 + $3,500).........................	$7,639.10

2. The disbursements are made up of three parts: (a) the real estate commission; (b) the check to the seller; and (c) expenses paid by the broker.

3. Expenses paid by the broker are drawn from entries on the buyer and seller statements. They do not include office expenses or expenses not shown on the buyer or seller closing statements.

ACCUMULATED DEDUCTION CLOSING STATEMENTS

For the most part, the accumulated deduction closing statement lists credits to the buyer and credits to the seller in cumulative form. Figure 9–7 illustrates this type of statement. Using the same closing information, note that the credits to the purchaser and the credits to the seller columns are identical to the entries on the debit and credit closing statement.

Under the "Escrow Memorandum" portion of the statement, the balance due the seller is increased by the amount of expenses borne by the purchaser. The $4,187.10 is identical to the amount due from the buyer shown on the buyer's closing statement, Figure 9–5.

The expenses paid by the seller are then totaled, shown as $3,265.05. The adjusting entry of $4,374.05 represents the final settlement to the seller. The total receipts to the seller of $7,639.10 equals the sum of the balance due the seller, $4,139.10, and the earnest money deposit of $3,500.

Deducting expenses paid by the seller, $3,265.05, from $7,639.10 gives the final settlement due the seller, $4,374.05. While mathematically correct, the accumulated deduction statement does not result in separate statements for the buyer and seller; nor does it provide the checks and balances provided by the cash reconciliation statement, and it does not follow conventional debit and credit accounting procedures. For these reasons most real estate professionals prefer debit and credit closing statements.

QUESTIONS FOR REVIEW

I. Answer the following questions on *debit and credit* closing statements.

A. General Closing Statement Questions

_____ 1. A second loan would be entered on the closing statements as
    a. a debit to the buyer and a credit to the seller.
    b. a debit to the buyer and no entry to the seller.
    c. a credit to the buyer and no entry to the seller.
    d. a debit to the seller and a credit to the buyer.

_____ 2. The price of personal property would appear as _____ if it is included in a real estate transaction.
    a. a credit on the buyer's statement
    b. part of the total purchase price of the real property on both statements
    c. a debit on the seller's statement
    d. a credit on the seller's statement

_____ 3. If the buyer obtains a new loan as part of the purchase price, the amount of the new loan

    a. does not appear on the closing statement.
    b. appears only on the seller's statement.
    c. appears as a debit on the buyer's statement.
    d. appears as a credit on the buyer's statement.

_____4. Earnest money paid by the buyer appears as

    a. a debit on the seller's statement.
    b. a credit on the buyer's statement.
    c. a disbursement on the cash reconciliation statement.
    d. neither a debit nor a credit if it was received before closing.

_____ 5. On the buyer's closing statement,

    a. prorated property taxes are entered as a debit.
    b. the earnest money deposit is a debit entry.
    c. the prorated insurance premium is a credit entry.
    d. the balance due from the buyer is a credit entry.

B. Prorating Property Taxes

_____ 6. If the property tax is due and payable on a fiscal year basis (July 1 to June 30), how much is the buyer's share of the taxes if the closing date is March 25? Assume actual calendar days, a tax rate of 2.55 percent on a $10,500 assessed value, and that property taxes have not been paid.

    a. $ 68.75.
    b. $ 71.16.
    c. $102.18.
    d. $196.59.

_____ 7. Assume closing is held on July 15, a tax rate of 3.25 percent on an assessed value of $10,500, and that property taxes are payable on a calendar year basis and have not been paid. What is the seller's prorated share of the property taxes? Use actual calendar days.

    a. $183.24.
    b. $141.25.
    c. $205.60.
    d. $158.01.

_____ 8. If taxes are payable on a fiscal year basis (July 1 to June 30), and have already been paid by the seller based on a millage rate of 31.75 on an assessed value of $12,400, what is the buyer's prorated share of the taxes if the closing date is March 25? Assume a 30-day month.

    a. $293.83.
    b. $103.89.
    c. $122.80.
    d. $ 96.75.

_____ 9. If the property taxes have been prepaid by the seller, and the tax rate is 2.43 percent on an assessed value of $10,500, the buyer's prorated share of the property taxes is _____. Assume a 30-day month, a closing date of March 25, and that property taxes are payable on a calendar-year basis.

    a. $ 60.23.
    b. $170.88.
    c. $125.55.
    d. $194.92.

_____10. Assume a tax rate of 3.25 percent on an assessed value of $10,500 and a closing date of March 25. If the property taxes have been prepaid and if they were based on a fiscal year (July 1 to June 30), the seller's prorated share of the taxes would be shown as a _____ on the seller's statement. Use actual calendar days.

    a.   credit of $250.55
    b.   credit of $90.70
    c.   debit of $250.55
    d.   debit of $90.70

C. Prorating Prepaid Insurance

_____11. If a $360 fire insurance premium for two years has been paid for a policy in effect since January 1 of the preceding year, what is the buyer's prorated share of the premium if closing is on March 25? Use actual calendar days.

    a. $138.59
    b. $221.41.
    c. $318.59.
    d. $ 41.41.

_____12. If closing is on March 25 and a 3-year premium of $425 has been paid for a fire insurance policy in effect since January 1 of the preceding year, what is the buyer's prorated share of the insurance premium? Assume a 30-day month.

    a. $141.67.
    b. $225.33.
    c. $249.90.
    d. $304.75.

_____13. If a 3-year fire insurance policy has been in effect since January 1 of the preceding year, how would the seller's prorated share of the premium be shown if the total cost of the policy is $360 and he has paid the insurance premium through the current year only? Assume a 30-day month and a closing date of March 25.

    a.   A debit of $91.67.
    b.   A credit of $91.67.
    c.   A credit of $28.33.
    d.   A debit of $28.33.

___14. If a 3-year premium of $360 has been paid for a fire insurance pol-
icy in effect since January 1 of the preceding year, the buyer's prorated share of the insurance premium is shown as a _____ if
closing is on March 25. Assume a 30-day month.
   a. credit of $211.67
   b. debit of $211.67
   c. debit of $148.32
   d. credit of $148.32

___15. The seller's statement would show a _____ for the insurance premium proration if closing is on March 25 and a 3-year premium of
$270 has been paid for a fire insurance policy in effect since Janu-
ary 1 of the preceding year. Assume actual calendar days.
   a. debit of $109.75
   b. credit of $160.25
   c. debit of $160.25
   d. credit of $109.75

D. Prorating Prepaid Rent

___16. If the sale includes an apartment which is currently rented for
$125 per month, what is the seller's prorated share of the March
rent if the rent is payable on the first day of each month and the
seller has collected the March rent payment? Assume a 30-day
month and a closing date of March 25.
   a. $ 75.00.
   b. $ 20.83.
   c. $ 83.33.
   d. $104.17.

___17. If closing is on March 15, what is the buyer's prorated share of the
March rent if the sale includes an apartment which is currently
rented for $125 per month and the seller has collected the March
rent payment? Assume a 30-day month.
   a. $62.50.
   b. $66.72.
   c. $50.00.
   d. $76.40.

___18. The buyer's statement would show a _____ as the entry for the
March rent proration if closing is held on March 20, the sale includes an apartment currently rented for $125 per month, and the
seller has collected the March rent payment. Assume a 30-day
month.
   a. debit for $41.67
   b. credit for $83.33
   c. credit for $41.67
   d. debit for $83.33

____19. If the sale includes an apartment which is currently rented for $125 per month, what is the seller's prorated share of the March rent if the rent is payable on the first day of each month and the seller has collected the March rent payment? Use actual calendar days and a closing date of March 25.

    a. $ 33.87.
    b. $141.13.
    c. $ 62.10.
    d. $112.90.

____20. If closing is on March 25 and the sale includes an apartment which is currently rented for $175 per month, rent is payable on the 15th of the month, and the seller has collected the March rent payment, what is the seller's prorated share of the rent? Use actual calendar days.

    a. $ 33.87.
    b. $141.14.
    c. $ 62.10.
    d. $112.90.

E. Prorating Mortgage Interest

____21. What is the buyer's prorated share of the monthly interest on the first mortgage if the remaining balance is $21,325 at the date of closing, monthly mortgage payments are $185.21 including principal and interest, the mortgage interest rate is 8.5 percent, and the closing date is March 25? Assume a 30-day month.

    a. $ 51.05.
    b. $125.87.
    c. $ 19.24.
    d. $ 25.18.

____22. If closing is on March 20, what is the buyer's prorated share of the monthly interest on the first mortgage if the remaining balance is $21,325 at the date of closing, monthly mortgage payments are $185.21 including principal and interest, and the monthly interest rate is 8.5 percent? Assume a 30-day month.

    a. $ 50.35.
    b. $ 40.50.
    c. $100.70.
    d. $ 15.15.

____23. If the remaining balance on the outstanding first mortgage is $23,768.14 at the date of closing, the interest rate is 8 percent, the monthly mortgage payments are $185.21 including principal and interest, and the closing date is March 25, what is the buyer's share of the mortgage interest? Use actual calendar days.

    a. $ 58.45.
    b. $ 31.67.

    c. $127.78.
    d. $158.45.

_____24. Assume an outstanding first mortgage with a remaining balance of
$21,325 at the closing date, monthly mortgage payments of $185.21
including principal and interest, and an interest rate of 9 percent.
If closing is on March 25, the seller's statement shows a _____
as the entry for prorated interest. Use a 30-day month and assume
interest is paid at the end of the month.
    a. debit of $159.94
    b. credit of $133.28
    c. credit of $159.94
    d. debit of $133.28

_____25. If the remaining balance on the outstanding first mortgage is
$21,325 at the date of closing, the interest rate is 7.75 percent, the
monthly mortgage payments are $184.21 including principal and
interest, and the closing date is March 22, the buyer's statement
shows a _____ as the entry for prorated interest. Use actual
calendar days.
    a. debit of $97.74
    b. credit of $97.74
    c. credit of $39.98
    d. debit of $39.98

II. Read the following report of a real estate sale. Note the facts necessary to
prepare closing statements.

On March 10, 19_____, Mr. and Mrs. John K. Rich signed a contract
for sale to purchase the property of Mr. and Mrs. Jerry W. Best at 1042 River
Drive. Mr. and Mrs. Rich gave Mr. Jack Dee, a salesman for Eastern Realty,
Inc., a check for $3,000 as earnest money.

The Bests accepted an offer of $28,500 and agreed to pay a real estate
commission of 6 percent of the sales price. Mr. and Mrs. Rich will assume an
outstanding first mortgage with a remaining balance of $21,325 at the date
of closing. Monthly mortgage payments of $185.21, including principal and
interest, are due on the first day of each month. The mortgage interest rate
is 8.5 percent.

The seller agrees to accept a second loan of $3,175 at 9 percent interest
for a term of five years with monthly payments of $65.92 due on the first
day of each month. The balance of the purchase price is to be paid at the
time of closing, March 25, 19_____.

The buyer agrees to have the outstanding fire insurance policy on the property assigned to him. The policy has been in effect since January 1 of the
preceding year. A three-year premium of $360 was paid on the effective date.
Property taxes for the current calendar year have not been paid. The taxes are
based on a total millage rate of 32.5 mills and an assessed value of $10,500
(1 mill = $0.001).

The sale includes a one-bedroom garage apartment which is currently rented
for $125 per month. The rent is payable on the first day of each month. The

seller has collected the March rent payment. In addition, there is an outstanding street assessment of $450 against the property. The seller agrees to pay the street assessment at closing. Property taxes, insurance, mortgage interest, and rent are to be prorated at the date of closing.

Mr. and Mrs. Rich will pay $175 for an owner's title insurance policy, $25 for the preparation of the second mortgage and promissory note, recording fees of $15 for the warranty deed and $15 for the mortgage, an intangible tax of $3 per $1,000 on the second loan, and a legal fee of $50.

Mr. and Mrs. Best are obligated to pay the state transfer tax of 10 cents per $100, or fraction thereof, on the difference between the sales price and the remaining balance of the first mortgage. The seller will also pay a fee of $10 for the preparation of the warranty deed and a legal fee of $50.

III. Prepare a debit and credit closing statement for the seller and buyer. Prepare the broker's cash reconciliation statement based on the debit and credit closing statements. Check your work with statements illustrated in the Answer Key. Answer the following questions based on this transaction.

A. Closing Statements to the Sellers

_____26. The purchase price of real and personal property would be shown as a
  a. debit of $28,500.
  b. debit of $25,500.
  c. credit of $28,500.
  d. credit of $25,500.

_____27. The first mortgage would be shown as a
  a. debit of $21,325.
  b. credit of $21,325.
  c. debit of $24,500.
  d. credit of $24,500.

_____28. Under the assumptions of the problem, the street assessment would be entered as a
  a. debit of $450.00.
  b. debit of $106.25.
  c. credit of $106.25.
  d. credit of $450.00.

_____29. The property tax prorate would be shown as a
  a. credit of $80.57.
  b. debit of $80.57.
  c. debit of $341.25.
  d. credit of $341.25.

_____30. On the seller's statement the insurance would be shown as a
  a. debit of $211.67.
  b. credit of $211.67.

    c. credit of $360.00.
    d. debit of $120.00.

_____31. The interest on the first mortgage would be
    a. entered as a debit of $125.88.
    b. shown as a credit of $125.88.
    c. omitted from the closing statement to the seller.
    d. shown only on the buyer's closing statement.

_____32. On the statement to the seller, the real estate commission would be entered as a
    a. credit of $1,710.
    b. debit of $1,710.
    c. debit of $1,530.
    d. credit of $1,530.

_____33. The deposit receipt would be shown on the closing statement of the seller as a
    a. debit of $3,000.
    b. credit of $3,000.
    c. debit of $1,500.
    d. none of the above.

_____34. The state transfer tax will be shown as a
    a. debit of $7.20.
    b. credit of $7.20.
    c. debit of $7.20 and a credit of $3.60.
    d. debit of $3.60 and a credit of $7.20.

_____35. The balance due the seller would be entered as a
    a. credit of $1,757.19.
    b. credit of $2,100.96.
    c. debit of $1,757.19.
    d. debit of $2,196.00.

B. Closing Statement to the Buyer

_____36. The purchase price would be shown as a
    a. debit of $28,500.
    b. debit of $25,500.
    c. credit of $28,500.
    d. credit of $25,500.

_____37. On the closing statement to the buyer, the mortgage assumption would be shown as a
    a. credit of $21,325.
    b. debit of $3,175.
    c. credit of $24,500.
    d. debit of $24,500.

_____38. In preparing the closing statement to the buyer, you would enter the property tax prorate as a
   a. debit of $80.57.
   b. credit of $80.57.
   c. debit of $161.04.
   d. credit of $161.04.

_____39. Prepaid rent is entered as a
   a. $20.83 debit.
   b. $20.83 credit.
   c. debit of $125.88.
   d. credit of $125.88.

_____40. The balance due from the buyer is shown as a
   a. credit of $1,273.92.
   b. debit of $1,273.92.
   c. debit of $29,001.21.
   d. credit of $29,001.21.

C. The Cash Reconciliation Statement

_____41. The earnest money deposit of $3,000 is shown as
   a. a disbursement.
   b. a receipt.
   c. part of the real estate commission on the statement to the seller.
   d. a credit after deducting the real estate commission.

_____42. The check for the balance from the buyer
   a. of $1,273.92 is entered as a receipt.
   b. is entered as a disbursement of $4,273.92.
   c. is entered as a disbursement of $1,757.19.
   d. is entered as a receipt of $4,757.19.

_____43. Expenses listed on the cash reconciliation statement are added to other disbursements and total
   a. $1,757.19.
   b. $4,273.92.
   c. $4,167.52 less prepaid taxes.
   d. $4,167.52 in addition to prepaid taxes.

_____44. Expenses entered on the cash reconciliation statement
   a. include office expenses incurred by the broker.
   b. include salesman's share of the real estate commission.
   c. are copied from entries on the seller and buyer closing statements.
   d. are prepared for distribution to both the buyer and seller.

_____45. According to the cash reconciliation statement, the

    a. net real estate commission earned is $4,273.92 less the check to the seller of $1,757.19.

    b. real estate broker earns a commission of $1,273.92 plus the $3,000.00 deposit.

    c. net commission is equal to $1,710.00 plus the check for the balance of $1,273.92.

    d. none of the above.

IV. *Closing Statement: Accumulated Deduction Method.*

Using the same problem, answer the following questions based on the accumulated deduction closing statement. Prepare a closing statement following the accumulated deduction method. See the Answer Key.

_____46. The balance due the seller is shown as

    a. a credit to purchaser of $984.39.

    b. a credit to the seller of $984.39.

    c. a credit to purchaser of $1,757.19.

    d. a debit to the seller of $1,757.19.

_____47. Under the "Escrow Memorandum," you would

    a. credit the amount received from the seller of $984.39.

    b. record the total received from the purchaser of $984.39.

    c. enter the total received from purchaser as $1,273.92.

    d. enter the total received from purchaser as $2,227.20.

_____48. The amount received from the seller will include the first mortgage less the

    a. real estate commission of $1,710.00.

    b. title insurance expense of $135.00.

    c. recording fees for the warranty deed and second mortgage of $30.00.

    d. none of the above.

_____49. Credits to the seller would include the

    a. purchase price of $28,500.00 and prepaid insurance of $211.67.

    b. purchase price of $28,500.00 and the earnest money of $3,000.00.

    c. prepaid insurance of $211.67 and mortgage liens of $24,500.00.

    d. credit to the purchaser of $28,711.67.

_____50. The check to the seller for the balance of the purchase price equals

    a. the balance due to the seller and the earnest money deposit of $3,000.00.

    b. the total received of seller, $2,227.20 less total received from the purchaser of $1,273.92.

    c. the total received from the purchaser.

    d. $1,757.19.

ANSWER KEY

1. (d)	14. (b)	27. (a)	39. (b)
2. (d)	15. (b)	28. (a)	40. (a)
3. (d)	16. (d)	29. (b)	41. (b)
4. (b)	17. (a)	30. (b)	42. (a)
5. (d)	18. (c)	31. (a)	43. (b)
6. (b)	19. (b)	32. (b)	44. (c)
7. (a)	20. (b)	33. (d)	45. (d)
8. (b)	21. (d)	34. (a)	46. (d)
9. (d)	22. (a)	35. (c)	47. (c)
10. (b)	23. (b)	36. (a)	48. (d)
11. (a)	24. (d)	37. (a)	49. (a)
12. (c)	25. (b)	38. (b)	50. (d)
13. (b)	26. (c)		

Closing Statement for Seller

Name of Seller: Mr. and Mrs. Jerry W. Best
Legal Description:
Closing Date: March 25, 19＿＿

Real and Personal Property	Debits	Credits
Purchase price of real and personal property..........................		$28,500.00
Mortgages and Liens		
First mortgage................................	$21,325.00	
Second mortgage............................	3,175.00	
Street assessment...........................	450.00	
Prorated Charges		
Property taxes................................	80.57	
Insurance.....................................		211.67
Rent...	20.83	
Interest on mortgage........................	125.88	
Closing Expenses		
Real estate commission......................	1,710.00	
Preparation of warranty deed................	10.00	
Transfer tax..................................	7.20	
Legal fees....................................	50.00	
Balance due seller...........................	1,757.19	
Total................................	$28,711.67	$28,711.67

Closing Statement for Buyer

Name of Buyer: Mr. and Mrs. John K. Rich
Legal Description:
Closing Date: March 25, 19 _____

Real and Personal Property	Debits	Credits
Purchase price of real and personal property...................................	$28,500.00	
Earnest money deposit........................		$ 3,000.00
Mortgages and Liens		
First mortgage................................		21,325.00
Second mortgage.............................		3,175.00
Prorated Charges		
Property taxes................................		80.57
Insurance....................................	211.67	
Rent..		20.83
Interest on mortgage.........................		125.88
Closing Expenses		
Title insurance...............................	175.00	
Preparation of second mortgage and promissory note............................	25.00	
Recording warranty deed.....................	15.00	
Recording mortgage..........................	15.00	
Intangible tax................................	9.53	
Legal fees....................................	50.00	
Balance due from buyer......................		1,273.92
Total.................................	$29,001.20	$29,001.20

Cash Reconciliation Statement

Name of Seller: Mr. and Mrs. Jerry W. Best
Name of Buyer: Mr. and Mrs. John K. Rich
Legal Description:
Date of Closing: March 25, 19 _____

From the Buyer	Receipts	Disbursements
Earnest money deposit......................	$3,000.00	
Check for balance...........................	1,273.92	
To the seller.................................		$1,757.19
Expenses		
Street assessment...........................		450.00
Real estate commission......................		1,710.00
Warranty deed...............................		10.00
Transfer tax.................................		7.20
Title insurance..............................		175.00
Preparation of second mortgage and promissory note............................		25.00
Recording warranty deed....................		15.00
Recording mortgage..........................		15.00
Intangible tax................................		9.53
Legal fees, buyer............................		50.00
Legal fees, seller............................		50.00
Total.................................	$4,273.92	$4,273.92

Accumulated Deduction Closing Statement

Jerry W. Best   John K. Rich
_____   _____
Seller   Buyer

1042 River Drive
_____

		Property Description	
		Credit to Purchaser	Credit to Seller
1.	Purchase Price:...........................		$28,500.00
2.	Earnest Money............................	$ 3,000.00	
3.	Outstanding Liens assumed by purchaser:		
	(a) First Mortgage.......................	21,325.00	
	(b) Second Mortgage....................	3,175.00	
4.	Adjusted (Pro-rated) Items:		
	(a) Accrued property taxes for present year......................	80.57	
	(b) Prepaid insurance....................		211.67
	(c) Prepaid rent.........................	20.83	
	(d) Interest on mortgage.................	125.88	
5.	Balance due seller........................	984.39	
	Totals.............................	$28,711.67	$28,711.67

Escrow Memorandum

Received from *Purchaser* money for the following purposes:
1. Balance due seller as per statement.................... $ 984.39
2. Title insurance... 175.00
3. Preparation of second mortgage and promissory
   note... 25.00
4. Recording warranty deed................................ 15.00
5. Recording second mortgage............................. 15.00
6. Intangible tax... 9.53
7. Legal fees... 50.00

    Total Received from Purchaser.................... $1,273.92

Received from *Seller* money for the following purposes:
1. Real estate commission................................. $1,710.00
2. Preparation of warranty deed........................... 10.00
3. Transfer tax.. 7.20
4. Legal fees... 50.00
5. Street assessment..................................... 450.00

    Total Received of Seller........................... $2,227.20
    Check to Seller for balance of purchase
      price.. 1,757.19
    Total ($984.39 + $3,000.00)........................ $3,984.39

SUGGESTED ADDITIONAL READING

Galaty, Fillmore W.; Allaway, Wellington J.; and Kyle, Robert C. *Modern Real Estate Practice*. 6th ed. Chicago: Real Estate Education Corp., 1973, chaps. 23 and 24.

O'Donnell, Paul T., and Maleady, Eugene L. *Principles of Real Estate*. Philadelphia, Pa.: W. B. Saunders Co., 1975, Appendix A.

Semenow, Robert W. *Questions and Answers on Real Estate*. 8th ed. Englewood Cliffs, N.J.: Prentice-Hall, Inc., 1975, chap. 12.

Unger, Maurice A. *Real Estate*. 5th ed. Cincinnati, O.: South-Western Publishing Co., 1974, chap. 23.

10

Commercial and Residential Leases

It is difficult to operate in the real estate business without a working knowledge of leases. In this chapter we will describe leases, rental adjustment clauses, techniques of appraising leased estates, and the more common lease terms. Finally, the chapter closes with a discussion of new landlord-tenant legislation. Familiarity with these points is necessary to the successful management, development, and marketing of real estate under lease.

THE ROLE OF LEASES

There are circumstances in which either the owner or the prospective tenant are virtually compelled to use leases. The owner may be restrained by institutional policy, or legal restrictions on the sale of property; income tax regulations may recommend leases as an alternative to a sale. During periods of capital shortages, tenants use leases as a financing device. In still other instances, the tenant has no alternative to leasing—if he or she wants the right to use a selected property that meets his or her needs. Then there are certain financial advantages of leasing that contrast to the ordinary sale and mortgage. In this respect, owners and tenants view leases quite differently, depending on the financial effect of leases on their operation.

Owner-Lessor Objectives

Certain owners must lease. The landed estates of Hawaii that are legally prohibited from selling land, for example, must lease. Much of the land owned by individual Indians and tribes held in trust by the federal government is similarly restricted. An act of Congress is required before tribes may sell part of an Indian reservation. Public utilities and timber companies hold extensive acreages in support of their operations. If the land is adaptable to multiple-purpose use, these companies may lease land for recreational and urban use. Besides these institutional and policy restraints, there are significant advantages to leasing property.

Owners avoid capital gains by leasing. If the property is sold, the individual or corporation (assuming appreciation on the site and improvements) is subject to a federal capital gains tax. If the land has been held for a long period and the property has substantially appreciated, then the maximum capital gain tax will apply against the sales price. Hence, leasing is a means of postponing or avoiding the capital gains tax.

With leases, owners may create incomes comparable to an annuity. The owner may select a tenant who meets his or her investment criteria. Rather than develop a commercial site for his or her own business purposes, an owner may lease a site to a reputable nationwide company. The financial status of the tenant determines the stability of income.

Tenant-constructed improvements benefit leased property. The owner acquires title to improvements (with or without paying some compensation) when the lease terminates. For example, a warehouse constructed on leased land reverts to the owner at the end of a 25-year lease. In this case, part of the inducement to lease includes the improvements to be constructed by the tenant as negotiated in the lease. In other words, the owner looks not only to rental income but to property betterment realized at the end of the lease. Agricultural property is frequently leased to tenants who agree to construct complex and expensive irrigation and drainage systems as part of the rental agreement. Title to the land improvements reverts to the owner when the lease ends.

Competent tenant operation enhances the value of property. In fact, the owner may be advised to subsidize a tenant who agrees to risk capital in a new site if it improves the potential of surrounding property. In this respect, the owner utilizes the expertise of the tenant and minimizes his or her own management responsibility. It is much easier, and even prudent, to let a knowledgeable tenant develop a new shopping center, for example, than to attempt to master the intricacies of such an involved operation.

Leases create direct financial advantages. First, vacant land may be more marketable if it is leased by a nationally-known reputable tenant who occupies the premises under a long-term lease. In effect, the potential buyer buys land with a paying tenant, not merely vacant land that requires development. The lease converts a vacant, unproductive property interest to an identifiable income property.

Second, the owner secures the benefit of tenant capital and financing ability. If the site is a potential shopping center or industrial site, it may be advantageous to work with an experienced tenant who has the knowledge and capital resources to improve the property and thus earn the highest possible land income.

Third, for buildings subject to a lease, tenant improvements, maintenance and repair, in a sense, are a form of income in that the tenant maintains the property and indirectly enhances property value. In contrast to an owner operation, tenant expenses and maintenance are recoverable by the owner in the form of capital gains. Conversely, if the owner is responsible for repairs and maintenance, they are deductible expenses, even though their expenditure tends to maintain or even increase capital value. While the main lease advantages to the owner recommend leasing, advantages accruing to the tenant encourage leasing even more strongly.

Tenant-Lessee Objectives

In real estate transactions, the main objective is to acquire exclusive rights to use real property. For the most part, the two main alternatives are (1) a purchase with mortgage financing, or (2) a long-term lease. Provided the terms of the lease are fair, the lease may be the better financing alternative.

Tenants secure the equivalent of a 100 percent loan equal to the value of the leased property. If the site in question covers land of high value, this fact in itself recommends a lease. Institutional lenders are restricted by legally enforceable loan-to-value ratios. In addition, institutional lenders —with few exceptions—are prohibited from lending money on vacant land. An owner willing to accept a long term lease on land gives the tenant a financial advantage largely unavailable from other sources. In sum, the lease is equivalent to a 100 percent loan: the rent substitutes for the mortgage payment.

Rent is deductible as an expense. In essence, businesses recover occupancy costs because of the rental allowance. Suppose, for example, the lease in question covers a $1,000,000 site and $100,000 land improvement (such as paving for a parking lot). If a prospective client purchased the property, he could only depreciate, for income taxes, the $100,000 cost of the land improvement. Only a small proportion of the site and building value would be income tax deductible. By leasing, the rent would be totally deductible as an operating expense. The financial advantages of rent deductibility constitute a major incentive to negotiate long-term leases.

Leases minimize tenant equity. If a tenant combines mortgage financing with the lease, he minimizes his equity and increases the rate of return on invested capital. For example, assume a building cost of $225,-000 and a land value of $75,000. Assume also that the owner is willing to subordinate the land to a first mortgage to construct a building. With a mortgage of 20 years, 9 percent interest, and a 66⅔ percent mortgage, the return on equity may increase substantially under a lease.

Table 10–1 reveals that under conventional mortgage financing, the return on an equity investment of $100,000 is 23.1 percent. The example is based on a net income to the owner of $45,000. Without a lease subordination clause, the loan is restricted to a maximum of $150,000 (⅔ of $225,000). In this case the return on equity increased by 5 percentage points. However, with lease subordination, the equity amount is reduced to $25,000, with a consequence that the return on an equity

TABLE 10–1

Leasehold Financing Compared to Conventional Financing

Item	Mortgage Financing	Leasing without Subordination	Leasing with Subordination
1. Minimum Loan...............	$200,000	$150,000	$200,000
2. Equity........................	100,000	75,000	25,000
3. Net Income to owner.........	45,000	45,000	45,000
4. Ground rent..................	—	7,500	7,500
5. Mortgage Service (20 years, 9% rounded).........	21,909	16,431	21,909
6. Total Charges.................	21,909	23,931	29,409
7. Net after rent and mortgage..................	23,091	21,070	15,591
8. Return on Equity.............	23.1% ($ 23,091/ $100,000)	28.1% ($ 21,070/ $ 75,000)	62.4% ($ 15,591/ $ 25,000)

investment of $25,000 increases substantially—to 62.4 percent during the first year.

Add to these advantages the fact that a *leased location may represent the best site available.* Comparable sites of poorer quality may represent a less desirable option even though the purchase price is quite favorable. Furthermore, with a shortage of capital, the tenant may devote scarce capital to business or commercial operations without committing capital to a long-term real estate investment. Given these advantages of leasing, the next relevant issue relates to rental adjustment clauses.

RENTAL ADJUSTMENT CLAUSES

With the expectation of rising rents, owners hesitate to commit high-valued real estate to long-term contracts providing for fixed annual rents. As a result, rental adjustment clauses in their various forms are incorporated into most long-term lease agreements, say over five years. Such clauses have a two-fold objective: (1) they provide for higher rent as the value of the dollar declines, and (2) the owner recoups higher rents as site productivity increases over the lease. Examples follow of the more widely-used clauses and their objectives.

Graduated Rents

Graduated rent clauses, sometimes referred to as step-rate rents, provide for a fixed rent schedule adjusted upward (or downward) at stated intervals. The rationale behind specific increases rests on some estimate of the manner in which rents and prices will change over a long-term lease, say 25 years or more. As applied to property under development, the owner (and tenant) anticipate that the value of the site, and therefore rents, will increase as the property undergoes development.

To demonstrate, consider the step-rate ground rent proposed for a 6,359-acre development in Colorado that was set up on a schedule of rents over 25 years. Rents graduated steeply from $22,200 per year over the first five years to $193,900 per year for each of the last five years. The graduated rent schedule is shown below.

Term	Annual Rent
1st 5 years	$ 22,200
2nd 5 years	41,300
3rd 5 years	60,400
4th 5 years	98,500
5th 5 years	193,900

It was anticipated that the value of the property would increase with development to justify the proposed rent schedule.

Though based on a rational premise, step-rate leases may be hazardous both to the owner and tenant. Rents based on some anticipated change in the price level are risky. The risk increases with each additional year. Tenants and owners are gambling that the rent level proposed in a step-rate lease will move in sympathy with price levels.

Rents graduated according to the Colorado example just given further assume that development progresses to a point that justifies the proposed schedule. This is also a hazardous assumption. If the development is underestimated, the tenant secures the advantage and the owner has not accomplished his lease objectives. If development estimates are too optimistic, the tenant defaults; the rent schedule has not served its purpose.

Probably the best application of a step-rate rent clause covers newly-developed property which is unproductive in its early years. Suppose, for example, that the fair market rent of a site is $10,000 per year. The de-

veloper proposes a 25-year lease. Economic studies show that it is unlikely that the property will realize minimum expectations before the end
of the third year of development. In this instance the owner may elect
to subsidize the tenant during the initial, unproductive years of the
enterprise. A rent constituting a fractional return to the owner would
be appropriate, say $1,000 or $3,000 per year, for the first three years,
after which time the rent would increase to $10,000 per year, with other
rental adjustment techniques to be used over the succeeding 22 years.

Index Leases

So-called index leases provide for rents adjusted according to changes
in a price index. Initially, the rent is negotiated on the basis of current
property values and rents acceptable at the beginning of the lease. From
this point on, rents are adjusted according to a selected price index such
as the consumer price index, the wholesale price index, the implicit price
deflator, or an index of construction costs.

A price index is a relative number showing the change in purchasing
power of money over time. In the simplest case, assume that in the base
year—the year chosen to start—a commodity sells for $1 per unit. If a
year later, the price changes to $1.10 per unit, the price increase is equal
to 10 percent [($1.10 − $1.00) (price increase)/$1.00 (base period)]. The
corresponding index would be 110. Another way of showing price changes
is to calculate the decline in purchasing power. In the preceding example,
$1 at the beginning of the year would purchase 1 unit. A year later the
same $1 would purchase .91 of the same unit. The declining purchasing
power is found by the reciprocal of the price index, in this case 1.00/1.10
= .91.

In practice, price adjustments are made only if the selected price index
moves a material amount, say 5 percentage points or so. In other cases,
the rent is subject to readjustment according to a selected price index at
intervals of three years, five years or other relatively short periods. The
language used to adjust monthly rent in a 99-year lease beginning in
December 1972 is shown below. In this example, taken from a Palm
Springs, California lease, changes in the consumer price index control the
rent adjustment.

> The BASIC MONTHLY RENT shall be adjusted in the following
> manner to reflect increases and decreases in the cost of living as set forth
> in said Index, or if there be no such Index, then by the most nearly
> comparable successor to the Index, adjusted to the December 1972
> base: The amount of the increased or decreased rental shall be deter-
> mined by multiplication of the BASIC MONTHLY RENT provided
> for in Paragraph 5.1 by a fraction of which the numerator shall be the
> Index number for the October preceding each January 1st, or the May
> preceding each July 1st, whichever is applicable, and the denominator

shall be the Index figure for December 1972. The product of such multiplication shall be the amount of the monthly sums to be paid hereunder for the succeeding year until the next computation provided for hereunder shall be made. Any increase in the BASIC MONTHLY RENTAL so obtained shall be payable in addition to and with the BASIC MONTHLY RENTAL.

The price index maintains the relative purchasing power effective at the beginning of the lease. Local real estate values and rents move independently of general price levels. With a price index lease there is no allowance for anticipated changes in land productivity that vary from general price changes. Such leases tend to maintain the status quo of the tenant and owner with respect to their position at the time of lease negotiation.

Revaluation Leases

Some authorities strongly reject reappraisal leases. They call for periodic appraisals to adjust rent over a long-term lease. Normally the lessor and lessee each select an appraiser and the two appraisers select a third. The rent recommended by the three-member board serves as the basis of negotiation.

A possible conflict arises because the owner may believe that location determines the rent. As the location assumes greater value over the life of the lease, he or she attributes the increase in rent as a normal reward for ownership. In contrast, the tenant believes his or her capital and management contribute to the success of the development and that he or she alone is entitled to benefits of increased land productivity. The failure of the parties to accept findings of the arbitration board can lead to expensive litigation.

The conflict tends to be minimized if revaluation is postponed for a fairly long period. Because lenders are reluctant to accept revaluation leases over the life of the mortgage, revaluation clauses may restrict revaluation at the end of 25 years or more. The rental adjustment clause effective for FHA financing of long-term residential leases in Hawaii provides for the following revaluation clause:

> Whenever this lease provides that the annual rent payable by Lessee for any period of the term hereof shall be determined by appraisal, such rent shall be the product of the then prevailing rate of return for similar lands (but not less than the then prime rate of interest in Hawaii) multiplied by the then market value of the demised land exclusive of improvements thereon, first deducting from such market value the then unamortized cost to Lessee of $_____ as the prorata share attributable to said premises for off-site subdivision improvements such as streets, sewers, water facilities and utilities in the tract

of which said premises constitute part, amortized on a straight-line basis over 75 years from the date of commencement of this lease, and such return and market value shall be determined by three recognized real estate appraisers, one to be appointed by each of the parties hereto, and Lessor and Lessee shall each promptly name one such appraiser and give written notice thereof to the other party, and in case of failure of either party so to do within ten days after such notice by the other the party naming the first appraiser may apply to any person then sitting as judge of the Circuit Court of the First Circuit of the State of Hawaii for appointment of a second appraiser, and the two appraisers thus appointed in either manner shall appoint a third appraiser, and in case of their failure so to do within ten days after appointment of the second appraiser either party may have the third appraiser appointed by such judge, and the three appraisers so appointed shall proceed to determine the matters in question, and the decision of said appraisers or a majority of them shall be final, conclusive and binding on both parties hereto, and Lessor and Lessee shall each pay one-half of all proper costs and expenses of such appraisal other than attorneys' fees.

A long-term lease approved by the Secretary of the Interior provides for rental adjustment at the end of 35 years and at each 10-year interval thereafter: "Rent shall be increased or decreased upon a reappraisal provided that the basic rental shall not exceed 35 percent of the base period and that the increase or decrease in subsequent rents at the end of each 10 year period shall exceed 10 percent of the previous rental period." In other words, rental adjustments are restricted to a 1 percent per year change.

Rental revaluation clauses tied to a given percentage increase defeat the purposes of a revaluation clause. Similar lease adjustments based on reappraisals limit the rental increase to a stated percentage of the reappraisal value. Though reappraisal adjustment clauses are subject to many variations, there appears to be a tendency to postpone revaluation to fairly long periods (i.e., 10, 15 or 25 years).

Percentage Rental Clauses

Commercial leases frequently tie rents to gross receipts. Usually some minimum rent is established after which a percentage of gross receipts is paid to the owner.

On its face, a percentage lease seems quite workable. As gross receipts increase, the owner secures added benefits of site productivity. At the same time, the tenant pays increased rents only as his receipts and profits rise. Both parties benefit.

Note, however, that percentage rents are not particularly adapted to short-term leases. There is little point in undertaking the administrative burden of percentage rents if the rent is renegotiable over relatively short periods; for example, in leases limited to three years. Percentage rents require auditing procedures and therefore are difficult to apply to small businesses, one-man shops, and the like. They are difficult to enforce and they do not apply to businesses based on personal services.

Custom and the economics of retailing have led to percentage rents being classified according to the type of business. Generally speaking, the *high-volume*, low mark-up retailers pay relatively low percentage rents in contrast to *low-volume*, high mark-up businesses, who pay a higher percentage of gross receipts. The following sample list of percentage rents applying to selected businesses shows how percentage rents vary by type of business in community shopping centers (the source is the Urban Land Institute):

Tenant	Median Percentage Rent
Supermarket	1.29
Meat	3.60
Bakeries	6.00
Costume Jewelry	9.52
Liquors and Wines	4.00
Key Shops	18.77
Gifts	7.98
Camera Shops	5.25

There have been notable applications of percentage rents to net ground leases. Suppose the owner dedicates vacant land to a long-term development, and the tenant agrees to construct a building for sublease to multiple tenants. As part of such an agreement, the owner generally requires a minimum rent in addition to a stated percentage of subrents. The subrents may apply to office buildings, motel-hotel operations, and other tenants. For example, a 40-acre resort development constructed on leased land in Palm Springs, California, provided for percentage rents as follows:

Minimum Annual Rent
1st 2 years:	$13,000
Next 3 years:	$20,000
Next 55 years:	$26,000

Percentage Rents on Subleases
Apartment rents: 5%
Subleases of residential lots: 35%
Liquor bar receipts: 2.5%
Restaurant sales: 2%
Hotel room rents: 5%

On balance, percentage rents are preferred to other rental adjustment clauses. They are objective, they are based on the tenant's ability to pay, and they tend to move with the changing value of the dollar and land productivity. Against these advantages are the costs of administration (e.g., auditing the tenant books, annual accounting reports, and the like). Further, they are not applicable to numerous businesses not engaged in retail sales.

THE VALUATION OF LEASED ESTATES

The real estate expert contributes to his client's welfare if he understands calculations for the valuation of estates under lease. In actual practice, most cases fall into one of six categories. Knowing the six categories of lease valuation enables the practitioner to handle complexities of lease negotiation. The first four cases relate to valuation of the owner's estate identified as the leased fee. The interest of the tenant or lessee is represented by the leasehold estate. The last two cases deal with two common examples of leasehold estate values.

Valuation of the Leased Fee

Case 1 below is followed by cases covering graduated leases and improvement leases. The last case below discusses leases calling for payments of the rent in advance.

Case 1. Leased Fee Valuation. For valuation purposes, the owner has two economic rights: (1) the right to collect contract rent, and (2) the right to recapture the property at the end of the lease—the reversionary value. The leased fee value is equal to the present worth of these rights.

To illustrate, assume that the owner grants a five-year lease on a $100,000 site for a net annual rent of $10,000. Assuming a capitalization rate of 9 percent, the value of the leased fee would be equal to (1) the present worth of contract rent, and (2) the present worth of the reversion—the right to a $100,000 site postponed for five years. The present worth of an income over five years is found by multiplying the annual rent times the present worth of 1 per annum factor for five years (explained in Chapter 13). It will be recalled also that the present worth of a sum postponed is found by multiplying the sum times the present worth of $1. Accordingly, the value of the leased fee is $103,887. Here are the calculations:

1. The present worth of the contract rent:
   $10,000 × 3.8897 (the present worth of $1 per annum
   for 5 years, 9 percent).................................. $ 38,897

2. The present worth of the reversion:
   $100,000 × .6499 (the present worth of $1, 5 years,
   9 percent)... 64,990

   Value of leased fee...................................... $103,887

The example shows that the right to $10,000 over five years has a present worth of $38,897. Added to this is the value of the property that reverts to the owner at the end of the lease. The sum of $100,000 today postponed five years is worth $64,990. The two calculations produce the present worth of the leased fee estate, $103,887.

Case 2. Graduated Leases. To illustrate this case, assume that the rent schedule is graduated over 20 years in 5-year increments according to the following schedule:

```
$10,000.................. 1st  5 years
 20,000.................. 2nd  5 years
 40,000.................. 3rd  5 years
 50,000.................. 4th  5 years
  Total..................      20 years
```

Using a 9 percent capitalization rate and assumed value of $100,000 for the site at the end of 20 years, the value of the leased fee is calculated as follows:

1. Value of contract rent:
    $10,000 × 3.8897.. $ 38,897
    20,000 × (6.4177 − 3.8897)............................... 50,560
    40,000 × (8.0607 − 6.4177)............................... 65,720
    50,000 × (9.1285 − 8.0607)............................... 53,390
                                                              $208,567

2. Add value of land reversion:
    $100,000 × .1784 (present worth of $1 postponed 20
      years, 9 percent)...................................... $ 17,840
                    Value of leased fee...................... $226,407

The innovation introduced in this example is the calculation of present worth of 1 per annum factors. The 3.8897 factor, representing the present worth of 1 per annum, means that you would pay $3.89 for the right to a dollar income payable at the end of the year over five years. However, income received over the next five years is postponed for five years. To find the value of the right to receive $20,000 annually over five years—but postponed for five years—the factor for five years must be subtracted from the factor for 10 years (6.4177 − 3.8897). The same procedure is used in dealing with incomes in succeeding five-year increments. These calculations show that the lease income has a present worth of $208,567. Adding the reversionary value gives the value of the leased fee estate, $226,407. The assumption must be made that the land and improvements have a value at the end of the lease.

Case 3. Improvement Leases. Suppose the owner leased land for ten years at which time tenant constructed improvements which revert to the owner. With a $10,000 annual rent payable over ten years, a present land value of $100,000, and a building with an estimated worth of $100,000 at the end of ten years, one additional assumption is necessary.

If the building is worth $100,000 ten years from now, that sum is postponed for ten years. Therefore, the problem is to calculate the present worth of $100,000 postponed for ten years. Use a 9 percent discount rate.

1. Value of contract rent:
   $10,000 × 6.4177 (present worth of an annual income
   of $1 for 10 years discounted at 9 percent)........... $ 64,177

2. Land Reversion:
   $100,000 × .4224 (present worth of $1 postponed 10
   years, 9 percent discount)......................... $ 42,240

3. Improvement value at end of ten years:
   $100,000 × .4224...................................... $ 42,240
   Value of leased fee............................... $148,657

The right to the contract rent of $10,000 per year has a present worth of $64,177. Adding the present worth of the right to land of $100,000 and a $100,000 improvement reverting to the owner at the end of the lease, produces the value of the leased fee estate, $148,657. In this improvement lease, value was given to the improvement that reverted to the owner at the end of the lease. The discounted value of this sum is part of the leased-fee value.

Case 4. Advanced Rent.   To help in explaining leased-fee values, it was assumed that rents are payable at the end of the year. This is seldom the case. Most leases provide for rent in advance. Hence, to calculate the value of a leased fee, an adjustment must be made for rent payable in advance. Assume the facts of the preceding example and assume that the $10,000 annual rent is payable at the beginning of the year. The leased fee value is $112,192.

1. Value of $10,000 received at the beginning of the year.... $ 10,000

2. Value of $10,000 received for 9 years, $10,000 × 5.9952
   (present worth of $1 per annum received over 9
   years, 9 percent discount)............................. $ 59,952

3. Value of reversion:
   $100,000 × .4224 (present worth of $1 discounted
   for 10 years, 9 percent).................................. $ 42,240
   Value of leased fee............................. $112,192

Because $10,000 is paid on the effective date of the lease, add the $10,000 to the leased fee calculation. In other words, the present worth of $100,000 now is $10,000. With this initial payment, the owner has the right to nine additional $10,000 payments. The 5.9952 multiplier in the second step represents the present worth of the right to $1 payable at the end of the year for nine years. Add to these sums the value of the reversion, $42,240.

The rule to follow with advance rent payments includes three steps: (1) reduce the period of discount by one year; (2) add the rent for the first period and discount the present worth of rent received for the balance of the term (one year less than the lease term); and (3) add the reversionary value of land and building.

The Valuation of Leasehold Estates

The two main valuation problems cover the conventional leasehold valuation and the valuation of subleases. In the first instance, the value relates to property purchased and sold subject to a lease, while the second issue covers the valuation of a sandwich lease. Cases 5 and 6 illustrate the valuation of these lease estates.

Case 5. Leasehold Estate Valuation. The typical problem in valuing the tenant's interest relates to the value of his estate over the unexpired time remaining under the lease. The issue is further complicated by tenant improvements which have value in use over the lease and which do not revert to the owner until termination of the lease. To illustrate this case, assume a contract rent of $10,000, a tenant-constructed building of $100,000 with an economic life of 20 years and economic rent of $20,000 and a 9 percent discount rate with ten years remaining on the original lease. What is the value of the leasehold interest?

Recall that the tenant has exclusive right to use the property over the remaining term of the lease. If the market or economic rent is $20,000 per year and the lease calls for an annual payment of $10,000, the tenant receives the equivalent of a $10,000 annual income. Though not receiving this income directly, he or she has the use of property with a use value of $20,000 which has economic value.

Moreover, the tenant has the right to use a building which under our assumptions has another ten years of remaining life. In this case we are assuming that the value of unexpired improvements is worth $50,000 (the depreciated value). Here is calculation of the leasehold interest:

The present worth of the difference between
economic rent and contract rent:
($20,000 − 10,000) × 6.4177............................... $ 64,177
Value of unexpired improvements..................... $ 50,000
Value of leasehold interest........................... $114,177

Under these assumptions the tenant's right to use the property for an additional ten years has a present worth of $64,177. This value follows since market rent is considerably above the contract rent provided by the lease. In addition, he has the right to use a $50,000 structure for another ten years. Adding the market value of the structure produces a leasehold interest value of $114,177.

Case 6. Sublease Valuation. If the original tenant subleases to a second tenant, a new estate is created. The original tenant is said to hold the sandwich lease—he or she is sandwiched between the owner and the second tenant. To value the sandwich lease, assume the following facts: a 50-year lease requiring a contract annual rent of $10,000, a land value of $100,000, and a tenant who subleases the premises for a net rent of $20,000. What is the value of the sandwich lease with *10 years remaining* in the master or 50-year lease? To value the sandwich lease calculate the difference between the original rent and the rent to the subtenant.

$$(\$20,000 - \$10,000) \times 6.4177 \ldots \$64,177$$

Since the original tenant has the right of exclusive use for the remaining ten years, he enjoys a net $10,000 advantage each year. Under a 9 percent capitalization rate, the value of this right (the sandwich lease) is $64,177. It is assumed that the original tenant has no reversionary interest at the expiration of the lease.

In each example, the same capitalization rate was applied. In reality, the capitalization rate is subject to an appraisal opinion. Frequently the rate must be varied to reflect the differences in the certainty and stability of income with respect to the interest of the lessee, lessor and subtenants. It is also assumed that the terms of the lease do not affect the valuation of the leased estates.

COMMON LEASE TERMS

The format of long-term leases follows no set pattern. Much depends on the type of property and negotiations between owner and tenant. Some corporations enter into complex leases with a four-page document. In other cases the parties negotiate leases taking up to 90 pages of type-written copy. Even the order of presentation follows no final pattern. Lease terms fall in six subject groups. For convenience, we will discuss them in these groups, though the presentation of materials in an actual lease may be in different order.

Further comments are directed only to general practices: The comments do not constitute universal legal acceptance. Leases are prepared by legal counsel—the broker only negotiates the terms of agreement—but familiarity with the most common terms encountered in leases is essential to the lease negotiator.

Introductory Terms

The better leases define technical terms used in the lease. For income properties it is critical to define gross receipts for leases using percentage rents. For example, income accruing from credit transactions should be defined. The definition of "gross" usually excludes sales and excise taxes, merchandise returns, cash refunds, and the sale of business equipment and fixtures. Other technical terms influencing rent interpretation should also be included.

The land description is critical to the lease. In this respect the description should meet all qualifications of deeds and other conveyance documents. The introductory portion identifies parties to the lease, their titles, and their interests.

Financial Terms

A considerable portion of a commercial lease covers the rent liability and circumstances of its collection. In the beginning the lease will state the effective and termination date, the place of rent payment, and the time of payment. Succeeding terms will identify the amount of rent. If percentage rents are provided, considerable attention is paid to annual accounting procedures, which usually require written statements of a certified public accountant and rights to inspect accounting records.

Other financial terms give the owner added security. For fairly large projects the owner may require a corporate surety bond or a penal sum of not less than one year's minimum rent. As an alternative, the tenant may be allowed to deposit government bonds in escrow equal to a year's rent and give power of attorney to dispose of such bonds in the event of default. Bonds are viewed as liquidated damages for the benefit of the owner, subject to the tenant's curing the default.

A related issue covers performance bonds. These apply to leases requiring the tenant to construct buildings on leased ground. The tenant will be asked to provide security guaranteeing completion of the building and the payment of all claims for work performed and materials furnished for construction. This requirement will be satisfied by posting a corporate surety bond in an amount equal to the cost of the building, such a bond to be in effect until the building is completed. As an alternative, the tenant may be allowed to deposit in escrow bonds or cash sufficient to pay the costs of building construction required by the lease. Normally the escrow will provide that not less than 15 percent of such funds will be withheld by the escrow holder until the time for filing of mechanic's and materialmen's liens has expired.

To insure observance of these clauses, the bonding company must be rated as AAA or better according to Best's Insurance Guide. Usually there will be a clause guarding holding over by the tenant. That is, if the tenant does not vacate the premises after termination of the lease, such holding over will not constitute a renewal or extension of the lease.

Terms Relating to Building Improvements

Property developed under a lease creates the maximum income under the highest and best land use. Accordingly, leases control the type of building, its construction, maintenance, and repair. A tenant proposing to lease land over a long term will ordinarily be required to submit architectural plans for approval. In this way the owner insures that the property is developed to its maximum potential.

Plan approval may even include landscaping. A typical clause is illustrated by a long-term lease development in Gleneden, Oregon (Lincoln County), that states:

> It is the desire of Salishan, Inc. to preserve the natural vegetation of Salishan to the greatest extent possible and to preclude the planting of trees, shrubs, lawns and other vegetation therein not indigenous to Salishan.
>
> The lessee shall neither remove from the leased premises any tree, shrub or other vegetation nor shall they plant any new tree, shrub or other vegetation without having first obtained permission in writing of one member of the architectural committee.

Lease terms relating to improvements may include a dollar requirement; that is, the tenant agrees to construct a building at a cost of not less than $1,000,000 to be completed by a stated time. Performance bonds will be required to guarantee completion. This section of the lease will also cover the use of the property which may not be changed without permission of the owner. Generally speaking, these clauses attempt to preserve the character of the property and to insure maximum land use.

Other Financial Rights

A critical issue in lease negotiation relates to the right to sublease. The tenant and the lender will negotiate for the unrestricted right to transfer the leasehold interest or to sublease as required. Most owners prefer to reserve the right of approving subleases. Control over the tenant's right to sublease helps guarantee that only responsible tenants will use the property and that the use of the property will not be in violation of the lease.

The same reasoning applies to an assignment. An assignment represents the transfer of the leasehold interest to another party. In this respect the owner has a similar interest, he or she wants to insure that a new tenant will be financially responsible and will manage the property according to the lease agreement. In an assignment no new estate is created. The assignee assumes the rights and obligations of the assignor. In a sublease, however, the lessee remains responsible to the lessor. Similarly, the sublessee, holding a new estate, is responsible to the original tenant or lessee.

Other miscellaneous financial rights relate to the agreement for utility lines and streets. The tenant generally is required to permit easements for public utilities as required by local agencies. Clauses dealing with property taxes in long-term leases usually hold the owner free from property taxes on leased land and buildings. In some states property taxes must be paid on the leasehold interest, termed the possessory interest, in California.

Insurance Requirements

In ground leases, the lessee is generally required to insure against loss or damage by fire with extended coverage endorsements in an amount equal to the insurable value of buildings. Some leases require the proceeds of insurance funds to be deposited in an escrow with instructions that the deposited funds shall be used to repair, restore, or replace building structures.

Tenants will normally be required to maintain and carry personal liability insurance for property damage and personal injury. A related clause will hold the lessor free from liens and claims resulting from tenant operations.

Other Legal Requirements

The more common lease terms not included in the above categories will include clauses covering the following topics.

Eminent domain	No partnership clause
Arbitration	Obligations of lessee
Default of tenant	Status of subleases
Attorney fees	Payments and notices

Some of these legal qualifications are quite significant. For example, controversies arise if the property is subject to an eminent domain taking. The leasehold interest may have substantial value because of the difference between the economic and contract rent or because of the value of tenant-constructed improvements. In the usual case, the taking authority is not required to divide the award between the lessor and the lessee. The clause dealing with eminent domain tends to anticipate these problems by an agreement covering division of the award in eminent domain.

For partial takings, the question arises as to whether the lease will be continued or, if the property use is affected, a reduction in rent may be justified. Typically, the lease will state that compensation shall be awarded and paid to the lessee or lessor, as their interests may appear. For partial takings, "the lease shall continue as to the remainder thereof, the rent thereafter payable hereunder for the remainder of the term hereof shall be reduced in the proportion that the area of land so taken shall bear to the area hereby leased." Alternatively, the lessee may be given the option to terminate the lease if the taking affects the use and occupancy.

The arbitration and default clauses define the owner-tenant relationship..

In the event of disagreement over terms of the lease and its interpretation, an arbitration board is sometimes provided. The default clause defines terms of the default and describes the rights of the parties in the event of default. The lease will fix liability of attorney fees in the event of litigation, it will state that the lease does not create a partnership between owner and tenant, and it will preserve the status of subleases if the lease is assigned. The clause related to payments and notices identifies a time and place of payment and other notices required by contract.

LANDLORD AND TENANT LEGISLATION

Recent landlord-tenant laws have revised the relationship between landlord and tenants. Residential leases are traced to feudal property law of the middle ages when most leases dealt with rural land. Beginning in the year 1235, tenants were treated as owners of an estate in land. At this time, tenants gained the right to repossession after being ejected by a new purchaser. Leases were considered a conveyance of an estate in land rather than a contract between two parties with mutually dependent covenants of an enforceable contract.

Consequently, as these concepts were carried over to residential leases, under common law it was held (1) the owner had no duty to deliver and maintain premises in a safe and habitable condition. The doctrine of *caveat emptor* (let the buyer beware) prevailed. The tenant could inspect the premises and enter into a rental agreement or look elsewhere. (2) Further, the landlord was under no obligation to repair or keep the premises in a certain condition—unless the lease expressly covered this point. Moreover, if the tenant occupied the premises, he or she continued to be liable for the rent. (3) In addition, courts have held that landlords could mingle security deposits with personal funds because security deposits were believed held under a relationship of debtor and creditor. (4) And finally, at common law the landlord had the right to seize personal property of the tenant as security until the rent was paid. In some jurisdictions the landlord could sell personal property and keep the proceeds.

Proposals to modernize common law developed from the growing concern over the dependency of poor households on rental housing, the inability of low-income families to seek suitable housing because of rising rents, and the unequal bargaining power of landlord and tenant. The problem is illustrated in North Carolina where according to the 1970 census one third of all occupied rental units had one or more plumbing deficiencies —among rental units occupied by nonwhites the proportion reached 46 percent (see Michael A. Stegman and Howard J. Sumka, "The Economics of Landlord/Tenant Reform in Smaller Cities," *Popular Government*, vol. 40, no. 3 (Winter 1975), p. 7).

Accordingly concern over these issues led the National Conference of Commissioners on Uniform State Laws to publish the *Uniform Residential Landlord and Tenant Act* (1972). This publication, referred to as URLTA, served as a model statute for several states. Among the states recently enacting new landlord-tenant acts are Tennessee, Georgia, New York, Alaska, Arizona, Florida, Hawaii, Nebraska, Oregon, and Virginia. These new laws significantly changed landlord and tenant duties.

Landlord Duties

The new landlord-tenant laws that followed URLTA abandoned the view that the landlord-tenant relationship rests on property law. The new view considers the rental agreement as establishing enforceable contractual rights and duties between the landlord and tenant.

Habitable Premises. New legislation such as the Kentucky law enacted in 1975 (*Ky. Rev. Stat. Ann.* Sections 383.505–383.715 [1975]) requires the landlord "to comply with all applicable building and housing codes, to make repairs and to do whatever is necessary to maintain the premises in a fit and habitable state." In addition, the landlord has an obligation to keep all common areas in a clean and safe condition and to maintain in a good and safe working order all electrical, plumbing, sanitary, heating, ventilating, air conditioning, and other mechanical appliances.

By law the landlord must provide running water during the rental term and supply reasonable amounts of heat during the cold season. The implied warranty provisions continue as the landlord's obligation unless the tenant agrees to excuse the landlord's duties in writing, the transaction is made in good faith, and the contract changes are not made to evade statutory duties. Such new statutes represent an *express warranty of habitability* and an enforceable *covenant to repair*.

Security Deposits. The Georgia Landlord-Tenant Act illustrates new legislation affecting security deposits (*Uniform Residential Landlord-Tenant Act*, Senate Bill 472 [1976]). If the lease calls for payment of a security deposit, the landlord must either place the deposit in an escrow account or post a security bond with the Clerk of the Superior Court in the county where the dwelling is located.

Security deposits are defined as money or any other form of security given by a tenant to a landlord to be held by the landlord on behalf of a tenant by virtue of a residential rental agreement. Security deposits include damage deposits, advance rent deposits, and pet deposits. The landlord must notify the tenant in writing of the location and the account number of the escrow account.

Moreover, before tendering a security deposit, tenants must be given a list of any existing damages to the premises. The tenant, after inspecting the dwelling to ascertain the accuracy of the list, then signs the list with the landlord—the list becomes conclusive evidence of existing damage. Tenants may refuse to sign the list but must state in writing the specific items which are in question. Failure to sign either statement precludes the tenant from recovering security deposits.

After termination of occupancy, the landlord must inspect the premises and compile a list of damages. In this instance, the tenant has five days from the date of termination to inspect. Again, both parties must sign the final damage list. In cases of disagreement, the tenant must sign a specific statement detailing items in disagreement. After signing a statement of dissent, the tenant is entitled to file an action to recover that portion of the deposit which he believes to have been wrongfully withheld.

Moreover, within one month the landlord must return the full deposit of the tenant after the lease termination date. Failure to return the deposit requires that the landlord give the tenant a written statement of reasons for withholding the deposit. Landlords improperly withholding deposits are liable for triple the amount plus reasonable attorney fees.

Tenant Duties

Under common law, tenants had an implied obligation to protect the rented premises from waste. Tenants were required to return the premises to the landlord in a substantially undamaged condition except for ordinary wear and tear and free from the willful or neglectful conduct of the tenant.

Tenant Uses. On this point the Kentucky law requires tenants to keep the leased premises clean and safe, to dispose properly of garbage and waste, to keep plumbing facilities as clean as their condition permits, and to use heating, plumbing, sanitary, ventilating, electrical, and other facilities and appliances in a reasonable manner. Similarly, tenants must observe provisions of local building and housing codes that materially affect health and safety.

Similarly the model URLTA prohibits tenants and other persons from disturbing other tenants' peaceful enjoyment of their premises. Disturbed neighboring tenants may bring action against the offending tenant. In short, these laws make all tenants subject to a uniform duty not to disturb other tenants and give all landlords and tenants uniform remedies against tenants who cause disturbances. This provision substitutes for the common law arrangement under which tenants who caused disturbances were subject to eviction by a landlord under terms of a properly drafted lease.

Access. Under common law that considered the lease a conveyance instrument, the landlord had no right to enter premises to make repairs or to inspect premises. The model URLTA imposes a duty on tenants to allow reasonable access by the landlord to make inspections, repairs, alterations, or show premises to prospective tenants, purchasers, or contractors. It requires landlords to give tenants two days' advance notice before entering premises except in emergencies. The tenant's refusal to allow reasonable entry or the landlord's abuse of access rights allows either party to seek injunctive relief, terminate the lease, or sue for damages and reasonable attorneys' fees.

The Payment of Rent. States that follow the common law rule recognize the fundamental obligation of the tenant to pay rent. In the absence of agreement on rent, common law implics that the tenant must pay a reasonable rent. The Uniform Residential Landlord-Tenant Act codifies this rule, providing that the tenant shall pay as rent "the fair rental value for the use and occupancy of the dwelling unit."

(1) *Time of Payment.* Further, if the parties have not agreed as to the time of rent payment, the common law rule held that rent is neither due nor payable until the end of the rental period. New legislation usually states that if the parties have not agreed as to the time for payment of rent, "periodic rent is payable at the beginning of any term of one month or less and otherwise in cqual monthly installments at the beginning of each month."

Further, under common law the duty to pay rent was independent of any obligation of the landlord. That is, the tenant's duty to pay rent continued even if the premises were untenable either at the beginning of the lease or later on. The rent obligation could be suspended only if the tenant could prove that he was "constructively evicted" from the premises —an act or omission by the landlord that interfered with the tenant's use of the premises. Generally, as long as the tenant continued to occupy the premises, he was obligated to pay rent.

(2) *Rent Withholding.* Acts in various states tend to increase tenant bargaining power by allowing total or partial rent withholding to coerce the landlord to make needed repairs. For example, in Massachusetts, tenants may withhold rent after a landlord is notified that an inspection has shown the premises to be below the prescribed standard of livability (*Mass. Gen. Laws Ann. Ch. 239*, Section 8a, 1974, as amended). The landlord loses rights to rent until the premises are restored. In comparison, the comparable New York statute requires that the tenant's complaint be on record with the housing department for six months before sanctions may be imposed. After that time, a tenant has no obligation to pay rent until the violation is corrected.

In still other states, rent suspension utilizes escrow accounts. Under this arrangement, needed repairs are accomplished if rental payments are collected by courts or municipal agencies in some form of a rent escrow account (Pennsylvania and Rhode Island). For example, the tenant may be required to pay all rent into an escrow account that is released to the landlord after the required repairs have been made. In Pennsylvania, the landlord has a six-month deadline for completing required repairs. Failure to make repairs allows the court to return escrow funds to the tenant depositors. A variant in giving tenants enforcement rights against landlords for needed repairs is found in states that sanction tenant rent strikes (New York).

Retaliatory Eviction.   Under common law it was generally ruled that the landlord could evict tenants if the tenant violated a duty. More recent tenant laws, however, prohibit retaliatory eviction, for example, the states of Massachusetts, Ohio, Pennsylvania, and Missouri.

To illustrate, consider the case of Mr. and Mrs. Leon Fulcher, mobile home owners who leased space in a mobile home park. They reported to public health authorities that their sewage system was defective, causing back-up and resulting in unsanitary conditions. Their local health department investigated and issued an order requiring the park owner to remedy the problem. The next day the Fulchers were evicted by the park owner. The Fulchers brought suit in superior court which granted a temporary restraining order and later a preliminary injunction.

It was undisputed in court that the motivating factor behind the eviction was the complaint filed with the health department (see Craig J. Tillery, "Landlord and Tenant," *North Carolina Law Review*, vol. 54 (June 1976), pp. 86–102). In agreement with this decision the new tenant laws on retaliatory eviction are based on the theory that the tenant should not be punished for acting in the public interest and within their rights by reporting legal violations.

Indeed, legislation protecting tenants would be of little effect if tenants were afraid of retaliatory acts by the landlord. For instance, under Kentucky law, retaliatory action by the landlord includes increasing rent, decreasing utility services and eviction. The Act states that the action is retaliatory if it follows:

1. a tenant's complaint to a governmental agency that the landlord is not in compliance with building and housing codes; or
2. a tenant's complaint to a landlord concerning a material noncompliance; or
3. a tenant's joining of a tenant's union (George Wm. Moss III, "The Kentucky Uniform Residential Landlord and Tenant Act: Tenants' New Lease on Life?" *Journal of Family Law*, vol. 14, 1975–1976, p. 623).

Some courts have barred retaliatory eviction. In the case of *Edwards v. Habib* (397 F. 2d 687 D.C. Cir. 1968) the tenant reported sanitary code violations to public health authorities. The landlord was required to remedy 40 violations. In retaliation, the landlord gave the tenant 30 days' notice to vacate. When the tenant refused to vacate, the landlord brought suit for eviction. The court noted that the landlord had no duty to give reasons for his eviction. However, the court continued, "while the landlord may evict for any legal reason or for no reason at all, he is not, we hold, free to evict in retaliation for his tenant's report of housing code violations to the authorities. As a matter of statutory construction and for reasons of public policy, such an eviction cannot be permitted."

Under the *Tennessee Code Annotated,* Section 64–2854 (Supp. 1975), the landlord is forbidden from bringing retaliatory increases in rent or decreases in services in certain circumstances. Tenancy law further provides that the tenant cannot be dispossessed or otherwise penalized for bringing an action under the *Tennessee Code Annotated,* Section 53–5501. The law provides that the tenant may either recover possession or terminate the rental agreement and recover actual damages or punitive damages where appropriate plus reasonable attorney fees.

In agreement with these cases, the model *Uniform Residential Landlord and Tenant Act* prohibits the landlords from initiating an action to recover the dwelling unit, demand an increase in rent or decrease in services to which a tenant is entitled for one year after (1) the tenant has complained to a government agency over a code violation, (2) the tenant has complained to the landlord of the condition of the premises, or (3) the tenant has organized or joined a tenant's unit union or similar organization.

In short, members of the real estate industry must carefully review standard lease clauses, new legislation and review with counsel relations with tenants and landlords. In most states practices formerly condoned by common law are no longer legally acceptable.

QUESTIONS FOR REVIEW

_____ 1. Which of the following statements is correct?
   a. The tenant is known as the lessee; the tenant has an interest in the leased fee.
   b. The owner leasing property is the lessor; he acquires the leasehold estate.
   c. The tenant is the lessee; he acquires the leasehold interest.
   d. An owner executing a lease becomes the lessor; he or she acquires the leasehold estate.

_____ 2. A property owner may be advised to lease property as an alternative to selling because
   a. under a long-term lease the total rental received is greater than the sales price.
   b. income tax regulations may make leasing more profitable than selling.

     c. leases are based on lower property values than sales prices.
     d. leasing decreases the risk of inflation.

_____ 3. By leasing instead of selling, an owner may
     a. avoid personal net income taxes.
     b. avoid federal estate taxes.
     c. convert ordinary income to a capital gain.
     d. postpone capital gain taxes.

_____ 4. If the tenant improves a leased building, the
     a. owner acquires title to the improvements when the lease terminates.
     b. tenant retains title to the improvements when the lease terminates.
     c. owner must pay the tenant for building improvements.
     d. tenant may deduct the cost of improvements from the rent.

_____ 5. Which of the following statements is incorrect?
     a. Vacant land may be less marketable if it is leased by a nationally known tenant.
     b. Vacant land may be more marketable if it is leased by a nationally known tenant.
     c. The leasehold interest may have a value greater than the leased fee.
     d. The leased fee may have a value greater than the leasehold estate.

_____ 6. Which of the following statements describes an advantage of a net ground lease to a tenant?
     a. A net ground lease is equivalent to a 100-percent loan equal to the value of the leased property.
     b. Rent is equivalent to a deferred expense.
     c. Leases increase the equity required of tenants.
     d. Tenants benefit from an increase in the value of a leased fee.

_____ 7. To compensate for the effects of inflation and increases in site productivity, a _____ clause is generally included in a long-term lease.
     a. cancellation
     b. repurchase agreement
     c. rental adjustment
     d. 50-year renewal option

_____ 8. Graduated rents are disadvantageous to the lessee if future projections are
     a. not realized.
     b. underestimated.
     c. based on economic data.
     d. based on projections of the quantity of money.

_____ 9. Index leases provide for rents that are adjusted according to changes in

    a. a price index.
    b. an index of property values.
    c. annual property taxes.
    d. the oil price index.

_____10. Revaluation clauses may be undesirable because

    a. the tenant believes his capital and management contribute to the success of the development.
    b. the owner believes the location determines the rental value.
    c. arbitration can lead to expensive litigation.
    d. all of the above.

_____11. An owner of a leased fee has a right to the

    I. contract rent.
    II. reversionary value.

    a. I only.
    b. II only.
    c. Both I and II.
    d. Neither I nor II.

_____12. Assume that an owner grants a five-year lease on a $100,000 site for an annual rent of $10,000. Assume a capitalization rate of 9 percent. The value of the leased fee would be equal to

    a. $150,000 less a 9-percent discount.
    b. the present worth of $150,000 deferred ten years and discounted by 9 percent.
    c. the present worth of the contract rent and the present worth of the reversionary value discounted at a rate of 9 percent.
    d. the present value of the contract rent and the present worth of the reversionary value discounted at a rate of 18 percent.

_____13. Assume a property value of $100,000, an annual rent of $70,000, a capitalization rate of 9 percent and a five-year lease (the present worth of one per period for five years at 9 percent is 3.89; the present worth of $1 for five years at 9 percent is 0.65). What is the value of the leased fee?

    a. $337,300.
    b. $338,600.
    c. $428,200.
    d. $450,000.

_____14. Suppose the owner leased land for ten years at an annual rate of $8,000. If the present land value is $120,000 and the tenant constructed a building with a value of $100,000 at the end of ten years, what is the value of the leased fee assuming a 9-percent discount rate (the present worth of one per period for ten years at 9 percent is 6.42, the present worth of one, ten years at 9 percent is .42).

     a. $ 93,360.
     b. $101,760.
     c. $143,760.
     d. $200,000.

_____15. Assume that rent of $8,000 per year is paid in advance. The property is worth $100,000. What is the value of the leased fee assuming a 9-percent capitalization rate? (present worth of one per period at 9 percent, 9 years, is 6.00; the present worth of one for ten years at 9 percent is .42).

     a. $ 56,000.
     b. $ 90,000.
     c. $ 98,000.
     d. $180,000.

_____16. To value a leased fee with advance rent payments
     a. increase the period of discount by one year.
     b. add the rent for the first period and discount the present worth of the rent received for the balance of the term (one year less than the lease term).
     c. subtract the reversionary value from the current value.
     d. increase the capitalization rate by one.

_____17. To find the value of a leasehold interest,
     a. compute the present worth of the difference between economic rent and contract rent and add the present value of the unexpired improvements.
     b. add the market value of the structure and the present worth of the contract rent.
     c. subtract the market value of the structure from the present worth of the difference between economic rent and contract rent.
     d. compute the present worth of improvements that revert to the owner when the lease terminates and add the present value of the land.

_____18. If the original lessee subleases, the
     a. sublessee holds the leased fee interest.
     b. original lessee has a "sandwich lease."
     c. lessee has a reversionary interest.
     d. value of the lessor interest equals the present worth of the difference between contract and economic rent.

_____19. Gross receipts for lease purposes refer to
     a. sales and excise taxes.
     b. merchandise returns.
     c. cash refunds.
     d. none of the above.

_____20. Index leases provide for
  a. an estimate of the manner in which rents and prices will change over a long-term lease.
  b. anticipated changes in land productivity that vary from general price changes.
  c. adjustments in the rent according to changes in a selected price index.
  d. the independence of local real estate values and rent in relation to general price changes.

_____21. Revaluation leases are preferred because the
  I. owner often believes that location determines rent.
  II. tenant often believes that his capital and management contribute to the success of the development.
  a. I only.
  b. II only.
  c. Both I and II.
  d. Neither I nor II.

_____22. A business may secure the equivalent of a 100-percent loan on a property by
  a. purchasing vacant land with mortgage financing.
  b. negotiating a long-term lease on land.
  c. purchasing vacant land for lease to a reputable nationwide company.
  d. leasing improved land to a long-term tenant.

_____23. A long-term lease
  a. may not be used on properties subject to the federal capital gains tax.
  b. conveys title to any tenant improvements on the land to the tenant at the end of the lease.
  c. maximizes tenant equity.
  d. to a reputable nationwide company may create income comparable to an annuity.

_____24. Graduated rent clauses
  I. tend to be highly risky to the owner and tenant.
  II. call for periodic appraisals to adjust rent over a long-term lease.
  a. I only.
  b. II only.
  c. Both I and II.
  d. Neither I nor II.

_____25. Which of the following items should be included in a percentage lease?
  a. A description of the property subject to lease and an estimate of the building cost.

    b. Identification of the parties to the lease and their net worth.

    c. A definition of gross receipts and the percentage rate used to calculate average rent.

    d. A beginning and ending date, the rental value of the land, and the rental value of the building.

_____26. It is common for a lessor to require a(n) _____ equal to the minimum rent for one year.

    a. letter of credit
    b. binder fee
    c. escrow bond
    d. corporate surety bond

_____27. A tenant may be required to secure a(n) _____ to insure the lessor that improvements required by the lease will be completed.

    a. performance bond
    b. cosigner
    c. lease partner
    d. insured mortgage

_____28. Good practice for property developed under a lease dictates that the

    a. maximum rental income should be increased as the cost of the leased building decreases.
    b. lessor manage the leased premises.
    c. lessee submit architectural plans to the lessor for approval.
    d. rent should be at least 10 percent above the market value.

_____29. A(n) _____ represents the transfer of the leasehold interest to another party.

    a. sublease
    b. assignment
    c. life estate
    d. written notice of termination.

_____30. In a _____ lease, the lessee is generally required to insure against loss or damage by fire with extended coverage endorsements in an amount equal to the insurable value of the buildings.

    a. net ground
    b. percentage
    c. general liability
    d. mortgage

_____31. The _____ clause covers compensation to the lessor and lessee if the leased property is taken by the county.

    a. default of tenant
    b. obligations of lessee
    c. eminent domain
    d. status of subleases

_____32. The _____ clause defines the term of default and describes the rights of the parties in the event of default.

    a. no partnership default
    b. obligations of lessee
    c. arbitration default
    d. default

____33. The value of a leased fee is equal to the

    a. reversionary value of the contract rent plus the reversionary value of the property at the end of the lease.
    b. present worth of the contract rent plus the present worth of the property at the end of the lease.
    c. value of the land plus the value of the building minus the present worth of the contract rent.
    d. present worth of the difference between economic rent and contract rent.

____34. In valuing leasehold estates, the

    I. same capitalization rate must be applied to the interests of the lessee, lessor, and subtenants.
    II. terms of the lease may affect the final valuation judgment.
    a. I only.
    b. II only.
    c. Both I and II.
    d. Neither I nor II.

____35. Property owners may be induced to execute a long-term lease because

    a. they may create incomes comparable to an annuity by proper tenant selection.
    b. the discounted value of rental income is always greater than the present market value of leased property.
    c. rental income from leases is always capitalized at a lower rate than the market rate of capitalization.
    d. income from leases is preferred over income from other types of tangible and intangible property.

____36. The owner of vacant land may

    a. enhance the value of the property by leasing it to a knowledgeable tenant for development as a new shopping center.
    b. increase its marketability by leasing it to a nationally known reputable tenant who occupies the premises under a long-term lease.
    c. earn the highest possible land income by working with an experienced tenant who has the knowledge and capital resources to improve the property.
    d. all of the above.

____37. Under the common law, it was held that

    a. the landlord had no duty to maintain premises in a habitable condition.
    b. landlords could mingle security deposits with personal funds.

     c. landlord had the right to seize personal property as security for rent.

     d. all of the above.

_____38. The Model Uniform Residential Landlord and Tenant Act requires

     a. tenants to pay two months' advance rent for leases twelve months and over.

     b. the landlord to comply with all applicable building and housing codes and to maintain premises in a habitable state.

     c. the landlord to seek injunctive relief for nonpayment of rent.

     d. tenants to assume responsibility for repairs and maintenance.

_____39. The new residential landlord and tenant acts generally

     a. regard the duty to pay rent as independent of any obligation of the landlord.

     b. recognize the tenant's duty to pay rent even if the premises are untenable.

     c. as long as the tenant continues to occupy premises he or she is obligated to pay rent.

     d. none of the above.

_____40. Retaliatory eviction includes eviction resulting from a tenant's complaint

     a. to a governmental agency.

     b. to a landlord about needed repairs.

     c. about inadequate heating.

     d. all of the above.

ANSWER KEY

1. *(c)*	11. *(c)*	21. *(d)*	31. *(c)*
2. *(b)*	12. *(c)*	22. *(b)*	32. *(d)*
3. *(d)*	13. *(a)*	23. *(d)*	33. *(b)*
4. *(a)*	14. *(c)*	24. *(a)*	34. *(b)*
5. *(a)*	15. *(c)*	25. *(c)*	35. *(a)*
6. *(a)*	16. *(b)*	26. *(d)*	36. *(d)*
7. *(c)*	17. *(a)*	27. *(a)*	37. *(d)*
8. *(a)*	18. *(b)*	28. *(c)*	38. *(b)*
9. *(a)*	19. *(d)*	29. *(b)*	39. *(d)*
10. *(d)*	20. *(c)*	30. *(a)*	40. *(d)*

SUGGESTED ADDITIONAL READING

Friedman, Milton R. *Friedman on Leases.* vol. I and II. New York: Practising Law Institute, 1974.

Hoagland, Henry E.; Stone, Leo; and Brueggeman, William B. *Real Estate Finance.* 6th ed. Homewood, Ill.: Richard D. Irwin, Inc., 1977, chaps. 6 and 8.

Semenow, Robert W. *Questions and Answers on Real Estate.* 8th ed. Englewood Cliffs, N.J.: Prentice-Hall, Inc., 1975, chap. 7.

Shenkel, William M. "The Case for Index Leases," *Journal of Property Management*, vol. 40 (January 1975), pp. 156–61.

Shenkel, William M. "The Valuation of Leased Fees and Leasehold Interests," *The Appraisal Journal*, vol. 33 (October 1965), pp. 487–98.

11

Condominium Ownership

C ondominium ownership is established by a deed that conveys the fee
simple estate to a designated unit within a building and an undivided interest in the common elements. The common elements include the halls, elevators, the walls, the land area, and other property
shared in common with other condominium owners. In essence, a condominium combines ownership in severalty with ownership in common.
While this type of ownership is more common in residential property, it
is also found in office buildings, shopping centers, and industrial property.
Condominium ownership is growing, and competence in the real estate
industry calls for an understanding of condominium ownership, its
characteristics, its limitations, and its main features. The discussion in
this chapter concentrates on residential condominiums.

THE EARLY DEVELOPMENT OF CONDOMINIUMS

The condominium plan is a popular way of acquiring housing both in
Europe and South America. Its current appeal in the United States lies
in protecting households from inflation relative to rental occupancy.
Income tax laws further favor condominium ownership over rental occupancy.

Condominiums in the United States may be traced to the 1958 horizontal property law of Puerto Rico. The Act referred to horizontal property because an apartment unit typically occupied one floor level, requiring
a separate legal description for property divided horizontally by floors.
In Puerto Rico, condominiums helped solve the scarcity of apartment sites
in the face of an expanding population. The movement was aided by

agreement of the Federal Housing Administration to insure mortgages on condominium units constructed under the Puerto Rican Act.

This experience led to Section 234 of the Housing Act enacted into law in 1961. The availability of FHA financing led to widespread adoption of condominium housing. Today, they are found in the 50 states, United States territories, and Puerto Rico. Housing authorities have predicted that 50 percent of the United States population will live in some form of condominium housing within 20 years.

CONDOMINIUM OWNERSHIP EVALUATED

Condominium ownership introduces two changes in property ownership. The first innovation requires a means of recording legal descriptions not in the form of a flat, two-dimensional plane, but in a three-dimensional form. Some means had to be developed to permit the recording, the writing, and the identification of each ownership space. Section 234 of the 1961 Housing Act permitted FHA financing only if state laws provided for the new condominium description.

The second innovation required that property tax assessors—state, county and local—allocate property taxes of a composite apartment building to individual unit owners. Before condominiums, property taxes were levied on legal descriptions of land allocated only between land and the buildings of the project. The assessor, under the condominium statutes, must allocate the value of the common elements and the individual unit value to each unit owner. At the present time, the laws of the 50 states provide for both of these innovations.

Characteristics of Condominium Ownership

A condominium converts ownership conveyed in a single deed to individual estates within an original fee simple estate. Land and the structural parts of buildings of other apartments become part of the common estate owned jointly by owners of the individual estates. Moreover, a condominium unit is not complete without its undivided interest in the larger common estate. Each individual owner owns exclusive use and possession of the cubic space. The cubic area of the dwelling space with the undivided common interest may be purchased, sold, mortgaged, and willed like other ownership interests. (See Figure 11–1 for an illustration of a condominium ownership.)

Simply stated, the developer starts with a fee simple estate in a proposed condominium site. After filing the necessary documents, he constructs an apartment building with each apartment unit sold to individual owners. Under the condominium plan, the developer conveys title in a separate deed to each buyer covering a fee interest in an in-

FIGURE 11–1

A Diagram of Apartment Condominium Ownerships

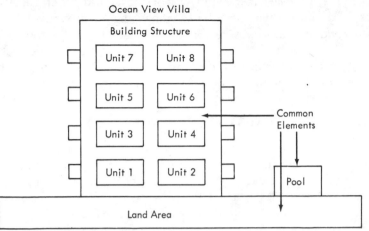

Ocean View Villa

Condominium ownership
1. Fee interest in an individual apartment unit.
2. Undivided fee interest in common elements.

dividual unit with an undivided interest in land and other apartment facilities used jointly with other owners. The developer of a 100-unit condominium would convey 100 deeds to 100 buyers if he or she sold all units.

Condominium ownership introduces a new vocabulary describing rights of the parties. Condominium terms must be defined to understand condominium ownership. The more important terms include the following items:

1. *Unit owner.* The purchaser who holds title to an individual apartment with an undivided interest in the common elements is a unit owner.
2. *A unit.* The portion of a condominium designed and intended for individual ownership and use. If the boundaries of units consist of walls and ceilings, Virginia law defines their finished surfaces as part of the unit (1974 c. 416).
3. *Common elements.* The individual interest in the common elements typically includes (*a*) floors, walls, ceilings (except finished surfaces) of each unit, and (*b*) chutes, flues, ducts, conduits, and bearing walls serving more than one unit. A common element is regarded as any portion of the condominium other than the units.
4. *Limited common elements.* A portion of the common elements reserved for the exclusive use of those entitled to the use of an in-

dividual unit. Limited common elements may include shutters, awnings, porches, balconies, patios, or other items designed to serve a single unit but lying outside the boundaries of a unit.

As an owner of a condominium unit, occupants derive certain advantages from the condominium concept. The same income tax advantages enjoyed by single-family dwelling owners are shared by condominium owners. The main advantage lies in the income tax deductibility of property taxes and mortgage interest. In effect, the purchaser of a condominium unit receives an indirect subsidy in comparison to renters. Judged strictly on financial grounds, after taxes, it is generally cheaper to own a condominium than to rent the same unit. Of course the final decision to rent or buy will be affected by other relevant issues.

Economic Advantages

Most condominiums are operated as nonprofit organizations. To the extent that the owner profits are omitted, condominium owners benefit over comparable rental space operated as an investment. Some authorities have further claimed that condominium units show lower rates of turnover and lower vacancy rates, and, therefore, lower vacancy and debt losses. The operating efficiencies per unit are reduced by reason of the higher occupancy rate.

It should be noted that unit owners invest only in their individual unit with its prorata share in the common elements. Indeed, the owner's interest is limited, the value of his interest largely turning on the type of unit he has purchased. Though the owner shares an interest in other property of the condominium not included in individual units, he is not a group investor—the value of his interest varies with the value of his individual interest. In this regard, he stands with owners of single family dwellings.

The condominium unit may be separately financed according to the requirements of the buyer and seller. In this respect, the condominium is treated as a single-family dwelling ownership in which each owner pays his prorata share of a single mortgage based on the total value of a condominium unit. For financing condominiums, appraisal, title searches and foreclosure procedures conform closely to practices common to single family dwellings.

Proponents of condominiums point out that compared to rental occupancy the condominium owner has a voice in the management of his property. The bylaws of the corporation provide a means to select officers, employ professional management, and operate the building in the best interest of the owners. These are privileges normally not extended to renters.

It is also reasonable to say that condominiums give the owner-occupant the advantages associated with multiple-family dwellings and at the same time provide for advantages of fee ownership. Further, an economic advantage is gained from high-density land use. The land cost per condominium unit is usually less than the land cost of comparable space invested in a single-family dwelling. This means that single-family occupancy and its advantages accrue to the condominium owners for normally highly expensive, central locations. This is especially appealing to occupants who prefer the apartment "life style" and the associated benefits of owner occupancy.

In contrast to cooperative ownership, the personal liability of each unit owner is restricted to a stated percentage of his or her ownership. Hence, the owner-occupants know that their personal liability will be limited for maintenance, fees, property taxes, mortgage, and other charges that might be levied against the structure. This is an element not found in cooperative apartment ownerships.

Today probably the leading reason for buying a condominium relates to the protection afforded against progressive rent increases. In a period of rising prices—as experience in other countries has shown—renters face a continuing, progressive rise in housing costs. For the condominium owner, out-of-pocket housing costs are determined by normal maintenance and operating costs, and financing charges if his or her property is mortgaged. Added to these features are the usual amenities associated with condominium apartments that are often more appealing than conventional apartment properties operated for profit. Against these advantages lie certain limitations of condominium ownership.

Limitations of Condominium Ownership

Some authorities stress the point that condominium owners are highly dependent on the proper maintenance of the common areas. In the first instance, the individual owner must conform to interests of other owners. Compared to single-family occupancy, the owner loses much of his or her independence as a fee owner. For some purchasers, this dependence could be a disturbing disadvantage. In other respects, the maintenance of the common areas, rehabilitation, remodeling, and upkeep are charges against each owner. Consequently, as the record shows, it is difficult to provide for the replacement and rehabilitation of common areas since charges and the approval of these charges turns on the voting membership. To some extent the management firm may have sufficient authority delegated by the board of directors to offset these deficiencies.

Another aspect of condominium ownership concerns the enforceability of rules, regulations, and decisions of a central management. The interdependence of individual owners involves a central management, and the equitable sharing of common facilities, the preservation of the character of common areas, and strict observance of land use controls. If these rules are not enforced, many of the expected amenities of condominium ownership remain unrealized.

LEGAL ELEMENTS

To establish a condominium, a minimum of three documents control the rights and obligations of individual unit owners. (1) The first requirement is a *declaration*. (A number of other names may be used to refer to the same document, i.e., the master deed, a declaration of conditions, covenants and restrictions, or the plan of condominium ownership.) However described, the declaration is the most important of condominium documents. (2) The second legal instrument controls the internal government of the condominium: the organization *bylaws*. (In some areas they are called secondary laws to differentiate them from the primary or constitutional laws of the declaration.) Occupants of condominiums are subject to regulations described in the bylaws. (3) The third item is the deed conveying the property, in some instances called the *description and purchase agreement*, which constitutes a conditional sales contract for properties under development.

The Declaration

The declaration is the legal document which places the property described under authority of the condominium law. At the same time the declaration provides for the administration of the condominium property. It describes the rights of individual owners with regard to maintenance of the apartment and outlines the obligations of individual unit owners. Though varying in detail by states, the declaration generally covers the following topics:

1. Purpose.
2. Legal description.
3. Description or improvements.
4. Definition of terms.
5. Interest in common elements. Boundaries of units, parking, and storage areas.
6. Restriction against further subdividing of units.
7. Easements.
8. Common expense; common surplus.
9. Administration of the condominium: the membership association, member voting.
10. Use and occupancy.

11. Maintenance and repair; alterations and improvements.
12. Apportionment of taxes or special assessments.
13. Maintenance of community interests.
14. Insurance provisions.
15. Assessments; liability, liens and enforcement.
16. Termination.
17. Amendments.
18. Long-term lease.
19. Management agreement.
20. Remedies in event of default.

A declaration with all of its necessary exhibits could easily run over 100 legal-sized typewritten pages. Their complexity may recommend an interpretation by an attorney before purchase.

Undivided Interest in the Common Elements. Of particular interest in the declaration is the provision covering the method of calculating the undivided interest in the common elements. A typical clause is illustrated in a declaration for a condominium in Fort Lauderdale, Florida, which reads:

> Each unit owner shall own, as an appurtenance to his unit, an undivided interest in the common elements as assigned thereto in Exhibit 1. The percentage of undivided interest of each unit shall not be changed without the unanimous consent of all owners of all of the units. No owner of any unit shall bring an action for partition or division of his undivided interest in the common elements.

In this instance, the percentage of ownership in the common elements in each unit's share of common expenses is determined by the relative floor area of each unit. With three floor plans identified as A, B, and C, these shares are listed as:

A type unit......3.343%
B type unit......3.951%
C type unit......4.585%

The stated share of the undivided interest controls (1) an owner's percentage of the undivided ownership interest in the common elements, (2) the share of maintenance and operating expenses, (3) the real estate tax assessed against the individual units, and the (4) appraisal of the condominium units for mortgage purposes. For example, if total operating expenses for the year amount to $100,000, the owner of a type C unit would pay $4,585 as his or her share of operating expenses. Similarly, the property tax assessor would place a value on the total property and then assign the assessed value to individual units according to the percentage ownership in common elements.

Typically the percentage interest in common elements is based on the proportion that the floor area of each unit bears to the total area of the project.

An alternative method establishes the original price of each condominium unit. The ratio of the value of individual units to the total value of the property determines the prorata share of the operating expenses and ownership in common elements. The condominium statute of Virginia (one of the more comprehensive state statutes dealing with condominiums) defines the value of individual units in terms of "par value":

> (u) *"Par value"* shall mean a number of dollars or points assigned to each unit by the declaration. Substantially identical units shall be assigned the same par value, but units located at substantially different heights above the ground, or having substantially different views, or having substantially different amenities or other characteristics that might result in differences in market value, may, but need not, be considered substantially identical within the meaning of this subsection. If par value is stated in terms of dollars, that statement shall not be deemed to reflect or control the sales price or fair market value of any unit, and no opinion, appraisal, or fair market transaction at a different figure shall affect the par value of any unit, or any undivided interest in the common elements, voting rights in the unit owners' association, liability for common expenses, or rights to common profits, assigned on the basis thereof (Condominium Act [1974 c. 416]).

Note that the appraisal of each unit may vary according to the view, height above ground, and other differences that affect market value. The Virginia statute distinguishes between par value and sale value of individual units. Par value controls the share of liabilities, expenses, and ownership in the common elements. Similarly, the sale price or subsequent appraisal opinion does not affect voting rights, interest in common elements, or liability for common expenses.

In some states such as Alaska and the state of Washington, condominiums must arrange for a periodic reappraisal of apartment units to establish the undivided share in the common elements. As the properties are resold, their proportionate value to the total property may change and, therefore, require a revision of the relative shares owned in the common elements.

Condominium Administration. Some of the other elements of the declaration should be noted, especially the administration of condominium owner rights and the management agreement. To govern the operation of the condominium, the declaration provides for an association with the power and authority to enforce provisions of the declaration. Each unit owner automatically becomes a member of the association with one vote assigned to each unit owner. The association has the power and authority to employ a manager or to delegate management to a management firm for the administration, maintenance, and repair of the condominium property.

To accomplish these ends, the declaration provides for a management agreement. The management agreement delegates certain powers and duties of the association to the management firm, primarily the power to employ operating personnel, spend money for maintenance, purchase insurance and supplies, and assume other custodial duties of a multiple-family unit manager. The management agreement may initially provide for a management contract of three to five years, with options for succeeding renewals. (The management agreement is dealt with in greater detail in a succeeding section.)

While other provisions of the declaration are largely self-explanatory, in some areas it is a common practice to construct a condominium building on leased land or to provide central facilities such as a swimming pool and a recreational area under a long-term lease. In the latter case, the developer retains ownership of recreational facilities such as a swimming pool and a recreation hall and leases these improved properties to the condominium association under a long-term lease. Monthly charges are levied on a predetermined basis for each condominium unit, with provision for rental adjustment clauses over the life of the lease. Some long-term leases tie lease payments to the consumer price index.

Corporation Bylaws

Given the corporation establishing the condominium, bylaws provided by the declaration relate to the administration of condominium affairs. The first portion of the bylaws qualifies voting members and provides for a quorum. For example, a quorum would typically be 50 percent of the total votes of the association plus one vote. Usually one vote is provided per unit owner.

The bylaws must provide for the initial board. Usually the board is designated by the sponsor-builder and prevails until a designated number of units have been sold. In the Century Village East, Inc., a condominium in Fort Lauderdale, Florida, a three-member board of directors has all the powers and duties of the association. Such powers include the right to levy and collect assessments against member units; to expend funds on the maintenance, repair, replacement, operation, improvement, and management of the condominium; to provide rules and regulations governing the condominium; to enter contracts for the condominium; to enforce the declaration and regulations; and to pay utility charges. The board may also delegate these responsibilities to a management firm under a management agreement. The bylaws must include the other requirements necessary for governing a voluntary association; for instance, the election of officers, amendments to the bylaws, accounting of funds, and the like.

The content of the bylaws may be governed by statute as, for example, the Florida Condominium Law. In Florida the bylaws must be set forth in the declaration or annexed to the declaration and shall provide for:

1. The form of administration, indicating the officers and board of administration, specifying their powers, duties, and their manner of election or removal.
2. The procedure in calling for meetings of unit owners and specifying their voting rights and defining the quorum.
3. The manner of collecting common expenses from unit owners.
4. The method of amending bylaws.

While not specifically required, the Florida law allows for bylaws that may provide:

1. The method of adopting and amending administrative rules and regulations.
2. Restrictions respecting the use and maintenance of common elements.

A special section of the bylaws relate to the use of individual units and restrictions on the use of common elements. Bylaws pertaining to condominium properties are shown in Figure 11–2.

FIGURE 11–2

Condominium Bylaws

---

a. The sidewalk, entrances, passages, elevators (if applicable), vestibules, stairways, corridors, halls and all other COMMON ELEMENTS must not be obstructed, encumbered or used for any purpose other than ingress and egress to and from the premises. No carriages, velocipedes, bicycles, wagons, shopping carts, chairs, benches, tables, or any other object of a similar type and nature shall be stored therein. Children shall not play or loiter in halls, stairways, elevators, or other COMMON ELEMENTS.

b. The personal property of all UNIT OWNERS shall be stored within their CONDOMINIUM UNITS or the specific LIMITED COMMON ELEMENTS assigned to them for storage purposes, provided, however, that no UNIT OWNER may store any personal property on, or make any use of, the porch within the boundaries of his UNIT, which is unsightly nor shall he make any use of the same which interferes with the comfort and convenience of other UNIT OWNERS.

c. No garbage cans, supplies, milk bottles, or other articles shall be placed in the halls, on the balconies, or on the staircase landings, nor shall any linens, cloths, clothing, curtains, rugs, mops or laundry of any kind, or other article, be shaken or hung from any of the windows, doors or balconies, or exposed to or on any part of the COMMON ELE-

FIGURE 11–2 (continued)

MENTS or porches within any UNIT. Fire exits shall not be obstructed in any manner and the COMMON ELEMENTS shall be kept free and clear of rubbish, debris, and other unsightly material.

d. No UNIT OWNERS shall allow anything whatsoever to fall from the window, balcony or doors of the premises, nor shall he sweep or throw from the premises any dirt or other substance into any of the corridors, halls or balconies, elevators, ventilators, or elsewhere in the building or upon the grounds.

e. Refuse and garbage shall be deposited only in the area provided therefor.

f. Employees of the ASSOCIATION shall not be sent out of the building by any UNIT OWNER, except in the UNIT OWNER's capacity as an officer or director, at any time, for any purpose. No UNIT OWNER or resident shall direct, supervise, or in any manner attempt to assert any control over the employees of the ASSOCIATION.

g. Servants and domestic help of the UNIT OWNERS may not gather or lounge in the public areas of the building or grounds.

h. The parking facilities shall be used in accordance with the regulations adopted by the ASSOCIATION. No vehicle which cannot operate on its own power shall remain on the CONDOMINIUM premises for more than twelve hours, and no repair, except emergency repair, of vehicles shall be made on the CONDOMINIUM PROPERTY. No commercial vehicle owned or driven by a CONDOMINIUM OWNER shall be parked on the CONDOMINIUM PROPERTY. No boat trailer, camper or like vehicle shall be left or stored on the CONDOMINIUM PROPERTY and no UNIT OWNER's boat may be used, stored or left on the lakes, canals and drainage systems within CENTURY VILLAGE, Deerfield Beach, Florida. Bicycles shall be parked in the areas, if any, provided for that purpose.

i. No UNIT OWNER shall make or permit any disturbing noises in the building by himself, his family, servants, employees, agents, visitors and licensees, nor do or permit anything by such persons that will interfere with the rights, comforts or convenience of other UNIT OWNERS. No UNIT OWNER shall play upon or suffer to be played upon, any musical instrument, or operate or suffer to be operated, a phonograph, televisions, radio or sound amplifier, in his UNIT, in such manner as to disturb or annoy other occupants of the CONDOMINIUM.

j. No sign, advertisement, notice or other lettering shall be exhibited, displayed, inscribed, painted or affixed in, on, or upon any part of the CONDOMINIUM UNIT that is visible from outside the UNIT or CONDOMINIUM PROPERTY.

k. No awning, enclosure, canopy, shutter, or like item, except removable hurricane shutters, shall be attached to, or placed upon, the porch within any unit, outside walls or roof of the building except as provided in the DECLARATION.

l. The ASSOCIATION shall retain a pass key to all UNITS. No

FIGURE 11–2 (continued)

UNIT OWNER or occupant shall alter any lock or install a new lock without the written consent of the BOARD. Where such consent is given the UNIT OWNER shall provide the ASSOCIATION with an additional key for use of ASSOCIATION, pursuant to its right of access to the UNIT.

m. No cooking shall be permitted on any porch or terrace or COMMON ELEMENT nor shall any goods or beverage be consumed outside of a UNIT except in areas designated for that purpose by the BOARD.

n. No inflammable, combustible or explosive fluid, chemical or substance shall be kept in any UNIT except those required for normal household use.

o. Each UNIT OWNER who plans to be absent from his UNIT during the hurricane season must prepare his UNIT prior to his departure by (1) removing all furniture, plants and other objects from his terrace or porch prior to his departure; and (2) designating a responsible firm or individual to care for his UNIT, should the UNIT suffer hurricane damage, and furnishing the ASSOCIATION with the name of said firm or individual. Such firm or individual shall contact the ASSOCIATION for clearance to install or remove hurricane shutters.

p. No UNIT OWNER shall keep or harbor any walking pet or animal on the CONDOMINIUM PROPERTY or within the confines of his unit. No other pets may be kept without the written consent of the ASSOCIATION. Such consent may be given upon such conditions as the ASSOCIATION may prescribe and shall be deemed provisional and subject to revocation at any time. No animal or pet shall be maintained or harbored within a UNIT that would create a nuisance to any other UNIT OWNER. A determination by the BOARD that an animal or pet maintained or harbored in a UNIT creates a nuisance shall be conclusive and binding upon all parties.

q. No UNIT may be occupied by any person under eighteen (18) years of age, except that any relative of a UNIT OWNER under 18 may be permitted to visit for reasonable periods not to exceed two (2) consecutive weeks or thirty (30) days in any calendar year. However, any such visitor under the age of 18 may only use the DEMISED PREMISES pursuant and subject to such RULES AND REGULATIONS concerning such use that are established by the LESSOR.

r. No UNIT may be used for any commercial or business purpose. No UNIT OWNER may actively engage in any solicitations for commercial purposes within CENTURY VILLAGE, Deerfield Beach, Florida, nor shall any solicitor of a commercial nature be allowed on the CONDOMINIUM PROPERTY without the prior written consent of the BOARD.

s. No radio or television installation or modification or other wiring shall be accomplished by a UNIT OWNER without written permis-

FIGURE 11-2 (concluded)

---

sion of the BOARD. No antenna may be placed on the exterior of the CONDOMINIUM PROPERTY.

t. Each UNIT OWNER shall park his automobile in his assigned space. All parking spaces not assigned shall be used by guests of the UNIT OWNERS only, except such spaces as may be designated for the temporary parking of delivery vehicles.

u. Complaints concerning the use of the CONDOMINIUM PROPERTY and/or service to the same shall be made in writing, signed by the complaining party, and delivered to the MANAGEMENT FIRM, and thereafter the BOARD, who, if necessary, will forward the same to the appropriate party.

v. Until further notice, all payments of assessments, monthly or otherwise, shall be made at the office of the MANAGEMENT FIRM as designated in the MANAGEMENT AGREEMENT. Checks should be made payable to: CEN-DEER MANAGEMENT, INC. Payments shall be made on the first day of each month, without notice, and if more than ten (10) days late, they shall be subject to late charges as provided in THE DECLARATION and BYLAWS.

A review of the restrictions shown in Figure 11-2 shows that rules governing use are intended to preserve the amenities of the condominium. Restrictions go far beyond the public and private restraints exercised against owners of the conventional single-family dwelling.

Conveyance Instruments

Given the declaration and the articles of a corporation and their bylaws, the next significant instrument is the deed conveying the individual ownership and the undivided interest of the common elements. In most respects the deed will be common to conveyance instruments normally used for conveyance of the simple estate. The legal description may refer to the designated unit number established by the declaration. The declaration, in turn, will include the legal description common to the condominium project and will show the plot plan, floor plan, and a detailed legal description of the individual unit.

The conveyance instrument may refer to the legal descriptions entered in the declaration by reference. While the deed operates to convey the property interest, it is important to note that the use and enjoyment are governed also by the declaration, the bylaws, and the contracts made part of the condominium: namely, the management agreement and ground leases.

If the condominium is purchased under an agreement of sale and purchase, certain minimum information should be included. This is the first document the buyer has signed and is similar to a contract for sale. As the buyer signs this instrument, he or she makes an earnest money deposit on a specific condominium. Items to be included in the agreement cover the following points:

1. The date of the agreement.
2. The buyer's name and address.
3. The name of a developer or developing corporation.
4. The apartment identified by number; name and address of the condominium property.
5. The total purchase price.
6. The amount of the mortgage and the mortgage terms; principal and interest payments.
7. The total equity required by the time of closing.
8. The estimated date of building completion.
9. Monthly assessment for maintenance and operation.
10. Estimated property taxes on the individual unit.
11. Provision for placing the money in escrow. If the money deposited may be used for construction, this should be disclosed with an agreement on conditions on which the deposit may be returned.
12. A list of closing documents to be completed at the time of closing.
13. The estimated closing costs to be assumed by the purchaser.

Real estate agents, developers, and others selling condominiums under certain state laws are required to make full disclosures prior to the sale. Full disclosure under the Florida statute requires that the respective buyer be furnished a copy of the following documents.

1. The declaration.
2. The articles of incorporation or charter of the association.
3. The bylaws.
4. The ground lease if the property is constructed on leased land.
5. The management agreement.
6. The projected operating budget including details on monthly payments for the condominium unit, charges for maintenance or management of the condominium, and the monthly charge for use of leased recreational facilities.
7. The sales brochure and floor plan to be purchased by prospective buyers.

If these required documents are not given the purchaser prior to execution of the contract for sale, the contract must provide that it shall be voidable at the option of the buyer up to 15 days after the last item of required information is furnished to the buyer. The required documents shall be delivered not later than 90 days before the final closing date. Other violations of the full disclosure rule entitle the buyer to rescind the contract for sale at any time prior to making the final settlement. Rescission requires the developer or sponsor of the condominium to refund all deposit monies with interest.

THE MANAGEMENT OF CONDOMINIUMS

The association of individual owners has final responsibility for management, including the responsibility for hiring employees, contracting for services, maintenance, and repairs. Normally this authority is delegated to a professional management firm. Initially, however, the sponsor—the developer or contractor—is given this responsibility under terms of the declaration or bylaws. At some point these responsibilities must be transferred to the association. In some cases the management agreement provides for sponsor management until all condominium units are sold.

Terms of the management agreement are fairly critical to the success of the project. The management agreement prevails until the point is reached where management responsibilities are assumed by the association. It typically extends over three to five years, with options for renewal unless the management agreement is terminated at the end of the contract period by act of the board of directors or the membership.

If the management agreement concerns the initial management of a condominium prior to the time that the unit owners' association (the "board") is organized, the agreement must clearly define the authority of the agent. On this point, the model condominium management agreement prepared by the Institute of Real Estate Management reads as shown in Figure 11–3.

For a new condominium, the agreement provides for a one-year contract with termination by the developer or agent with notice. This clause provides for eventual authority over management by the unit owners' association as the units are sold.

The management agreement also specifies the maximum sum that can be spent for maintenance and repairs without special approval of the board of directors or membership. Usually this sum is large enough to enable the management firm to undertake nominal repairs. An exception to this are emergencies that may require immediate and costly expenditures to protect and preserve property.

The management firm assumes responsibility to keep records of the association and approved accounting forms for periodic audit. In this regard, the management firm collects common expenses for operation and for this service is paid a specified fee. Fees may be calculated by the monthly cost per individual unit or may be based on the percent of operating costs and expenses. If the percentage arrangement is used, 3 percent of operating expenses is common for condominium operation in Florida.

FIGURE 11–3

Condominium Management Agreement

THIS AGREEMENT, made and entered into this_____day of

_____, 19____, by and between_____

_____

(the "DEVELOPER"), not individually but on behalf of all of the owners

from time to time of units in_____(the
"Condominium") and on behalf of the owners' association to be organized
pursuant to Section_____
_____or the not-for-profit corpora-
tion to be organized pursuant to Section_____
of said Act (the "OWNERS"), and_____
(the "AGENT");

WITNESSETH:

WHEREAS, under the provisions of the purchase contract with the
purchaser of each condominium unit, the Declaration of Condominium
Ownership and the By laws required under the provisions of the_____

Condominium Property Act, the OWNERS delegate the authority to manage
the Condominium initially to the DEVELOPER and thereafter to an elected
Board of Managers, which may be the Board of Directors of a not-for-profit
corporation organized by the Owners (the "BOARD"); and

WHEREAS, under the provisions of the purchase contract with the purchaser of each condominium unit, the Declaration of Condominium Ownership and the By-laws required under the provisions of the_____

Condominium Property Act, the DEVELOPER is authorized to engage a
management agent on behalf of the OWNERS under a contract to expire not
later than_____years after the first unit is occupied; and

WHEREAS, the DEVELOPER, on behalf of the OWNERS, desires to
employ the AGENT to manage the Condominium, and the AGENT desires
to be employed to manage the Condominium;

NOW, THEREFORE, it is agreed as follows:

1. The DEVELOPER, on behalf of the OWNERS, hereby employs the
AGENT exclusively to manage the Condominium for a period of_____
years, beginning on the date the first unit in the Condominium is occupied,
and thereafter for yearly periods from time to time, unless on or before sixty
days prior to the expiration of the initial term or on or before thirty days prior
to the expiration of any such renewal period, either party hereto shall notify
the other in writing that it elects to terminate this agreement, in which case
this agreement shall be terminated at the end of said period.

Another issue arises in the case of transient occupancy. If all units are
not sold, the sponsor has an incentive to rent the property for transient
or hotel purposes. For projects financed under a federally insured mortgage
(Federal Housing Administration), a family unit cannot be rented for
transient or hotel purposes. A rental is defined as any period of less than
30 days or any rental if the occupants of a family unit are provided customary hotel services. Such a requirement may not prevent owners from
leasing their units for residential purposes subject to restrictions of the
declaration or bylaws.

In judging a condominium unit, it should be determined if there are restrictions on the right to resell. Some condominium associations reserve the right of first refusal. In the event of a proposed sale, the unit must be first offered to the condominium association for a stipulated period of time. This practice is against current Federal Housing Administration regulations for units financed with federally insured mortgages.

APARTMENT CONVERSION TO CONDOMINIUMS

If households continue to favor condominium ownership over rental, apartment owners may find it economic to convert an existing apartment building to a condominium. The main difficulty in doing this is the fact that apartment buildings are not constructed for condominium use. Generally, apartment buildings of the past do not have the amenities associated with the modern condominium; older buildings show substantial obsolescence; they are subject to deferred maintenance; further, their location may not be as desirable as newly-developed condominium projects.

There is the added problem of dealing with long-term standing tenants. If these obstacles are overcome, the sponsor must proceed according to four steps: (1) the condominium entity must be legally established; (2) each apartment must be physically adapted to condominium use; (3) there must be an organized plan for transition from rental occupancy to condominium occupancy; (4) the owner must arrange for building operations during the conversion and subsequent condominium management.

Physical Changes

After a building is committed to conversion to a condominium, the conversion starts with remedying the physical depreciation of the roof, the exterior walls, and the landscaping, and the rehabilitation or remodeling of the lobby entrance. In the case of individual apartment units, rehabilitation may not be advisable. For instance, if 30 to 60 percent of condominium sales are made to existing tenants, extensive rehabilitation of apartments showing deferred maintenance may not be desired by the present tenants. (Quite possibly the cost of rehabilitation may price the units out of reach of present tenants.) In still other instances, tenants may be unwilling to change their life style and expenditure patterns brought about by a remodeled apartment.

In fact, the conversion of individual apartments to condominiums may be a method of shifting rehabilitation costs to the tenants, particularly if the cost of rehabilitation cannot be recovered in the sale price. That is, it may be more economical to shift the cost of rehabilitating the kitchen to the tenant. Such costs might include replacement of floor coverings, wall surfaces, new cabinets, drainboards, dishwashers, ranges, overhead fans, and the like. If the kitchen requires remodeling, typically the bathroom would show some obsolescence in the form of outdated medicine cabinets, bathroom vanities, and plumbing fixtures. Updating such apartments to compete with new condominium units may be prohibitively expensive.

Consider also the rehabilitation of building equipment—namely, the heating system, air conditioning, and electrical systems. Each of these utility systems may be obsolete. A carefully undertaken feasibility analysis is necessary.

Experience has shown that conversion is more successful if the rental apartments have balconies and patios. Other sponsors have reported that sales tend to be limited for apartments without basement space that can be converted to extra storage and community recreation rooms. Without basements, generally, it is impractical to provide recreation and additional storage space in existing buildings.

Conversion Feasibility

The location largely dictates the probability of successful condominium sales. Conversion tends to be less successful in districts dominated by tenancy occupancy. Moreover, buildings constructed in the shape of letters (E, H, U) have restricted views; they are acceptable for tenant occupancy but unsatisfactory for owners of condominium units who seem to prefer an open-air view. Conversions tend to be more successful if the apartment complex to be converted appeals to buyers in upper-income groups. Ordinarily, eligible apartment buildings would be luxury apartments in central locations of large cities (Park Avenue in New York; The Gold Coast in Chicago) or in prestige suburban locations.

Judging the feasibility of conversion introduces other unique problems: For example, tenants who occupy buildings during the conversion increase costs not encountered in new units. Engineering and legal surveys necessary for the declaration are difficult and costly for existing buildings. Hostile tenants may delay the detailed reproduction of the floor plans for each apartment.

Offsetting these costs, however, are tenants with leases that provide income during the conversion—a source of income not available for new condominium units. If conversions are sufficiently staggered, the building will earn income until the end of each lease, at which time the apartment may be converted to a sale unit. Lease occupancy during conversion helps reduce holding costs.

If conversion of the condominium unit is viewed from the standpoint of the real estate agent, clients should be advised against acquiring individual units in a building with equipment and utility facilities that may need replacement over the life of the property. Replacement of the heating system, or air conditioning, or plumbing would call for heavy assessments not anticipated by the condominium purchaser. The danger here is to avoid condominium units used as a dumping ground for undesirable properties with little marketability for rental or investment.

In brief, conversion involves two types of cost: (1) restoration and (2) improvements that enhance marketability. The restoration should restore the building to a like-new condition, correcting for deferred maintenance. The improvements include additions that enhance the livability and marketability of the property: new clubhouse facilities, swimming pool, community facilities, and structural changes to individual apartments.

THE CONDOMINIUM PURCHASE: A SUMMARY

It is fairly easy for a real estate agent to damage his reputation by dealing with condominium listings. In contrast, the agent may serve as a valuable consultant to clients contemplating a purchase. To serve in this latter capacity, the client should be warned of the main pitfalls confronting the uninitiated condominium purchaser.

1. The buyer of the condominium (and certainly the agent) should be familiar with the main points of the (a) declaration, (b) bylaws, (c) operating budget, (d) management agreement, and (e) purchase agreement. State law may even require these documents to be furnished to purchaser.

2. The operating budget should be reviewed for accuracy. Monthly assessments should be sufficient to cover maintenance and related expenses of the project.

3. The prospect should understand the calculation of ownership assessments and voting rights and how they are determined. If the property is constructed on leased land, the terms of the lease and their monthly rental cost to the individual owners should be clear.

4. The insurance policy should insure individual units against loss from fire and other perils. Such policies may contain a condominium property endorsement that recognizes that condominium units have a multiple number of beneficiaries. Such an endorsement should be part of the insurance package. Condominium projects should have liability coverage for the entire condominium development which names a board of directors and each unit owner individually as co-owner.

5. The degree of control held by the developer or sponsor before and after the condominium is legally constituted should be known by the prospect.

6. Prospective purchasers should be informed on their right to resale. If the bylaws give the association the right of first refusal, this should be clearly explained.

7. The management agreement should be such that the board has

authority to hire the management agent, who then remains under association control.

8. The basis for governing and operating the condominium should be reasonable and equitable to individual owners. Restrictions on the use of individual units and rules of conduct should be uniformly administered and reasonable.

Sales of condominiums may be expected to come under increasing regulation. For example, real estate license law officials in Virginia are charged with enforcing the provisions of the state condominium act. They are empowered to subpoena records and witnesses, conduct investigations, and issue cease and desist orders. Persons guilty of a misdemeanor may be subject to a fine of $1,000 to $50,000 and six months imprisonment. (Condominium Act [1974 c. 416].)

QUESTIONS FOR REVIEW

_____ 1. Which of the following statements is correct?
   a. A condominium unit is jointly owned by owners of the common elements.
   b. A condominium unit may be conveyed without the undivided interest in common elements.
   c. A condominium converts ownership conveyed in a single deed to individual estates within an original fee simple estate.
   d. The undivided common interest of a condominium may be mortgaged separately from each condominium unit.

_____ 2. The unit owner of a condominium may be defined as
   a. the owner of an undivided interest in the common elements.
   b. an owner who holds title to an individual apartment with an undivided interest in the common elements.
   c. an owner of an individual apartment with no interest in the common elements.
   d. the developer of a condominium complex.

_____ 3. Which of the following items would not be included in the common elements of a condominium?
   a. The floors, walls, and ceilings of each condominium unit.
   b. Party walls serving more than one condominium unit.
   c. Any portion of the condominium other than individual units.
   d. The cubic foot area of each condominium unit.

_____ 4. Which of the following items illustrates limited common elements?
   a. Patios and the furniture of a single condominium unit.
   b. Porches, balconies and the cubic foot area of each condominium unit.
   c. Shutters, awnings, porches, balconies and patios.
   d. An undivided interest in the swimming pool.

_____ 5. Part of the general appeal of condominiums lies in the fact that
  a. the condominium owner enjoys advantages associated with multiple-family dwellings and advantages of the fee ownership of single-family dwellings.
  b. the land cost per condominium unit is usually more than the land cost of comparable single-family dwelling space.
  c. condominium units are free of the disadvantages associated with single-family occupancy.
  d. in a condominium, each unit owner pays his prorata share of the condominium project mortgage.

_____ 6. Which of the following statements is correct?
  a. In a condominium unit, the personal liability of each owner is restricted to a stated percentage of his ownership.
  b. In a cooperative the personal liability of each cooperative owner is restricted to a stated percentage of his ownership.
  c. A condominium unit owner is responsible for an unlimited share in the mortgage covering the condominium project.
  d. In a cooperative unit, the owner knows that his personal liability for operating expenses, property taxes, and mortgage payments will be limited to a specific share.

_____ 7. Which of the following statements refers to a disadvantage of condominium ownership?
  a. The condominium owner loses much of the independence enjoyed by an owner of a single-family dwelling.
  b. The cost of condominium amenities is difficult to justify economically.
  c. The condominium owner must act in a custodial capacity in managing the project.
  d. The condominium owner must provide for his own maintenance of common areas.

_____ 8. Which of the three documents listed below control the rights and obligations of individual condominium owners?
  a. The declaration, the abstract of title, and the corporation bylaws.
  b. The corporation bylaws, the property tax agreement, and the declaration.
  c. The first mortgage and promissory note, the declaration, and the description and purchase agreement.
  d. The declaration, the organization bylaws, and the description and purchase agreement.

_____ 9. The powers delegated to a management firm by the condominium association through a management agreement include the
  a. power to spend money for maintenance and to establish the rental value of each condominium unit.

    b. right to redecorate each condominium unit and to assume other custodial duties of a multiple-family unit manager.

    c. right to refinance individual condominium units and the power to employ operating personnel.

    d. power to employ operating personnel and spend money for maintenance, insurance, and supplies.

_____10. Condominium ownership is established by a deed that conveys a _____ estate in the designated unit within the building and an undivided interest in the common elements.

    a. fee simple

    b. detailed

    c. freehold

    d. leasehold

_____11. Condominium ownership was first introduced in the United States by the

    a. 1946 Housing Act.

    b. 1954 Fair Housing Act.

    c. 1958 Horizontal Property Law of Puerto Rico.

    d. 1972 Fair Housing Act.

_____12. Income tax laws favor _____ over _____.

    a. single-family residence ownership; condominium ownership

    b. condominium ownership; single-family residence ownership

    c. condominium ownership; rental occupancy

    d. rental occupancy; condominium ownership

_____13. Unit owners in a condominium project have the right to the exclusive use and possession of a(n)

    a. square foot area.

    b. area described by a metes and bounds description.

    c. cubic area.

    d. property described by metes and bounds plus an undivided interest in the common elements.

_____14. A condominium owner may deduct _____ for federal personal net income tax purposes.

    a. property taxes

    b. mortgage principal payments

    c. rental income

    d. all of the above

_____15. Compared to comparable rental units, successful condominiums are generally subject to

    a. higher rates of tenant turnover.

    b. higher vacancy rates.

    c. lower bad debt losses.

    d. federal rent controls.

_____16. In comparing condominiums with single-family dwellings, a major advantage of condominiums is the
  a. income tax deductibility of property taxes and interest payments.
  b. lower rate of occupancy turnover.
  c. higher density of land use.
  d. lower density of land use.

_____17. The purchaser of a condominium unit is entitled to the following documents:
  a. The declaration.
  b. The articles of incorporation or charter of the association.
  c. The bylaws and the management agreement.
  d. All of the above.

_____18. The model condominium management agreement prepared by the Institute of Real Estate Management for a new condominium provides for
  a. a one-year management contract with termination by the developer or agent with notice.
  b. a five-year contract with a renewal option for an additional five-year term.
  c. a five-year management contract with automatic renewal for one-year periods unless terminated by legal notice.
  d. authority over management by the developer until all units are sold.

_____19. Which of the following statements is correct?
  a. Management agreements give the managing agent an unlimited allowance for maintenance and repairs without board approval.
  b. Management fees are based on a percent of gross rental income.
  c. Responsibility for keeping records and preparing accounting statements is assigned to the management firm by the management agreement.
  d. The management agreement restricts unit owners from reselling within two years.

_____20. Condominium bylaws provide for
  a. the determination of the assessed value for property taxes on each unit.
  b. collecting common expenses from unit owners and listing their custodial duties.
  c. the procedure in calling for meetings of unit owners and the method of amending bylaws.
  d. voting rights of unit owners and their liability for the condominium project mortgage.

_____21. In contrast to cooperative ownership, the personal liability of a condominium owner for maintenance expenses is limited to *a.* his stated ownership percentage.

    b. a share equal to the total liability divided by the total number of unit owners.

    c. a fixed dollar amount as specified in the corporation bylaws.

    d. the total liability as a percentage of the consumer price index.

_____22. In a condominium property, the description and purchase agreement constitutes a(n) _____ for properties under development.

    a. unconditional sales contract

    b. conditional sales contract

    c. bargain and sale deed

    d. fee simple estate to the deed

_____23. The declaration is a legal document that

    a. places the property described under the authority of the condominium law.

    b. provides for the administration of condominium property.

    c. describes owner duties in maintaining the common elements.

    d. outlines the obligations of unit owners.

_____24. In converting an apartment house to a condominium, which of the following problems must be resolved?

    a. The condominium entity must be legally established with apartment units priced 25 percent below current construction costs.

    b. The owner must arrange for building operations during conversion and for long-term leases on each condominium unit.

    c. The apartment building must be physically adapted to condominium use and the condominium unity must be legally established.

    d. There must be an organized plan for transition from rental to condominium occupancy and property taxes must be paid two years in advance.

_____25. Apartment-house conversion to condominiums seems more successful if the

    a. apartment building converted is adapted to low-income buyers.

    b. apartment building is located in a district dominated by tenant occupancy.

    c. building converted is a luxury apartment in a central location of a large city.

    d. apartment to be converted is at least 30 years old.

_____26. Buyers of condominiums are advised to be familiar with the

    a. declaration, the bylaws, and the net worth of the developer.

    b. management agreement, the purchase agreement, and the reversionary agreement of the condominium unit.

    c. operating budget, the purchase agreement, and the state law governing property taxes.

    d. declaration, the bylaws, and the operating budget.

_____27. Prospects contemplating purchase of a condominium should understand the calculation of

    a. quantity survey methods of estimating construction costs.

    b. ownership assessments, voting rights, and how they are determined.

    c. the land value based on the price per condominium unit.

    d. the terms of the lease and the rental value of each condominium unit.

_____28. The share of the undivided interest in the common elements does not control the

    a. interest in common elements.

    b. maintenance of each unit.

    c. property tax liability of the individual owners for the common elements.

    d. appraisal of condominium units for mortgage purposes.

_____29. Suppose a condominium project consisted of three floor plans, A, B and C, with a share of the undivided interest of 3.3 percent (A unit), 3.9 percent (B unit) and 4.5 percent (C unit). If annual maintenance costs totaled $100,000, an owner of a C unit would be liable for the following share:

    a. $900.

    b. $9,000.

    c. $2,750.

    d. $4,500.

_____30. The most common method of apportioning condominium maintenance costs and taxes is based on the

    a. floor area.

    b. age of property.

    c. rates of the original price of each unit to the total current price of the condominium project.

    d. location of the condominium unit.

_____31. The voting rights of a condominium owner are determined by

    a. weighing each vote by the unit share of total property taxes.

    b. weighing each vote by the amount of equity in the condominium unit.

    c. assigning one vote per unit owner.

    d. weighing each vote by the amount of the mortgage on the condominium unit.

_____32. Which of the following items found in a condominium agreement of sale and purchase agreement would not be found in the sales contract of a single-family dwelling?

    a. The name of the developer or seller.

    b. The monthly assessment for maintenance and operation.

    c. The estimated property taxes on the individual unit.

      d. A list of closing documents to be completed at the time of closing.

____33. Some states provide that if a developer or sponsor of a condominium is unable to complete the terms of the contract of sale, the purchaser is

      a. entitled to a refund of all monies plus interest.
      b. liable for taxes only for the second year.
      c. excused from interest payments for one year.
      d. excused from principal payments for one year.

____34. The _____ has the final responsibility for management including the responsibility for hiring employees, contracting services, maintenance and repairs.

      a. individual owner
      b. developer
      c. association of individual owners
      d. condominium board appointed by the state legislature

____35. Initially the responsibilities for maintenance and repairs do not fall on the

      a. sponsor.
      b. developer.
      c. contractor.
      d. association of condominium owners.

____36. Conversion of an apartment to a condominium involves

      a. restoration and maintenance.
      b. improvements and maintenance.
      c. restoration and improvement.
      d. structural changes and new tenants.

____37. Which of the following items would not be included in the declaration?

      a. The operating budget.
      b. The basis for calculating ownership assessments.
      c. A description of insurance coverage against fire and other perils.
      d. The resale value.

____38. Which of the following is prohibited if mortgages on condominium units are insured by the Federal Housing Administration?

      a. The assumption of responsibility for keeping records.
      b. The management agreement specifying the maximum expenditure for maintenance and repair without association approval.
      c. An agreement giving the condominium association the right of first refusal for all resales.
      d. A prohibition against subletting.

____39. The condominium association is made up of all

      a. unit owners with one vote assigned to each unit owner.

    b. unit owners with one vote assigned to each member of the family over age 16.

    c. condominium residents with one vote assigned to each unit owner.

    d. unit owners with one vote given for each percentage (rounded to the nearest percent) of the common element ownership they have been assigned.

_____40. Which of the following statements is correct?

    a. Conversion to condominiums tends to be most successful for apartment buildings constructed in the shape of the letters *E*, *H* and *U*.

    b. Condominium projects financed under a federally-insured mortgage may be rented for transient or hotel purposes if all units are sold.

    c. In some areas, it is a common practice for condominium developers to provide a swimming pool and a recreational area under a long-term lease.

    d. Condominium regulations may not restrict the use of an individual condominium unit.

ANSWER KEY

1. (*c*)	11. (*c*)	21. (*a*)	31. (*c*)
2. (*b*)	12. (*c*)	22. (*b*)	32. (*b*)
3. (*d*)	13. (*c*)	23. (*a*)	33. (*a*)
4. (*c*)	14. (*a*)	24. (*c*)	34. (*c*)
5. (*a*)	15. (*c*)	25. (*c*)	35. (*d*)
6. (*a*)	16. (*c*)	26. (*d*)	36. (*c*)
7. (*a*)	17. (*d*)	27. (*b*)	37. (*d*)
8. (*d*)	18. (*a*)	28. (*b*)	38. (*c*)
9. (*d*)	19. (*c*)	29. (*d*)	39. (*a*)
10. (*a*)	20. (*c*)	30. (*a*)	40. (*c*)

SUGGESTED ADDITIONAL READING

Atteberry, William; Pearson, Karl; and Litka, Michael. *Real Estate Law.* Columbus, O.: Grid, Inc., 1974, chap. 17.

Downs, James C., Jr. *Principles of Real Estate Management.* 11th ed. Chicago: Institute of Real Estate Management, 1975, chap. 12.

Hebard, Edna L., and Meisel, Gerald S. *Principles of Real Estate Law.* Cambridge, Mass.: Schenkman Publishing Co., 1967, chap. 6.

Lusk, Harold F., and French, William B. *Law of the Real Estate Business.* 3d ed. Homewood, Ill.: Richard D. Irwin, Inc., 1975, chap. 4.

Part III

The Practice of Real Estate

12

Real Estate Mathematics

R eal estate practice includes mathematical problems concentrated in
four subject areas: property taxes, land and building area calculations,
real estate commissions, and interest rates. The examples in this chapter
are taken directly from real estate operations. They should give the
reader a workable knowledge of the most common types of real estate
mathematical problems.

PROPERTY TAXES

Property taxes are administered by local agencies: counties, cities,
townships, and similar local jurisdictions. Many local agencies have the
right to levy or place a tax on local property in their district. For example,
there are special districts formed for schools, fire fighting, drainage,
sewerage systems, county roads, mosquito control, ports, and others.
Usually there is a county or city assessor whose responsibility is to value
local real estate for property tax purposes. To understand how to calculate
property taxes, it is necessary to understand two terms: the assessed value
and the millage rate.

Assessed Value

The office charged with placing a value on local real estate for
property tax purposes must estimate the "true and fair value," just value,
or a like value. These statutory values have been interpreted to mean
market value. The laws of the various states may require an estimate of
assessed value based in some cases on a percentage of the market value.

The assessed value is the value used to calculate annual property taxes. In Florida, county assessors must place property on the local property tax roll at 100 percent of the true value, meaning market value. In this case, the assessed value entered on the property tax roll presumably is the market value.

There is much confusion over the calculation of assessed values. While the law calls for assessed values equal to just value, just and fair value, or fair market value, experience shows that assessed values are based on a system of "fractional" values. Fractional values follow from the practice of applying cost of reproduction estimates (less depreciation) to all properties in an assessment district. Suppose for example, that the cost manual used to calculate assessed values results in building valuation equal to $15 per square foot for a new building. With a 1,500-square–foot building, the cost value would be $22,500. If the land is valued at $2,500, the total assessed valued of the land and buildings would be $25,000.

Assuming that the property sells for $40,000, the assessed value is equal to roughly 60 percent of the current market value as indicated by the sales price ($25,000/$40,000). If this 60 percent ratio between the assessed value and the current sales price (market value) prevails generally, local assessments would be based upon a fractional assessment of 60 percent. Alternatively the assessments may be described as based on an assessment ratio of 60 percent (assessed value/sales price).

Knowing the mechanics of assessing and taxing real estate helps to estimate property tax payments. In most local jurisdictions, land is assessed separately from buildings. Every property theoretically is valued as of a given date, usually the first of January. For example, a subdivision completed *after* January 1st, will probably have lot values determined as of the first of January of the following year. A house which is started in February and completed in June may not be entered on the tax roll until the succeeding year. Therefore, care must be taken in calculating the property taxes of new property; the current property tax may be calculated on the assessed value of land only.

There is the further point that the assessed value may have only a remote relation to market value. Property is infrequently appraised by the local assessor. Moreover, the assessor must usually rely on reproduction costs to value a building. The resulting figure may or may not be close to the current market value. Wide discrepancies in value between and among similar properties, recommend against using assessed values as substitutes for market value. The assessed value serves only as the base against which property taxes are levied.

The Millage Rate

The tax levy or the rate at which property is taxed is calculated in mills. A mill is one tenth of a cent. In tax terminology, the tax rate may be expressed in mills, for example, 45.63 mills. Since a mill is one tenth of a cent, the equivalent here in dollars is $.04563. This rate is multiplied times the assessed value. Assume an assessed value of $20,400:

Annual property tax = Assessed value × Tax levy (in mills)
= $20,400 × .04563
= $930.85

Local officials often express the tax rate as so many dollars in thousands and hundreds. For instance, a 45.63 millage rate would be equivalent to a tax rate of $45.63 per $1,000 of assessed value. Alternatively, in some areas the millage rate is shown as so many dollars per $100. The same millage rate would be expressed as $4.563 per $100 of assessed value.

To estimate the annual property tax in dollars, determine the total assessed value of the property, land and buildings, from the records of the local tax office. Make sure that the reported assessed value covers both land and the buildings. Make sure also that the assessed value applies to the current property value. The next step is to multiply the assessed value times the tax rate in mills.

There is one other point: the tax levy is determined by government officials charged with the responsibility of approving the local budget and fixing the tax rate. Given the total assessed value of the district, and the budget required to support local government, the budget authority—the city council, the county commissioners, township officials, or other authorities—divides the total required budget by the total assessed value in the tax district. The result is the millage rate.

The millage rate is then applied against individual properties to determine the allocation of property taxes between and among individual property owners. To show how the local tax rate is calculated, consider the following case.

```
Required annual budget............................ $ 21,563,000
Total assessed value................................. $408,768,000
Annual tax levy $21,563,000/$408,768,000...............     0.05275
                                                       (52.75 mills)
```

The example shows a required annual budget of $21,563,000. The total assessed value of all properties in the tax jurisdiction is some $408,768,000. The local agency determines the tax rate to be applied to individual properties, in this case 52.75 mills. This is equivalent to a tax of 5.275 percent on the assessed value (52.75 mills = .05275 or 5.275 percent).

The next issue is to show how the levy is applied to selected property types. The examples that follow indicate how property taxes are imposed on land. Generally speaking, land is taxed on a per acre, per front foot, or per square foot basis. Subdivision lots showing unusual shapes may be assessed at so many dollars per lot. See the following example of land taxes:

Assessed value per acre

25.6 acres at $750 an acre..................	$ 19,200
Annual tax levy, 54.65 mills...............	.05465
Annual property tax, 19__.................	$1,049.29

Assessed value per front foot

156.3 front feet at $35.00..................	$5,470.50
Annual tax levy, 30.63 mills...............	.03063
Annual property tax, 19__.................	$ 167.56

Assessed value per square foot

106,583 square feet at $.45..................	$ 47,962
Annual tax levy, 100.35 mills..............	.10035
Annual property tax, 19__.................	$4,812.99

Note that the unit of valuation is applied to the unit measure used to value land (e.g., the price per acre times the number of acres). The resulting assessed value serves as the tax base. The property owner will pay taxes on the assessed value according to the annual tax levy, in this case, expressed in mills. (Recall that a mill is equal to $0.001.)

Buildings are assessed separately. The same procedure will be used to value the land, then the assessed value of the building is added to derive the total assessed value, land and buildings. Building valuation follows normal appraisal practices usually resulting in an estimate of the reproduction cost less depreciation. Calculations applied to building and land are shown in the following example.

Property taxes on land and building

Land assessed value.....................	$ 11,550
Building assessed value.................	206,300
Total assessed value.....................	$ 217,850
Annual property tax levy (20.36 mills)......	× .02036
Annual property tax, 19__................	$4,435.42

The annual property tax levy of 20.36 mills results in an annual property tax of $4,435.42.

The property taxes for a given year will probably vary in succeeding years. First, property in the local jurisdiction is subject to periodic revaluation of land and buildings, and as the tax base or assessed value changes, the annual property tax will change. Second, local officials may change the tax levy from year to year. The tax levy is a function of the budgets adopted by local governments, which are financed from local property taxes. Inquiries to local officials may help in projecting property taxes for succeeding years.

There is one further point. Local assessors generally follow accepted appraisal techniques, which are explained in a later chapter. For the present, it should be noted that reliance is placed on the estimate of cost new less the depreciation, comparisons with the sale of like property, and capitalization of net income. If accepted appraisal techniques are applied, the initial value will tend to equal current market value. Here the law of the respective states is controlling. In Georgia, local assessors are directed to value property 40 percent of the current market value. In Montgomery County, Pennsylvania, the assessor values property at 30 percent of market value.

For instance, suppose a shopping center has a value based upon its capitalized net income of $2,000,000. The assessor arrives at this figure by estimating net income and capitalizing this value to give present worth or market value. To illustrate, assume a net income of $250,000. If this income is capitalized with a .125 percent capitalization rate, the property would have an indicated market value of $2,000,000 under the income technique ($250,000/.125). Actually, a shopping center appraisal would be considerably more complicated. But assuming that the $2,000,000 produces an estimate of market value by the income approach, and that the assessor applies the 30 percent assessment ratio to his value estimate, the assessed value would be $600,000, or equal to 30 percent of the market value. The same treatment would be given to a building that was ap-praised by the cost of reproduction and by comparison with prices of recently sold properties.

CALCULATION OF LAND AND BUILDING AREAS

The ability to calculate land and building areas avoids embarrassing errors. Problems are frequently encountered requiring the conversion of area and volumes to units of a different measure: for example, square feet to square yards or cubic feet to cubic yards. A review of the standard methods of calculating land area, building area, and cubic volume provides a useful background to solve the more common real estate area and volume problems.

Land Area

Most problems relating to land area calculations may be solved by formulas that apply to the rectangle, the triangle, the trapezoid, and circle. Only arithmetical methods of calculating these areas are described here. Technical training in trigonometry and surveying and the knowledge of drafting equipment would be used for more precision.

The simplest cases start with land shaped in a rectangle. Assuming that the rectangle has 90-degree corners, the area is found by multiplying width times length. The illustration of Figure 12–1 shows an area of 5,000 square feet. The perimeter is important in calculating the lineal feet for fencing and walls and is found by summing the sides or multiplying the sum of length and width by two.

Knowing how to calculate the area of a triangle is helpful in calculating the area of an oddly-shaped area. The area of a right triangle is found

FIGURE 12–1
Example Calculations

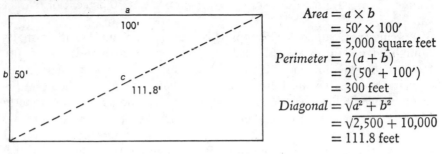

$$Area = a \times b$$
$$= 50' \times 100'$$
$$= 5{,}000 \text{ square feet}$$
$$Perimeter = 2(a + b)$$
$$= 2(50' + 100')$$
$$= 300 \text{ feet}$$
$$Diagonal = \sqrt{a^2 + b^2}$$
$$= \sqrt{2{,}500 + 10{,}000}$$
$$= 111.8 \text{ feet}$$

by multiplying its base times its height and dividing the product by two. To find the perimeter, add the distance of the legs. To use this method, two dimensions of the triangle must be known, as shown in Figure 12–2.

Rarely do subdivided lots have the regular dimensions of perfect rectangles or triangles. In the majority of cases, the land area will resemble a trapezoid. A trapezoid calls for the type of calculations shown in Figure 12–3.

FIGURE 12–2
Example Calculations

$$Area = \frac{a \times d}{2}$$
$$= \frac{200' \times 50'}{2}$$
$$= 5{,}000 \text{ square feet}$$
$$Perimeter = a + b + c$$
$$= 200' + 111.8' + 111.8'$$
$$= 423.6 \text{ feet}$$

FIGURE 12–3
Example Calculations

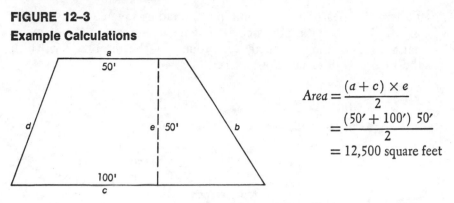

$$Area = \frac{(a+c) \times e}{2}$$
$$= \frac{(50' + 100')\ 50'}{2}$$
$$= 12,500 \text{ square feet}$$

The formula for the area starts with the average length of *a* and *c* and multiplies this times the height. For a residential lot, the area would be the result of multiplying the average lot depth times the lot width. If the width varies, draw a scale diagram so that the odd-shaped area can be divided into right-angled triangles. See Figure 12–4 for an illustration of this technique.

FIGURE 12–4
Example Calculations

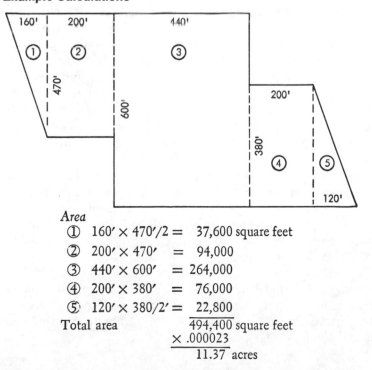

Area
① 160′ × 470′/2 =   37,600 square feet
② 200′ × 470′   =   94,000
③ 440′ × 600′   = 264,000
④ 200′ × 380′   =   76,000
⑤ 120′ × 380/2′ =   22,800
Total area   494,400 square feet
                        × .000023
                        11.37 acres

To find the area of a circle, multiply the radius squared times pi (π). Pi (3.14159) is the ratio of the circumference of a circle to the diameter Given the radius, the circumference is found by the formula $2\pi r$, which in the Figure 12–5 equals 314.159 feet.

FIGURE 12–5
Example Calculations

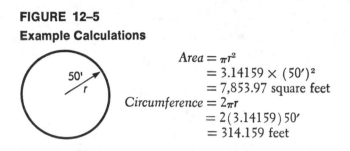

$$Area = \pi r^2$$
$$= 3.14159 \times (50')^2$$
$$= 7,853.97 \text{ square feet}$$
$$Circumference = 2\pi r$$
$$= 2(3.14159)50'$$
$$= 314.159 \text{ feet}$$

Building Areas

There are certain conventions which guide the calculation of building areas. The building area may refer to the ground floor area or the total floor area. The ground floor area usually agrees with the area enclosed by the foundation. For single-family dwellings, the ground floor is measured from outside dimensions of the exterior wall. Total floor area includes the heated living area, attic rooms (but not attic space), floors above the first-floor level, and basement areas if they are finished as separate rooms. Houses with unfinished basements are usually reported as houses of given square-foot floor area reported for the first floor and above with basements. For split-level houses, which are usually improved on three or more floor levels, total floor area includes the square foot floor area of each level. (Omitted in these floor-area and ground-floor calculations are nonliving areas, such as unheated utility spaces, garages and carports, unenclosed porches, roofed or unroofed, unimproved attic space, and unfinished basements.

The most common errors in calculating floor areas, given these omissions, occur with the courts of irregularly shaped houses. The easiest way to measure floor area is to take the maximum dimensions of a house, length and width, and subtract the odd-shaped areas or courts. Garages, open porches, and utility space, which are not part of the living area, would be shown separately.

Figure 12–6 shows how to calculate ground-floor area by taking the maximum width and length dimensions. The floor area (enclosed living space) is found by deducting the court areas shown. (Roofs, porches, patios, car ports, and outside unheated utility space would be shown separately from the floor area.)

FIGURE 12–6

Ground-floor Area Calculations

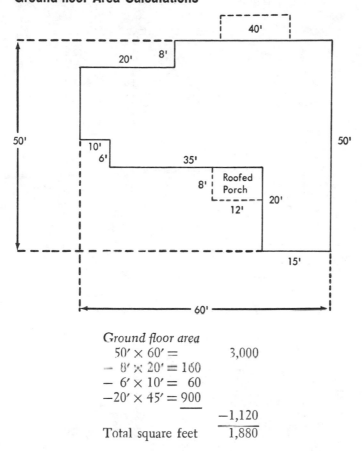

Ground floor area

$$50' \times 60' = \qquad 3{,}000$$
$$- 8' \times 20' = 160$$
$$- 6' \times 10' = 60$$
$$-20' \times 45' = 900$$
$$\overline{}$$
$$-1{,}120$$

Total square feet $\qquad \overline{1{,}880}$

In dwellings with gable roofs, the floor area includes only rooms with a minimum ceiling height of seven feet. Attic rooms are calculated as 50 percent of the ground floor space, unless they have a steep pitch. For buildings of two stories or more, the area of the upper stories must be added to the ground floor area.

For certain structures the cubic foot area is more relevant. Commercial and industrial property with varying ceiling heights are measured in cubic feet rather than square feet. Because of higher ceilings and the special construction found in auditoriums and other buildings with varying ceiling heights, such as industrial buildings, certain accepted rules apply to cubic-foot calculations. Figure 12–7 shows calculations for a two-story building with a gable and flat roof. Since cubic foot construction costs are related to outside dimensions, measurements are taken from the floor

FIGURE 12–7

The Calculation of Cubic Feet

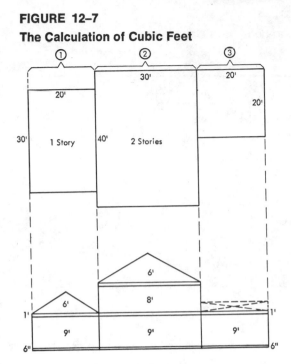

Cubic feet calculations
        Area ①
            20′ × 30′ × 10′6″ =   6,300
            20′ × 30′ × 6′/2   =   1,800
        Area ②
            30′ × 40′ × 10′6″ = 12,600
            30′ × 40′ × 9′   = 10,800
            30′ × 40′ × 6′/2   =   3,600
        Area ③
            20′ × 20′ × 10′6″ =   4,200
            Total Cubic feet 39,300

area measured from its base to the top of the roof. Note that the attic space is included.

SQUARE FOOT AND CUBIC FOOT CONVERSIONS

On occasion, measurements must be converted to alternative units of measure. Here are equivalents for linear and surface area measurements:

Linear Measures
    12 inches = 1 foot
    3 feet   = 36 inches

```
36 inches = 1 yard
1 mile    = 5,280 feet
5,280 feet = 1,760 yards
```
Area Measurements
```
144 square inches = 1 square foot
9 square feet      = 1 square yard
43,560 square feet = 1 acre
640 acres          = 1 square mile
1 square mile      = 1 section
36 sections        = 36 square miles
36 square miles    = 1 township
¼ section          = 160 acres
```

In real estate, land measurements are often given in lineal feet, which must be converted to acreage values. A shortcut method of converting from square feet to acres uses the reciprocal of 43,560 (1/43,560). The decimal or the reciprocal of the number of square feet per acre is .000023 (or the number of acres per square foot is .000023). Multiplying square feet by 23 and pointing off 6 decimal places is easier than dividing the number of square feet by 43,560. For example, here is the number of acres in 161,654 square feet:

$$\frac{\begin{array}{r} 161,654 \text{ square feet} \\ .000023 \end{array}}{3.718042 \text{ acres}}$$

The product shows an approximate acreage of 3.72 acres (rounded).

Other common problems require conversion of square feet to square yards. The most frequently used volume measures are listed below:

Cubic Measures
```
1,728 cubic inches = 1 cubic foot
27 cubic feet      = 1 cubic yard
128 cubic feet     = 1 cord of wood
                     (a pile 8′ × 4′ × 4′)
```

Asphalt paving is often priced according to square yard calculations. Suppose, for example, that a driveway measuring 12 feet by 50 feet must be converted to square yards.

$$12' \times 50' = 600 \text{ square feet}$$
$$\frac{600}{9} = 66.67 \text{ square yards}$$

A surface measuring 12 feet by 50 feet, or 600 square feet, is equivalent to 66.67 square yards.

Similar problems require the conversion of cubic feet to cubic yards, as in estimates of excavation and concrete requirements. A block of concrete measuring 3 feet wide by 3 feet long and 3 feet high constitutes one cubic yard, or 27 cubic feet. Given the 27-cubic foot equivalent, calculate the number of cubic yards in an area measuring 125 feet by 63 feet with an average depth of 8 feet.

$$125' \times 8' \times 63' = 63,000 \text{ cubic feet}$$
$$63,000/27 = 2,333.3 \text{ cubic yards}$$

REAL ESTATE COMMISSIONS

Real estate commissions follow a varied pattern. While a flat percentage commission based on the sales price is the most common procedure, other arrangements complicate the calculation of real estate commissions.

Commissions based on net listings are one variation. In other instances the commission will be graduated. That is, the commission will be the result of different commission rates applied to different value portions of the sale. Graduated rates are common for commercial property sales, and leases quite often call for a different method of calculating commissions, since there is no final sale price.

Besides the calculation of the commission, its distribution requires additional calculation. Commissions are shared with cooperating brokers. If multiple listing services are used, the commission must be divided between the listing agency, the salesman, and the employing broker. Additionally, interoffice arrangements call for special formulas to cover draws against commissions, straight commissions, and allowable expenses.

If a commission is based on a stated percentage of the sales price, the first step is to determine if personal property sold with real estate is considered part of the sales price for commission purposes. After this problem is resolved the next step is to multiply the price times the commission rate. For example:

$$\$35,000 \times .06 = \$2,100$$

The only other qualification turns on the commission rate. Commission rates follow local custom and are subject to negotiation between the broker and the seller. In some cases the broker is employed by the buyer, or in special circumstances he may collect from both the buyer and the seller if both parties agree to this arrangement. For the marketing of highly specialized properties such as industrial properties, the broker may charge agreed-upon advertising expenses in addition to a straight commission. Industrial properties that are marketed on a national scale may call for a commission rate of 150 percent of customary commissions. The additional 50 percent is paid to the selling broker, while the listing broker who supervises a national marketing plan will earn the customary full commission.

The first variation of a real estate commission is calculation of the recommended listing price. Assume that the seller wants to recover his equity, selling expenses and real estate commissions. To proceed on this basis, the real estate commission and selling expenses and the net selling price must be given. To illustrate assume the following facts:

100%	gross sales price
9%	commission rate
91%	gross to owner
$40,000	net to owner
800	estimated closing expenses of seller
$40,800	gross to owner

In this example, the owner desires $40,000 net from the sale. With closing expenses of $800, this means the property must sell for $40,800 after payment of real estate commission. Dividing $40,800 by the gross percentage to the owner, 91 percent, gives the listing price that allows a 9 percent commission on the sales price, $40,000 net to the owner, and an allowance of $800 for closing expenses.

$$\$40,800/.91 = \$44,835 \text{ minimum listing price}$$

If the property sells for $44,835 the sale proceeds would be distributed as follows:

$44,835	sales price
−4,035	9% sales commission
$40,800	gross to owner
− 800	closing expenses
$40,000	net to seller

The example offers a proof of the recommended minimum listing price if the owner is to net $40,000 under these conditions.

Graduated commissions are calculated by dividing the sales price into sales brackets. Suppose the commission schedule called for the following schedule:

10% on the first	$100,000
8% on the next	$500,000
4% on the next	$400,000
2% on the amount over	$1,000,000

If the listed property sells for $1,500,000, the commission would total $76,000.

1st	$ 100,000 × .10 =	$10,000
next	500,000 × .08 =	40,000
next	400,000 × .04 =	16,000
next	500,000 × .02 =	10,000
	$1,500,000	$76,000 total commission

Long-term leases usually call for a commission schedule graduated according to the annual rent payment. For a 25-year lease calling for an annual minimum rent graduated by 5-year intervals, suppose the commission was also graduated according to the following schedule.

Lease Commission Schedule	Minimum Rent Schedule	
8% 1st year	1st 5 years	$10,000
2% each year for 4 years	2d 5 years	12,500
1% each year thereafter	3d 5 years	15,000
	4th 5 years	20,000
	5th 5 years	25,000

Commission Calculation

1st year	$10,000 × .08.............	$ 800
Next four years	10,000 × (4) × .02........	800
Next five years	12,500 × (5) × .01........	625
Next five years	15,000 × (5) × .01........	750
Next five years	20,000 × (5) × .01........	1,000
Next five years	25,000 × (5) × .01........	1,250
	Total commission..................	$5,225

With a graduated rent and commission schedule as shown, the total commission amounts to $5,225.

Other problems relate to the division of the commission between salesmen and the broker, listing salesman, multiple-listing service, or co-operating brokers. Naturally the shares to each party should not total more than full commission. After calculating separate shares, they should be added to permit verification with the total commission.

INTEREST RATE PROBLEMS

When solving interest rate problems, much time can be saved with compound interest tables. Compound interest is interest earned on a principal sum which is increased each year. Unless interest is paid annually, interest is compounded. Compound interest tables are labeled as the compound amount of one (dollar).

S = Compound amount $(i + P)$
i = Rate of interest per period
P = Principal or amount of money
    borrowed or invested

The compound amount at the end of the first year is given by the formula:

$$S_1 = P(1 + i)$$

At the end of the second year, the compound amount is given by:

$$S_2 = S_1(1 + i)$$

This is equivalent to:

$$S = P(1 + i)^2$$

Succeeding periods can be calculated by multiplying the compound amount at the end of each year by $1 + i$. For any given number of periods (n), the general formula would be:

$$S = P(1 + i)^n$$

To avoid tedious calculations for additional periods, compound amounts in Table 12–1 show the values of $1 calculated at different in-

TABLE 12–1

Compound Interest, 6 Percent, 5 Years

Beginning of Year	Principal (P)	6 Percent Interest Added at End of Year (i)	Compound Amount End of Year (S)	Amount of $1 Compound Interest $S = (1 + i)^n$
1...............	$1,000.00	$60.00	$1,060.00	1.06000
2...............	1,060.00	63.60	1,123.60	1.12360
3...............	1,123.60	67.42	1,191.02	1.19102
4...............	1,191.02	71.46	1,262.48	1.26248
5...............	1,262.50	75.75	1,338.23	1.33823

terest rates by periods. Table 12–1 reproduces calculations assumed for a five year, 6 percent compound interest table. The table shows that $1,338.23 would be paid at the end of five years, compounded at 6 percent interest annually. To find out how much $1,000 would accumulate compounded at 6 percent per year for five years, you would multiply the principal by the factor 1.33823. This factor is the value of $1 compounded annually for five years at 6 percent.

$$1.33823 \times \$1,000 = \$1,338.23$$

To illustrate the use of these tables, assume that A loans B $10,000 for five years at 6 percent interest compounded annually. If interest and principal are due at the end of the term, how much will A receive at the end of 5 years? The answer is found by applying the compound interest formula, $S = P(1 + i)^n$ and the compound interest factor of 2.33823:

$$S = \$10,000(1 + .06)^5$$
$$S = \$10,000(1.33823)$$
$$S = \$13,382.30$$

Compound interest tables are used to determine the principal, given the payment of a debt over a stated time and the interest rate. For instance, if A collects $11,910.16 on a debt that was repaid at the end of three years at 6 percent compound interest, what was the principal? In this case solve for P:

$$S = P(1.06)^3$$
$$\$11,910.16 = P(1.06)^3$$
$$P = \frac{\$11,910.16}{1.191016}$$
$$P = \$10,000$$

To calculate principal and interest payments for more frequent compounding, different interest tables and periods must be used. Suppose a loan is compounded at an interest rate of 6 percent for one year. The compound amount of one factor would be calculated by the compound interest formula:

$$S = (1.00 + .06)^1$$
$$= \$1.06$$

But if interest is compounded *semi-annually* at an *annual* interest rate of 6 percent, the formula would be changed to read:

$$S = (1.00 + .03)^2$$
$$= 1.0609$$

A $1,000 loan compounded semi-annually at an annual 6 percent rate would require an interest and principal payment of $1,060.90 at the end of one year ($1,000 × 1.0609).

Thus, to calculate the compound amount of $1 for more frequent compounding, divide the annual interest rate by the number of periods compounded. Using the annual interest rate of 6 percent compounded for more frequent periods, use the rule to adjust periods and interest rates as here:

Compound Period	Interest Rate	Numbers of Periods Compounded
Annual....................	.06	1
Semi-annual............	.03	2
Quarterly...............	.015	4
Monthly.................	.005	12

In the example, a 6 percent compound interest rate, compounded semi-annually, would be found by using the 3 percent compound interest table for two periods.

In real estate, simple interest must often be calculated over odd periods of time. As applied to the mortgage, the interest is calculated on the outstanding monthly balance. To illustrate, let us suppose that the outstanding mortgage balance of $34,531 calls for monthly payments under a 25-year mortgage with 9 percent annual interest rate. Monthly amortized mortgages are based on interest payments calculated on the remaining balance each month. Given the remaining balance, interest can be calculated for the first month. A 9 percent monthly amortized mortgage has a monthly interest rate of .0075 (.09/12). The interest for the next month would be

$$\$34,531 \times .0075 = \$258.98$$

If mortgage payments were $420, then the amount of the amortized principal for a given month would be found by subtraction.

$420.00 monthly payment
−258.98 interest
$161.02 principal amortization

With a $420 monthly payment, the mortgage in the following months would be reduced by $161.02.

The Mortgage Constant

It is useful to determine annual monthly interest and principal payments, given the interest rate and length of the mortgage and the amount of the loan. Since most real estate loans provide for monthly amortization, this figure must be taken from mortgage installment tables.

To illustrate, suppose a loan requires repayment of mortgage and interest at the end of the year over the five-year term. The mortgage installment table shows the amount of the annual payment required at the end of the year:

Mortgage Installment Table
9 Percent, Five Annual Payments
1.090000
.568469
.395055
.308669
.257092

The table shows that a loan of $1 for one year at 9 percent requires a mortgage and interest payment of $1.09 at the end of the year. If a loan of $1 is repaid in two annual installments, the two payments would equal $.568469; five annual payments would equal $.257092.

Table 12–2 shows the way in which these payments may be applied to a loan of $3,889.65 in five annual payments at a 9 percent capitalization rate. Since $.257092 is the amount necessary to repay $1, a loan of $3,889.65 would call for annual payments of $1,000 (.257092 × $3,889.65).

With a constant annual payment of $1,000, the interest rate paid at the end of the year would be $350.07 ($3,889.65 × .09).

The assumption is that the lender is entitled to a 9 percent return on his remaining balance for each payment. Note that with a constant annual payment of $1,000, only $350.07 goes to interest, representing 9 percent of the remaining balance. The difference between the $1,000 payment and interest of $350.07 is the principal repayment. At the end of the first year, the principal repayment of $649.93 results in a remaining balance of $3,239.72 at the end of the first year.

As this procedure is repeated at the end of the five years, payments total $5,000, of which $1,110.34 represents interest and the balance repre-

TABLE 12–2

The Amortization of $3,889.65, Five Years, 9 Percent Interest

End of Period	Installment to Amortize $1.00	Principal	Constant Annual Payment	Interest on Remaining Balance	Principal Repayment	Remaining Balance
1..........	0.257092	$3,889.65	$1,000	$ 350.07	$ 649.93	3,239.72
2..........	0.257092	3,889.65	1,000	291.57	708.43	2,531.24
3..........	0.257092	3,889.65	1,000	227.82	772.18	1,759.06
4..........	0.257092	3,889.65	1,000	158.32	841.68	917.38
5..........	0.257092	3,889.65	1,000	82.56	917.44	(.06 rounding error)
Total........	—	—	$5,000	$1,110.34	$3,888.66	—

sents the return of principal. The mortgage constant is taken from mortgage tables showing the amount necessary to amortize a loan of $1.00 given the interest rate and the term of the mortgage. A loan of 25 years at 9 percent requires 300 monthly payments (25 years × 12 months). If the loan is for $1, 300 payments of $.008391 would be required to repay it.

To calculate the *annual mortgage constant*, the monthly payment, including principal and interest, is multiplied by 12 months. The mortgage constant for a 9 percent, 25-year mortgage would be .1006, or in percent terms the mortgage constant would be described as 10.06 percent (.008391 × 12). Therefore, to repay a $100,000 loan over 25 years in 300 monthly installments at 9 percent interest, $10,060 is required each year.

The mortgage constant is a shorthand method of estimating how much money must be set aside on an annual basis to amortize a real estate loan. The mortgage constant is found by a partial payment or installment loan table based on monthly payments times 12. In the preceding example, it would probably be uneconomic to invest in a project that is expected to earn a net income of $10,000 if the property requires a $100,000 loan with a mortgage constant of 10.06 percent. In this instance, the mortgage payments would be greater than the net income.

Simple Interest Calculations

For some purposes, simple interest is based on a 360-day year and 30-day months. If this is the case, simple interest is calculated for the year. The interest rate per month and per year are found by division. For example, what is the interest charge for a $30,000 loan at a 8 percent simple interest for 7 months?

$$
\begin{array}{r}
30,000 \\
.09 \\
\hline
\$270 \text{ annual interest}
\end{array}
$$

$$
\frac{\$270}{12} = \$22.50 \text{ monthly interest}
$$

$$
\$22.50 \times 7 = \$157.50
$$

Assume further that the interest applies to 7 months and 21 days. The daily interest rate would be equal to $.75 per day ($22.50 per month/30). The interest for 7 months and 21 days would total:

$$
\begin{array}{lr}
7 \text{ months} & \$157.50 \\
21 \text{ days} \times \$.75 & 15.75 \\
\hline
7 \text{ months, 21 days} & \$173.25
\end{array}
$$

Contrast this technique with simple interest calculated according to the actual number of days. For this purpose, actual days in the calendar month are used based on a 365-day year. Table 12–3 provides a fairly easy method of calculating the actual number of days starting from any given date to any terminal date during the calendar year. The table follows the usual assumptions that the first day is not counted and that the terminal day is counted.

TABLE 12–3

Calculation of the Actual Number of Days within a 365-day Year

From Any Day of	To the Same Day of the Next											
	Jan.	Feb.	Mar.	Apr.	May	June	July	Aug.	Sep.	Oct.	Nov.	Dec.
January......	365	31	59	90	120	151	181	212	243	273	304	334
February.....	334	365	28	59	89	120	150	181	212	242	273	303
March........	306	337	365	31	61	92	122	153	184	214	245	275
April.........	275	306	334	365	30	61	91	122	153	183	214	244
May..........	245	276	304	335	365	31	61	92	123	153	184	214
June.........	214	245	273	304	334	365	30	61	92	122	153	183
July..........	184	215	243	274	304	335	365	31	62	92	123	153
August.......	153	184	212	243	273	304	334	365	31	61	92	122
September...	122	153	181	212	242	273	303	334	365	30	61	91
October......	92	123	151	182	212	243	273	304	335	365	31	61
November....	61	92	120	151	181	212	242	273	304	334	365	30
December....	31	62	90	121	151	182	212	243	274	304	335	365

From Table 12–3, select a date in January to the same date in January of the following year. The table will show 365 days. In other words, from any date to the same date a year later gives 365 days (i.e., 365 days expire from January 15 to the same date in January of the following year).

Suppose you want the number of days from January 15 to January 5 of the following year. Since Table 12–3 shows 365 days from the same date in January of the following year, subtract 10 days (15 − 5) for the correct answer: 355 days. The exact number of days from August 5 to October 23 is found by finding 61 days opposite August on the horizontal line under the column under October. Since there are 61 days between August 5 and October 5, add 18 days for the correct answer: 79 days. By adding or subtracting the actual number of days required from one month to any other given month, the number of days may be readily calculated.

With the actual number of days, simple interest is given according to the proportion of that the actual number of days bears to 365 days. For example, the amount of interest earned on a $10,000 debt for 79 days, at 9 percent interest would be equal to

$$\text{Interest} = \frac{\$10,000}{1} \times \frac{.09}{1} \times \frac{79}{365}$$

$$= \$900 \times \frac{79}{365}$$

$$= \$194.79$$

In effect, calculation of simple interest starts with the interest for the full year, $900 times the actual fraction of the year that earns interest, in this example.

QUESTIONS FOR REVIEW

_____ 1. A rectangular lot measuring 74.6 front feet by 147 feet deep represents _____ of an acre.
  a.   9.9 percent
  b.   12.5 percent
  c.   25.2 percent
  d.   27.5 percent

_____ 2. A farm has ⅝ of its acreage under cultivation; ¼₄ of the acreage is unusable; the remainder is in standing timber. The standing timber represents 90 acres. How many acres are in the entire farm?
  a.   360.
  b.   420.
  c.   247.
  d.   505.

_____ 3. How many square feet would be contained in a sidewalk 6 feet wide around the outside of a corner lot measuring 60 by 110 feet?

    a. 1,020.
    b.   940.
    c. 1,120.
    d. 1,056.

_____ 4. Dave has decided to build a flat-roofed building and has received two estimates for the job. The first contractor can build the building for $19.50 per square foot; the second contractor estimates a $1.05 per-cubic-foot cost. If the building is to measure 65 feet wide by 40 deep by 18 feet high, which contractor should Dave select and how much will he save?

    a. The first contractor would save $747.00.
    b. The second contractor would save $507.50.
    c. The second contractor would save $1,560.00.
    d. The first contractor would save $1,056.00.

_____ 5. How many acres are contained in a land parcel measuring 1,250 feet by 900 feet (rounded to the nearest tenth of an acre)?

    a. 17.5.
    b. 25.8.
    c. 32.3.
    d. 20.5.

_____ 6. If land is priced at $1,200 per acre, what is the price of land measuring 600 feet by 750 feet?

    a. $ 9,855.60.
    b. $18,750.00.
    c. $24,600.00.
    d. $12,396.00.

_____ 7. If a house that measures 54 feet by 36 feet cost $36,500 to construct, what was the cost per square foot (rounded to the nearest cent)?

    a. $18.78.
    b. $19.44.
    c. $17.57.
    d. $16.48.

_____ 8. Ed purchased 12 acres of land for subdivision into lots 110 feet by 150 feet deep. If one fourth of the total area is unusable, how many lots will be available for sale (rounded to the nearest whole number of lots)?

    a. 18.
    b. 24.
    c. 36.
    d. 42.

_____ 9. Compute the tax on a property assessed at $25,600 with a millage
          rate of 64.5 mills.
          a. $ 640.50.
          b. $2,118.75.
          c. $1,066.30.
          d. $1,651.20.

_____10. If the county levies 24 mills, the city 10 mills and the school district
          17.5 mills, what would be the tax for a property assessed at
          $18,000?
          a. $1,800.00.
          b. $ 927.00.
          c. $ 467.50.
          d. $ 754.60.

_____11. The total assessed value of taxable property in the city of Greenville
          is $50,000,000. If the city budget calls for expenditures of $1,250,-
          000, what would the annual property tax be on property assessed at
          $35,000?
          a. $ 875.00
          b. $ 350.50.
          c. $1,236.00.
          d. $ 940.00.

_____12. Assuming a fair market value of $36,800 and an assessment ratio of
          40 percent, calculate the property tax under a tax levy of 42.75
          mills.
          a. $427.75.
          b. $368.57.
          c. $852.34.
          d. $629.28.

_____13. If an $80,000 property is assessed at 60 percent of its value, what
          is the annual property tax if the tax rate is $17 per thousand?
          a. $1,360.00.
          b. $ 136.45.
          c. $ 918.20.
          d. $ 816.00.

_____14. A residential lot is assessed at $3,500; the tax rate is $.0075. If the
          owner constructs a house on the lot with an assessed value of
          $29,200, what is the annual property tax?
          a. $359.20.
          b. $245.25.
          c. $194.63.
          d. $546.83.

_____15. If a property is assessed at $10,100 with a tax rate of $2.50 per
          $100, how much would the owner need to put into a monthly
          escrow account to cover the annual property taxes?

a. $21.04.
b. $25.25.
c. $15.75.
d. $36.00.

____16. A broker manages a 200-unit apartment house with an average rental of $220 per month. His management contract calls for 6 percent of the actual rent collected. Assuming an annual vacancy rate of 10 percent, what is his annual management fee?

a. $38,125.
b. $28,512.
c. $42,812.
d. $22,215.

____17. An owner wants $10,500 from the sale of his property. If he pays the listing broker a 6-percent commission, how much must the broker list the property for to net $10,500 (round to nearest dollar)?

a. $11,130.
b. $10,560.
c. $12,136.
d. $11,170.

____18. Salesperson Ames receives 60 percent of the total commission on all sales he makes. If he sells a property for $42,300, how much will he receive in commission if the total brokerage fee is 6 percent?

a. $2,538.00.
b. $1,769.00.
c. $1,522.80.
d. $1,354.00.

____19. By agreement, salespersons for the Ajax Realty Company receive a listing fee of 10 percent of the gross commission, and the selling salesperson shares the remaining commission equally with the firm. If a salesperson sells a $35,000 property, which he did not list, how much will he receive with a brokerage commission of 7 percent?

a. $1,102.50.
b. $1,245.00.
c. $1,225.00.
d. $1,050.50.

____20. Frank leased a store on a percentage basis. The lease calls for a minimum of $425 per month plus 3.5 percent of the annual gross receipts in excess of $50,000. If at the end of the year sales totaled $120,000, how much is the annual rent?

a. $ 7,000.
b. $12,750.
c. $ 5,100.
d. $ 7,550.

_____21. Broker Ames negotiated a sale for $175,000. The listing called for a 10 percent commission on the first $100,000, 7.5 percent on the next $50,000 and 5 percent on the balance. What was the total commission?

    a. $13,750.
    b. $15,000.
    c. $10,000.
    d. $12,500.

_____22. A property-manager negotiated a 20-year lease at an annual rental of $11,500. By agreement the leasing commission was 6 percent of the rental the first year, 5 percent of the yearly rent for each of the next 12 years and 1 percent of the rent for each of the remaining years. What is the total leasing commission for the 20-year lease?

    a. $8,395.
    b. $6,500.
    c. $7,475.
    d. $5,600.

_____23. The sales manager receives 25 percent of the salesperson's 60 percent share of the real estate commission. If a property is sold for $84,000 with a commission of 8 percent, how much will the sales manager receive?

    a. $1,008.
    b. $2,426.
    c. $1,720.
    d. $1,680.

_____24. What is the brokerage fee on the sale of a lot with frontage of 125 feet sold at $85 per front foot with a 9 percent commission on the first $3,000 and 3 percent on the balance of the sales price?

    a. $498.75.
    b. $954.80.
    c. $370.00.
    d. $762.50.

_____25. What is the simple interest on $1,100 for 2 years, 8 months, and 15 days at 7 percent per annum?

    a. $157.20.
    b. $131.45.
    c. $285.14.
    d. $208.54.

_____26. Charles has a $10,000 mortgage on his house at 8.5 percent interest per annum. Total mortgage payments are $92.53 per month including principal, interest, taxes, and insurance. Taxes and insurance amount to $144 per annum. What would the unpaid mortgage balance be after Charles made his first mortgage payment?

    a. $9,919.47.

b. $9,929.17.
c. $9,988.00.
d. $9,990.30.

_____27. There is a balance of $15,400 on a real estate contract which requires monthly payments of $105 plus interest on the remaining balance at 8 percent per annum, payable monthly. What will be the monthly payment for the third month?
  a. $210.00.
  b. $151.90.
  c. $206.27.
  d. $215.40.

_____28. A $25,000 loan calls for payments of $209.80 per month. If the first payment included a payment of $22.30 on the principal, what was the annual rate of interest on the loan?
  a. 7.4.
  b. 8.6.
  c. 9.0.
  d. 10.2.

_____29. Monroe borrowed $1,500 at 7 percent interest per annum. At the end of each year for 5 years he paid the interest on the loan and $300 on the principal. How much total interest did he pay on the loan?
  a. $315.
  b. $484.
  c. $363.
  d. $210.

_____30. Smith deposited $800 into a savings account paying simple interest at 5 percent per annum. If Smith withdraws his money in 18 months, how much interest will he have earned?
  a. $40.
  b. $80.
  c. $60.
  d. $50.

_____31. Jackson borrowed $25,000.00 at 8 percent interest per annum for 25 years. If after the 25 years Jackson had made a total repayment of $56,713.42, how much were his monthly payments (round to nearest cent)?
  a. $290.47.
  b. $189.04.
  c. $212.50.
  d. $147.33.

_____32. Which of the following statements is correct?
  a. The mortgage constant is equivalent to the installment of one.

b. The mortgage constant is equivalent to 12 times the monthly installment of one.
c. The mortgage constant is equal to 12 times the annual installment of one.
d. The mortgage constant refers to a constantly amortized mortgage.

_____33. A lender has agreed to lend $25,600 for the purchase of a new house. However, the lender requires the seller to pay a 4-percent discount on the loan. How much will the discount be?
a. $1,024.
b. $ 400.
c. $4,000.
d. $1,536.

_____34. A buyer agreed to purchase an outstanding contract for $5,800 if the seller would discount the contract $696. What rate of discount is represented by the $696?
a. 10.5 percent.
b. 12.0 percent.
c. 14.3 percent.
d. 15.0 percent.

_____35. The square foot area of a single-family dwelling is calculated by
a. including the garage or carport area with the living area.
b. calculating the square foot area (outside dimensions) of the total enclosed heated living area.
c. including the square foot area of the ground floor only.
d. including unenclosed porches, carports, and garages.

_____36. What is the minimum sale price required if the owner realizes a net of $50,000, if closing costs to the seller are $1,000, and if a 10-percent commission is paid to the broker?
a. $51,000.
b. $56,667.
c. $56,000.
d. $55,000.

_____37. If you borrow $12,000 discounted by 5.5 points, how much will you actually receive?
a. $12,550.
b. $11,450.
c. $10,950.
d. $11,340.

_____38. A 6-percent interest note compounded semiannually for 1 year is equivalent to
a. 1.5 percent interest compounded for 4 periods.
b. .5 percent interest compounded for 12 periods.

      c.   3 percent interest compounded for 2 periods.

      d.   12 percent interest compounded for 2 periods.

_____39.   An FHA insured loan for $21,300 requires a 10-point discount. If the buyer agrees to pay 40 percent of the discount, how much will he or she have to pay?

      a. $1,065.00.

      b. $ 547.20.

      c. $ 852.00.

      d. $ 956.00.

_____40.   The compound amount of $1, compounded at 6 percent semiannually for 1 year, is

      a. $1.0609.

      b. $1.0600.

      c. $1.12.

      d.   none of the above.

ANSWER KEY

1. (c)	11. (a)	21. (b)	31. (b)
2. (b)	12. (d)	22. (a)	32. (b)
3. (d)	13. (d)	23. (a)	33. (a)
4. (c)	14. (b)	24. (a)	34. (b)
5. (h)	15. (a)	25. (d)	35. (b)
6. (d)	16. (b)	26. (d)	36. (h)
7. (a)	17. (d)	27. (c)	37. (d)
8. (b)	18. (c)	28. (c)	38. (c)
9. (d)	19. (a)	29. (a)	39. (c)
10. (b)	20. (d)	30. (c)	40. (a)

SUGGESTED ADDITIONAL READING

Brown, Robert Kevin. *Essentials of Real Estate.* Englewood Cliffs, N.J.: Prentice-Hall, Inc., 1970, Appendix 2.

Brown, Robert Kevin. *Real Estate Economics, An Introduction to Urban Land Use.* Boston, Mass.: Houghton Mifflin Co., 1965, chap. 17.

Semenow, Robert W. *Questions and Answers on Real Estate.* 8th ed. Englewood Cliffs, N.J.: Prentice-Hall, Inc., 1975, chap. 12.

Sirota, David. *Essentials of Real Estate Finance.* Chicago: Real Estate Education Co., 1976, chap. 16.

13

Real Estate Appraisal

I n one sense, a personal opinion of value represents an appraisal. But while personal opinions may be expedient, most industry demands call for a formal report that documents, explains, and offers evidence in support of the value judgment. Though appraisal reports give personal opinions of value, a professional opinion is based on a thorough analysis of value-determining factors that verify the market value estimate.

A formal, professionally prepared appraisal report is required for many real estate transactions. Among the more common uses are appraisal reports used for condemnation of private property for public use, feasibility studies, partnership liquidation, mortgage financing, property taxes, purchase and sale, personal income taxes, state inheritance taxes, counseling for investment, federal estate taxes, FHA and VA mortgages, long-term leases, liquidation, and property insurance. In each instance the appraisal constitutes a written report that follows an organized procedure called the *appraisal process*.

THE APPRAISAL PROCESS

The appraisal process starts with property identification. Next appraisal data is acquired, classified, and analyzed. The final value estimate represents the appraiser's personal opinion of market value submitted after analysis of the appraisal information. Each appraisal report, if it is to conform to professional standards, has certain minimum requirements.

Definition of the Problem

The definition of the appraisal problem helps to interpret appraisal data and narrows the analysis to the most relevant facts. For instance, the

362

valuation of a power-line easement leads to an appraisal analysis quite different than that for the analysis prepared for an apartment building. As part of the definitional requirement, the legal description will state the property to be appraised.

If the fee simple estate (total ownership) is the property interest to be appraised, the appraisal process follows a fairly formal procedure of analyzing income, cost, and sales data. If, however, the property to be valued covers only property rights of the tenant or property subject to a long-term lease, appraisal data must relate not only to the property described, but also to the title associated with the legally described real estate. In appraisals for eminent domain, the legal requirements and the property rights depart markedly from the fee simple estate.

Appraisal Data

Economic conditions affect real estate values. For this reason, part of the appraisal process deals with regional and local conditions that bear on trends in real estate values. The main points covering regional analysis relate to prospects for economic growth or decline. They can be grouped in the following categories:

1. Population characteristics (in-migration, number of households, age groups, education, personal income).
2. Employment (major industries, the labor supply, educational level, skills, wage rates).
3. Retail trade (per capita expenditures by retail categories, trends in retail sales).
4. Transportation facilities.
5. Taxation (corporate income taxes, business taxes, personal income taxes, property taxes, sales taxes).
6. Educational facilities.

A review of this data will help project economic growth, especially as it relates to local real estate values. Supplementing this data are comparable figures on local activities that affect economic opportunity, such as:

1. Government services—their quality and relative cost.
2. Local schools.
3. Recreation.
4. Sources of employment.
5. Housing facilities.
6. Access (air, highway, rail, and water).

It is not enough to cite statistics on these topics. The written appraisal report shows how changes in economic conditions contribute to growing real estate values.

Valuation Approaches

Conventional appraisals concentrate on three approaches to value. First, is the cost approach. The cost to reproduce or replace a building is estimated subject to a deduction for depreciation. The cost less depreciation value is added to the land value, giving an indication of market value. This value is compared with the value derived from market-sale comparisons and a value based on net income. With three possible market value estimates, the appraiser arrives at his final opinion of value as of a specific appraisal date.

THE COST APPROACH

The cost approach starts with the land value estimate. The land value is added to the estimated building cost, less an allowance for depreciation. The main elements of this appraisal method focus on the land value, the estimate of cost new, and the depreciation allowance.

The Land Value Estimate

In practice, appraising land by the cost approach is no small task. For example, how would you value a downtown commercial site if there are no land sales that are reasonably similar to the property appraised? What value would you place on land under a wharf, a pier, or a large industrial warehouse? It is unlikely that comparable land has recently sold that would provide an accurate comparison. The same problem is encountered in valuing land improved with public buildings, or schools, and churches.

Under the cost approach, land is valued separately and independently of the building. For commercial property, land is valued on a per square-foot basis. If the land is platted in lots of equal depth, commercial (and residential) land is priced on a per front-foot basis. Acreage prices are usually applied to agricultural, industrial, and potential subdivision property.

The Cost New Estimate

At the outset, the basis of the cost estimate must be selected—either *reproduction* or *replacement* costs. The reproduction cost refers to the cost of reproducing an exact new building. An exact building means that the cost covers identical materials, the same level of workmanship, and the same architectural features. Reproduction costs refer to an identical image of the building under appraisal.

Replacement costs apply to a building that serves the same function, but assumes more modern and readily available materials. A contemporary architectural design, and different methods of construction lie behind the replacement cost estimate. The concept of replacement costs is required to value buildings that are no longer economically feasible to reproduce in their exact image.

Take, for example, a four-story industrial building with solid brick walls, 36 inches thick at their base. Such buildings typically have relatively low ceilings and floor space, interrupted by load-bearing posts 20 feet on center. As a practical matter, an industrial building would not be reproduced in precisely the same way. To appraise this type of building, the replacement cost standard would give the estimated construction cost of an industrial building constructed under modern standards that would serve the same function. An identical problem is encountered in appraising houses constructed before 1900, old-style office buildings, warehouses, and public buildings.

Per Unit Costs

After a deciding on the cost basis, one of three cost-estimating procedures can be followed. The most accurate and precise method of estimating building costs is the *quantity-survey method*. Building contractors who submit bids on new construction use this more detailed method. It requires a list of building materials and their prices. This requirement, in itself, is time consuming, detailed, and if competently done, quite accurate. The labor costs of construction, given the building to be appraised, must also be broken down by categories to report the amount of labor and its price for the work required to complete the building.

While this method is accurate, it is expensive to administer and requires considerable technical knowledge. In appraising an existing building under this method, the appraiser follows virtually the same steps as the contractor would follow in estimating the cost of a proposed building.

Two time-saving shortcuts substitute for quantity surveys. It is common practice to use *unit-in-place* costs, which include both materials and labor. For example, a structural wall would be priced according to the cost per lineal foot, or a floor would be priced as a unit cost per square foot or per square yard (labor and materials). Ordinarily, an estimate based on unit-in-place costs also requires a practical knowledge of the construction industry and is more time-consuming than per square foot or per cubic foot cost estimates.

For appraisal purposes, costs based on a *price per square foot* of the building (or per cubic foot) adequately serves the appraisal task. If this method is used, the appraiser is guided by commercial cost services that provide cost manuals showing the cost per square foot for different types of construction. Alternatively, the appraiser may rely on his or her own cost study, which is based on costs of recently completed buildings. Properly researched, costs per square foot have sufficient accuracy and save considerable time.

The Depreciation Allowance

The cost approach depends on the estimated replacement or reproduction cost of a building appraised as if it is in new condition. Yet most existing buildings are not worth their cost new value—they are subject to depreciation. Depreciation in this sense is defined as *a loss in value from any cause.* It falls into three types: physical depreciation, functional depreciation, and economic obsolescence. By treating depreciation in these three groups, the appraiser minimizes the subjectivity inherent in estimating depreciation.

Physical Depreciation. Virtually every structure is subject to some form of observed depreciation from physical causes. Buildings physically depreciate because of *catastrophic events* such as floods, hurricanes, earthquakes, and fire. Building exteriors show physical deterioration through *action of the elements*—rain, snow, hail, wind, and the sun. The interior of a building will experience loss by reason of *wear and tear.* Besides these easily observable items, the building structure itself deteriorates (floor and ceiling joists, beams, roof rafters, and other structural members not exposed to view).

Of the two most common ways of adjusting for physical depreciation, the simplest relies on an annual straight-line percentage deduction from reproduction or replacement cost new. A five-year-old house with an estimated reproduction cost new of $50,000 might have physical depreciation equal to 1 percent per year or 5 percent (in dollars $2,500). If this figure represents the total depreciation estimate, the building would have a cost new less depreciation value of $47,500.

A more reliable method is to base physical depreciation on (1) some allowance for the general loss in value of structural members, and (2) a lump sum deduction representing the hypothetical cost of remedying observed physical deficiencies. For example, if the structural members of a house represent 40 percent of the reproduction cost new of $50,000, an appraiser might deduct, say, 1 percent per year against the 40-percent proportion. In this illustration, a 40-percent allowance for the structural frame of the house is equal to $20,000. A 1-percent loss in value over five years would be reported as $1,000.

The remaining physical depreciation would be estimated by calculating the hypothetical cost of correcting for observed deficiencies. If repainting of a deteriorated exterior is estimated to cost $800, it follows that the house has a cost new of $50,000 less $800 representing the loss by reason of the deteriorated exterior. Other physical deficiencies may be estimated in the same way. The cost to cure observed physical defects reduces the reproduction cost new by the loss in value (physical depreciation).

Functional Depreciation. Buildings lose value from functional depreciation more than from any other single cause. While buildings may last over several generations, if they are properly maintained, they become obsolete in comparison with new construction. New materials, new design standards, and changing public preferences operate to lower the value of existing buildings. In this respect, buildings lose value much as last year's automobile model loses value as it is replaced by the current model. An older house with a 10-foot ceiling is functionally obsolete compared to a new house with a 7-foot, 6-inch ceiling. A two-bedroom house without a family room loses value from functional depreciation relative to a three-bedroom house with a family room. In some neighborhoods a house without central air conditioning will be obsolete if new houses are constructed with this feature.

The best method of calculating functional obsolescence is to relate the depreciation deduction to the cost of remedying the deficiency. The hypothetical cost of replacing a linoleum drainboard with formica would give an estimate of functional obsolescence for this item. If the cost to remedy the defect is not economic, appraisers tend to deduct an allowance for functional depreciation by estimating the difference in prices of houses showing older features relative to the prices of current construction. A comparison of rental differences provides another basis for adjusting the cost new for functional depreciation.

Economic Obsolescence. Economic obsolescence is a form of depreciation that is not correctable by the property owner. It comes about by the general decline of property values in a neighborhood (for example, a dwelling may lose value by virtue of construction of a commercial building next door, which causes the dwelling to have less utility as a single-family dwelling). Factors that lower the popularity of a neighborhood fall in this category. An appraiser calculates the loss of value from economic obsolescence by estimating the proportionate decline in rents or real estate prices.

The Cost Approach Evaluated

The cost approach is virtually the only appraisal method available for highly-specialized properties (industrial properties, public buildings, churches, and property infrequently sold and not owned by investors for income purposes). Moreover, the method tends to be fairly accurate for new buildings not subject to much depreciation. In addition, the cost method is a good one by which to compare the cost of a proposed project with its estimated value under the income or sales approach.

Yet the cost approach is appropriate only if the property is used for its highest and best use. There is no point in valuing a dilapidated, single-family dwelling on a site that is best used for a neighborhood shopping center. The cost approach is also a weak method for appraising older buildings or other properties showing considerable depreciation, or if the land value cannot be determined by sales prices. Finally, the cost approach is highly subjective relative to other valuation techniques. Cost estimates are subject to error, and the depreciation allowance is based on a high degree of personal judgment.

For an illustration of the cost technique, see Figure 13–1. In this instance, the cost technique applies to a 361-unit, eight-story apartment building. The building is only three years old. Construction costs were taken from recently built apartments in the same city. Note that the cost per square foot is supplemented by lump sum calculations covering engineering, legal, and financing fees. The depreciation is based on a 1 percent per year allowance believed suitable to record physical depreciation only. The land value is taken from recent sales of similar apartment house sites. This reproduction cost appraisal is only one indication of value, however. Market comparison and income techniques are used in conjunction with the $11,284,000 market value estimate.

THE MARKET COMPARISON APPROACH

The rationale of the market comparison approach rests on the opinions of many buyers and sellers negotiating freely in the open market. Repeated

FIGURE 13–1

Indicated Market Value, Cost Approach for a High-rise Apartment Building

Main building, 455,890 square feet.........	@ $19.48	$ 8,880,737
Parking, deck and covered area, 35,105 square feet.............................	@ 6.50	228,183
Site improvements.......................		164,269
		$ 9,273,189
Architect and engineer.................... $9,273,000 @ .02		185,460
Tests: Soil, concrete......................		3,500
Land surveyor............................		1,000
Insurance on completion portion.......... 361 units @ $75.00		27,075
Title insurance........................... $9,273,000 @ $ 2.25/M		20,864
Construction mortgage Fee, 3%........... 9,273,000 @ $ .03		278,190
Construction loan Interest, 12%, 1 year.................... 5,750,000 @ $ .12		690,000
Mortgage recording tax.................... 9,273,000 @ $ 2.00/M		18,546
Document tax............................ 9,273,000 @ $ 1.50/M		13,909
Total reproduction cost....................		$10,511,733
Less depreciation, 2% per year, 3 years....		630,704
Total reproduction cost less depreciation..		$ 9,881,024
Add land value............................ 200,400 S.F., @ $7.00		1,402,800
Market value, cost approach..............		$11,283,824
	(rounded)	$11,284,000

observations of similar properties recently sold lead to the market value, the main task being to interpret real estate values from bona fide transactions. Real estate sales that do not qualify as normal market transactions have to be eliminated. Real estate sales, unusable for real estate appraisal purposes, would include transactions in the following groups:

Sales to and from
government agencies

Bankruptcy sales

Mortgage foreclosure sales

Sales in lieu of bankruptcy
or foreclosure

Sales between individuals

Sales between interrelated
corporations

Tax foreclosure sale

Sales between relatives

Sales to and from
charitable organizations

Given a selection of fairly current sales of similar property, prices are converted to per unit values: square-foot, front-foot, per-acre, or per-cubic foot. Real estate appraisals require considerable care in documenting prices. The motives of the buyer and seller and other circumstances of the transaction must conform to market practices if the sale is to be accepted. Consequently, considerable importance should be attached to comparable sales information. Figure 13–2 shows the minimum information listed for a comparable sale used to value an apartment building.

FIGURE 13 2

Comparable Sale Data for a High-rise Apartment Building

Grantor................... Zuckerman-Vernon Corporation.

Grantee................... Dupont Commercial Enterprises, Inc.

Date of Sale.............. January 6, 19__.

Recorded................. Deed Book 3831, page 214, Broward County, Florida.

Legal Description........ Lots 1 and 2 in Block 19 of The Landing, First Section, Broward County, Florida, and Parcel "A" of Replat of Block 5, amended Plat of Coral Ridge Commercial Boulevard Addition, Broward County, Florida.

Lot Area................. 30,535 square feet in Parcel 1; Building site Parcel 2, 37,500 square feet; Total, 68,035 square feet.

Location................. The intersection of N.E. 33rd Avenue and N.E. 51st Street, Fort Lauderdale, Florida.

Zoning................... R3, High Density, Multiple Family.

Sale Price............... Total, $3,641,000; per apartment, $26,007.14; per room; $7,500; per square foot building area, $16.82.

Verified................. Broward Real Estate Company.

Remarks................. The 11-story building, the Dupont Towers, illustrates highly comparable features to the property appraised. The 140-unit apartment building fronts on the Intercoastal Waterway. The seller reported a gross income of $475,000, 216,341 square feet and a gross income multiplier of 7.7.

The purpose of presenting information in the format of Figure 13–2 is to document the sale price and to permit a review of the sale-price information. Appraisals are undertaken for decision-making purposes and often must be presented in court testimony. The information cited provides the minimum information for these purposes.

Note in Figure 13–2 that the buyer and seller are listed with the date of sale and the deed book and page to permit verification of those facts. The legal description locates the property and supports the accuracy of the land sales value per unit. The sale price is listed in total amount and per unit (i.e., the price per apartment, per room, and per square foot). Sales prices are verified from the selling broker. The remarks direct attention to the main items of comparison.

Comparable sales data are accompanied by (1) a map showing the land area and the street plan of each sale, (2) a photograph of the building sold, and (3) a map of the neighborhood or city showing the location of properties sold and selected for comparison. An appraisal explaining this information in narrative form proves that appraisal judgment is based on actual observation of the market and not mere hearsay or biased opinion data.

Real estate properties are unique. Buildings and locations show much variation in size, condition, and age. Even the date of sale may be considered in reporting the current market value. As a result, the technique of evaluating each transaction in relation to the property appraised calls for "sales adjustments." Table 13–1 shows how each sale is adjusted to the property appraised.

In Table 13–1, the five sales have been especially selected for direct

TABLE 13–1

Sales Adjustment of Single-family Dwelling Sales

	Sale Number				
Adjustment Item	1	2	3	4	5
Floor area....................	$ −800	$−1,000	$−1,500	$ −500	$ +100
Present condition...........	+200	+1,500	+1,000	—	+500
Lot area......................	—	+500	−100	—	+1,000
Fireplace.....................	—	—	—	+500	—
Garage.......................	+500	—	+300	—	+200
Landscaping.................	+200	−600	+500	—	−1,000
Extra plumbing..............	—	−400	−600	+600	−600
Air conditioning..............	+900	—	+1,200	+800	—
Location.....................	+500	—	−300	+900	—
Architectural appeal.........	+300	+950	−900	+500	+1,000
Time of sale.................	+800	+400	+500	—	+300
Total Net Adjustments...	+$ 2,600	+$ 1,350	+$ 100	+$ 2,800	+$ 1,500
Sale price....................	$58,900	$51,400	$50,400	$50,200	$51,400
Indicated market value......	$61,500	$52,750	$50,500	$53,000	$52,900

comparison to the property under appraisal. Eleven characteristics have been selected for direct adjustments. These are the most significant property characteristics that affect value. For example, the first example has a larger square foot area than the property appraised. The $58,900 sale price, therefore, shows a value of $58,100 for the property appraised. Turning to the second item (present condition), the property appraised is considered in better condition than Sale 1. Therefore, if Sale 1 sold for $58,900, the superior condition of the property appraised, in comparison, would show a value of $59,100 ($58,900 + $200). Each of the characteristics are judged separately to produce a net adjustment. If there are no differences observed between the property sold and the property appraised for the selected characteristics, no adjustment factor is shown.

Field Data Sources

When the real estate transaction is completed, the buyer or escrow agent normally records the conveyance instrument (the deed or other title document). Consequently, the local county recording office is the best source for legal details of sales, but there are two difficulties in using this source: First, recording regulations do not always require a listing of the sales price. Document stamps are not universally required and, if used, they are subject to wide variation. Second, recorded documents are filed alphabetically by last name of buyer and seller. For larger communities, there is no way of identifying the type of property sold without access to other record systems.

In some areas, sales-reporting services will provide information in tabulated form. The Society of Real Estate Appraisers, for example, supports a sales file in selected cities for subscribing members. Active real estate brokers, savings and loan associations, mortgage bankers and, in some cases, property tax assessors maintain sales data files. Even given the sales data, however, the importance of selecting bona fide sales calls for more than a sales data file. Qualified appraisers will interview the buyer and seller or other knowledgeable parties to verify sale details, the price, and circumstances of negotiation that might have affected the price.

Advantages of Market Comparisons

If the appraisal is to follow the dictates of the market, sales comparisons will constitute the best source of valuation evidence. Because:

1. Provided sales are available in sufficient number and representative of the property appraised, they provide a current value that agrees with opinions of buyers and sellers.

2. The method is easily understood and accepted by the public and the courts.
3. The method gives an objective estimate of value to the extent that values are derived from the market as interpreted by qualified appraisers.
4. The method is highly adapted to properties frequently sold.

While these points argue strongly for the market comparison approach, that approach must not be used without reservations. First, prices change over time. A sale completed two years ago may not be indicative of value today. While the need for adjusting past sales to current values may be recognized, the data may not be at hand to objectively determine how much real estate prices have increased or decreased. But for properties frequently exchanged, data is becoming increasingly available. In a recent survey in Montgomery County, Pennsylvania, for example, the tabulation of 1,106 dwellings that resold within a four-year period showed average price increases per month of 1.3 percent. As sales records become increasingly maintained by government agencies, these data will be more widely available.

Second, it is not always clear how financing terms affect real estate prices. More favorable terms—longer-term mortgages and lower down payments or lower interest rates—may increase the price relative to a cash price. Appraisers must make some adjustment for terms of sale if they think it affects the price. The evidence supporting sale adjustments for terms of sale tend to be subjective.

Third, there is always the difficulty of evaluating characteristics of the property sold against those of the property appraised. Adjusting for differences between the properties is another subjective element in the appraisal which, however, can be overcome partly by experience, training, and competent judgment. In the final analysis, market comparisons are preferred for properties frequently sold.

THE INCOME APPROACH

The income approach is justified by a single point: market value is equal to the present worth of future income. Real estate is viewed as something that generates income. It is the right to the income that is purchased and not the land and the building. Only to the extent that land and the buildings on it contribute to earning capacity, do they affect market value. Under this concept, market value follows from three factors: (1) the annual gross income; (2) annual expenses of operation, and (3) the rate of capitalization. The capitalization rate is a discount that converts the right to an income to market value. In other words, an investor is willing to pay $100,000 for the right to an income of $10,000, received in perpetuity. To put it differently, the right to a future income of $10,000 is "capitalized" to give market value. The basic formula underlying the income approach is

$$\text{Market value} = \frac{\text{Annual net income}}{\text{Capitalization rate}}$$

The market value of property earning an annual income of $10,000 would be

$$\text{Market value} = \$10,000/.10$$
$$= \$100,000.$$

The method's practical advantages turn on three points:

1. The income approach is the best method to value real estate bought and sold on the basis of annual net income.
2. It is preferred for income properties that are old and highly depreciated.
3. The method avoids the subjective interpretation of comparable sales, costs and depreciation.

The records show that certain properties are purchased and developed primarily to earn net income. This fact, in itself, endorses the income approach. Acceptance of the first point, however, does not mean that the method has universal application to all income properties. Income from residential duplexes, small retail property, and marginal farms are diffi cult to appraise by reference solely to net income. For the smaller properties, the labor of the owner complicates the calculation of income and expense data. The method, however, has universal acceptance if economic operation for income purposes is used as the strict rule.

Further, older properties, which are also bought and sold for net income, automatically show the effect of depreciation in reduced rental income and higher expenses of operation. These market adjustments provide an automatic means of adjusting for loss of value because of age, obsolescence, and location. In this respect, the income technique is the preferred valuation procedure.

Against these observations are major limitations. Small changes in the capitalization rate make substantial differences in the final value estimate. Income data is difficult to justify for certain properties; it is not applicable to smaller income properties of uneconomic size. Moreover, the method of capitalization substantially affects the value estimate.

The Gross Income Estimate

As one of the three factors that affect market value, the gross income estimate is highly critical. There is much misunderstanding of gross income estimates used for valuation purposes. Recall that income property is purchased on the basis of anticipated income, not past nor current income. To be sure, anticipated income is closely related to past and present net income, but the real problem lies in the difference between contract and economic rent.

Contract rent is the actual rent received. In a shopping center, the contract rent is set forth in lease terms, and in an apartment lease, the contract rent will be specified in the lease document. For downtown retail property, rented on a month to month basis over the last five years, the actual rent collected is contract rent. In contrast, *economic rent* refers to the market rent assuming the property is used in its highest use.

On this issue laypersons and unqualified appraisers are often led to erroneous value conclusions. Typically, lease or contract rents lag behind the current market rent. This being so, then past gross incomes are understated for appraisal purposes. So this leads to a first rule in valuing income property: Compare current rents with economic rent. There are occasions when the appraiser must use a higher gross income estimate than the property owner reports on a current profit-and-loss statement.

It should also be noted that gross income is the income that would accrue if the property were fully rented. If you are appraising a 400-unit apartment, for example, the gross income is reported as if all apartments were rented at their market rent. With this figure in hand, you calculate the *effective gross income* (the gross income less allowance for vacancies and bad debts). Though the property may show 100 percent occupancy, some downward adjustment must be made in gross income for anticipated losses in rent from any cause. At this point the valuation starts with gross income as adjusted for economic rent and as adjusted downward for vacancies and bad debts.

Net Operating Income

With the effective gross income at hand, the next step is to calculate net operating income by deducting annual operating expenses from effective gross income. Here again laypersons often incorrectly include certain expenses that must be eliminated before reporting net operating income. Invalid expenses are avoided by observing four rules:

1. Do not include mortgage principal or interest payments as annual operating expenses.
2. Eliminate corporate net income and personal net income tax payments.
3. Omit depreciation allowances for the building.
4. Do not include as expenses payments which are more properly listed as additions to capital.

Mortgage payments are omitted because they are not operating expenses. To include mortgage payments would vary net operating income according to the mortgage terms. Conventional appraisal methods assume that property is free and clear of all mortgage debt. Mortgage payments are accounted for in more specialized income appraisal techniques that show the return on the equity or down payment and the cash flow remaining after net income taxes and mortgage payments.

Likewise, corporate and personal net income taxes are personal to the taxpayer and are not associated with expenses of operating an income building. Depreciation is part of real estate capitalization process. Net operating income is reported before allowances for depreciation.

Property owners may pay substantial sums which are listed as expenses but which are more properly classified as additions to the investment. A new carport, for example, that costs $50,000 in a 100-unit apartment adds to property value but the $50,000 is a one-time payment which is not an annual expense of operation. Only recurring normal expenses of operation are listed in the income statement.

Added to this list are other items frequently omitted by the apartment owner. For instance, lobby furniture in an apartment, kitchen ovens and range tops, and refrigerators are short-lived items that require replacement on a three- to five-year cycle. The annual expense of replacement must be converted to an annual operating expense.

Suppose also that the property is owner-operated. In this case the owner performs the management function, which has an economic value. Make sure that the income statement allows for the customary management

FIGURE 13–3

Net Income Estimate: High-rise Apartment

Annual gross income	$1,088,640	
Other income	13,000	
Gross possible income		$1,101,640
Less vacancy and rent loss, 3%		− 33,049
Effective gross income		$1,068,591
Less expenses		
Property taxes	$ 166,376	
Insurance	15,200	
Maintenance, repairs	34,900	
Management	45,000	
Payroll expenses	45,900	
Electricity	37,891	
Gas	779	
Water	14,800	
Heating	13,000	
Administrative costs	78,000	
Supplies	12,000	
Reserves for replacements	25,000	
Total Expenses		−$ 488,846
Net operating income		$ 579,745

operating expense. An income statement prepared according to these requirements is shown in Figure 13–3.

The Capitalization Rate

The capitalization process converts an income to market value. Actually the capitalization rate is a rate of discount applied to future incomes. Present goods are preferred to future goods. Hence, future incomes are discounted in the present. The market value estimate for income properties is a capital sum representing the present worth of rights to discounted future incomes.

After the net income is calculated, the capitalization rate largely controls the appraised value. Because this value is highly sensitive to the capitalization rate, its selection is based on well-defined appraisal rules.

If available, appraisers base the capitalization rate on a study of market transactions. For example, property selling for $100,000 that shows a net operating income of $12,000 illustrates an overall capitalization rate of 12 percent ($12,000/$100,000). If the property includes a depreciating building, the 12 percent rate provides for the return of invested capital in the building and a return on the investment in the land and building. A study of net operating incomes of property recently sold provides the capitalization rate determined from market data.

Sales prices and net incomes are subject to much interpretation and such data are not always available in the quality and frequency required for appraisal. An alternative method of selecting the capitalization rate relies on the rate of return earned on interests or shares in real estate. For instance, if interest rates on first and second mortgages are available and the rate required on invested capital (the equity), a weighted average of these returns produces a valid capitalization rate. This technique may be illustrated by assuming a first and second mortgage of $750,000 and $150,000

Property Interest	Percent of Total	Weighted Interest (%)
1st mortgage, $750,000, 9.0% interest rate.............. .75		6.75
2nd mortgage, $150,000, 12.0% interest rate............ .15		1.80
Equity, 25% rate of return........................... .10		2.50
Weighted capitalization rate..........................		11.05

To apply this method, the typical mortgage loan to value ratio and the going rate on first mortgages provides the first weighted interest rate (in the illustration 6.75—9 percent × .75). Weighting the second mortgage interest rate of 12 percent by its proportionate share of the total property value, and adding the weighted share going to equity (25 percent), produces a capitalization rate of 11.05 percent. On this last point, note that the equity rate is given if the interest rate on the first and second mortgages are known.

In addition to these two methods, the capitalization rate may be compared to the rate of return on alternative investments. Usually the capitalization rate will be above the interest rate charged on the first mortgage. The risks are greater on the whole property ownership than the risks assumed by the lender, who loans only a portion of the property interest. In real estate, values tend to be adjusted to earn the rate of return which is competitive with other investments of equal income quality, stability and risk.

CAPITALIZATION TECHNIQUES: RESIDUAL METHODS

Depreciation is not a part of the income statement, but real estate buildings are known as wasting assets. They depreciate each year of their economic life. Assume that a property loses value at a constant rate each year. A building with an estimated economic life of 50 years loses value equal to 2 percent of its cost on an annual basis. To find the straight-line rate of depreciation, divide the estimate of economic life into one. The annual straight-line depreciation for buildings with lives varying from 50 years to 20 years shows the amount that the property depreciates annually under straight-lines assumptions:

Straight-Line Rates of Depreciation

$\frac{1}{50}$	2.0%
$\frac{1}{40}$	2.5
$\frac{1}{30}$	3.3
$\frac{1}{25}$	4.0
$\frac{1}{20}$	5.0

Because buildings depreciate and land does not depreciate, net income is capitalized under the land-residual, building-residual, or property-residual techniques.

Land-Residual Capitalization

Under residual methods of capitalization, income must be allocated separately to land and buildings (see Figure 13–4). Figure 13–4 assumes a building value of $200,000, a building life of 50 years, a return on capital of 9 percent and a return of capital of 2 percent. The latter figure provides for straight-line return of the $200,000 building cost over its 50-year life.

FIGURE 13–4

Land-Residual Capitalization

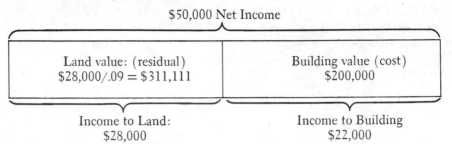

$50,000 Net Income

| Land value: (residual) | Building value (cost) |
| $28,000/.09 = $311,111 | $200,000 |

Income to Land: Income to Building
$28,000 $22,000

With a $50,000 net operating income, the market value under the land residual technique would be $511,000.

Net income...	$ 50,000
Less income to building ($200,000 × .11).................	−22,000
Income to land......................................	$ 28,000
Land value ($28,000/.09)..............................	$311,111
Add building value...................................	200,000
Estimated market value, land-residual..................	$511,111
(rounded)...	$511,000

The land-residual example allocates $22,000 of the net operating income to the building, which provides a 9 percent return on invested capital and provides, further, for the recovery of the building investment on a straight-line basis at the rate of 2 percent per year. The residual income allocated to the land, some $28,000, is capitalized on a straight-line basis at 9 percent. Adding the capitalized value of the land and the building value gives an indicated market value of $511,000, land residual.

Here is a summary of steps in capitalizing income by the land-residual technique:

1. Estimate the building value from local construction costs (i.e., $20,000 square foot and a 10,000 square-foot building = $200,000).
2. Estimate the economic life of the building (for example, 50 years).
3. Calculate the capitalization rate: (*a*) Determine the return on capital (for example, 9 percent). (*b*) Add the return of capital: divide economic life of building into 1. For example, $\frac{1}{50}$ = 2 percent. In the example, the overall capitalization rate is equal to .09 + .02, or 11 percent.
4. Calculate the return on the building ($200,000 × .11 = $22,000).
5. Subtract income allocated to building from the assumed annual net income ($50,000 − $22,000 = $28,000).
6. Capitalize income to land ($28,000/.09 = $311,111).

7. Add the building and land value $311,111

200,000

Estimated market value $511,000 (rounded)

Building-Residual Capitalization

Building-residual capitalization parallels the preceding example, with one difference. The appraisal starts with a market value estimate of the land. The building value represents the capitalization of income allocated to the building. To illustrate this method, assume a land value of $100,000, a capitalization rate of 9 percent, a remaining building life of 40 years and a net income of $20,000.

```
Net income........................................ $ 20,000
Less income to land, $100,000 × .09.............. −9,000
Income to building............................. $ 11,000

Building value, $11,000/.115 (.09 + .025)........... $ 95,652
Add land value.................................. $100,000
Estimated market value........................ $195,652
    (rounded)................................... $195,600
```

If land of $100,000, as estimated from comparable sales, warrants a 9 percent return, then $11,000 of the net income represents the income derived from the building. A 9 percent return of capital and a 2.5 percent straight-line depreciation rate produces an overall capitalization rate of 11.5 percent. The $95,652 is the capitalized value of income allocated to the building. The land and building added produce a market value estimate, building residual of $195,600. Here is a summary of these steps for the building-residual capitalization:

1. Estimate market value of the land from comparable sales.
2. Estimate the capitalization rate for the return of capital.
3. Calculate the annual return to the land.
4. Subtract the annual return to the land from annual net operating income.
5. Estimate the economic life of the building.
6. Estimate the overall capitalization rate. For example:

.090 return on capital
.025 return of capital ($\frac{1}{40}$ = .025)
.115 overall capitalization rate

7. Capitalize income to the building to give the building value (e.g., $11,000/.115 = $95,652).
8. Add the land value to the building value.

In some instances, the land and building residual are not appropriate because they often call for an arbitrary division of value between land

and building. This problem is minimized under the property-residual method.

Property-Residual Capitalization

To understand property-residual technique, two common capitalization tables must be reviewed. The first refers to the *present worth of one per annum* table and the second is called the *present worth of one*. The first table gives capitalization factors to determine the present worth of an income earned over a limited period. Appraisers using this table frequently refer to it as an annuity table applicable to incomes having characteristics of an annuity. Reference to the formula used to calculate present worth of one per annum tables shows how this table is used for the property residual technique. These tables help value property under lease. (See chap. 10 on leases for illustrations of lease valuation.)

Because present goods are preferred to future goods, $100 now would be preferred to $100 a year from now. In other words, $100 postponed one year from now must be discounted. If an 8 percent discount is acceptable, then $100 today is equivalent to $92.59 one year later. This calculation is based on the present worth of one per annum formula:

$$p \text{ (present worth)} = f \text{ (future amount)}/(1 + \text{rate})$$

$$p = \frac{f}{(1 + r)}$$

$$p = \frac{\$100}{1.08}$$

$$p = \$92.59$$

In short, if you invested $92.59 today at 8 percent interest, you would have $100 one year later and you would have earned 8 percent on your investment ($92.59 × .08 = $7.40).

The present worth of $100 2 years from now is found by the same formula.

$$p = \frac{f}{(1 + r)^2}$$

$$p = \frac{\$100}{(1 + .08)^2}$$

$$p = \frac{100}{1.1664}$$

$$p = \$85.73$$

An income of $100 per year payable over 2 years has a present value equivalent to $92.59 + $85.73 or $178.32.

TABLE 13–2

Present Worth of One and Present Worth of One per Period: 8 percent

Periods	Present worth of One	Present Worth of One per Period
1	.9259259259	.9259259259
2	.8573388203	1.7832647462
3	.7938322410	2.5770969872
4	.7350298528	3.3121268400
5	.6805831970	3.9927100371
6	.6301696269	4.6228796640
7	.5834903953	5.2063700592
8	.5402688845	5.7466389437
9	.5002489671	6.2468879109
10	.4631934881	6.7100813989
11	.4288828593	7.1389642583
12	.3971137586	7.5360780169
13	.3676979247	7.9037759416
14	.3404610414	8.2442369830
15	.3152417050	8.5594786879
16	.2918904676	8.8513691555
17	.2702689514	9.1216381069
18	.2502490291	9.3718871360
19	.2317120640	9.6035992000
20	.2145482074	9.8181814740/4
21	.1986557476	10.0168031550
22	.1839405070	10.2007436621
23	.1703152843	10.3710589464
24	.1576993373	10.5287582837
25	.1460179049	10.6747761886
26	.1352017638	10.8099779524
27	.1251868183	10.9351647707
28	.1159137207	11.0510784914
29	.1073275192	11.1584060106
30	.0993773325	11.2577833431
31	.0920160487	11.3497993918
32	.0852000451	11.4349994368
33	.0788889306	11.5138883674
34	.0730453061	11.5869336736
35	.0676345427	11.6545682163
36	.0626245766	11.7171927928
37	.0579857190	11.7751785119
38	.0536904806	11.8288689925
39	.0497134080	11.8785824004
40	.0460309333	11.9246133337

TABLE 13–2 *(concluded)*

Periods	Present Worth of One	Present Worth of One per Period
41	.0426212345	11.9672345683
42	.0394641061	12.0066986743
43	.0365408389	12.0432395133
44	.0338341101	12.0770736234
45	.0313278797	12.1084015032
46	.0290072961	12.1374087992
47	.0268586075	12.1642674067
48	.0248690810	12.1891364877
49	.0230269268	12.2121634145
50	.0213212286	12.2334846431

Therefore it follows that the present worth of an income is merely the summation of the present worth of a sum of discounted annual payments. This leads to the use of present worth of one per period tables. The second column in Table 13–2 gives a present worth of one per period, 8 percent discount, which is a summation of the first column. The present worth of one per period shows that an income of $1 payable at the end of the year for 50 years discounted at 8 percent is worth $12.23. Capitalization tables are always expressed in terms of $1.

The first column in Table 13–2, the present worth of one, shows a present worth of $1 postponed for a given period; $1 discounted at 8 percent payable 50 years from now has a value of $.02.

With these ideas in mind, we may now turn to the property residual technique. This capitalization procedure is advised by some appraisers who argue that income cannot be divided between land and buildings. They hold that the net income should be allocated to the property as a whole. The example below shows the market value of an apartment earning a net income of $100,000 with an estimated life of 50 years. It is assumed further that the land today has a present value of $50,000. Applying the factors from the 8 percent capitalization table, the market value is estimated as $1,224,000.

Total net (annual income)................................	$ 100,000
Present worth of $100,000 annual income received for 50 years, 8 percent ×12.2334 (present worth of one per annum factor).....................................	$1,223,340
Land reversion, $50,000, 50 years, 8 percent ×.02132 (present worth of one factor)...........................	1,066
Market value...	$1,224,406
(rounded)...	$1,224,000

Steps in appraising property under the property residual capitalization method can be summarized in this way:

1. Estimate the economic life of the building.
2. Multiply the net operating income by the present worth of one per annum factor for a period equal to the remaining building life at a given capitalization rate.
3. Multiply the present worth of land by the present worth of one factor for a period equal to the remaining building life at the stated capitalization rate.
4. Add the present worth of the income to the discounted value of land postponed to the end of the building's economic life.

With this technique of capitalization, income is treated as if it is earned from the whole property, land *and* building. Given the economic life of the building, it is presumed that income will terminate at the end of that life. This method assumes that the building has no value at the end of its economic life; the land has value since it is not a wasting asset. The method treats the land as if it is equal to the present value which is postponed to the end of the building life.

QUESTIONS FOR REVIEW

_____ 1. The main reason for covering regional analysis is to
   a. estimate the prospects for economic growth or decline.
   b. conform with requirements of the narrative appraisal report.
   c. eliminate the need for comparable sales data.
   d. none of the above.

_____ 2. In the cost approach to value,
   a. land values are not required to estimate market value.
   b. the method focuses on the land value, the estimate of cost new and the depreciation allowance.
   c. the market value estimate is superior to estimates derived from other methods of valuation.
   d. the resulting value estimate is preferred for income properties.

_____ 3. Which of the following statements is correct?
   I.   The reproduction cost estimate refers to the cost of reproducing an exact new building.
   II. The replacement cost applies to a building serving the same utility.
   a. I only.
   b. II only.
   c. Both I and II.
   d. Neither I nor II.

_____ 4. In estimating the building cost, most appraisers would prefer the quantity survey method because
   a. the quantity survey method requires less time than alternative cost-estimating methods.

    b.   the quantity survey method requires little technical training.

    c.   most appraisal clients require quantity survey estimates.

    d.   none of the above.

_____ 5. In estimating market value, depreciation in value has been defined as

    a.   the depreciation allowable for federal net income tax purposes.

    b.   a loss that is irrelevant in valuing a new building.

    c.   a loss in value from any cause.

    d.   an allowance that may be used only in valuing multiple-family dwellings.

_____ 6. Which of the following statements is correct?

    a.   Physical depreciation is probably the least important cause of a loss in value.

    b.   Functional depreciation arises from wear and tear and action of the elements.

    c.   A poor floor plan represents a loss in value from physical causes.

    d.   Functional depreciation is not correctable by the property owner.

_____ 7. Which of the following statements is *incorrect?*

    a.   Economic obsolescence arises from forces external to the property.

    b.   Economic obsolescence is not correctable by the property owner.

    c.   A poorly constructed building is an example of economic obsolescence.

    d.   A single-family dwelling may lose value by construction of a commercial building next door.

_____ 8. The cost technique has been criticized on grounds that

    a.   cost new estimates are subject to considerable error.

    b.   depreciation allowances are based on a high degree of personal judgment.

    c.   it is a weak method of appraising older property showing considerable depreciation.

    d.   all of the above.

_____ 9. The main support for the market comparison approach to value rests on

    a.   the opinions of many buyers and sellers negotiating freely in the open market.

    b.   the ready availability of real estate sales for all property types.

    c.   the acceptance of a market comparison approach for publicly-owned buildings.

    d.   the high validity of all real estate sales.

____10. Which of the following real estate transactions would generally be unacceptable for market comparison purposes?

    a. Single-family dwellings sold through the multiple listing service.

    b. Sales to and from the charitable organizations.

    c. Real estate sales evidenced by a warranty deed.

    d. Sales for investment purposes.

____11. Sales adjustments of comparable sales are required because

    a. by adjusting sales, virtually any type of sale may be used.

    b. sales adjustments are acceptable if more than 15 property characteristics are adjusted.

    c. even though sale properties are fairly similar, buildings and locations show sufficient variation to justify sales adjustments.

    d. none of the above.

____12. The main advantage of market comparisons lies in the fact that

    a. they provide a current value that agrees with opinions of many buyers and sellers.

    b. the method rests solely on informed opinion.

    c. by using comparisons, other valuation approaches are unnecessary.

    d. the method applies primarily to income-producing property.

____13. Erroneous market value estimates may follow for the market comparison approach if

    a. the sale is not sufficiently current to indicate market value.

    b. financing terms unique to each sale may distort real estate prices.

    c. property characteristics of the property sold vary widely from the property appraised.

    d. all of the above.

____14. The income approach is justified by a single point:

    a. The method rests on the analysis of the location.

    b. The income approach is appropriate for properties showing little or no depreciation.

    c. Market value is equal to the present worth of future income.

    d. The method is ideal for appraising property in growth areas.

____15. The capitalization process is a

    a. method of stabilizing net income.

    b. procedure used to discount income from properties showing high vacancies.

    c. procedure to value income only from intangible property.

    d. procedure to convert rights to an income to market value.

____16. Under the concept of the income approach to value, market value follows from

    a. location analysis, the cost approach, and adjustment of annual gross income.

    b. annual expenses of operation, the vacancy allowance, and site valuation.

    c. the annual gross income, annual expenses of operation, and the rate of capitalization.

    d. the rate of capitalization, building costs, and the annual gross income.

_____17. Which of the following statements is correct?

    a. Contract rent is the actual rent received.

    b. Economic rent refers to the income shown on the income statement prepared for net income taxes.

    c. Economic rent refers only to the market rent for property not used for its highest use.

    d. Typically, economic rent lags behind contract rent.

_____18. Which of the following indicates an overall capitalization of 10 percent?

    a. Gross income, $10,000; sale price, $100,000.

    b. Net income after depreciation, $10,000; sale price, $100,000.

    c. Net income, $10,000; sale price, $100,000.

    d. Net income, $10,000; reproduction cost, $100,000.

_____19. Derivation of the capitalization rate by the band of investment method is based on

    a. the relation between net income and sales price.

    b. the rate of return earned on alternative investments.

    c. the value of present goods compared to the value of future goods.

    d. the rate of return earned on component shares in real estate.

_____20. The straight-line rate of depreciation for a building with an estimated remaining life of 33 years is

    a. 3.3 percent.

    b. 33.0 percent.

    c. 3.0 percent.

    d. 0.33 percent.

_____21. Under the land- and building-residual methods of capitalization, which of the following statements is correct?

    a. Income is allocated to the property.

    b. Income must be allocated separately to land and buildings.

    c. Income to buildings is capitalized at a lower rate than income to land.

    d. Income is not divided between land and buildings.

_____22. Assume the following facts: net income, $100,000; building value, $200,000, return on capital, 10 percent; building life, 50 years. The estimated market value under straight-line capitalization would be (round to the nearest $1,000)

    a. $ 280,000.
    b. $ 666,000.
    c. $ 960,000.
    d. $1,000,000.

____23. Under the land-residual technique, the appraiser must
    a. estimate the land value from comparable sales analysis.
    b. estimate the building value from local construction costs.
    c. calculate the return on land before valuing the building.
    d. subtract income allocated to the land from the annual net income.

____24. Under the building-residual technique of capitalization, the
    a. appraisal starts with a market value estimate of land.
    b. appraisal starts with a markct value estimate of the building.
    c. land value represents the capitalization of net income allocated to the land.
    d. building value is based on replacement costs.

____25. The property-residual capitalization technique, annuity capitalization, relies on
    a. the compound of one table.
    b. the installment of one table.
    c. the accumulation of one tablc.
    d. the present worth of one per period table.

____26. The capitalization table identified as the prcsent worth of one per pcriod is used to calculate
    a. the present worth of a postponcd sum.
    b. the compound amount of $1.00.
    c. the present worth of an income.
    d. mortgage payments.

____27. Under the property-residual technique of valuation, the appraiscr must
    a. multiply the net operating income by the present worth of one per period factor for a period equal to the remaining building life at a given capitalization rate.
    b. multiply the present worth of the building by the present worth of one factor.
    c. add the present worth of net income to the discounted value of the building.
    d. multiply the present worth of one factor times the economic life of the building.

____28. Select the group below which enumerates the three types of depreciation that affect property values.
    a. Functional obsolescence
       Gross obsolescence
       Physical deterioration

     b. The theoretical method
        The quantity survey method
        Sinking fund approach
     c. Straight-line method
        Sinking fund method
        Physical deterioration
     d. Physical deterioration
        Functional obsolescence
        Economic obsolescence

____29. Net income is determined by deducting operating expenses from the
     a. effective gross income.
     b. net income after depreciation.
     c. net operating income after mortgage payments.
     d. gross income.

____30. No depreciation is allowed for federal net income taxes on
     a. a 15-year-old improvement.
     b. land.
     c. temporary buildings.
     d. buildings with an age of 25 or more years.

____31. An appraiser
     a. determines value.
     b. computes value.
     c. sets value.
     d. estimates value.

____32. Which of the following is not a valid expense in capitalizing net income?
     a. Real estate taxes.
     b. Vacancy and bad debts.
     c. Management expense.
     d. Interest payments.

____33. In capitalizing net income, what is the effect of lowering the capitalization rate from 10 percent to 8 percent?
     a. The value would increase.
     b. The value would decrease.
     c. The value would decrease because of higher risk.
     d. The value would increase only for new buildings.

____34. In determining effective gross income, which one of the following would be deducted from gross income?
     a. Insurance and taxes.
     b. Repairs.
     c. Physical depreciation. .
     d. Vacancy and bad debts.

____35. The loss of value because of deferred maintenance is called _____ depreciation.

a. functional
b. economic
c. physical
d. straight-line

____36. A report setting forth an estimate and conclusion of value is

a. an abstract.
b. a title report.
c. an appraisal.
d. a contract.

____37. The period over which a property may be profitably utilized is called its _____ life.

a. economic
b. physical
c. contract
d. income

____38. A complete narrative appraisal report would *not* include

a. a legal description of the property.
b. a title abstract.
c. the purpose of the appraisal.
d. a definition of value.

____39. Which of the following is a type of depreciation?

a. Capital deterioration.
b. Straight-line obsolescence.
c. Economic obsolescence.
d. Equity amortization.

____40. The cost approach includes an estimate of

a. reproduction cost new at the time of the appraisal.
b. accrued depreciation.
c. market value equal to the land value plus the depreciated reproduction cost new.
d. all of the above.

ANSWER KEY

1. (*a*)	11. (*c*)	21. (*b*)	31. (*d*)
2. (*b*)	12. (*a*)	22. (*c*)	32. (*d*)
3. (*c*)	13. (*d*)	23. (*b*)	33. (*a*)
4. (*d*)	14. (*c*)	24. (*a*)	34. (*d*)
5. (*c*)	15. (*d*)	25. (*d*)	35. (*c*)
6. (*a*)	16. (*c*)	26. (*c*)	36. (*c*)
7. (*c*)	17. (*a*)	27. (*a*)	37. (*a*)
8. (*d*)	18. (*c*)	28. (*d*)	38. (*b*)
9. (*a*)	19. (*d*)	29. (*a*)	39. (*c*)
10. (*b*)	20. (*c*)	30. (*b*)	40. (*d*)

SUGGESTED ADDITIONAL READING

The Appraisal of Real Estate. 5th ed. Chicago: American Institute of Real Estate Appraisers, 1967, chap. 19.

North, Lincoln W. *Real Estate Investment Analysis and Valuation*. Winnipeg, Canada: Saults and Pollard, Ltd., 1973, chap. 3.

Ring, Alfred A. *The Valuation of Real Estate*. 2d ed. Englewood Cliffs, N.J.: Prentice-Hall, Inc., 1970, chap. 19.

Shenkel, William M. *Modern Real Estate Appraisal*. New York: McGraw-Hill Book Co., 1978, chaps. 7 and 8.

Smith, Halbert C. *Real Estate Appraisal*. Columbus, O.: Grid, Inc., 1976, Chaps. 5 and 6.

14

Evaluating Energy Conservation Techniques

The original energy law proposed by the current administration declared that the United States faces an increasing shortage of nonrenewable energy resources. According to the proposed law:

1. The United States faces an increasing shortage of nonrenewable energy resources.
2. This energy shortage and our increasing dependence on foreign energy supplies present a serious threat to the national security of the United States and to the health, safety, and welfare of its citizens.
3. A strong national energy program is needed to meet the present and future energy needs of the nation consistent with overall national economic, environmental and social goals.

The proposed legislation was to:

> . . . create an awareness of, and responsibility for, the fuel and energy needs of rural and urban residents as such needs pertain to home heating and cooling, transportation, agricultural production, electrical generation, conservation, and research and development. . . . (*Public Law 95–91*, August 4, 1977).

Because of the developing energy shortages, proposals have been offered to deregulate natural gas prices, encourage industries to convert from oil and gas to coal, to restrict production of low gas mileage automobiles, to set standards for utility rates that encourage conservation, and to provide tax incentives that encourage energy conservation construction.

Private interest in energy conservation is illustrated by recommendations of the United States League of Savings Associations. According to the League:

391

We believe that the energy crisis is both real and permanent, a belief unfortunately not yet shared by the majority of the American public.

We are concerned that the shortage and high cost of energy may curtail the production of new housing and make home ownership too burdensome for many Americans.

Among the ten recommendations made to their membership are six points that especially illustrate the growing importance of energy conservation techniques.

1. The U.S. League and its affiliates should initiate an educational campaign to increase the energy awareness of their staffs and memberships through publications, workshops, conferences, and other appropriate means.
2. The U.S. League should develop energy recommendations for application by member associations in their underwriting and appraisal processes.
3. The U.S. League should cooperate with the National Association of Realtors in developing a system of disclosure to buyers of utility costs for the preceding 12 months separating space heating and cooling costs to the extent practicable.
4. Associations should adopt underwriting procedures which give full consideration to utility (energy) costs.
5. Associations should encourage appraisal procedures which adequately reflect thermal characteristics of properties.
6. Associations should make every effort to extend additional credit for energy improvement through open-end mortgage and similar devices ("Real Estate Trends," *The Real Estate Appraiser*, vol. 43, no. 3 [May–June 1977], p. 49).

Indeed, it has been held that because of the acceptance of energy conservation construction, existing structures will become economically obsolete.

According to one authority, "there can be no doubt whatsoever that rising energy costs, translated into rising operating expenses will have a detrimental effect on the property value of existing structures (Hans Isakson, "The Real Estate Appraiser and the Energy Crisis," *The Real Estate Appraiser*, vol. 43, no. 5 [September 1977], p. 9). Since virtually all structures were built during the cheap energy era, the highly inefficient energy buildings will consume more fuel and suffer depreciation as new buildings are built with more efficient heating and cooling systems. Some experts have also predicted that the rising cost of transportation may change land use densities and even cause commercial and industrial firms to favor more central locations (Ibid).

To provide an insight into current developments in energy conservation techniques, the chapter covers (1) common methods of retrofitting single-family dwellings, (2) measures to make apartment buildings more energy efficient, and (3) present methods of evaluating energy conservation construction. (4) The chapter closes with a discussion of solar heating.

RETROFITTING SINGLE-FAMILY DWELLINGS

Retrofitting techniques refer to measures that improve the thermal efficiency of buildings. The most common techniques include:

1. Attic insulation
2. Wall insulation
3. Floor insulation
4. Insulating the ducts in unheated spaces
5. Storm windows and doors
6. Weatherstripping

These measures generally prove profitable since most of the 70,000,000 residences in the United States listed in the 1970 census were constructed in periods of relatively low energy costs. As a result, these buildings consume more energy than newer buildings constructed during periods of high and rising energy costs. Because of the higher costs of heating and cooling, energy conservation techniques which were not economic before 1974 are feasible today.

Moreover, it will be appreciated that energy conservation includes certain operating innovations: adjustments to furnaces to make them more efficient; caulking cracks in openings around window and door frames; and relamping—changing high-wattage light bulbs for lower wattage bulbs or fluorescent lighting. Other operating efficiencies are widely discussed in other sources. Here, only retrofitting techniques are included that require new construction.

Retrofitting Feasibility

Energy conservation techniques increase the resistance of heat transfer in the building, providing more efficient heating, ventilating, and air conditioning. In fact, some studies have reported the annual energy consumption of a single-family residence may be reduced 36 percent without affecting the occupants' life-style. The general profitability of retrofitting techniques depends partly on the number of degree days and cooling hours.

Degree Days. The profitability of retrofitting techniques tends to increase with the number of degree days. The degree day is based on the proposition that the amount of heat used per day is proportional to the number of degrees the average outside temperature falls below 65 degrees. For a specific day, the number of degree days is equal to 65 degrees less the daily mean temperature for that date. The sum of individual degree days gives the number of degree days per year. For a given location, if the daily mean temperature on January 1 is 61 degrees as reported by the local weather bureau, the number of degree days for that day is four (65–61). The sum of degree days for the year gives the annual number of degree days (Clifford Strock and William B. Foxhall, eds. *Handbook of Air Conditioning, Heating and Ventilating* [New York: The Industrial Press, 1959], pp. 4–27).

Figure 14–1 illustrates the number of degree days per year for the main regions of the United States. More specific data may be obtained from local weather bureaus. Note that the number of degree days ranges from 500 in central Florida to 10,000 degree days in northern North Dakota and Minnesota. The calculation of the local degree days makes it possible to estimate the optimum energy conservation techniques given the energy cost for heating. To calculate savings in air conditioning, consult similar tables and maps showing the number of *cooling days* for selected locations.

Annual Energy Savings. The feasibility of energy conservation techniques is determined by first converting heating and cooling costs to the cost per 100,000 British Thermal Units (BTU). (One BTU is the amount

FIGURE 14–1

Normal Number of Degree Days per Year

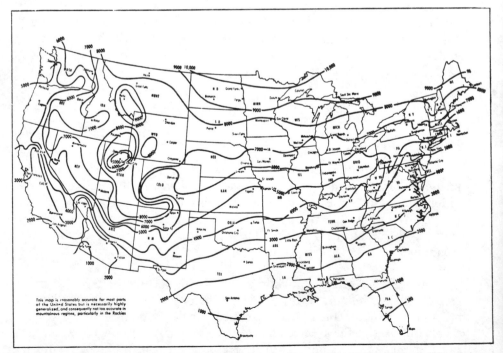

Source. *Retrofitting Existing Homes for Energy Conservation: An Economic Analysis.* Building Science Series 64 (Washington, D.C.: U.S. Government Printing Office, 1974), p. 52.

of heat required to heat one pound of water one degree Fahrenheit.) One report has shown that if natural gas costs 30 cents per 100,000 BTU and if the heating system operates under an efficiency rate of 50 percent, the heating cost amounts to $.075 per 100,000 BTU. The energy savings realized depends on the initial investment cost given the expected payback period. For example, assuming a 4,000-degree day, attic insulation of five inches (loose-filled glass fiber) would take eight years to pay back. The potential savings realized would be considerable since loose attic insulation has an expected life equal to the life of the house.

To estimate savings gained from insulation, experts refer to insulation R values, which measure resistance to heat loss. Technically R factors measure thermal resistance in terms of Fahrenheit degrees per hour per BTU. The higher the R value, the greater the thermal resistance. (The complex formula to calculate R values is given in *Handbook of Fundamentals.* New York: American Society of Heating, Refrigerating and Air-Conditioning Engineers, Inc., 1972.) In northern cities, insulation with a rating of R–38 is recommended for ceilings. Even in Atlanta, Georgia, ceiling insulation with a rating of R–30 is recommended for air conditioned houses. Table 14–1 shows representative R values for selected insulation materials.

TABLE 14–1

Loose-Fill Insulation Materials Showing R-Values

	Loose-Fill Thickness in Inches		
R-Value	Glass Fiber	Rock Wool	Cellulosic Fiber
R–11................	5	4	3
R–19................	8–9	6–7	5
R–22................	10	7–8	6
R–30................	13–14	10–11	8
R–38................	17–18	13–14	10–11

Source: *In the Bank or Up the Chimney* (Washington, D.C.: U.S. Department of Housing and Urban Development, 1975), p. 44.

To carry this analysis further, consult local utilities for approximate costs of heating a dwelling for different fuels. For example, in the Atlanta, Georgia area an average frame house of 1,600 square feet with an uninsulated ceiling loses 54,400 British Thermal Units an hour or more when temperatures fall below freezing. With natural gas fuel, this amounts to a cost of $1.20 per day. An electrically heated house would cost $5.25 per day. Ceiling insulation with an R–30 value in such a house would reduce natural gas heating costs to $.06 per day.

To illustrate further, suppose ceiling insulation costs $.25 a square foot installed for a ceiling of 1,500 square feet, and assume heating experts estimate savings of 49,500 British Thermal Units an hour. With an outside temperature 60 degrees colder, the actual cost-savings may be calculated. For natural gas heat, convert British Thermal Units to therms by multiplying by .0173—in this example, 856 therms. If the local gas utility reports a cost of $.18 a therm, the annual savings equals $154. With a cost of ceiling insulation of $375, the initial cost will be repaid in 2.4 years ($375/154). As fuel costs increase, the payback period decreases.

These savings are financially feasible even under relatively high interest rates of home improvement loans. Assume, for example, a 12-percent interest rate and a 25-percent marginal income tax rate. The effective interest rate cost would be 9 percent. Furthermore, if the consumer price index shows an inflationary rate of 6 or 7 percent per year, in *real* terms the interest rate would decrease even further, for example, the borrower pays the loan back with cheaper dollars, lowering the effective interest cost (see Stephen R. Petersen, *Retrofitting Existing Housing for Energy Conservation: An Economic Analysis.* [Washington, D.C.: U.S. Government Printing Office, 1974], pp. 29–30).

A layman's guide to energy-saving home improvements has been published by the Department of Housing and Urban Development (*In the Bank . . . Or Up the Chimney?* [Washington, D.C.: U.S. Department of Housing and Urban Development, April 1975], 73 pp.). In this report the heating factors are given for selected communities. For example, the heating factor for natural gas heat in cents per 100 cubic feet for Los Angeles is .07. The report recommends that heating factors be obtained from local utility companies which report the true cost including fuel adjustment factors and taxes. Heating multipliers are given for gas, oil, electric, and coal heat which is multiplied times the local fuel costs to give the heating factor. Heating and cooling factors, fuel costs, and heating multipliers are reported for major cities in various states (Ibid, p. 29).

This report provides a means of calculating net savings realized over the life of an investment in energy conservation. For a one-time investment, such as new ceiling insulation, data needed include the

Savings factor.
Heating factor.
Cooling factor.
Investment cost.

To illustrate what is the total net savings realized by adding six inches of attic insulation for a 1,200 square foot attic located in Los Angeles and heated with natural gas? The formula giving this answer is:

Net savings realized
    over the life of
    the project   = [savings factor × (heating factor
                            + cooling factor) × 13] − investment cost

From the report, data for this formula indicates:

> Savings factor, $473
> Heating factor, 0.07
> Cooling factor, 0.09
> Investment cost, $216

Therefore (heating and cooling factors total .16):

> Net savings realized
> over the life of
> the project $= [\$473 \times 0.16 \times 13] - \$216$
> $= \$767.84$

The factor 13, according to this source, approximates the annual yearly savings and the expected rate of inflation. Similar tables are available for estimating savings from other energy conservation techniques to give the total savings for numerous energy-saving techniques.

It will be realized that these tabular results *serve only as general guides.* Since source data are based on past years, utility rates must be secured from local utility sources and insulation and construction costs from local building suppliers and contractors. The method of analysis, however, indicates a convenient way of testing the feasibility of conservation techniques.

Energy Cost Reduction for Apartments

According to the Institute of Real Estate Management, the energy cost for apartment buildings averages about 27 percent of total operating costs. For a 100-unit garden court apartment, these energy costs approximate $400 per apartment, or in northern cities, $550 per apartment unit in a total electric building. It is claimed that the efficient management of energy in apartment buildings reduces energy costs by 20 to 30 percent.

Table 14-2 summarizes energy savings for 11 recommended ways to reduce energy costs. In one example, replacing high-flow rate showerheads (four gallons per minute capacity) with low-flow showerheads, restricting water flow to 2.3 gallons per minute, reduced the annual water cost by $943. Similar cost-saving measures include installing flow-limiting aerators in kitchen and bathroom faucets. It is reported that the new showerheads and aerators paid for themselves in less than two months.

Relamping apartments with lower wattage light bulbs and replacing incandescent bulbs with fluorescent lights produced further savings. Correcting for overheated and overcooled apartments required the installation of thermostats with set upper and lower temperature limits. In the example cited, the cost of thermostats averages $30 an apartment and, in an all-electric 184-unit complex, amounted to first-year savings of $6,522.

TABLE 14-2

A Summary of Annual Savings Realized from Energy Conservation Techniques for Selected Apartments

Recommendation	Cost to Implement	Payback Period (years)	First-year Energy Cost Reduction	10-year Savings
Savings on Hot Water:				
1. Replace showerheads and sink aerators....................	$ 1,094	0.1	$ 9,570	$147,818
2. Reduce hot water temperature..	No Cost	Immediate	7,837	121,946
3. Install timer on hot water circulating pump...............	16	0.3	61	911
Savings on Lighting:				
4. Relamp apartments............	1,623	0.6	3,215	39,632
Relamp common areas........	98	0.1	1,886	29,249
Savings on Heating and Cooling:				
5. Correct overheating............	39,000	0.8	48,583	715,616
6. Limit temperature..............	5,465	0.8	6,522	96,019
7. Set back temperature (1).......	6,000	1.1	5,558	80,484
Set back temperature (2).......	3,000	2.7	971	16,030
8. Improve and maintain boiler efficiency......................	100	0.8	225	2,787
9. Install storm windows..........	7,700	3.8	1,671	23,668
10. Insulate pipes and tanks.......	200	2.9	60	921
11. Add roof insulation.............	3,456	2.6	1,143	18,945
Other Potential Savings:				
Repair water leaks				
Install time switches in rooms which are used irregularly				
Minimize energy waste in vacant apartments				
Shut off pilots in gas furnaces				
Caulk and weatherstrip doors and windows				

Note: The first-year energy cost reduction figure is the *gross* amount saved. The 10-year savings figure is the projected *net* amount saved over a 10-year period, before taxes. It takes into account the initial implementation expense, annual maintenance costs (if any), estimated rate of inflation, and anticipated increases in energy costs.

Source: *Energy Cost Reduction for Apartment Owners and Managers* (Chicago: Institute of Real Estate Management of the National Association of Realtors, 1977), p. 5.

Temperature-limiting thermostats were paid back in less than ten months. In this example, the ten-year savings totaled $96,020. See Table 14-3.

The studies by the Institute of Real Estate Management show that energy reduction is a good low-risk investment. Measures that reduce energy consumption allow apartment owners to survive the long term and become more competitive in the short run. These conclusions even apply to apartment units in which tenants pay their own utilities. For it follows that higher costs to tenants mean higher costs to the apartment owners. That is, tenants who have the option of living in comparable apartments for less money have incentives to move—increasing tenant turnover and higher vacancy rates. While the examples cited here may not apply to individual apartment buildings, the savings documented in Table 14–2 suggest the potential dollar savings for leading energy-saving recommendations.

TABLE 14–3

Annual Savings Realized by Installing Temperature Limiting Thermostats: 184-Unit Apartment

Assumptions	
1. Initial Investment...............................	$5,465
2. Units of Savings.................................	191,822 KWH
3. Current Price per Unit...........................	$.034/KWH
4. First-year Pretax Savings........................	$6,522
5. Payback, before Taxes (Years)...................	0.8
6. Projected Energy Price Rise, Years 1–5..........	3%
7. Projected Energy Price Rise, Years 6–10........	3%
8. Projected Annual Inflation Rate.................	6.5%

	(A) Pretax Savings	(B) Implementation/ Maintenance Costs	(C) Pretax Cash Flow (A) − (B)
Initial investment.....		$5,465	
Year			
1...............	$ 6,522		$ 6,522
2...............	7,142		7,142
3...............	7,820		7,820
4...............	8,563		8,563
5...............	9,376		9,376
6...............	10,267		10,267
7...............	11,243		11,243
8...............	12,311		12,311
9...............	13,480		13,480
10...............	14,761		14,761
Total.............	$101,485	$5,465	$96,020

Source: *Energy Cost Reduction for Apartment Owners and Managers* (Chicago: Institute of Real Estate Management of the National Association of Realtors, 1977), p. 31.

SOLAR HEATING

The continued depletion of fossil fuel resources, leading to shortages, curtailments, and dependence on foreign sources of energy, has encouraged the installation of domestic solar hot water and space heating systems. It has been stated that approximately 25 percent of the total energy consumed in the Southwest is used for heating buildings and domestic water supplies—an area suitable for expansion of solar systems. Not only would solar energy for domestic purposes conserve fossil fuels, solar energy minimizes environmental consequences of nonrenewable forms of energy.

The interest in solar energy follows from its abundant source. Authorities have stated that sunlight falling on the surface of Lake Erie in a single day is greater than the current annual U.S. energy consumption. Further, the amount of solar radiation striking only 1 percent of the land area each year is more than projected national energy needs to the year 2000 (John Hamer, "Solar Energy," *Editorial Research Reports*, vol. 2, no. 18 [November 12, 1976], p. 825).

The Energy Research Development Administration predicts that solar energy will provide about 25 percent of the nation's needs by the year 2020. In fact, the state of Florida has enacted legislation that states "no single family residence shall be constructed within the state, unless the plumbing therein is designed to facilitate the future installment of solar water heating equipment" (*Fla. Stat. Ann.* Section 553.065 [Supp. 1974]).

Problems in utilizing solar energy handicap its more widespread adoption. Consider only a few of the more serious problems: *First*, solar energy varies greatly with latitude, season, time of day, and weather. *Secondly*, solar energy cannot be stored easily for later use or transported to other areas. And *thirdly*, solar systems are still burdened with technical problems and, *finally*, the economics of solar systems depend largely on assumptions over future fuel costs and general inflation.

To explain future solar system prospects, it is proposed to describe the state of the art and then indicate under what circumstances solar systems are feasible. Finally, solar systems have introduced a new element in property ownership: solar property rights, a topic that ends the chapter.

Solar Systems for Domestic Heat

Solar heating systems may be designed for (1) heating domestic water, (2) space heating, and (3) heating both space and domestic hot water. The systems that employ air heating collectors transfer hot air from roof panels to a bin full of rocks heated by hot air from the collector. Space heating is accomplished by blowing cooler air from the room through the heated rock bin or directly through the collector. An auxiliary space heater supplements room temperature during periods of peak demand.

Domestic solar hot water heaters transfer hot water through roof-mounted collector panels which are heated by the sun to an electrically heated hot water tank. Some more advanced systems incorporate an air-to-liquid heat exchanger that circulates water through the air heating system. Under favorable conditions, water is circulated through tubes on collector panels which are covered by glass that trap heat like a greenhouse. Such units mounted on the roof, facing the sun, may heat water to 100 to 200 degrees on sunny days. Other systems transfer solar heat either to water or air which is pumped or blown into the heating system's radiators or ducts.

A limited amount of heat may be stored (in hot water tanks or in a bin of hot rocks) for release during the night or cooler weather. Figure 14–2 illustrates a combination domestic hot water and space heating system.

It will be appreciated that operating costs of these systems are fairly nominal—the main cost lies in the initial investment which must be amortized (or allocated) over the expected life of the system. Their feasibility will improve as components of solar systems are mass produced.

FIGURE 14–2

Solar Space Heating and Domestic Hot Water System

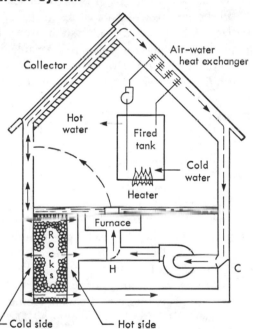

Source: William D. Schulze, Shaul Ben-David, and J. Douglas Balcomb, *Economics of Solar Home Heating* (Washington, D.C.: U.S. Government Printing Office, 1977), p. 39.

Currently, observers have reported the cost of solar collectors at $10.00 per square foot or more. As a consequence, the payback period may extend over five to ten years, depending on the future price of fuel, financing costs, and projections of future solar equipment costs. As more states and the federal government provide subsidies in the form of low-interest financing, and tax incentives, these systems will appear even more financially feasible.

Solar System Feasibility

The high capital investment of solar systems tends to be offset by incentives that include tax credits, low-interest loans and property tax abatement. Among the states that have provided property tax exemption for solar equipment are Arizona, Colorado, Connecticut, Hawaii, Illinois, Indiana, Kansas, Maryland, Massachusetts, Michigan, Montana, New Hampshire, North Dakota, Oregon, and South Dakota.

Numerous other states provide state income tax incentives for solar devices or exempt solar equipment from state or local sales taxes. For instance in New Mexico the solar system tax credit allowed on state income tax returns is equal to 25 percent of the cost of solar equipment, not to exceed $1,000 on the taxpayer's principal residence. Arizona allows the taxpayer to amortize the cost of the solar system over a 60-month period effectively deducting the total cost from net taxable income. Arizona further exempts solar systems from property taxation.

To test the feasibility of a solar system, the initial cost of the collector and its associated equipment would include

1. Storage costs.
2. Pipes and fittings.
3. Motors and pumps.
4. Heat exchanger.
5. Controls.

Storage costs in terms of 1975 dollars experienced in the southwest part of the United States have been equal to $0.065 per pounds of water required for heat storage times the collector area in square feet. In part, these costs are sensitive to the supply and demand for heat, the size of the home, the local climate, architectural characteristics and location of the home (Thomas H. Stevens, "The Economics of Solar Home Heating Systems for the Southwest Region," *Journal of Energy and Development*, vol. 2, no. 2 [Spring 1977], p. 283).

Given these variables for the southwest part of the United States, the optimum solar system would satisfy 75 percent of the heat demand with the remaining 25 percent supplied by conventional systems. In one study, the cost of the solar system was estimated for a new 2,000-square-foot home over 20 years. At current fuel prices the present value of savings under solar systems in selected cities of the Southwest were negative for electricity and natural gas. However, the system proved feasible for electricity, assuming a 10-percent annual price increase in fuel and the assumption of natural gas price deregulation.

In considering the long-run implications of solar energy systems, observers have noted that because of the practice of pricing gas or electricity at declining rates as increasing blocks of power are consumed, users of solar systems, who use less natural gas or electricity, pay higher per unit fuel costs. Some authorities argue that block pricing of utilities at declining marginal rates should be discontinued—a recommendation which would penalize high-volume users.

One authority, while noting that property tax incentives make solar systems more competitive, believes that present tax incentives at the state or federal level are not sufficient to stimulate investment in solar systems. This source recommends low-interest rate loans as the best means to encourage solar investment. Finally, if natural gas prices are deregulated, homeowners will find it even more advantageous to install solar systems.

To illustrate, see Figure 14–3 that projects solar feasibility by states, according to certain well-defined assumptions. The data for this map has been prepared assuming fixed costs of $1,100 and variable costs of $9.50 a square foot (1976), decreasing to $8.00 a square foot by 1990; a system life of 30 years and annual operating and maintenance costs of .75 percent.

The map indicates that the solar space heating is currently feasible in the northern tier of states. In the midsouthern states solar feasibility is postponed to 1985 or 1990. In short, solar feasibility begins in the north-

FIGURE 14–3

Solar Feasibility—Residential Space Heating Standard Air System (real interest rate—2.5%)*

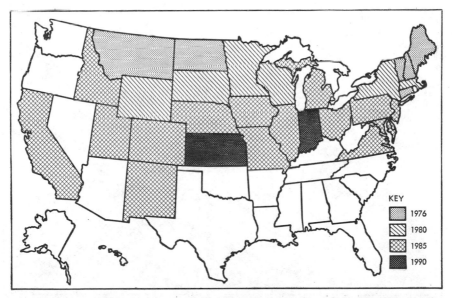

KEY

▨	1976
▨	1980
▨	1985
■	1990

* Fixed costs: $1100; variable costs: $9.50/ft² in 1976, decreasing to $8.00/ft² in 1990; operation and maintenance: 0.75% annually; system life: 30 years.

Source: Shaul, Ben-David, et al., "Near Term Prospects for Solar Energy: An Economic Analysis." Reprinted with permission from 17 *Natural Resources Journal* 185 (1977), published by the University of New Mexico School of Law, Albuquerque, N.M. 87131.

ern tier of states and systematically moves southward. Projections are based on current energy prices.

Figure 14–4 shows similar data for the solar feasibility of a domestic hot water system. Note that fixed costs, system life, and operation and maintenance costs are much lower. (See Ben-David Shaul, William D. Schulze, et al., "Near Term Prospects for Solar Energy: An Economic Analysis," *Natural Resources Journal*, vol. 17 [April 1977], p. 186.)

The real interest rate of 2.5 percent assumed for data of Figures 14–3 and 14–4 deserves added comment. The real interest rate refers to annual loan payments in constant dollars. For example, if an individual borrows $1,000 for 30 years at 8.5 percent interest, the yearly payment would be $92.20. Next, assume a 6.0-percent inflation rate. The annual payment in the 30th year—in base year dollars—would be $15.24. In other words, assuming some rate of inflation, the real interest rate on long-term loans moves toward zero and effectively reduces the burden of repayments.

Observers have noted another factor limiting investment in solar systems. It is reported that financial institutions are reluctant to lend money for solar systems which may not add to the market value of the house. This reluctance has led some authorities to recommend federal interest

FIGURE 14–4

Solar Feasibility—Domestic Hot Water (real interest rate—2.5%)*

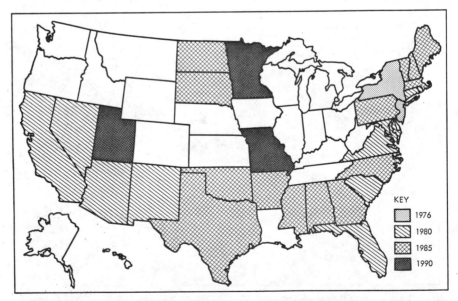

KEY
1976
1980
1985
1990

*Fixed costs: $300; variable costs: $11.00/ft²; operation and maintenance: 1.0% annually; system life: 20 years.

Source: Shaul, Ben-David, et al., "Near Term Prospects for Solar Energy: An Economic Analysis." Reprinted with permission from 17 *Natural Resources Journal* 190 (1977), published by the University of New Mexico School of Law, Albuquerque, N.M. 87131.

rate subsidies and loan insurance for solar equipment, in this way reducing risks to lending institution.

The Midland Federal Savings Association of Denver, Colorado, has developed certain policies in granting 90 percent mortgages that include the cost of solar systems. Residential loans, including solar systems proposed for existing houses, must conform to the following requirements:

1. The solar system must be properly engineered by a registered professional engineer selected by the Association.
2. The cost of verifying the solar system analysis is paid by the prospective borrower.
3. Solar heating systems must have a conventional back-up system verified by a registered engineer.
4. Solar easements to protect the loan security must be included with the mortgage application.

Moreover, loan officers advise borrowers to secure insurance on glass panels required for solar systems. All solar heated homes must conform to minimum construction standards established for solar heated homes.

Solar Property Rights

Investment in solar collectors would be largely worthless if a neighbor constructed a two-story structure or planted trees that shaded the collector. As a consequence the law is beginning to recognize solar property rights. This extension of common law stems from the historic right of property owners to the free flow of light and air across adjoining land. This right is inherent in zoning requirements that govern building setbacks from the street, maximum building height, and other types of density controls.

The Right to Solar Energy. Traditionally, the courts have held that zoning to provide adequate light and air were valid. According to one ruling, "In the exercise of police power, a local government can impose restrictions on the maximum height of buildings for the purpose of securing adequate sunlight to promote public health in general" (Melvin M. Eisenstadt and Albert E. Utton, "Solar Rights and Their Effect on Solar Heating and Cooling," *Natural Resources Journal,* vol. 16, no. 2 [April 1977], p. 385). Solar rights, however, go beyond the traditional zoning regulation.

Solar rights have been defined as the right to "solar energy that would fall in one's property if the path of sunshine were not impeded by one's neighbors." A zoning code that follows this definition adopted by the city of Albuquerque, New Mexico, states

> tall or massive structures which would dominate their environment shall
> be located in urban centers to provide visual variety and functional

diversity while preserving pleasing vistas and *solar access* (see Melvin M. Eisenstadt and Albert E. Utton, "Solar Rights and Their Effect on Solar Heating and Cooling," p. 387).

With the increasing recognition of solar rights, its value depends on the price of energy and the location. Presumably, solar rights could be sold, leased, and conveyed by easement as other property rights. To pursue this point, the difference must be recognized between solar light and solar energy.

1. *Solar Light.* Experts have noted that the right to light and air does not necessarily convey rights to the direct rays of the sun. Adequate light might be reflected or diffused and yet be adequate under standards of the right to light and air set by zoning regulations or by common law. However, reflected or diffused radiation would be of minor value for purposes of capturing solar energy.

2. *Solar Energy.* Solar energy refers to more than visible light. Technically, solar energy refers to all of the energy in the solar wavelength band including infrared light, ultraviolet and gamma rays. Thus a landowner seeking rights to solar energy must have the right to the *unobstructed* light over the property of another. In fact, the concept of solar rights could be extended to property owners over whole neighborhoods. In new subdivisions, each owner would, in effect, grant solar rights across his air space to all of his neighbors. In this way a group of property owners would have mutual access to solar energy. These rights would be created by zoning regulations and mutual grants of private easements.

Protection of Solar Rights. The trend seems to favor creation of solar rights and their protection by zoning regulations or by private easements. The first requires an exercise of the police power, the second requires a conveyance of private property rights that "run with the land."

1. *Solar Rights under Zoning Regulations.* Zoning regulations that deal with solar rights extend the police power under the theory that zoning regulation makes the best use of the land resources. Zoning regulations that protect solar rights require a property owner give up part of his air space in return for similar solar rights granted by adjoining property owners. In this sense, solar rights are similar to grants from others for light and air.

The planning commission of Albuquerque, New Mexico, recommended that to protect solar access building structures should be limited to 26 feet and must fall within a 45-degree angle measured from the property boundary line or public right of way center line.

> Structure height up to 26 feet is permitted at any legal location. The height and width of the structure over 26 feet shall fall within 45-degree angle planes drawn from the horizontal at the main grade along each internal boundary of the premises and each adjacent public right-of-way center line.

These provisions recognize that solar rights effectively guarantee access to solar energy. While zoning may appear to be valid, others rely on zoning easements.

2. *Zoning Easements.* It is well established that easements for light, air, view, and access are valid property rights that have a definite value and that may be sold and conveyed as other property rights. Accordingly, easements for unobstructed light give the dominant estate the right to light coming directly from the sun. The servient estate must not obstruct light coming from the sky to the dominant estate—the estate that benefits from the solar easements. Easements for solar energy refer to the light originating from the sun that strikes the earth in a straight line.

The grant of a solar energy easement rests on the voluntary conveyance of private owners. Developers, however, in conveying deeds to property owners in a new subdivision may include the solar easement as a deed covenant. Under this arrangement each land owner grants solar rights across his or her air space to all neighbors such that every lot owner has access to solar energy. In this respect, solar rights protected by zoning regulations avoid requirements that solar rights conveyed by easements be acquired voluntarily or by mutual grants of adjoining property owners.

QUESTIONS FOR REVIEW

_____ 1. The purpose of new energy legislation is to
   a. increase revenue to finance public transportation.
   b. promote mass transportation.
   c. create an awareness of fuel and energy needs of rural and urban residents.
   d. subsidize private and public transportation.

_____ 2. Which of the following statements is correct?
   a. Mortgage lenders have no interest in energy conservation techniques.
   b. The United States League of Savings Associations has encouraged adoption of underwriting procedures which give full consideration to utility costs.
   c. Lenders do not recognize energy conservation techniques in granting home loan mortgages.
   d. Energy conservation techniques are not feasible in new dwellings.

_____ 3. Which of the following are believed consequences of higher energy costs?
   a. Energy inefficient buildings will suffer increased depreciation.
   b. More central locations will be preferred as the cost of transportation increases.
   c. Property values of existing structures will decrease.
   d. All of the above.

_____ 4. Retrofitting techniques to improve the thermal efficiency of buildings generally prove profitable because
   a. future energy costs in the United States will probably decrease.
   b. most of the existing dwellings in the United States were constructed in periods of relatively low energy costs.
   c. the future cost of retrofitting will decline.
   d. new buildings consume more energy than older buildings.

_____ 5. The degree day is
   a. the annual sum of degree days defined as the difference between 65 degrees and the daily mean temperature less than 65 degrees.
   b. the number of days in which the average temperature is above 65 degrees.
   c. the annual average number of days in which the temperature falls between 65 and 72 degrees.
   d. the annual average number of days in which the temperature falls below 65 degrees.

_____ 6. The potential savings realized from attic insulation
   a. would be relatively insignificant for a house heated by electricity.
   b. decreases with declining fuel prices.
   c. depends on the number of British Thermal Units required annually.
   d. would be considerable since loose attic insulation has an expected life equal to the life of the house.

_____ 7. In financing energy conservation improvements in existing dwellings,
   a. continued inflation increases financing costs over the life of a loan.
   b. continued deflation increases the interest rate in real terms.
   c. an increase in the consumer price index decreases interest costs in real terms.
   d. none of the above.

_____ 8. To estimate savings realized from attic insulation,
   a. utility rates must be secured from local utility sources.
   b. insulation and construction costs must be obtained from local suppliers and contractors.
   c. savings and cooling factors must be secured from published tables.
   d. all of the above.

_____ 9. Energy costs for apartment buildings tend to
   a. be relatively insignificant as a proportion of total operating costs.
   b. average about 27 percent of total operating costs.
   c. be less significant than energy costs of homes since energy costs may be shifted to tenants.

     d. be lower in northern cities and more in southern cities of the United States.

_____10. Relamping refers to

     a. replacing existing bulbs with lower wattage bulbs and with fluorescent lights.

     b. methods of compensating for overheated and overcooled apartments.

     c. the practice of charging tenants for excessive electrical costs.

     d. the installation of electric meters for each apartment unit.

_____11. In the operation of apartment buildings, studies by the Institute of Real Estate Management show an investment in energy reduction

     a. is a risky investment.

     b. makes apartments relatively noncompetitive in the short run.

     c. is a good low-risk investment.

     d. is uneconomic for apartment units in which tenants pay their own utilities.

_____12. Generally, for apartment buildings investment in energy reduction techniques are advised even if tenants pay their own utilities because

     a. lower costs to tenants mean higher costs to apartment owners.

     b. higher costs to tenants mean higher costs to apartment owners.

     c. differences in energy costs among apartments provide no incentives for tenants to move.

     d. higher costs to tenants mean lower costs to apartment owners.

_____13. Which of the following has encouraged interest in solar heating systems?

     a. The continued depletion of fossil fuel resources.

     b. Solar energy minimizes environmental consequences of non renewable forms of energy.

     c. Solar energy is abundantly available.

     d. All of the above.

_____14. Solar energy will

     a. provide about 25 percent of the nation's needs by the year 2020.

     b. provide 50 percent of the required energy in the United States by the year 2000.

     c. be relatively uneconomic at the present time because of rising construction costs.

     d. provide less than 10 percent of the nation's needs by the year 2020.

_____15. The main reasons for the limited adoption of solar energy is that

     a. solar energy varies greatly with latitude, season, time of day, and weather.

     b. solar energy cannot be stored easily for later use.

     c. economics of solar systems depend largely on assumptions over future fuel costs and general inflation.

     d. all of the above.

_____16. Solar heating systems have

     a. high operating costs and high initial investment costs.

     b. a minimum economic life of 40 years.

     c. fairly nominal operating costs; the main cost lies in the initial investment.

     d. none of the above.

_____17. The payback period for solar heating systems depends on

     a. the future price of fuel and local regulations.

     b. financing costs and availability of technically trained operators.

     c. future solar equipment costs and future land prices.

     d. the future price of fuel, financing costs, and projections of future solar equipment costs.

_____18. The high capital investment of solar systems tends to

     a. be offset by incentives that include tax credits, low-interest loans, and property tax abatement.

     b. increase the market value of solar equipped dwellings.

     c. be accepted by buyers of new dwellings.

     d. all of the above.

_____19. Which of the following would *not* be a cost of a solar heating system?

     a. Storage costs and the cost of motors and pumps.

     b. The cost of heat exchangers and controls.

     c. The cost of pipes, fittings, and storage costs.

     d. Land prices judged on a front-foot basis.

_____20. Solar system costs depend on

     a. supply and demand for heat.

     b. the size of the home.

     c. the local climate.

     d. all of the above.

_____21. In the southwest part of the United States it is claimed that the ideal solar heating system will

     a. satisfy 75 percent of domestic heating demands.

     b. supply at least 50 percent of domestic heat.

     c. be feasible only for luxury dwellings.

     d. supply domestic heat for more than 75 percent of all dwellings.

_____22. Which of the following statements is true regarding utility rates?

     a. Declining utility rates as added blocks of power are used favors small utility users.

     b. Block pricing of utilities at declining marginal rates penalizes small volume users.

    c. To conserve energy, large users of utilities should pay lower per unit utility rates.

    d. Utility rates graduated by volume of use have no bearing on energy use.

_____23. Authorities have concluded that the best means to encourage solar energy investments is to

    a. provide for property tax abatement.

    b. provide income tax incentives at the present level.

    c. maintain price controls on natural gas.

    d. provide low-interest rate loans to encourage solar investment.

_____24. Which of the following statements is correct?

    a. Deregulation of natural gas prices would encourage investment in solar heating systems.

    b. Continued price controls on natural gas prices encourages rapid investment in solar energy systems.

    c. Cheaper electricity rates would lower operating costs of solar energy systems and encourage significant increases in solar energy investments.

    d. Financing terms have no effect on incentives to install solar energy heating systems.

_____25. According to the available information,

    a. solar space heating is feasible in the state of Florida.

    b. solar domestic hot water systems are feasible in such states as Florida.

    c. solar domestic hot water systems are not workable in extreme northern states.

    d. at current energy prices, solar space heating is universally feasible.

_____26. The available evidence suggests that

    a. solar space heating is currently feasible in selected northern states.

    b. feasible solar domestic hot water systems are confined to northern states.

    c. fixed costs, system life, and operating costs of solar systems are much lower in the northern states.

    d. solar domestic hot water systems are presently feasible only in the most northern states.

_____27. Policies that minimize lender risk in financing solar equipped dwellings include

    a. solar systems properly engineered.

    b. solar heating systems with a conventional back-up system.

    c. solar easements to protect loan security.

    d. all of the above.

_____28. A 6-percent general inflation rate

     a. tends to increase the real financing costs of solar energy systems.
     b. has no effect on decisions to finance solar energy systems.
     c. tends to decrease real interest rates in constant dollars.
     d. tends to increase the burden of loan repayments on solar energy systems.

____29. What are the factors that limit investment in solar energy systems?
     a. the reluctance of lending authorities to lend money on untested solar energy systems.
     b. solar energy systems decrease market value.
     c. high operating costs of solar energy systems.
     d. all of the above.

____30. Solar property rights are
     a. inherent property rights originating in feudal property law.
     b. an extension of common law based on the right to the free flow of light and air.
     c. rights created by local zoning codes.
     d. rights conveyed by warranty deeds.

____31. Traditionally, courts have held that
     a. zoning may not be used to protect the right to adequate light and air.
     b. local governments can impose land use restrictions for the purpose of securing adequate sunlight.
     c. solar rights must be conveyed by deed.
     d. solar rights must be established by statute.

____32. Solar rights have been defined as
     a. energy that would fall on one's property if a path of sunlight were not impeded by one's neighbors.
     b. the right to diffused light.
     c. the right to sunlight on at least 25 percent of an owner's land.
     d. the right to sunlight less ultraviolet light and gamma rays.

____33. The value of solar rights depends on
     a. the location and land area.
     b. the price of energy and the value of the property.
     c. building value and location.
     d. the price of energy and the location.

____34. Which of the following statements is correct?
     a. Solar light refers to direct rays of the sun.
     b. Solar light includes reflected or diffused light.
     c. Solar light has no bearing on property value.
     d. None of the above.

_____35. Solar energy is restricted to
  a. indirect, reflected, or diffused light.
  b. all of the energy in the solar wavelength band including infra-
      red light, ultraviolet and gamma rays.
  c. rights established by subdivision regulations.
  d. rights as defined in zoning regulations.

_____36. Zoning regulations that protect solar rights
  a. require a property owner to give up part of his air space in
      return for similar solar rights granted by adjoining property
      owners.
  b. require that solar rights be recorded.
  c. require an easement deed to adjoining property owners.
  d. are based on the right of eminent domain.

_____37. Zoning regulations protect solar rights by
  a. prohibiting buildings or other obstructions within 50 feet of
      the property line.
  b. prohibiting building or other structures within a given angle
      measured from the property line or public right-of-way center
      line.
  c. basing solar rights on voluntary grants by property owners.
  d. creating solar rights that are voidable at the option of adjoining
      property owners.

_____38. Easements for solar energy refer to
  a. diffused light originating from sunlight.
  b. indirect sunlight.
  c. light originating from the sun that strikes the earth in a
      straight line.
  d. establishing solar rights by local regulation.

_____39. Developers in conveying land in a new subdivision provide solar
          rights by
  a. restricting development density.
  b. relying on local zoning regulations to create solar rights.
  c. reserving solar rights that may be purchased by individual lot
      owners.
  d. granting solar rights to air space so that every lot owner has
      access to solar energy.

_____40. Which of the following would *not* help conserve energy?
  a. Set standards for utility rates that penalize high volume users.
  b. Tax incentives for investors in energy conservation techniques.
  c. Maintain present natural gas prices.
  d. Mortgage underwriting procedures that give full consideration
      to energy costs.

ANSWER KEY

1. (c)	11. (c)	21. (a)	31. (b)
2. (b)	12. (d)	22. (b)	32. (a)
3. (d)	13. (d)	23. (d)	33. (d)
4. (b)	14. (a)	24. (a)	34. (b)
5. (a)	15. (d)	25. (b)	35. (b)
6. (d)	16. (c)	26. (a)	36. (a)
7. (c)	17. (d)	27. (d)	37. (b)
8. (d)	18. (a)	28. (c)	38. (c)
9. (b)	19. (d)	29. (a)	39. (d)
10. (a)	20. (d)	30. (b)	40. (c)

SUGGESTED ADDITIONAL READING

The Economics of Solar Home Heating. Washington, D.C.: U.S. Government Printing Office, January 1977.

Energy Cost Reduction for Apartment Owners and Managers. Chicago: Institute of Real Estate Management, 1977.

Hamer, John. "Solar Energy," *Editorial Research Reports,* vol. 2, no. 2 (November 1976), pp. 825–42.

"How to Conserve Energy," *Realtors Review,* vol. 1, no. 5 (May 1977), pp. 4–8.

In the Bank . . . Or Up the Chimney? Washington, D.C.: U.S. Department of Housing and Urban Development, April 1975.

Life Cycle Costing Emphasizing Energy Conservation. Springfield, N.J.: National Technical Information, May 1977.

Peterson, Stephen R. *Retrofitting Existing Housing for Energy Conservation: An Economic Analysis.* Washington, D.C.: U.S. Government Printing Office, December 1974.

15

Real Estate Finance

Real estate finance is one of the more complex real estate specialities. It requires a knowledge of savings and loan procedures, practices of mortgage bankers, and mortgage regulations controlling commercial banks, insurance companies, and mutual savings banks. Other mortgage policies vary among pension funds, real estate investment trusts, individuals, and government agencies. A comprehensive treatment of the subject is beyond the scope of this work, but, to proceed without explaining the most relevant topics would leave a serious gap in an introductory survey of real estate practices, since an understanding of the elements of real estate finance is essential to a successful career in real estate.

GOVERNMENT INTERVENTION IN THE MORTGAGE MARKET

The real estate industry is highly dependent on the flow of funds into the mortgage market. The flow of savings in the national economy is channeled into investments that pay the highest interest rate. For real estate, the difficulty lies in mortgages that provide a fixed rate of return on relatively long-term investments. Investors tend to place funds where the interest rates are the highest. In periods of high interest rates, funds are withdrawn from mortgages to higher paying investments (i.e., government securities, private bonds and other relatively high-yield, short-term securities).

The federal government plays the dominant role in the flow of funds, primarily because the government controls the supply of money. Fiscal policy also influences the demand and supply of loanable funds; taxation lowers spending, investment, and savings; government spending adds to incomes, spending, and savings. To the extent that government agencies vary the supply of money and influence the interest rate, the supply of mortgage money may be adversely affected. Taxation and government spending are other factors that affect the availability of credit. A brief explanation of how these changes take place will show how real estate mortgage money is vulnerable to federal policy.

The Supply of Mortgage Money

The amount of money available for mortgages changes as the Federal Reserve Board increases or decreases the quantity of money. The amount of money available in the economy is closely related to fluctuations in the interest rate. For the economy generally, with a fixed supply of goods and services available at any one time, an increase in the quantity of money leads to higher prices. Conversely, a decrease in the supply leads to lower prices. The Federal Reserve Board, a quasipublic institution with regulatory power over the commercial banking system, affects the money supply through the purchase and sale of government bonds, changes in the discount rate, and varying reserve requirements.

If the Federal Reserve Board decides to purchase government bonds held by banks, banks exchange bonds for money, making more money available for loans. If the Federal Reserve elects to sell bonds to commercial banks, this means that money which would normally go into the economy as loanable funds is unavailable for loans, mortgages, and other purposes.

The other techniques used by the Federal Reserve Board—changing the discount rate and reserve requirements—have a similar impact on the money supply. The discount rate is the interest rate charged to commercial banks for borrowing from the Federal Reserve Bank. As the discount rate increases, banks charge higher interest rates on loans to their customers. This can discourage some borrowers from borrowing money. By lowering the discount rate, banks are induced to lower their interest rates on loans, which in turn tends to have an expansionary effect.

Likewise, reserve requirements regulate the amount of money that must be held in reserves, which in part controls the amount of loanable funds an individual bank can make available to its customers.

These operations that affect the supply of money for investment purposes also affect the interest rate on savings. Suppose, for example, that the interest rate increases on treasury bills (short-term government bonds). As these rates go up, savings tend to flow from financial institutions that supply money for mortgages. Savings and loan associations that only pay 5½ percent interest on passbook deposits would be expected to lose savings from customers that invest in government bonds yielding a higher return. Other financial institutions, such as commercial banks, life insurance companies, and mutual savings banks either lose funds on these competing investments or they invest funds in nonmortgage investments paying higher yields (for instance, life insurance companies). The crucial problem for real estate is that long-term borrowers in the market for new mortgages must compete with other investments that pay higher yields.

The Demand for Loanable Funds

While the supply of loanable funds varies according to national policy, the demand for loanable funds may be expected to vary with economic conditions. Suppose, for example, that businesses anticipate price increases. Under these circumstances it may be prudent to borrow money in the short run to purchase new equipment and inventories before price increases take effect. This places pressure on available funds for investment even to the point that savings are used to supply short-term commercial credit in preference to lower-paying yields on long-term mortgages.

Consider also certain institutional restraints that bear on the availability of mortgage credit. Some states limit by statute the maximum interest rate that may be paid on mortgages. If the mortgage interest rate increases to 9 percent nationally but state law limits the maximum rate to 8 percent, then institutional funds tend to move toward states having more liberal or no interest rate ceilings. Further, Congress has imposed interest rate ceilings on government-insured and guaranteed mortgages. Even though the face value of the mortgage may be discounted by the lender, funds may be placed in nonmortgage investments because of higher yields and fewer regulatory restrictions.

To some extent, developers of commercial properties are able to shift higher mortgage interest rates in the form of higher rents and prices. For the buyer of a single-family dwelling, this option is not available. As financing costs increase, buyers are unable (or unwilling) to meet monthly payments at higher interest rates on home mortgages. Therefore, higher interest rates tend to decrease the demand for single-family dwellings.

Federal policies, then, directly affect the availability of mortgage funds. As mortgage funds become less available and as real estate financing costs rise, the demand for real estate, especially housing, decreases.

REAL ESTATE MORTGAGES

Mortgages are instruments that convey real estate as security for a debt. The debt is evidenced by a promissory note or bond representing a personal promise to repay. In some states the mortgage conveys title to the lender with the provision that if the debt is paid according to the terms of the mortgage, the conveyance is void (a title state). In other states (called the lien states), the borrower retains title, the mortgage creates a lien against the real estate in favor of the lender. Mortgages are adapted to different types of real estate and vary according to the repayment plan and the purpose of the mortgage.

Mortgages Classified by the Repayment Plan

The repayment plan is adapted to the ability of the borrower to meet equity requirements and to make the required payments. Several types of mortgages have proven acceptable to lenders. In some transactions a mortgage is issued with the understanding that over the life of the loan the mortgage will be converted to more permanent financing. Mortgages identified with the method of repayment cover three main types.

Term Mortgages. Term mortgages were popular before the depression of 1930. In the simplest case, term mortgages provided for interest payments on a monthly or annual basis or on a schedule acceptable to the borrower and lender. The principal is repaid at the end of the term. At the end of the term if the principal was not paid, the lender might elect to grant another term mortgage and continue to collect interest on the original debt. No provision for principal repayment is provided by the term mortgage.

Amortized Mortgages. A mortgage providing for the repayment of principal over the term of the mortgage qualifies as an amortized mortgage. Principal and interest payments, typically paid monthly, provide for interest payments on the remaining balance as the principal is reduced with each payment. In the early years the proportion going to interest is high, decreasing with each level payment. This schedule is common to *level payment* mortgages.

A less popular amortization provides for a fixed monthly payment to the principal. Since interest declines with each payment the monthly payments are higher at the beginning of the mortgage, decreasing in final years. These mortgages are referred to as *variable payment* mortgages. In both plans payments are arranged so that at the end of the term the principal is repaid.

Partially Amortized Mortgages. The partially amortized mortgage, also termed a balloon mortgage, provides principal repayment down to a given amount and then requires a lump sum payment for the balance of the principal. In practice the balloon payment is not made since the amortization schedule increases the equity to the point that the property qualifies for refinancing under a fully amortized loan. The effect of the balloon mortgage is to reduce the amount of the monthly payment without reducing interest rates and without extending loan terms beyond legal maximum limits.

Special-Purpose Mortgages

Besides varying by the method of repayment, mortgages are adapted to different types of security and to alternative financing techniques. The legal rights of the borrower and lender serve as another common basis of classification.

Package Mortgages. Custom provides that certain types of personal property included in the sale of a single-family dwelling be added to the mortgage. Real estate developers may add washing machines, dryers, refrigerators, and other items normally regarded as personal property to the mortgage. Mortgages that include personal property or chattels are called package mortgages. Their appeal lies in the advantage of financing high-valued personal property with a limited down payment under long-term financing, with interest paid on the remaining balance and not on the original debt typical of consumer installment loans. Under a package mortgage, a purchaser of a new house may acquire expensive personal property with a minimum of capital.

Purchase Money Mortgages. In effect, sellers substitute purchase money mortgages for cash. In most states it does not include a promissory note and is secured only by the real estate and not the personal promise of the buyer. Sellers may accept a down payment and a purchase money mortgage that provides for repayment as other amortized mortgages. No third party lender is included. Like other mortgages, the purchase money mortgage takes priority over other subsequent claims against the borrower. A purchase money mortgage may be subordinate to a mortgage granted by a lending institution.

To illustrate, suppose A agrees to sell a dwelling to B for $60,000. A agrees to accept $5,000 cash, a purchase money mortgage of $7,000, 9 percent interest, repayable in monthly installments over 15 years. The balance of the purchase price is financed with a conventional first mortgage of $40,000, 9 percent interest, 25 years. In this case, B makes monthly payments to the lender on the $48,000 first mortgage and monthly payments to the seller who holds a purchase money mortgage. Since the purchase money mortgage is subordinate to the $48,000 first mortgage, A actually holds a second mortgage.

Participation Mortgages. To reduce risk, some lenders participate in mortgages in which more than one lender conveys money secured by a single mortgage. The participation agreement entered into by the lenders governs the share of each lender. This procedure is followed if institutional lenders are legally restricted in the amount they may loan, or if they wish to diversify their risks.

Blanket Mortgages. The blanket mortgage is secured by more than one parcel of real estate. Typically used to finance subdivisions, the blanket mortgage includes a clause that releases title to a particular house and lot if the seller pays a proportion of the lot value to the original land owner. As individual homes are sold, a separate loan is executed to the new buyer and part of the proceeds of this loan are used to pay the blanket loan covering all lots of the subdivision. The buyer of the house and lot secures a release of his or her lot from the blanket mortgage covering remaining unsold lots.

Trust Deeds. In certain states such as California and Arizona, the trust deed substitutes for the mortgage. In a mortgage there are two parties: a borrower and a lender. In a trust deed there are three parties: the borrower becomes the *trustor*, the lender becomes the *beneficiary* of the trust, and a third party operates as the *trustee*. The borrower conveys title to the trustee which is held "in trust" as security for the lender or beneficiary of the trust. The trustee conveys the title back to the borrower when the debt is repaid. If the debt is in default the trustee is instructed to foreclose and sell the property at public sale for the benefit of the lender. The trust device circumvents the more restrictive foreclosure laws that unduly delay transfer of title to the lender. Trust deeds appeal to lenders, since the property may be foreclosed and recovered more rapidly than foreclosure on mortgages governed by state redemption statutes.

Open Mortgages. The open mortgage provides for future advances secured by the same mortgage. Thus, owners holding an open mortgage may obtain additional funds for repairs, alterations or additions. It substitutes for the second mortgage that might finance additions and betterments and it reduces financing costs of the borrower if the only other alternative would be to refinance with a new mortgage.

Construction Loan Mortgages. Institutional lenders generally are legally prevented or unwilling to grant loans secured by vacant land. Contractors, however, require a means of financing buildings pending their completion and long-term financing by institutional lenders. Construction loans meet this need. Local financing agencies such as savings and loan associations and commercial banks may advance short-term credit, say for 18 months, at relatively high interest rates for construction purposes. As a further protection, the construction lender may require a firm commitment by a lender to loan under a long-term mortgage to a qualified buyer. The contractor pays the construction loan from proceeds of the long-term loan. The construction lender advances money after making building inspections at agreed upon stages of building completion. The lender withholds final payment until the building is inspected for completion and for verification that the contractor has paid for materials and labor.

Security Deeds.   Widely used in Georgia, this instrument constitutes a conveyance of land by warranty deed with the provision that:

1.   The deed secures payment of a debt.
2.   It grants power of attorney to sell the property upon default.
3.   Payment of the full debt cancels the deed.

The security deed substitutes for the mortgage, which in Georgia creates only a lien. Lenders prefer the security deed since it gives the lender more rights than he would have under a mortgage and promissory note in the event of the borrower's default.

Wrap-around Mortgages.   The wrap-around mortgage may be arranged if (1) an existing property is subject to a loan under relatively low interest payments, and (2) the borrower wishes to borrow additional money. Or the borrower may be a buyer who finances a new purchase with a wrap-around mortgage. Given these conditions, a second lender advances a new mortgage based on the current property value, advancing the difference between the principal of the new mortgage and the principal of the outstanding first mortgage. The second lender makes the mortgage payments on an existing mortgage. He or she makes these payments from the payments of the borrower on the new mortgage. The lender keeps the difference between the payment on the old mortgage and the new mortgage.

Though the originator of the wrap-around mortgage actually holds a second mortgage, the effective yield is higher than the going rate on new mortgages. The borrower usually gains additional financing at a lower rate than could be obtained by refinancing, because he or she retains the below market interest rate of the original mortgage.

Rights of the Mortgagor

The courts and statutes give the borrower certain remedies in the event of default. Though varying in detail, most of these rights are common to all states.

Equity of Redemption.   The right of a defaulting borrower to pay his debt and remedy his default is known as the equity of redemption. Even though the mortgage payments are in arrears, the borrower may still retain possession if he or she makes payment according to the redemption statute. Some states provide for a *statutory* equity of redemption that gives the borrower the right to redeem the property even after a foreclosure sale. In California, the mortgagor, for example, has the right to redeem property sold under mortgage foreclosure procedures 12 months after the sale by paying the mortgage debt, accumulated interest, unpaid tax assessments, insurance and maintenance and repairs. The period of redemption ranges from six months in Wisconsin to two years in Arkansas. In some states the borrower may remain in possession over the statutory redemption period, though the new purchaser of the foreclosed property is entitled to rents and profits.

Estoppel Certificates. Suppose a purchaser buys a dwelling and agrees to continue payments on an existing mortgage. Suppose also that the purchaser acts on representations by the lender that the remaining mortgage balance is $50,000. If it is later discovered that the remaining balance is more than $50,000, the purchaser would be subject to a greater liability than he or she anticipated. To overcome this difficulty, a buyer who assumes a mortgage may ask for an estoppel certificate: a written statement from the lender showing the remaining balance. If subsequently this amount is proven incorrect, the lender is barred or estopped from recovering a larger amount.

Prepayment Privileges. Lenders enter into mortgages with the expectation of earning interest on a long-term investment. Before the mortgage is executed, the lender assumes administrative costs, legal fees, appraisal fees, and other expenses. Consequently, lenders restrict the right of the borrower to prepay the loan. The lender may require prepayment penalties if the buyer proposes to prepay the debt over the first five years. Another common arrangement is to restrict prepayment privileges to an amount not to exceed 20 percent of the principal in any given year. Other lenders impose an interest penalty equal to three months interest if the loan is prepaid.

Satisfaction Piece. If the borrower repays a loan as required by the mortgage, he or she has a right to written evidence of the repayment. If the lender returns the promissory note and mortgage with a signed inscription that the debt has been fully paid, this may serve as sufficient evidence of repayment. Some states require that the mortgage be presented to the recording officer with a separate instrument of release which gives legal notice of satisfaction of the mortgage. The instrument of release, where it is required, is called a satisfaction piece or satisfaction of mortgage.

A satisfaction of mortgage must definitely prove the lender's intention to discharge the mortgage. The mortgage must be identified. The party holding the mortgage who has authority to release it should be shown on the satisfaction instrument. In other respects, the satisfaction instrument or piece must conform to contract law and the recording statutes.

Rights of the Mortgagee

Certain terms of the mortgage historically favor the lender and his or her right to foreclosure against a defaulting borrower.

Deficiency Judgment. Because the loan is secured by a mortgage on real estate and a personal promise—a promissory note—the lender may foreclose under the mortgage and proceed against personal assets of the borrower under the promissory note. The latter right may be exercised if the lender forecloses on a $30,000 mortgage but only realizes $20,000 out of the foreclosure sale. In this instance, if deficiency judgments apply, the lender may secure a deficiency judgment under the promissory note and collect the balance of the $30,000 against personal assets. Deficiency judgments are prohibited in some states and limited in others.

Power of Sale. In still other states, lenders have used a power of sale clause in the mortgage or deed of trust. For example, in California if the power of sale is used, the lender has no right to a deficiency judgment. Lenders proceed under the power of sale to avoid delay in repossessing the property because of the equity of redemption.

Acceleration Clauses. In almost all mortgages, the lender operates under an acceleration clause that gives the lender the right to the total mortgage debt if payments are in default. Other common provisions allow the lender to proceed under the acceleration clause for the failure to pay taxes, assessments, insurance premiums, or to keep buildings in repair.

Mortgage Recording. Though a mortgage is enforceable if it complies with contract law, the mortgage is valid against subsequent purchasers or encumbrances provided it is recorded. Thus, without recording the mortgage is void against the subsequent purchaser or lender who acts in good faith for valuable consideration. Lenders take care in recording a new mortgage to establish a prior lien position. To this extent, recording constitutes constructive notice substituting for actual notice because the lender does not ordinarily enter the premises and take possession.

Mortgage Assumption. If a purchaser agrees to assume an outstanding mortgage, the parties must enter into an agreement defining the terms in which the purchaser agrees to assume the mortgage. The difficulty arises in placing the personal liability of an existing mortgage debt on a new purchaser. The purchaser must show intent to assume the obligation. Additionally, the original borrower-seller (the mortgagor-grantor) should secure a release from the lender. Without such an agreement, the lender in most states has the right to obtain a deficiency judgment against the original borrower or against the new purchaser.

If the lender releases the original borrower from his liability for the mortgage indebtedness, the substitution must be evidenced by an agreement between the three parties. The agreement that releases the previous borrower is termed a *novation*: it substitutes one borrower for another, evidenced by a release from the lender.

Some institutional lenders charge an assumption fee for a novation agreement. Where they apply, the fees may range from $25 to a percentage of the sales price. In other instances the lender stipulates in the mortgage or trust deed that the debt cannot be assumed without consent of the lender. These terms give the lender the opportunity to increase the interest rate or charge an assumption fee.

"Subject to" Mortgages. If the buyer of a $50,000 property pays $20,000 cash and buys subject to an existing $30,000 loan, he or she does not personally assume the debt. If the new purchaser defaults on the mortgage, the lender may not proceed against the buyer. The lender exercises his or her rights under mortgage foreclosure laws and recovers the property pledged by the mortgagor.

NEW MORTGAGE PLANS

Rising interest rates, particularly on long-term mortgages, have two effects. First, higher interest, increasing monthly payments, raises the cost of mortgages beyond the reach of a large segment of the home-buying public. Coupled with inflationary increases in land and building costs, the minimum required mortgage has magnified the effect of higher mortgage interest.

The second issue relates to the loss of deposits among thrift institutions, primarily savings and loan institutions and mutual savings banks. Together these lenders historically have accounted for about 60 percent of all mortgages on one- to four-family, nonfarm dwellings. The main problem stems from the movement of short-term interest rates above the saving deposit dividends paid by the thrift institutions. Thrift institutions are burdened by relatively low yields on existing mortgages that do not return enough to pay depositors a competitive interest rate. Further, even if they were able to pay their depositors competitive rates, regulatory agencies have controlled the interest which institutions pay depositors.

To counteract the shortage of funds moving into the mortgage market, several flexible plans have been adopted. Since these innovations promise to be increasingly important, a short explanation of the main elements of new financing plans seems worthwhile.

Flexible-Payment Mortgages

In February 1974, the Federal Home Loan Bank Board (the agency regulating savings and loan associations) authorized savings and loan associations to make flexible-payment mortgages (FPM). These mortgages allow initial monthly payments below those required by a level payment, amortized mortgage. Regulations allow mortgage payments based on interest only up to five years, with full amortization effective in the sixth year.

Depending on the initial interest rate and the length of the loan,

FPM payments may range from 5 percent to 25 percent below the level payment amortized mortgage. For instance, assume an interest rate of 9 percent and a loan of 20 years. Restricting the maximum monthly mortgage payment to 20 percent of income, a monthly income of $1,350 would be required to finance a $30,000 mortgage. Under an FPM with interest only payable for the first five years, the required monthly income would be reduced to $1,125 or $225 below that needed for an amortized mortgage.

Or to put it differently, with an income of $1,125 a month a buyer could qualify for a 9 percent, 20-year mortgage of $25,000. With an FPM, he could qualify for a loan of $30,000. While this advantage serves the interest of the buyer, the lenders may not advance such a loan because of the risk that at the end of the five years, the borrower under the example above may not be able to meet the increase of $79 in monthly payments after the fifth year. Conversely, if the buyer's income does not rise proportionally with the increase in payments, the borrower would probably suffer a handicap in meeting the higher mortgage monthly payments.

Variable Rate Mortgages

The central problem in financing single-family dwellings relates to the shortage of mortgage capital. Since about 95 percent of new homes are acquired with long-term mortgages, the shortage of deposits in savings and loan associations and mutual savings banks seriously restricts the availability of mortgage credit. Because savings and loan associations must live with the average yield earned on the *total* mortgage portfolio created in periods when interest rates were much lower, they are unable to pay depositors much more than the average yields on the mortgage portfolio. Moreover, when other short-term interest rates go up—for example on treasury bills—large depositors tend to withdraw savings deposits. Variable rate mortgages tend to counteract the outflow of funds from savings institutions.

Under the variable rate mortgage (VRM), interest rates would change according to some index—the rate of interest on government bonds, the prime interest rate charged by banks, the cost of mortgage funds, or the consumer price index. If the index adopted as a reference point increases, then mortgage rates would rise by a similar amount. With the higher interest, the savings banks would be able to pay depositors a higher return on savings and effectively decrease the loss of deposits to other, higher-yielding investments. With a decrease in the index, borrowers would pay lower interest on mortgages. As the market rate of interest declined, depositors would earn lower interest dividends. It is argued that VRMs would minimize the boom and bust characteristics of the housing market.

It will be understood that under the present system of level-payment mortgages, the risk of *higher* short-term interest rates and *lower* long-term mortgage interest rates rests on the mortgage lender. Without the variable rate mortgage, in periods of declining interest rates, the borrower may prepay the loan and refinance under more favorable interest rates. The lender, on the other hand, assumes the final risks, for he must continue to accept mortgage payments on long-term, below-market interest rates.

Variable rate mortgages have not been widely adopted because certain states still impose restrictive statutory ceilings on interest rates. Borrowers also tend to resist higher monthly payments as the variable interest rate increases mortgage payments. In practice, variable rate mortgages are increased over infrequent periods.

Some states have imposed restrictions on variable rate mortgages. California requires that variable rate mortgages be flexible downward in the same way that they are flexible upward. Increases in interest rates are restricted to one-quarter of 1 percent semiannually. The borrower, moreover, may prepay the mortgage within 90 days of a change in interest rates without penalty. While these mortgages are relatively new in the United States, they have had wide acceptance in Switzerland, Sweden, England, and South America—countries that have experienced relatively long periods of inflation.

Partially Amortized Mortgages

While popularly termed "balloon payment mortgages," these mortgages call for periodic installments of interest or principal with only partial amortization. For example the 20-year mortgage might be arranged with principal payment amortized over a 30-year basis. At the end of 20 years, the borrower is required to make a balloon payment, which will amortize the remaining principal. The purpose of this loan is to reduce the monthly payments. In actual experience, it is unlikely that the balloon payment will be made, since the life of a mortgage seldom runs more than 10 to 12 years before the property is refinanced.

If the balloon payment is due, the borrower usually has the option of making the lump sum payment or refinancing. Because he has repaid a substantial portion of principal, he usually qualifies for a smaller loan amortized under the conventional level-payment plan.

Some lenders have financed single-family dwellings with partially amortized mortgages over the first five years with a balloon payment due at the end of five years. It is anticipated that the partially amortized principal will qualify the buyer for a longer-term, conventionally-amortized mortgage when the balloon payment is due. The borrower who enters into this agreement risks the possibility of more expensive financing if he is unable to make the balloon payment.

SOURCES OF MORTGAGE FUNDS

Financial institutions active in mortgage markets vary in their policies, regulations, and geographical range of operation. Some financial organizations have more freedom than others in granting loans because they are relatively unrestricted by state and federal regulations. Some institutions are chartered only by state governments, while others are chartered by both state and federal agencies. For the most part, each institution must observe a special set of statutory and regulatory laws. Besides restrictive regulations, unfavorable economic conditions may further restrict their willingness to lend.

Savings and Loan Associations

The 4,858 U.S. savings and loan associations promote thrift and home ownership, and together they account for over one half of all outstanding mortgages on one- to four-family nonfarm dwellings. Over one quarter of the loans secured by multiple-family units (27.6 percent) are held by savings and loan associations. Their role in mortgage finance is evidenced by the fact that 85 percent of their total assets are invested in mortgages, which makes them vulnerable to changes in the real estate market.

Approximately 81 percent of the mortgage loans held by savings and loan associations are secured by one- to four family dwellings. Historically, these thrift institutions have favored conventional loans.

Savings and loan institutions are highly dependent on the growth of local savings. Their prime interest is in pooling the savings of the local community and reinvesting savings in local mortgages. With certain exceptions, they are restricted to loaning money on dwellings within a 100-mile radius. Since thrift institutions must compete with other saving depositories, they are highly sensitive to changes in the interest rate. As the yield on short-term investments increases, namely United States obligations, corporate bonds, and certificates of deposits, investors withdraw funds from savings and loan associations.

Moreover, savings and loan institutions are restricted in the payment of deposit interest by regulatory agencies. At the present time, they are unable effectively to compete with market interest rates since their source of income is derived from long-term mortgages based on lower interest rates of the past. Thus the average yield earned by savings institutions since 1969 has ranged from 6.3 percent to 7.95 percent. It is clear that without further subsidies savings and loans are unable to attract monies that go to relatively short-term securities paying simple interest of 8 percent or more. Proposals before Congress, including income tax exemption of interest on savings deposits, are directed to increasing the deposits in savings and loan institutions.

Mutual Savings Banks

As a source of mortgage funds, mutual savings banks are particularly important to the housing market. Their competitive advantage in the residential mortgage market rests on two main characteristics:

1. They are state chartered institutions and not subject to national regulations typical of federally chartered institutions.
2. They may grant mortgages without respect to geographic limits— unlike savings and loan associations.

The 476 U.S. mutual savings banks are concentrated in the Middle Atlantic and New England states. Over one half of the savings bank assets are concentrated in New York. With the right to place mortgages in other parts of the country, the Northeastern banks provide a source of funds to the capital shortage states of the Southeast, Southwest, and West.

This geographic diversity creates a need for mortgages with the highest possible liquidity. To meet this requirement, mutual savings banks have been an important supply of credit for Federal Housing Administration and Veteran Administration loans. The federal insurance and guarantees of these mortgages allow mutual savings banks to sell their portfolio of FHA and VA mortgages in periods of capital shortage. The sale of a mortgage enables the banks to place additional loans. Recently the availability of private mortgage insurance has encouraged placement of conventional mortgages unsecured by federal insurance or guarantees.

As a source of mortgage funds, the mutual savings banks hold approximately 10.4 percent of the total outstanding mortgages. Of their total mortgage portfolio, FHA and VA loans account for about 35 percent. By type of property, residential loans constitute 83 percent, while conventional, nonresidential loans amount to 17 percent of their mortgage portfolio. The trend is toward conventional loans because of the growth of private mortgage insurance, improved opportunities to sell conventional mortgages, and the administrative restrictions of government programs. Like the savings and loan associations, however, mutual savings banks are faced with a loss of deposits to higher yielding investments.

Life Insurance Companies

Life insurance companies in recent years have placed between 20 and 30 percent of their assets in mortgages (28.5 percent today). Most of these loans are concentrated in nonfarm conventional loans. In the latest year for which figures are available, they have increased their mortgage investments on farms and conventional nonfarm mortgages. Multiple-family dwellings financed through conventional mortgages have shown a slight decrease. Nonfarm, nonresidential loans, primarily commercial properties such as office buildings, shopping centers, and industrial properties, have recently shown about a 10 percent increase over the preceding year.

In other respects, life insurance companies have pioneered in the construction of large-scale apartment complexes under their direct ownership. They have participated in construction of shopping centers by purchasing the centers from developers and leasing them back for management.

Their ability to enter the mortgage market is partly because of the absence of direct federal control. They operate under state charters and state regulations. As a consequence, they have the mobility to invest in geographic areas showing the highest yield consistent with minimum mortgage security.

The main problem faced by life insurance companies is to place a continuous inflow of funds which fluctuates very little into income-earning assets. For this reason, insurance companies have favored mortgages on conventional income property loans. Varying by state, the maximum loan to appraised value varies from 66.6 percent to 75 percent. In addition, New York-chartered companies may grant loans on leasehold mortgages with an unexpired term of at least 21 years which are fully amortized within the lesser of 35 years or the unexpired leasehold term. The maximum amortization period may be more liberal compared to other institutions, though maximum maturities of 25 years seem more common for policy reasons

Mortgage Bankers

Mortgage banker operations differ significantly from other financial institutions. Subject to a minimum of regulation, they generally work under the corporate laws of their home state. Their main function is to act as a go-between for institutional investors and the primary borrower. A mortgage banker becomes a specialist in knowing the requirements of various financial institutions that place local real estate loans. As compensation for his services, the mortgage banker earns a fee from the borrower for placing the loan with an institution and a monthly servicing fee generally equal to one-half of 1 percent of the outstanding loan. Mortgage bankers specialize in the placement of FHA and VA mortgages, income properties, and even local construction loans. Since they use little of their own capital, they are dependent on funds committed by life insurance companies, mutual savings banks, pension funds, and others with funds for long-term investments.

If they are active in placing FHA loans, they must be qualified by establishing a minimum net worth of at least $100,000 and by proving that stockholders are of excellent character. They must have practical mortgage lending experience and an organization capable of servicing a mortgage portfolio. The main contribution of the mortgage banker lies in providing a smooth flow of capital from institutional investors to local mortgage markets.

Commercial Banks

In terms of the total mortgage debt outstanding today, commercial banks hold 18.8 percent of all mortgage debt outstanding. Their volume is second only to savings and loan associations. Approximately half of this amount (57 percent) is placed in one- to four-family mortgages. Because they prefer the liquidity and security of FHA insurance and VA mortgages, they are important suppliers of funds for one- to four-family FHA and VA loans. Approximately 90 percent of FHA-insured and VA-guaranteed residential mortgage debt is held by commercial banks. Under the Housing and Community Development Act of 1974, the laws governing terms on which national banks may make loans secured by real estate have been significantly liberalized. These changes promise to increase participation of commercial banks in mortgage markets.

Under the 1974 Act commercial banks operate under new rules:

1. Banks may grant real estate loans equal to 100 percent of time and savings deposits.
2. Ten percent of the real estate loans are exempt from individual loan restrictions of the statute.
3. Loans secured by other than first mortgages may be granted providing that the total lien does not exceed the permissible ratio of loan to appraised value. Loans of this type are limited to 20 percent of capital surplus.
4. Banks may loan money on land up to 66⅔ percent of the appraised value and up to 75 percent of the appraised value if there are off-site improvements on it or if the property includes a building either planned or under construction.
5. Loans secured by land and a building may be granted up to 90 percent of the appraised value. If the loan requires no amortization, the loan may not exceed 75 percent of the appraised value or if the security consists of a one- to four-family dwelling. Amortization is based on the maximum 30-year term.
6. The bank is exempt from real estate loan restrictions for any loan covered by an agreement of a third party to pay the loan within 60 months from the date of making the loan. This latter provision will allow the bank to make construction loans without observing real estate mortgage restrictions.

Commercial banks may be expected to be more active in land development and particularly in income-producing property. Loans on single-family dwellings under conventional mortgage terms, are limited to 75 percent of the appraised value. With no amortization, banks will be able to compete with other lenders who have more stringent amortization requirements. This probably means that banks will make such loans if they are well-secured by credit of the borrower and provide for a premium interest rate.

Other Loan Sources

Pension funds, real estate investment trusts, and miscellaneous sources constitute the remaining sources of loanable funds. The concentration of capital in pension funds has opened a new source of mortgage money. In the past, pension funds favored corporate bonds and common stocks. The unfamiliarity with mortgages on the part of the pension fund administrators has not encouraged the development of mortgage investments. The depressed value of common stocks and the attractiveness of mortgages and real estate investments with participation clauses will encourage real estate investments from this source.

In addition, the mortgage principal repayment feature leads to investment management problems not found in stocks and bonds. These objections to real estate investments in real estate have been partly overcome by securities issued by Government National Mortgage Association (GNMA) that are backed by FHA and VA mortgages. Under these arrangements, the pension fund may buy a mortgage backed security from GNMA and receive the proceeds from the mortgages pledged as security. The pension fund only collects the proceeds from a block of mortgages. A lending institution holding the pledged mortgages, services each loan and collects monthly payments for a fee. By this device GNMA attracts pension funds into financing FHA and VA loans.

Real estate investment trusts have assets totaling over $20 billion, divided among some 210 different trusts. Their appeal lies in providing large and small investors with a diversified ownership in a professionally managed portfolio of real estate investments. Their importance as a source of mortgage capital is shown by the proportion of mortgages held in their total portfolio: 82.3 percent. Since their organization in 1961, they have attracted capital to the real estate industry that would flow to other types of investment.

GOVERNMENT ASSISTANCE

Of the many agencies active in real estate finance, five bear importantly on the housing market: (1) The Federal Housing Administration, (2) the Veterans Administration, (3) Federal National Mortgage Association, (4) the Government National Mortgage Association, and (5) the Federal Home Loan Bank Board. The Housing and Community Act of

1974 affects programs administered by each of these agencies. Administrative rules and new legislation can be expected to revise their practices in future years.

Federal Housing Administration

Originally formed as a new agency to attract capital in the mortgage market and to increase employment, the Federal Housing Administration is now part of the United States Department of Housing and Urban Development. Its responsibilities range from insuring mortgages on single-family dwellings, multiple-family units, cooperatives, condominiums, nursing homes, mobile homes, and land developments. Its programs now include certain forms of subsidy to low-income families. Of the total debt outstanding on one- to four-family nonfarm dwellings, loans insured by FHA have amounted to about 17.1 percent. It is uncertain how extensively FHA will be used by lenders and home buyers in the future.

FHA Terms. The main appeal of an FHA mortgage lies in the minimum down payment requirements. Under the Housing and Community Development Act of 1977, Congress increased the loan ceiling on FHA mortgages and lowered down payment requirements for unsubsidized home mortgages. The maximum loan to appraised value ratio provides for a minimum of 97 percent of the first $25,000 and 95 percent for that portion of the mortgage between $25,000 and $65,000. The new act allows a buyer of a $50,000 home to purchase under an FHA mortgage with a down payment of $2,000 in contrast to a $4,750 down payment prevailing before the new 1977 Act.

Loan Amount		Down Payment	Total Down Payment
First.................. $25,000	×	.03	$ 750
Next.................. 25,000	×	.05	1,250
Total loan........... $50,000			$2,000

The property mortgaged and the borrower must meet standards of FHA. The appraisal form used by FHA, shown in Figure 15–1, shows the required appraisal detail for a single-family dwelling.

Discount Points. In earlier years Congress has fixed the maximum interest rate to be paid on FHA mortgages. The rates effective on FHA mortgages have lagged behind the market rate on conventional mortgages and other financial securities. To make mortgages more attractive to institutional lenders that invest in FHA mortgages, the mortgages have been subject to discounts by lending institutions. With a fixed yield of 8.5 percent, for example, the lender may be unwilling to accept an FHA mortgage without buying subject to a 5-percent discount. For example, a dwell-

FIGURE 15-1
FHA Appraisal Form

Form Approved
OMB No 63-R1087

FHA MORTGAGEE NO *(Please Verify)*	U.S. DEPARTMENT OF HOUSING AND URBAN DEVELOPMENT FEDERAL HOUSING ADMINISTRATION	FHA CASE NO.

MORTGAGEE'S APPLICATION FOR PROPERTY APPRAISAL AND COMMITMENT FOR MORTGAGE INSURANCE UNDER THE NATIONAL HOUSING ACT

PROPERTY ADDRESS

☐ SEC. 203(b)   ☐ SEC. _____

MORTGAGEE Name and Address including ZIP Code *(Please Type)*
(Please locate address within corner marks)

⌐ ¬

∟ ⌟

Telephone No.

This form is a request for an appraisal and a commitment to insure a loan on an individual property.

We cannot process incomplete applications.
Rejecting them is costly.
Please help by giving us well prepared applications.
Keep all entries within alloted spaces.

EXISTING HOUSE ☐ | Name of Occupant *(or person to call if unoccupied)* | Tel. No. | Key Encl. ☐ *(If unfurnished)*

Mon. & Yr. Completed _____ ☐ Never Occup. ☐ Vacant   Occupied by ☐ Owner ☐ Tenant at $ _____ Per Mo. ☐ Furn. ☐ Unfurn.

PROPOSED SUBSTAN. REHAB. UNDER CONSTR. ☐☐☐ | Builder's Name & Address Including ZIP Code | Tel. No. | Model Identification

Plans: ☐ First Subm.   Prob. Repeat Cases ☐ Yes ☐ No   ☐ Prev. Proc. as FHA Case No.

DESCRIPTION							
☐ Detached	☐ Wood siding	__ Stories	__ Bedrooms	☐ Store Rm.	Mineral Rights Reserved		Type of Heating
☐ Semi-det.	☐ Wood shingle	☐ Split Foyer	__ Liv. room	☐ Util. Rm.	☐ No ☐ Yes *(Explain)*		
☐ Row	☐ Asb. shingle	☐ Bi-Level	__ Din. room	☐ Garage	Util-ities:	Public Comm. Individual	☐ Cent. Air Cond.
☐ Frame	☐ Fiber board	☐ Split Level	__ Kitchen	☐ Carport	Water ☐ ☐ ☐		☐ Wall Air Cond.
☐ Masonry	☐ Brick or stone	☐ Full Basement	__ No. rms.	No cars	Gas ☐ ☐ ☐		Type of Paving (Str.)
☐ Concrete	☐ Stuc. or c. blk.	__ % Basement	__ Baths	☐ Built-in	Elect. ☐ ☐ ☐		☐ None
Factory Fabricated	☐ Aluminum	☐ Slab on Gr.	__ ½ Baths	☐ Attached	☐ Underground Wiring	Sept. Cess	☐ Curb & Gutter
☐ Yes ☐ No	☐ Asph. siding	☐ Crawl Space	% Non-res.	☐ Detached	Sanitary: tank Pool	☐ Sidewalk
	☐ _____	Living Units			Sewer ☐ ☐ ☐		☐ Storm Sewer

EXTRA FEATURES	☐ Fireplace	☐ Rec. Room	☐ Sw. Pool	☐ Enclosed Porch	☐ Breezeway	☐ Fence
	☐ Extra Fire Pl.	☐ Expand Attic	☐ Fin. Attic			

SPEC. ASSESS. Prepayable.$_____ Non-Prepay.$_____   LOT _____ × _____ ☐ Irr. ☐ Acres _____ Sq. Ft.

Int. ___% Ann. Pay.$_____ Unpd. Bal. $_____ Rem. Term ___ Yrs.   GENERAL LOCATION:

ANN. R. EST. TAXES $ | ANN. FIRE INS. $ | SALE PRICE $

EQUAL OPPORTUNITY IN HOUSING

Federal laws and regulations prohibit discrimination because of race, color, religion, or national origin in the sale or rental of residential property. Numerous state statutes and local ordinances also prohibit such discrimination. In addition, section 805 of the Civil Rights Act of 1968 prohibits discriminatory practices in connection with the financing of housing.

If FHA finds there is noncompliance with any applicable antidiscrimination laws or regulations, it may discontinue FHA business with the violator.

LEGAL DESCRIPTION *(Attach one page if necessary)*

SHOW BELOW: Shape, location, distance from nearest intersection and street names. Mark N at NORTH point.

Please consider the following TITLE EXCEPTIONS in value:

Please consider the following Equipment in value:

LEASEHOLD Ground Rent *(Per Yr)* $ _____ Lease is: ☐ 99 years ☐ Renewable ☐ FHA Approved Expires

BUILDER/SELLER'S AGREEMENT: All Houses: The undersigned agrees to deliver to the purchaser FHA's statement of appraised value. Proposed Construction: The undersigned agrees, upon sale or conveyance of title within one year from date of initial occupancy, to deliver to the purchaser FHA Form 2544, warranting that the house is constructed in substantial conformity with the plans and specifications on which FHA based its value and to furnish FHA a conformed copy with the purchaser's receipt thereon that the original warranty was delivered to him. All Houses: In consideration of the issuance of the commitment requested by this application, I (we) hereby agree that any deposit or downpayment made in connection with the purchase of the property described above, whether received by the undersigned or an agent of the undersigned, shall upon receipt be deposited in escrow or in trust or in a special account which is not subject to the claims of my creditors and where it will be maintained until it has been disbursed for the benefit of the purchaser or otherwise disposed of in accordance with the terms of the contract of sale.

Signature: ☐ Mortgagee ☐ Builder ☐ Seller ☐ Other   19

MORTGAGEE'S CERTIFICATE: The undersigned mortgagee certifies that to the best of its knowledge all statements made in this application and the supporting documents are true, correct and complete.

Signature/Title of Mortgagee Officer: 19

WARNING: Section 1010 of Title 18, U.S.C., provides: "Whoever, for the purpose of . . . influencing such Administration . . . makes, passes, utters, or publishes any statement, knowing the same to be false . . . shall be fined not more than $5,000 or imprisoned not more than two years, or both."

FHA FORM NO. 2800 - 1 Rev. 12/72

ing financed with an FHA $40,000, 8.5 percent mortgage, may be given credit for $39,000. In other words the buyer would repay the lender for a $40,000 mortgage for which the lender paid $39,000. In this way the cost of credit is shifted to the seller. In the trade, a point is equivalent to a 1-percent discount on the mortgage amount. Depending on the condition of the market, the seller offering a property financed with an FHA loan attempts to shift the cost of the discount to the buyer in the form of a higher asking price.

Veterans Administration

Under the Servicemen's Readjustment Act of 1944, loans guaranteed by the Veterans Administration are available to eligible veterans serving in World War II, the Korean Conflict, or in the armed forces for 180 days or more since January 1955. Unlike the FHA mortgage, the Veterans Administration guarantees mortgages up to 60 percent of the original mortgage or $17,500, whichever is less. The loans may be for purchasing, constructing, improving, or repairing dwellings or farm homes. The appeal of a VA loan lies in certain advantages extended to both the lender and veteran purchaser:

1. Veterans Administration mortgages require no down payment.
2. The mortgage origination fee is limited to a maximum of 1 percent of the loan.
3. Loan closing costs, including title fees, appraisal fees, and prepaid items, must be approved by the Veterans Administration.
4. Veterans Administration loans provide for prepayment of the loan without penalty.
5. The maximum loan term extends to 30 years for dwellings and for farm loans to 40 years.
6. The loan is subject to a certificate of reasonable value issued by the Veterans Administration.
7. In practice the Veterans Administration pays the lender the unpaid mortgage loan balance in default, though the agency has other options.

Interest rates on Veterans Administration loans tend to follow FHA rates and consequently the mortgage is subject to point discounts which are charged to the seller. As a total of mortgage loans outstanding, VA loans account for 13 percent of the total one- to four-family nonfarm mortgages outstanding.

Federal National Mortgage Association

The explanation of the mortgage market, up to this point, has dealt with the primary market—a market consisting of the borrower and the lender. This market is supported by a *secondary* market in which the original lender may convert the mortgage loan to cash. In the secondary market institutional investors buy and sell blocks of mortgages meeting certain characteristics. Buyers of mortgages in the secondary market have no direct contact with the original borrower. In fact, the borrower may continue to make monthly payments to the original lender who sells the mortgage and continues to service the mortgage for a fee, generally one half of 1 percent of the loan.

The Federal National Mortgage Association purchases mortgages only in the secondary market. Started in 1938, FNMA ("Fannie Mae") was a government agency that purchased FHA insured mortgages from private lenders. By manipulating the price at which mortgages were bought and sold, FNMA increased or decreased the supply of available mortgage funds. In addition, Fannie Mae was directed to support mortgages insured under special FHA programs.

Today the Federal National Mortgage Association under a 1968 act is a private corporation which has maintained a quasi-public function. The Board of Directors includes five members appointed by the President of the United States with ten remaining directors elected by shareholders. Financial policies of FNMA must be approved by the Secretary of Housing and Urban Development. Its operations are supported by the Secretary of the Treasury who has authority to purchase debt obligations of FNMA. Funds to implement their operations come from the sale of stock, borrowing through the sale of bonds, fees, and proceeds from sales of mortgage loans.

In actual practice, FNMA periodically offers to purchase mortgages having certain characteristics. Lenders with blocks of mortgages meeting the standards of FNMA may offer to sell mortgages at a stated bid price that meets the approval of the corporation. Originally covering only FHA and VA loans, FNMA is now authorized to purchase conventional loans provided the selling agency and the mortgage meets the corporation's stringent requirements. The most recent figures available show that FNMA has over $32 billion in mortgages in their portfolio.

The effect of FNMA is to increase the supply of loanable funds, since it sells bonds in the open market thereby raising capital among investors who normally would not be investing in real estate mortgages. In this manner funds are available for mortgages which would not ordinarily be channeled into thrift institutions. FNMA makes mortgages a highly liquid form of investment which also attracts lenders who are willing to advance funds, knowing that mortgages may be readily converted to cash.

Governmental National Mortgage Association

This government agency, created under the Housing Act of 1968, purchases mortgage loans from private lenders under special assistance programs of the Department of Housing and Urban Development. Some 22 mortgage financial assistance programs are supported by GNMA ("Ginnie Mae"), some of which are being phased out. Lenders are induced to participate in mortgages on subsidized rental projects, rehabilitated housing, below-market interest rate mortgages, housing for the elderly, and similar programs. With interest rates fixed on FHA-insured mortgages, GNMA offers to purchase mortgages at a discount. On application, GNMA may offer to purchase mortgages under a specific program at a stated discount.

This forward commitment attracts private lenders who in turn make commitments to contractors and others participating in housing projects. Funds to support GNMA's special function are supported from borrowing from the Treasury and the resale of mortgages in the open market or to FNMA. Though GNMA may sell mortgages at a loss to FNMA, the sale makes more money available than if FNMA held mortgages in their own portfolio. This plan involving FNMA purchases is known as a tandem operation in which GNMA is out of pocket for only the difference between the purchase price and the selling price. The GNMA program through the sale of bonds reaches new sources of mortgage capital such as pension funds and credit unions—agencies who would not typically invest in real estate mortgages.

Federal Home Loan Bank Board

Savings and loan associations relate to the Federal Home Loan Bank Board (FHLB) as nationally chartered commercial banks relate to the Federal Reserve System. The FHLB is governed by three members appointed by the President with the consent of the Senate. Administrative tasks are under 12 regional banks that serve the savings and loan membership. The 4,238 members include all nationally chartered savings associations and qualified state-chartered associations, mutual savings banks, and life insurance companies.

The main function of the FHLB system is to provide funds to member savings and loan associations. The system transfers funds from capital surplus areas to areas experiencing capital shortage. In this respect the organization supplements the resources of its member institutions by providing a central credit facility. From the standpoint of the real estate borrower, the system serves a more basic function: It is a source of secondary financing to the member institutions in supplying funds to meet heavy withdrawals during seasonal peaks in savings and withdrawals.

By issuing consolidated obligations in large denominations, it provides a source of funds used to loan money to savings associations who in turn may place funds in additional mortgages. These activities act as a stabilizing influence on residential construction and financing. While the board has no direct contact with real estate markets, its operations closely control the availability of mortgage funds and their terms among savings and loan members.

More recently the FHLB established the Federal Home Loan Mortgage Corporation (FHLMC), known in the trade as the "Corporation." It is empowered to buy and sell FHA, VA loans, participation mortgages, and conventional loans. By offering to buy and sell conventional loans, savings and loan institutions have a system of financing parallel to the Federal National Mortgage Association and the Government National Mortgage Association.

PRIVATE MORTGAGE INSURANCE

Since 1957, more than six private mortgage insurance companies have been organized to provide private mortgage insurance. Today private mortgage insurance may be obtained for new and existing dwellings on qualified first mortgages. Private lenders, mainly savings and loan associations, use mortgage insurance for loans that exceed 80 percent of market value. One of the larger companies insures such loans on the last 20 percent of the mortgage loan to a maximum of 95 percent of the appraised value. This arrangement encourages lenders to grant loans above maximum loan-to-value ratios observed as a matter of policy.

If a loan which is covered by private mortgage insurance has been in default for four months, notice must be given to the insurer within ten days. The lending institution then proceeds to foreclose under state law. Eventually title is conveyed to the insurer, with the loss payable to the lender limited to the unpaid principal, accrued interest, taxes, insurance, and other legal expenses. The alternative allows the insurer to limit liability to 20 percent of the claim, effectively shifting the risk on 80 percent of the appraised value to the lender. In this case the lender retains title to the foreclosed property.

Fees for private mortgage insurance, which are paid by the borrower, typically are 1 percent of the amount of the loan over the first year, decreasing to one fourth of 1 percent of the declining balance of the loan over succeeding years. Other variations of the plan allow for a single premium paid to provide insurance over a limited term, say 10 years. It is reported that private mortgage insurance companies are extending insurance protection to commercial and industrial properties. The impact of these plans is placing greater importance on conventional lending and decreasing the appeal of FHA and VA loans. Lower administrative costs, more expeditious processing of mortgages and foreclosure claims, and lower costs account for the growing popularity of private mortgage insurance.

QUESTIONS FOR REVIEW

_____ 1. Which of the following statements is correct?

    a. The real estate industry operates independently of the mortgage market.

    b. The demand and supply of real estate is unrelated to the volume of savings.

    c. The real estate industry is highly dependent on the flow of funds into the mortgage market.

    d. Land and building costs govern the amount of mortgage money available.

_____ 2. Federal policy affects mortgage interest rates by

    a. raising and lowering interest rates on investments that compete with mortgages and savings.

    b. rationing goods and services.

    c. fixing bond prices.

    d. influencing corporation dividend policy.

_____ 3. A mortgage creates a lien in favor of the

    a. lender.

    b. borrower.

    c. seller.

    d. mortgagor.

_____ 4. In a term mortgage, the

    a. principal is reduced periodically with the payment of interest for that period.

    b. principal is paid at the end of the term.

    c. lenders have greater security compared to an amortized mortgage.

    d. loan-to-value ratio does not exceed 30 percent.

_____ 5. A level-payment mortgage is characterized by

    a. a balloon payment.

    b. interest-only payments.

    c. variable payments.

    d. fixed payments including both principal and interest.

_____ 6. Mortgages are legal instruments that

    a. convey real estate.

    b. transfer title of property.

    c. convey real estate as security for a debt.

    d. convey debt for both real and personal property.

_____ 7. A state in which a mortgage conveys title to the lender is known as a _____ state.

    a. lien

    b. title

    c. conveyance

    d. community property

_____ 8. A state in which a borrower retains title to the real property is a
_____ state.
   a. lien
   b. title
   c. conveyance
   d. community property

_____ 9. A partially amortized mortgage is characterized by
   a. a balloon payment.
   b. interest payments only.
   c. principal payments only.
   d. fixed interest and variable principal payments.

_____10. A mortgage that includes the financing of washers, dryers, refrigerators, and other equipment is commonly termed a
   a. package mortgage.
   b. purchase money mortgage.
   c. participation mortgage.
   d. blanket mortgage.

_____11. A purchase money mortgage usually
   a. includes a promissory note.
   b. is secured by real estate and the personal promise of the buyer.
   c. requires third-party financing.
   d. is secured only by real estate.

_____12. A participation mortgage
   a. reduces the risk of the lender.
   b. reduces the risk of the borrower.
   c. substitutes for the borrower's equity.
   d. includes real and personal property.

_____13. A blanket mortgage is secured by
   a. real and personal property.
   b. a purchase money mortgage.
   c. more than one parcel of real estate.
   d. a warranty deed.

_____14. In a trust deed the lender serves as a
   a. trustor.
   b. beneficiary.
   c. trustee.
   d. litigant.

_____15. An open mortgage serves the interest of the borrower because it
   a. provides for future advances secured by the same mortgage.
   b. does not set a final date for the payment of the principal.
   c. does not become a primary lien on the property.
   d. allows the lender to adjust the interest rate.

_____16. A short-term mortgage granted in anticipation of a long-term mortgage represents a(n)
    a. open mortgage.
    b. trust mortgage.
    c. blanket mortgage.
    d. construction mortgage.

_____17. A wraparound mortgage may be arranged if
    I. an existing property is subject to a loan under relatively low interest payments.
    II. the borrower is willing to refinance at a higher interest rate.
    a. I only.
    b. II only.
    c. Both I and II.
    d. Neither I nor II.

_____18. The main advantage of a wraparound mortgage is that the
    a. effective interest rate is lower than the prevailing rate on new mortgages.
    b. borrower gains additional financing at a higher rate than the market interest rate.
    c. originator of a wraparound mortgage is the primary mortgage holder.
    d. wraparound mortgage is specifically to finance subdivisions.

_____19. The right of a borrower to redeem foreclosed property is the
    a. estoppel certificate.
    b. satisfaction piece.
    c. equity of redemption.
    d. power of sale.

_____20. Upon repayment of a loan a borrower has the right to a(n)
    a. estoppel certificate.
    b. redemption of equity certificate.
    c. satisfaction piece.
    d. acceleration certificate.

_____21. To protect the rights of the mortgagor, which of the following would be used?
    a. A deficiency judgment.
    b. A power of sale.
    c. An acceleration clause.
    d. An estoppel certificate.

_____22. If a lender releases an original borrower from his liability for a mortgage, the substitution must be evidenced by an agreement called a(n)
    a. acceleration clause.
    b. power of sale clause.

    c. satisfaction piece.
    d. novation.

23. The purpose of recording a mortgage is to
    a. protect the borrower against subsequent liens.
    b. protect the purchaser against subsequent liens.
    c. give constructive notice which substitutes for actual notice.
    d. make the mortgage enforceable.

24. In February 1974 the Federal Home Loan Bank Board authorized savings and loan institutions to make
    a. FHA mortgages.
    b. FNMA mortgages.
    c. GNMA mortgages.
    d. FPM mortgages.

25. Flexible payment mortgages (FPM)
    a. decrease monthly payments over the life of the mortgage.
    b. increase buying power of the purchaser.
    c. decrease mortgage yields.
    d. decrease the mortgage term.

26. The balloon payment mortgage is a
    a. variable rate mortgage.
    b. fixed rate mortgage.
    c. flexible payment mortgage.
    d. partially amortized mortgage.

27. The competitive advantage of mutual savings banks in the residential mortgage market rests on which of the following characteristics?
    I. They are state chartered institutions and not subject to national regulations.
    II. They may grant mortgages without respect to geographic limits.
    a. I only.
    b. II only.
    c. Both I and II.
    d. Neither I nor II.

28. Life insurance companies in recent years have placed 20 to 30 percent of their assets in mortgages. Mortgages financed by life insurance companies have been concentrated in
    a. farm loans.
    b. condominiums.
    c. single-family dwellings.
    d. nonfarm conventional loans.

29. Which of the following statements is correct?
    a. The originator of a wraparound mortgage holds a first mortgage.

    b. The second lender in a wraparound mortgage makes the mortgage payments on the existing mortgage.

    c. A wraparound mortgage may be arranged if an existing property is subject to a loan at an interest rate above the current market rate.

    d. The effective yield on wraparound mortgages is lower than the effective yield on new mortgages.

_____30. Discount points

    a. decrease yields to the lender.

    b. increase yields to the lender.

    c. increase yields to the seller.

    d. decrease yields to the seller.

_____31. Which of the following statements describes an advantage of a VA-guaranteed mortgage?

    a. VA mortgages require no down payment.

    b. The mortgage origination fee is waived.

    c. Loan closing costs, including title fees, appraisal fees, and prepaid items are not subject to VA approval.

    d. The VA loan provides for prepayment of a loan with a 1-percent penalty.

_____32. The Federal National Mortgage Association is active in the

    a. primary mortgage market.

    b. secondary mortgage market.

    c. tertiary mortgage market.

    d. *a* and *b.*

_____33. The federal agency that purchases mortgage loans from private lenders under special assistance programs is called the

    a. GNMA.

    b. FNMA.

    c. GMAC.

    d. FHA.

_____34. The main function of the Federal Home Loan Bank Board is to regulate

    a. mortgage bankers.

    b. commercial banks.

    c. savings and loan associations.

    d. "Fannie Mae" organizations.

_____35. The _____ is empowered to buy and sell FHA, VA, participation, and conventional mortgages.

    a. Federal Home Loan Bank Board

    b. Federal Home Loan Mortgage Corporation

    c. FNMA

    d. GNMA

_____36. Mortgage bankers
   a. secure funds from small investors generally within 100 miles of the mortgage banker.
   b. do not loan their own money for long-term mortgages.
   c. loan money only for conventional mortgages.
   d. deal only with government-subsidized loans.

_____37. Mortgage bankers
   a. are subject to regulations of the Federal Reserve System.
   b. are regulated by federal, not state, corporation laws.
   c. act as primary lenders.
   d. earn fees paid by new borrowers and lenders.

_____38. Commercial banks
   a. hold approximately 80 percent of the total mortgage debt.
   b. prefer the liquidity and security of FHA and VA mortgages.
   c. hold 10 percent of FHA and VA mortgages.
   d. place approximately 97 percent of the total mortgages on 1- to 4-family dwellings.

_____39. Since 1974, commercial banks may
   a. grant real estate loans equal to 125 percent of time and savings deposits.
   b. have 10 percent of their real estate loans exempt from loan restrictions.
   c. loan money on land up to 75 percent of the appraised value.
   d. loan money on land up to 100 percent of the appraised value if off-site improvements are under construction.

_____40. The availability of credit is related to
   I. The supply of goods and services available at any one time.
   II. government spending and taxation.
   a. I only.
   b. II only.
   c. Both I and II.
   d. Neither I nor II.

ANSWER KEY

1. (c)	11. (d)	21. (d)	31. (a)
2. (a)	12. (a)	22. (d)	32. (b)
3. (a)	13. (c)	23. (c)	33. (a)
4. (b)	14. (b)	24. (d)	34. (c)
5. (d)	15. (a)	25. (b)	35. (b)
6. (c)	16. (d)	26. (d)	36. (b)
7. (b)	17. (c)	27. (c)	37. (d)
8. (a)	18. (a)	28. (d)	38. (b)
9. (a)	19. (c)	29. (b)	39. (b)
10. (a)	20. (c)	30. (b)	40. (b)

SUGGESTED ADDITIONAL READING

Atteberry, William. *Modern Real Estate Finance.* Columbus, O.: Grid, Inc., 1972, chap. 1.

Hoagland, Henry E.; Stone, Leo D.; and Brueggeman, William B. *Real Estate Finance.* 6th ed. Homewood, Ill.: Richard D. Irwin, Inc., 1977, chap. 14.

Maisel, Sherman J., and Roulac, Stephen E. *Real Estate Investment and . Finance.* New York: McGraw-Hill Book Co., 1976, chap. 3.

Shenkel, William M. *Real Estate Finance.* Washington, D.C.: American Bankers Assn., 1976, chaps. 6 and 7.

Wiedemer, John P. *Real Estate Finance.* Reston, Va.: Reston Publishing Co., Inc., 1974, chap. 4.

16

Real Estate Management

Property management is a growing business. In recent years the management of public and private housing projects has assumed increasing importance—and with the growth of shopping centers, techniques of managing retail property has grown highly professional. In addition, the continuing demand for multiple-family units and condominiums has created a shortage of professionally trained property managers.

Moreover, real property management is compatible with other real estate operations. A Realtor who offers management services has an operation that will earn a steady income to cover his fixed overhead. The truly professional real estate broker will organize management departments for investors who buy their listed income properties and who want their properties under professional management. This is one of the more invaluable services provided by brokers. For income properties, special knowledge is required of management personnel: They must be skilled in human relations, they must be familiar with management, accounting, and reporting techniques. They must know rental practices common to commercial, industrial and residential properties. Besides these skills, they must know basic real estate principles.

FUNCTIONS OF A REAL ESTATE MANAGER

A real estate manager is more than a rent collector. Since rent collection is more of a custodial operation, this responsibility is delegated to the resident manager. In specialized firms offering a full range of management skills, managers know real estate appraising, legal responsibilities of the managing agent, accounting procedures, feasibility analysis, and the economics of real property operation. In short, the real estate manager performs a function not served by other real estate specialties.

Marketing and Budgeting

Like the broker who markets property for sale, a property manager markets space. The manager's job is to maximize net income over the economic life of the property. Merchandising techniques are directed to securing tenants that produce the maximum net income, especially for apartment buildings, office buildings, and shopping centers. Each property type is sufficiently complex to allow specialization in property management. For example, to sell office space, the manager must have detailed knowledge of the building and a close familiarity with the local market for office space. In office buildings, there are companies that lease an entire floor, arranging space for their particular requirements. Office space is also leased to individual firms on terms based on square-foot rents of competing space, the length of the lease, and management services supplied such as parking, janitorial service, security protection, and monthly utilities.

In the case of residential property, management functions are controlled largely by the lease agreement. As a rule, managers attempt to keep rents at the current market level without overpricing individual apartments, causing prohibitive vacancies. In the face of rising and continuing vacancies, managers recommend tenant concessions in the form of free occupancy for one to three months, free utilities, television cable service, and the like.

On balance, it is the job of the manager to market space in competition with other properties. Hence the manager plans an optimum advertising and promotional campaign, merchandises the space, and operates the property. Normally a manager is responsible for purchasing supplies and equipment up to a stated dollar amount. Typically expenditures over some given sum require owner approval. Expenses of operation are under the full control of the manager and, in this respect, he works toward the least costly operation that will provide an adequate level of tenant services. He is responsible for negotiating service contracts, for window washing, elevator service, landscaping, and janitorial service. Providing for normal repairs and maintenance, adds to the manager's responsibility.

Rehabilitation, Modernization, and Conversions

These responsibilities require considerable technical know-how. But while the task is complex, the rewards are substantial. The main problem is to decide on the best course to produce the highest new income. If the property undergoes *rehabilitation*, the manager maintains the present use, making no changes in design, and restores the building to a like-new condition.

More than likely most problem buildings must undergo *modernization* without changing the property use. This step is recommended if the equipment is wearing out or is functionally obsolete. The replacement of the heating system, lighting fixtures, and plumbing are common examples of modernization. The purpose of modernization is to extend the useful life of the building and at the same time maintain or increase net income. While the rent level may not increase as a result of modernization, net income may be prevented from decreasing as a result of continued deterioration.

Property *conversions* require more investigation. Though a change in design or use introduces a higher risk factor, conversion is advised if the current use is no longer profitable. That is, if the net income is insufficient to continue the present use. Conversion of an apartment building to a motel or the conversion of rental apartments to condominium units are common examples of conversion. Downtown industrial property newly renovated for retail and warehouse use constitutes other popular property conversions. In sum, property managers are skilled in determining the highest and best use, and in estimating the cost of rehabilitation, modernization, or conversion.

Rent Collection

Much of the work of the property manager would fail without establishment of a rental collection policy. Tenant relations are set by the property manager, who is responsible for training employees in rent collection. In one respect, delinquent rents are more harmful than vacancies because nonpaying tenants subject the premises to wear and tear. A system of minimizing delinquent rental payments and educating tenants to pay promptly is one of the key duties of the trained property manager.

THE MANAGEMENT AGREEMENT

As observed in other real estate contracts, the management agreement gives the managing agent limited or exclusive agency to rent, lease, or operate and manage the property for a stated term, usually one year with renewal options. The agreement describes the duties of the agent and the authority granted to the agent by the owner. The final section of the management agreement authorizes the manager to pay mortgages, insurance premiums, and worker's compensation.

Duties of the Managing Agent

Typical of the law of agency, the agreement states that the agent will use diligence in managing the premises. One of the main responsibilities is the provision for statements of receipts and expenses given to the owner each month. While the manager normally will give the owner all receipts less disbursements, the owner agrees to pay losses promptly upon demand of the agent. In this respect the manager has a more difficult task than the broker who handles escrow payments of a buyer. The typical management office will have hundreds of building accounts covering several thousand individual rentals. A separate owner account must be kept for each property under management. In some instances the rent account—at the request of the owner—must be placed in a specific bank.

The record-keeping responsibility, one of the critical issues in property management, must be administered so that statements are rendered soon after the first of the month. Like all real estate brokers, receipts accepted in the name of the owner must be held in a trust account separate and apart from the personal business account of the managing agent. The more responsible management companies provide for fidelity bonds for all employees responsible for owner money.

Owner Grant of Authority

The management agreement delegates certain authority to the agent. For example, the manager may advertise rentals, display signs, and as part of the lease administration, sign, renew, and cancel leases. These duties include the responsibility to collect rents, give receipts, and terminate tenancies in the name of the owner. The power to evict and sue in the name of the owner are delegated by the agreement. Most managers will ask the owner for authority to lease up to a given period, say three years for apartment houses.

Management includes responsibilities for maintenance and repairs. Depending on the property size, expenditures for repairs and alterations usually will not require owner approval below a stated amount. In this portion of the agreement the agent has authority to protect the property from damage and maintain services to the tenant as called for in leases without prior approval.

To insure professional operation, the manager has the authority to hire, discharge, and supervise employees required for operation and maintenance. He has authority to contract for services such as electricity, gas, fuel, water, telephone, window cleaning, garbage collection, elevator service, janitorial services, and the like.

The final part of the management agreement provides that the manager will be held harmless from damage suits. The owner agrees to carry public liability, worker's compensation, and insurance commensurate with the property under management. The agent may be instructed to make mortgage payments, and to pay insurance, taxes, and special assessments from funds of the owner. If there are restrictions in these responsibilities, the management agreement will provide for written exceptions.

Of considerable interest to the property manager is the clause stating that if the property is offered for sale while subject to the management agreement, the agent be recognized as the listing broker.

The management fee calling for special management responsibilities will be listed in the management agreement. These fees may cover separate payments for:

1. Management.
2. Leasing fees.
3. Modernization.
4. Refinancing.
5. Broker's commission (if sold by manager).
6. Fire restoration.
7. Other fees.

A management agreement published by the Institute of Real Estate Management illustrating these points is shown in Figure 16–1. The legal requirements of the different states may call for special terms not included in this form.

While the exact form of the management agreement may vary, the main purpose is to establish compatible owner relations. In each instance the management agreement should be a written contract covering a minimum of seven subjects:

1. A legal description of the property to be managed.
2. The names of the parties of the agreement.
3. The rate of compensation paid to the manager with the schedule of rates for different services.
4. A statement of authority of the manager with limitations imposed on management operations.
5. Hold harmless clauses, bonding requirements of management employees to protect the agent-principal relationship from normal risks of agency.
6. The beginning date, the termination date and provision for renewal options or termination.
7. An agreement to render periodic statements.

TENANT-OWNER RELATIONS

Some observers regard tenant-owner relations as the most critical part of management. Today added complications result from new legislation that imposes new duties on the owner and from militant tenant organizations. Certainly, even for the problem properties, the manager must maintain good public relations. This seems even more essential today than formerly, in view of the growing conflicts between tenants and landlords and the public.

FIGURE 16–1

A Property Management Agreement

Between

OWNER_____

and

AGENT_____

for Property located at_____

Beginning_____19_____

Ending_____19_____

MANAGEMENT
AGREEMENT

In consideration of the covenants herein contained,_____

_____(hereinafter called

"OWNER"), and_____(hereinafter called "AGENT"),
agree as follows:

    1. The OWNER hereby employs the AGENT exclusively to rent and
manage the property (hereinafter called the "Premises") known as_____

_____

_____

upon the terms hereinafter set forth, for a period of_____years beginning

on the_____day of_____, 19_____, and ending on

the_____day of_____,19_____, and there-
after for yearly periods from time to time, unless on or before _____ days
prior to the date last above mentioned or on or before   _____ days prior
to the expiration of any such renewal period, either party hereto shall notify
the other in writing that it elects to terminate this Agreement, in which case
this Agreement shall be thereby terminated on said last mentioned date.
(See also Paragraph 6(c) below.)

Institute of Real Estate Management—1974

FIGURE 16–1 (*continued*)

2. THE AGENT AGREES:

(a) To accept the management of the Premises, to the extent, for the period, and upon the terms herein provided and agrees to furnish the services of its organization for the rental operation and management of the Premises.

(b) To render a monthly statement of receipts, disbursements and charges to the following person at the address shown:

Name   Address

_____   _____

_____   _____

and to remit each month the net proceeds (provided Agent is not required to make any mortgage, escrow or tax payment on the first day of the following month). Agent will remit the net proceeds or the balance thereof after making allowance for such payments to the following persons, in the percentages specified and at the addresses shown:

Name   Percentage   Address

_____   _____   _____

_____   _____   _____

_____   _____   _____

In case the disbursements and charges shall be in excess of the receipts, the OWNER agrees to pay such excess promptly, but nothing herein contained shall obligate the AGENT to advance its own funds on behalf of the OWNER.

(c) To cause all employees of the AGENT who handle or are responsible for the safekeeping of any monies of the OWNER to be covered by a fidelity bond in an amount and with a company determined by the AGENT at no cost to the OWNER.

3. THE OWNER AGREES:

To give the AGENT the following authority and powers (all or any of which may be exercised in the name of the OWNER) and agrees to assume all expenses in connection therewith:

(a) To advertise the Premises or any part thereof, to display signs thereon and to rent the same; to cause references of prospective tenants to be investigated; to sign leases for terms not in excess of _____ years and to renew and or cancel the existing leases and prepare and execute the new lease without additional charge to the OWNER; provided, however, that the AGENT may collect from tenants all or any of the following: a late rent administrative charge, a non-negotiable check charge, credit report fee, a subleasing administrative charge and/or broker's commission and need not account for such charges and/or commission to the OWNER; to terminate tenancies and to sign and serve such notices as are deemed needful by the AGENT; to institute and prosecute actions to oust tenants and to recover possession of the Premises; to sue for and recover rent: and, when expedient, to settle, compromise and release such actions or suits, or reinstate such tenancies.

Institute of Real Estate Management—1974

FIGURE 16–1 (*continued*)

(b) To hire, discharge and pay all engineers, janitors and other employees; to make or cause to be made all ordinary repairs and replacements necessary to preserve the Premises in its present condition and for the operating efficiency thereof and all alterations required to comply with lease requirements, and to do decorating on the Premises; to negotiate contracts for non-recurring items not exceeding $_____and to enter into agreements for all necessary repairs, maintenance, minor alterations and utility services; and to purchase supplies and pay all bills.

(c) To collect rents and/or assessments and other items due or to become due and give receipts therefor and to deposit all funds collected hereunder in the Agent's custodial account.

(d) To refund tenants' security deposits at the expiration of leases and, only if required to do so by law, to pay interest upon such security deposits.

(e) To execute and file all returns and other instruments and do and perform all acts required of the OWNER as an employer with respect to the Premises under the Federal Insurance Contributions Acts, the Federal Unemployment Tax Act and Subtitle C of the Internal Revenue Code of 1954 with respect to wages paid by the AGENT on behalf of the OWNER and under any similar Federal or State law now or hereafter in force (and in connection therewith the OWNER agrees upon request to promptly execute and deliver to the AGENT all necessary powers of attorney, notices of appointment and the like).

4. THE OWNER FURTHER AGREES:

(a) To indemnify, defend and save the AGENT harmless from all suits in connection with the Premises and from liability for damage to property and injuries to or death of any employee or other person whomsoever, and to carry at his (its) own expense public liability, elevator liability (if elevators are part of the equipment of the Premises), and workmen's compensation insurance naming the OWNER and the AGENT and adequate to protect their interests and in form, substance and amounts reasonably satisfactory to the AGENT, and to furnish to the AGENT certificates evidencing the existence of such insurance. Unless the OWNER shall provide such insurance and furnish such certificate within _____ days from the date of this Agreement, the AGENT may, but shall not be obligated to, place said insurance and charge the cost thereof to the account of the OWNER.

(b) To pay all expenses incurred by the AGENT, including, without limitation, attorney's fees for counsel employed to represent the AGENT or the OWNER in any proceeding or suit involving an alleged violation by the AGENT or the OWNER, or both, of any constitutional provision, statute, ordinance, law or regulation of any governmental body pertaining to fair employment, Federal Fair Credit Reporting Act, environmental protection, or fair housing, including, without limitation, those prohibiting or making illegal discrimination on the basis of race, creed, color, religion or national origin in the sale, rental or other disposition of housing or any services rendered in connection therewith (unless the AGENT is finally adjudicated to have personally and not in a representative capacity violated such constitutional provision, statute, ordinance, law or regulation), but nothing herein contained shall require the AGENT to employ counsel to represent the OWNER in any such proceeding or suit.

(c) To indemnify, defend and save the AGENT harmless from all claims, investigations and suits with respect to any alleged or actual violation of state or federal labor laws, it being expressly agreed and understood that as between the OWNER and the AGENT, all persons employed in connection

FIGURE 16–1 *(continued)*

with the Premises are employees of the OWNER not the AGENT. The OWNER's obligation under this paragraph 4(c) shall include the payment of all settlements, judgments, damages, liquidated damages, penalties, forfeitures, back pay awards, court costs, litigation expense and attorneys' fees.

(d) To give adequate advance written notice to the AGENT if payment of mortgage indebtedness, general taxes or special assessments or the placing of fire, steam boiler or any other insurance is desired.

5. TO PAY THE AGENT EACH MONTH:

(a) FOR MANAGEMENT: _____ per month or _____

percent (_____ %) of the monthly gross receipts from the operation of the Premises during the period this Agreement remains in full force and effect, whichever is the greater amount.

(b) APARTMENT LEASING _____

_____

_____

(c) FOR MODERNIZATION (REHABILITATION/CONSTRUCTION)

_____

_____

(d) FIRE RESTORATION _____

_____

_____

_____

(e) OTHER ITEMS OF MUTUAL AGREEMENT _____

_____

_____

_____

_____

6. IT IS MUTUALLY AGREED THAT:

(a) The OWNER expressly withholds from the AGENT any power or authority to make any structural changes in any building or to make any other major alterations or additions in or to any such building or equipment therein, or to incur any expense chargeable to the OWNER other than expenses related to exercising the express powers above vested in the AGENT without the prior written direction of the following person:

Name   Address

_____   _____

Institute of Real Estate Management—1974

FIGURE 16–1 (*continued*)

except such emergency repairs as may be required because of danger to life or property or which are immediately necessary for the preservation and safety of the Premises or the safety of the tenants and occupants thereof or are required to avoid the suspension of any necessary service to the Premises.

(b) The AGENT does not assume and is given no responsibility for compliance of any building on the Premises or any equipment therein with the requirements of any statute, ordinance, law or regulation of any governmental body or of any public authority or official thereof having jurisdiction, except to notify the OWNER promptly or forward to the OWNER promptly any complaints, warnings, notices or summonses received by it relating to such matters. The OWNER represents that to the best of his (its) knowledge the Premises and such equipment comply with all such requirements and authorizes the AGENT to disclose the ownership of the Premises to any such officials and agrees to indemnify and hold harmless the AGENT, its representatives, servants and employees, of and from all loss, cost, expense and liability whatsoever which may be imposed on them or any of them by reason of any present or future violation or alleged violation of such laws, ordinances, statutes or regulations.

(c) In the event it is alleged or charged that any building on the Premises or any equipment therein or any act or failure to act by the OWNER with respect to the Premises or the sale, rental or other disposition thereof fails to comply with, or is in violation·of, any of the requirements of any consititutional provision, statute, ordinance, law or regulation of any governmental body or any order or ruling of any public authority or official thereof having or claiming to have jurisdiction thereover, and the AGENT, in its sole and absolute discretion, considers that the action or position of the OWNER or registered managing agent with respect thereto may result in damage or liability to the AGENT, the AGENT shall have the right to cancel this Agreement at any time by written notice to the OWNER of its election so to do, which cancellation shall be effective upon the service of such notice. Such notice may be served personally or by registered mail, on or to the person named to receive the AGENT's monthly statement at the address designated for such person as provided in Paragraph 2(b) above, and if served by mail shall be deemed to have been served when deposited in the mails. Such cancellation shall not release the indemnities of the OWNER set forth in Paragraphs 4 and 6(b) above and shall not terminate any liability or obligation of the OWNER to the AGENT for any payment, reimbursement or other sum of money then due and payable to the AGENT hereunder.

7. This Agreement may be cancelled by OWNER before the termination date specified in paragraph 1 on not less than __ days prior written notice to the AGENT, provided that such notice is accompanied by payment to the AGENT of a cancellation fee in an amount equal to __% of the management fee that would accrue over the remainder of the stated term of the Agreement. For this purpose the monthly management fee for the remainder of the stated term shall be presumed to be the same as that of the last month prior to service of the notice of cancellation.

This Agreement shall be binding upon the successors and assigns of the AGENT and their heirs, administrators, executors, successors and assigns of the OWNER.

FIGURE 16–1 *(concluded)*

IN WITNESS WHEREOF, the parties hereto have affixed or caused to be affixed

their respective signatures this_____day of_____, 19_____.

WITNESSES: OWNER:

_____   _____

_____   _____

_____   _____

                                              _____

                                              AGENT:

                                              Firm_____

_____   By_____
Submitted by

POWER OF ATTORNEY

KNOW ALL MEN BY THESE PRESENTS, THAT

_____
                        (Name)

_____located at
       (State whether individual, partnership or corporation, etc.)

_____.has made,
                    (Address)

constituted and appointed. and. by these presents does hereby make, constitute and appoint._____ , a resident of
the United States, whose address is _____ , (its)
true and lawful attorney for (it) (me) in (its) (my) name. place and stead to

execute and to file any Tax Returns due on and after _____

_____

under the provisions of the Social Security Act, now in force or future
amendments thereto.

Dated at _____ this____ day of _____ , 19____

                              _____
                              Signature of Taxpayer

                              _____
                              Title

Executed in presence of: _____
                              Signature of Taxpayer

                              _____
                              Title

Witness _____   _____
                              Signature of Taxpayer

Witness _____   _____
                              Title

        Acknowledged before me this_____day of_____ , 19____
        NOTARIAL
        SEAL

Tenant Relations

Property managers are generally agreed that controversies are avoided by communicating tenant rules before possession is granted. It will be appreciated that the rules posted by management work toward the welfare of all tenants. Generally, individual tenants are restricted in activities that might cause other tenants to suffer inconveniences, that cause nuisances, or that restrict the rights of other tenants. In other instances, tenant rules minimize operating expenses and reduce repair expenses which, again, benefit tenants in the form of lower rents.

Figure 16–2 illustrates a set of regulations applying to a condominium development. The main rules posted for the benefit of tenants relate to use of the apartment, insuring that the tenant areas are maintained for the common good. Tenants are required to observe the rights, comforts, or the convenience of other tenants; harmful noises or other annoyances to building occupants are prohibited. The storage of property in the public way, restriction on the keeping of pets, and the use of building equipment are controlled by tenant rules. Property managers specializing in this type of property make certain that tenants understand rules of the building, their enforcement, and reasons for their adoption.

Professional managers work constantly to be sympathetic with complaining tenants. Promises that cannot be kept should not be made. The

FIGURE 16–2
Condominium House Rules

1. The public halls, sidewalks, and stairways shall not be obstructed or used for any other purposes than for ingress to and egress from the apartments.
2. No occupant shall make or permit any disturbing noises in the building by himself, his family, friends or servants; nor do or permit anything to be done by such persons that will interfere with the rights, comforts or convenience of other tenants. No occupant shall play upon or suffer to be played upon any musical instrument in the demised premises between the hours of 11 P.M. and the following 8 A.M. if the same shall disturb or annoy other occupants of the building.
3. Occupants will not be allowed to put their names in any entry, passageway, vestibule, hall or stairway of the building, except in the proper place or in the mail box provided for use of the apartments occupied by them respectively.
4. No rugs shall be beaten on the porches, fire escapes or in the halls or corridors, nor dust, rubbish or litter swept from the demised premises or any room thereof into any of the halls or entryways of the building containing said premises, except under the direction of the janitor.

FIGURE 16–2 (continued)

5. Children shall not be permitted to loiter or play on the stairways or in the halls, lobbies and elevators.
6. The water closets and other water apparatus shall not be used for any purpose other than that for which they were constructed, and no sweeping, rubbish, rags, paper, ashes or other substance shall be thrown therein. Any damage resulting to them from misuse of any nature or character whatever shall be paid for by the tenant who shall cause it.
7. All damages to the building, caused by the moving and carrying of articles therein, shall be paid by the occupant, or person in charge of such articles.
8. Nothing shall be thrown or emptied by the occupants or their servants out of the windows or doors, or down the passages, courts or in the building areas, nor shall anything be hung from the outside of the windows or fire escapes or placed on the outside window sills.
9. Dogs, cats, parrots or reptiles are not allowed in the demised premises.
10. The lobby, stairway and other public areas shall not be used for the storage of furniture or other articles.
11. The water shall not be left running any unreasonable or unnecessary length of time in the demised premises.
12. No occupant shall interfere in any manner with any portion either of the heating or lighting apparatus in or about the demised premises nor in or about the building containing the same.
13. Laundry work shall be done only in the areas provided for such purposes in the demised premises. Electric washing machines, mangles and apparatus shall be used and operated only in the place provided by the Council of Co-owners for this purpose.
14. No shades, awnings or window guards shall be used except such as shall be put up or approved by the Council of Co-owners.
15. The Council of Co-owners reserves the right to make such other rules and regulations from time to time as may be deemed needful for the safety, care and cleanliness of the premises and for securing the comfort and convenience of all of the occupants thereof.
16. No radio aerial or connection shall be installed by the occupants outside of their respective apartments without the written consent of the Council or Co-owners or its agent.
17. Unless the Council of Co-owners gives advance written consent in each and every instance, occupants shall not install or operate in the premises any machinery, refrigerating or heating device or air conditioning apparatus, or use any illumination other than electric lights, or use or permit to be brought into the building any inflammable oils or fluids such as gasoline, kerosene, naptha or benzine, or other explosives or articles deemed extra hazardous to life, limb or property.

object is to reduce complaints by giving the tenant the highest possible level of services.

Good management should provide uniform policies applied equally to each tenant. Such policies cover how and when rent is to be paid, the requirements for landlord and tenant maintenance, and rules restricting the use of public areas, playgrounds, landscaping, and building equipment. Policies adopted should be in writing as illustrated in Figure 16–2. Furthermore, these points seem more relevant to the low-income housing tenant, who often must live with restricted housing choices. The high-income occupant, rather than voice complaints, may elect to vacate the premises.

MANAGEMENT ACCOUNTING SYSTEMS

The larger property manager offices have developed computer systems to list individual payments, receipts, disbursements, and delinquent rents, and to calculate the monthly and annual operating statements. For smaller management offices, a set of accounting forms provides the necessary detail and control. A talent for maintaining detail is essential to this phase of property management responsibilities. Probably the most

FIGURE 16–3

Summary of Receipts and Disbursements

BAIRD & WARNER
CHICAGO

SUMMARY OF RECEIPTS AND DISBURSEMENTS

OWNER: 1234 MAIN STREET BUILDING CORP.

ACCOUNT NO. 0-000

PROPERTY: 1234 MAIN STREET
CHICAGO ILLINOIS

PERIOD: JAN THRU DEC 19

CLASS NO.	DESCRIPTION	CURRENT YEAR AMOUNT	%	PREVIOUS YEAR AMOUNT	%
	INCOME				
1	RENT INCOME	59,340.00CR		59,055.00CR	
4	SUNDRY INCOME	109.96CR		135.11CR	
	A TOTAL INCOME	59,449.96CR	100.00CR	59,190.11CR	100.00CR
	OPERATING EXPENSES				
	BUILDING SERVICES				
10	ELECTRICITY	806.91-	1.4-	794.91-	1.3-
13	GAS	311.31-	.5-	294.36-	.5-
14	HEATING FUEL	3,302.91-	5.6-	3,245.04-	5.5-
15	INSPECTION FEES & PERMITS	88.25-	.1-	62.00-	.1-
17	PAYROLL	6,206.49-	10.4-	6,106.49-	10.3-
18	PAYROLL TAXES	163.47-	.3-	145.96-	.2-
19	SCAVENGER SERVICE	180.00-	.3-	180.00-	.3-
20	SUPPLIES	160.69-	.3-	259.21-	.4-
22	WATER	391.05-	.7-	326.13-	.6-
	TOTAL BUILDING SERVICES	11,611.08-	19.6-	11,414.10-	19.2-
	ADMINISTRATIVE & GENERAL EXPENSES				
31	INSURANCE	891.75-	1.5-	651.09-	1.1-
33	MANAGEMENT FEE	2,967.00-	5.0-	2,952.75-	5.0-
34	PROFESSIONAL SERVICES	61.42-	.1-	60.10-	.1-
	TOTAL ADMINISTRATIVE & GENERAL EXPENSES	3,920.17-	6.6-	3,663.94-	6.2-
	MAINTENANCE & REPAIRS				
41	APPLIANCES	74.62-	.1-	115.85-	.2-
42	CARPENTRY	51.65-	.1-	52.39-	.1-
43	DECORATING - PUBLIC	313.14-	.5-	115.85-	.2-
44	DECORATING - TENANT	2,523.00-	4.2-	2,485.98-	4.2-
45	ELECTRICAL	89.53-	.1-	96.07-	.2-
46	ELEVATORS	497.02-	.8-	432.83-	.7-
47	FLOORS	117.00-	.2-	42.00-	.1-

MANAGING OFFICE COPY

FIGURE 16–3 (continued)

SUMMARY OF RECEIPTS AND DISBURSEMENTS

OWNER: 1234 MAIN STREET BUILDING CORP.

PROPERTY: 1234 MAIN STREET
CHICAGO ILLINOIS

ACCOUNT NO. 0–000

PERIOD: JAN THRU DEC 19

CLASS NO.	DESCRIPTION	CURRENT YEAR AMOUNT	%	PREVIOUS YEAR AMOUNT	%
48	FURNITURE, FURNISHINGS & CARPETS	150.00-	.3-	312.80-	.5-
50	HEATING	314.01	.5-		
53	PLASTERING & WALL TILE	270.59-	.5-	85.69-	.1-
54	PLUMBING & SEWERS	346.80-	.6-	530.78-	.9-
55	ROOFS & GUTTERS			4.77-	
57	SHADES, RODS & BLINDS	93.18-	.2-	203.74-	.4-
	TOTAL MAINTENANCE & REPAIRS	4,840.54-	8.1-	4,478.75-	7.6-
B	TOTAL OPERATING EXPENSES	20,371.79-	34.3-	19,556.79-	33.0-
C	NET OPERATING INCOME – LINE A MINUS LINE B	39,078.17CR	65.7CR	39,633.32CR	67.0CR
	OTHER CHARGES & CREDITS				
71	PRINCIPAL PAYMENTS	11,395.92-	19.1-	10,062.30-	17.0-
72	INTEREST	4,210.08-	7.0-	5,386.29-	9.1-
74	NEW EQUIPMENT	121.68-	.2-	82.50-	.1-
75	REAL ESTATE TAXES	12,413.00-	20.7-	12,649.00-	21.2-
78	SUNDRY			36.00-	.1-
D	TOTAL OTHER CHARGES & CREDITS	28,140.68-	47.0-	28,216.09-	47.7-
	NET RECEIPTS FOR PERIOD – LINE C MINUS LINE D	10,937.49CR	18.7CR	11,417.23CR	19.3CR
	OWNERSHIP ACCOUNTS				
91	BALANCE AT BEGINNING OF PERIOD				
94	PAYMENTS TO OWNER	10,937.49-		11,417.23-	
99	BALANCE AT END OF PERIOD				

important document given the owner is the list of monthly rental payments, with a summary statement showing total rentals, miscellaneous receipts, less disbursements, and the management fee. If there is a net balance, the amount remitted to the owner is disbursed according to the monthly summary statement. At the end of the accounting year, the owner is provided a summary profit and loss statement as shown in Figure 16–3.

Starting with the total income from rent and sundry income, operating expenses are deducted. In the form illustrated in Figure 16–3, expenses are listed with building services. The special advantage of the accounts listed in Figure 16–3 lies in the comparison of current year figures with data for the previous year. The separation of administrative and general expenses, including insurance, the management fee and other professional services, gives the owner a basis for evaluating management efficiency. The list of maintenance and repairs, starting with appliances and carpentry and ending with expenses of maintaining the roof, gutters, shades, rods and blinds, provides detail for monitoring total maintenance and repair expenses. Note that the net operating income is shown as a percentage of income, in this case 65.7 percent.

Another section of the report indicates other charges and credits which primarily relate to principal payments, interest, and real estate taxes. These serve as a basis for personal income tax reports. It should be added that property management accounts are usually evaluated in terms of their cost per apartment unit. Some managers report that automated records cost from $1 to $2 per unit, depending on the financial detail covered. As a rule, the larger management office with 3,000 units or more under management will show lower accounting costs per unit than the manager who is limited to 1,000 units or less.

THE MANAGEMENT SURVEY

Managers rely on the management survey as appraisers rely on the narrative appraisal report. According to the Institute of Real Estate Management, the management survey is a comprehensive analysis of the economic aspects of real property. The report is prepared for purposes of buying or selling for refinancing, or for redeveloping or changing the property use. The end objective is to show the owner how to increase net income.

By maximizing net income, it is not implied that the recommended management program resulting from the management survey would necessarily lead to higher rents. Tenants may already be paying the maximum rent. Instead, the management survey may point out benefits of modernization, rehabilitation, or conversion to the end that the economic life of the property is extended, that vacancies decrease, or that operating expenses decline. In addition, the recommended financing plan may increase cash flow. If the management survey leads to expectations of increased income or a longer economic life, then the market value of the property may also increase.

While the management survey calls for technical skills, a brief outline of its requirements will prove helpful to the general practitioner. To carry out the management survey, the expert must concentrate on a six-part analysis:

1. Physical real property inventory.
2. Neighborhood analysis.
3. Market analysis.
4. Gross income analysis.
5. Operating expense analysis.
6. Economic analysis of alternative plans.

After reviewing these points the property manager submits final conclusions and recommendations.

PHYSICAL REAL PROPERTY INVENTORY

Without special training and considerable experience, few real estate owners and developers are qualified to inspect the property physically. Even contractors and architects, while knowing construction details, are

FIGURE 16–4

Inspection Report

THE INSTITUTE OF REAL ESTATE MANAGEMENT   Form '40A
of the
NATIONAL ASSOCIATION OF REALTORS®   ———————— 19——

APARTMENT BUILDING INSPECTION REPORT

Name of Property.. Address................................

Type of Property..

No. of Stories..

Report Submitted by..

| No. of Apts.: 1's........................ 1½'s........................ |
| 2's............ 2½'s............ 3's............ 3½'s............ |
| 4's............ 4½'s............ 5's............ 5½'s............ |
| 6's............ 7's............ 8's............ Total............ |

EXTERIOR

Items	Character and Condition	Needs	Estimated Expense Involved
Grounds			
1. Soil			
2. Grass			
3. Shrubs			
4. Flowers			
5. Trees			
6. Fences			
7. Urns			
8. Walks			
9. Cement flashings			
10. Parking curbs			
Brick and Stone			
11. Front walls			
A. Base			
B. Top			
C. Coping			
D. Tuck pointing			
E. Cleanliness			
12. Court walls			
A. Base			
B. Top			
C. Coping			
D. Tuck pointing			
E. Cleanliness			
13. Side walls			
A. Base			
B. Top			
C. Coping			
D. Tuck pointing			
E. Cleanliness			
14. Rear walls			
A. Base			
B. Top			
C. Coping			
D. Tuck pointing			
E. Cleanliness			
15. Chimneys			

FIGURE 16–4 (*continued*)

GENERAL INTERIOR

Items	Character and Condition	Needs	Estimated Expense Involved
Vestibules			
1. Steps			
2. Risers			
3. Floors			
4. Marble slabs			
5. Walls			
6. Ceilings			
7. Door mats			
Vestibule Doors			
8. Glass			
9. Transoms			
10. Hinges			
11. Knobs			
12. Door checks			
13. Door finish			
14. Kick plates			
15. Handrails			
Mail Boxes			
16. Glass			
17. Doors			
18. Locks			
19. Name plates			
20. Speaking tubes			
21. Signal buttons and connections			
Stair Halls			
22. Steps			
23. Landings			
24. Handrails			
25. Woodwork			
26. Carpets			
27. Walls			
28. Ceilings			
29. Skylights			
30. Windows			
31. Shades			
Rear Halls			
32. Steps			
33. Landings			
34. Walls			
35. Ceilings			
36. Handrails			
37. Garbage cans			
38. Waste-paper receptacles			
39. Windows			
40. Shades			

FIGURE 16–4 (continued)

Items	Character and Condition	Needs	Estimated Expense Involved
Elevators			
41. Signal buttons			
42. Doors			
43. Cab floors			
44. Cab walls			
45. Cab ceilings			
46. Control mechanism			
47. Cables			
48. Pulleys			
49. Motor			
50. Shaft walls			
51. Shaft ceiling			
52. Shaft floor			
53. Floor numbers on doors			
Public Light Fixtures			
54. Entrance			
A. Brackets			
B. Fixtures			
C. Bulbs			
D. Switch			
55. Vestibule			
A. Brackets			
B. Fixtures			
C. Bulbs			
D. Switch			
56. Halls			
A. Brackets			
B. Fixtures			
C. Bulbs			
D. Switch			

BASEMENT

Items	Character and Condition	Needs	Estimated Expense Involved
Laundries			
1. Floors			
2. Walls			
3. Ceilings			
4. Stoves			
5. Driers			
6. Tubs			
7. Faucets			
8. Toilet bowls			
9. Lavatories			
10. Drains			
11. Windows			
12. Doors			
13. Shades			
Boiler Room			
14. Floor			
15. Pipes			
16. Fuel bin			
17. Fire hazards			

FIGURE 16–4 (concluded)

Items	Character and Condition	Needs	Estimated Expense Involved
Boiler Room (cont'd)			
18. Ceiling			
19. Walls			
20. Windows			
21. Doors			
22. Cleanliness			
23. Shades			
24. Ash cans			
Boiler			
25. Flues			
26. Tubes			
27. Valves			
28. Diaphragms			
29. Flange unions			
30. Grates			
31. Ash pits			
32. Pointing on brickwork			
33. Motors			
34. Draft controls			
35. Chimney			
36. Thermostats			
37. Hydrostats			
38. Stoker			
39. Insulation			
40. Combustion chambers			
41. Water level			
Hot-Water Heater			
42. Tank			
43. Insulation			
44. Ash pit			
45. Incinerator			
46. Submerged system			
47. Hydrolator			
Pumps			
48. Motors			
49. Sump			
50. Pressure			
51. Circulating			
Lockers			
52. Floors			
53. Walls			
54. Ceilings			
55. Doors			
56. Fire hazards			
57. Aisles			
Refrigeration Units			
58. Motors			
59. Cleanliness			
60. Accessibility			
General			
61. Plaster			
62. Trash and junk			
63. Screens			

not always able to relate property characteristics to market demands and the potential for alternative uses. The property manager looks at the building from the standpoint of its economic use. To guide this inspection, forms are prepared that record inspection results.

Figure 16–4 illustrates such a form for an apartment house inspection. As the illustration shows, physical inspection calls for a detailed examination and a description of the exterior wall and roof condition, including flashing, windows, downspouts, and gutters. Turning to the interior, special attention is given public areas (mainly, the lobby and corridors). Next in importance are the tenant-occupied areas including walls, ceiling, and floor coverings. A review of the mechanical equipment, including the electrical system, elevators, plumbing, heating, and air conditioning, may call for outside counsel and advice. If furniture and furnishings are part of the property operation, these will be reviewed in the light of their current condition and style.

The physical inventory points out areas of deferred maintenance and examples of obsolescence: obsolescence which may be remedied and obsolescence which is uneconomic to remedy—unusually wide corridors, high ceilings, obsolete floor plans and old style architecture. The form shows compliance with building, housing, and zoning codes and the present use and occupancy, conforming or nonconforming to local ordinances.

Neighborhood Analysis

An exceptionally well-maintained building showing good construction and modern features will be affected by the surrounding property even to the point that a change in use may be advised. Points deserving attention cover physical aspects of the neighborhood, including general judgments on the appearance of surrounding property and the effect on continued property operation.

In this portion of the survey the neighborhood pattern and its characteristics are judged according to the type of surrounding buildings, the types of tenants, and comments on whether, in the judgment of the investigator, the neighborhood is declining or improving. These trends will be shown by the condition and quality of parking and transportation, evidence of new construction, and the impact of neighborhood trends on net income expectation.

Market Analysis

For purposes of property management, the market analysis goes beyond the analysis of comparable sales and profit and loss statements. Analysis begins with a study of each lease, its terms, and renewal options. Considerable importance is attached to the vacancy rate and the experience with credit losses. If these seem excessive, a review of them will probably disclose managerial deficiencies. A related issue concerns leases, their renewal, and tenant turnover. If they seem above or below normal, then the property manager may suspect the quality of tenant services or the presence of below- or above-market rents. In either case, by studying tenant arrangements, deficiencies in the rent and lease structure are revealed.

The net income potential of a given property is associated with external developments. That is, what is the economic base of the city? What are the employment trends of tenant occupants and what are prospects for the future? For instance, recommendations covering an apartment house in a hospital district serving primarily medical personnel would be quite different from recommendations covering an apartment building occupied by tenants employed at a local military base. An economic study of the neighborhood and the source of tenant income support final manager recommendations.

Gross Income Analysis

The current income is documented to reveal distortions in the rental pattern. By reducing gross income to the rent per square foot of rentable area, per apartment, and per room, the manager can accurately compare experience of the property with other like properties. The issue is complicated by the variation in services provided by different building owners, however. Parking, extra storage, and extra features such as swimming pools, sauna baths, air conditioning, and utilities included in the rent usually require adjustments if gross income is to agree with the current rent level.

Operating Expense Analysis, Short and Long Term

Ordinarily the owner of a nonprofessionally managed property will not have a statement of operating expenses for *management* purposes. The profit and loss statement, though showing sufficient detail for income tax purposes, will lack the classifications important to management decisions. To illustrate, the management survey requires a distinction between *current* expenses and *stabilized* expenses. The current expense statement shows actual disbursements as made by the property owner. Accordingly, some of the expenses will be randomly entered as property operations require. For instance, the stabilized expense list will set aside an annual sum to cover the replacement of lobby carpets, say on a three-year cycle. Likewise, other equipment and furnishings for the property will require periodic replacement or repair.

By setting aside funds representing their average annual cost or replacement, a true income statement will result. Hot water heaters, refrigerators, dishwashers, washing machines, dryers, and lobby furniture are typical of items needing periodic repair-replacement. A current expense list showing actual cash output for income tax purposes will not show the true economic cost of the operation.

Another issue is the division of expenses between *recurring* and *nonrecurring* expenses. Recurring expenses are monthly operating expenses such as utility costs, wages, and property taxes. By separating nonrecurring costs from repetitive monthly expenses, the true cost of operation is found more accurately. Interior painting, floor refinishing, and new window blinds fall into the nonrecurring cost category. In this way the management may determine if the property has been maintained on an adequate level and if these nonrecurring expenses must be increased over the economic life of the property. The end result of these calculations provides an estimate of the expected net income.

Economics of Alternative Plans

A problem property may be corrected by more than one management plan. Starting with the question of what can be done to maximize income, the property manager will present a capital improvement budget. The budget may include different types of plans ranging from low-cost modernization to rehabilitation or conversion to a different use. The cost of adding capital improvements—if these are necessary—will be shown in detail.

The extent of physical depreciation which may be corrected and the economic feasibility of correcting obsolete features of the building will be shown in this part of the report. Income tax aspects of capital improvements, to the extent that they remedy physical and functional obsolescence, are also explained. If the property requires substantial capital investment, a schedule of proposed improvements and the way in which they may change expected net income will be scheduled in a proposed management program. Techniques of financing the cost, the recommended leasing program, and suggested reserves for replacements help make the management survey more practical.

The six-part survey leads to a set of final recommendations. The management survey reports the most economical plan of operation in the light of the revised operating expense schedule (as stabilized). It includes estimates of expected net income, explains the income tax effects of the proposed plan, and details a schedule for implementation. The preparation of the management survey encompasses a study of the local market, real estate finance and taxation, and the more technical parts of real property management. Clearly, the property manager serves a function not covered by other real estate specialists.

MANAGEMENT OF INCOME PROPERTIES

To demonstrate management techniques, three types of property have been selected: apartments, shopping centers, and office buildings. In each case, the vocabulary associated with each property, its net income analysis, and the unique problems of management associated with it are covered. While this review is not comprehensive, it introduces the practical content of management believed useful to beginning management agents.

Managing Apartment Properties

Familiarity with the terms common to apartments helps understand apartment operations. A net income statement developed and used by property managers precedes a discussion of financial ratios common to multiple-family income properties. By learning these points the managing agent may judge a given property against accepted, uniform financial reports of like properties.

Types of Apartments. Techniques of management, income analysis, and merchandising space vary by the type of apartment building. Custom has led to a four-part classification: First, *high-rise elevator buildings*. To fall in this category, a building must be four stories or more and must be equipped with one or more elevators. Second, *low-rise buildings under 25 units*. Buildings in this group have three stories or less. They may or may not have an elevator. Third, *low-rise buildings of 25 units or more*. This category is similar to the preceding group; they vary only by the number of apartment units. Fourth, *garden apartments*. An apartment complex consisting of more than one building on a land-scaped area, usually a group of low-rise apartment buildings, qualifies as a garden apartment.

To be sure, apartment buildings may be classified by type of construction, age, or architectural style and the level of services: high-income or low-income. But the definition used by the management specialist is highly workable. As a group, high-rise elevator buildings show higher operating expenses than low-rise buildings under 25 units. Even in this latter group, management techniques vary by the number of units, accounting for the two divisions of low-rise apartments. Garden type apartments, of large scale, require more formal, project-oriented management.

Certain other technical definitions should be noted. For example, the floor area consists of the space measured from outside walls, including the rentable area, corridor, lobbies, stores, offices, garages within the building, basement, and public areas on all floors. Outside court areas are excluded. The rentable floor area is measured by the total square foot area within individual apartment units, stores, and offices. Care must be taken in comparing incomes and expenses reported by per unit values for the two-floor area measurements.

Because apartments are leased on the basis of the number of square feet and number of rooms, common agreement must be reached on the definition of a room. For example, a combined dining and living room is counted as one room if there is less than 260 square feet. The same combination in more than 260 square feet is counted as 1.5 rooms. Similarly, a breakfast room is counted as a separate room if it is 100 square feet or more.

Likewise a separate walk-in kitchen is counted as a full room, but if the kitchen and dining room are combined, then other rules prevail. For instance, if the total combined dining and kitchen area is less than 105 square feet, it is counted as one room. An area between 105 to 140 feet is listed as 1.5 rooms, while a two-room area would be more than 140 square feet. Bathrooms, porches, halls, closets, and storage space are not counted as separate rooms. By following these rules, financial ratios and income statements may be broken down by the listed categories for accurate comparisons.

Apartment Net Income. Apartment net income is calculated from the gross possible rental income and miscellaneous income earned from coin machines, parking, or forfeited rents, damage deposits, and other fees. From this figure will be deducted an allowance for vacancies and bad debts. For management purposes, these are actual records and not an estimate of expected income. Operating expenses are then deducted from *effective gross income*, which includes a reserve for replacements. In addition to the expenses listed in Table 16–1, other administrative costs, supplies, contract services (e.g., elevator service contracts, and window washing services), landscaping costs, and other taxes would normally be included.

The manager, while concerned with absolute costs recorded over the year, evaluates operating expenses from per unit costs. This explains why rental income and expenses are converted to a per room and per square foot basis. Additional columns showing expenses and vacancies as a percentage of gross possible income provide a means of comparing the current year with the past years and with other comparable properties. The income statement following the outline of Table 16–1 permits further comparisons with annual published reports of apartment house income and expenses prepared by the Institute of Real Estate Management.

Apartment Financial Ratios

If the property manager is asked to supply information to appraise property on the basis of capitalized net income, it is useful to prepare a series of financial ratios that show relative performance. Table 16–2 illustrates a breakdown of apartment house incomes, expenses, and valuation including mortgage ratios for five apartment buildings.

In the first case, the valuation enables the professional manager to compare the relative risk of ownership, given the value and the mortgage.

Expressing the first mortgage as a multiple of gross income, in Table 16–2 this ranges from 4.73 to 4.99, indicating that the first mortgage and gross income are in proper relation. A figure above 5.0 would indicate a relatively high loan-to-value ratio or an unusually low appraised value. With the mortgage payment for apartment number 5 as a percentage of net income, 95.76 percent, note that the owner undertakes a considerable risk

TABLE 16–1
Apartment Annual Income and Operating Expenses

Income and Expenses*	Total	Per Room	Per Square Foot	Percent of Gross Income†
Gross possible rental income............	$459,792	$579.08	$2.64	99.5
Miscellaneous other income.............	2,400	3.02	0.01	0.5
Gross possible income..................	$462,192	$582.11	$2.66	100.0
Less vacancies and bad debts...........	−22,990	−28.95	−0.13	5.0
Effective gross income..................	$439,202	$553.15	$2.52	95.0
Less expenses				
Total payroll expenses.................	34,202	43.08	0.20	7.4
Electricity.............................	24,034	30.27	0.14	5.2
Gas (excluding heating fuel)...........	8,782	11.06	0.05	1.9
Water.................................	14,790	18.63	0.09	3.2
Heating fuel...........................	15,715	19.79	0.09	3.4
Management............................	23,110	29.11	0.13	5.0
Painting and decorating...............	4,160	5.24	0.02	0.9
Maintenance and repairs..............	5,084	6.40	0.03	1.1
Miscellaneous expenses...............	924	1.16	0.01	0.2
Insurance.............................	5,546	6.99	0.03	1.2
Real estate taxes......................	51,765	65.20	0.30	11.2
Reserves for replacements............	25,883	32.60	0.15	5.6
Total Expenses.........................	$213,995	$269.51	$1.23	46.3
Net Operating Income..................	$225,208	$283.64	$1.29	48.7

* Number of apartments, 160; number of rentable rooms, 794.
† Totals may not add to 100 percent because of rounding.

—if gross income decreases by a small amount, monthly net income is less than monthly mortgage payments.

The next series of ratios shows whether or not the properties are operated according to the prevailing gross income and expenses. The valuation ratios of Table 16–2 test the accuracy of the valuation relative to other apartments. The series of assessment ratios helps to determine the fairness and uniformity of property taxes. In short if the ratios of Table 16–2 vary markedly from typical ratios for the same type of property, the property manager should correct out-of-line income or expenses.

TABLE 16–2

Selected Financial Ratios on Five Apartment Buildings

Financial Ratios	Apartment Buildings				
	1	2	3	4	5
Loan ratios (first mortgage)					
Loan-to-value ratio..................	0.84	0.82	0.82	0.80	0.79
Loan per unit.......................	$15,000.00	$15,277.78	$16,968.32	$14,958.45	$14,488.63
Loan per room......................	3,472.67	3,536.98	6,019.26	3,463.76	4,344.12
First mortgage as a multiple of gross income.....................	4.90	4.99	4.83	4.89	4.73
Percent of mortgage payment to net income.......................	83.42	81.72	87.29	72.28	95.76
Income and expense ratios					
Gross possible income					
Per unit........................	3,062.89	3,060.11	3,513.25	3,062.05	3,062.50
Per room.......................	709.09	708.45	1,246.27	709.04	918.23
Per square foot..................	2.33	2.32	2.27	2.33	2.13
Expenses					
Per unit........................	1,438.53	1,357.91	1,625.85	1,350.33	1,384.24
Per room.......................	333.04	314.37	576.75	312.68	415.04
Per square foot..................	1.09	1.03	1.05	1.03	0.96
Percent of gross possible income....	46.97	44.37	46.28	44.10	45.20
Net Income					
Per unit........................	1,523.47	1,610.40	1,782.00	1,619.86	1,586.38
Per room.......................	354.78	372.83	632.14	375.09	475.64
Per square foot..................	1.16	1.22	1.15	1.23	1.10
Valuation ratios					
Percent of land value to total value....	21.69	1.05	12.24	1.91	10.08
Land value					
Per unit........................	3,858.26	195.20	2,527.74	358.39	1,852.67
Per room	893.23	45.19	896.68	82.99	555.49
Per square foot..................	2.93	0.15	1.63	0.27	1.29
Building value					
Per unit........................	13,930.95	18,433.33	18,124.92	18,382.27	16,526.05
Per room.......................	3,225.17	4,267.52	6,429.55	4,256.57	4,955.00
Per square foot..................	10.58	14.00	11.71	14.00	11.51
Land and building value					
Per unit........................	17,789.21	18,628.53	20,652.66	18,740.66	18,378.73
Per room.......................	4,118.40	4,312.71	7,326.22	4,339.56	5,510.48
Per square foot..................	13.51	14.15	13.35	14.27	12.80
Gross rate of return, percent........	17.22	16.43	17.01	16.34	16.66
Gross income multiplier.............	5.81	6.09	5.88	6.12	6.00
Overall capitalization rate...........	8.61	8.64	8.63	8.64	8.63
Assessment ratios					
Taxes paid per sq. ft. of building area.............................. $	0.35 $	0.35 $	0.30 $	0.35 $	0.33
Property taxes as a percent of market value......................	2.60	2.48	2.21	2.44	2.58
Property taxes paid per room......... $	107.00 $	107.00 $	162.00 $	106.00 $	142.00
Property taxes paid per apartment.... $	463.00 $	462.00 $	457.00 $	457.00 $	475.00
Property taxes as a percent of gross income......................	15.12	15.10	13.01	14.93	15.50
Total assessed value as a percent of market value....................	100.73	102.92	104.97	99.04	116.57
Number of apartment units...........	360	360	221	361	176

Shopping Center Management

The principal task of the shopping center manager is to select a compatible group of tenants. Indeed, a center may not survive unless a major tenant is committed to the project. With the major tenant attracting customers, the next task is to assemble a group of tenants who offer supplementary goods and services to customers who patronize the major tenant. The major tenants vary by the type of shopping center:

Type of Center	*Major Tenants*
Regional	Full-line department store
Community	Junior department store
Neighborhood	Supermarket

It should be noted that neighborhood centers tend to specialize in stores offering convenience goods and services such as laundry and dry cleaning, barber shops, drug stores, and beauty shops.

The importance of the leading tenant is such that the gross income produced by major tenants is shown separately. In addition, the manager tends to negotiate leases based on a minimum square-foot floor rental, with a provision that the tenant pays an overage rent based on a percentage of annual gross sales. As the shopping center prospers (increased sales volume), the owner receives minimum rent plus a percent of gross sales. For supermarkets this may be in the order of 1 percent to 1.5 percent, while for high-markup, low-turnover sales of a jewelry store, an overage rent of 8 percent of gross sales is fairly common.

Shopping Center Expenses. An income statement detailed in this way is illustrated in Table 16–3. The income is shown separately for major tenants, since on a per square-foot basis this is usually the lowest rent in a shopping center. The bargaining power of the major tenant is

TABLE 16–3
Shopping Center Income Statement

Gross Income		
Big discount store............................		$ 80,400
Supermarket....................................		48,000
Other retail space (@ $3 per sq. ft.)............		13,800
Overage rent...................................		30,000
Total Gross Income......................		$172,200
Less vacancy and collection loss		
Big discount (rent abatement assumed		
to be exercised in first 6 months of		
20-year term)................................	$5,400	
Supermarket and other (approx. 5%)........	3,100	
Total Vacancy Allowance......................		−8,500
Effective gross income estimate..............		$163,700
Operating expense estimate		
Estimated Total Expenses....................		−65,200
Estimated Net Operating Income.............		$ 98,500

such that the owner is usually willing to grant rent concessions to it. The overage rent is shown separately also, since it is dependent upon the volume of retail sales which depends largely on per capita income and competitive shopping centers. The expenses of operation, shown in summary form, are dominated by real estate taxes. Expenses of shopping center operation, shown as a percent of total receipts, would include:

Expenses	Percent of Total
Total receipts................................	100.0
Operating expenses:	
Building maintenance.......................	2.2
Parking lot, mall and other public areas...............................	7.1
Maintenance and housekeeping expenses.................................	14.1
Advertising and promotion.................	1.6
Real estate taxes..........................	20.8
Insurance.................................	1.0
General and administrative................	3.6
Total Operating Expenses....................	45.5*
Net Income.................................	54.5

* Totals do not agree since median percents from many centers are reported.
Source: Urban Land Institute.

The expense ratios are taken from current reports of regional centers in the Midwest. After property taxes, maintenance and administrative expenses tend to stand out, with expenses of operating the parking lot and public areas ranking next in importance. Before depreciation, regional centers (on the average) show a net income of 54.5 percent of total operating receipts. Since this is an average figure, experience of individual shopping centers may be expected to vary from these data.

The Merchants Association. The Merchants Association is a required management tool of the shopping center operator. Each tenant is required to participate in the Merchants Association—an organization that promotes the shopping center as an institution. Promotional plans are directed toward institutional types of advertising. In monthly meetings, member tenants review sales reports of each store so they may compare their own operation with neighboring tenants. The association works for uniform store hours and days of operation.

Tenants support the promotional expenses of the association usually according to their respective square foot floor areas. In some cases association charges are levied on a per front-foot basis or as a percentage of gross rent. The Urban Land Institute recommends allocation of association expense according to each tenant's sales volume. The association is governed by tenants in cooperation with the management, which usually retains a minority voting right.

Office Management

Like apartment properties, the gross income of an office building is governed by the utility of the rentable space. Utility, in turn, is dependent on special features important to the office tenant. Of prime importance is the site. In most cities the site must be adequate for office purposes, including space for a parking garage, preferably separate from the office building. Moreover, the site should be in the path of development. In this regard, the cost of land on a per square-foot or acre basis should be related to the density of use. Higher-priced land will be offset by a higher-use density so that the land price per square foot of office space tends to decline.

Furthermore, office buildings will be more rentable if they are built with compatible neighbors and with convenient access to present and future transportation facilities. There seems to be a premium placed on office locations near public buildings, federal, state, county and city.

A location in an established office district enables tenants to maintain a person-to-person contact with management offices, financial institutions, and professional offices serving business headquarters. A large body of businesses that have frequent contact with public officials are willing to pay a premium for these more convenient locations.

The rent structure of an office building, and therefore net income, relates to the building itself. While the older buildings conform to the alphabet shape, newer buildings are of the tower type, with open landscaped grounds. Both types of buildings are dependent on the appearance of surrounding structures. The appearance of the building itself, the exterior, the attractiveness of the lobby, and elevator service and corridors are other relevant features. Elevator service should provide for service at intervals of not more than 30 seconds. Newer office buildings have corridors meeting the current six-foot-wide standard and a lighting system of at least 75-foot candlepower.

Certain other factors control office building management. It is unwise to mix medical and dental tenants with business tenants. Their clients are inconsistent with normal business operations; medical offices generate noxious smells and require special-purpose construction, besides burdening utility and service facilities.

Another aspect of office buildings deserving mention relates to the efficiency of the building. In office management, rents are based on the net rentable area—the area leased by tenants measured from the middle of adjoining partitions. A 100,000-square–foot office building with a net rentable area of 76,000 square feet would indicate a 76-percent efficiency. By and large, the higher the ratio, the more profitable the building. Net income statements for office buildings follow accounting procedures used for apartments and shopping centers. They vary only in the importance attached to the net rentable area.

QUESTIONS FOR REVIEW

_____ 1. A property manager must
    a. market space in competition with other properties.
    b. provide the highest level of tenant services, without regard to cost of operation.
    c. keep rents slightly above the current market level to avoid overcrowding.
    d. increase gross receipts in a period of rising and continuing vacancies.

_____ 2. Rehabilitation
    a. requires changes in design.
    b. increases the risk factor.
    c. restores the building to a like-new condition.
    d. changes property use.

_____ 3. Property conversions
    a. change the use of the property.
    b. merely replace worn out equipment.
    c. require no changes in design.
    d. refer to modernization programs.

_____ 4. Receipts accepted in the name of the owner
    a. may be kept in the personal business account of the managing agent.
    b. must be held in a trust account.
    c. must be held in the owner's personal account.
    d. may be placed temporarily in the agent's savings account.

_____ 5. The management agreement should include
    a. a legal description of the property to be managed.
    b. the names of the parties to the agreement.
    c. the rate of compensation paid to the manager.
    d. all of the above.

_____ 6. Which of the following statements is correct?
    a. It is unnecessary to publish and distribute tenant rules.
    b. Property managers prefer to let tenants establish their own rules.
    c. Tenant rules benefit tenants and the owner.
    d. Tenant rules should be varied for each tenant.

_____ 7. Which of the following statements is correct?
    a. Generally owners do not require monthly income and expense statements.
    b. Gross income minus total operating expenses equals the management fee.
    c. Net receipts after fixed payments to the owner are paid to the property manager.
    d. None of the above.

_____ 8. Which of the following statements is correct?
   a. Rehabilitation refers to replacement of the heating system, lighting fixtures, and other building equipment.
   b. Rehabilitation requires a change in the design and use.
   c. Rehabilitation maintains the present use, restoring the building to a like-new condition.
   d. None of the above.

_____ 9. Which of the following statements describes a duty of the managing agent?
   a. The managing agent must use diligence in managing the premises.
   b. The managing agent is responsible only for annual statements of receipts and expenses.
   c. As part of the management agreement, the agent accepts responsibility for losses.
   d. The management's responsibility covers only normal operation of a building.

_____10. Under the owner grant of authority
   a. only the owner is given the authority to discharge and supervise employees.
   b. the managing agent has no authority to contract for services such as electricity, gas, fuel, water, and other utilities.
   e. owners delegate authority to lease premises up to a maximum lease term.
   d. the agent is generally prohibited from making mortgage payments from funds of the owner.

_____11. Which of the following items would be included in a management agreement?
   a. A legal description of the property, hold harmless clauses, and an agreement to render periodic statements.
   b. A statement of authority of the manager and an agreement to pay net income taxes of the owner.
   c. Provision for renewal options and a rate of compensation based on a percentage of net income.
   d. Names of the parties to the agreement and a clause holding the manager responsible for damage claims.

_____12. The management survey
   a. supports the market value estimate.
   b. is a comprehensive analysis of the economic aspects of real property.
   c. gives an estimate of local property taxes.
   d. is prepared for net income tax purposes.

_____13. If implemented, the recommended management program
   a. increases gross income.
   b. reduces the economic life of the property.

   c. reduces cash flow.
   d. typically maximizes net income.

_____14. A neighborhood analysis
   a. is irrelevant to property management plans.
   b. has no bearing on expected net income from an apartment.
   c. may indicate that the property use should be changed.
   d. determines the age and income of the surrounding tenants

_____15. Market analysis includes a study of
   a. original reproduction costs.
   b. vacancy rates and credit losses.
   c. balance sheet ratios.
   d. income tax factors.

_____16. Gross income analysis
   a. reports gross income in terms of the rent per square foot, per apartment, and per room.
   b. compares the gross income of the subject property with the gross income of other like properties.
   c. is complicated by the variation in services provided by the building owners.
   d. all of the above.

_____17. Management plans for a problem property should include a(n)
   a. capital improvement budget.
   b. analysis of income tax factors.
   c. recommended leasing program.
   d. all of the above.

_____18. Income and expense statements prepared by property managers

   a. do not include financial data on principal payments, mortgage interest, and real estate taxes.
   b. are usually evaluated in terms of their total cost over the management agreement.
   c. of larger management offices with 3,000 units or more generally show lower accounting costs per unit than accounting costs of management offices limited to 1,000 units or less.
   d. are inadequate for monitoring maintenance and repair expenses.

_____19. The management survey includes which of the following items?
   a. Real property inventory, gross income analysis, and a cash flow report.
   b. Market analysis, operating expense analysis, and a net income tax projection.
   c. Neighborhood analysis, an economic analysis of alternative plans, and operating expense analysis.
   d. Gross income analysis, market analysis, and an engineering construction survey.

_____20. The physical real property inventory points out
  a. deferred maintenance and examples of obsolescence.
  b. when the property should be sold for maximum gain.
  c. advantages of maintaining a poor level of maintenance.
  d. economic benefits of maintaining an obsolete building.

_____21. Which of the following items would be covered in a market analysis?
  a. An analysis of vacancy rates and credit losses.
  b. A review of leases, lease renewal options, and tenant turnover.
  c. The net income potential of a given property.
  d. All of the above.

_____22. The management survey requires a distinction between current and stabilized
  a. gross income.
  b. property taxes.
  c. net income taxes.
  d. expenses

_____23. Final recommendations included in the management survey would report
  a. the advisability of an immediate sale.
  b. a program of deferred maintenance.
  c. the most economical plan of operation in the light of the revised operating expense schedule as stabilized.
  d. the advantages of rent control.

_____24. High-rise elevator buildings
  a. include garden apartments.
  b. have four stories or more and are equipped with one or more elevators.
  c. may have three stories.
  d. have two stories or more and an elevator.

_____25. Garden apartments
  a. must have more than one building of at least four stories with elevators.
  b. consist of a one-unit building of more than one story with no elevator.
  c. consist of one or more buildings on a landscaped site.
  d. have at least one building of four stories.

_____26. The total floor area of an apartment building includes
  I. garages within the building.
  II. corridors and lobbies.
      a. I only.
      b. II only.
      c. Both I and II.
      d. Neither I nor II.

_____27. Apartment net income is calculated from the
   a. gross possible rental income and miscellaneous income.
   b. average gross income of the preceding three years.
   c. net operating income less federal net income taxes.
   d. net rental.

_____28. _____ is subtracted from gross possible income to arrive at net income.
   a. An allowance for vacancies and bad debts
   b. Operating expense
   c. A reserve for replacements
   d. All of the above

_____29. The principal task of the shopping center manager is to
   a. control the merchant association.
   b. supervise tenant advertising.
   c. select a compatible group of tenants.
   d. supervise custodial operations.

_____30. The shopping center manager often negotiates leases based on a
   a. minimum rent plus a percentage of gross sales.
   b. per square-foot rent.
   c. step-up rent.
   d. fixed rent.

_____31. Major tenants in a shopping center
   a. have no more drawing power than minor tenants.
   b. usually pay more rent per square foot than other tenants.
   c. usually rent on a lower per square-foot basis than other tenants.
   d. are required to subsidize shopping center advertising.

_____32. Before depreciation, regional shopping centers (on the average) show a net income of _____ percent of total operating receipts.
   a. 10.5
   b. 75.5
   c. 54.5
   d. 18.5

_____33. The merchant's association of a shopping center
   I. is governed by the shopping center management.
   II. promotes the shopping center as an institution.
      a. I only.
      b. II only.
      c. Both I and II.
      d. Neither I nor II.

_____34. Newer office buildings conform to the
   a. alphabet shape.
   b. cone shape.
   c. tower shape.
   d. cylindrical shape.

_____35. Which of the following is not considered in establishing rental fees for a tenant in a large office complex?
  a. Ratio of total space to rental space.
  b. Square foot area.
  c. Special services furnished (e.g., parking, security, and utilities).
  d. Cubic foot area.

_____36. _____ is recommended if building equipment is functionally obsolete.
  a. Rehabilitation
  b. Modernization
  c. Conversion
  d. Capitalization

_____37. Which of the following statements is correct?
  a. A full-line department store represents a major tenant for a community shopping center.
  b. A supermarket is a major tenant in a community shopping center.
  c. A regional center will have at least one full-line department store as a major tenant.
  d. A junior department store and a supermarket are major tenants of a neighborhood shopping center.

_____38. Percentage rents used in shopping center management are usually
  a. less than 1 percent of sales for stores with a high mark-up, high-sales turnover.
  b. 1 percent to 1.5 percent of sales for high-turnover, low mark-up stores.
  c. as high as 8 percent of sales for low mark-up, low-turnover stores.
  d. relatively low for low mark-up, low-turnover stores.

_____39. Which of the following statements is correct?
  a. Tenants may be required to support the promotional expenses of a shopping center merchant association according to their respective square-foot areas.
  b. Tenants manage the merchant association with funds supplied by the shopping center management.
  c. Tenants are given a minority voting right in a merchant association sponsored by shopping center management.
  d. Tenants must subscribe to shopping center management associations which are funded and controlled by shopping center management.

_____40. The net rentable area of an office building is calculated by
  a. computing the square foot area of each floor using outside dimensions.
  b. taking the inside measurements of heated space.

    c. computing the area leased by tenants as measured from the middle of adjoining partitions.

    d. calculating the square foot floor area from outside dimensions less the square foot area in halls and stair wells.

ANSWER KEY

1.	(*a*)	11.	(*a*)	21.	(*d*)	31.	(*c*)
2.	(*c*)	12.	(*b*)	22.	(*d*)	32.	(*c*)
3.	(*a*)	13.	(*d*)	23.	(*c*)	33.	(*b*)
4.	(*b*)	14.	(*c*)	24.	(*b*)	34.	(*c*)
5.	(*d*)	15.	(*b*)	25.	(*c*)	35.	(*a*)
6.	(*c*)	16.	(*d*)	26.	(*c*)	36.	(*b*)
7.	(*d*)	17.	(*d*)	27.	(*a*)	37.	(*c*)
8.	(*c*)	18.	(*c*)	28.	(*d*)	38.	(*c*)
9.	(*a*)	19.	(*c*)	29.	(*c*)	39.	(*a*)
10.	(*c*)	20.	(*a*)	30.	(*a*)	40.	(*c*)

SUGGESTED ADDITIONAL READING

Bowman, Arthur G. *California Real Estate Principles.* Pacific Palisades, Calif.: Goodyear Publishing Co., Inc., 1972, chap. 13.

Downs, James C., Jr. *Principles of Real Estate Management.* Chicago: Institute of Real Estate Management, 1975, chaps. 12 and 22.

Hines, Mary Alice. *Principles & Practices of Real Estate.* Homewood, Ill.: Richard D. Irwin, Inc., 1976, chap. 13.

Shenkel, William M. *Modern Real Estate Principles.* Dallas, Tex.: Business Publications, Inc., 1977, chap. 18.

17

Selling Real Estate

Few occupations are as demanding as the job of selling real estate. Not only does the salesperson require a technical knowledge of real estate matters, but the salesperson earns commissions only if the office has an adequate inventory of property listed for sale. As a consequence, a successful sales program requires two selling tasks: to the seller-client, sale of the *listing service*, and to the buyer-prospect, the sale of *real estate*.

In selling the listing service, the real estate broker competes with other brokers for available listings and with owners who elect to sell their own property. In both instances, the broker must show that (1) among competing brokers, he or she offers the best available service, and (2) to earn a commission, the broker performs an economic function. Consequently, successful brokers organize campaigns to sell listing services.

The real estate sales process shown in Figure 17–1 emphasizes, first, the problem of selling the listing and, secondly, selling the prospect. In the first part of the chapter, suggestions for selling the listing, unsolicited and solicited listings, precede recommendations for selling the prospect.

SELLING THE LISTING

The successful firm capitalizes on unsolicited listings. The public relations of the firm and their reputation develops listings from unsolicited sources. In addition, careful campaigns are organized to solicit listings actively. The soliciting program is especially important to the new firm that competes in new real estate markets.

482

FIGURE 17–1

The Real Estate Sales Process

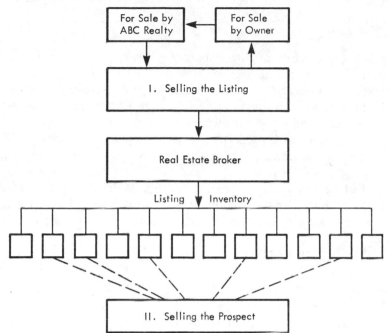

Unsolicited Listings

Unsolicited listings depend on a favorable office reputation. To exploit this advantage, qualifications of the firm are continually advanced. If the firm is a member of the local real estate board, the meaning of Realtor membership deserves continual public advertising. Prospective clients should know the general content of the Code of Ethics observed by Realtor members.

A public relations program should advertise prominent real estate sales and the appointment of new salespersons. The appearance of the office should denote professional activity. New listing inquiries should be furnished information on houses recently sold in the neighborhood.

Sales staff members further promote the organization by holding active memberships in community, civic, and professional associations that result in listings gained from acquaintances and friends familiar with the personal integrity of the firm and its staff. In addition, the established firm gains listings from former buyers and listings from friends and neighbors of former clients. Word-of-mouth advertising and the effective use of "sold" signs on property listed and successfully sold call attention to the selling broker. Some offices send out cards to "introduce your new neighbor" which is an effective way to advertise the fact that the firm was the successful selling agent.

Solicited Listings

Besides capitalizing on their reputation, brokers organize formal listing campaigns. In this respect the main object is to list property at a saleable price, inspect the property, and prepare the listed property for prospect inspection. Finally, meeting objections of the "for sale by owner" cases supplies an added source of new listings. A solicited listing system includes the highly organized farm system, telephone canvassing, and related listing techniques. Particular attention is given listings gained from "for sale by owner" cases.

The Listing Farm. This system refers to a deliberately planned listing campaign in a selected neighborhood. The neighborhood is selected for personal canvassing on an orderly basis by one salesperson for the listing canvass.

Neighborhoods selected for a farm must meet certain qualifications. Ideally, the neighborhood should consist of 400 to 500 houses with a suitable rate of turnover that qualifies as a listing farm. As a minimum, the neighborhood should illustrate:

1. A turnover factor of eight or less—meaning that, on the average, houses in the neighborhood will sell every eight years.
2. An area reasonably close to the sales office.
3. A homogeneous conforming neighborhood (Bruce T. Mulhearn, "The Listing Farm," in *In Search of Agreement* [Los Angeles, Calif.: California Real Estate Assn., 1974], p. 8).

The turnover factor is estimated from the total number of dwellings in the area and the number of properties sold in the preceding year. Such information may be gained from a count of for sale signs in the neighborhood and, in some communities, from sales recorded on local property tax records. In other instances, multiple listing offices identify sales activity by neighborhoods. By counting the properties for sale and by comparing the number of past sales per year, the salesperson makes an estimate of the anticipated average turnover factor by the following formula.

$$\text{Turnover factor} = \frac{\text{Total number of houses}}{\text{Total number of annual sales}}$$
$$= \frac{500}{80}$$
$$= 6.25$$

If the neighborhood qualifies, subdivision maps are divided into groups of 25 houses. The person assigned to the farm visits 25 houses daily so that in about a month's time personal knowledge will be gained over the listing possibilities of 500 houses.

In direct canvassing, the salesperson introduces the firm by stating firm qualifications, for example, number of houses recently sold in the neighborhood, size of the sales staff, and services rendered by the office. Each household is asked if there is a possibility of listing the house at the present time. Each call is recorded on a specially prepared form, listing the owner's name, phone number, the day they purchased the house, whether the property is rented or owned, whether it is owner-occupied, the number of children, and the time and date of call.

The canvassing record provides space for a code indicating whether the owner reacts positively to the canvass. Best results have been reported by late afternoon visits, avoiding weekends and evenings. Some salespersons distribute small gifts such as note pads, pencils, pens, or other give-aways to introduce their prepared approach.

Telephone Solicitation. As a source of listings, telephone solicitations assume two forms. The first represents a follow-up on an expired listing; the other concentrates on "cold" telephone canvassing. Though opinion seems divided on telephone solicitations for listings, sources recommending telephone solicitations advise salespersons to make telephone solicitations a regular part of their daily activities.

The follow-up on expired listings assumes that the staff has knowledge of an expired listing with another broker or an expired multiple listing exclusive. Some real estate boards regulate the solicitation of expired multiple listings; such regulations should be followed. If the local board approves soliciting expired listings, it is usually recommended that listings expire at least 24 hours before calling. The telephone inquiry—after an appropriate introduction—starts with a query on whether the home is still for sale. If the property remains unsold and is withdrawn from the market, the salesperson asks why the home was withdrawn. If there seem prospects for listing the property, the agent then asks permission to inspect the property. During the inspection, the seller is treated as a potential listing prospect.

Cold telephone canvassing for listing depends on prospective buyers who may be searching for a dwelling in a neighborhood in question. Here the agent calls a homeowner who is approached with the problem of the agent: namely, that the agent has a prospective buyer with an urgent desire to purchase a dwelling in that neighborhood. Each prospect is approached with the question "Do you know of houses that may be for sale in this neighborhood?" Though the person telephoned may not be a selling prospect, they may know neighbors planning to sell because of pending job transfers or other reasons.

Other Listing Sources. The range of listing sources covers a long list. Some offices regularly invite listings by classified advertisements. In the course of frequent contacts, brokers personally solicit listings from financial institutions and carefully canvass home builders. These methods are supplemented by direct-mail campaigns and follow-up telephone canvassing. Some Realtors read local newspapers closely for owners selling furniture in classified advertisements, announcements of company transfers and notices of divorces, weddings, and advertisements by owners who attempt to sell houses directly to buyers.

For Sale by Owner. These cases require a special approach. The special approach deals with owners who want to avoid commissions or who have had poor experiences with real estate brokers. In either case, the selling owner faces formidable obstacles. (1) The owner has no way of qualifying the buyers. (2) He or she must be ready to show the house without appointments. (3) The seller faces buyer prospects who want to buy the house free of the commission. (4) Few buyer prospects will voice objections to the seller, preventing the seller from responding to objections and stressing property advantages. (5) Moreover, the owner is generally unfamiliar with real estate financing arrangements and the price of competitive houses.

To overcome objections to paying commissions, one leading reference explains:

> There are several items besides the brokerage that you must be aware of when you sell a house. There are title insurance fees, escrow fees (or attorney fees), there are pro-rate taxes, insurance, and so on. There are recording fees and possibly loan payoff penalties. If the buyer is getting a government insured loan, there could be loan "points" that you would be required to pay, and then there are tax stamps, charges for paper work, and so forth.
>
> The total brokerage fee on this house at the price you have listed is $_____. This is divided between the listing and selling offices, and it's divided again between the brokers and the salesmen involved. In addition to that, the brokers pay the charge for putting the property on the Multiple Listing Service, and, of course, the listing broker pays for all of the advertising (Reprinted from *Using the Magic of Word Power to Multiply Real Estate Sales* by Les Davidson by permission of Executive Reports Corp. © Copyright 1972 by Executive Reports Corp., Englewood Cliffs, N.J., 07632).

This speech is followed by an offer to show the owner-seller how to calculate his net cash after sale.

It is probably universally true that sellers have exaggerated ideas of their property worth. Usually their concept of value is related to original cost plus the value they place on improvements made during their ownership. Or, they contemplate purchase of a larger dwelling, believing that the value of their house goes up commensurate with the increased cost of a new and better dwelling—which is usually in a better location.

The problem is resolved by suggesting that the buyer—not the seller—determines the market. By pointing out competitive houses for sale and recent sales or offering prices, the listing broker helps the buyer reach a realistic market price.

The consequences of an overpriced house are well known. Real estate sales personnel are reluctant to waste time on property overpriced to a point that discourages buyers. Brokers are unwilling to advertise over-priced property, and soon the unsold dwelling gains a reputation as un-saleable.

Preferably, the listing price should be within 5 percent of the sales price. Five percent is believed to be a reasonable margin of error in establishing comparable sales price. It is presumed that if the listing is properly merchandised, a dwelling should sell within the 5 percent margin. If comparable sales in the neighborhood have been secured, the listing agent should point out

1. Recent sales of listings of comparable properties in the same neighborhood.
2. That a properly priced property does not justify acceptance of a below-market offer from buyer prospects.
3. That financing terms may help evaluate the final offer—an FHA or VA financing plan may justify a higher price to compensate for mortgage discounting.
4. That, alternatively, a conventional loan without discount points in some circumstances may warrant an acceptance of an offer below the listed price.

Property Inspection. Assuming that the listing has been obtained, the initial inspection performs two functions: It acquaints the agent with features of the property, and it allows the agent to suggest ways in which the homeowner may help the sales. The seller should be instructed that the house will be shown by appointment. At this time the agent explains the importance of vacating the premises during the presence of buyer prospects. Further, the agent suggests small repairs that should be made and arrangements that make the house more attractive, for example, trim shrubbery, repair leaks, gutters, downspouts, paint trim, interior rooms, and the like. The owner is encouraged to place the property in the best possible condition.

Listing Aids. Regardless of the technique used to acquire new listings, the agent makes frequent use of two helpful aids: a *competitive market analysis* and the *listing presentation kit*. The competitive market analysis, illustrated in Figure 17–2, shows that the agent is familiar with the local real estate market. Of equal importance is the listing presentation kit that highlights qualifications of the sales office.

Note that the competitive market analysis gives listing information on

FIGURE 17–2

COMPETITIVE MARKET ANALYSIS
CALIFORNIA REAL ESTATE ASSOCIATION STANDARD FORM

PROPERTY ADDRESS_____ DATE_____

FOR SALE NOW:	BED-RMS.	BATHS	DEN	SQ. FT.	1ST LOAN	LIST PRICE	DAYS ON MARKET	TERMS

SOLD PAST 12 MOS.	BED-RMS.	BATHS	DEN	SQ. FT.	1ST LOAN	LIST PRICE	DAYS ON MARKET	DATE SOLD	SALE PRICE	TERMS

EXPIRED PAST 12 MOS.	BED-RMS.	BATHS	DEN	SQ. FT.	1ST LOAN	LIST PRICE	DAYS ON MARKET	TERMS

F.H.A. ---- V.A. APPRAISALS

ADDRESS	APPRAISAL	ADDRESS	APPRAISAL

BUYER APPEAL   MARKETING POSITION
(GRADE EACH ITEM 0 TO 20% ON THE BASIS OF DESIRABILITY OR URGENCY)

1. FINE LOCATION_____%   1. WHY ARE THEY SELLING_____%
2. EXCITING EXTRAS_____%   2. HOW SOON MUST THEY SELL_____%
3. EXTRA SPECIAL FINANCING_____%   3. WILL THEY HELP FINANCE...............YES____NO____%
4. EXCEPTIONAL APPEAL_____%   4. WILL THEY LIST AT COMPETITIVE MARKET VALUE..YES____NO____%
5. UNDER MARKET PRICE_____YES____NO____%   5. WILL THEY PAY FOR APPRAISAL...........YES____NO____%

       RATING TOTAL _____%   RATING TOTAL _____%

ASSETS_____
DRAWBACKS_____
AREA MARKET CONDITIONS_____
_____
RECOMMENDED TERMS_____

TOP COMPETITIVE MARKET VALUE.................................... $_____

PROBABLE FINAL SALES PRICE.. $_____

SELLING COSTS

BROKERAGE	$
LOAN PAYOFF	$
PREPAYMENT PRIVILEGE	$
FHA — VA POINTS	$
TITLE AND ESCROW FEES: IRS STAMPS, RECORDS, RECORDING	$
TERMITE CLEARANCE	$
MISC. PAYOFFS: 2ND T.D., POOL, PATIO. WTR. SFTNR., FENCE, IMPROVEMENT BOND.	$
	$
	$
TOTAL	$

TOTAL........$_____

NET PROCEEDS $_____   PLUS OR MINUS $_____

For these forms address California Association of Realtors,
505 Shatto Place, Los Angeles 90020. All rights reserved.

FORM CM 14
REV. 9/64

Source: *How to Negotiate in Listing and Selling Homes* (Los Angeles, Calif.: California Assn. of Realtors, 1977), p. 5.

dwellings presently for sale in the immediate vicinity. Sufficient detail allows the seller to compare local prices with the dwelling proposed for listing. In addition the form provides similar data on sales and expired listings of the past 12 months. Space is provided for judging the property proposed for listing. Even selling costs are summarized, showing the expected net sale proceeds for the property listed. Data on this form support the listing recommendation. Factual data establish credibility and discourage an overpriced listing.

The listing presentation kit covers a wide variety of brochures, examples of real estate advertisements, and lists of recently sold dwellings in the neighborhood. The E. G. Stassens, Inc., Realtors of Portland, Oregon, use a specially prepared 10-by-14 inch loose-leaf manual for presentation to prospects. Colorfully illustrated, the brochure outlines major professional affiliations, local memberships in real estate organizations, and states that the firm includes over 150 sales associates in ten area offices. The brochure illustrates the competitive market analysis form, the sales inspection report, and illustrates how net proceeds are calculated for the seller. The buyer qualification form, the buyer's move-in cost estimate, and services provided by the firm are reproduced in this presentation.

One of the last pages advises the seller on the recommended price:

> *Let's talk about the price of your home.* Your home is going to sell at market value: which is the amount a buyer is going to pay. The price range we recommend for your home is based on the following values:

1. Assessed value from the tax rolls.
2. Actual value to reproduce your home.
3. Loan value from the lending institution.
4. Market value of comparable homes.
5. The buyer's value . . . what he will pay today.

From a six-year survey of 3,000 dwelling sales, the brochure includes data showing the relation between the final sales price and the original asking price.

Average Days on Market	Percentage of Final Sales Price below Original Asking Prize (percent)
30 days	0–5
75 days	6–10
105 days	11–15
More than a year	Over 15

It will be appreciated that the listing kit promotes services of the Realtor and establishes the organization as a highly trained, professional real estate staff. Information is arranged to help the seller list at the market price under the most advantageous conditions.

QUALIFYING THE BUYER

With an inventory of saleable listings, the actual sale begins by expertly qualifying the buyer. Suppose the initial contact for the buyer prospect is in the office. Knowing that a successful sale results if the buyer is matched with the right house, a salesperson must learn the buyer's preferences and ability to finance a purchase. These steps are particularly critical if a buyer is purchasing a home for the first time. Such buyers are unlikely to be very knowledgeable on the mechanics of buying a house, real estate vocabulary, and prices, terms, and locational advantages. In these first contacts it is especially important not to use technical real estate terms unfamiliar to the layman. FHA points, easements, trust deeds, earnest money, and other trade jargon cause confusion and suspicion.

Buyer Qualification Forms

Most real estate offices use forms to qualify prospects. The form recommended by the McLennan Company of Park Ridge, Illinois, is shown in Figure 17–3. Space is provided for a written statement of the special requirements desired by the prospect, family information, income, occupation, and amount of money available for down payments. Other similar forms list hobbies of the owner which may dictate housing requirements.

The main advantage in working with the buyer to complete the form is that the salesperson learns the family's needs and desires. The buyer must be shown the house the family needs and can finance—the agent ignores the family's expressed dream, especially common for first home buyers. Some brokers advise visiting the buyer's home since buyers usually want to stay in the same environment. At any rate, it must be remembered that frequently home buyers express preferences for houses that they may not finance. Consider the salesperson that showed a prospect houses in the $50,000 to $60,000 price range only to discover that the financial position of the buyer restricted the family to a $40,000 dwelling. Questions that help identify buyer motives and residential preference (and financial ability) include

1. Do you own your own home? Where?
2. Must you sell your home before you buy?
3. Do you own other real estate? Where?
4. Have you owned many properties in the past?
5. Is any of your property currently for sale? Please describe it.
6. How long have you been looking for a home?
7. Why do you want to buy?
8. Have you seen anything you like?
9. What hobbies do you have?

FIGURE 17–3

RESIDENTIAL PREFERENCE FORM

NAME	☐ BUY ☐ RENT
ADDRESS	DATE
	HOME PHONE
BUS ADDRESS	BUS PHONE

NO OF CHILDREN	AGES OF GIRLS	AGES OF BOYS	

CASH DOWN	PRICE RANGE	MONTHLY PAYMENTS	GI	FHA	CONV.
TYPE OF HOUSE DESIRED		ROOMS NEEDED	BATHS NEEDED	BEDROOMS NEEDED

SPECIAL REQUIREMENTS (LOCATION DESIRED, ETC.)

_____

_____

_____

_____

_____

_____

_____

_____

PRESENT HOME ☐ OWN? ☐ RENT?	INCOME	OCCUPATION	

HEARD OF US FROM ☐ TRIBUNE ☐ DIRECT MAIL ☐ REFERRAL ☐ SIGN ☐ SUN-TIMES ☐ HERALD ☐ NEWS RELEASES ☐ OTHER	SALESMAN

RECORD OF PROPERTIES SHOWN OR SUBMITTED TO THIS PROSPECT

DATE	ADDRESS	BY	REMARKS

McLENNAN COMPANY ADHERES TO THE LAWS AND/OR REGULATIONS OF: THE NORTHWEST SUBURBAN REAL ESTATE BOARD, THE NATIONAL ASSOCIATION OF REALTORS, THE ILLINOIS DEPARTMENT OF REGISTRATION AND EDUCATION, AND THE U.S. DEPARTMENT OF HOUSING AND URBAN DEVELOPMENT.

Source: McLennan Company, Park Ridge, Illinois.

10. What did you like most about your last property?
11. What did you like least about your last property?
12. What style home do you like?
13. Do you want a large lot?
14. Do you want a swimming pool?
15. What is the maximum cash investment you can make in a home?
16. Do you have this money available now?
17. How much rent payments do you make now?
18. How much can you spend monthly for housing?
19. What area do you work in?
20. Do you have auto payments, other payments? Balance due? (Gael Himmah, *Real Estate Selling Magic*. rev. ed. [Creek, Calif.: Gael Himmah Publishing Co., 1974] p. 170.)

To help buyers reach decisions on these points some brokers prepare a statement of buyer's costs and payments. Such a tentative statement, adapted to VA, FHA, or conventional loans, is reproduced in Figure 17–4. Note that the down payment, closing costs, and monthly charges are shown. Increasingly Realtors add the after tax costs of home ownership, showing the advantage of property tax and mortgage interest income tax deductions for homeowners.

Showing the Prospect

It is presumed that salespersons are intimately familiar with their listing inventory. Some small feature that makes the property outstanding should be noted for further reference. With this background, the salesperson carefully plans the property inspection. Sellers are phoned in advance for appointments and instructed to leave the premises during the buyer inspection. During the tour, prospects are given detail on neighborhood advantages, schools, shopping, transportation, and recreation facilities. It is helpful to point out houses that have been recently sold and their sale price.

The Burke Agency with offices in several states advises that the first two or three houses shown to prospects should be progressively higher priced but lower than the prospect can realistically afford. At this point, they are shown a house that is considered best suited to their requirements. If this property is rejected, then the agency recommends showing higher priced houses until they locate a house that the prospect prefers.

In the house, prospects are shown the best room first, making certain that every room is open and visited by the prospect. The salesperson, alert to buyer attitudes, may inquire what it is they like best about this particular house. Finally, rules guiding the inspection may be summarized in three points.

FIGURE 17–4

Estimate Buyers' Costs and Payment

ESTIMATE BUYERS' COSTS & PAYMENT

Property Address: _____ Date: _____

V.A.		F.H.A.		OTHER	
Loan Origin. Fee	$ _____	Loan Origin. Fee	$ _____	Loan Fee	$ _____
Appraisal Fee	_____	Appraisal Fee	_____	Appraisal Fee	_____
Credit Report	_____	Credit Report	_____	Loan Tie-In Fee	_____
ALTA Title Policy	_____	ALTA Title Policy	_____	Credit Report	_____
Tax Impounds	_____	Tax Impounds	_____	ALTA Title Policy	_____
Fire Ins. Policy (1 yr.)	_____	Fire Ins. Policy (1 yr.)	_____	Tax Impounds	_____
Interest	_____	Interest	_____	Fire Ins. Policy	_____
Tax Service	_____	Tax Service	_____	Interest	_____
Misc. (Notary, Recording)	_____	Escrow Fee	_____	Tax Service	_____
	_____	Misc. (Notary, Recording)	_____	Escrow Fee	_____
	_____		_____	Draw 2nd T.D.	_____
	_____		_____	Misc. (Notary, Recording)	_____
TOTAL	$ _____	**TOTAL**	$ _____	**TOTAL**	$ _____
EST. MONTHLY PYMT.		**EST. MONTHLY PYMT.**		**EST. MONTHLY PYMT.**	
Purchase Price	$ _____	Purchase Price	$ _____	Purchase Price	$ _____
Loan Amount	_____	Loan Amount	_____	Loan Amount	_____
Down Payment	_____	Down Payment	_____	Down Payment	_____
Total Est. Costs	_____	Total Est. Costs	_____	Total Est. Costs	_____
Total Cash Inv.	$ _____	Total Cash Inv.	$ _____	Total Cash Inv.	$ _____
_____ % Interest _____ Yr. Loan		_____ % Interest _____ Yr. Loan		_____ % Interest _____ Yr. Loan	
Principal & Interest	_____	Principal & Interest	_____	Principal & Interest	_____
1/12 Annual Taxes	_____	1/12 Annual Taxes	_____	1/12 Annual Taxes	_____
1/12 Fire Ins. Prem.	_____	1/12 Fire Ins. Prem.	_____	1/12 Fire Ins. Prem.	_____
EST. PAYMENT	$ _____	**EST. PAYMENT**	$ _____	**EST. PAYMENT**	$ _____

This sheet has been prepared to assist the buyer in computing his charges. Whenever possible we have used the MAXIMUM charges that can be expected. Lenders and escrow companies will vary in their charges; therefore, these figures cannot be guaranteed.

I have read the above figures and acknowledge receipt of a copy of this form.

Presented by: _____

BUYER _____   ADDRESS _____

BUYER _____   OFFICE PHONE _____

BUYER'S ADDRESS _____ PHONE _____   APPROVED BY: _____

Source: *How to Negotiate in Listing and Selling Homes* (Los Angeles Calif.: California Assn. of Realtors, 1977), p. 58.

1. Ask questions to arouse interest.
2. Show houses that the prospect may visualize as the proper setting for his family.
3. Be sincere, emphasizing how the home you are showing answers his or her needs.

Salespersons are advised not to take a defensive attitude toward prospect objections; the agent responds to objections by emphasizing positive features of the property.

MEETING BUYER OBJECTIONS

Presuming that the buyer is motivated, the next issue is to respond to prospective buyer objections. It is natural for buyers to have objections concerning specific problems, and by responding to objections, the salesperson helps convince the prospect that he has selected the right house. Usually, it is necessary to compromise some of the buyer's requirements. Compromise is reached by stressing good points of the house that overcome minor problems. Some of the more common objections are met with commonsense replies.

1. *The Monthly Payments Are Too High.* The monthly payment schedule is divided into principal payments, mortgage interest payments, real estate taxes, and homeowner's insurance. Compare the effective monthly mortgage payment after taxes, and then add the probable utility expenses to show total monthly housing expense. The effective monthly payment (after income taxes) will reveal the advantage of homeownership over rental occupancy. The total housing expense should be compared to annual earnings, showing how much of the monthly paycheck goes to housing.

2. *The Prospect Considers a New House a Better Buy Than a Used One.* This response is countered by indicating that an existing house avoids costs encountered in buying a new house. Landscaping and other items such as curtain rods and drapery rods are seldom offered by a contractor of a new home but included in existing homes.

3. *The Prospect Would Rather Continue to Rent.* In showing the effective monthly payment after income tax deductions, explain further that a portion of the monthly payment adds to their equity every month. Indicate also that construction costs are continually rising and that land prices have shown a substantial rise over the last ten years.

4. *The Prospect Wants to Think It Over.* If you have shown the proper house and it is clearly to the benefit of the buyer to purchase, insist that they think it over now, and make a decision while the salesperson is available to answer questions. If the prospect declines to purchase houses shown, a revisit to selected houses reinforces the fact that a

particular house meets buyer needs within the required price range. Failing here, the salesperson is advised to make a future definite appointment to inspect other houses which may be available next week.

A request to "think over" the decision indicates that the buyer has a hidden objection which the salesperson must find by asking further questions. If the response is that the price is too high, refer to other houses in the neighborhood that have recently sold in the same price range.

At some point, the buyer may suggest an offering price below the listing price. If it is unrealistically low, the salesperson should point out that the seller is unlikely to consider the offer made in good faith and will refuse to negotiate further. Explain further than the seller cannot be honestly advised to consider such an offer. While not suggesting an offering price, the salesperson should discourage unrealistic offers that would not interest the selling owner. If the buyer's income qualifies for the purchase of the selected house, encourage the buyer to make a realistic offer. In short, salespersons realize that a listed house sold at the market price benefits both buyer and seller.

5. Interest Rates Are Too High. There are two responses to this objection. The first requires that the salesperson work out monthly payments under the most probable financing plan. For example, a 30-year loan for $40,000 at 9 percent interest requires a monthly payment of $322. A one percentage point decline in the interest rate (8%) would reduce payments to $293.60 per month—a monthly savings of $28.40. Therefore, even if interest rates dropped by one percentage point, monthly savings would be less than 10 percent of the total mortgage payments. This difference would be reduced by the income tax deductibility of mortgage interest rates.

A related point is that construction costs are likely to increase at a greater rate than the savings in the interest rate—assuming interest rates go down which, in itself, is an uncertain proposition. Or, if the value of the dollar declines, i.e., inflation continues, the buyer has a fixed obligation that is paid back in cheaper dollars.

The more important consideration is the forecast in local real estate values. If the record suggests a continual long-run increase in property values, a purchase today avoids higher prices of later years—or even next year. By postponing a decision to buy on grounds that interest rates may drop exposes the prospect to the risk of higher future prices with their higher monthly and down payments.

6. Housing Prices Will Decline. This is really an objection against high prices. If the salesperson has knowledge of price trends in the neighborhood, it would be prudent to show evidence of resales in the neighborhood indicating how past housing prices have increased. Moreover, reference to local building costs shows average construction cost increases of 7 to 10 percent over the last ten years. While it is difficult to predict future prices realistically, it is fairly clear that if past trends continue, postponing a decision in the belief that prices will come down is probably more risky than purchase today at relatively low prices. Moreover, if the party is a renter, housing costs increase with higher rents, placing the prospect in an even more unfavorable position.

7. *The Location Is Too Far to Commute.* Prospects unfamiliar with the location judge the dwelling by the distance from employment. By reviewing the actual driving time from the house to source of employment, it may be readily apparent that, compared to the present housing, the new house represents only a few minutes a day in additional commuting time. By establishing the time differential, the salesperson may then ask if the additional few minutes a day in commuting does not justify the purchase of a suburban dwelling with all its features attractive to the buyer prospect. Emphasize driving time, not distance.

The main point in answering objections is that buyers may mask true reasons for not accepting the offer. By responding to objections with probing questions, the salesperson learns the true objections permitting the agent to respond by (1) explaining main features of the property or (2) showing other suitable housing that more nearly meets buyer needs and financial capacity. There is no substitute for the searching, questioning probe to identify true buyer objectives.

NEGOTIATING THE SALE

Suppose the buyer makes a reasonable offer in terms of the price, financing, and date of possession. Acceptance of the offer partly depends on advance preparation of the salesperson. If the offer is below the listing price, the agent must review the competitive market analysis as support for the offer. Points of comparison, prices, and housing features are made with the property listed. Next the salesperson prepares a statement of seller costs showing net proceeds of the sale resulting from this offer. The net proceeds show the price, terms, the date of closing, possession, and the conditions affecting the transfer of personal property. The salesperson covers the advantages and disadvantages of the offer to the seller.

If your competitive market analysis is up to date, you should be able to advise buyers what price a particular type of house should be selling for, and if they don't want to lose the house, they must make their offer at the fair market value. Convince the buyer that the offer should be written with the suitable deposit.

Adequately prepared, the offer is presented at the earliest possible appointment with the seller. Telephone calls are ineffective at this point. A copy of the listed offer is explained to the seller without being negative, i.e., "though the price is less than you expected, it's the best I can negotiate." Or, in equally bad form, "it is the highest price the buyer would consider."

Realistic Offers

Explain further that the offer is realistic in terms of other available properties. Point out the competition the seller faces in asking for a higher price or waiting for other possible offers. Suppose the listed price is $50,000 and the prospects offered $42,000. If your analysis shows that the offer is reasonable, indicate to the seller that a counteroffer of $46,000 may jeopardize the sale. In effect, the seller would be risking $42,000 for the off-chance that he would gain an additional $4,000.

Again, if the offer is reasonable, most sellers would see the risk of a counteroffer. After your presentation of competitive market analysis, and a careful review of the costs incurred by the seller showing his net proceeds, ask for acceptance.

The seller will respond in one of three ways: I'll take it, I'll think it over, or I believe the offer is too low. If he accepts, have the seller sign and depart quickly. If the seller delays, discover the real objection. Is it the price, sale terms, date of possession, or transfer of personal property? After identifying the objection, the salesperson must continue to explain and negotiate, pointing to the buyer's bargaining position.

In the last analysis, successful salespersons approach the seller with considerable enthusiasm about the fact that they have obtained the best possible offer. In the preparation, the salesperson studies answers to possible seller objections. The presentation depends partly on how long the property has been on the market, the seller's motivation, and the reasonableness of the offer relative to market value. Some brokers advise agents to remind sellers that if they do not accept the offer the prospective buyer has instructed the broker to withdraw the offer, void the contract, and return the check.

Counteroffer

The dissatisfied seller opens the door to a counteroffer. The counteroffer by the seller should represent the lowest price the seller is willing to accept. Consider the case of a realistic offer on a highly overpriced listing. Sellers should realize from the agent's explanation why the offer is good, why the terms of the agreement are fair, and why the seller cannot expect to get above market price. Emphasizing net proceeds of the sale helps the seller to reach a decision.

Negotiations on counteroffers are more successful if buyers and sellers work to split the difference. Counteroffers should be presented immediately with least possible delay in written form. Both parties should be given honest advice on a realistic negotiated price.

To sum up, the buyer is made to realize that he will purchase a prop-erty at the fair market price. The seller must be convinced of the reason-ableness of the offer by reference to the competitive market analysis and the statement of the net proceeds realized from the sale. In the negoti-ation, the agent has the obligation to sell property at the highest reason-able market value on terms acceptable to a buyer and seller. The buyer completes the transaction understanding that the purchase is at the fair market value paying only for improvements to the dwelling that contrib-ute to the market value.

CLOSING THE SALE

Closing the sale may require that the salesperson convince the seller to accept an offer below the listing. Usually the final presentation is made in the seller's home. It may be appropriate to explain, for example, that the buyers have offered $50,000 which is the maximum that they can finance in down payment and monthly costs. The salesperson, knowing that the buyer has other options, may indicate that they are unwilling to pay more than $50,000 since they carefully considered purchasing a house in the same neighborhood for $45,000 which is more nearly within their budget.

Presenting the Final Offer

After going through this analysis, the salesman calculates the balance to the seller referring to the final offering price. A work sheet for this purpose is shown in Figure 17–5. Final figures would be worked out in advance so that the estimate of net proceeds is reasonably accurate. If estimated net proceeds are in error, the error should be above the actual cost.

In dealing with the seller, present the buyer's offer as quickly as possi-ble. Until the contract is signed and delivered, both parties have the right to withdraw offers and counteroffers. The seller is approached with the idea that the agent has secured the best possible sales price. The seller should not be made to feel that the buyer will accept counteroffers or contract changes.

Some brokers prefer to present the final offer to sellers in the real estate office rather than the home. In moving to the closing, the seller should be told something about the buyers—their search for a house, their prefer-ences, what good neighbors they will make, and the high probabilities of their credit approval.

Closing Negotiations

Occasionally, the seller honestly does not desire to sell, which is ex-pressed in an overpriced listing. Or, since the listing date, the seller may

FIGURE 17–5

Estimate of Seller's Closing Costs

SELLER'S NAME _____ DATE _____

PROPERTY ADDRESS _____

SALESMAN: _____ SELLING PRICE $ _____

ENCUMBRANCES:

First Trust Deed .... $ _____

Second Trust Deed .... _____

Other Encumbrances .... _____

TOTAL ENCUMBRANCES .... $ _____

GROSS EQUITY $ _____

ESTIMATED EXPENSES

Policy of Title Insurance .... $ _____

State & County Tax Stamps .... _____

Estimated Escrow Fees .... _____
   (Use VA $200)

Termite Inspection & Report .... _____

Prepayment penalty if any:

VA: none, FHA: none .... _____

Cal-Vet: 2% within 2 years .... _____

Conv: figure 6 months interest on unpaid balance .... _____

Lender's Demand or Beneficiary.. _____
   Average $25

Reconveyance Fee (loan Payoff)... _____
   Average $25.

Proration of interest on existing loan (1 month's) .... _____

Miscellaneous: (Avg. $100.) .... _____

FHA or VA loan fee _____ % of new loan .... _____

Sales Fee _____% of sales price .... _____

Home Warranty .... $ _____

APPROXIMATE TOTAL COSTS .... $ _____ $ _____

APPROXIMATE NET CASH TO SELLER .... $ _____
   (Gross equity less total costs)

POSSIBLE CREDITS OR DEBITS:

Proration of tax

Return balance on impound account, proration or cancellation of fire insurance.

This sheet has been prepared to assist the seller in computing charges. Lenders & Escrow Companies will vary in charges, therefore, these figures cannot be guaranteed.

I have read the above figures and acknowledge receipt of same.

_____   _____

Seller

Source: *How to Negotiate in Listing and Selling Homes* (Los Angeles, Calif.: California Assn. of Realtors), p. 79.

have changed his mind about selling. The agent should determine if the seller is really serious about selling and the strength of his motivations. In presenting the offer lower than the quoted price, the salesperson must be certain that the offer is in writing with the buyer's check, representing the highest offer attainable. The buyer's reasons for arriving at the price must be explained to the seller, and with the competitive market analysis at hand, the chances of acceptance are high.

Finally, in the counteroffer the agent must make certain that the counteroffer is the lowest figure attainable from the seller. The buyer should understand the rationale of the seller in presenting the counteroffer and that it is the last compromise available from the seller. In all these negotiations, the agent works toward a fair solution with a positive and constructive attitude.

By asking both parties to restate their reasons for their offers and counteroffers, the agent attempts to reduce the difference between offer and counteroffer to so many dollars per month. And, too, it is made clear that both parties undertake risks in allowing the house to remain on the market while both buyer and seller are exploring other options.

QUESTIONS FOR REVIEW

_____ 1. The successful sales program requires
   a. the sale of listing services and the sale of real estate.
   b. the sale of real estate and an effective office program.
   c. the sale of listing services and an understanding of legal matters.
   d. a college trained sales staff.

_____ 2. Unsolicited listings depend on
   a. the listing farm operation.
   b. a large sales staff.
   c. a favorable office reputation.
   d. none of the above.

_____ 3. Which of the following statements is correct?
   a. Neighborhoods selected for a listing farm should not have more than 100 houses.
   b. The neighborhood should have a turnover factor of eight or less.
   c. The turnover factor refers to the total number of new dwellings constructed in a neighborhood.
   d. A neighborhood considered for a listing farm should show a wide diversity of dwellings.

_____ 4. Telephone solicitations assume two forms:
   a. Solicitations of listings held by other brokers and cold telephone canvassing.

    b. Follow-ups on expired listings and telephone canvassing of contractors.

    c. Cold telephone canvassing and telephone canvassing of newly married couples.

    d. A follow-up on an expired listing and cold telephone canvassing.

_____ 5. Which of the following are obstacles faced by the selling owner?

    a. The owner has no way of qualifying buyers.

    b. Buyer prospects are unlikely to voice objections to the seller.

    c. The owner is unfamiliar with real estate financing arrangements.

    d. All of the above.

_____ 6. To prevent buyers from overpricing their houses, brokers should point out

    a. recent sales of comparable properties in the same neighborhood.

    b. distress sales in the same neighborhood.

    c. houses that have sold considerably above the house listed.

    d. houses that have sold considerably less than the house listed.

_____ 7. In accepting a listing, the broker should instruct the seller

    a. that the house will be shown only by appointment.

    b. of the importance of vacating the premises during the presence of buyer prospects.

    c. of ways to make the house more attractive.

    d. all of the above.

_____ 8. In listing houses for sale

    a. the seller determines the market.

    b. the broker determines the market.

    c. the buyer determines the market.

    d. none of the above.

_____ 9. Which of the following are elements of the competitive analysis?

    a. Property for sale now.

    b. Property sold over the last 12 months.

    c. Listings that have expired in the past 12 months.

    d. All of the above.

_____10. The purpose of the competitive market analysis is to:

    a. give the listing broker information on property available for sale.

    b. allow the seller to compare local prices with the dwelling proposed for listing.

    c. show the seller how to reduce selling costs.

    d. encourage underpriced listings.

_____11. Listing kits:

    a. outline major professional affiliations.

      b.   illustrate the sale inspection report.

      c.   demonstrate how net proceeds are calculated for the seller.

      d.   all of the above.

_____12.   In recommending a listing price, the listing broker would refer **to:**

      a.   the actual value to reproduce the house.

      b.   market value of comparable houses.

      c.   the dwelling's insurable value.

      d.   all of the above.

_____13.   In qualifying the buyer,

      a.   the salesperson must learn the buyer's preferences and abilities to finance purchase.

      b.   the salesperson eliminates prospects buying houses for the first time.

      c.   the salesperson educates the buyer on technical real estate terms.

      d.   none of the above.

_____14.   Which of the following questions help identify buyer motives?

      a.   Do you own your own home?

      b.   Must you sell your home before you buy?

      c.   How long have you been looking for a home?

      d.   All of the above.

_____15.   To expedite the sale of houses, Realtors often emphasize:

      a.   neighborhood appreciation.

      b.   local property taxes.

      c.   the after-tax cost of homeownership.

      d.   neighborhood incomes.

_____16.   In responding to buyer objections, the salesperson is advised to

      a.   ignore the objection.

      b.   explain how the buyer is wrong in voicing objections.

      c.   ask reasons for the objection.

      d.   emphasize positive features of the property.

_____17.   Which of the following statements is correct?

      a.   It is usually necessary to compromise some of the buyer's requirements.

      b.   Compromise is reached by stressing good points of a house that overcome minor problems.

      c.   It is natural for buyers to have objections concerning specific problems.

      d.   All of the above.

_____18.   If the buyer-prospect believes the monthly payments are **too high,** you are advised to

      a.   abandon the prospect.

> *b.* indicate the effective monthly mortgage payment after income taxes.
>
> *c.* show the prospect a house financed under federally subsidized mortgages.
>
> *d.* compare monthly payments to monthly rent for luxury apartments.

_____19. Which of the following statements is correct?

> *a.* New houses are always a better buy than older houses.
>
> *b.* New houses appreciate faster than older houses.
>
> *c.* An existing house avoids the costs encountered by purchasers of a new house.
>
> *d.* Existing houses are usually in a better location than newer houses.

_____20. Which of the following is a recommended response to prospects who want to "think it over?"

> *a.* Encourage the prospect to think it over now while the salesperson is available to answer questions.
>
> *b.* Revisit other houses to reinforce the fact that a particular house meets buyer's needs.
>
> *c.* Make a future definite appointment to inspect other houses which may be available next week.
>
> *d.* All of the above.

_____21. If the buyer prospect makes an unrealistically low offering price

> *a.* point out that the seller is unlikely to consider the offer made in good faith and refuse to negotiate further.
>
> *b.* explain that the seller cannot be honestly advised to consider such an offer.
>
> *c.* discourage unrealistic offers that would not interest the selling owner.
>
> *d.* all of the above.

_____22. If the buyer-prospect objects on grounds that interest rates are too high,

> *a.* work out a monthly payment schedule under the most probable financing plan.
>
> *b.* show that construction costs are likely to decrease at a greater rate than savings and interest rates.
>
> *c.* show that fixed mortgage payments are paid back in more expensive dollars.
>
> *d.* none of the above.

_____23. Buyers who object that the location is too far to commute should be told

> *a.* the actual driving time from the house to source of employment.

b. that more house per dollar may be purchased at more distant locations than more centrally located housing.

c. the driving time, not distance to shopping and employment.

d. all of the above.

_____24. By responding to objections with probing questions, the selling agent may

a. respond by explaining the main features of the property.

b. show other suitable housing that more nearly meets buyer needs and capacities.

c. learn true buyer objections.

d. all of the above.

_____25. Which of the following is preferred in presenting an offer below the listing price?

a. Though the price is less than you expected, it is the best the buyer is able to negotiate.

b. It is the highest price I can obtain.

c. Present the offer two weeks after the buyer submits the offer.

d. None of the above.

_____26. The average turnover factor is calculated by

a. dividing the total number of houses by the total number of annual sales.

b. dividing the total number of houses by the total newly constructed dwellings.

c. dividing the total number of sales by the number of real estate brokers.

d. calculating 10 percent of the total number of houses.

_____27. Which of the following would not be included in estimating buyer's closing costs?

a. Appraisal fees and credit report charges.

b. Fire insurance policy and escrow fees.

c. The real estate commission and title policy.

d. Loans, origination fees, and appraisal fees.

_____28. Which of the following items would be included in estimating the buyer's monthly payments?

a. Monthly principal and interest.

b. One twelfth of estimated annual property taxes.

c. One twelfth of estimated fire insurance premiums.

d. All of the above.

_____29. In showing the prospect a house, leading brokers recommend that

a. salespersons ask questions to arouse interest.

b. salespersons show houses that prospects may visualize as the proper setting for family.

c. salespersons be sincere.

d. all of the above.

_____30. Which of the following would *not* be included in estimating the closing expenses assumed by the seller?
    a. Escrow fees.
    b. Termite inspection costs.
    c. The real estate sales commission.
    d. Monthly costs for fire insurance.

_____31. Which of the following statements is correct?
    a. The listing kit promotes services of the Realtor and establishes the organization as a highly trained, professional real estate staff.
    b. The listing kit shows services offered to the buyer.
    c. The listing kit helps the seller list the house 10 percent above the market value.
    d. The listing kit shows the buyer how to negotiate for the lowest possible price.

_____32. In qualifying the buyer,
    a. the selling agent must learn buyer housing preferences without reference to their financial capacity.
    b. the agent must learn the dominant buying motives by asking the right questions.
    c. salespersons are careful not to reveal buyer's costs and payments.
    d. the selling agent shows the house to a prospect before buyer qualifications are established.

_____33. Which of the following statements is *not* correct?
    a. It is natural for buyers to have objections concerning specific problems.
    b. Buyers' requirements are seldom compromised.
    c. The salesperson should not respond to buyer objections.
    d. The salesperson is advised not to take defensive attitudes toward prospect objections.

_____34. Postponing a decision to buy on grounds that interest rates may drop
    a. exposes the prospect to the risk of higher future prices.
    b. is always in the best interest of the buyer-prospect.
    c. is an action that favors both buyer and seller.
    d. shows the advantages of renting over a housing purchase.

_____35. There is no valid substitute for
    a. homeownership.
    b. an open listing.
    c. the searching, questioning probe to identify true buyer objectives.
    d. all of the above.

_____36. In presenting an offer to the seller,
  a. and the seller delays, discover the real objection.
  b. and after identifying seller objections to the offer, the sales-
        person must continue to explain and negotiate.
  c. approach the seller with considerable enthusiasm that the
        buyer has made the best possible offer.
  d. all of the above.

_____37. Unsolicited listings depend on
  a. the size of the sales staff.
  b. the length of time the business is in operation.
  c. a favorable office reputation.
  d. the size of the community.

_____38. Which of the following help maximize unsolicited listings?
  a. Announcement of new salesperson appointments.
  b. A professional-appearing office.
  c. Active membership in community, civic, and professional as-
        sociations.
  d. All of the above.

_____39. In responding to a buyer who makes an unrealistically low offer,
          the salesperson should
  a. show the buyer other houses.
  b. hope that the seller makes a counteroffer.
  c. discourage unrealistic offers that would not interest the selling
        owner.
  d. none of the above.

_____40. Suppose the buyer makes a reasonable offer,
  a. acceptance of the offer partly depends on the advance prepa-
        ration of the salesperson.
  b. if the offer is below the listing price, the agent must review the
        competitive market analysis to support the offer.
  c. the salesperson prepares a statement of seller costs showing
        net proceeds of the sale.
  d. all of the above.

ANSWER KEY

1. (*a*)	11. (*d*)	21. (*d*)	31. (*a*)
2. (*c*)	12. (*d*)	22. (*a*)	32. (*b*)
3. (*b*)	13. (*a*)	23. (*d*)	33. (*c*)
4. (*d*)	14. (*d*)	24. (*d*)	34. (*a*)
5. (*d*)	15. (*c*)	25. (*a*)	35. (*c*)
6. (*a*)	16. (*d*)	26. (*a*)	36. (*d*)
7. (*d*)	17. (*d*)	27. (*c*)	37. (*c*)
8. (*c*)	18. (*b*)	28. (*d*)	38. (*d*)
9. (*d*)	19. (*c*)	29. (*d*)	39. (*c*)
10. (*b*)	20. (*d*)	30. (*d*)	40. (*d*)

SUGGESTED ADDITIONAL READING

Davidson, Les. *Using the Magic of Word Power to Multiply Real Estate Sales.* Englewood Cliffs, N.J.: Executive Reports Corp., 1976, chap. 4.

How to Negotiate in Listing and Selling Homes. Los Angeles, Calif.: California Assn. of Realtors, 1977, chap. 1.

In Search of Agreement. Los Angeles, Calif.: California Real Estate Assn., 1974, chap. 5.

Rybka, Edward F. *The Number One Success System to Boost Your Earnings in Real Estate.* Englewood Cliffs, N.J.: Prentice-Hall, Inc., 1971, chap. 7.

Wigginton, F. Peter. *The Complete Guide to Profitable Real Estate Listings.* Homewood, Ill.: Dow Jones-Irwin, 1977.

Part IV

Real Estate and the Community

18

Subdivision Regulations

Subdivision regulations solve two problems: they insure that subdivision lots conform to physical standards required by local and state laws, and they help prevent misrepresentations, fraud, and deceit in the sale of subdivided land. Before land can be sold as a recorded lot, it must have streets that conform to the local traffic pattern and it must meet other requirements of a planned residential subdivision. In addition, state laws usually call for approval of subdivided land before it may be sold. The intent is to prevent the sale of land for residential purposes if the land is physically unsuitable for residential use; for example, swampy or mountainous land. To this end even advertising material comes under the review of certain state agencies that govern subdivision sales.

Subdivision regulations requiring minimum standards of design, utility, and other physical characteristics contribute to better neighborhoods. In subdivisions developed before regulations were provided, street width and layout was often nonconforming to the street plan of adjoining subdivisions, and street and drainage facilities were often so inadequate that constant repair and maintenance raised government expenses and led to higher local taxes. Inadequate water and sewer systems that must be replaced because of faulty original construction represent a waste that is shifted to the general taxpayer in the form of deteriorating neighborhoods or higher costs of maintenance.

In the more urban areas, it is no longer possible to subdivide single-family dwelling lots with a width of 17.5 feet, typical of the downtown fringe area in Tampa, Florida, before urban renewal projects led to redevelopment. In this respect, subdivision regulations restrict residential density to acceptable levels.

State regulations require approval of a subdivision before land is offered for sale and, in general, prevent shady practices of the past. Misleading advertising or the purchase of lots that have no access are prevented by the restrictive state regulations such as those in California and other states. The sale of lots over interstate boundaries by mail and telephone, and the inadequacy of state laws respecting interstate sales has led to control of interstate land sales by a federal agency. Because of the growing importance of subdivision regulations, real estate agents are required to observe local, state and federal laws governing the sale of recorded lots.

For a recorded subdivision to be acceptable, local regulations must be such that each lot may be identified by a metes and bounds description as filed and shown in a map recorded in the appropriate county office. Subdivisions that are unrecorded have no force or effect.

The real issue in working with recorded subdivisions lies in understanding regulations governing their development and sale. The practitioner must observe local ordinances and regulations, state laws governing the sale of subdivisions, and—in the case of interstate land sales—general provisions of the Interstate Land Sales Full Disclosure Act. A land sale might be illegal or voidable if these regulations are not observed.

LOCAL SUBDIVISION REGULATIONS

The following discussion covers typical procedures applying to new subdivisions. Variations occur, according to the local ordinances of each community. The purpose of these regulations, administered by local agencies, are directed to the planning function. Before the owner may describe land by lots and blocks, or even sell newly subdivided property, he must conform to local subdivision regulations controlling the physical aspects of each lot. A review of typical requirements will show how recorded subdivision regulations affect the purchase, sale, and development of new subdivisions.

Local Approval

At the outset, local regulations, which conform to state law governing local ordinances, usually define subdivisions as "the division of a parcel of land into five or more lots or parcels for the purpose of transfer of ownership or building development. . . ." The number of lots defining a subdivision may vary between jurisdictions. There is usually a provision to exempt agricultural land, which is typically defined as parcels of five acres or more that do not involve a new street. Because subdivision regulations must conform to local land use controls, subdivisions must be approved by several offices.

The Planning Commission. The local planning commission is responsible for approving all proposed developments as they relate to the general or master plan. The planning commission coordinates the review of the subdivision by local officials so that the proposed subdivision conforms with zoning, building, and other regulations that affect their sale and development. The planning commission has the ultimate responsibility for approving the design of the plan. The layout of roads, public spaces, and lots should conform to the existing street pattern and utility layout.

The County Engineer. The local official responsible for the water supply, sewer, and drainage systems must pass on the adequacy of the utility system. This office is also responsible for the construction of streets, roads, and the proper location, construction, and size of utilities, so that the subdivision will be developed on a sound basis leading to economy in construction and maintenance.

Fire and Police Protection. The fire department reviews the street plan to insure that streets and utilities permit the movement of emergency equipment. The water supply must be available at appropriate access points and available at proper pressures. Likewise, the street plan should provide for safe traffic control, school patrol, and pedestrian traffic.

Local School Boards. The school board reviews the new subdivision as it may affect school planning. Approval from this agency helps school officials program construction of school facilities and anticipate space requirements.

Parks and Recreation. These agencies look to the health, stability, and welfare of the residential community. They require a careful balance of the anticipated child age composition, attempting to estimate the need of a recreation program for the whole community. They may negotiate with the subdivider for the reservation or dedication of space for playground and park space.

Other Agencies. The subdivider may be required to work closely with transportation and transit officials. There may be a need to minimize the volume of traffic or to reserve space for off-street parking or provide mass transit facilities. Though not directly involved, the office of the assessor or the local tax department has a vested interest in revising records and plans for an equitable valuation of the proposed subdivision.

The county recorder or clerk only accepts subdivisions that conform to legal descriptions showing exact boundaries and clear title. The recording of the plat must be in accordance with state law and local county municipal codes.

The Preliminary Plan

The tentative map is reviewed by the local planning agency (a board of trustees or a special committee according to local ordinances) for conditional approval. The agency grants conditional approval if the plan generally conforms to subdivision standards. Approval is subject to conditions and other requirements noted in the approval letter. In this step, the local agency negotiates with the subdivider on advisable changes and the extent of improvements to be made. Conditional approval does not constitute final approval of the subdivision plan.

Preparation of the Final Plat

With conditional approval, the subdivider stakes out the plat in accordance with the preliminary plan as approved. A bond to certify completion of improvements as stipulated will be submitted with the final map. The final map is prepared and submitted as revised to the planning agency. The final plat will not be approved until requirements of the survey and final map have been met. For example, in Oregon final plat approval requires that the plat of a subdivision cannot be recorded until all the requirements for the survey and final map have been met. The requirements are as follows:

1. The survey for the plat of the subdivision must be of such accuracy that the error of closure does not exceed 1 foot in 4,000 feet.
2. That the survey and plat of the subdivision be made by a surveyor who is a registered engineer or a licensed land surveyor.
3. The plat of the subdivision must be of such a scale that survey and mathematical information and other details can be easily obtained from it. All of the streets must be named. Each block must be lettered or numbered and all the lots numbered. The length and width of all lots must be clearly shown.

Certain additional requirements must be met before approval of the final subdivision map. Local regulations usually require that (1) the streets must be laid out to conform with adjoining plats as to their general direction and construction; (2) they must be dedicated to public use without reservation or restrictions; (3) the name of this plat must agree with planning rules governing subdivision designations; (4) all taxes and special assessments must be paid.

The Recording of Plats

Assuming that the final map of the subdivision has been approved, the designated local county official must examine the subdivision for its compliance with state and local law. For instance, most state laws require an affidavit from a licensed surveyor that the surveyor made a correct survey of the land and marked it with monuments as prescribed by law. It identifies the initial point of the survey, the type of monument used to designate the point, and further locates the point of reference to a corner established by a U.S. survey or two or more objects for identifying the location.

Regulations ordinarily require identification of all corners with monuments of galvanized iron pipe not less than one-half inch thick. Meeting these requirements, the subdivision map is filed with the date and other pertinent information, and recorded with maps of like character in a plat book. Copies of the map are frequently distributed to other local agencies.

The acceptance of the final map and its recording does not itself constitute final approval. The developer will usually be required to post a performance bond or a certified check in a sufficient amount to assure completion of all required streets and public utilities. Moreover, state subdivision laws controlling the sale of subdivided lots must also be observed.

The act of recording subdivision plats constitutes a public dedication of streets, playgrounds, or other public areas. However, the dedication is not complete until the plat is recorded and formally accepted by local authorities. To gain acceptance, requirements of the local authorities must be met with respect to utilities, completion of streets, sidewalks, and other provisions required under local ordinances.

STATE ADMINISTERED SUBDIVISION CONTROLS

State laws do not ordinarily deal with physical improvements of subdivisions. The only requirement is that they conform to local ordinances. Subdivision laws administered by real estate commissioners protect the public from misrepresentation, deceit, and fraud in the sale of subdivision lots. Such laws provide for investigation by state officials of each proposed new subdivision and a publication of facts important to prospective purchasers. State subdivision laws frequently extend to out-of-state subdivisions if lots are sold within the regulated state. Generally the point of sale, not the location of the subdivision, controls the jurisdiction of state subdivision laws.

A review of state subdivision legislation shows that if the law informs the buyer of the relevant facts, there can be no fraud or basis for complaint. Therefore, if the buyer has reasonable knowledge of the transaction, he is protected. Brokers and salesmen who sell subdivision lots without giving the purchaser full information or who misrepresent the facts are in violation of state laws. Their licenses are subject to revocation or suspension.

Before subdivided land may be sold, notice of the proposed subdivision must be given to the state agency administering a subdivision act. In California a questionnaire must be filled out by the subdivider. In other instances, the subdivision application must give information necessary for state review:

The name and address of the title owner.

The name and address of the subdivision.

The legal description of acreage or subdivision map.

The statement of title including encumbrances and unpaid taxes.

The proposed sale terms and conditions.

A statement covering the provision for sewage disposal and public utilities.

Evidence of conformity with local regulations.

With this information in hand, investigating agencies will issue a public report. A public report is issued only upon approval of the subdivision. This report must be delivered to the prospective purchaser on a form approved by the state agency. In some cases, subdividers must furnish copies of advertising material, brochures, radio transcripts, and other promotional material.

Assuming that the subdivision and its administration conform to the appropriate laws, the supervising agency will issue a report, providing reasonable steps have been made to assure completion of the subdivision as advertised. Arrangements must be made for liens and a satisfactory completion bond to assure completion of these improvements free of liens. Deed conveyances and instruments of assignment should be adequate to protect purchasers. Approval of the subdivision will be forthcoming providing these provisions are fulfilled and providing certain other deficiencies are avoided. Most states restrict the sale of subdivided lots unless recommended procedures are added.

Blanket Encumbrances

At the start, a subdivision usually is pledged as security for a development loan. This means that each lot is subject to a lien covering all the property. Since it is difficult to obtain an unconditional release of individual lots free of the blanket encumbrance, the owner or subdivider cannot sell lots in a new subdivision unless he complies with requirements of state regulations.

For example, California and Georgia law permit lot sales subject to a blanket encumbrance only if the developer agrees to (1) an impoundment of monies sufficient to protect the interest of the purchaser; (2) the owner may elect to place title to the subdivision property in trust under an agreement providing for proper release of each lot from the blanket encumbrance; (3) the subdivider may furnish a bond to the state in an amount and form approved by the real estate commissioner. The bond provides for the return of monies paid or advanced by the purchaser if proper release from the blanket encumbrance is not obtained.

Contracts of Sale

The danger in contracts of sale lies in the fact that usually contracts may not be recorded. Further, title remains with the seller. In certain states regulations prohibit a title holder or seller from encumbering a lot sold under a contract of sale. Moreover, payments made under the sales contract in California must apply first to payments which might be due under the blanket encumbrance. Other provisions affecting the contracts of a sale are the legal description, statement of all encumbrances outstanding at the date of the contract, and the specific terms of the contract.

Grounds for Denial of Public Report

Investigation of the proposed subdivision may lead to denial of the public report. In this event no offer or sales of subdivided property can be made until the subdivider has remedied the unsatisfactory conditions. A review of state subdivision laws shows several grounds for denying the public report:

1. Failure to comply with provisions of the state subdivision act.
2. The lot sales constitute misrepresentation, deceit or fraud.
3. Inability to deliver title.
4. Inability to demonstrate that off-site improvements will be completed.
5. Failure to demonstrate that the recreational facilities included in the offering will be completed.
6. Failure to show that the parcels can be used for the purpose for which they are offered.
7. Failure to state uses for which the parcels are offered.

These points are illustrative of regulations preventing fraud, deceit, and misrepresentation. For example, under grounds for the denial of the public report, a subdivider could not offer a lot proposed for a single-family dwelling that was on the side of a mountain and obviously unusable for its intended purpose. It should be added that these provisions generally apply to sales of lots outside of the state of jurisdiction. In certain other states—Georgia, for example—these provisions would be waived if the purchaser inspected the property. It is reasoned that the buyer, by inspecting the site, cannot be defrauded because he has reasonable knowledge of the property purchased.

SUBDIVISION COVENANTS

Subdivision covenants are termed restrictive or protective covenants. Their purpose is to preserve the character of the neighborhood, reduce property depreciation and add to the amenities of a community. They supplement local zoning codes, ordinances, housing codes and building codes. The developer may introduce controls on use and other matters that affect the aesthetic qualities of a subdivision which may not be enforceable by public ordinances.

Subdivision covenants have the added advantage of being more permanent than zoning codes that may be subject to change by political pressure. Besides, subdivision covenants may be sufficiently flexible to conform to land use trends and at the same time preserve the character of the neighborhood. This is provided by covenants that may be changed by a majority of property owners in the subdivision. A review of the main points of restrictive covenants illustrated here indicates how these covenants benefit the purchaser of lots subject to private (not public) subdivision controls.

Initially, it should be noted that covenants and restrictions run with the land for a specific period, say for 25 years. In a Florida subdivision, which includes waterfront lots, covenants are effective for 30 years, with provision for successive periods of 10 years. Within this term, a favorable vote by the majority of owners will change the original covenants. Rights of way for utility easements are established in perpetuity.

Land Use and Aesthetic Covenants

The main subdivision covenants relate to land use and architectural controls. If the subdivision is developed solely for residential use, it will be restricted to single-family dwellings. Such covenants provide that only one detached dwelling of two stories in height with attached carport or garage may be placed on the property. Further, covenants typically prevent the use of a dwelling for any purpose other than a private dwelling. No business of any kind nor offensive activity may be carried on upon any lot so as to cause an annoyance or nuisance to the neighborhood. In the more restrictive cases, owners are prohibited from parking, storing, or garaging trailers, campers, motor homes, and similar vehicles on the site.

Architectural control is provided by plan approval by an architectural committee formed by the developer before any structure may be constructed. The committee must act normally within a specified period, say 30 to 45 days after a written request for approval; after construction is started, exteriors must be completed within a specified time (e.g., six months). A related issue provides for the placement of buildings calling for setback lines from the streets, a minimum lot size, and a minimum building area. With these standards, the developer may guide the open appearance of the subdivision. Usually such restrictions go beyond the local zoning code and in this way provide for a higher level of amenities.

In some instances, residents are prohibited from erecting antennaes or placing air conditioning units in view of the street or allowing any outside storage. In some instances, the landscaping must be approved by the architectural committee. Further concern over the environment of the subdivision may prohibit the erection of fences more than three feet high (in effect prohibiting "spite" fences on the property line), and control the type of lawn fertilizer that may be used so that it is not injurious to surface waters.

A group of miscellaneous covenants prohibit the disposition of refuse, trash, or waste materials into waterways or waterfront lots. Restrictions on the placement of billboards and signs are further controls that preserve the character of the subdivision. In selected cases, subdivisions do not allow direct exterior lighting. The architectural committee may also restrict the size of signs for sale or rent to not more than five square feet. In addition, pets may be allowed but only provided they are not maintained for commercial purposes.

Enforcement

Covenants give the developer or the owner of lots the right to bring action at law or in equity to enjoin violations of the recorded covenants. Note that failure of parties to proceed against the violators does not constitute a waiver of restrictive covenants.

(a) Violations of any covenant or restriction may be remedied by the Company, and the reasonable expenses thereof shall be chargeable to the then owner of the lot and be payable upon demand. The foregoing shall be alternative, or in addition, to the enforcement provisions of sub-paragraph (b).

(b) Enforcement shall be by proceedings at law or in equity brought *by the Company*, its successors and assigns, or *by the owner* of any lot, against any person or persons violating or attempting to violate any covenants to enjoin such violations or attempted violations or to recover damages or both (Emphasis supplied).

(c) The failure of the Company to enforce any covenant or restriction herein or to remedy any violation thereof, at any time, or from time to time, shall not constitute a waiver by the Company of those or other provisions of these restrictive covenants.

In sum, restrictive covenants, which restrict private rights in real estate, tend to benefit property owners by (1) tending to preserve the environment of the subdivision, (2) retarding neighborhood depreciation by enhancing the openness and general appearance of the subdivision, and (3) minimizing the loss in value from neighborhood obsolescence. While the restrictive covenants restrict rights of property owners, each property owner benefits from the land use restrictions imposed uniformly on his neighbors. The purchase of a lot subject to restrictive covenants protects property owners from acts of their neighbors which may cause nuisances or otherwise limit the enjoyment of residential districts.

THE INTERSTATE LAND SALES
FULL DISCLOSURE ACT

The Interstate Land Sales Full Disclosure Act discourages fraud, misrepresentation, and deceit in the sale of subdivision lots over interstate boundaries. It is believed that if a purchaser has adequate information on the property he is purchasing, no fraud is committed. The provisions of Public Law 90–48, August 1, 1968, apply to subdivisions divided into 50 or more lots offered for sale or lease as part of a common promotional plan. For land subject to this regulation, it is unlawful for any developer or agent to use any means of transportation or communication in interstate commerce unless he conforms to the act. The exceptions to this legislation reveal the general purpose of the full disclosure principle:

1. Sales to contractors required to construct buildings within two years.
2. Real estate sold under court order.
3. The sale of mortgages or deeds of trust.
4. Securities issued by a real estate investment trust.
5. The sale of real estate owned by government or its administrative agencies.
6. Cemetery lots.
7. Sales to a person for purposes of constructing buildings.
8. Sales of real estate which are free of all encumbrances if the purchaser has inspected the lots which he proposes to purchase.
9. Lots of five acres or more.

With these noted exceptions, lots coming under the Act may not be sold unless a statement of record has been registered with the Secretary of Housing and Urban Development and a copy of the property report has been given to the purchaser in advance of the contract or agreement for sale. Any act which is interpreted as fraud or deceit is unlawful. Failure to issue the proper report to the purchaser is grounds for considering the contract of sale voidable at the option of the purchaser.

Statement of Record

In short, the sales of subdivision lots over interstate lines is unlawful unless the subdivision is registered with the Secretary by issuing a statement of record. The statement of record must include:

1. The name and address of each person having an interest in the lots of the subdivision.
2. The legal description of the total area included in the subdivision and a statement of the topography, including a map showing block dimensions and streets.
3. A statement of the condition of title to the land.
4. A statement of the present condition of access to the subdivision,

availability of sewage disposal facilities, the location of the subdivision with respect to nearby municipalities, the nature of improvements to be installed and the schedule for completion.

5. If there is a blanket encumbrance, a statement of the consequences
    for an individual purchaser of a failure to fulfill obligations of the
    encumbrance.
6. Copies of articles of incorporation, instruments by which the trust
    is declared or created, copies of articles of partnership, and related
    papers showing ownership.
7. Copies of the deed establishing title to the subdivision.
8. Copies of all forms of conveyances to be used in selling lots.
9. Copies of instruments creating easements or other restrictions.
10. Certified financial statements as required by the Secretary.
11. A statement of terms, conditions, prices and rents.

The Property Report

Upon receipt of the statement of record, the property report relating
to lots in a subdivision is issued stating information the Secretary believes
important to a prudent purchaser. The Act specifies that the report should
not be used for promotional purposes nor may the seller advertise or
represent that the Secretary approves or recommends the subdivision.

Enforcement is provided by allowing the purchaser to bring suit to
recover his purchase price, the cost of improvements, and reasonable
court costs. Moreover, the Secretary has the right, upon proper showing,
to issue a permanent or temporary injunction or restraining order to enjoin such acts or practices. Evidence may be referred to the Attorney
General for appropriate criminal prosecution. The power to subpoena
witnesses, books, and papers constitutes other enforcement measures.
Further, a violation of the Act is subject to a fine of not more than $5,000,
imprisonment of up to five years or both.

In practice the property report tends to be quite complete. Besides
the normal questions on title, recording, and encumbrances, the developer
is required to list unusual conditions relating to the location of the subdivision. For example, the existence of an air corridor and sonic booms
may be noted in the property report. Air pollution from local plants or
the possibility of floods will be noted. Considerable detail will be added
on the availability of water, electricity, telephone service, and sewage
disposal.

A detailed list of municipal services to the subdivision, including fire
and police protection, garbage collection, public schools, medical and
dental facilities, public transportation, and postal service will be covered
in the property report. Even special risk factors will be listed. For
example, the property report may state that "the future value of land is

FIGURE 18–1

Acknowledgment of the Receipt of a Public Report

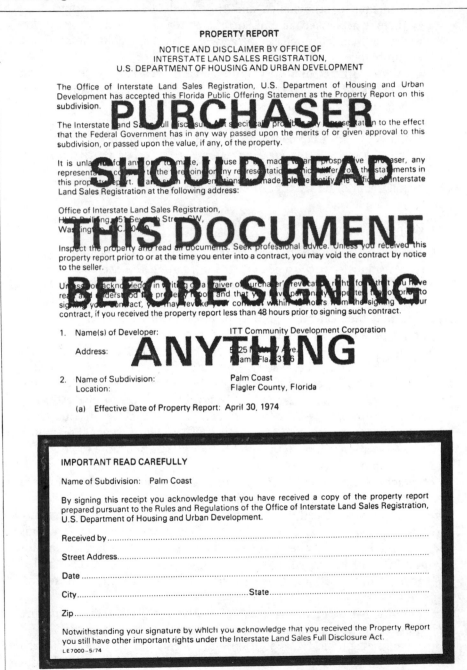

PROPERTY REPORT

NOTICE AND DISCLAIMER BY OFFICE OF
INTERSTATE LAND SALES REGISTRATION,
U.S. DEPARTMENT OF HOUSING AND URBAN DEVELOPMENT

The Office of Interstate Land Sales Registration, U.S. Department of Housing and Urban Development has accepted this Florida Public Offering Statement as the Property Report on this subdivision.

The Interstate Land Sales Full Disclosure Act specifically prohibits any representation to the effect that the Federal Government has in any way passed upon the merits of or given approval to this subdivision, or passed upon the value, if any, of the property.

It is unlawful for any person, to induce or attempt to make any prospective purchaser, any representation contrary to the foregoing or any representation which differs from the statements in this property report. If any such representations are made, please notify the Office of Interstate Land Sales Registration at the following address:

Office of Interstate Land Sales Registration,
HUD Building, 451 Seventh Street, S.W.,
Washington, D.C. 20410

Inspect the property and read all documents. Seek professional advice. Unless you received this property report prior to or at the time you enter into a contract, you may void the contract by notice to the seller.

Unless you acknowledge in writing a waiver of purchaser's revocation rights for that you have read and understood the property report and that you have personally inspected the lot prior to signing your contract, you may revoke your contract within 48 hours from the signing of your contract, if you received the property report less than 48 hours prior to signing such contract.

1. Name(s) of Developer: ITT Community Development Corporation

     Address: 5525 N.W. 7 Ave.
                               Miami, Fla. 33156

2. Name of Subdivision: Palm Coast
    Location: Flagler County, Florida

    (a) Effective Date of Property Report: April 30, 1974

IMPORTANT READ CAREFULLY

Name of Subdivision: Palm Coast

By signing this receipt you acknowledge that you have received a copy of the property report prepared pursuant to the Rules and Regulations of the Office of Interstate Land Sales Registration, U.S. Department of Housing and Urban Development.

Received by...

Street Address...

Date ....

City...State...

Zip...

Notwithstanding your signature by which you acknowledge that you received the Property Report you still have other important rights under the Interstate Land Sales Full Disclosure Act.

LE 7000–5/74

very uncertain; do not count on appreciation." Further, the property report may add: "You may be required to pay the full amount of the obligation to a bank or third party to whom the developer assigns your contracts or note, even though the developer may have failed to fulfill promises he has made."

These and other issues demonstrate that the full disclosure law helps prevent fraud and misrepresentation by requiring the developer to reveal facts that affect the property use, future liability and the value of the purchase. Figure 18-1 shows the receipt acknowledging that the prospective purchaser has received a copy of the property report. This cover document which is attached to the property report advises the purchaser to read the document before signing and prohibits the representation that the federal government has passed on the merits of the subdivision or its value.

Purchasers are advised that unless they acknowledge a waiving of revocation rights the purchaser has 48 hours after signing to revoke the contract. Under the Interstate Land Sales Registration Act, property owners have certain rights that deserve repeating:

1. With a few exceptions, developers of land sold interstate must have a property report.
2. A purchaser who is not given a property report more than 48 hours before signing has the right to cancel and the developer must return earnest money—unless the purchaser waived his right to cancel in writing.
3. If a property is misrepresented by the purchaser, he may sue under federal law.

To avoid litigation, purchasers of land sold interstate are advised to (1) take copies of the property report home before signing. If in doubt about property rights, purchasers should consult an attorney before signing. (2) Purchasers are advised not to sign contracts before reading the property report. Signing a contract may also include a waiver of the purchaser's right to cancel within 48 hours. (3) The purchaser should be aware that the federal government has not inspected, investigated, appraised or endorsed the land offering. Federal agencies rely on information provided by the developer; federal officials do not check the authenticity of statements by the developer. (4) It is not necessarily true that the land always appreciates or that it will appreciate to the point of offsetting financing charges and property taxes. (5) Purchasers should not rely on oral representations. A written contract controls contractual terms.

QUESTIONS FOR REVIEW

_____ 1. Subdivision regulations help to
   a. protect purchasers from being "overcharged" in real estate transactions.
   b. prevent misrepresentation.
   c. facilitate the sale of residential property.
   d. direct urban growth patterns.

_____ 2. In subdivisions developed before regulations were provided,
   a. street width and design are highly conforming.
   b. street improvements are usually substandard.
   c. utilities are superior to newer subdivisions.
   d. costs of maintenance are relatively low.

_____ 3. Without subdivision regulations
   a. local government expenses for street repair and maintenance tend to be high.
   b. brokers are unprotected from litigation over titles.
   c. purchasers pay higher land prices.
   d. subdivision land tends to be wisely used.

_____ 4. Subdivision regulations restrict
   a. the volume of advertising.
   b. interest payments.
   c. residential density.
   d. cash sales only.

_____ 5. Unrecorded subdivisions
   a. must conform to local ordinances regulating their development.
   b. have no force or effect.
   c. may legally provide for higher residential density.
   d. may only be sold by mail.

_____ 6. The legislation preventing fraud in interstate land sales is commonly known as the
   a. Fair Housing Act.
   b. Real Estate Recovery Act.
   c. Interstate Land Sales and Full Disclosure Act.
   d. Truth in Lending and Investment Sales Act.

_____ 7. The agency which is ultimately responsible to ensure conformity in existing street patterns and utility layouts is the
   a. county commissioner.
   b. district attorney.
   c. building permit department.
   d. planning agency.

_____ 8. Generally, the _____ controls state jurisdiction over subdivision sales.

       a. location of the subdivision
       b. residence of the purchaser
       c. residence of the seller
       d. point of sale

_____ 9. If the purchaser is provided with _____ the seller is protected against complaints of fraud or misrepresentation.

       a. an ample opportunity to inspect the property,
       b. a reasonable knowledge of the transaction,
       c. a certificate of "reasonable value,"
       d. a subdivision map and a copy of subdivision covenants,

_____10. State subdivision laws do not deal with

       a. the protection of the public from misrepresentation and deceit or fraud in the sale of lots.
       b. the physical planning of subdivisions.
       c. out-of-state subdivisions.
       d. compliance with local subdivision ordinances.

_____11. In some states, such as California, a public report

       a. is only issued after subdividers provide detailed information to the state real estate commission.
       b. is always issued after a detailed investigation by the state real estate commission.
       c. must be included in all mailed advertisements.
       d. must be published in a newspaper circulating in the county where the subdivision is located.

_____12. Which of the following is not a ground for denying the public report in states that regulate the sale of subdivision property?

       a. Failure to itemize uses for which parcels are offered.
       b. Failure to show that parcels can be used for the purpose under which they are offered.
       c. Failure to document land values.
       d. Failure to demonstrate that adequate financial arrangements have been made for community facilities and off-site improvements.

_____13. Restrictive covenants tend to benefit property owners by

       a. changing the environment of the subdivision.
       b. expediting neighborhood appreciation.
       c. minimizing the loss in value from neighborhood obsolescence.
       d. permitting individual owners to change covenants with respect to their own land.

_____14. The Interstate Land Sales and Full Disclosure Act was designed to discourage fraud, misrepresentation, and deceit in the sale of

       a. real estate sold under court order.
       b. mortgages or deeds of trust.

    c. cemetery lots.
    d. lots of less than five acres.

_____15. Which of the following statements is incorrect?
    a. Purchasers should not rely on oral contracts.
    b. Purchasers arc advised not to sign contracts before reading the property report thoroughly.
    c. The federal government investigates and endorses land offered interstate.
    d. Land does not always appreciate.

_____16. John C. Stone purchased 25 acres of land for development as a subdivision. He must comply with local subdivision regulations controlling the physical aspects of each lot before
    I. describing land by lots and blocks.
    II. selling the newly subdivided property.
    a. I only.
    b. II only.
    c. Both I and II.
    d. Neither I nor II.

_____17. Phillis Fortner owns 50 acres of land bordering a large reservoir. To develop a subdivision, she must have her plans reviewed by
    a. the local chamber of commerce.
    b. a major industry that is willing to guarantee that its employees will buy at least 25 percent of the lots.
    c. the local school district.
    d. the county engineer.

_____18. The county engineer must pass on the adequacy of the proposed location, construction, and size of the subdivision's
    a. playground and park space.
    b. utility system.
    c. emergency equipment.
    d. off-street parking.

_____19. Which of the following is usually not a requirement for recording a subdivision?
    a. The survey and plat of the subdivision must be made by a surveyor who is a registered engineer or a licensed land surveyor.
    b. The plat of the subdivision must be scaled so that survey information can be easily determined.
    c. The survey for the plat of the subdivision must be of such accuracy that the error of closure does not exceed 1 foot in 4,000 feet.
    d. The map of the survey must be scaled to 1 inch equals 100 feet.

_____20. State law in some states permits lot sales subject to a blanket encumbrance only if the developer agrees to

    a. an impoundment of monies sufficient to protect his interest.

    b. release the lot from the blanket agreement.

    c. furnish a bond to the state in an amount and form approved by the real estate commission.

    d. return any monies paid or advanced by the purchaser if proper release from the blanket encumbrance is not obtained.

_____21. Emory Mullins contracted to buy a retirement lot in another state. He did not inspect the property, and the selling broker did not give him a copy of the property report. What are the remedies available to Mullins if he discovers that his lot is unsuitable for residential use?

    a. He may declare the contract void and bring suit to recover his purchase price and reasonable court costs.

    b. He should not tell anyone about his discovery and should try to sell the property.

    c. He must fulfill the terms of the contract.

    d. He should advertise a notice of default in the official county paper within 30 days of his purchase.

_____22. Which of the following items is not included in a statement of record?

    a. The name and address of each person having an interest in the lots of the subdivision.

    b. The legal description of the total area included in the subdivision and a statement of the topography.

    c. A statement of the title status.

    d. A statement of the professional qualifications of the developer or corporate officers.

_____23. A detailed list of municipal services available in a subdivision will be covered in the

    a. statement of record.

    b. property report.

    c. preliminary plan.

    d. recorded plat of the subdivision.

_____24. Copies of the deed establishing title to the subdivision, copies of all forms of conveyances to be used in selling lots as required by the Secretary of Housing and Urban Development would be included in the

    a. statement of record.

    b. property report.

    c. preliminary plan.

    d. plat book.

_____25. The purpose of the Interstate Land Sales and Full Disclosure Act is to

I. help prevent fraud and misrepresentation in the sale of sub-division lots over interstate boundaries.

II. enable the buyer to obtain the lowest possible price for the property he is purchasing.

a. I only.

b. II only.

c. Both I and II.

d. Neither I nor II.

____26. Mr. and Mrs. Simmons signed a contract to purchase a lot on the oral promise that within a few years the development would be a thriving retirement village. They signed the purchase contract after inspecting the lot with the listing broker. Six months later the Simmons discovered that their lot was under water three months of the year. If the broker and developer complied with all regulations, what remedies would Mr. and Mrs. Simmons have?

a. The Simmonses would be reimbursed for all monies paid on this contract.

b. Since the Simmonses made an on-site inspection there is little they can do in the way of litigation.

c. The broker is guilty of misrepresentation and is liable under "puffing of goods" portion of the Interstate Land Sales and Full Disclosure Act.

d. The Simmonses could recover damages because they did not have reasonable knowledge of the real estate.

____27. In defining a nonconforming use, which of the following items would be disregarded?

a. The quality of landscaping in a middle-income residential district.

b. A neighborhood grocery store in a single-family district.

c. An auto repair garage in a motel district.

d. A welding shop in a commercial retail district.

____28. Which of the following officials would a subdivider probably not be required to consult for approval of a subdivision?

a. The planning commission.

b. The county engineer.

c. The local school board.

d. The city tax commissioner.

____29. The sale of subdivision lots over interstate lines is prohibited unless the subdivision is registered with the Secretary of Housing and Urban Development by issuing a statement of record. The statement of record is not required to include

a. the names and addresses of each person having an interest in the lots and subdivisions.

b. copies of the deed establishing title to the subdivision.

c. copies of an environmental impact study.

d. a statement of terms, conditions, prices, and rents.

_____30. The property report issued by the Secretary of Housing and Urban Development would not include
   a. detailed information on the availability of water, electricity, telephone service, and sewerage disposal.
   b. information on titles and encumbrances.
   c. the proposed ethnic background of the neighborhood.
   d. the proximity of an air corridor and jet aircraft noise.

_____31. The Interstate Land Sales and Full Disclosure Act allows a wronged purchaser to bring suit for all of the following except
   a. the purchase price.
   b. the down payment.
   c. reasonable court costs.
   d. lost profits from foregone opportunities.

_____32. The purpose of the property report is to
   a. show that the Secretary approves the subdivision.
   b. give the seller promotional material for direct-mail advertising.
   c. recommend subdivisions for sale.
   d. provide relevant information to prospective purchasers.

_____33. A subdivision developer may guide the open appearance of a subdivision by requiring that
   a. houses in the subdivision follow the same floor plan.
   b. landscaping be executed by the same firm.
   c. architectural plans be approved before construction.
   d. the county planning commission approve all floor plans.

_____34. _____ would restrict type of construction, height of buildings, and fences.
   a. The Interstate Land Sales and Full Disclosure Act
   b. City ordinances
   c. Subdivision covenants
   d. The first mortgage

_____35. The purpose of subdivision covenants is to
   a. restrict the use of property by the seller.
   b. restrict the enjoyment of residential districts while increasing the tax base.
   c. provide for expenses of local government.
   d. preserve the neighborhood character, reduce property depreciation, and add to residential amenities.

_____36. Which of the following are excluded from the Interstate Land Sales and Full Disclosure Act?
   a. Subdivisions of more than 50 lots sold interstate.
   b. Lot sales to a person for purposes of constructing buildings.
   c. Subdivisions of more than 100 lots sold interstate.
   d. All of the above.

_____37. To the buyer, a disadvantage of a land contract is that
  a. either party may revoke the contract before title is conveyed.
  b. in some states contracts may not be recorded.
  c. some states prohibit the seller from encumbering a lot sold under contract.
  d. title is conveyed before the contract is fulfilled.

_____38. Which of the following acts constitutes a public dedication of streets?
  a. Recording the plat.
  b. Acceptance of an affidavit from a licensed surveyor attesting to the acceptability of the subdivision survey.
  c. Approval of the final map.
  d. Formal acceptance of the recorded plat by local authorities.

_____39. Before land may be sold as a recorded lot in a planned residential subdivision,
  I. it must have streets that conform to the pattern established by the State Highway Department.
  II. it must be approved by the Secretary of Housing and Urban Development.
  a. I only.
  b. II only.
  c. Both I and II.
  d. Neither I nor II.

_____40. Which of the following represents the final step that a developer must take before he may offer lots for sale?
  a. He must secure acceptance of the final map by local authorities.
  b. He must record the subdivision plat.
  c. He must publicly dedicate the streets, playgrounds, and other common areas.
  d. He must post a performance bond covering the cost of streets and public utilities.

ANSWER KEY

1. (*b*)	11. (*a*)	21. (*a*)	31. (*d*)
2. (*b*)	12. (*c*)	22. (*d*)	32. (*d*)
3. (*a*)	13. (*c*)	23. (*b*)	33. (*c*)
4. (*c*)	14. (*d*)	24. (*a*)	34. (*c*)
5. (*b*)	15. (*c*)	25. (*a*)	35. (*d*)
6. (*c*)	16. (*c*)	26. (*b*)	36. (*b*)
7. (*d*)	17. (*d*)	27. (*a*)	37. (*b*)
8. (*d*)	18. (*b*)	28. (*d*)	38. (*d*)
9. (*b*)	19. (*d*)	29. (*c*)	39. (*d*)
10. (*b*)	20. (*c*)	30. (*c*)	40. (*d*)

SUGGESTED ADDITIONAL READING

Barlowe, Raleigh. *Land Resource Economics, The Economics of Real Property.* 2d ed. Englewood Cliffs, N.J.: Prentice-Hall, Inc., 1972, chaps. 16 and 17.

Bowman, Arthur G. *California Real Estate Principles.* Pacific Palisades, Calif.: Goodyear Publishing Co., Inc., 1972, chap. 14.

Kratovil, Robert. *Real Estate Law.* 6th ed. Englewood Cliffs, N.J.: Prentice-Hall, Inc., 1974, chaps. 28, 29 and 35.

Land Development Manual. Washington, D.C.: National Assn. of Home Builders of the United States, 1974, chaps. 1 and 2.

Lusk, Harold F., and French, William B. *Law of the Real Estate Business.* 3d ed. Homewood, Ill.: Richard D. Irwin, Inc., 1975, chaps. 13 and 16.

19

Land Use Controls

Virtually all real estate is subject to land use control. The controls operate against a wide range of property uses—from the high rise condominiums of Ft. Lauderdale, Florida to the desert tracts of Coachella Valley near Palm Springs, California. Land owners encounter both public and private controls. It is difficult to own real estate, to use real estate, to develop or manage real estate without observing restrictions on property use. Property owners hold exclusive rights of use but the right is not absolute.

Probably most owners are aware of public controls. Such controls rest on the inherent powers of the state. Public controls include the general plan, zoning ordinances, building and housing codes, subdivision regulations, and more recently, ecological controls. Private developers impose land use restrictions in deeds, subdivisions, housing associations, and "planned unit developments." An explanation of land use controls is helpful to understanding the modern concept of private property ownership.

PUBLIC LAND USE CONTROLS

As used here, the "state" refers to federal, state and local governments with all of their numerous agencies. While local governments have no direct constitutional powers, they work under a delegation of authority from their respective state. The states, in turn, can enforce land use controls if they are not preempted by the federal Constitution.

532

General Powers of the State

Government controls come under the constitutional authority covering the police power, the right of eminent domain, the power of escheat, and taxation. The more important restrictions on land use follow from the police power and eminent domain. An explanation of these four inherent rights reveals the effect of land use controls on real estate development and value.

The Police Power. The police power refers to the inherent power of government to regulate land use for the public interest, health, morals, convenience, and safety. This inherent right permits municipalities to enact and enforce building codes, regulate housing occupancy and restrict property uses by zoning districts. With these tools, local municipalities restrict private rights and interests in real estate. Among local regulations, the following controls are more commonly encountered by property owners:

The general plan	Electrical codes
Zoning ordinances	Plumbing codes
Building codes	Subdivision regulations
Housing codes	

Originally, the police power suppressed dangerous property uses or controlled nuisances. Typical colonial ordinances protected residential districts from land uses such as gunpowder houses, livery stables, and slaughter houses. Today police power assumes a more positive role. Land use is now guided by a set of local, state, and federal laws presumably administered for the general benefit. The real question relates to the economic burden of regulatory restrictions. On the one hand, it is argued that land use regulations, like child labor laws, are socially beneficial. On the other hand, the more onerous regulations are believed to be of limited general benefit and, in effect, constitute the taking of private property under the guise of public regulation.

If police power is exercised, no compensation is paid the owner even though substantial losses may result. For example, the construction of a center line barrier on a highway may be justified on grounds of public safety. The center line barrier prevents dangerous left turns on a busy arterial—even though retail businesses depending on left turn traffic for patronage may suffer substantial financial losses which are not compensationable.

To illustrate further, a zoning classification calling for a conservation district may prevent construction of multiple-family or condominium dwelling units. Such a zoning restriction would probably lower property value. Because the restriction follows from the police power, the owner is not entitled to compensation. Generally speaking, the police power cannot be arbitrary or discriminatory. It must be reasonable. The right of eminent domain is exercised under a different set of circumstances.

The Right of Eminent Domain. The right of eminent domain provides for the taking of private property by public authorities upon payment of just compensation. Private power companies, the telephone company and other publicly regulated utilities are granted the right of eminent domain. Eminent domain comes under the Fifth Amendment of the federal Constitution and the constitutions of 49 states (excepting North Carolina). Just compensation generally means market value.

Originated in colonial times, the right of eminent domain was exercised to acquire land for public use such as buildings, towns and forts, water mills and ferry sites. Today providing for public highways constitutes the largest public consumption of land. Currently about 22 million acres of land are in highway rights-of-way for a road system of 3½ million miles. In describing eminent domain, it is difficult to generalize. Governments vary widely in their handling of public land acquisition. Yet certain facts seem fairly common to agencies that exercise the right of eminent domain.

There is an almost universal principle that owners losing land taken for public purposes are entitled to compensation for the actual land (and buildings) taken. The only issue is the value of the taking, which is subject to judicial review. However in most cases, public acquisition of private property constitutes a partial taking. Technically if only part of the property is acquired, the owner is left with the "remainder" after the taking. In these partial takings land remaining after the taking may suffer a loss in value by reason of the taking. These damages are viewed as *severance damages:* damages to land remaining after the taking.

Probably the most frequent method of measuring damages is the before and after rule. Land and buildings subject to eminent domain will be value *before* the taking and *after* the taking. The difference between the two values represents just compensation. Failure of the property owner and the taking authority to agree on just compensation results in a court review of the proposed award to the property owner. Just compensation payments may always be appealed to the courts.

Figure 19–1 illustrates a fairly typical case showing severance damages in a right-of-way taking. In this instance some 0.828 acres is taken for a 100-foot wide highway right-of-way across a 10.017 acre parcel. As a result of the taking, Parcel B of .239 acres is severed from the main tract, Parcel C. Moreover, Parcel C, formerly a rectangular shape, after the taking, assumes an odd shape and suffers damage because of the .828 acre right-of-way. The estimate of just compensation follows the before and after rule.

FIGURE 19–1

Right-of-way Taken Showing Severance Damage

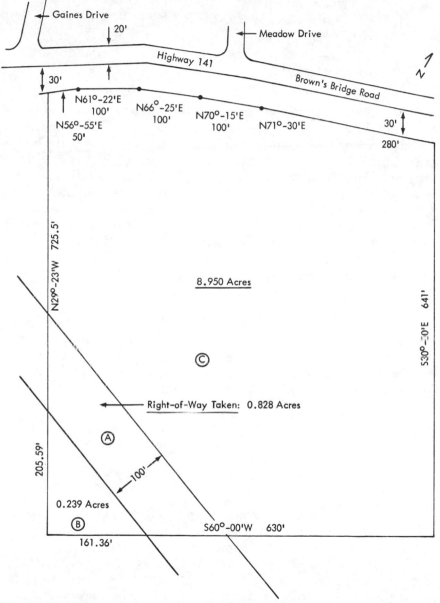

Note: Drawn to scale.

Value before taking
    10.017 acres, @ $25,000 .... $250,425
Value after taking
    9.189 acres, @ $20,000 183,780
Just compensation .... $ 66,645
    Less value of part taken, 0.828
    acres, @ $25,000 20,700
Severance damages .... $ 45,945

Before the taking, the property had an estimated market value of $250,425. With the proposed improvement in place, parcels B and C are separated and lack utility compared to the whole property before the taking. Subtracting the $183,780 value of the 9.189 acres remainder after the taking (parcels B and C) gives an estimate of just compensation: $66,645. The just compensation represents the value of the *part taken* and *severance damages*.

To show the loss in value to the remainder after the taking (parcels B and C), the value of the part taken is subtracted from the total estimate of just compensation—in this instance, $20,700. Thus, the final award includes severance damages of $45,945 and the value of the part taken, $20,700. The severance damages represent the loss in value to parcels B and C after the taking.

As a general rule, property owners are entitled to the market value of the part taken. But to receive compensation for severance damages, damages to the property remaining must be definite and not merely remote and speculative. Severance damages occur if property is affected by specific conditions that qualify for severance damages:

The remaining property is uneconomic in size or shape.

Deep cuts or high fills that limit utility and accessibility.

Water pollution.

Injury to irrigation, drainage, or water facilities.

Change in property use.

In the last analysis, compensation for damages to the remainder depends on court review. Statutory law and constitutional provisions, which vary among the states, govern the payment of just compensation.

Not all property damages are compensable. The courts have refused compensation for certain losses arising from eminent domain which, under the law, are not compensable. The list of damages which my occur under an eminent domain taking includes:

Loss of good will.

Loss of business profit.

Diversion of traffic.

Circuity of travel.

Noise, fumes and nuisances of traffic.

Changing use of a street or highway.

Loss of right of way on property abutting the right of way.

Interruption of business during construction.

Establishment of one way streets.

Cost of moving personal property.

Under specific legislation, limited moving expenses have been allowed for personal property. The Uniform Relocation Assistance and Real Property Acquisition Policies Act of 1970 affects more than 50 federally-assisted programs that acquire private property for public use. Property owners subject to the act may recover reasonable moving expenses, or accept a financial relocation expense not exceeding $500. Under like conditions, businesses are eligible for up to $10,000 compensation for relocation expenses. Other provisions provide for just compensation and provision for substitute housing for displaced persons. With these exceptions, eminent domain awards are normally restricted to damages for the property taken and the remainder. So the point is that eminent domain calls for just compensation, but not all losses are compensable.

The Power of Escheat. In colonial times, land was forfeited for failure to plant crops or to pay rents or taxes. The legal term for such a forfeiture is escheat. Land in the United States is owned by private entities (e.g., a person or corporation, or an agency of state, local, or federal government). If a property owner dies without a will or known heirs, property reverts to the state under the power of escheat. While one of the public rights imposed on private property, it is relatively unimportant. It is unusual for property owners to die without a will or legal heirs.

Power of Taxation. The right to tax was first exercised by colonial governments, much as state and local governments currently exercise their right of taxation. Even today the federal government does not tax real estate and the states do not tax federally-owned real estate. The property tax, usually administered on the local level, represents a delegation of taxing power from the state. Proceeds of the property tax generally support services of local government and schools. The critical property tax problem concerns the uniformity of property tax assessments between and among individual properties.

The most common method of testing the fairness of local tax assessments is to compare the sales price with the current assessed value. It is reasoned that properties selling for the same price should have pretty much the same assessed value. If the assessment ratio (assessed value divided by the sales price) varies between properties selling for the same amount, one property owner pays more than his fair share of local taxes. For example, two houses selling for $30,000 may have assessments equal to 20 percent and 30 percent of the price: $6,000 and $9,000. With an annual tax rate of 60 mills ($0.060), annual taxes for the properties would be $360 and $450. The latter property owner pays $90 more than his neighbor, though the properties have the same value.

Nonuniform assessments among higher-priced properties result in even greater distortions of annual property taxes. In illustration, two apartment houses sold for $780,000 and $460,000 were assessed at *25.4 percent* and *13.6 percent* of their sales price. With a tax rate of 50 mills, property taxes for the second apartment were $3,128. If the same percentage assessment of 25.4 percent was applied to the second apartment, property taxes would amount to $5,842. In other words, the owner of the $460,000 apartment paid $2,714 taxes less than would have been paid if the assessment was on the same sales assessment ratio of the $780,000 apartment.

Because property tax assessors are unable to revalue property except in five- or ten-year or longer cycles, these discrepancies may pass undetected for years. The result is to discriminate between and among taxpayers. An assessment below the current level of assessment constitutes an unwarranted subsidy. Conversely, an overassessment represents unjust tax discrimination.

The General Plan

The general plan precedes other land use controls. It sometimes goes under other labels such as "the master plan," "the comprehensive plan," or "the city plan." Whatever the local name, the plan is a statement of community goals covering physical development of the community in the light of social, economic, and political goals. It guides the use of private land for commercial, industrial and residential purposes. It attempts to maximize social and economic benefits for the people in the community. To accomplish these objectives, planning consists of three general characteristics: (1) planning is closely related to government policy; (2) it is a means of coordinating local government agencies; and (3) it is a continuous process.

Each community evolves its own plan. The general plan for Miami Beach emphasizes tourism. The land use controls oriented to the tourist industry will follow from the general plan. A general plan for Seattle, Washington, emphasizes the physical attractiveness of the area and promotes a specialized economic base. In short, the general plan is directed to balanced community growth.

The general plan is presented only after a comprehensive survey.

The survey first describes *physical* characteristics of the community. Land characteristics, natural resources, topography, climate and the present land use will undergo detailed study. The next part of the survey deals with the *economic base*—the activities in which people earn their living. This part of the general plan analyzes the source of employment, labor skills, transportation, and other economic advantages. As part of the general plan, a *social* survey details population characteristics, education, and other social aspects of community.

With this information at hand, the general plan may be used to guide and develop, making the most efficient use of available private and public land. The development is guided by suggestions on the most appropriate areas for public buildings, recreational centers, street improvements, and private land use. In this way the general plan works to minimize the effect of blight and other nonconforming land use. On a grand scale the general plan assures the optimum use of local real estate. The objectives of the general plan help insure community welfare and, in part, encourage the type of land use controls that meets local needs.

First, the general plan supports the economic base. Therefore, the general plan is unique to each area. As an expression of community goals, it will vary from area to area and between communities. The second goal relates to its comprehensiveness. It must meet all aspects of community growth. And, third, the general plan must be adapted to special requirements of the area, maximizing the social, economic, and natural advantages of the community. Fourth, the general plan accounts for the character and probable growth of the community by coordinating land use controls, public, and private land use.

Given these objectives, the land use controls in their various forms tend to promote the general plan. Hence, they are secondary to the general plan. Of first importance are the zoning regulations that provide for the orderly growth of the community according to goals of the master plan. Subdivision regulations, building codes, and housing codes are part of the devices available to the local community. Among the various controls, probably zoning regulations have the most direct influence in expediting the general plan.

Zoning Regulations

Zoning, regulating the use of property, is an exercise of the police power. Present-day zoning, usually administered by the city or county, divides land into detailed land use districts. Zoning includes restrictions on the bulk and height of buildings and controls the density of land use by property use.

Towns first began to ban dangerous uses and nuisances from residential districts. In 1916 Los Angeles enacted an ordinance establishing

FIGURE 19–2

The Intent and Purpose of Zoning Codes

This comprehensive amendment to the Cook County Zoning Ordinance is adopted for the following purposes:

1. To promote and to protect the public health, safety, morals, comfort, convenience, and the general welfare of the people
2. To zone all properties in such a manner as to reflect their best use and to conserve and enhance their value
3. To check existing congestion and to prevent future congestion by limiting the development of land to a degree consistent with the capacity of the county to furnish adequate public services
4. To prevent overcrowding of land with buildings and thereby insure maximum living and working conditions and prevent blight and slums
5. To protect residential, business, and manufacturing areas alike from harmful encroachment by incompatible uses and to insure that land allocated to a class of uses shall not be usurped by other inappropriate uses
6. To fix reasonable zoning standards to which buildings or structures shall conform
7. To prevent such additions to, and alterations or remodeling of, existing buildings or structures as would not comply with the restrictions and limitations imposed hereinafter
8. To insure high standards of light, air, and open space in areas where people live and work
9. To relieve street congestion through adequate requirements for off-street parking and loading facilities
10. To foster a more rational pattern of relationships between residential, business, and manufacturing for the mutual benefit of all
11. To isolate or control the location of unavoidable nuisance-producing uses
12. To provide protection against fire, explosion, noxious fumes, and other hazards, in the interest of the public health, safety, comfort, and the general welfare
13. To define the powers and duties of the administrative officers and bodies, as provided hereinafter
14. To prescribe penalties for the violations of the provisions of this ordinance, or of any amendment thereto

exclusive residential districts that prohibited commercial and industrial buildings. Not until 1926 was comprehensive zoning firmly established by the Supreme Court in *Village of Euclid* v. *Ambler Realty*, 272 U.S. 365. As originally enacted, comprehensive zoning established districts for different types of land use, and controlled the bulk of buildings by restricting the number of stories. Density is controlled with land coverage ratios, set-back requirements, restrictions on the number of residential units per lot, acre, or square foot.

Today zoning has much broader application. Figure 19–2 lists the intent and purposes of the Cook County, Illinois, zoning ordinance. An explanation of the main components of the usual zoning ordinance shows how the 14 purposes listed in Figure 19–2 are enforced.

General Provisions. The main elements of general provisions normally cover

The scope of regulations.
Regulations for specific uses covering sewage disposal, water supply, and number of buildings on a lot.
Accessory buildings.
Bulk regulations.
Off-street parking and loading.
Height regulations.
Existing special uses.

General provisions under scope of regulations extend the zoning controls to all uses of land or buildings and deal with the alteration and relocation and enlargement of building additions. Specific uses are exempt in the case of agricultural buildings and distribution facilities of electric power utilities. The zoning code requires conformity with plumbing and health codes of the county, city, and state.

With respect to buildings, zoning ordinances generally provide for only one principal residential building on each zoning lot. Accessory buildings are restricted in numerous ways: They cannot cover more than a stated percentage of a lot, and are restricted in height and in their sideyard requirements. Bulk regulations vary in the type of zoning district, and include required setbacks, sideyards, and floor-area ratios. Off-street parking and loading facilities apply to each zoning district.

Nonconforming Uses. Every zoning ordinance controls nonconforming buildings and structures. They are not conforming in the sense that they are inconsistent with the type of district or land use provided by the zoning ordinance. Usually nonconforming uses may not be enlarged or remodeled so as to increase bulk unless such remodeling changes the structure to a conforming use.

Zoning Administration. Enforcement of the zoning ordinance is usually placed in the hands of an administrator who is responsible for issuing zoning certificates and for undertaking inspections. An appeals board is established to hear and decide appeals on any order or decision of the zoning administrator. The board of appeals passes on applications for zoning variances, special uses, and other matters.

Public hearings are required to determine and vary regulations of the zoning ordinance. Special provisions guide standards for authorizing variances. These rules provide for the granting of variations, if such variations are not detrimental to the public welfare or injurious to other property improvements in the neighborhood. The zoning board hears appeals from the decisions of the zoning executive office or administrator.

Zoning Districts. Probably because zoning developed from nuisance controls, zoning districts begin with residential districts. The owner of a site zoned for single family dwelling use, frequently identified as an R-1 district, can use the property only for single family dwelling purposes. In an R-1 or comparable district, some localities allow churches, schools, and a limited number of other compatible institutional uses. In effect, the R-1 zoning is an exclusive use in the typical zoning ordinance. Succeeding districts tend to allow accumulative land uses. The resulting system of zoning has been referred to as *progressively inclusive districts.*

Progressively inclusive districts refer to the practice of allowing preceding uses in succeeding districts. For example, if R-2 is the multiple-family low-density area, multiple-family units may be allowed in addition to uses of the preceding district which would include single-family dwellings of the R-1 district. As the zoning ordinance deals with each type of district—residential, commercial, and industrial—it becomes progressively inclusive to the point that districts reserved for industry can also be devoted to commercial and residential use. The result is that districts subject to uses of preceding districts tend to become mixed districts.

This is especially true if the zoned district creates a land supply greater than the current amount of land demanded. If industrial land use is not in sufficient demand, some owners sell property for commercial and other purposes. As a consequence, the district becomes neither a good industrial district nor a good commercial district.

Exclusive districts for particular purposes avoid the progressively inclusive districts of the typical zoning ordinance. The planned industrial park, which reserves land specifically for a select group of industries, is a case in point. Included also would be planned unit developments in which land is carefully allocated by land use type, avoiding inharmonious land use and minimizing incompatible land uses. Cluster housing and shopping centers are other instances in which zoning deficiencies are corrected.

On this point, ideally zoning accomplishes four objectives:

Separates inharmonious uses.

Groups compatible land uses.

Provides space for undesirable uses.

Establishes minimum building standards within districts.

It is fairly clear that zoning separates residential property districts from industrial districts. In other respects, zoning provides space for uses that have a mutual attraction: the apartment district, motel districts, hospital districts, and shopping districts among others. Moreover, virtually every locality needs space for sanitary fills, mortuaries, and sewage disposal plants, for example. Building standards relate to the minimum size of a dwelling (e.g., no residential building of less than 600 square feet). Other similar zoning regulations provide building standards suitable for each district.

Certain administrative practices relate to "variances" and "spot zoning." Variances refer to the practice of allowing a variation in land use. For example, an owner of a lot may be issued a variance to permit construction of a house on a lot that has a stream or water-front location, making it impossible to observe building set-back regulations. Or a variance may permit construction of a hospital in a residential district.

Spot zoning occurs under amendments to the zoning code that change land zoned, say, from residential to commercial use. To be sure, zoning districts must be flexible to adapt to current needs. However, if the zoning districts are amended indiscriminately (and without reference to the general plan), they create haphazard development unsatisfactory to district residents. District boundary changes, the result of friendship, politics, and influence are administrative deficiencies and against the purpose of zoning.

Housing Codes

Housing codes are another example of the exercise of police power. They are limited by the constitutional protection from deprivation of life, liberty, and property, without due process of law. Housing regulations are valid as long as they bear a demonstrable relationship to public health, safety, and welfare.

Housing codes deal with the responsibility to keep housing in conformity with the code. Their main requirements cover several common regulations: They restrict the number of persons legally permitted for a given dwelling; housing must be kept in proper repair; they provide for maintenance of the house in a sanitary condition and establish minimum ventilation and lighting standards. Under the usual code, housing must have acceptable facilities for fire protection; machinery and services such as water and heat; hot and cold water must be furnished in accordance with the code.

In short, housing codes refer to municipal ordinances adopted under special enabling legislation of the state legislature. In a few states—primarily Connecticut, Iowa, Massachusetts, Michigan and Minnesota, New Jersey, and Pennsylvania—state housing codes operate over the entire state or apply state codes only to certain cities. California and New York are examples of states that have enacted extensive housing legislation but that allow municipalities to adopt codes that are not inconsistent with state law. It is estimated that almost 30 percent of some 18,000 local governments have enacted a housing code.

Many communities have enacted housing codes by adopting a uniform national code. Such a code has been widely adopted as published by the International Conference of Building Officials. According to this source, housing codes

> . . . provide minimum requirements for the protection of life, limb, health, property, safety, and welfare of the general public and the owners and occupants of residential buildings. The provisions of this Code shall apply to all buildings or portions thereof used or intended to be used, for human habitation.

The enforcement of a housing code starts with an inspection by a local housing code inspector. The inspector may inform the owner of conditions that violate the housing code and request correcting of the violation. Administrative and judicial pressures are brought to bear against the responsible owner. In some instances the municipality has the right to remedy the deficiency and charge the cost to the owner. For the most part, the shortage of housing for low-income families has not encouraged rigid enforcement of the housing code.

Building Codes

Building codes are directed to the public safety. They regulate the kinds of materials that go into a building and they regulate the standards of construction that provide for a safe structure. Building codes may be separately listed to include plumbing codes controlling the type of plumbing hardware and sanitary disposal of sewage, and electrical codes that regulate wiring and the type of equipment to be put into a building and its manner of connection and insulation. Thus, the building code covers only the construction of a building. The housing code deals more with the use, occupancy, and maintenance of existing buildings. Both controls depend on the judicious exercise of police power.

The uniform building code as prepared by the International Conference of Building Officials describes the purpose of building codes in the following terms:

> . . . to provide minimum standards to safeguard life or limb, health, property, and public welfare by regulating and controlling the design, construction, quality of materials, use and occupancy, location and maintenance of all buildings and structures within the city and certain equipment specifically regulated herein.

The scope of the building code is illustrated by other provisions of the uniform building code.

This Code shall apply to the construction, alteration, moving, demolition, repair, and use of any building or structure within the city, except work located primarily in a public way, public utility towers and poles, mechanical equipment not specifically regulated in this Code, and hydraulic flood control structures.

The enforcement of building codes is implemented by a permit system. Before a permit for new construction is issued, the applicant must demonstrate compliance with local building code requirements.

PRIVATE CONTROLS

While the main concern here is with public land use controls, real estate developers, investors, and owners may impose private restrictions equally enforceable. Their main purpose is to maintain the character of property uses. In some respects, they are more effective because design, planning, and property use may be more rigidly controlled than would be possible under the police power. The main instruments for exercising private controls are found in deed restrictions, subdivision covenants, and provisions governing property uses in special-purpose developments such as planned unit developments, housing associations, shopping centers, and industrial parks.

Deed Restrictions

An owner of extensive acreage may control developments by terms of the sale. For example, the purchaser of a 20-acre tract may buy subject to the restriction that buildings constructed on the purchased property must be constructed of brick veneer exteriors or that the property is to be used only for single-family dwellings of not less than 2,500 square feet. Condominiums transferring a fee interest contain special restrictions aimed at preserving the character of the condominium development.

Though deed restrictions may be more restrictive than public controls, they do not give the same protection. For example, an owner may relax restrictions in deeds indiscriminately as competition for sales increases. There are pressures to lower restrictions to widen the market. Moreover, the enforcement of deed restrictions depends on private action and not public enforcement.

Subdivision Covenants

Private subdivision restrictions apply mainly to high-valued, exclusive residential neighborhoods. One of the first subdivisions using private controls to shape the character of a whole neighborhood was the Roland Park Company of Baltimore of 1887. Similar controls were used in the

"Garden District" of Baltimore. The Palos Verdes Estates of California is another well-known subdivision restricted by private covenants. Subdivision covenants restrict property use to preserve the value and character of the neighborhood. Private subdivision regulations required by Levitt and Sons illustrate the more restrictive nature of private controls. For example,

> You may add a detached room or garage to your house. It must be similar in architecture, color, and material to the original dwelling and the addition must not project in front of the dwelling at all.

Restrictive covenants often control residential signs; they restrict ownership of pets to two household pets; no businesses are permitted; and, laundry may be hung only in the rear yard. Subdivision restrictions may even include a prohibition against fences and shrubs over three feet high. For example:

> You may plant a shrub or other growing fence but don't let it grow higher than three feet. No fabricated fences (wood, metal, etc.) will be permitted. In designing the blocks and lots at Levittown we have achieved the maximum open and spacious appearance. Fences will cut this in small parcels and spoil the whole effect no matter how good-looking the fence material itself may be—and some of it is or can become pretty terrible! This item is of prime importance.

It would not be possible publicly to enact and enforce the more restrictive private covenants applying to subdivision regulations. Compared to public controls, the danger lies in their nonenforcement or relaxation by subsequent purchasers. Again, enforcement depends on private legal action. Usually subdivision covenants of this type will be enforced by adjoining property owners bringing private legal action against the offending owner. (See Chapter 18 on subdivision regulations for additional illustrations of subdivision covenants.)

Planned Unit Developments

Traditional zoning regulations have been tied to the purchase and development of individual lots. While satisfactory to control scattered development of individual lots, controls directed to a single parcel lack the flexibility for planning of larger-scale developments. Planned unit developments provide for greater flexibility in planning communities or even new towns.

Ordinances permitting planned unit developments are specific on the procedures for plan approval but less detailed in substantive requirements. Official approval, where permitted, requires the submission of plans and in other respects leaves other detail open for negotiation between the developer and the local agency. Specific standards of the typical zoning ordinance are replaced by approval of the concept of land unit development. Considerable discretion is given local agencies for final land approval. Discretionary authority anticipates that the developer will employ a competent planner who submits a comprehensive plan for the area in mind.

The zoning ordinance of the city of San Francisco authorizes planned unit development provided (1) the developer submits an overall development plan showing land use provision for public and open space; (2) it includes an area of at least three acres or adjoins open space; (3) the plan produces an environment of a stable and desirable character and provides standards of open space. These provisions may include shopping centers and office buildings compatible with the overall plan.

A related concept are the new towns which incorporate residential, commercial and industrial land use with open space and recreation suitable to the local area. The more prominent projects are relatively large.

Location	Number of Acres
Reston, Virginia	7,180
Laguna Niguel, California	7,100
El Dorado Hills, California	9,800
Clear Lake City, Texas	50,000
Irvine Ranch, California	93,000

In the planned development, less land is lost for streets and public highways. The street plan, originally developed for horses and buggies may absorb up to 23 percent of the land area. In the newer development, with curvilinear streets and super blocks, only 8 to 10 percent of the area is taken for streets. The more efficient layout provides more land for parks and open space.

The basic concept of these developments is illustrated by the purpose of planned unit residential development stated in the model act published by the National Association of Home Builders in collaboration with the Urban Land Institute:

Section 3. PURPOSE OF PLANNED UNIT RESIDENTIAL DE-VELOPMENT CHAPTER.

The City, being confronted with increasing urbanization, and acknowledging that the technology of land development and the demand for housing are undergoing substantial and rapid changes, and recognizing the applicability of the objectives set forth in Section 1 of the Act [Model Act], intends to encourage (1) that variety and flexibility in land development for residential purposes, and uses ancillary thereto, that are necessary to meet those changes in technology and demand and that will be consistent with the best interests of the entire City; (2) the more efficient allocation and maintenance by private initiative of Common Open Space ancillary to new residential areas; and (3) the more efficient use of those public facilities required in connection with new residential development; and, determining this means of providing for residential and ancillary uses to be in the best interest of the City, does hereby adopt this ordinance for application to areas of land which are to be developed as Planned Residential Developments, as herein defined (*Legal Aspects of Planned Unit Residential Development*, Technical Bulletin 52, Urban Land Institute, Washington, D.C.).

Supporters of this type of regulation contend that the police power guides development consistent with the new community requirements. The legalities and restrictions imposed on conventional regulations are avoided in favor of professionally planned projects that promote the community interest.

ENVIRONMENTAL CONTROLS

The police power has been increasingly exercised to enact environmental controls dealing with air, water, coastal zones and land use that affects the surrounding environment. Such legislation began with enactment of the National Environmental Policy Act of 1969. An indication of Congressional intent is provided by Section 101 that defines a National Environmental Policy. Succeeding legislation may be expected to follow the policy as set forth in the act. The main points, as stated in the act, explain that it is the federal responsibility to improve and coordinate federal plans, functions, programs, and sources so that the nation may

1. Fulfill the responsibilities of each generation as trustee of the environment for succeeding generations;
2. Assure for all Americans safe, healthful, productive, and esthetically and culturally pleasing surroundings;
3. Attain the widest range of beneficial uses of the environment without degradation, risk to health or safety, or other undesirable and unintended consequences.
4. Preserve important historic, cultural, and natural aspects of our national heritage, and maintain, wherever possible, an environment which supports diversity and variety of individual choice;
5. Achieve a balance between population and resource use which will permit high standards of living and a wide sharing of life's amenities; and
6. Enhance the quality of renewable resources and approach the maximum attainable recycling of depletable resources.

More recently the Land Use Policy and Planning Assistance Act has been proposed by Congress. Currently, approximately 25 states have enacted land use controls covering planning environmental controls. A review of these proposals shows that the police power is increasingly used on a national or state-wide basis. The directions that these controls are taking may be summarized in five points.

1. *Control of large-scale developments.* Private property planned for urban use will be subject to more stringent state or federal control. State planning acts in some areas have already covered this point. For example, the Department of Environmental Protection in Maine reserves final approval on all projects of 200 acres or more.

2. *Control over land use density.* These controls will probably substitute for the sideyard setbacks and minimum area requirements of the conventional zoning ordinance. In Vermont, for instance, it has been proposed to regulate density in various land districts by area zoning around standard metropolitan statistical areas. The more distant bands would require lower land use densities.

3. *All private land to be subject to planning.* Pending legislation, some already in effect, will control land by regional, state, or federal agencies in jurisdictions that have no land planning requirement. Proposals have been introduced in Congress to require an integrated land use plan over the respective states. Communities too small or without professional planning staffs will probably be subject to nonlocal restrictions.

4. *Waterfront areas.* Land use problems covering coastal zones, rivers and lakes will be subject to special building and sewage standards. The effect of any proposed land use on waterfrontage will probably be reviewed by environmental agencies.

5. *Location of public facilities.* Federal agencies will examine the location of public facilities, including public highways, bridges, public buildings, and other installations, relative to the environmental impact of the proposed construction. Such steps are already required for some projects.

It has been reported that the Environmental Protection Agency proposes to approve construction of parking facilities exceeding 1,000 parking spaces within urban areas. The effect of such controls will probably (1) increase development costs, and (2) restrict the supply of land for urban development. To the extent that controls lead to compatible open and attractive land use, land values will probably increase. But the increase may be at the expense of individual property owners.

The main issue turns on common objections to the police power; namely, restricting individual property rights for the general benefit. It is probably true that there is some general benefit in restricting dwelling units, for example, to two units per acre in a selected project. But if the effect of this restriction, which is for the general benefit, operates to lower the productive capacity of the land and, therefore, its value, the private property owner is bearing the final burden. The sacrifice is especially noticeable if the land was acquired in anticipation of more intensive development. Later, if public controls are exercised against land which was acquired for more intensive use, the owner suffers a loss which, under our present rules, is usually not compensable.

Therefore the issue turns on whether the exercise of police power is reasonable and not discriminatory and is not in violation of the equal protection clause. The law must be reasonable, not arbitrary, and must bear a rational relationship to a stated objective. In the last analysis, ecological controls will bear heavily on property owners—subject to court review.

QUESTIONS FOR REVIEW

_____ 1. The police power refers to the
   a. public right to take private property.
   b. right to tax private property.
   c. inherent power of government to regulate land use for the public interest, health, morals, convenience, and safety.
   d. right to regulate federal land in the public interest, health, morals, convenience, and safety.

_____ 2. Which of the following statements is correct?
   a. The right of eminent domain is provided by the federal Constitution.
   b. Under eminent domain proceedings, private property owners are entitled to just compensation.
   c. Public utilities under state and federal regulation are granted the right of eminent domain.
   d. All of the above.

_____ 3. Which of the following is associated with the right of eminent domain?
   a. Building codes.
   b. Severance damages.
   c. Subdivision regulations.
   d. The general plan.

_____ 4. Land use planning should be based on a comprehensive local survey which would not include
   a. a physical survey.
   b. an economic survey.
   c. a social survey.
   d. a political survey.

_____ 5. Which of the following items illustrates severance damages?
   a. Damages to land remaining after a public taking.
   b. A ten-acre tract taken for highway right of way purposes.
   c. The value of land before a taking.
   d. An easement for an electrical distribution line.

_____ 6. Which of the following statements is correct?
   a. Losses of property owners arising from eminent domain are fully compensable.
   b. Loss of business profits is compensable under eminent domain.
   c. In a taking, damages will be paid for the interruption of business during construction.
   d. Not all property damages are compensable under eminent domain.

_____ 7. The forfeiture of private property to the state owned by persons dying interstate and without heirs is known as the
   a. power of lis pendens.
   b. power of escheat.
   c. right of inheritance.
   d. power of taxation and eminent domain.

_____ 8. The right to regulate private land use differs from eminent domain in that
   a. property owners vote on eminent domain proceedings.
   b. public control of private land use forces a change in property ownership.
   c. property owners are reimbursed for the loss of rights under land use controls.
   d. property owners are reimbursed for certain losses under eminent domain.

_____ 9. _____ insure that buildings are constructed according to minimum safety standards.
   a. Zoning ordinances
   b. Housing controls
   c. Building codes
   d. Health codes

_____10. Zoning regulations generally
   a. retard neighborhood depreciation.
   b. tend to protect residential areas from incompatible land uses.
   c. contribute to the best use of land.
   d. all of the above.

_____11. Housing codes control
   a. land used for public buildings.
   b. minimum standards of dwelling occupancy.
   c. private investment in public lands.
   d. the density of single-family dwellings.

_____12. Local land use controls generally promote the objectives of the
   a. chamber of commerce.
   b. state revenue department.
   c. general plan.
   d. local school district.

_____13. Land use controls are justified under the right of government to use

    a. police power.
    b. eminent domain.
    c. laws of inherent right.
    d. ordinances of beneficial interest.

_____14. Guiding the use and development of land to maximize social and economic benefits is called

    a. police power.
    b. pollution control.
    c. land use planning.
    d. building code regulation.

_____15. Eminent domain requires

    a. permission of the property owner.
    b. legislative action.
    c. payment of just compensation.
    d. special purpose legislation.

_____16. Which of the following terms increases the optimum use of local real estate?

    a. The general plan.
    b. Tax equalization.
    c. Improved highway access.
    d. New sewer and utility systems.

_____17. Which of the following statements is correct?

    a. Zoning creates property values.
    b. Zoning has no relation to land use density.
    c. Zoning does not create property values.
    d. Zoning increases neighborhood depreciation.

_____18. The property of a person who dies intestate, leaving no heirs, passes to the state under power of

    a. respondent superior.
    b. reversionary estoppel.
    c. escheat.
    d. each state constitution.

_____19. Planned unit developments

    a. provide variety and flexibility in land development.
    b. reduce the possibility of an eminent domain taking.
    c. circumvent objectives of the general plan.
    d. provide low-income housing.

_____20. The zoning of a particular property is called

    a. a nonconforming use.
    b. an easement.
    c. "spot" zoning.
    d. aesthetic zoning.

_____21. Which of the following statements is correct?

    a. A planned unit development increases the amount of land necessary for streets.

    b. Planned unit developments are seldom suitable for areas greater than 200 units.

    c. Planned unit developments refer to industrial acreage.

    d. The more efficient layout of a planned unit development reduces the area taken for streets.

_____22. Private subdivision covenants generally

    a. increase local property taxes.

    b. tend to preserve the value and character of the neighborhood.

    c. are enforced by public agencies.

    d. are less restrictive than local subdivision regulations.

_____23. If industries meet _____ they are acceptable under the zoning ordinance regardless of the type of industry.

    a. minimum building standards

    b. density controls

    c. performance standards

    d. the approval of surrounding property owners

_____24. The right of eminent domain is *not* available to which of the following?

    a. A private business.

    b. A state agency.

    c. A federal agency.

    d. A pipeline company.

_____25. In reference to escheat of real property to the state, which of the following statements is *incorrect*?

    a. Escheat resembles the feudal concept of sovereignty under which the king owned all land.

    b. Upon the death of an intestate property owner without heirs, title vests immediately in the state by operation of law.

    c. Judicial action is necessary for the state to acquire property by escheat.

    d. It is the responsibility of the federal district attorney to prove that there are no heirs.

_____26. Local land use planning is justified under

    a. police power.

    b. federal laws.

    c. eminent domain.

    d. escheat.

_____27. The exercise of police power cannot be

    a. reasonable.

    b. discriminatory.

    c. restrictive.

    d. exercised by local government agencies.

_____28. Police powers exercised by local governments are generally not

    a. granted by local statutes.

    b. designed to promote orderly growth.

    c. explicit in their design and implementation.

    d. designed to restrict land use by ethnic groups in the public interest.

_____29. The right to regulate _____ gives local agencies the right to approve street width, drainage, and public utilities.

    a. deed recordings

    b. subdivisions

    c. city growth

    d. mortgage lending practices

_____30. Historically, zoning regulations have provided for exclusive _____ land use.

    a. commercial

    b. industrial

    c. residential

    d. urban

_____31. Which of the following statements is correct?

    a. Building codes control the use and occupancy of dwelling units.

    b. Building codes affect the land use pattern.

    c. Building codes relate to standards of building construction.

    d. Building codes govern severance damages.

_____32. Progressively inclusive zoning districts are

    a. desirable innovations of the zoning code.

    b. techniques that separate inharmonious land uses.

    c. land use practices enforced by the Environmental Protection Agency.

    d. zoning methods that encourage incompatible land uses.

_____33. Property tax discrimination is illustrated by a(n)

    a. high annual tax rate measured in mills.

    b. high assessment ratio.

    c. assessment ratio that varies between properties selling for the same amount.

    d. high level of assessed value to the sales price among all taxable properties.

_____34. Which of the following statements is correct?

    a. The general plan is closely related to government policy and is a means of coordinating local government agencies.

    b. The general plan is a continuous process directed by the state legislature without public intervention.

    c. The general plan permits local government agencies to comply with federal directives.

    d. Planning is closely related to local government policy, it is a continuous process, and it is a necessary part of the local property tax administration.

_____35. Owners suffering substantial losses from the exercise of the police power will

    a. receive only partial compensation for their losses.

    b. receive only severance damages.

    c. receive payment of just compensation for their losses.

    d. not receive compensation for their losses.

_____36. The right of eminent domain provides for the taking of private property by public authorities

    I. upon payment of just compensation.

    II. for the public interest, health, morals, convenience, and safety.

    a. I only.

    b. II only.

    c. Both I and II.

    d. Neither I nor II.

_____37. The system of zoning referred to as progressively inclusive districts

    a. allows only one type of land use within each district.

    b. prevents districts subject to uses of preceding districts from becoming mixed districts.

    c. allows preceding uses in succeeding districts.

    d. prevents the creation of a land supply greater than the current amount of land demanded.

_____38. Objectives of zoning include

    a. separation of inharmonious land uses, grouping of compatible land uses, provision of space for undesirable uses, and establishment of standards within districts.

    b. grouping of inharmonious land uses, separation of compatible land uses, and establishment of standards within districts.

    c. grouping of sanitary fills, mortuaries, and sewage disposal plants, building standards relating to the maximum size of a dwelling, and separation of inharmonious land uses.

    d. separation of inharmonious land uses, grouping of apartments, motels, hospitals, and shopping districts, and provision of land for exclusive land use districts.

_____39. Housing codes

    a. are valid as long as they bear a demonstrable relationship to public health, safety, and welfare.

    b. may not restrict the number of persons who occupy a given dwelling.

      c. allow municipalities constitutionally to deprive persons of life.
          liberty and property, without due process of law.
      d. are always strictly enforced.

_____40. Housing codes
      I. are enforced by use of a permit system.
      II. regulate the kinds of materials that go into a building.
      a. I only.
      b. II only.
      c. Both I and II.
      d. Neither I nor II.

ANSWER KEY

1. (*c*)	11. (*b*)	21. (*d*)	31. (*c*)
2. (*d*)	12. (*c*)	22. (*b*)	32. (*d*)
3. (*b*)	13. (*a*)	23. (*c*)	33. (*c*)
4. (*d*)	14. (*c*)	24. (*a*)	34. (*a*)
5. (*a*)	15. (*c*)	25. (*c*)	35. (*d*)
6. (*d*)	16. (*a*)	26. (*a*)	36. (*a*)
7. (*b*)	17. (*c*)	27. (*b*)	37. (*c*)
8. (*d*)	18. (*c*)	28. (*d*)	38. (*a*)
9. (*c*)	19. (*a*)	29. (*b*)	39. (*a*)
10. (*d*)	20. (*c*)	30. (*c*)	40. (*d*)

SUGGESTED ADDITIONAL READING

Environmental Quality, The Fifth Annual Report of the Council on Environmental Quality. Washington, D.C.: U.S. Printing Office, December 1974.

Land Development Manual. Washington, D.C.: National Ass. of Home Builders, 1974.

Meisel, Gerald S., and Hebard, Edna L. *Principles of Real Estate Law.* Cambridge, Mass.: Schenkman Publishing Co., 1967, chap. 7.

Smith, Wallace F. *Urban Development, the Process and the Problems.* Berkeley, Calif.: University of California Press, 1975, chaps. 14 and 15.

20

Federal Legislation
Affecting Real Estate

In earlier years real estate operations were considered local affairs, not involving interstate commerce and subject at the most to local zoning and building codes. Today, real estate developers and others must comply with new legislation dealing with *fair housing, equal credit opportunity* legislation and federal *flood insurance* regulations. In still other instances, federal *environmental laws* are such that real estate developments and their operation encounter a growing number of federal and state administered controls. Even some new local environmental controls parallel and even exceed state and federal land use restrictions. Surely, the more significant elements of federal legislation—for the serious real estate professional—warrant careful study.

FAIR HOUSING ADMINISTRATION

An executive order issued by President Kennedy, November 20, 1962, prohibited discrimination in housing provided with federal financial assistance, i.e., FHA, VA, and public housing. Later Title VI of the *Civil Rights Act of 1964* extended the executive order by prohibiting discrimination in housing that received federal financial assistance. Then as a result of a Supreme Court decision (*Jones* v. *Mayer*, 392 U.S. 409 1968), it was held that a 1866 civil rights law, under authority of the *13th Amendment*, prohibited racial discrimination in housing, both private and public.

The 1866 law stated:

> . . . citizens, of every race and color . . . shall have the same right, in every State and Territory in the United States, . . . to inherit, purchase,

557

lease, sell, hold, and convey real and personal property (42 U.S.C. Section 1982 [1970]).

The Supreme Court ruling followed from a complaint by Joseph Lee Jones that the Alfred H. Mayer Company refused to sell him a home in the Paddock Woods community of St. Louis County for the sole reason that he was a Negro. The court ruled that the 1866 law "bars all racial discrimination, private as well as public, in the sale or rental of property, and that the statute, thus construed, is a valid exercise of the power of Congress to enforce the 13th Amendment."

While the act requires observance of fair housing rules, the decision did not include discrimination on grounds of religion or national origin, and it did not prohibit advertising or discrimination in house financing, nor did it provide for discrimination in offering brokerage services. Unlike the Fair Housing Act, it made no provision for intervention by the Attorney General. Moreover, no provisions were made for a federal court to order payment of damages.

Fair housing regulation is much broader under Title VIII of the Civil Rights Act of 1968 (Fair Housing Title [Title VIII] of the *Civil Rights Act of 1968*, Pub. L. 90–284, 82 Stat. 81). As a consequence of this Act, real estate brokers are required to observe fair housing requirements, and builders and sponsors of FHA-financed housing must prepare affirmative fair housing marketing plans for HUD approval.

Fair Housing Regulations

The *Civil Rights Act of 1968*, as amended by the *Housing and Community Development Act of 1974*, makes discrimination based on race, color, religion, sex, or national origin illegal in the sale or rental of most housing and any vacant land offered for residential construction or use. Title VIII of the Civil Rights Act of 1968 stated "it is the policy of the United States to provide, within constitutional limitations, for fair housing throughout the United States." Acts prohibited by the fair housing law cover several types of discrimination.

1. Refusing to sell or rent to, deal, or negotiate with any person.
2. Discriminating in terms or conditions for buying or renting housing.
3. Discriminating by advertising that housing is available only to persons of a certain race, color, religion, sex, or national origin.
4. Denying that housing is available for inspection, sale, or rent when it really is available.
5. "Blockbusting" for profit, persuading owners to sell or rent housing by telling them that minority groups are moving into the neighborhood.
6. Denying or making different terms or conditions for home loans by

commercial lenders, such as banks, savings and loan associations, and insurance companies.

7. Denying to anyone the use of or participation in any real estate services, such as brokers' organizations, multiple listing services, or the facilities related to the selling or renting of housing.

Observers have estimated that the Act applies to 80 percent of residential properties. More specifically, the Act covers single-family housing owned by private individuals which are listed with a broker for sale or rent. The Act covers houses owned by persons who own more than three houses or who in a two-year period sell more than one house in which the individual was not the most recent resident. Apartments of five or more units are automatically included while apartments of less than five units are covered if the owner does not reside in one of the units.

Exemptions. The exemptions under the Act are fairly limited. An individual owning three or fewer single-family dwellings does not fall within the purview of the Act if a broker is not used, and if discriminatory advertising is avoided; provided, that no more than one house in which the owner was not the most most recent resident is sold during any two-year period.

Further, if discriminatory advertising is not used, the Act exempts rentals of rooms or units in owner-occupied dwellings of two to four families. Dwellings owned by religious organizations, which are operated for other than a commercial purpose, are exempt if the religion is not restricted on account of race, color, or national origin. Similarly, private clubs that own and operate residential property for other than a commercial purpose have the right to rent or sell residential property to its own members.

Enforcement. The Act is enforced by complaints filed with the Secretary of Housing and Urban Development or directly to federal, state, or local courts. The courts are authorized to grant permanent or temporary injunctions, temporary restraining orders, or other appropriate relief. Actual damages may be awarded, and not more than $1,000 in punitive damages are provided by the Act.

Real estate brokers are subject to regulations that require the display of a fair housing poster. According to the Act, real estate brokers or others selling or renting dwellings, shall post and maintain a fair housing poster at their place of business where a dwelling is offered for sale or rental. Figure 20–1 illustrates the fair housing poster available from the Department of Housing and Urban Development.

According to current law, all fair housing posters shall be prominently displayed so as to be readily apparent to all persons seeking housing accommodations or brokerage services. Failure to display the fair housing poster is deemed prima facie evidence of a discriminatory housing practice. (37 *Federal Register* 3429, February 16, 1972).

FIGURE 20–1

Fair Housing Poster

Real estate brokers offering dwellings for sale are required to post this 11x14-inch poster prominently in their place of business.

**EQUAL HOUSING
OPPORTUNITY**

We Do Business in Accordance With the Federal Fair Housing Law

(Title VIII of the Civil Rights Act of 1968, as Amended by the Housing and Community Development Act of 1974)

IT IS ILLEGAL TO DISCRIMINATE AGAINST ANY PERSON BECAUSE OF RACE, COLOR, RELIGION, SEX, OR NATIONAL ORIGIN

- In the sale or rental of housing or residential lots
- In advertising the sale or rental of housing
- In the financing of housing
- In the provision of real estate brokerage services

Blockbusting is also illegal

An aggrieved person may file a complaint of a housing discrimination act with the:

U.S. DEPARTMENT OF HOUSING AND URBAN DEVELOPMENT
Assistant Secretary for Fair Housing and Equal Opportunity
Washington, D.C. 20410

Affirmative Marketing Plans

Beginning in 1972, the Department of Housing and Urban Development (HUD), enforced affirmative fair housing marketing regulations. According to HUD:

> It is the policy of the department to administer its FHA housing programs affirmatively, so as to achieve a condition in which individuals of similar income levels in the same housing market area have a like range of housing choices available to them regardless of race, color, religion or national origin (*HUD Guide to Evaluating Affirmative Fair Housing Market Plans.* vol. III. Washington, D.C.: Department of Housing and Urban Development, 1975, p. 1).

These regulations require developers of federally assisted or insured housing to attract "those persons who traditionally would not have been expected to apply for the housing, primarily blacks, Spanish-Americans, Orientals, and American Indians." The marketing plan, required of all federally subsidized and unsubsidized housing developments, including rehabilitation projects, require developers to

Establish and maintain an equal opportunity hiring policy with respect to staff engaged in the sale or rental of housing.

Display the HUD logo or slogan in any printed material used in connection with sales or rentals.

Post a sign on all FHA project sites displaying prominently the HUD equal opportunity statements.

Hence developers must practice affirmative fair housing marketing that complies with HUD regulations. The marketing plan must be approved as a condition for federal assistance. Such a plan must show the direction of marketing activity, the target minority group, and the marketing program. Advertising media, frequency of use, and copies of brochures that will be used must be submitted for approval. Even a written copy of radio announcements must be submitted for approval as part of the marketing plan. Further, the sales staff will be reviewed for their experience in marketing to racial and ethnic groups.

EQUAL CREDIT OPPORTUNITY

The Federal Reserve Board enforces Regulation B controlling financial institutions that grant mortgage credit. The regulation follows requirements of the *Equal Credit Opportunity Act* of October 20, 1975. This legislation provides that

> it shall be unlawful for any creditor to discriminate against any applicant on the basis of sex or marital status with respect to any aspect of a credit transaction.

In short, Congress has enacted laws ensuring that financial institutions will exercise their responsibility to make credit available with fairness, impartiality, and without discrimination on the basis of sex or marital status. Under the amendments of 1976, Congress added *race, color, religion, national origin,* and *age* as areas in which lenders may not practice discrimination.

That portion of Regulation B that affects mortgage processing covers

1. *Credit scoring on the basis of marital status.* The Regulation forbids the use of sex or marital status in credit-scoring systems.
2. *Reasons for denying credit.* Upon the request of an applicant, creditors are required to provide the reasons for terminating or denying credit.
3. *Childbearing.* Creditors may not inquire into birth control practices or into childbearing capabilities or intentions, or assume from her age that an applicant or an applicant's spouse may drop out of the labor force due to childbearing and thus have an interruption of income.
4. *Income.* A creditor may not discount part-time income but may examine the probable continuity of the applicant's job. A creditor may ask and consider whether and to what extent an applicant's income is affected by obligations to make alimony, child support or maintenance payments. Further, a creditor may ask to what extent an applicant is relying on alimony or child support or maintenance payments to repay the debt being incurred. *But the applicant must first be informed that no such disclosure is necessary if the applicant does not rely on such income to obtain the credit.* Where an applicant chooses to rely on alimony, a creditor shall consider such payments as income to the extent the payments are likely to be made consistently. [emphasis supplied].
5. *Recordkeeping.* Creditors must keep applications and related materials, including any written charges submitted by the applicant alleging discrimination for 15 months following the date the creditor gives the applicant notice of action. For all accounts established on or after November 1, 1976, the creditor must identify, for consumer reporting agencies or others to whom the creditor furnishes information, those accounts that both spouses may use or for which they are both liable, so that the credit history can be utilized in the name of each spouse. No later than February 1, 1977, the creditor is required to inform holders of accounts existing prior to November 1, 1976, of a similar right to have credit history reported in both names.

Lenders are required to give mortgage applicants the following notice:

> The Federal Equal Credit Opportunity Act prohibits creditors from discriminating against credit applicants on the basis of sex or marital status. The federal agency which administers compliance with this law

concerning this (insert appropriate description—bank, store, etc.) is (name and address of the appropriate agency). (For additional detail see William M. Shenkel, *Real Estate Finance* [Washington, D.C.: American Bankers Assn., 1976], pp. 295–98.)

Treating an applicant less favorably than other applicants on the basis of sex or marital status constitutes discrimination. An aggrieved applicant may sue creditors for actual and punitive damages up to $10,000, and they have the right to bring a class action lawsuit on behalf of a group of aggrieved applicants. Moreover, married persons are entitled to the credit history of the account where both are contractually liable for the account or allowed to use it. Credit applicants are entitled to a statement of the reasons for denial or termination of credit on request.

While not directly affecting real estate brokers, the law probably makes more single persons eligible for mortgage credit. Moreover, some married borrowers may be eligible for higher-valued mortgages by the more liberal treatment of the wife's income.

TRUTH IN LENDING

The Truth in Lending Act requires that lenders and real estate brokers make certain disclosures in advertising credit terms. Failure to make the required disclosures permits customers to sue for twice the amount of finance charges—a minimum of $100 to a maximum of $1,000—plus court costs and attorney fees. Conviction of willful disregard for the law or regulation Z subjects the offender to a fine of up to $5,000 or one year imprisonment or both.

Regulation Z, prepared by the Board of Governors of the Federal Reserve System, sets forth rules that must be observed in certain real estate transactions. In this respect the regulation applies to any individual organization that extends or arranges credit for which a finance charge is or may be payable or which is repayable in more than four installments (*What You Ought to Know about Federal Reserve Regulation* [Washington, D.C.: Board of Governors of the Federal Reserve System, 1969], p. 4).

The 1969 Act which has been amended several times was enacted to increase competition among various financial institutions by informing consumers on consumer credit terms. Enforcement of the Act is divided among nine federal agencies. For example, the Comptroller of the Currency insures enforcement of the Act among national banks. The Federal Trade Commission enforces advertising rules, especially by real estate brokers. Thus, the purpose of the Act is to assure a meaningful disclosure of credit terms so that the consumer will be able to compare various credit terms and avoid the uninformed use of credit.

The more important points relating to real estate cover (1) the right to rescind credit terms and (2) the disclosure of credit terms. The Act covers all real estate credit to individuals not financing real estate for business purposes.

The Right of Rescission

Borrowers generally have the right to cancel a transaction three business days after loan approval. However, the right of cancellation does *not apply to a first mortgage to finance the purchase of a customer's residence.* First mortgages on dwellings *not purchased as a residence* and second mortgage liens may be cancelled within the three-day limit.

Real estate is subject to other exceptions: persons extending real estate credit are not required to show the total dollar amount of finance charges for dwelling purchases. Further, it is not necessary to show total mortgage payments in the case of first mortgages on dwellings. And while other lenders must show the total cash price, total financing, and other charges, this requirement does not apply to the sale of a dwelling.

Advertising

According to the Act, which applies to real estate brokers,

> No advertisement to aid, promote, or assist directly or indirectly any credit sale including the sale of residential real estate, loan, or other extension of credit, other than open end credit, subject to the provisions of this Part, shall state (1) The rate of a finance charge unless it states the rate of that charge expressed as an "annual percentage rate," using that term (Ibid., p. 19).

Under this requirement, real estate brokers may not advertise that a buyer may "assume an 8 percent mortgage." The latter paragraph requires the advertisement to read "assume 8 percent *annual percentage rate* mortgage." Abbreviations are not permissible. If the dwelling is purchased *subject* to an outstanding mortgage, the advertisement should read "may be purchased subject to a 6 percent mortgage." Brokers are advised that in mentioning specific credit terms, the advertisement is subject to full disclosure requirements. If the advertisement reads "no down payment," or states the amount of monthly payments, the Act requires that the advertisement disclose:

1. The selling price (cash).
2. The dollar amount of the down payment.
3. The number of monthly payments, the dollar amount, and payment periods.
4. The mortgage interest shown as an annual percentage rate.

Again, note that the law excepts a first lien for a dwelling sold to persons buying a dwelling as their residence. Note further than the annual percentage rate should be expressed after discount points if applicable. Lenders have tables that show annual percentage rates under different discount and mortgage interest rates.

THE NATIONAL FLOOD INSURANCE PROGRAM

Under the Flood Disaster Protection Act of 1973, as amended, flood insurance is required for FHA and VA mortgages in flood hazard areas. The Federal Insurance Administration (FIA) of the Department of Housing and Urban Development has identified some 21,000 flood-prone communities which have a risk of at least one flood every 100 years.

Insurance Coverage

Flood insurance is administered by the Federal Insurance Administration which notifies communities that they are in a flood-prone area. After this notification, the community (city, town, or village) has one year to adopt flood plain management measures. These measures might include zoning to prevent new construction in special flood hazard areas. Typically, new buildings permitted in special flood hazard areas must be placed on stilts, piling, or additional land fill. After adopting flood hazard measures, residents may purchase flood insurance at subsidized rates under the *emergency program*. Maximum insurance rates are shown in Table 20–1.

Subsequently, the FIA prepares flood hazard boundary maps that identify special flood hazard areas. See Figure 20 2 showing a flood hazard boundary map for a portion of Atlanta, Georgia. Special flood hazard

TABLE 20–1

Emergency Flood Insurance Coverage and Annual Premiums

	Emergency Program			
Structure	*Building (each)*	*Annual Premium Per $100*	*Contents (each)*	*Annual Premium Per $100*
Single-family dwellings (all states except Alaska, Hawaii, Guam, Virgin Islands).....................	$ 35,000	$.25	$ 10,000	$.35
Other residential (all states except Alaska, Hawaii, Guam, Virgin Islands).....................	100,000	.25	10,000	.35
Small business.....................	100,000		100,000	
Any other structure.................	100,000	.40	100,000	.75

Source: *The Lender and Flood Insurance* (Washington, D.C.: American Bankers Assn., no date), p. 10.

FIGURE 20-2
A Flood Hazard Map in the Atlantic Area*

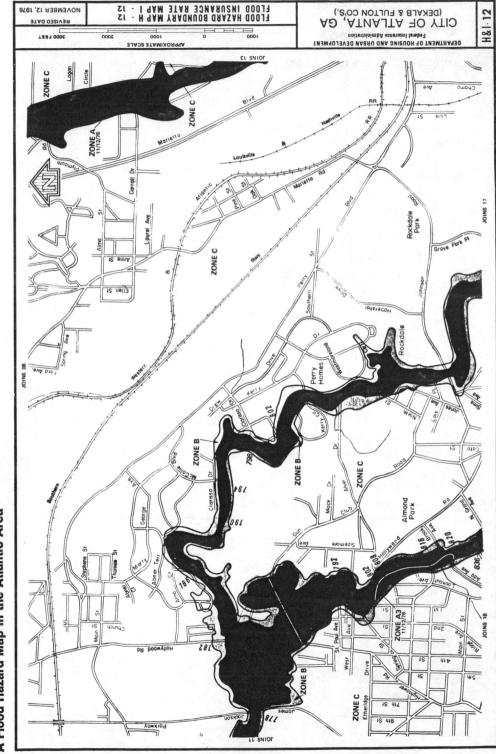

FIGURE 20–2 (continued)

EXPLANATION OF ZONE DESIGNATIONS

A flood insurance map displays the zone designations for a community according to areas of designated flood hazards. The zone designations used by FIA are:

Zone	Explanation
A	Areas of 100-year flood; base flood elevations and flood hazard factors not determined.
A0	Areas of 100-year shallow flooding; flood depth 1 to 3 feet; product of flood depth (feet) and velocity (feet per second) less than 15.
A1–A30	Areas of 100-year flood; base flood elevations and flood hazard factors determined.
A99	Areas of 100-year flood to be protected by a flood protection system under construction; base flood elevations and flood hazard factors not determined.
B	Area between limits of 100-year flood and 500-year flood; areas of 100-year shallow flooding where depth is less than 1 foot.
C	Areas outside 500-year flood.
D	Areas of undetermined, but possible, flood hazards.
V	Areas of 100-year coastal flood with velocity (wave action); base flood elevations and flood hazard factors not determined.
V0	Areas of 100-year shallow flooding with velocity; flood depth 1 to 3 feet; product of depth (feet) and velocity (feet per second) more than 15.
V1–V30	Areas of 100-year coastal flood with velocity (wave action); base flood elevations and flood hazard factors determined.

areas are the shaded areas with elevations given for each area. After FIA makes a rate survey study, residents are eligible for the *regular program* with higher insurance limits and insurance rates determined by actuarial studies. These rates and coverage under the regular program are shown in Table 20–2.

Under the 1977 amendments the maximum insurance limit for single-family dwellings was increased to $185,000. Insurance limits on other buildings and their contents were also increased. The first layer and second layers shown in Table 20–2 refer to differential premiums that

TABLE 20–2

Maximum Insurance Coverage: Regular Program

	First Layer	Second Layer	Total Maximum Insurance
Building			
Single-family (all states except Alaska, Hawaii, Guam, Virgin Islands)	$ 35,000	$150,000	$185,000
All other residential (all states except Alaska, Hawaii, Guam, Virgin Islands)	100,000	150,000	250,000
Small business	100,000	100,000	250,000
Any other structure	100,000	100,000	200,000
Contents			
Residential	10,000	50,000	60,000
Small business	100,000	200,000	300,000
Any other structure	100,000	100,000	200,000

apply to different shares of property value. For example the $35,000 first layer on single-family dwellings will carry a different premium than the amount insured over $35,000 (the second layer). Premiums are based on actuarial studies and must be determined from local sources.

The insurance covers damages from water overflow, the runoff of surface waters, mud slides, and the subsidence of land along shorelands caused by erosion or waves. The insurance does not cover accounts, bills, money, security, manuscripts, stamps, or coin collections. Also excluded are fences, swimming pools, wharves, piers, docks, walks, driveways, and landscaping. Animals and personal property such as motor vehicles, trailers, aircraft, and boats are not covered.

Administrative Requirements

Dwellings in communities that fail to participate may not be financed by FHA, VA or other federally assisted loans. Lenders in nonparticipating communities may make conventional loans without purchasing flood insurance. Flood insurance is not available in nonparticipating communities. Further, federal financial assistance would not be available for flood damages in these communities.

The Flood Insurance Agency has designated representatives in each state that provide forms and other information to local insurance agencies. Flood control maps may be secured from the designated state agency. For example, the Fireman's Fund Insurance Companies of Los Angeles are the designated representative for the state of California. Flood insurance may be purchased from any licensed insurance agent who in turn works through the state designated representative. Further information may be secured from regional offices of the Flood Insurance Administration.

ENVIRONMENTAL LAWS

Historically land use controls were largely confined to local building codes, zoning codes, and subdivision regulations. Gradually, these local restrictions were supplemented by federal legislation that controlled land uses on a regional basis. Present federal laws were enacted to resolve a particular problem on a piece-by-piece basis—requiring real estate developers to observe numerous laws and to cope, at all levels of government, with many different agencies. There is no national land use policy.

And there is one other change. Formerly real estate was subject only to *preregulatory* land use controls. For instance, a zoning ordinance establishes regulations that control future projects. Property owners could determine in advance regulations that restricted land use; that is, land use was preregulated.

The new legislation, in contrast, employs *case-by-case* regulation. As a consequence, costly presentations precede construction approval which later may be denied. Under the case-by-case method of regulation, the proposed development remains uncertain until final approval. The more important regulations affecting local real estate development include the National Environmental Protection Act, coastal zone management, and legislation that controls air, water, and noise pollution.

The Environmental Protection Agency

In the National Environmental Policy Act of 1969, Congress established national environmental policy. In the words of the Act

> . . . it is the continuing policy of the Federal Government, in cooperation with State and local governments, and other concerned public and private organizations, to use all practicable means and measures, including financial and technical assistance, in a manner calculated to foster and promote the general welfare, to create and maintain conditions under which man and nature can exist in productive harmony, and fulfill the social, economic, and other requirements of present and future generations of Americans.

And further,

> The Congress recognizes that each person should enjoy a healthful environment and that each person has a responsibility to contribute to the preservation and enhancement of the environment.

Environmental policy is interpreted by the Council on Environmental Quality, composed of three members appointed by the President with the advice and consent of the Senate. The council is directed to analyze environmental trends and to appraise environmental programs of the federal government. The Act requires federal agencies to prepare an *environmental impact statement* for federal actions that significantly affect the quality of the human environment. Environmental impact statements include a detailed explanation of

1. The *environmental impact* of the proposed action.
2. Any adverse environmental effects which cannot be avoided should the proposal be implemented.
3. *Alternatives* to the proposed action.
4. The relationship between local *short-term uses* of man's environment and the maintenance and enhancement of *long-term productivity*.
5. Any *irreversible* and *irretrievable* commitments of resources which should be involved in the proposed action should it be implemented (*emphasis supplied*).

Though the Act relates only to federal agencies, virtually every state has enacted similar legislation or has proposed similar environmental restrictions. For example, California requires environmental impact statements on private and government actions. The Massachusetts Act applies to any work, project, or activity that may cause damage to the environment.

The scope of an environmental impact statement is illustrated by the type of data required to construct a 20-story office building that replaces tenement housing. Data measuring the impact describes the anticipated effect on the local economy. Air pollution, local transportation, the change in the housing stock, as well as neighborhood stability and aesthetics, are other factors that "significantly affect the environment." Additional relationships are suggested by the Urban Land Institute that lists groups affected by such a land use project.

Physical proximity
  Persons living or working on the land proposed for development.
  Persons living or working immediately adjacent to the proposed development.
  Persons in neighborhoods surrounding the proposed development.
  Persons within commuting distance (one hour by public transit, for example) from proposed commercial and industrial developments.
Business relationship
  Realtors, builders, bankers, and others directly involved in the development.
  Owners and managers of businesses or property in the neighborhood.
Political jurisdiction
  Citizens of the local jurisdiction containing the development.
  Citizens of immediately adjacent jurisdictions and of the entire metropolitan area.
  Citizens of the state and nation.
Socioeconomic and demographic
  Age groups.
  Racial and ethnic groups.
  Persons of various income levels from poor to affluent.
Other interest groups
  Tourists.
  Landowners.
  Others.
The long-term public interest
  All present groupings over time.
  Future generations.

As a result of these detailed studies that must precede actual project approval, the Environmental Protection Agency has been criticized for delaying project approval and for increasing project costs. Environmental Impact Studies cost as much as $25,000 for a 500-unit subdivision (California).

There is also the problem of overlapping agency jurisdiction. Consider, for example, the agencies concerned with approving a new electric power generation unit. Because of the water required for cooling, steam generating plants locate near large bodies of water. The Fish and Wildlife Service, the Corps of Engineers, the Federal Power Commission, and state and local government offices must approve the project that affects separate areas of their responsibility. The impact of environmental controls is made even more complex under other laws affecting specific aspects of the environment.

Air Pollution

The Environmental Protection Agency was given added responsibility under the *Clean Air Amendments of 1970*. This is the act causing controversies over new car exhaust emissions. The Act provides grants to states to initiate air quality controls. Each state is required to submit an implementation plan for assuring air quality within their geographic area. The Act provides for establishing air quality standards throughout the United States.

The Environmental Protection Agency continuously analyzes air quality data at 247 air quality control regions. Controls over air pollution are concentrated on emissions of particulate matter both *uncontrollable*, for example, from wind erosion, forest fires, volcanos, and other natural phenomena, and *controllable emissions*.

Controllable emissions refer to burning fuels, chemical dust, and spray-producing activities. Under authority granted by the Act, highway locations, mass transportation projects, new industrial developments, and even parking lots that concentrate automobiles are subject to case-by-case review to measure their probable impact on local air pollution.

Water Pollution

Water pollution legislation seeks to restore and maintain the chemical, physical, and biological integrity of the nation's waters. The *Federal Water Pollution Control Act Amendments of 1972* stated it is the national goal that

1. The discharge of pollutants into the navigable waters be eliminated by 1985.
2. Wherever attainable, an interim goal of water quality which provides for the protection and propagation of fish, shellfish, and wildlife and provides for recreation in and on the water be achieved by July 1, 1983.
3. The discharge of toxic pollutants in toxic amounts be prohibited.
4. Federal financial assistance be provided to construct publicly owned waste treatment works.

5. Areawide waste treatment management planning processes be developed and implemented to assure adequate control of sources of pollutants in each state.
6. A major research and demonstration effort be made to develop technology necessary to eliminate the discharge of pollutants into the navigable waters, waters of the contiguous zone, and the oceans.

Before discharging pollutants, permits must be secured that specify the allowable amount of effluent. Approved water quality standards determine whether additional pollution reduction is necessary for particular stretches of water. Municipal treatment plants must provide secondary treatment; industrial plant discharges must meet standards based on the best practicable means currently available. Congress has made the federal government responsible for navigable waters for the protection of aquatic life and for encouragement of recreational activities such as boating and fishing. Environmental impact statements must be prepared for waste treatment plants.

Observers have noted that EPA's construction grant program for waste water treatment is probably the largest public works program ever undertaken. The federal government provides 75 percent of the construction costs with state and local governments contributing the balance of 25 percent. It is particularly significant to the real estate industry because the availability of waste treatment plants largely dictates the location and rate of community growth. If waste treatment facilities are not available, growth may be postponed (or prohibited).

The *National Pollutant Discharge Elimination System,* a program administered by EPA, suggests the impact of water pollution control. Some 58,000 industrial water users and municipal sewages treatment plants in 13,000 communities fall under this legislation. The discharge of pollutants is denied if the discharge is in conflict with the approved water quality management plan.

Areawide Waste Treatment Management Plans regulate the location, modification, and construction of any facility that contributes to water pollution. A narrow interpretation of this section of the water pollution control act would cover construction of a single-family dwelling or new construction that causes soil erosion and water runoff. Even farming, mining, forestry, and earth-moving activities are regulated by areawide waste treatment management plans.

The Coastal Zone Management Act

Some 30 states, which are affected by the *Coastal Zone Management Act of 1972,* administer land use and water plans. The main purposes of the Act are three-fold:

1. To preserve, protect, develop, and where possible, to restore coastal resources.
2. To assist states in the wise management of their coastal resources to the formulation of effective management programs.
3. To encourage federal agencies engaged in activities in coastal areas to work closely with the designated state agencies responsible for coastal zone management.

The program is based on a system of development grants to participating states; namely, the coastal states and states bordering the Great Lakes. Coastal zones extend inland from shorelines covering the necessary land uses that have a direct and significant impact on coastal waters. States must identify coastal zone boundaries and develop authorities to control land and water uses that have a significant impact on coastal waters. Management plans coordinate local, areawide, and interstate agencies.

Population and economic development of coastal areas must protect and preserve living marine resources and wildlife. Further, the Act controls the ecological, cultural, historic and aesthetic values in coastal zones deemed "essential to the well-being of all citizens." Special natural and scenic characteristics fall under protection of the Act.

The main thrust of the legislation encourages states to exercise full authority over lands and waters in the coastal zones for the protection of land and water resources. Clearly these controls go much further than the customary building permit, zoning, and other local controls coming under the police power.

Noise Pollution

The Environmental Protection Agency established the office of noise abatement and control to administer the *Noise Pollution and Abatement Act of 1970.* Legislation directs the agency to identify sources of noise and more specifically to determine

1. The effects at various noise levels.
2. Growth of noise levels in urban areas to the year 2,000.
3. The psychological and physiological effects on humans.
4. The effects of sporadic extreme noise (such as jet noise near airports) as compared with constant noise.
5. The effect on wildlife and property (including values).
6. The effect of sonic booms on property (including values).
7. Such other matters as may be of interest to the public welfare.

Real estate projects that create noise, for instance, airports, industrial operations, highways, or other transportation equipment or facilities, must observe noise controls. Restrictions administered as part of this law provide that the environment surrounding residential property must be relatively free of noise. The Department of Housing and Urban Development is prohibited from providing federal assistance for dwellings subject to the impact of high noise levels.

THE FEDERAL IMPACT ON LOCAL ENVIRONMENTAL CONTROLS

Federal legislation has spawned local environmental controls that parallel and often exceed federal and state restrictions. Growth communities have been forced to construct new sewage treatment plants, protect water sources, and provide for clean air. To limit further pressure on local facilities, such communities have frequently imposed moratoriums on new development. These moratoriums, generally temporary in nature, give communities time to study and enact controls that variously restrict population growth and lower the rate of real estate development. An important aspect of this type of control is exercised through new zoning regulations.

Zoning Environmental Controls

A list of zoning devices uncovers many innovations to control the environment:

1. Zoning that prohibits construction in sensitive areas (flood plains, steep slopes, potential earthquake and slide areas).
2. Down zoning.
3. Open space zoning.
4. Large lot zoning.
5. Low density zoning.
6. Agricultural zoning.

The first type of zoning discourages construction where it is desired to preserve drainage, watershed, or rainwater overflow areas. Down zoning, a highly controversial technique, lowers the allowable land use density from a previously more intensively zoned land use. For example, a community wishing to restrict population growth may reduce minimum land area per apartment unit from one unit per 1,000 square feet to one unit per 5,000 square feet of land area.

Open space zoning may be justified on ecological grounds or even for social and aesthetic reasons. More intensive land use may be allowed for new construction, provided that open space is preserved. Large lot zoning is similar in its effect: By increasing the ratio of dwelling to land area the number of households will be correspondingly reduced. For example, one dwelling per acre compared to one dwelling per five acres.

Low density zoning, another version of large lot zoning, preserves the character of established neighborhoods. Similarly, agricultural zoning saves rich agricultural land and effectively prohibits population growth that encroaches on agricultural land.

Other Local Controls

The range of environmental controls available to local communities covers an impressive number of restrictions. Public purchases to preserve land in its natural state for an indefinite period (preserving the green belt area) represents one of the more restrictive practices. Areas regarded as environmentally sensitive may be subject to local authorities that designate special preservation districts which, in the public interest, are directed to protect the environment.

In other cases, developers, as compensation for public services in a new development, may be required to contribute land or money for environmental purposes. Or, alternatively, developments may be prohibited unless public services such as sewer lines, water lines, schools, fire protection, street, and playground construction are planned as part of the proposed development.

Concern over the local environment has led still other communities to establish population limits. For instance, the local jurisdiction may restrict new construction by issuing a fixed number of building permits, a method reported to be upheld by the U.S. Supreme Court in the city of Petaluma, California (*Environmental Controls, a Handbook for Realtors* [Chicago: National Assn. of Realtors, 1977], p. 42). Another proper practice is the designation of certain areas or buildings as historic landmarks that must be preserved. If a building is placed on the National Register of Historic Places, demolition or alteration of the building or site is prohibited.

Some states have provided for the transfer of development rights as an alternative to down zoning. Where this program is authorized, the landowner sells or transfers his or her rights to develop land to a local agency that seeks to preserve open space. In some instances, the development rights restricted on one parcel may be transferred or sold to others for more intensive development in less restricted areas.

In sum, real estate ownership and the right to use privately owned land is now subject to a wide variety of regulations—and the weight of opinion predicts even more stringent controls. Growth control methods result from overcrowded highways and schools, overburdened public facilities, and concern over air, water, and noise pollution. The cost of environmental protection has been partly shifted to property owners in higher costs of compliance. Inevitably, real estate prices increase under measures that restrict the supply of land and buildings.

QUESTIONS FOR REVIEW

_____ 1. The Civil Rights Act of 1968
   a. made it unlawful to discriminate in the sale or rental of housing.
   b. provided for fair housing throughout the United States.
   c. made it unlawful to discriminate in the sale of rental housing on dwellings provided with the aid of loans, advances, grants, or contributions by the federal government.
   d. all of the above.

_____ 2. The following are exempt from provisions of the Fair Housing Act:
   a. Single-family dwellings sold or rented by an owner without services of a real estate broker.
   b. Units and dwellings occupied by more than ten families.
   c. Dwellings owned by religious organizations which are restricted on account of race, color, or national origin.
   d. All of the above.

_____ 3. Which of the following acts are prohibited by fair housing legislation?
   a. Refusal to sell to any person because of race, color, religion, or national origin.
   b. Denying that housing is available for inspection when it really is available.
   c. Persuading owners to sell or rent housing by telling them that minority groups are moving into the neighborhood.
   d. All of the above.

_____ 4. Which of the following acts are prohibited by the fair housing law?
   a. Refusing to sell or rent to, deal or negotiate with any person.
   b. Discriminating in terms or conditions for buying or renting housing.
   c. Denying that housing is available for inspection, sale, or rent when it is really available.
   d. All of the above.

_____ 5. Which of the following are exempt under Title VIII of the Civil Rights Act of 1968?
   a. Provided discriminatory advertising is not used, rental units in owner-occupied dwellings of two to four families.
   b. Provided discriminatory advertising is not used, rental of units in owner-occupied dwelling of five units or more.
   c. Dwellings owned by religious organizations operated for commercial purposes.
   d. Luxury apartments.

_____ 6. Affirmative fair housing marketing plans enforced by the Department of Housing and Urban Development require developers *a.* to give preference to minority groups in the sale of FHA-financed dwellings.

    b. to sell subsidized housing only to minority groups.

    c. of federally assisted or insured housing to attract persons who traditionally would not have been expected to apply for the housing.

    d. to market housing only to low-income groups.

_____ 7. Affirmative marketing plans require developers to

    a. establish equal opportunity hiring policies.

    b. display the HUD logo in advertising material.

    c. post signs on project sites displaying prominently the HUD equal opportunity statement.

    d. all of the above.

_____ 8. Which of the following statements is correct?

    a. Affirmative marketing plans must be approved as a condition for federal assistance.

    b. Advertising media and copies of brochures are exempt from affirmative marketing plans.

    c. It is not necessary to seek approval of radio announcements to comply with affirmative marketing regulations.

    d. It is unnecessary to identify the target minority group to comply with affirmative marketing policies.

_____ 9. Equal credit opportunity legislation as amended makes it unlawful for creditors to discriminate on the basis of

    a. occupation, income, race, color, and neighborhood.

    b. race, color, religion, national origin, and age.

    c. age, national origin, income, wealth, and color.

    d. sex, marital status, race, color, education, job status, and annual income.

_____10. Regulation B of the Federal Reserve Board

    a. forbids the use of sex or marital status in credit-scoring systems.

    b. requires creditors to provide reasons for terminating or denying credit.

    c. prohibits mortgage lenders from inquiring into birth control practices or into childbearing capabilities or intentions as a condition for mortgage approval.

    d. all of the above.

_____11. Under equal credit opportunity regulations,

    a. a creditor may ask and consider to what extent an applicant's income is affected by obligations to make alimony or child support payments.

    b. mortgage lenders are required to inform applicants that creditors are prohibited from discriminating against credit applicants on the basis of sex or marital status.

        c.   treating an applicant less favorably than other applicants on the basis of sex or marital status constitutes discrimination.

        d.   all of the above.

_____12. Which of the following statements is correct?

        a.   First mortgages on dwellings not purchased as a residence may be rescinded by the borrower three days after loan approval.

        b.   The right of rescission three days after loan approval applies to first mortgages to finance purchase of a customer's residence.

        c.   Second mortgages on single-family dwellings may not be cancelled within three business days after loan approval.

        d.   None of the above.

_____13. Which of the following advertisements by a real estate broker conforms to the Truth in Lending Law?

        a.   The buyer may assume an 8 percent mortgage.

        b.   The purchaser may assume an 8 percent annual percentage rate mortgage.

        c.   The purchaser may buy with no down payment.

        d.   The house may be purchased with monthly mortgage payments of $251.

_____14. Which of the following statements is correct?

        a.   Flood insurance is voluntary for FHA loans in some 21,000 flood-prone communities.

        b.   Flood-prone communities are identified by the Corps of Engineers.

        c.   Flood-prone communities are areas that have special flood-hazard risks of at least one flood every 100 years.

        d.   None of the above.

_____15. Under the "regular" flood insurance program

        a.   a single-family dwelling may be insured to a maximum of $185,000.

        b.   all buildings in the community are automatically insured at subsidized rates.

        c.   buildings are not eligible for federal financing assistance.

        d.   new construction is prohibited in special flood-hazard areas.

_____16. Creditors must keep applications and related materials for _____ following the date the creditor gives the applicant notice of action.

        a.   five months

        b.   ten months

        c.   one year

        d.   15 months

_____17. Lenders are required to give mortgage applicants a notice that creditors are prohibited from discriminating against applicants on the basis of

        a.   annual income.

        b.   total current assets.

     c.   sex or marital status.

     d.   employment or education.

_____18. Under the Federal Equal Credit Opportunity Act, aggrieved applicants may

     a.   force creditors to approve previously denied credit.

     b.   sue creditors for actual punitive damages up to $10,000.

     c.   bring a class action suit on behalf of a group of aggrieved applicants.

     d.   both *b* and *c.*

_____19. Which of the following statements is correct?

     a.   Historically, land use controls were largely confined to local building codes, zoning codes, and subdivision regulations.

     b.   Federal environmental laws were enacted to resolve problems on a piece-by-piece basis.

     c.   In the past real estate was subject only to preregulatory land use controls.

     d.   All of the above.

_____20. New environmental legislation

     a.   is based on preregulation controls.

     b.   employs the case-by-case system of regulation.

     c.   allows new developments to precede environmental presentations.

     d.   provides that environmental approval will not be denied if new construction has commenced.

_____21. Which of the following statements best describes our national environmental policy?

     a.   Private property rights have precedence over enhancement of the environment.

     b.   Unrestricted private development fosters and promotes the general welfare.

     c.   Each person has the responsibility to contribute to the preservation and enhancement of the environment.

     d.   Public and private organizations should use all practical means and measures to promote new real estate projects.

_____22. The National Environmental Protection Act requires

     a.   federal agencies to prepare environmental impact statements for federal actions that significantly affect the quality of the human environment.

     b.   environmental impact statements for new construction that costs over $100,000.

     c.   state legislatures to enact environmental laws for states to require environmental impact statements for new housing construction.

     d.   a system of preregulation environmental controls.

_____23. Environmental impact statements include an explanation of
      a. environmental impact and adverse environmental effects.
      b. short-term and long-term relationships between the environment and productivity.
      c. alternatives to the proposed action and any irreversible commitments of resources.
      d. all of the above.

_____24. The Environmental Protection Agency has been criticized for
      a. failure to protect coastal areas.
      b. delaying project approval, increasing project costs, and creating overlapping agency jurisdictions.
      c. concentrating too heavily on water pollution.
      d. promoting private special interests.

_____25. New car exhaust emissions are administered under
      a. the Federal Water Pollution Control Act Amendments of 1972.
      b. zoning environmental controls.
      c. Noise Pollution and Abatement Act of 1974.
      d. Clean Air Amendments of 1970.

_____26. Controllable air pollution emissions refer to
      a. wind erosion.
      b. forest fires and volcano eruptions.
      c. burning fuels, chemicals, dust, and spray-producing activities.
      d. none of the above.

_____27. Water pollution legislation seeks to
      a. preserve the coastal environment.
      b. restrict the use of potable water supplies.
      c. restrict the use of ground water for drinking purposes.
      d. restore and maintain the chemical, physical, and biological integrity of the nation's waters.

_____28. According to the Federal Water Pollution Control Act Amendments of 1972, it is the national goal that
      a. the discharge of pollutants into the navigable waters be eliminated by 1985.
      b. the discharge of toxic pollutants in toxic amounts be prohibited by 1980.
      c. water for recreation purposes takes precedence over the propagation of fish, shellfish, and wildlife.
      d. waste water treatment works be financed exclusively from local funds.

_____29. Developments subject to the Water Pollution Control Act must secure permits that specify the allowable amount of effluent before
      a. starting construction.
      b. discharging pollutants.

   c.   construction is completed.
   d.   beginning operations.

_____30. Which of the following statements is correct?
   a.   Local governments are responsible for the protection of aquatic life and encouragement of recreational activities.
   b.   Waste treatment plants do not require environmental impact statements.
   c.   The federal government is responsible for navigable waters for the protection of aquatic life and encouragement of recreational activities.
   d.   Congress has delegated responsibility for water pollution controls to state governments.

_____31. Water pollution treatment plants are particularly significant to the real estate industry because
   a.   such plants dictate the location and rate of community growth.
   b.   waste treatment plants depreciate surrounding property.
   c.   residential property may not be constructed within two miles of waste treatment plants.
   d.   waste treatment plants serve only residential developments, not industrial projects.

_____32. Which of the following represent purposes of the Coastal Zone Management Act of 1972?
   a.   To preserve, protect, and develop coastal resources.
   b.   To assist states in the wise management of coastal resources.
   c.   To encourage federal agencies to work closely with state agencies in coastal areas.
   d.   All of the above.

_____33. Coastal zones extend
   a.   from the high tide mark inland for five miles.
   b.   from two miles along bordering shorelands.
   c.   inland from shorelines covering the necessary land uses that have a direct and significant impact on coastal waters.
   d.   from shorelines to mountainous areas.

_____34. Under the Coastal Zone Management Act of 1972, the states must
   a.   enforce federal regulations governing coastal zone management areas.
   b.   identify coastal zone boundaries and develop authorities to control land and water uses in coastal zone areas.
   c.   delegate coastal zone management to local agencies.
   d.   delegate coastal zone management to federal agencies.

_____35. Which of the following describes provisions of the Coastal Zone Management Act of 1972?
   a.   The Act controls the ecological, cultural, historic, and aesthetic values in coastal zones.

b. The Act protects special, natural, and scenic characteristics.
c. The legislation encourages states to exercise full authority over lands and waters in the coastal zones.
d. All of the above.

____36. Restrictions under the Noise Pollution and Abatement Act of 1970 provide that
a. the environment surrounding residential property must be relatively free of noise.
b. federal mortgage subsidies are available for dwellings subject to high impact noise levels.
c. federal assistance is available for residential property near airports.
d. all of the above.

____37. To help preserve the environment, local communities have
a. delegated environmental controls to the federal government.
b. frequently imposed moratoriums on new development.
c. provided local assistance to real estate developers.
d. subsidized new construction to preserve the local environment.

____38. Which of the following represent environmental controls enacted as part of zoning controls?
a. Down zoning.
b. Open space zoning.
c. Housing codes.
d. a and b.

____39. Low density zoning tends to
a. increase environmental problems.
b. increase population density.
c. preserve the character of established neighborhoods.
d. prohibit population growth that encroaches on agricultural land.

____40. Which of the following represent local controls that preserve the environment?
a. Public purchase of open land.
b. Contributions by developers to compensate for the cost of public services.
c. Restrictions on the number of building permits.
d. All of the above.

ANSWER KEY

1.	(d)	11.	(d)	21.	(c)	31.	(a)
2.	(a)	12.	(a)	22.	(a)	32.	(d)
3.	(d)	13.	(b)	23.	(d)	33.	(c)
4.	(d)	14.	(c)	24.	(b)	34.	(b)
5.	(a)	15.	(a)	25.	(d)	35.	(d)
6.	(c)	16.	(d)	26.	(c)	36.	(a)
7.	(d)	17.	(c)	27.	(d)	37.	(b)
8.	(a)	18.	(d)	28.	(a)	38.	(d)
9.	(b)	19.	(d)	29.	(b)	39.	(c)
10.	(d)	20.	(b)	30.	(c)	40.	(d)

SUGGESTED ADDITIONAL READING

Burchell, Robert W., and Listokin, David. *The Environmental Impact Handbook.* New Brunswick, N.J.: Rutgers University, 1975.

Environmental Controls: A Handbook for Realtors. Chicago: National Assn. of Realtors, 1977.

The Federal Government Fair Housing 1976. Washington, D.C.: U.S. Department of Housing and Urban Development, 1977.

Listokin, David. *Fair Share Housing Allocation.* New Brunswick, N.J.: Rutgers University, 1976.

Shenkel, William M. *Modern Real Estate Principles.* Dallas, Tex.: Business Publications, Inc., 1977, chap. 4.

What You Ought to Know about Federal Reserve Regulation Z: Truth in Lending, Consumer Credit Cost Disclosure. Washington, D.C.: U.S. Board of Governors of the Federal Reserve System, 1969.

Appendix

How to Take Real Estate
License Examinations

Recall the purpose of real estate license examinations: to qualify persons to act as salespersons or real estate brokers. Consequently, license examinations cover certain essential topics to protect the public from unqualified persons. Real estate license law officials, who are experienced in preparing, grading, and administering examinations, have eliminated confusing questions—examinations are professionally prepared; there are no trick questions. These examination refinements make it easier for a licensee to study and complete examinations successfully.

To pass a real estate license examination, the prospective licensee, *first*, must know subjects covered by the examination. The subject matter is divided between (1) real estate topics that apply generally and (2) questions particularly appropriate to each state. *Secondly*, there are widely accepted rules developed for taking tests based on machine-graded, multiple-choice questions—the type of test usually given by real estate commissions.

To serve as the best possible guide for examination preparation, this discussion deals with the subject matter common to the most frequently given examinations—(1) the *multistate examination* prepared by the Department of Real Estate, State of California and (2) the *uniform examination* prepared and graded by the Educational Testing Service of Princeton, New Jersey. Guides are offered for studying that portion of the examination dealing with a particular state. Finally, suggestions on how to prepare for examinations and a review of rules for answering multiple-choice questions will prove helpful to persons unfamiliar with machine-graded tests.

584

LICENSE EXAMINATION CONTENT

At present most license agencies administer two tests: examinations for salespersons and a more comprehensive examination for real estate brokers. Both the multistate examinations prepared by the California Department of Real Estate and the Educational Testing Service make this distinction.

The California Multistate Examinations

For salespersons multiple state examinations consist of 150 multiple-choice questions. The first 100 questions test the applicants' familiarity with general real estate topics. The last 50 questions relate to laws and practices of the particular state. In the state of California applicants have three hours and fifteen minutes to complete the 150 questions.

The real estate broker examination is more inclusive. The first part of the examination, 100 multiple-choice questions, applies to general topics common to real estate brokerage practice. The second part of the examination of 100 multiple-choice questions concerns real estate law and brokerage practices for a specific state. Most jurisdictions allow two and a half to three hours for each part of the examinations. While the greatest proportion of questions cover real estate law, the topics covered are taken from five main fields:

Topic	Percent of Total Questions
1. Real estate law	50
2. Real estate regulations	10
3. Real estate valuation	15
4. Real estate finance	10
5. General questions	15

A review of these topics suggests the broad coverage of the examination.

1. *Real Estate Law.* Because of the importance of agency-principal relationships, examinations are heavily weighted with questions on real estate law. Laws covering deeds, contracts, and state license laws will be covered in this portion of the test. Expect questions on listing agreements and deposit receipts. The test for real estate brokers requires an interpretation of law applied to hypothetical cases presented in the test.

2. *Real Estate Regulation.* This portion of the examination covers federal, state, and local land use controls. The questions on local regulations concern zoning, eminent domain, police power, and subdividing. Questions on federal legislation include main provisions of the Real Estate Settlement Procedures Act, Interstate Land Disclosure Act, the Truth in Lending Act, and the Fair Housing Law.

3. *Real Estate Valuation*. Prospective licensees will be examined on the three approaches to value. Questions may cover the market approach to value, cost estimating, depreciation, the capitalization of net income including land, and building residual capitalization methods.

4. *Real Estate Finance*. This portion of the test requires a review of FHA regulations on single-family dwellings, the main features of a Veteran's Administration loan, and significant points governing institutional lenders. In the case of conventional mortgages, expect numerous questions on the calculation of mortgage interest.

5. *General Questions*. The knowledge required of real estate salespersons and brokers extends over numerous other subjects. In the multistate examination, there will be questions on the income tax treatment of real estate, capital gain taxes on residential property, installment sales, corporations, and even real estate investment trusts.

The Code of Ethics of the National Association of Realtors is almost certain to be represented by more than one question. In a related area, questions deal with *property management*—the management agreement, management policies, and new tenant-landlord laws that change the common law treatment of landlords and tenants.

Still other questions concern escrow agreements, title insurance, and local land use controls covering subdivision approval based on adequate water sewage treatment, streets, and community facilities.

In preparing for these five areas, plan on answering questions on real estate arithmetic, totaling about 10 percent of all questions. Review methods of calculating interest, property taxes, real estate commissions, sales prices, building areas, land areas, and the estimation of building perimeter. For that portion of the broker's test prepared for a particular state, the examination will present two narrative case studies. The first narrative describes data and negotiations that lead to a sales contract and an earnest money deposit. Questions relate to the interpretation of the rights of parties under stated assumptions given changing circumstances of the narrative.

A second narrative on a real estate closing requires calculation of prorates, the debit and credit of expenses and completion of a buyer's and seller's closing statement. A Real Estate Settlement Procedures Act form will be supplied for this purpose. Though the test on the closing statement is based on multiple-choice questions, selecting the correct answers requires that the prospective licensee make closing statement entries and calculations.

The Educational Testing Service Examinations

Both the salesperson and broker's examination consists of 130 questions. Four hours is allowed for the real estate salesperson examination while the broker's examination extends up to four and one-half hours. A review of their examination content shows that the salesperson examination covers a broader range of subjects; the broker's examination has more arithmetic problems and concentrates more heavily on state practice.

Real Estate Salesperson Examination. The 130 questions are divided between the *uniform test* of 100 questions and the *state* test of 30 questions. The material covered by the uniform test, like the multistate test prepared in California, consists of five main subjects. The concentration of questions within these five areas shows their wide diversity:

	Topic		Percent of Total Questions
1.	Real estate contracts......................		26
2.	Real estate finance........................		20
3.	Real estate ownership.....................		19
	Deeds...................................	6	
	Real property interest.....................	8	
	Condominiums............................	2	
	Fair housing..............................	3	
4.	Real estate brokerage......................		20
	Agency law...............................	10	
	Property management.....................	2	
	Settlement procedures....................	8	
5.	Real estate valuation......................		15
	Valuation principles......................	6	
	Planning, zoning, and public land use controls...................	3	
	Legal descriptions........................	3	
	Property taxes, liens.....................	3	

1. *Real Estate Contracts.* Among the contracts dealt with in this portion of the test are leases, listing agreements, sales contracts, offers to purchase agreements and options. Licensees are first given a listing contract and sales contract to be filled out based on information presented in the case example. The questions on listing and sales contracts are taken from these two contracts (applicants for the salesperson license are not required to calculate closing costs).

2. *Real Estate Finance.* Questions on this topic are evenly divided between financing instruments and methods. In the first instance, questions refer to regulations of the Federal Housing Administration, Veteran's Administration, and the Truth-in-Lending Act. Other questions deal with types of mortgages, loan fees, term loans, junior financing, and the rights of parties under default and foreclosure.

3. *Real Estate Ownership.* Included in the deed questions are queries on recording, acknowledgment, and differences between the main types of deeds. That portion of the test on real estate interests relates specifically to differences in title between various estates, private rights to real prop-

erty, public powers over real property, and certain special interests such as easements, licenses, life estates, and the like.

Condominium questions require an understanding of the ownership of common and separate elements, the duties and responsibilities of condominium owners and the homeowner association. Know also grievance procedures, penalties, and practices required by the Federal Fair Housing Act.

4. *Real Estate Brokerage.* The law of agency refers to rights and responsibilities common to the principal-agent relationship. Questions on property management cover the property management function and its general scope. Settlement procedures concern common settlement charges, credits and debits, adjusting entries, and prorating.

5. *Real Estate Valuation.* Some 6 percent of the questions require knowledge of the definition of value, the approaches to value, appraisal process, terminology, and valuation of partial interests under leases, easements, and eminent domain. The final 3 percent of this portion of the exam tests the prospective licensee's knowledge of real property taxes and their calculation, special assessments, lien law, and related taxation topics.

For the state test of 30 questions applicants must demonstrate a knowledge of real estate practices, laws, and license laws and regulations of the particular state. Generally, reasons for license suspension, revocation, and administrative hearing procedures are covered in this section.

The Broker Examination. Currently, the 100 questions of the uniform test concentrate on five subject areas.

Topic	Percent of Total Questions
1. Real estate instruments	30
2. Real estate values, deeds, and contracts	20
3. Leases, property management, and real estate financing	20
4. Legal and governmental aspects of real estate	10
5. Arithmetic functions	20

In the section on real estate instruments, the applicant must interpret a listing contract and a sale contract (or offer to purchase agreement). A settlement statement worksheet based on these instruments must be completed by the applicant. A copy of the real estate sales contract is shown in Figure A–1. The blanks are filled out on the basis of facts presented in the examination booklet. The settlement statement follows the debit-credit closing system (see Chapter 9).

The appraisal of partial interests, the three approaches to value and appraisal terminology are covered in this portion of the test. The essential elements of a deed, types of deeds, and the law relating to transfer of

FIGURE A–1

Real Estate Sales Contract for Real Estate Broker Examination

REAL ESTATE SALES CONTRACT (OFFER TO PURCHASE AGREEMENT)

This AGREEMENT made as of_____, 19_____,

among_____(herein called "Purchaser"),

and_____(herein called "Seller"),

and_____(herein called "Broker"),
provides that Purchaser agrees to buy through Broker as agent for Seller, and Seller agrees to sell the following described real estate, and all improvements
thereon, located in the jurisdiction of_____,
(all herein called "the property"):_____

_____, and more commonly known as_____

_____(street address).

    1. The purchase price of the property is_____

Dollars ($_____), and such purchase price shall be paid as follows:

_____

    2. Purchaser has made a deposit of_____Dollars ($_____)
with Broker, receipt of which is hereby acknowledged, and such deposit shall be held by Broker in escrow until the date of settlement and then applied
to the purchase price, or returned to Purchaser if the title to the property is not marketable.

    3. Seller agrees to convey the property to Purchaser by Deed with the usual covenants of title and free and clear from all monetary encumbrances,
tenancies, liens (for taxes or otherwise), except as may be otherwise provided above, but subject to applicable restrictive covenants of record. Seller further
agrees to deliver possession of the property to Purchaser on the date of settlement and to pay the expense of preparing the deed of conveyance.

    4. Settlement shall be made at _____on or before

_____, 19_____, or as soon thereafter as title can be examined and necessary documents prepared, with allowance of
a reasonable time for Seller to correct any defects reported by the title examiner.

    5. All taxes, interest, rent, and impound escrow deposits, if any, shall be prorated as of the date of settlement.

    6. All risk of loss or damage to the property by fire, windstorm, casualty, or other cause is assumed by Seller until the date of settlement.

    7. Purchaser and Seller agree that Broker was the sole procuring cause of this Contract of Purchase, and Seller agrees to pay Broker for services
rendered a cash fee of_____per cent of the purchase price. If either Purchaser or Seller defaults under such Contract, such defaulting party shall
be liable for the cash fee of Broker and any expenses incurred by the non-defaulting party in connection with this transaction.
Subject to:

_____

_____

    8. Purchaser represents that an inspection satisfactory to Purchaser has been made of the property, and Purchaser agrees to accept the property in
its present condition except as may be otherwise provided in the description of the property above.

    9. This Contract of Purchase constitutes the entire agreement among the parties and may not be modified or changed except by written instrument
executed by all of the parties, including Broker.

    10. This Contract of Purchase shall be construed, interpreted, and applied according to the law of the jurisdiction of_____and shall
be binding upon and shall inure to the benefit of the heirs, personal representatives, successors, and assigns of the parties.

All parties to this agreement acknowledge receipt of a certified copy.

WITNESS the following signatures:

_____   _____
                      Seller   Purchaser

_____   _____
                      Seller   Purchaser

_____
                      Broker

Deposit Rec'd $_____

Personal Check   Cash

Cashier's Check   Company Check

Sales Agent:

title to real property represent other portions of this section. Other questions deal with real estate contracts, types of contracts, and their application.

Landlord and tenant rights, types of tenancy, and the types of leases besides the use of different types of mortgages, and deeds of trust must be reviewed for this portion of the test. Applicants are expected to be familiar with the Federal Housing Administration and Veteran's Administration loans and the main financial institutions active in real estate finance.

Federal laws dealing with federal housing, the Truth in Lending Act (Regulation Z) the law of agencies, Statute of Frauds, planning, zoning, taxes and assessments cover 10 questions out of the 100 questions in the uniform test. Basic arithmetic problems common to real estate account for 20 questions.

In the state portion of the test, condominiums, subdivisions, fair housing practice, and administrative hearing procedures are covered according to state law. Know also real estate law, rules and regulations of the license agency, and other real estate practices unique to each state. The importance of the state portion of the license test, both for salespersons and brokers, warrants added explanation.

STATE TEST QUESTIONS

Because of the variation in state license law regulations and differing state laws relating to real estate instruments, titles, and conveyances, it is convenient to detail the type of questions covered in license examinations. From your local real estate manual, issued by real estate commissions or other published sources, material may be extracted that is especially important to license preparation.

Topics for review conveniently fall in three categories: (1) license law and state regulations, (2) real estate instruments and (3) real estate law. In the following pages the most significant topics covering each of these three areas is identified. Note that space is provided to fill in a summary of state law for each of the three main topics. It is recommended that from local references you fill in the questions dealing with these topics. In this way you will have a convenient source to review license questions taken from your state.

State Real Estate License Laws

Questions on this topic examine familiarity with the regulatory agency, and the minimum requirements that a salesperson's or broker's license must meet before taking the examination. You should know the grounds for suspension or revocation of real estate licenses and penalties imposed for violation of the real estate license law. The license examination may ask other details as indicated in the following outline.

The Real Estate License Agency. Examination questions may be expected to include information provided by answers to these questions.

1. Identify the agency responsible for administering real estate license law. _____

   _____
   _____

2. How many members are appointed to the licensing agency? _____

   _____

3. What are their qualifications? _____

   _____

4. How are they appointed? _____

   _____

5. What are their terms of office and compensation? _____

   _____
   _____

Minimum Qualifications of Salespersons and Brokers. Before taking the examination you should be familiar with the following points in your state.

1. Real estate salespersons.
   a. Minimum age. _____

   b. Citizenship required? _____

   c. State residency required (minimum period). _____

   d. Minimum education. _____

   e. Special real estate courses required (number and hours/credit).

   _____

   f. Number and nature of personal recommendations. _____

   g. Required bond. _____

   h. How is a salesperson defined? _____

   _____

i. List the activities that require a salesperson's license.

_____

_____

_____

_____

_____

j. What activities or persons are exempt from a real estate sales-person license? _____

_____

_____

_____

_____

k. When does a salesperson's license expire? _____

l. When must salespersons renew their licenses? _____

_____

m. Does your state provide for inactive salesperson licenses? If so, explain. _____

_____

_____

n. What is the examination fee for a salesperson? _____

_____

o. What is the fee for a salesperson's original license?

_____ ;

for a renewal application? _____

2. Real Estate Brokers.
   a. What is the minimum legal age for real estate brokers? _____

_____

b. Is citizenship required? _____

_____

c. What are residency requirements? _____

_____

d. What is the minimum experience required? _____

_____

e. State education requirements. _____

_____

f. What special real estate education courses are required? _____

_____

_____

_____

g. Define a real estate broker; what activities fall under the definition of real estate broker in your state? _____

_____

_____

_____

_____

h. What activities are exempt from the real estate license law?

_____

_____

_____

_____

_____

i. What is the examination fee for a real estate broker? _____

j. What is the original license application fee? _____

k. What is the license renewal fee? _____

l. Are bonds required for a real estate broker (give amount)?

_____

m. For what period are real estate broker licenses issued? _____

n. When do real estate broker licenses expire? _____

o. What date must real estate broker licenses be renewed? _____

p. What are regulations governing real estate broker pocket cards, office signs, addresses? _____

_____

_____

_____

q. What duties are required of a broker in terminating and hiring salespersons? _____

_____

_____

r. What responsibilities does the broker have in changing the location of his office or terminating his agency? _____

_____

_____

State License Law Provisions. Questions on the state license law account for a significant part of the license examinations. Questions deal with administrative procedures and grounds for suspending or revoking licenses.

1. Grounds for license suspension or revocation. List below the grounds stated for suspending or revoking real estate licenses. _____
    _____
    _____
    _____
    _____
    _____
    _____

2. What action may be taken by the real estate regulatory agency against violators of the license law? _____
    _____

3. What provisions are provided for hearings before an administrative agency? _____
    _____

4. What other penalties are provided by the real estate license law against illegal acts of licensed salespersons or real estate brokers?
    _____
    _____

5. What are the provisions governing the issuance of *nonresident* brokers' licenses? _____
    _____

6. What are the requirements for maintaining escrow accounts? _____
    _____

Real Estate Instruments

1. What instruments are used in your state for accepting earnest money deposits? For example, binder receipts, contract for sale, earnest money deposit? _____
    _____

2. What deeds are commonly used in your state: For example, grant deed (California), security deed (Georgia)? _____
    _____
    _____

3. Is your state a mortgage *title* or *lien* state? _____

4. What period of time is allowed for the exercise of the equity of redemption? _____ ; statutory equity of redemption? _____

5. Does your state provide for a deed of trust in lieu of mortgages? If so, describe the main features. _____

_____

_____

_____

6. Are net listings permitted? _____

_____

7. Are listing agreements required to be in writing? _____

8. What provision does your state make for the following rights: joint tenancy, tenancy in common, dower, curtesy, homestead rights, and community property? _____

_____

_____

_____

_____

9. What period of time is allowed for the filing of mechanic's and materialmen's liens? _____

_____

10. What are the main provisions of landlord-tenant laws recently enacted in your state? _____

_____

_____

_____

_____

11. Does your state provide for a recovery fund in lieu of the bonding of salespersons and brokers? If so, what are the maximum limits of the recovery fund? _____

_____

12. What fees must the salesperson and broker pay to maintain the recovery fund? _____

_____

13. What rights does the public have in filing claims against the recovery fund? _____

_____

14. Explain other state laws important to real estate licensees. ————

_____

_____

_____

HOW TO TAKE MULTIPLE-CHOICE EXAMINATIONS

In part, passing multiple-choice examinations depends on familiarity with examination procedures—this is especially true for adults who have not undertaken examinations for several years. Even for the more initiated, there are certain agreed-upon rules that help ensure a passing grade. To this end, it is recommended that prospective licensees concentrate on (1) examination preparation and (2) the examination technique.

Examination Preparation

At the outset it is presumed that the applicant knows the subject. If the subject is new, it is usually necessary to read chapter material more than once. In this text, the multiple-choice questions should serve as a guide for examination preparation. After reading the chapter, give yourself a self-test, and for those questions missed, again review the appropriate text pages.

Do not memorize questions. Examinations are more often cast in a manner that requires an interpretation of an example or a case narrative forcing the student to apply his knowledge of the subject to a specific case. The self-test questions at the end of each chapter help you determine if you are prepared. Pay particular attention to vocabulary and arithmetic examples common to real estate practice.

There is one additional point. Arrange matters so that you are in the best possible frame of mind as the examination begins. Most agencies prohibit notes, books, or other personal effects to be taken into the examination room. It would be wise to determine in advance if the testing agency allows pocket calculators. While the problems presented in the examination are easily solved by hand, pocket calculators save time in solving problems. It is good practice to arrive at the point of examination several minutes early. If you are not familiar with the area, allow for delays in traffic and parking.

The Examination Technique

On entering the examination room, you will probably be given pencils that must be used on the answering sheet. Some agencies provide working paper and forms in addition to the examination booklet which must be turned in at the examination completion. Expect that the time for the examination to be strictly enforced. You will be told when to begin the examination and the precise time at which all the examinations must be turned in to the proctors.

Because license agencies must keep records of the examination, follow the initial directions carefully. Since the examinations are machine processed, the identifying entries on your examination should conform to requirements for machine record processing.

When you have been given permission to begin the examination, quickly review the contents of the examination so that you may properly allocate time to different portions of the examination. The next task is to program your answers in the best possible way for the multiple-choice format.

1. *Each question has only one correct answer.* Examination instructions usually state that you should select the best possible answer. Some choices may be only partly correct.
2. *Do not leave questions unanswered.* Though you do not know the correct choice, be sure that you have answered each question. Since you are given credit for correct answers in a four-part multiple-choice question, you have once chance in four of guessing the correct answers. Questions left blank are automatically counted wrong.
3. *Do not ponder for an unduly long time over a difficult question.* Answer the easy questions first and leave the more difficult questions to the end. You should plan on answering about 50 questions every 30 minutes. Go back to the more difficult questions after completing the easier questions.
4. *If you have time for reviewing your answers, change answers only with caution.* Studies have shown that the initial response is more likely to be the correct response. If you do decide to change an answer, erase carefully so that the machine will not read two responses for the same question and mark the question wrong.
5. *Do not assume additional facts.* You must read each question carefully and not assume other facts that are not noted in the question.
6. *Make certain that your answers apply to the proper question.* Cases have occurred where applicants have checked answers for the wrong

question, resulting in a failing grade. Be sure to match the question number on the answer sheet with the corresponding question number on the examination.

The Multistate Examination Procedure. To illustrate, note Figure A–2, an answer sheet used in the state of California. Suppose, for example, that question 1 reads:

1. You accept an exclusive right to sell listing at a price of $9,000, but you sell the property for $13,000, based on an unsolicited offer to purchase:
   a. You have violated the laws of agency;
   b. You have been guilty of no wrongdoing;
   c. You have violated your fiduciary obligation to your principal;
   d. You have violated the terms of your exclusive right to sell listing.

If you select answer (*b*) as the correct answer, you would mark the space for question 1 identified as the (*b*) response. Blanks for question 1 would be shown as

$$1 \quad [a] \quad \boxed{[b]} \quad [c] \quad [d]$$

In the answer sheet format of Figure A–2 note that the questions are grouped in blocks reading three or four responses vertically and then horizontally in groups of 15 questions. The answer sheet for the salesperson's and broker's examination administered in the state of Georgia follows a different format but requires the same type of entry for each question.

In selecting the correct answer, first, eliminate the obviously incorrect choices. After narrowing the choices, then select the best answer. For instance in question 1 above, which is directed at the agency-principal relationship, you know that the broker must act in the best interest of his principal. Answer (*a*) is incorrect since the offer of $13,000 is considerably above $9,000. Answer (*c*) is incorrect since the $13,000 sale is evidence that the broker has acted in the best interest of his clients in getting the best price. Answer (*d*) on the facts stated, does not show that terms of an exclusive right to sell listing have been violated. Therefore, you would conclude that (*b*) is the best possible answer. Hence, in eliminating the responses that you are reasonably sure are wrong, you narrow your choice to one or two remaining answers and increase your chances of being right.

Uniform Examination Procedure. Each applicant for a license in states using the Educational Testing Service examination receives a 15-page information pamphlet entitled *Bulletin of Information for Applicants.* The bulletin describes procedural rules for taking the examination. It further explains that the supervisor of the examination will give instructions for entering your identification on the answer sheet.

FIGURE A-2

Multiple Choice Answer Sheets Prepared by the Department of Real Estate, California

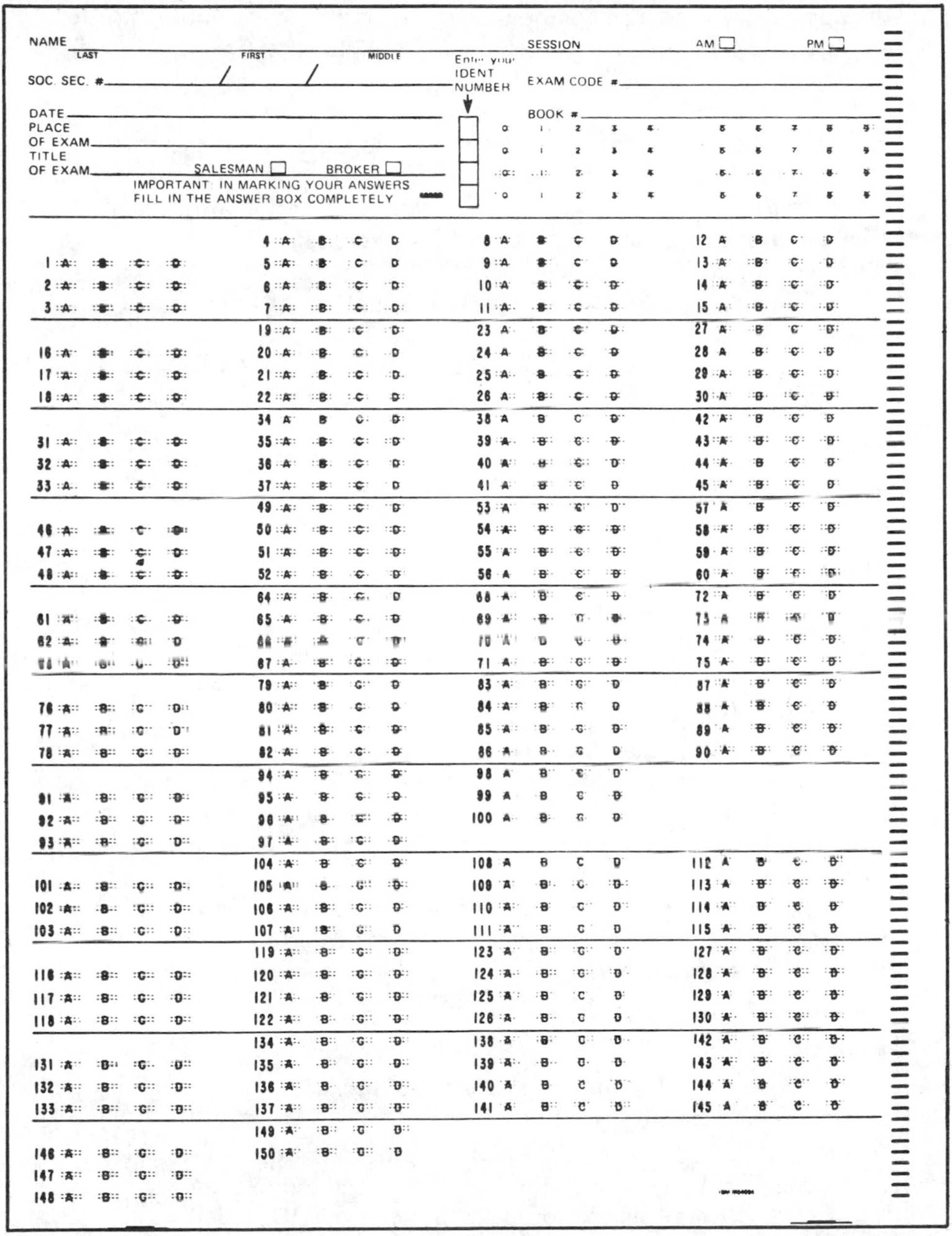

The examination form requires that the applicant mark spaces provided for the first 12 letters of the last name, the first 8 letters of the first name, the middle initial, and the examination number printed on the admission ticket. The appropriate spaces under each number or letter are blackened in pencil. This enables the testing service to read the identification by machine.

In the information bulletin published by the Educational Testing Service, it is explained that both the salesperson and broker examinations include only multiple-choice questions. Generally, the questions consist of two types: (1) an incomplete statement or question which requires selection of four suggested answers or (2) a question which refers to two statements or possibilities, identified as I and II.

(1) To illustrate, consider two possible variations of the first type.

SUGGESTED COMPLETIONS OR ANSWERS

Example 1

The main feature of _____ is the right of survivorship.

a. joint tenancy
b. tenancy in common
c. tenancy at will
d. ownership in severalty

Among the choices offered, answer (a) is correct since joint tenancy is the only form of ownership with the right of survivorship. Choice (b) is incorrect because tenants in common may sell, partition, and will their interest as tenants in common. No right of survivorship is associated with this estate. Tenancy at will refers to the estate held by a tenant which is revocable at will by the lessor or lessee; eliminate (c) as an option. The last possible answer, (d), referring to ownership in severalty, is incorrect since this form of ownership consists of ownership by one person—here the right of survivorship is not relevant.

Applicants to the Educational Testing Service Examination will confront a second example that gives three correct choices and one incorrect choice. The question is worded so that the incorrect answer must be selected. This type of question is shown in Example 2.

Example 2

To earn a real estate commission, real estate brokers must meet all of the following requirements except

a. The broker must be licensed and the procuring cause of the sale.
b. A completed sale entitles the broker to a real estate commission.
c. The broker must be employed by the principal, the seller.
d. The broker must secure a willing and able buyer able to purchase on terms acceptable to the seller.

The answer to Example 2 is (*b*). Do not select (*a*) because to enforce payment of a commission, license laws specify that the broker must be licensed and that he or she was the procuring cause of the sale. Answer (*b*) is the correct selection since a completed sale does not necessarily entitle a broker to a real estate commission. Answer (*c*) is one of the requirements for earning a commission—even though the broker may have influenced the buyer to purchase, the broker is not entitled to commission unless he or she was employed by the owner. Finally, (*d*) is incorrect since a commission has not been earned unless he or she finds a buyer willing and able to purchase under terms acceptable to the seller.

(2) The second type of question, referring to two possible statements, is illustrated by Example 3. The two possibilities are identified as I and II. Though there are two possibilities, the question is followed by four answer choices (*a*), (*b*), (*c*), and (*d*). This type of question requires careful reading.

Example 3

The Truth in Lending Act applies to operations of
- I. Only mortgage lenders.
- II. Only real estate brokers.
  - *a.* I only.
  - *b.* II only.
  - *c.* Both I and II.
  - *d.* Neither I nor II.

From the two statements I and II, four possibilities are presented. Determine which statement has the greatest probability of being right; initially, it must be determined if I is right or wrong and then if II is right or wrong.

Choice (*a*) should be selected only if you think that the Truth in Lending Act applies only to mortgage lenders. Select (*b*) if you think the act applies only to real estate brokers. In this instance, you should select (*c*) since under the act real estate brokers and lenders must state the annual percentage rate interest in advertising, lending, and purchasing terms. Answer (*d*) is not correct since the act applies to operations of real estate brokers and mortgage lenders in their advertising and other operations.

The uniform test for brokers deals with the interpretation of the listing contract, a sales contract, and a settlement statement worksheet. Sample questions on these forms are unavailable. The type of question on the uniform test for brokers on the valuation of residential property is indicated by the following example.

1. Concerning the valuation of residential property, which of the following is (are) true?

I. The value of the ordinary single-family residential property should be based on the income it is capable of producing if rented.

II. In valuing a residence, functional accessories (such as a built-in china closet or breakfast set) are seldom taken into consideration.

   a. I only.

   b. II only.

   c. Both I and II.

   d. Neither I nor II.

In this instance, selection (*d*) is most correct. Questions for the state portion of the test are comparable to questions given salespersons.

A Glossary of Common Real Estate Terms

Abstract of title—A written history from the original source of title to the present that summarizes all instruments of public record that affect a land title.

Acceleration clause—A clause authorizing the lender to collect the total debt if a borrower defaults in his mortgage payments.

Accumulated deduction form—A closing statement that lists credits to the buyer and seller in cumulative form.

Acknowledgment—A declaration usually made before an official who has power to acknowledge, such as a notary public, who attests to the validity of signatures to a contract.

Acre—A measure of land equaling 160 square rods, or 4,840 square yards, or 43,560 square feet, or a tract about 208.71 feet square.

Administrator—A person appointed by a court to manage and settle the estate of a deceased person who has left no will.

Adverse possession—A method of establishing valid title by occupation of land over a minimum period required by statute.

Affidavit—A statement or declaration reduced to writing and sworn to or examined by some officer who has authority to administer oaths or affirmation.

Affirmative marketing plans—A requirement enforced by the Department of Housing and Urban Development ensuring that individuals have a range of housing choices regardless of race, color, religion, or national origin.

Agency—A contract by which one person with greater or less discretionary power undertakes to represent another in certain business relations.

Agent—A person acting on behalf of another, called his principal.

Agreement of sale—A written agreement in which the seller agrees to convey an interest in real estate under certain sale terms and conditions.

Alienation—The conveyance of an interest in real estate.

Amortized mortgage—A mortgage providing for the repayment of principal over a mortgage term.

Annual percentage rate—The rate of a finance charge expressed in terms of an annual percent rate.

Annuity—A sum of money or its equivalent that constitutes one of a series of periodic payments.

Appraisal report—An estimate of value describing the real estate appraised, evidence of value, and other supporting information.

Assessed value—The value of real estate for property tax purposes.

Assignment—Transfer of a title or interest by writing.

Assignor—One who makes an assignment.

Attorney-at-law—A lawyer; an officer in a court of justice, who is employed by a party in a cause to manage the same for him.

Attorney-in-fact—One who is authorized to perform certain acts for another under a power of attorney; power of attorney may be general or limited to a specific act or acts.

Bargain and sale deed—A deed that conveys title without including warranties of title.

Beneficiary—A person designated as the recipient of funds or other property under a trust or insurance policy.

Bilateral contract—A mutual agreement between two parties.

Bill of sale—A written instrument transferring right, title, and interest in personal property to another.

Binder—An agreement to cover a down payment for the purchase of real estate as evidence of good faith on the part of the purchaser.

Blanket mortgage—A mortgage that pledges more than one parcel of real estate as security for a debt.

Blockbusting—Persuading owners to sell or rent housing by telling them that minority groups are moving into the neighborhood.

Breach—The violation of an obligation, engagement, or duty.

British Thermal Unit—The amount of heat required to heat one pound of water one degree Fahrenheit.

Building code—A locally enacted code that regulates building construction and the use of materials that provide for safe buildings.

Building residual—A method of valuing property that treats income to the building as a residual.

Bundle of rights—A theory that treats real estate interests as a bundle of sticks that may be bought and sold as individual sticks in a bundle of rights.

Capitalization rate—A rate of discount that converts income to a capital value.

Cash reconciliation statement—A statement showing the receipts and disbursements required to close a real estate sale.

Chattel—All personal property, which usually refers to furniture and other nonreal estate goods.

Cloud on the title—An outstanding claim or encumbrance, which, if valid, would affect or impair the owner's title; a deed of trust or judgment.

Co-brokerage—An informal arrangement in which brokers voluntarily share real estate commissions with other licensed brokers.

Color of title—A claim arising from a conveyance instrument that would appear valid to a person without legal training who might believe an actually defective instrument to be legal.

Common element—The undivided interest of a condominium owner in any portion of a condominium other than units.

Community property—Real estate acquired during marriage which is owned jointly by husband and wife with no right of survivorship.

Competitive market analysis—Current information showing houses listed for sale and recently sold showing the range of dwelling prices in selected neighborhoods.

Compound interest—The amount earned on a principal sum which is increased each year.

Condemnation—The right of government to take private property upon payment of just compensation under the right of eminent domain.

Condominium—An individual ownership with an undivided interest in the common elements.

Consideration—A promise to pay or do something that parties were not legally required to do at the time the contract was executed.

Construction mortgage—A relatively short-term mortgage secured by land and a building under construction, made in anticipation of long-term financing.

Constructive notice—Legal notice provided by the recording of documents in a public office and that substitutes for actual notice.

Covenant—A promise by one party to another promising certain performance or nonperformance of certain acts or a promise that certain conditions do or do not exist.

Covenant to repair—The obligation of a landlord to keep residential premises in a clean and safe condition and to maintain in good and safe working order all equipment and appliances.

Curtesy—The right of a surviving husband in real property owned during marriage.

Debit and credit closing statements—A method of preparing closing statements to the buyer and seller based on debit and credit accounting entries.

Declaration—A legal document that places property under authority of condominium law.

Decree—The judgment of a court of equity.

Deed restriction—A land use control initiated by the grantor in the deed of conveyance.

Default—The nonperformance of a duty.

Defendant—The party sued or called to answer in any suit, action, or proceeding.

Deficiency judgment—A judgment secured by a lender to attach personal assets in payment of an unsatisfied mortgage.

Degree days—The number of degree days is equal to 65 degrees less the daily mean temperature for that date. The sum of individual degree days gives the number of degree days per year.

Demise—The conveyance of an estate, chiefly by lease.

Depreciation—The loss in value from any cause.

Devise—A gift of real estate by will or last testament.

Domicile—The place where a person has his true, fixed, and permanent home and principal establishment, and to which whenever he or she is absent he or she has the intention of returning.

Dower—The interest of a widow in real estate owned by the husband during marriage.

Earnest money—A deposit given to bind the sale of real estate.

Easement—A nonpossessory interest in real estate to use property of another for a special purpose.

Easement appurtenant—A right to use land of another for a specific purpose that runs with the land receiving the benefit of the easement.

Easement in gross—A personal right acquired by one party to use land of another for a specific purpose.

Economic base—Activities in which people make their living.

Economic life—The period over which a property will yield a return on the investment, over and above the economic or ground rent due to land.

Economic obsolescence—Loss in value that occurs from forces external to a given property.

Effective gross income—Gross income less an allowance for vacancies and bad debts.

Ejectment—A form of action to regain the possession of real property, with damages for the unlawful retention.

Emblements—Things which grow on the land and require annual planting and cultivation.

Eminent domain—The right of government and regulated public utilities to take private property upon payment of just compensation.

Encroachment—A building improvement that illegally intrudes upon the property of another.

Encumbrance—A limitation on the fee simple title to real estate.

Environmental impact statement—A statement that is required by the National Environmental Policy Act of 1969 and certain state legislation that requires a detailed explanation of how a proposed project significantly affects the environment.

Equal credit opportunity—Federal legislation that prevents creditors from discriminating against applicants on grounds of race, color, religion, national origin, age, or sex.

Equity—An owner's interest representing the difference between property value and the outstanding debt.

Equity of redemption—The right of a defaulting borrower to pay his debts and remedy his default.

Escheat—The right of the state to take title to real estate of deceased persons who die without a will or legal heirs.

Escrow—A third party that has a fiduciary duty to the buyer and seller to deliver title on performance of all steps necessary to a real estate closing.

Estate—An individual ownership in real estate.

Estate for years—A lease for a fixed time, for example, a month, or a year.

Estoppel certificate—A written statement from a lender showing the remaining balance of an outstanding mortgage.

Eviction—The deprivation of the possession of lands or tenements.

Exclusive agency—A listing agreement in which the seller agrees not to list the property with other brokers during the listing period. The owner may sell the property by his own efforts without paying a real estate commission.

Exclusive right to sell—An exclusive listing agreement granted to a broker who has the right to a commission if the property is sold.

Executed contract—A contract which is completed.

Executory contract—A contract in which performance is incomplete.

Express contract—A written or oral contract created by acts of the parties.

Express warranty of habitability—The obligation of a landlord to keep premises fit and habitable.

Fair housing—Common and statute law that prevents discrimination in housing on grounds of religion, race, or national origin.

Federal National Mortgage Association—A privately owned, government regulated corporation that buys and sells mortgages to and from lending institutions.

Fee simple estate—The most complete form of ownership in real estate.

Fee tail—The right of inheritance granted only to lineal descendants of the owner.

Fiduciary—A person to whom property is entrusted, to hold, control, or manage for another.

Fixture—An item of personal property classified as real estate.

Flexible payment mortgage—Mortgages that allow initial monthly payments below those required by an amortized mortgage.

Flood hazard area—An area identified by the Flood Insurance Agency of the Department of Housing and Urban Development which is subject to floods at least once every 100 years.

Foreclosure—A legal remedy to collect a debt secured by a mortgage on property.

Freehold estate—A fee simple estate or life interest.

Functional depreciation—The loss in value from changes in design.

Government National Mortgage Association—A government agency that buys and sells mortgages on government subsidized projects to and from financial institutions.

Graduated rent—Rental payments that provide for rents that are adjusted upward or downward at stated intervals over the lease.

Grantee—The person to whom an interest in real property is conveyed.

Grantor—A person who conveys an interest in real property.

Gross income—Income received before deduction or net operating expenses, depreciation, vacancy, and bad debts or mortgage payments.

Gross leaseable area—The total floor area available for tenant occupancy—usually used in describing shopping center space.

Habendum clause—The "to have and to hold" clause which defines or limits the quantity of the estate granted in the premises of the deed.

Hereditaments—The term usually means real estate and all that goes with it as being incidental thereto; every sort of inheritable property, such as real, personal, corporeal, and incorporeal.

Highest and best use—That legal use which produces the highest net income to the land.

Homestead—A right created by state law protecting real estate owned by the head of the household from designated creditors.

Implied contract—A contract occurring as a result of a special circumstance existing between the agent and principal.

Income approach—A method of valuation based on the present worth of future net income.

Index leases—A lease that adjusts rents according to changes in a price index.

Interstate Land Sales Full Disclosure Act—An act that discourages fraud, misrepresentation, and deceit in the sale of subdivision lots over interstate boundaries.

Intestate—A person who dies, having made no will or one which is defective in form.

Joint tenancy—Ownership by two or more persons with the right of survivorship.

Junior mortgage—A mortgage second in priority to another, senior mortgage.

Land contract—An installment contract for the purchase of land providing for a deed upon payment of the last installment.

Land residual capitalization—A method of appraising property by treating income to the land as a residual.

Lease—A written or oral contract for the exclusive right to possess and use real estate upon payment of consideration, usually rent or other promises.

Leased fee—The estate of the lessor who conveys the leasehold interest to the tenant.

Leasehold interest—The estate held by the lessee or tenant.

Legal description—A land description that enables a particular parcel of real estate to be located and identified.

Lessee—A party who holds the exclusive right to possession under a valid lease.

Lessor—A party who leases property to a tenant.

Lien—A claim of one person on the property of another held in security for a debt.

Life estate—Ownership of property conveyed only during the lifetime of some person.

Listing agreement—A personal contract between a broker who acts as an agent and the principal who is usually a seller.

Listing farm—A method of obtaining listings by a personal canvass of a selected neighborhood.

Market comparison approach—A method of real property valuation that employs recent sales of similar property.

Marketable title—A title which a reasonable purchaser, well informed as to the facts and their legal bearing, willing and anxious to perform his contract, would in the exercise of that prudence which business people ordinarily bring to bear in such transactions, be willing and ought to accept; and which one is entitled to have.

Market value—The highest price in terms of money which a property will bring in the market, neither party acting under distress and with both parties having knowledge of all possible uses to which the property may be put.

Mechanic's lien—A lien created by statute which favors persons who have performed work or furnished materials in the erection or repair of a building.

Metes and bounds—A legal description describing land from a point of beginning with exact boundaries described by a series of linear measurements, directions, and monuments.

Millage rate—The property tax rate based upon a mill, which is one tenth of a cent.

Modernization—Restoration of the building which extends the useful life of the building without changing the property use.

Mortgage—An instrument that conveys real estate as security for a debt.

Mortgagee—A lender who advances funds in return for a mortgage.

Mortgagor—A borrower who conveys a mortgage to a lender as security for a debt.

Mortgage assumption—The assumption of a mortgage by a third party who personally promises to repay an existing mortgage debt.

Mortgage constant—The annual amount paid to interest and principal expressed as a percent of the original mortgage.

Multiple listing—A listing based on an exclusive right to sell which is shared by an association of cooperating brokers.

NAR—The National Association of Realtors, formerly the National Association of Real Estate Boards.

Net listing—A listing that provides for a net amount to the selling principal.

Net operating income—The effective gross income less the net operating expenses before depreciation and mortgage payments.

Open listing—A listing agreement in which the seller retains the right to list property with more than one broker.

Open mortgage—A mortgage that provides for future advances secured by the same mortgage.

Option contract—An exclusive right to buy or sell property at a given price within a stated period.

Package mortgage—A mortgage that includes personal property and real estate.

Parol evidence—A legal rule which prevents oral evidence from varying or adding to the terms of a written contract.

Partially amortized mortgage—A mortgage providing for principal repayment down to a given amount with a lump sum payment for the balance of the principal.

Participation mortgage—A mortgage that includes more than one lender.

Partition—The division of real estate made between copartners, tenants, and joint tenants.

Percentage lease—A lease in which rents are partially or completely based on a percentage of the gross receipts of a tenant.

Periodic tenancies—A tenancy that is renewed indefinitely from period to period.

Physical depreciation—The loss of value from action of the elements, wear and tear, and catastrophic events.

Planned unit development—A method of zoning that provides for a unified plan of developing residential, commercial, public, and industrial space.

Plat book—A public record of recorded plats in the municipality or county.

Points—A method of referring to the amount the lender discounts a government insured or guaranteed mortgage. One point is equal to 1 percent of the face value of the mortgage.

Police power—The inherent right of government to regulate property in the public interest, convenience, necessity, and health.

Power of attorney—An instrument authorizing a person to act as the agent or attorney of the person granting it.

Prepayment privileges—The right of a borrower to prepay a mortgage loan.

Property—The right or interest which an individual has in lands and chattels to the exclusion of all others.

Property conversion—Restoration of a building through a change in the design or use to a more profitable operation.

Property report—A report issued by the secretary of housing stating information important to a purchaser of land subject to the Interstate Land Sales Full Disclosure Act.

Property residual capitalization—The capitalization of net income by assuming that net income is derived from the building and land as one unit.

Purchase money mortgage—A mortgage that the seller accepts as a substitute for cash.

Quantity survey method—A method of estimating building costs by detailing the costs of materials and labor.

Quitclaim deed—A deed that conveys only an interest that a grantor may have in the property.

R values—Values that measure resistance to heat loss in terms of fahrenheit degrees per hour per British Thermal Unit.

Range—Common to U.S. governmental rectangular surveys, a range represents a strip of land six miles wide running north and south.

Real estate—Land, tenements, and hereditaments and all rights thereto and interests therein, other than a chattel interest; land and its attachments.

Real estate broker—Any person who sells or offers for sale or buys or offers to buy or negotiates real estate for compensation or promise of compensation. The term broker may be legally defined to include other real estate activities.

Real Estate Settlement Procedure Act of 1974—An act that requires lenders to disclose an estimate of closing costs and other details to the buyer and seller.

Realtor—A copyrighted designation referring to a member of the National Association of Realtors.

Rectangular survey system—A method of describing land from a base line and a principal meridian.

Regulation Z—A regulation prepared by the board of governors of the Federal Reserve System setting forth rules that must be observed under the Truth in Lending Act.

Rehabilitation—Restoration of a building in a like-new condition making no changes in design or use.

Remainderman—The party who acquires title on the death of a life tenant.

Replacement costs—The cost of a building that serves the same function and utility as the property under appraisal.

Reproduction costs—The cost of reproducing a new building identical to the building under appraisal.

Rescission of contract—The revocation or repealing of a contract by mutual consent by parties to the contract, or for cause by either party to the contract.

Restrictive covenant—A clause in a deed limiting the use of the property conveyed for a certain period of time.

Retaliatory eviction—Tenant eviction by a landlord in retaliation against tenant acts and which is usually prohibited by recent landlord-tenant statutes.

Retrofitting techniques—Measures that improve the thermal efficiency of buildings.

Revaluation lease—A lease that calls for periodic appraisals to adjust rent.

Right of rescission—The right of borrowers under certain circumstances to cancel a transaction three days after loan approval.

Right of survivorship—Right to acquire the interest of a deceased joint owner; distinguishing feature of a joint tenancy.

Satisfaction piece—A written statement which gives legal notice of satisfaction of a mortgage.

Section—Approximately one square mile or 640 acres, common to U.S. government rectangular surveys.

Security deed—A warranty deed that secures payment for a specified debt by granting a power of attorney authorizing the purchaser to sell the property upon default of a debt.

Setback—The distance from the property line, within which no buildings may be erected.

Severalty ownership—Ownership of real estate in one person.

Sheriff's deed—A deed that contains no warranties or guaranties of title.

Solar light—Refers to the right to adequate light which could be deflected or diffused.

Solar rights—The right to solar energy that falls on one's property if the path of sunshine were not impeded by one's neighbors.

Special warranty deed—A deed in which the grantor warrants title only against the lawful claims of all persons claiming by, due, or under him (her).

Statute of Frauds—Statutes that require certain instruments to be in writing.

Statutory equity of redemption—The right of a defaulting borrower to redeem property after a foreclosure sale.

Subdivision—A tract of land divided into lots suitable for building purposes.

Subdivision covenants—Land use controls that apply to all land in a recorded subdivision.

Subject to mortgages—The acceptance of an existing mortgage by a purchaser who makes no personal promise to repay the debt.

Tenancy at will—An agreement between the owner and tenant which may be terminated at the will of either party.

Tenancy by sufferance—A tenant who occupies premises without permission of the owner.

Tenancy by the entireties—Ownership by husband and wife with the right of survivorship as created by state law.

Tenancy in common—Ownership by two or more persons in an undivided interest in real estate without the right of survivorship.

Term mortgage—A mortgage that makes no provision for principal repayment.

Title insurance—A policy of insurance which indemnifies the holder for any loss sustained by reason of defects in the title.

Township—A part of the U.S. governmental rectangular survey system, a township consists of 36 square miles or sections. It also refers to a land area six miles wide running east and west.

Trust deeds—A deed that conveys real estate to a trustee as security for a debt.

Trustee—A person in whom some estate, interest, or power in or affecting property of any description is vested for the benefit of another.

Truth in lending—A 1969 act, as amended, which requires lenders and others to make certain disclosures in advertising credit terms.

Turnover factor—A ratio calculated by dividing the total number of houses by the total number of sales in a given year.

Unenforceable contract—A contract in which neither party may sue under terms of the contract.

Uniform Residential Landlord and Tenant Act—A publication prepared by the National Conference of Commissioners on Uniform State Laws (1972) which has served as a model statute for several states.

Unilateral contract—A promise given by one party to induce performance by another party.

Unit—A portion of a condominium designed and intended for individual ownership and use.

Unit-in-place costs—Construction costs based on the costs of building components in place, including labor and material.

Unit owner—The purchaser who holds title to a condominium unit with an undivided interest in the common elements.

Usury—The lending, or practice of lending, money at a rate of interest above the legal rate.

Valid—Having force, or binding force; legally sufficient and authorized by law.

Valid contract—A contract that contains all the essential elements of a contract as required by law.

Variable rate mortgages—Mortgages with interest rates that change according to a price index.

Vendee—A purchaser or buyer.

Vendor—The seller.

Void—That which is unenforceable; having no force or effect.

Void contract—A contract to commit an illegal act.

Voidable contract—A contract with all legal requirements of a contract which may be rejected by one or both parties to the contract.

Waiver—The renunciation, abandonment, or surrender of some claim, right, or privilege.

Warranty deed—A written instrument of conveyance that transfers an interest in real estate with covenants of title.

Will—A legal declaration of a person's wishes as to the disposition of his property after his death.

Wraparound mortgage—A second mortgage in which additional funds are granted at the same time an existing mortgage is continued and paid by the second lender.

Index

Index